More Praise for
CITY OF AMBITION

"Fascinating. . . . Williams tells the story of La Guardia and Roosevelt with insight and elegance. . . . [City of Ambition] succeeds impressively. . . . America's cities are the country's true economic heartland, and much of our most important past is urban. City of Ambition helps us to understand that past."
— Edward Glaeser,
New York Times Book Review

"An extraordinary book. In telling the story of how Roosevelt and La Guardia—men as fascinating as they were powerful—forged a mighty political collaboration, it brilliantly reinterprets the New Deal from the vantage point of the nation's greatest city. It also marks the remarkable debut of a gifted young historian." —Sean Wilentz,
author of The Rise of American Democracy: Jefferson to Lincoln

"This illuminating study offers a fresh vantage from which to comprehend key features of the New Deal and the history of New York. Moving between a vibrant portrayal of persons and incisive accounts of processes, City of Ambition is written with verve and imagination."
—Ira Katznelson,
author of Fear Itself: The New Deal and the Origins of Our Time

"An excellent account—well written and thoroughly researched—of how FDR and La Guardia, in an era of depression and war, channeled federal resources into crisis-ridden municipalities. Williams' recounting of their achievement is a salutary reminder of what was once possible, and could be again." — Mike Wallace,
coauthor of Gotham: A History of New York City to 1898

"[A] striking account. . . . Williams convincingly asserts that [New Deal] programs were vital and successful in stimulating a moribund economy and provided confirmation of the positive role that can be played by government at the local and national level."

—Jay Freeman, *Booklist*

"*City of Ambition* is important reading for anyone interested in the design of cities and particularly how plans and visions are translated to physical and social reality—or not. . . . The book comes at an appropriate time." —Phil Patton, *Designers and Books*

"[A] sweeping reinterpretation of the New Deal political economy. . . . Williams builds his analysis around vivid profiles of F.D.R. and especially of La Guardia, the colorful, pugnacious Republican reformer who roped union militants and socialists into his coalition. (The author's rich account of the era's crazy-quilt political alliances will astonish readers accustomed to today's rigid partisan lines.) Challenging conventional stereotypes about big government and local control, Williams highlights federalism as a revolutionary force." —*Publishers Weekly*

"Very readable, and highly informative history. It has a great deal to teach about the economics and politics of those watershed years, not just in New York but beyond." —Sanford Ikeda, *Reason*

CITY OF AMBITION

FDR, LA GUARDIA,
AND THE MAKING OF
MODERN NEW YORK

MASON B. WILLIAMS

W. W. NORTON & COMPANY
New York • London

For Alexis

For information about permission to reproduce selections from this book,
write to Permissions, W. W. Norton & Company, Inc.,
500 Fifth Avenue, New York, NY 10110

For information about special discounts for bulk purchases, please contact W. W. Norton
Special Sales at specialsales@wwnorton.com or 800-233-4830

Manufacturing by Courier Westford
Book design by Chris Welch Design
Production manager: Julia Druskin

Library of Congress Cataloging-in-Publication Data

Williams, Mason B.
City of ambition : FDR, La Guardia, and the making of modern New York / Mason B.
Williams. — First Edition.
pages cm
Includes bibliographical references and index.
ISBN 978-0-393-06691-3 (hardcover)
1. New York (N.Y.)—History—1898–1951. 2. New York (N.Y.)—Politics and
government—1898–1951. 3. New Deal, 1933–1939—New York (State)—New York.
4. Depressions—1929—New York (State)—New York. 5. Roosevelt, Franklin D.
(Franklin Delano) 1882–1945. 6. La Guardia, Fiorello H. (Fiorello Henry), 1882–1947.
I. Title.
F128.5.W73 2013
974.7'1—dc23

2013004481

ISBN 978-0-393-34898-9 pbk.

W. W. Norton & Company, Inc.
500 Fifth Avenue, New York, N.Y. 10110
www.wwnorton.com

W. W. Norton & Company Ltd.
Castle House, 75/76 Wells Street, London W1T 3QT

1 2 3 4 5 6 7 8 9 0

CONTENTS

Introduction   ix

PART I: FOUNDATIONS

1   Beginnings   3

2   A Season in the Wilderness   48

3   The Deluge   90

PART II: THE NEW DEAL

4   "Jobs Is the Cry"   135

5   The New Deal's "Lost Legacy"   175

6   From Fusion to Confusion   212

7   New Dealer for the Duration   250

PART III: WAR AND POSTWAR

8   The Local Politics of Foreign Policy   289

9   The Battle of New York   325

10   "I Hope Others Will Follow New York's Example"   362

Epilogue   395

Acknowledgments   407

Notes   411

Photo Credits   475

Index   477

Illustrations to follow page 206

In another few years, New York will have eight million people. It will do more than one-sixth of the business of all of the United States. As war tears the vitals out of the great cities of Asia and Europe, the countries of the world must look to New York as the center of progress, international culture, and advance. Maybe this ought not to be so; maybe the country ought to be centralized. But I know that is not happening.

You will see that New York has collectivized great masses of its enterprise. I am not arguing whether this is good or bad. I am merely pointing out that it must be so: eight million people crowded together do this automatically. . . .

New York's relations with Washington will be even closer than New York's relations with Albany. I don't know whether this will be a good or a bad [thing]; but I know that it will be so.

—*Adolf A. Berle, Jr., 1937*

These men certainly had tremendous advantages, one working with the other to accomplish similar purposes.

—*Reuben Lazarus, 1949*

INTRODUCTION

Today, many New Yorkers take the FDR to get to La Guardia. If their journeys originate in Manhattan north of 42nd Street, they may pass beneath Carl Schurz Park en route to the Triborough Bridge, which will carry them over the sites of the old Randall's Island Stadium and the Astoria Pool before depositing them on Long Island. If they leave from south of 42nd Street, they may cross under the East River by way of the Queens-Midtown Tunnel, entering the borough of Queens not far south of the Queensbridge Houses and passing within a few blocks of William Cullen Bryant High School. These and many similar structures are physical remnants of a time when the federal government under Franklin Roosevelt met the greatest domestic crisis of the twentieth century by putting unemployed men and women to work on public projects largely designed and carried out by local governments. In New York City, Roosevelt's partner was Mayor Fiorello La Guardia.

Other monuments from this time remain lynchpins of the city's infrastructure: the Lincoln Tunnel, Henry Hudson Drive, the Belt Parkway. Countless more, stretching from Orchard Beach in the Bronx to the Franklin D. Roosevelt boardwalk on Staten Island's south shore, have become part of the landscape within which life is lived in New York. In a city whose favorite amusements have long included putting up and pulling down, these projects have endured. And yet if the physical legacy of the New Deal still pervades the city, the history that produced it is only dimly understood. The public works projects of the 1930s stand today as mute testaments to an era of tumult and creativity, and to a conception of government which reached its apotheosis in interwar America and which shaped New York City profoundly—but whose history, obscured in turns by ideology and neglect, is too little known.[1]

This book is an account of the relationship between two of the most remarkable political leaders of the twentieth century: Franklin Roosevelt, the thirty-second president of the United States, and Fiorello La Guardia, the ninety-ninth mayor of New York City. The products of starkly different personal backgrounds and reform traditions, they rose in counterpoint through the ranks of New York politics before coming together in the 1930s to form a political collaboration unique between a national and a local official. Sworn in as the executives of America's two largest governments at the depths of the Great Depression, they kept the nation's biggest city together during one of the most trying periods in its history and helped to establish the course of its politics in the postwar decades.[2]

It is also a study of how government came to play an extraordinarily broad role in a quintessentially market-oriented city—of how the public sphere, embodied physically in the structures and spaces built up and carved out in the 1930s, was forged. This story has its roots in the Progressive Era, which marked the beginning of a decades-long debate over the ideal relationship among "individuals, society, and government."[3] In a modern, interdependent society, what rights did each of these groups possess, and what responsibilities? And how could collective action be deployed in the interest of social progress? Particularly in urban politics, the Progressive Era witnessed the introduction of a new set of policy approaches meant to improve the quality of life, mitigate the social costs of capitalist urban development, and render government more efficient and effective.

A crucial moment in this history came in the 1930s. During that turbulent decade, Franklin Roosevelt and his Democratic Party chose to channel the resources of the federal government through the agencies of America's cities and counties. Fiorello La Guardia's coalition of reformers, Republicans, social democrats, and leftists rebuilt New York's local state, chasing the functionaries of the city's fabled Tammany Hall political machine from power and implanting a cohort of technical experts committed to expanding the scope of the public sector. As depression gave way to war, the experience of total mobilization politicized market transactions, allowing grass-roots activists and political leaders alike to make fair employment and fair prices a central part of city politics.

THE BOOK'S TITLE, borrowed and adapted from Alfred Stieglitz's famous photograph of the lower Manhattan skyline, suggests its principal theme. New York in depression and war was a city of decidedly *public* ambitions: if Stieglitz's skyscrapers captured the ebullient commercialism of the early twentieth century, the New York of the thirties and forties was, as one of its sons has recalled it, a city of "libraries and parks."[4] It was also a city of municipal markets and public radio, of neighborhood health clinics and free adult education classes, of model housing, of bridges and tunnels and airports intended to integrate the five boroughs and to link the city to the metropolitan region and the wider world. Under La Guardia's leadership, the city built a physical infrastructure in which commerce could thrive and the interdependent processes of urban enterprise function efficiently. It also expanded the provision of public goods and services, envisioning these programs as means of lifting or mitigating constraints which impeded the happiness of individuals, families, and communities as they went about their lives—constraints such as unemployment, poverty, high prices, poor health, inadequate housing, a shortage of educational and recreational opportunities, and a stifling urban environment. During the Second World War, it sought to afford city dwellers protection from high prices and rents and to make available useful information to help them navigate consumer markets. These efforts were linked ideologically by the core belief that government should act as the mechanism by which the great productive energies and scientific and technological advantages of the age could be channeled to produce social progress. They were linked operationally by their self-conscious reliance on government as a technology of public action.[5]

This is, then, a history of "public economy"—a history of the ways in which government acted to produce wealth and shape the distribution of wealth in a society whose bedrock commitments include a separation between property and sovereignty, at a particular moment in time. That history took shape against the immediate background of the Great Depression and the Second World War, both national crises which forced Americans to search for new means of collective action. It was formed within the context of a broad shift in the American political landscape, as the lineaments of the American federal system, the relation between local and national authority, were being renegotiated.

At the time Roosevelt came to power, politics for many Americans remained primarily a local affair, with the municipality occupying a central position it would forfeit in the second half of the century. Even at the New Deal's high tide, the political scientist Samuel Beer recalled, New Deal reformers recognized the "great change in public attitudes" involved in their efforts to "persua[de] people to look to Washington for the solution of problems. . . ."[6] Yet under the influence of economic and social integration, the development of new forms of media, and such profound shocks as the two world wars and the Great Depression, American politics was also undergoing a process of nationalization. Local governments remained in many ways the strongest entities in the American governmental system (in their operational capacity and infrastructural presence, if not in their potential legal and fiscal authority). And as the Progressive reformer Frederic Howe had written a generation earlier, they were the governments primarily concerned with "the elevation of the standard of living, with equality of opportunity, with the uplifting of life, and the betterment of those conditions which most intimately affect mankind"—central concerns of American politics as it developed since the late nineteenth century.[7] Yet the national government, long a powerful (if unseen) presence in the American governmental system, was entering more fully and more visibly into what had been the domains of state and local governments, ushering in an age of "cooperative federalism" characterized by shared national, state, and local responsibility.[8] The equation was further complicated by the makeup of the New Deal coalition, which numbered a few genuine national state builders but many more men and women who endeavored to share political authority across the federal system. This was as true of Roosevelt, who valued American localism and sought to preserve and utilize it, as it was of the southern Democrats who ruled Congress and used the structures of American federalism to defend the low-wage regional economy and the system of racial discrimination which was inextricable from it. Under these conditions, it is hardly surprising that major shifts in national politics, such as those embodied in Roosevelt's New Deal, should implicate local governments, feeding back into local politics in powerful and sometimes surprising ways.[9]

The story of Roosevelt and La Guardia's relationship is the story of how these two political leaders maneuvered amidst the constraints of a system in flux, how they worked creatively to exploit that system's potentialities, and ultimately, how decisions taken at the national level reshaped the political landscape at the local level. Roosevelt and his administration, confronting the paramount problem of inadequate state capacity, responded by leveraging the particular strengths of the American polity—and local governments, with their infrastructural capacities and traditional responsibilities in public welfare and public health, represented one of these strengths. La Guardia became a major figure in the New Deal project because the New Dealers, finding few other options, designed programs that utilized local states for auxiliary capacity at a time when the national government's reach was exceeding its grasp. As a result, state and local governments played a vital role in some of the New Deal's greatest achievements: its bold and vigorous response to mass unemployment and its extensive contributions to the public wealth.

We tend to think of American federalism as a zero-sum game: power asserted by the federal government comes at the expense of state and local authority; power devolved to those governments "closest to the people" must be surrendered by Washington. In this reading, the expansion of national authority during Roosevelt's presidency produced a diminishment of "local government's role" in the American federal polity.[10] But New York's experience during the New Deal points in precisely the opposite direction: by pairing federal legal and fiscal resources with local operational capacity, the New Deal enabled local action rather than displacing it.[11] By injecting resources into local governments as a way of realizing national objectives, the New Dealers made possible a remarkable burst of public capital investment; they also allowed local officials to undertake scores of projects, most of them with origins in the various urban reform initiatives of the Progressive Era, which aimed to use the public sector as an instrument for improving the quality of urban life.

By making possible a kind of municipal government which would otherwise have been impossible, the New Deal became an integral part of a broader set of political changes within New York City.

Enabling local officials to intervene more effectively in everyday urban life, the New Deal helped to endow the project of municipal reform—the use of experts, the expansion of bureaucratic power—with a popular legitimacy that had previously eluded it. Linking New Yorkers to their government in new ways, it facilitated the incorporation of many thousands of people—immigrants and their children, working-class women, migrants from the American South and the West Indies, many of whom saw their own ideas and values reflected in New Deal social provision (and many of whom had been active in pressing for its enactment)—into the city's political life.[12]

Contenders for power in the post–La Guardia era would be forced to appeal to a far larger electorate, mobilized and incorporated into the city's politics during the 1930s, and to win the support of labor-based third parties which had been formed to advance the New Deal cause. If elected, they would preside over agencies which had grown larger, more professional, and more ambitious. More broadly, the city's politics would be conducted within a political culture shaped by the experience of the 1930s and 1940s. Having passed through a period in which the state had been, to an unusual degree, the driving force in urban social development, and in which it had done things it could not ordinarily do, New Yorkers became more cognizant of their governments. For several decades after the end of the Second World War, New Yorkers would reach instinctively for state-driven solutions to social problems. Though New York's municipal government would never again possess the sheer manpower the New Deal had given it, the political forces spawned during the 1930s, in the context of a singularly favorable local environment and extraordinary postwar growth, would prove capable of sustaining a robust local social politics—a "homegrown version of social democracy."[13]

Yet precisely because the New Deal represented a singular moment, it left New York's municipal state profoundly vulnerable. When the emergency ended, intergovernmental transfers would ebb.

And as national patterns of private and public investment shifted and more and more of the city's workforce spilled over its political boundaries, Gotham would lose the extraordinary advantage it had once enjoyed in local wealth and productivity. Under these conditions, the city's politics would become, as one New York State official has put it, a contest between "endless ambitions" and "finite resources."[14] This tension would constrain the possibilities of post–New Deal politics in the city even as the remarkable growth of the postwar decades sustained the development of the local state. When postwar growth gave way to the wrenching economic restructuring of the 1970s, much of the political legacy of the New Deal would be undone—though its physical legacy yet remains.

HISTORIANS HAVE LONG since discarded the old "great man" theory of political development that still passes for conventional wisdom in much of our day-to-day political discourse. Presidents and mayors do not possess carte blanche to shape policy according to their own visions (if they did, Roosevelt would have met the unemployment crisis of the 1930s by pulling industrial workers out of the great cities and resettling them in the country), or even according to the interests of their supporters. I trust readers will recognize that, in focusing upon Roosevelt and La Guardia's roles in "the making of modern New York," I am not seeking to revive the notion that political leadership alone constitutes the mainspring of American politics. On the contrary, one of this book's objectives is to show how patterns of social organization and developments within the American political system structured the kind of political leadership Roosevelt and La Guardia exercised.

Yet the careers of democratic politicians such as Roosevelt and La Guardia remain interesting, and we would do wrong to consign them to the margins of American political history (or to remand them solely to the care of biographers). Politicians make decisions that matter, and they do so by responding to forces and constraints—ideas, ideologies, cultures, contending parties and interest groups, social movements, institutional structures—which are themselves of interest. By examining the careers of politicians as they played out within the context of these shifting forces, I hope to present a more holistic picture of New York City's politics in depression and war, shaped as they were by national politics. In this conviction, we begin not among the six-story tenements of Manhattan nor the row houses and newly raised apartment buildings of the outer boroughs, but rather amid the rolling fields and riverfront vistas of Hyde Park, New York, and the open skies and baked earth of Prescott, Arizona.

PART I
FOUNDATIONS

1

Beginnings

In the summer in 1918, Franklin Delano Roosevelt, the young, energetic, and ambitious assistant secretary of the Navy, stepped off the train in Turin. He was en route to Rome, where he was to plead with Italian officials for action to combat the German U-boats that were sinking Allied ships in the Mediterranean Sea. He was greeted at the station by a young Italian American army captain, an aviator who was recently back from the front—Fiorello La Guardia. Born just eleven months and some ninety miles apart, the two men were nevertheless the products of different worlds. Roosevelt was the scion of Hudson Valley aristocracy; La Guardia the Greenwich Village–born, Arizona-raised son of an Italian father and a Sephardic mother: La Guardia would later refer to the pair of them as "the Son of the Revolution and the Son of the Steerage." On this day in 1918, they were two of the most promising young men in New York State politics. Chances were they would soon have met in the social circles of New York City, in the hotels where business was conducted in Washington, or in the legislative halls of Albany. But it was war that had brought them together for the first time, 4,000 miles from home. They chatted amiably for a few minutes, La Guardia telling

Roosevelt of the need for additional manpower to move supplies across the border between Italy and France. Both men remembered the conversation well enough that they could recall it twenty-three years later, when Roosevelt was president and La Guardia was mayor of New York, and war had once again engulfed the continent.[1]

I

Franklin Roosevelt was intensely proud of his family lineage—so proud that, when required to write an original thesis as part of the Harvard sophomore curriculum, he chose as his subject "The Roosevelt Family in New Amsterdam Before the Revolution." With the aid of records sent from the family estate at Hyde Park, he compiled enough research to fill more than one hundred pages. Why, he asked, had his own family proven so much more robust and durable than those "famous Dutch families" of colonial America whose prominence had declined to the point where they had "nothing left but their name"? "One reason—perhaps the chief—of the virility of the Roosevelts," he concluded, "is this very democratic spirit. They have never felt that because they were born in a good position they could put their hands in their pockets and succeed. They have felt, rather, that being born in a good position, there was no excuse for them if they did not do their duty by the community, and it is because this idea was instilled into them from their birth that they have in nearly every case proved good citizens."[2]

The heritage in which Roosevelt took such pride shaped his personality and worldview in profound ways. It provided him security of social status and financial wherewithal; these were in turn to foster in him an "extraordinarily sunny disposition and an abiding sense that all was right with the world," whatever the immediate challenges of the moment. The circumstances in which he was raised and the tradition he felt himself to be a part of gave him an assurance of the natural legitimacy of the power he was later to exercise—so long as he kept faith with the traditions and values that had been taught to him by his parents and his early teachers.[3]

Roosevelt was born on January 30, 1882, at his family's Dutchess County estate, perched atop a bluff on the east bank of the Hudson River in the small New York town of Hyde Park. He was born into a world of unassailable status and almost absolute security. The family's distinguished lineage made it a "solid Knickerbocker mainstay of New York society"; its fortune, though not tremendous by the standard of the Gilded Age, was sufficient to provide a life of privilege. Entry by birth into this quasi-aristocratic Anglo-Protestant world also presented Roosevelt with a fairly rigid set of expectations. It set him on a path from which he would not depart until he was twenty-eight years old.

Franklin was raised at the Hyde Park estate amidst tutors, nurses, cooks, butlers, coachmen, gardeners, and maids; his playmates were mostly relatives and children from neighboring estates. He enjoyed the abundant (and sometimes stifling) love of his mother and the steady company of his father, a former businessman who by the time of Franklin's birth was living in the manner of an English country gentleman. The young boy's daily life consisted of lessons and afternoons filled by gentlemanly hobbies—birding, sailing, riding. He learned the comportment expected of a young man of his background and upbringing: the ability to control one's emotions and to hide one's pain and suffering. He absorbed his family's belief that their social position entailed a broad civic responsibility. His father served as an example of the manner in which the wellborn and fortunate were to meet their responsibilities to the community—"sitting on boards and committees, being helpful in all good causes, and especially mitigating distress wherever it appeared."[4]

At fourteen, Roosevelt went away to Groton, a small-town Massachusetts boarding school that had recently been founded by an Episcopal priest and social humanitarian named Endicott Peabody. Rector Peabody's mission was to develop among the boys of America's "leading families" an ethic of public service comparable to that which permeated the English public schools in which he had been educated. Roosevelt absorbed Peabody's ethic of service, consonant with the lessons of *noblesse oblige* he had learned at Hyde Park, and also what Eleanor Roosevelt later described as the rector's "unwavering and direct" religious faith, a faith which held that "human beings were given tasks to perform and for those tasks the ability and strength to put them through." (Later, when Roosevelt held religious services in the White House, he often engaged Peabody to officiate.) From Groton, Roosevelt proceeded to Harvard. A member of the Mt. Auburn Street social elite, he devoted much of his time to a range of club and other extracurricular activities, the most notable of which was the *Daily Crimson*, of which he became the editor.[5]

Though his cheerful demeanor concealed the fact, Roosevelt's adolescence and early adulthood were more difficult than his happy and cloistered childhood had been. Rather over-eager, and only modestly endowed with the sporting abilities that brought prestige among his classmates, he did not enjoy great social success at Groton. He did somewhat better at Harvard, but he missed out on the association he most desired—election to the prestigious finals club, the Porcellian. Rexford Tugwell, an economist who worked with Roosevelt for several years before becoming one of the most penetrating of his biographers, concluded that the persistent "non-recognition" Roosevelt received at Groton and Harvard magnified his tendency to seek prestige for its own sake and made him willing to work with an "almost desperate energy" to achieve it: even as he sought election as vice president of the United States and as governor of New York, Tugwell believed, Roosevelt "was still trying to become stroke of the crew or end on the football team; still trying to rise from second to first" and to demonstrate to those who had slighted him early in his life that they had been mistaken. The columnist Joseph Alsop, a distant relative who observed Roosevelt throughout his career, speculated that Roosevelt's middling success at winning popularity within his own social circle may have led him to look outside it for approval—and thus pointed toward a career in democratic politics.[6]

By the time of his graduation in 1904, Roosevelt had become engaged to Eleanor Roosevelt, a very distant cousin whom he had known socially since childhood and had begun seeing more frequently several years earlier. Eleanor, whose own childhood had been as difficult as Franklin's had been idyllic, was serious, intelligent, and uncommonly mature; many Roosevelt biographers have concluded that Franklin saw qualities in her which he feared were lacking in himself. Marriage to Eleanor also gave Franklin direct access to the man who had become his hero: Theodore Roosevelt, whose late, troubled younger brother was Eleanor's father and whose meteoric career had culminated during Franklin's first year at Harvard when McKinley's death made him president. Franklin and Eleanor were married in March 1905 in an East 76th Street town house, their wedding date arranged so that the president, who was in town to review the St. Patrick's Day Parade, could give the bride away.[7]

Roosevelt had by then entered law school at Columbia University, where he would spend three years as an indifferent student before passing the bar in the spring of his third year and leaving without completing the requirements for a degree. He found a job as a clerk at the Wall Street corporate law firm of Carter, Ledyard & Milburn, where he would remain until 1910. This six-year interlude in New York City provided Roosevelt his first sustained encounters with big-city life. As a child, Roosevelt had experienced New York as a place of "parks, museums, and department stores"—yet even this attractive version of the late nineteenth-century city had not always appealed to him. "Can't you arrange to go to Hyde Park before Sunday?" he wrote his parents at the end of one term at Groton. "The less I have of N.Y. the better." As he had grown to adulthood, his deep joy in nature had developed into a belief, common among people of his background, that country living was a morally superior way of life—that it bred vitality, self-reliance, and spiritual balance. Cities, conversely, were but "a perhaps necessary nuisance." As a student at Groton, he had been involved with a group that hosted a summer camp in the country for the youth of New York and Boston. "Many boys from wretched homes arrive with pale faces looking worn, dirty, and old," the camp committee's officers claimed, "and go back after a fortnight completely transformed in appearance, and furthermore with a new idea of the possibilities of cleanliness, decency, and civilization."

Life in New York did not exactly challenge these squierarchical beliefs—indeed, they were to remain a core element of Roosevelt's social and moral thinking for many years—but it did engage him much more deeply in those aspects of city life his cosseted childhood had not permitted him to see firsthand. Here Eleanor Roosevelt played a particularly important role. She, unlike Franklin, had long been acutely aware of city people and how they lived. When she was five or six years old, she later recalled, her father had taken her to serve Thanksgiving dinner at a newsboys' clubhouse. "I was tremendously interested," she later wrote, "in all those ragged little boys and in the fact . . . that many of them had no homes and lived in little wooden shanties and in empty lots, or slept in vestibules of houses or public buildings." As a young woman she volunteered as a dance and calisthenics teacher at the Rivington Street Settlement House; shortly, her work as an investigator for the Consumers' League brought her into contact with sweatshops. Once married and established in New York, Eleanor arranged to have her husband meet her at Rivington Street, as she later told an acquaintance, "because I wanted him to see *how people lived*. . . . And it worked. He saw how people lived, and he *never* forgot." It was with Eleanor that Franklin first walked through the dark hallways of a Lower East Side tenement building. "My gosh," he exclaimed, "I didn't know anyone lived like that!"[8]

In 1910, at twenty-eight, Roosevelt left Carter, Ledyard & Milburn to pursue elective office. He had been contemplating a public career since college; he was now bored with the law, and moreover he had not proven particularly good at it. Like so much else, his party affiliation came to him by inheritance: his father had been a Tilden-Cleveland Democrat, and though he had adopted the Republican Roosevelt as his role model, FDR apparently never considered joining the GOP. A rare Democrat who possessed money, family status, and an upstate residence, political opportunities opened quickly for him. Soon after he made his interest known, he was given the Democratic nomination for state senate in a rock-ribbed Republican district encompassing Dutchess, Putnam, and Columbia counties—a nomination considered by the party to be of little value and typically bestowed on a wealthy aspirant who could carry a large share of the campaign expenses. Though there appeared to be little chance of victory, Roosevelt accepted. He hired an automobile—a red Maxwell capable of making twenty-two miles per hour at top speed—and toured across the district assailing "boss control" and advocating economy in government. Profiting from a national Democratic tide and the strains that had resulted from Theodore Roosevelt's effort to win control of the state Republican Party, he was elected with 52 percent of the vote.[9]

Roosevelt was to remain in Albany until 1913, when he would accept an offer to join the Wilson administration as assistant secretary of the Navy. During that time, he worked on behalf of agricultural legislation, environmental conservation (which became a life-long passion), and, somewhat belatedly, social insurance and other labor measures such as workmen's compensation and maximum work hours for women and children. But much of the attention

Roosevelt garnered during those years resulted from his confronta-
tions with the political bosses of New York City—men whose successors would become La Guardia's primary political antagonists.

The origins of the downstate machines ran back deep into the
nineteenth century, to the neighborhood- and ward-based political
clubs, tunnel gangs, and rings of the Antebellum Era, relatively small
and discreet organizations whose members were bound together by
"parochial loyalties and individual payoffs." Beginning in the late
1880s, the clubs had begun building permanent clubhouses; soon
they joined together to form a confederation: Tammany Hall. By
the early twentieth century, the modern political machine was fully
developed. Personal loyalties remained important within clubs, but,
as the political scientist Martin Shefter has detailed, devotion to the
party itself was now the force that held the organization together.
As the organization had matured, it had grown less dependent on
its candidates' independent standing and popularity; increasingly,
it elevated talented and loyal members from within its own ranks.
In each of the five boroughs, the assembly district leaders collectively made up the executive committee of the county organization; they elected a county chairman, usually a district leader. The
county chairmen decided nominations for public office and were
typically consulted on important governmental decisions. In theory,
the five county organizations that made up the Democratic Party in
New York City—New York, Kings, Queens, the Bronx, and Staten
Island—were independent and autonomous. But in fact, because of
tradition, population, superior resources, and a strategic alliance
arranged between New York County chairman Charles Francis
Murphy and his Kings County counterpart John H. McCooey, the
New York County organization—known colloquially as "Tammany
Hall"—ruled the roost.

The city machines had not traditionally exercised much power
in state affairs. But New York City's growth in relation to the state

population, the Democratic Party's reemergence as a competitor for state power in the early twentieth century, and a canny system of alliances with upstate urban Democrats had made it possible for the downstate leaders to exercise power in Albany. Charles F. Murphy, the shrewd Gashouse District saloonkeeper who assumed leadership of the New York County organization in 1902, became, one observer wrote, "the first Tammany chief who dared aspire above the Bronx." With the emergence of Murphy and Tammany Hall as major players in state politics, "boss control" became an issue no upstate Democrat could avoid.[10]

Roosevelt knew the Democratic Party could never succeed upstate if it was viewed as a mere extension of the city machines. Anti-Tammany sentiment—feeding on ethnic and cultural divisions as well as the real abuses of the political machines, and stoked by a strident anti-Tammany press both in New York City and upstate—was powerful in his district. He was also predisposed to New York City's anti-Tammany, independent Democrats—men whose social, educational, and professional backgrounds tended to be more like his own. He had made anti-bossism the primary note of his state senate campaign. "I accept the nomination with absolute independence," he had proclaimed. "I am pledged to no man; I am influenced by no specific interests; and so I shall remain." He even went so far as to denounce Charles Francis Murphy by name.[11]

When the state legislature convened in January 1911, it took as its first order of business the selection of a U.S. senator. (The ratification of the Seventeenth Amendment was still several years off.) With the Democrats in the majority, Murphy chose William F. ("Blue-eyed Billy") Sheehan, a former Buffalo party boss who had moved to New York City and amassed a fortune as a director of utilities corporations, and who had contributed generously to the party that year. Roosevelt and other anti-machine Democrats instead supported the Brooklyn corporate lawyer Edward M. Shepard, who was active in

New York City's good-government groups and whom Roosevelt considered "without question the most competent to fill the position."
Insisting that the Democratic Party was "on trial" with the upstate
voters upon whom the state party's majority status depended, and
could not "afford to surrender its control to the organization in New
York City," Roosevelt joined a group of insurgent Democrats who
refused to caucus with the party until Murphy withdrew Sheehan's
name and presented another, more acceptable candidate.

The contest dragged on for weeks, with Roosevelt serving as the
group's informal "presiding officer" and spokesman (partly because
his wealth had allowed him to rent a spacious house near the Capitol, which became the group's meeting place). The matter was
finally settled when Murphy and the upstate insurgents agreed on
a compromise candidate: New York State Supreme Court Justice
James A. O'Gorman, a Tammany sachem who possessed a strong
judicial record. O'Gorman was, if anything, more satisfactory to
Murphy than Sheehan would have been; but the result was ambigu-
ous enough that Roosevelt could declare victory in his district. The
"Blue-eyed Billy Sheehan affair" immediately made Roosevelt a well-
known figure in New York State politics, and it helped him appeal
to independent and Republican constituents in his district. It also
earned him a reputation outside the state as a fighter for clean government. Over time, it became part of the Roosevelt mythos that
the young senator had begun his career by staring down the greatest
boss of America's most notorious political machine and forcing an
acceptable compromise.[12]

By the end of his two-year term in Albany, Roosevelt had earned
the full enmity of the New York City delegation and the party leaders
who had sponsored them. Some came to believe his opposition to
Sheehan and to organization politics more broadly was motivated
by the anti-Irish, anti-Catholic prejudice common to his class. Some
viewed Roosevelt (as the biographer Geoffrey C. Ward has writ-

ten) as an "impractical 'damn fool,' a showy snob who could not be trusted, who talked too much and did too little, and was unwilling to work hard enough for the success he so nakedly craved." Even State Senator Robert F. Wagner, later Roosevelt's great ally in the U.S. Senate, noted with exasperation that the glamorous young man seemed more interested in newspaper headlines than governance.[13]

For a while, Roosevelt had little more use for the downstate machines than they had for him. In 1912, the young reformer gave his enthusiastic support to New Jersey governor Woodrow Wilson, a reform Democrat, for the party's presidential nomination; Tammany backed the more conservative Speaker of the House, Champ Clark of Missouri. When Wilson rewarded him with an appointment as assistant secretary of the Navy, a position with control of substantial federal patronage, Roosevelt sought to use this power to build up an anti-Tammany reform Democracy in upstate New York. In 1914, he launched a quixotic bid for an open U.S. Senate seat. Murphy cannily neutralized Roosevelt's association with the Wilson administration by naming Wilson's widely respected ambassador to Germany, the loyal Tammanyite James W. Gerard, as the organization's candidate, and Roosevelt lost the primary contest by nearly three to one.

More than anything else, this humiliating defeat—the only real electoral loss he would ever suffer—convinced Roosevelt that his political future depended on reaching a modus vivendi with Tammany Hall. Tammany and the Brooklyn organization were simply too powerful within the party to be circumvented with any regularity. It was a course made easier by the rise of a talented group of young machine-bred legislators—Murphy called them his "fair-haired boys"—who were passing a torrent of reform measures in Albany: ratification of the federal income tax amendment, the creation of public utilities commissions, direct election of U.S. senators and direct primaries, workmen's compensation, widows' pensions, and, in the wake of the Triangle Shirtwaist Company fire, a host of labor and factory safety regulations. After the 1914 primary, Roosevelt ceased his patronage war with Tammany and began delivering jobs at the Brooklyn Navy Yard to the machine. He halted his denunciations of Murphy, and in 1917 he accepted an invitation to address Tammany's Independence Day celebration, at which he was seen chatting with Murphy on the dais and was photographed with the Tammany sachems in full ceremonial regalia.[14]

While Roosevelt's service in the Navy Department raised his national profile, his cease-fire with Tammany Hall opened new political possibilities in New York. In 1918, several downstate Democrats floated his name for the gubernatorial nomination; Thomas J. ("The") McManus, for twenty-five years the "absolute political ruler" of Hell's Kitchen, was said to have pronounced Roosevelt a "corking good man" for the nomination. Roosevelt took himself out of consideration because he did not wish to leave the Navy Department during the war unless it was for active duty, and the downstate Democrats chose one of their own, Al Smith, who would go on to win the general election in an upset victory. Two years later, Roosevelt emerged during the Democratic National Convention as a contender for the vice-presidential nomination. Associated with Wilson but acceptable to a wide range of Democratic factions, possessed of the most famous name in American politics, he had advantages that counterbalanced his youth and relative lack of national recognition. The party's presidential nominee, Ohio governor James M. Cox, supported his bid, and with Murphy's assent, Roosevelt obtained the nomination.[15]

Cox and Roosevelt lost overwhelmingly, but Roosevelt suffered little damage to his prestige and emerged from the campaign with valuable experience, enhanced name recognition, and a national network of contacts with state and local politicians and party leaders. He now returned to a law partnership he had formed earlier that year and took a second job as the vice president of a Baltimore-based surety bonding firm, the Fidelity & Deposit, running the company's New York office and building its relations with state and local politicians. He professed a desire to make some money to support his ever-growing family, but in truth he was biding his time, intending to reenter politics at the next advantageous moment. The Republican landslide that had returned him to private life had also swept Governor Smith from office; Roosevelt assumed that the party would draw from this outcome the lesson that it could not win statewide on the strength of the New York City vote alone and would nominate an upstate figure in 1922. Both this assumption and the premise underpinning it would prove incorrect, but Roosevelt was not unrealistic in believing in the fall of 1920 that he would be the next Democratic nominee for governor of New York.

Then, in August 1921, several days after joining his family at their summer house on the Canadian island of Campobello, Roosevelt was suddenly struck by a strange and intense exhaustion. Within a few days he was running a high fever, had lost the use of many muscle groups, and was so acutely sensitive that visitors had to be careful not to touch his bedsheets lest they cause him excruciating pain. As the days passed, the fever abated; eventually he regained the use of all but his lower extremities. After several misdiagnoses, the disease was identified as poliomyelitis. Whatever mental and emotional anguish he might have felt, Roosevelt was upbeat in the presence of his family, visitors, and physicians. "He is very cheerful and hopeful," one of the doctors wrote, "and has made up his mind that he is going to go out of the hospital in the course of two or three weeks on crutches." In fact, he would never walk again—though, through a series of artifices, he would manage to hide his paralysis from much of the public.

Roosevelt's contemporaries, and his biographers, have offered many assessments of how this personal crisis shaped his character. Those who knew Roosevelt have often suggested that the experience

gave him a greater capacity for compassion and empathy, transforming an attractive but somewhat supercilious young man into a person
of much greater depth. The New York labor reformer Frances Perkins, who had thought the young Roosevelt haughty and arrogant,
believed the man who reemerged in the late 1920s had been purged
of these qualities. She believed, too, that the ordeal had deepened
Roosevelt's faith in a providential God, giving him a sense of inner
conviction during trying times. Historians and biographers have
emphasized the ways in which Roosevelt adapted his character and
personality to compensate for his physical disability. FDR developed "a talent for denial, a kind of forcefully willed optimism that
refused to dwell on life's difficulties," the historian David Kennedy
has written: this quality sometimes manifested itself in duplicity or
self-delusion, but at other times it "endowed him with an aura of radiant indomitability."[16]

Roosevelt was discharged from the hospital in November 1921. At
the insistence of Eleanor, who understood the mental and emotional
challenges her husband's condition would present, he began his convalescence not at Hyde Park (as his mother wished) but at the family's
East 65th Street town house—where, she believed, he would feel less
isolated from the life he had lived before the attack. By the following
spring he had returned to full health, above the waist. He plunged
into a demanding regimen of physical therapy, and within two years
of the attack he had regained as much usage of his legs and hips as he
would ever possess. For much of the 1920s he would devote himself
to one course of treatment after another—"massage, saltwater baths,
ultraviolet light, electrical currents. . . ." But as a practical matter, the
physical challenge Roosevelt faced after 1923 was essentially one of
deception. In time he learned to feign walking, to manage his entry
to buildings and his approach to stages, to control the dissemination
of images—all to conceal the extent of his handicap.

Though he went to extraordinary lengths to hide the fact, Roosevelt almost certainly dealt with bouts of depression, of anguish and hopelessness and despair for his condition and the life it had cost him. These, too, he learned to overcome, exercising a remarkable mental discipline, a kind of willful self-deception. He continued to believe he would walk again long after his physicians had told him it was all but certain he would not. And despite the fact that there was no precedent whatsoever in the American experience of so severely handicapped a man holding high public office, he refused to accept that his political career had come to an early end.[17]

II

In the 1920s, amidst a national debate on immigration policy, one national magazine condemned New York as an "alien city": even Gotham's congressional representatives, it opined, were not "real Americans." In response, the New York World, a voice for cosmopolitanism in the decade's culture wars, solicited from each member of the city's congressional delegation a family genealogy. Representative Fiorello La Guardia of East Harlem, the only Italian American in Congress and a well-known opponent of immigration restriction and the doctrines of "Nordic" supremacy that justified it, wrote only to offer his regrets: "I have no family tree. The only member of my family who has is my dog Yank. He is the son of Doughboy, who was the son of Siegfried, who was the son of Tannhäuser, who was the son of Wotan. A distinguished family tree, to be sure—but after all, he's only a son of a bitch."

This was the La Guardia of the twenties: iconoclastic, irreverent, quirky (Wagnerian dog names!), spectacular, vulgar, and pitiless in his denunciations of the decade's self-delusions and facile pieties. But the wisecrack was deceptively revealing. Years later, forced by the conventions of autobiography to discuss his family's history, he was only a little more forthcoming. His parents, he noted, were immigrants who passed through Castle Garden, the New York State immigration facility at the foot of Manhattan (soon to be superceded by Ellis Island) some three or four years before he was born. His mother, Irene, was from Trieste. His father, Achille, was a musician from Foggia. From what he learned later, their apartment in Greenwich Village, his birthplace, was modest but comfortable. As for himself, "I have a birth certificate to prove my birth in New York City on December 11, 1882. That should take care of that." A few years before he began work on the autobiography, he had confessed to a distant relative who wrote seeking information on Achille that he knew next to nothing.

If La Guardia's lack of interest in his family's history stood in sharp contrast to Roosevelt's detailed knowledge of his own lineage, this was suggestive of deeper differences. La Guardia was raised, and would live his adult life, on the margins of many different cultures: he was "half Jewish and half Italian, born in Greenwich Village but raised in Arizona, married first to a Catholic and then to a Lutheran, but himself a Mason and an Episcopalian." He did not possess the lattice of expectations that all but determined Roosevelt's first twenty-one years and that was available to guide him even after he started to transcend it. Born and raised between cultures on the edge of the American empire, an outsider on practically every level, La Guardia was, from the first, his own man.[18]

By the time Fiorello was born, Achille La Guardia was having trouble finding regular work. Rather than seek employment outside his profession, he enlisted in the Army and became a bandleader. The family left New York when Fiorello was three years old; they moved first to the Dakota Territory, then to Sackets Harbor, New York, then to Fort Huachuca in southern Arizona, and finally to Whipple Barracks near Prescott, Arizona. "All my boyhood memories," La Guardia later wrote, "are of those Arizona days."

Teachers remembered Fiorello—the name in English meant "little flower"—as headstrong, bright, precocious, and demanding. "He was not only stubborn about having his say, but he also knew what he was talking about. Everything interested him." "He was phenomenal," another teacher said, "a joy and a problem." Hot-tempered and acutely sensitive about his height—he would grow to only a little over five feet—he was quick to brawl and, as a classmate recalled, persisted long after most boys would have accepted defeat.

If Roosevelt was raised to believe that his estate entailed a certain civic custodianship, La Guardia exhibited an almost innate interest in public affairs. On school days, according to a teacher, he would "bolt his food" at lunchtime and "dash to the courthouse to listen to cases." He devoured the editorials and exposés of the *New York Sunday World*, which he bought at the drugstore when it arrived in Prescott the following Friday or Saturday. He later wrote that he received his "political education" from Joseph Pulitzer's crusading paper, and it was through the *World*'s coverage of the Lexow Committee's investigation of corruption in the New York Police Department that he first learned of Tammany Hall.

He also displayed an acute sensitivity to injustice, and his recollections of his childhood are filled with early exposures to exploitation, corruption, and discrimination. One passage from his autobiography recounts the experience of observing the progress of the Union Pacific Railroad as it was extended through Prescott to Phoenix: "The laborers were all immigrants, mostly Mexicans and Italians. If a laborer was injured, he lost his job. If he was killed, no one was notified, because there was no record of his name, address, or family. . . . As construction moved on, it left in its wake the injured, the jobless, and the stranded victims." Another recalls the poverty of the Native Americans who lived adjacent to him and the government corruption responsible for it. "I knew, even as a child, that the government in Washington provided food for all those Indians but that

'politicians' [Office of Indian Affairs patronage appointees] sold the
rations to miners and even to general stores, robbing the Indians of
the food the government provided for them."

"La Guardia," one perceptive New York City official later wrote,
"is understood most clearly if he is looked at as a Westerner." And
in fact, La Guardia's Arizona upbringing would continue to shape
his outlook even after he made himself into a leader and symbol of
America's greatest and most cosmopolitan city. A prospecting town,
trading outpost, and former territorial capital, Prescott remained a
primitive place during the years of La Guardia's upbringing: one of
Fiorello's grade school classmates recalled that life there consisted
of "school, a few chores, a little play, light the kerosene lamp, a little homework, and bed." But the Little Flower remembered it as a
child's paradise, "the greatest, the most comfortable and the most
wonderful city in the whole world," and many of his ideas of what
constituted a "proper American standard of living," a concept that
would be central to his politics throughout his career, were grounded
in the spacious housing and bounteous diet he had enjoyed as the
child of a middle-class Army family on this western outpost. His
western upbringing also bred in him a fierce sense of American identity which made it relatively easy for him to transcend both the paro-
chialism that existed in New York City and the boundary between
urban and national politics. In later years he often identified as an
Arizonan, and he took to wearing a talismanic black Stetson hat to
recall his southwestern roots.

In 1898, when the U.S. Congress declared war on Spain, Achille's
infantry unit was sent to Mobile, Alabama, for training, and then to
Tampa, Florida, where they were to embark for Cuba. While awaiting orders Achille fell ill from malaria, his condition complicated
by consuming "embalmed beef"—diseased meat that government
contractors had covered with spices and chemicals and sold to the
military. Discharged due to his illness, he moved the family to New

York City, but finding only manual work there (for which he was both too frail and too proud), he relocated the family again, this time to Trieste, where he built a profitable hotel business before dying of heart disease in 1904. Though the diseased meat represented only one cause of Achille's poor health, Fiorello always believed his father had died "because of crooked Army contractors"; the loss reinforced his already strong contempt for corruption and the corrupt, for profiteers, cheats, and chiselers. "That experience," he wrote tersely, "never left my mind."[19]

Through a friend of his father's, Fiorello, now eighteen, found a job as a clerk in the American consulate at Budapest. He remained in the Consular Service for over five years, first in Budapest, and then as the consular agent in Fiume, a semi-autonomous port city then under Austro-Hungarian jurisdiction. His official tasks involved certifying shipping invoices and overseeing the inspection of emigrants for infectious diseases. He spent his free time living rakishly and enjoying the sights and sounds of this cosmopolitan corner of Europe. His period in Fiume allowed him to cultivate his talent for languages: by the time he returned to America, he had a passable knowledge of Italian, Yiddish, French, Croatian, Hungarian, and German (the last, he later quipped to the German American publisher Victor Ridder, acquired as a result of his occasional proximity to houses of ill repute).

The Fiume years were among the happiest of La Guardia's life. But he soon grew anxious for promotion. In April 1904, he wrote the State Department requesting that Fiume be made a full consulate and he a consul. When this request was denied, La Guardia responded by asking to be made consul general in Belgrade, was turned down again, and decided (as he wrote the State Department) that "the service [was] not the place for a young man to work up." Later, he was more reflective: "There was a danger of becoming self-satisfied, not too industrious, and of acquiring too much of a

taste for idle social life." He told his mother, who pleaded with him
to stay in Europe, that he was going back to America to become a
lawyer and to "make something of [him]self." He sailed for New York
aboard a British ship, serving as an interpreter and assisting with
vaccinations to pay for his passage.[20]

After a short stay in Ohio, La Guardia moved to New York. Now
twenty-four years old, he had arrived without family or friends in
the city that was to become his adopted hometown. "Though he
was born on the lower East Side," an associate of La Guardia's wrote
shortly after his death, "he seemed to me to love New York as do
others who come here pursuing careers—as a prize, precious and
wonderful." He embraced the energy and diversity of the turn-of-the-
century city, and his tirelessness, stubbornness, and wits enabled
him to take advantage of the opportunities it offered. After taking
several short-term jobs, he acquired a high school equivalency certificate and enrolled in evening classes at the New York University
Law School in the fall of 1907. To support himself, he joined the Civil
Service as an Ellis Island interpreter. For two years, he took the 8:40
am ferry to work and returned at 5:30 pm, then took the IRT uptown
in time for a rushed dinner and a bit of studying before class.[21]

La Guardia received his LL.B. in June 1910 and passed the bar
that fall. He rented a small office on William Street, filled it with a
couple of pieces of used furniture and a six-inch bust of Napoleon,
and began taking deportation cases referred to him by his old Ellis
Island coworkers. Before long he was doing sundry legal work for
destitute East Siders who found their way to his office. He was, from
the beginning, more interested in building a political career than a
legal one. In 1913 he opened an office at 13th and Third with an Italian-born lawyer named Raimondo Canudo; a year later he opened
an office with two Jewish partners—Weil, La Guardia & Espen. Both
practices specialized in immigrant business, and it was through this
work that La Guardia had his first sustained encounters with life in

working-class immigrant communities. In 1914, while with Weil, La Guardia & Espen, La Guardia was assigned a secretary named Marie Fisher; she would work with him until 1929, when the Little Flower, then a widower, would ask her to marry him.

It was Canudo, a Sicilian immigrant, who served as La Guardia's point of entry into Italian New York, introducing him to a group of Italian-born intellectuals and artists that included the sculptor Attilio Piccirilli, the sculptor-poet-editor Onorio Ruotolo, the poet Antonio Calitri, the flutist Giovanni Fabrizio, and the brothers Giuseppe and August Bellanca. Though more radical in their politics than he, this circle adopted La Guardia's aspirations as their own, placing copies of his speeches in the Italian-language newspapers and taking him to meet the leaders of Italian fraternal and benevolent associations.

It was August Bellanca, an organizer in the men's clothing industry, who pulled La Guardia into the needle trades union movement. When the men's clothing workers went out on strike in late 1912 for higher wages and shorter hours, Bellanca enlisted La Guardia to defend picket cases in court and help thwart efforts to play Italian workers off against their Jewish counterparts. La Guardia took to walking the picket lines and addressed hundreds of meetings (making his first real public speeches); he was included in strategy meetings, and he served on the workers' negotiating committee. His participation, he wrote, "won me many friends and supporters in both Italian and Jewish labor circles," including many of the talented young organizers who would become leading figures in the Amalgamated Clothing Workers of America, which developed out of the strike and would, in time, become a powerful force in the city's politics. And in working closely with the garment unionists and Yiddish socialists of the Lower East Side, he learned to speak the political idiom of the city's largest ethnic community. It was on the picket lines in 1913 that he first met Thea Almerigotti, a Trieste-born dress designer more than a decade La Guardia's junior; they began dating in 1915 and were married in March 1919 in a Catholic ceremony in the rectory of St. Patrick's Cathedral.[22]

Even as he established himself among the city's immigrant communities, La Guardia worked to build his political career through more traditional means. Soon after he passed the bar, he joined the Madison Square Republican Club of Manhattan's 25th Assembly District, which covered a large area in the middle of Manhattan stretching north from Washington Square to 28th Street. Like Roosevelt's, La Guardia's choice of party bucked the sociological norm; insofar as they became involved in party politics, most "new ethnic" New Yorkers joined the Democratic Party. But to La Guardia, already averse to Tammany Hall, the GOP "seemed the only avenue I could choose at the time in order to carry out my boyhood dreams of going to work against corrupt government." Other factors may also have encouraged him to join the Republican Party. The GOP was the party of Robert Marion La Follette and Theodore Roosevelt, men La Guardia admired; it was also the party of choice for most upwardly aspirant Protestants, of which La Guardia was one. Perhaps he calculated, too, that he could advance more quickly in the Republican Party, for Tammany Hall, dominated by Irishmen, had not yet demonstrated a willingness to run Italian American candidates. As for the Socialist Party, then an ascendant force in the city's politics and a fount of policy ideas La Guardia would soon begin to draw upon, he would not come to know its most attractive figures until several years later, during the garment strike of 1913. More important; he wished to win public office, something he must have realized would be much more difficult as a Socialist than as a Republican.

"In his early days," recalled Frederick Tanner, the leader of the 25th Assembly District at the time La Guardia joined the Madison Square Club, the Little Flower "was one of the most thorough-going organization men that I have ever known." He served the Madison Square Republican Club, then in the hands of a group of young Ivy

League graduates, as a clubhouse lawyer, on call day and night to go to the Jefferson Market police court and lend his services to whatever unfortunate person had petitioned the GOP leaders for help. He was assigned as a lieutenant to a precinct captain who "boasted that he knew by sight and name every voter in the district." In 1912, he declined to bolt the Republican organization to join Theodore Roosevelt's Bull Moose campaign. The following year, when anti-Tammany forces coalesced to form a fusion ticket with the independent Democrat John Purroy Mitchel at the head, La Guardia refused to work for it, protesting that the nomination of a Democrat for mayor would hurt the Republican Party going into the 1914 elections. Mitchel would win that election and serve a single term, the last anti-Tammany mayor until La Guardia's own election in 1933.

"Somehow," La Guardia later wrote, "I did not know how—I had a feeling that somehow I would get into Congress." It was his great ambition to serve on Capitol Hill; by his own account he had subscribed to the *Congressional Record* upon arriving in New York, and he "kept abreast of activities in Congress," familiarizing himself with the legislation of the period in the hope that he could soon participate in the legislative game. "I kept my eyes open," he wrote, "but I felt that my chances in New York City were very slight. The Republican districts had their Congressmen, but it required a great deal more political influence than I had [at that time] to obtain a nomination in one of those districts, where nomination meant almost certain election. It was hard to break down the Democratic majorities in [the staunchly Democratic] districts. For a time I thought I might go West to a younger state, where the chances were better."

Like many ambitious young politicians at the margins of party power, La Guardia got his opportunity as a result of redistricting. In advance of the 1914 midterm elections, the downtown congressional districts, previously divided along the avenues, were redrawn as horizontal segments running river to river. The effect was to make what

had been relatively homogeneous districts into unusually diverse
ones. The new district in which La Guardia would run, the 14th
Congressional District (which stretched from 14th Street to Third
Street), contained Irish dockworkers, East Side garment workers and
socialists, Italians, Greenwich Village bohemians, and the wealthy
old-stock population around Washington Square. A Republican candidate could win by combining the votes of the affluent Washington
Square crowd with those of new ethnics and a respectable share of
the West Side Irish, but the nomination was not so obviously valuable as to be conferred on someone higher up in the Republican
Party pecking order. When La Guardia asked for the nomination, the
Republican leaders gave it to him, agreeing that he was the logical
candidate to run in the new district.

La Guardia waged a ferocious campaign; he did not win, but he
cut the Democratic margin to nearly a tenth of what it usually was
in a downtown congressional election. The state chairman recognized La Guardia's showing with an appointment as deputy attorney
general of the state of New York. La Guardia himself immediately
began to prepare for 1916. "There was not a meeting of five or ten
people in that congressional district that Fiorello and I didn't attend
for two solid years," one of his lieutenants later remarked. In 1916,
the party leaders renominated him. This time La Guardia was aided
by Irish and German dissatisfaction with Wilson's foreign policy
and a high turnout in the Republican precincts around Washington
Square (produced by the presidential candidacy of the popular former governor, Charles Evans Hughes). La Guardia and his volunteers
worked the district indefatigably, got up early on election day and
plied the boardinghouses with coffee and doughnuts, and enlisted
"school teachers, doctors, business men, longshoremen, and some
tough guys" to watch the polls. It was four in the morning before La
Guardia learned he had been elected to Congress by a slim margin of
357 ballots out of 18,670 cast.[23]

La Guardia served in the U.S. Congress from April 1917 until July 1917, when he left to join the military; he returned for the opening of the 66th Congress in May 1919 and remained until September 1919, when the Republican Party leaders in New York called him home to run for president of the city's Board of Aldermen. During his time in Congress he possessed little power and he did not occupy a distinctive position within the House. But some of his concerns and ideological commitments were already evident. La Guardia opposed the Espionage Act, which he considered "un-American and vicious," and the most powerful floor speeches of his first term were committed to the futile objective of killing it. He opposed Prohibition. He sought to safeguard the federal Treasury from the "profiteers buzzing around the capital" before and after the war.

And he displayed an acute interest in the standard of living. A little over two months before he took office, soaring food prices (a product of the curtailment of European agricultural production and wartime dislocations) had touched off protests in working-class neighborhoods across the city, including just south of La Guardia's own district. Immigrant housewives had overturned pushcarts, set fire to produce, implemented and enforced boycotts of highly priced items, and, eventually, marched to City Hall to demand a positive response from Mayor Mitchel. As the historian Dana Frank has suggested, these "food riots" were, in their essence, not a protest against imminent starvation, as was widely supposed, but rather a defense of the protesters' existing "American" standard of living. "We don't want oleomargarine," a cloakmaker's wife remarked. "I could buy butter once on my husband's wages—I don't see why I shouldn't have the same today." La Guardia, who made a "considerable and personal investigation" of the protests, seemed to understand what the women were after: a "proper American standard of living," he suggested, was a right of citizenship, and the working-class women of New York were justified in protesting the decline of their purchasing power amidst the war boom of 1917. Rising popular expectations struck him as one of the great democratic achievements of the age. "The trouble of the present," he suggested a few years later, explaining popular dissatisfaction with postwar politics, "lies in the fact that the average citizen believes that the inherent right of life, liberty and happiness includes something more than a bite to eat and a place to sleep in. It means a chance to play, a chance to educate himself and a chance to be happy."[24]

La Guardia took his seat on April 2, 1917, the first day of the special opening session of the 65th Congress, and had been a member for only a matter of hours when Woodrow Wilson asked Congress to declare war on Germany. Though a very sizable number of his constituents opposed American entry into the war, La Guardia voted in favor. The United States must take "a man's part in this war," he remarked. To this kind of machismo and bellicosity, he coupled a positive Wilsonian vision: the war had already "accomplished much good," he said, by bringing "liberty to Russia," and its successful prosecution might do the same for central Europe.[25]

During the floor debate on the Selective Service Act, when an anti-conscription member asked "how many members of the House who were going to send boys to war would go themselves," he, along with four colleagues, stood up. By midsummer, with the most important war and mobilization votes cast, La Guardia volunteered for service. Turned down by the National Guard on account of his height, he made his way to the aviation division of the Signal Corps. By September, already promoted to captain, he had taken temporary leave from Congress, had arranged to have a Republican colleague attend to constituent requests and his secretary Marie Fisher to his correspondence, and was on his way to Europe. For about twelve months he served as an administrator of the pilot training facility at Foggia, his father's hometown south of Rome; he also participated in bombing runs and did some flying of his own. By 1918, he had become a go-between for Italian cabinet ministers and military officials and their American counterparts. After the disaster at Caporetto caused American officials to fear that Italy might withdraw from the Allied effort as Russia had, the U.S. Embassy enlisted the Little Flower to give propaganda and morale speeches in city squares across Italy.

La Guardia had garnered some notice in the press as the first Republican to breach the Tammany citadel of lower Manhattan, but his war service as New York's "flying congressman" raised his public profile to a new level. His newfound stature was sufficient to garner him renomination in 1918 as part of a bipartisan Republican-Democratic slate engineered by Charles F. Murphy as a gesture of wartime unity and a move against the Socialist Party, which had reached its high-water mark in the previous year's mayoral election. La Guardia returned several weeks before the election and subjected his Socialist opponent, the noted economist (and Espionage Act victim) Scott Nearing, to what he called an "anti-yellow, anti-socialistic, anti-German and true blood American campaign." Victorious by an overwhelming margin, he returned to the House when the 66th Congress convened in May 1919. He had barely settled in when, two months later, the New York Republican leaders asked him to run for the presidency of the Board of Aldermen.[26]

III

Roosevelt and La Guardia came of age politically during the period of diverse and in some ways conflicting reform efforts commonly known as the Progressive Era. Neither identified closely with any single movement or faction; La Guardia, in particular, did not come to think of himself as being part of a progressive group or movement until after the First World War. But each absorbed the characteristic assumptions and beliefs of the men and women who led those efforts: that society could be improved through concerted human action; that advances in technology, engineering, and medicine had opened the door to unprecedented social progress; and that it was the task of government to help American society adapt to the new technological age. Each assimilated a robust conception of executive political leadership then in vogue in political theory and seeping into the broader political culture by way of Theodore Roosevelt, Woodrow Wilson, and a handful of progressive governors.[27]

More important, the reform efforts of the Progressive Era shaped the environment within which Roosevelt and La Guardia would eventually work. The reform ferment of the early twentieth century produced significant changes in what government did in urban America; it also reshaped how Americans envisioned the role of government in urban societies and economies. And it produced a toolbox of solutions upon which future policymakers would draw. One reason New Deal urban reform would prove so vibrant was that, at the moment when the federal government vastly expanded the resources available to local officials, a large body of ideas about how to use the power of the local state to improve the quality of urban life was already in circulation, waiting to be put into operation.

One of the most powerful impulses that drove reformers at the turn of the century was an embrace, particularly by a "new middle class" of university-trained and professionally accredited young people, of expert management as a means of achieving organizational efficiency and regularity. Nowhere was this so evident as in the efforts of a new generation of municipal reformers, who sought to improve city government by adapting the practices of private business management and social science to public administration. The "efficiency movement," as its proponents called it, arrived in New York via the Bureau of Municipal Research (BMR), an organization founded in 1906 by a group of young university and doctoral graduates with financial backing from some of the city's most prominent philanthropists. Within a few years the bureau had become practically an adjunct to New York's municipal government and a flagship for a broader movement that took root in many American cities.

The BMR, and the efficiency movement more broadly, had two overarching goals: first, to create a government that delivered, as their slogan had it, one hundred cents of service for every tax dollar collected; and second, to match the activities of government with social needs. Relying heavily on the model of private business, efficiency reformers called for the reorganization of municipal departments to remove redundancies and bottlenecks and alleviate the overloading and underloading of particular divisions; they called, too, for the implementation of business practices such as budget making, accounting, and centralized purchasing and such modern managerial techniques as the timesheet, work routines, service records, and efficiency tests.

But the efficiency movement did not focus solely on administrative reform. Its objective was not merely to spend as few tax dollars as possible for a given level of government output, but also to match that output to the actual needs of the community. Efficiency reformers gloried in data, and their preferred method was that of the investigation. The discovery of facts and the assembling of data, in the efficiency reformers' model of policy making, created social knowledge which revealed an undesirable condition and a sense of what factors contributed to it; experts with specialized training could then create and implement solutions. The typical charts produced by New York's Division of Child Hygiene exemplified this approach: in the left-hand column, they listed the division's activities before an investigation; in the center, the findings of the investigation; in the right-hand column, new activities undertaken in light of those findings.

For all its attention to the dry details of budgeting, work routines, and personnel systems, the efficiency movement seemed to many progressives to represent little short of a revolution in municipal reform politics. In comparison to nineteenth-century municipal reformers, who generally sought to keep government expenditures as low as possible (and not infrequently decried government spending as confiscation of property), the efficiency movement envisioned a more expansive, more positive role for government. In a modern city, its champions believed, community welfare could not be left to the laws of the market and to philanthropy and "scientific charity." "[T]he efficiency movement in cities," the BMR's founders wrote in 1912, "grew out of recognition of the dependence of community welfare upon government activity. It began . . . in an effort to capture the great forces of city government for harnessing the work of social betterment." Whereas nineteenth-century reformers had been suspicious of the urban immigrant masses and at times nakedly anti-democratic, the efficiency reformers, though wary in some ways of public passions, made it their avowed purpose to "make democracy work." Armed with a theory of government that sought to address social problems, they believed their task was to educate tenement dwellers to see that good government was in their own interest. The efficiency movement thus provided a language that enabled municipal reform to move beyond mere emphasis on honesty, economy, and rule by "good men": it provided a program to a new generation of reformers committed to democracy, to scientific progress, and to an expansion of the role of government in urban life.[28]

The efficiency movement's reconceptualization of the role of government dovetailed with the labors of other reformers—settlement house workers, social workers, technical experts, journalists, leaders of charity and philanthropic organizations, social scientists, liberal clergy, city bureaucrats, and others—more immediately concerned with the human costs of thriving market capitalism in the city. These "social reformers," as historians have categorized them, were connected at the broadest level by a common interest in big-city "slums"—the working-class, immigrant districts that had been chronicled so powerfully by the photojournalist Jacob Riis (whose stunning work *How the Other Half Lives* had been published in 1890). Unlike earlier reformers, who had tended to ascribe urban poverty to the habits and morals of immigrant tenement dwellers, the social reformers of the Progressive Era believed poverty was essentially circumstantial; they believed justice and social utility required some amelioration of the oppressive and unhealthy inner-city environment; and although they also worked through non-state institutions (such as the settlement houses), they considered it an obligation of the government to assure that citizens not be deprived of "the ordinary conveniences of living" (as the housing reformer Lawrence Veiller put it). Their technique of choice was "decommodification": because central-city neighborhoods were places where markets had conspicuously failed to produce socially acceptable outcomes, social reformers sought to "hold certain elements out of the market's processes, indeed to roll back those parts of the market whose social costs had proved too high"—either by enlisting state power to regulate private exchanges or by collective provision of particular goods and services by the government itself.

Not a movement in itself, this group of social reformers, tied together through networks of publications, schools, organizational memberships, and personal associations, provided much of the manpower for a series of discrete campaigns for specific projects intended to alleviate the tedium and squalor of the inner city. In New York and elsewhere, social reformers called for more small parks and play areas, for recreational piers, for more effective garbage collection and street cleaning, and for public bathhouses in neighborhoods where tenement apartments did not possess bathing facilities. Settlement house workers pushed responsive professionals within the Health Department to provide the country's first school nurses and to establish eye and dental clinics, health care centers, and milk stations. Housing reformers helped enact a tenement house law that required new residential buildings to meet higher ventilation standards and to provide private toilets and that established a municipal department to conduct inspections.[29]

To the left of the social reform cohort—though there was considerable overlap—was the socialist movement, which reached its peak in New York before and during the First World War. The more doctrinally committed socialists looked askance at the social reformers, who they believed dealt in palliatives: the slum, they believed, was endemic to wage-labor capitalism, and any real effort to raise the quality of life among the working class would necessarily entail broad changes in the basic economic structure. But the non-revolutionary wing of the Socialist Party had a reform program of its own—"immediate demands" intended to strengthen the working class so that it could act as an agent for the democratic realization of a cooperative commonwealth. The party's state and national programs called for reduced working hours and higher wages, the abolition of child labor, and social insurance—workers' compensation, unemployment insurance, and old-age pensions. Its municipal platforms proposed the provision of more parks and playgrounds in congested neighborhoods; the construction of municipal apartment houses and publicly owned terminal markets to reduce the cost of food; municipalization of public utilities (such as electricity and gas); the creation of municipal bakeries, milk depots, and iceworks; free maternity clinics and hospitals; free municipal nurseries; free medical care, food, and clothing for those who could not afford it; "seaside colonies and summer outings for all poor school children"; and "cultivation of the fine arts and dissemination of popular science among the adult workers, through the medium of municipal theatres, free concerts, public reading-rooms, and public lectures."[30]

New York (and other cities) also possessed a distinct political tradition that scholars of city politics have described as "municipal populism": a kind of urban politics whose practitioners spoke the populist language of opposition to powerful "interests"—private utilities corporations, their Wall Street investors, and the political bosses who, it was claimed, did their bidding. Municipal populists were driven by the linked issues of exorbitant monopoly profits, boss rule, and the cost of living; they espoused a program of municipal ownership which aimed both to break the link between boss politics and utility monopolies and to bring down the price of (and improve the quality of) life's necessities—especially "milk, ice, gas, and local transit."

In New York, the leading figure in this movement was the "*enfant terrible* of American journalism," William Randolph Hearst. With his inscrutable mix of demagogy and sincerity, Hearst broke into the New York newspaper market in 1895 and immediately made himself a scourge of the utility companies and their political allies—particularly the "gas trust," against which he waged a continuing war on multiple fronts, and Tammany Hall, which he accused of aiding the private utility corporations. In 1905, he ran for mayor on an independent Municipal Ownership ticket. His campaign galvanized labor unions as well as a group his opponent characterized as "the white-collar proletariat, the clerks, small employees, and small shopkeepers": the "upper strata of the working class," less dependent on the institutions of the Democratic machine and relatively well educated (and hence more easily mobilized by policy proposals presented through the medium of the newspaper, including Hearst's own). Hearst lost narrowly in an election that very likely turned on fraud, but not before his candidacy had publicized new demands and new policy solutions, demonstrating convincingly how a dynamic sector of the electorate could be won over by the means of public policy.[31]

Taken as a whole, the influence of Progressive Era reform upon the trajectory of New York City's politics and government was profound.

These reform efforts had extended the range of the municipal state, endowing it with new legal authorities and institutional capacities. Fiscal practices pushed by the efficiency movement had enabled the city to form a more effective partnership with the financial community, which in turn had made possible a veritable revolution in debt financing and public investment that encompassed everything from water supply to schoolhouses to new subway lines. Housing reformers had won the authority to mandate minimum standards and had secured the creation of a municipal department to enforce them. Public health advocates had built a highly professionalized department and had constructed a chain of child health clinics across the city. Social reformers had claimed public money for small parks and municipal bathhouses. Many other Progressive Era policy ideas had failed of enactment and would remain on the progressive agenda at the time of the New Deal—often having been adopted and further developed in the interim by the city's private philanthropic and charity institutions. They would constitute a valuable legacy of policy ideas, well formed, familiar, and ready should additional resources become available.

But the movements of the Progressive Era also did something more. Collectively, they had begun to reshape how policymakers and citizens thought about the role of government in an urban, liberal society. For all their differences, each of these reform projects sought to inject public considerations into urban societies built of "myriad private decisions," envisioning public action and collective initiative as ways to improve the quality of urban life and the functioning of the city as a whole. In pursuing these objectives, they began to construct an alternative vision to that of "the thoroughly commercial city" of the nineteenth century. Those interested in urban government, the Socialist Morris Hillquit wrote in 1913, were no longer apt to view the municipality as "first of all a business concern, instituted and maintained for the purpose of administering the corporate property of the city" and safeguarding the private property upon which urban commerce depended; they increasingly emphasized "the social functions of the municipality" and proposed to use local government to implement "measures based on the recognition of the social obligation of the community toward the citizens." The reformers of the Progressive Era had begun to carve out a new, more robust role for government in America's urban society.[32]

IV

La Guardia received the Republican leaders' invitation to run for city office with mixed emotions. He would have preferred to remain in Washington, but Thea wished him to return to New York—the young couple, by all accounts deeply happy, wished to start a family—and the party brought sufficient pressure to bear that La Guardia came to believe that he had "no choice in the matter." He won the support of both the good-government community and the Hearst press, and, profiting from the bitterness many ethnic nationalists felt toward Wilson as a result of the Versailles peace settlement—"We must have a Republican election this year," La Guardia told one audience, "to show the whole world that President Wilson is discredited at home"—he prevailed by a paper-thin margin. It was a striking victory for the Republican Party, which had never before won an election in the City of Greater New York without the support of independent Democrats.

The following two years were to be crucial ones in La Guardia's development. As president of the Board of Aldermen, he presided over the city's lower legislative body, which had been stripped by successive reform administrations of much of its power and now dealt mostly in mundane resolutions and local ordinances. But he also held a seat on the Board of Estimate, the city's chief lawmaking body, which had jurisdiction over budgeting and land use decisions; through this work, he came to understand the machinery of municipal government and the ins-and-outs of city politics—how the departments functioned, how the government was financed, and what levers had to be pulled to launch a desired project. He went around "day and night," Marie La Guardia later recalled, with the city charter under his arm; he would work a long day and then travel across the five boroughs at night to address any public meeting that agreed to hear him, gradually making himself known in neighborhoods outside Manhattan.[33]

La Guardia took office at the midpoint of the mayoralty of the Brooklyn Democrat John F. Hylan. Commonly regarded as a rank fool, a stooge for William Randolph Hearst, and a puppet of Charles Francis Murphy (who, to his relief, found that Hylan recognized his obligations to the party organizations far more faithfully than his two Democratic predecessors), Hylan had ridden to office upon the backlash against John Purroy Mitchel's progressive reform program of government-by-experts. Presenting himself as a majoritarian democrat and man of the people who would give no quarter to the privileged interests he believed had captured the city government during the Mitchel years, he vowed to "fill the outgoing trains" with Mitchel's efficiency experts. "We have had all the reform we want in this city for some time to come," he declared.

Yet Hylan himself was a kind of progressive, reflecting especially the municipal populism of his sponsor, Hearst. He became a hero to many working-class people through his outspoken and successful opposition to the pleas of the private corporations that ran New York's subways to adjust the traditional five-cent fare, stipulated in their contracts, in light of postwar inflation. He began construction of the Bronx Terminal Market, a grand project long advocated by socialists and municipal populists, which was intended to reduce the cost of living by improving the infrastructure upon which food distribution in the five boroughs depended. And he threw his support behind a state rent control law to protect tenants amidst a severe postwar housing shortage. Progressives such as Walter Lippmann chided Hylan for pursuing a "dull, suspicious, hysterical and foolish kind of class war"; yet in 1921, the working people of New York reelected him in a landslide. "Anyone who caught the spirit of the crowds on election night knows how the victors interpreted the event," *The New Republic* editorialized. "A great popular victory had been won" by men and women uneasy about their jobs or small businesses, preyed upon by profiteers, trodden upon by the big men in business and politics. . . ."[34]

It was both a demonstration of the complexity of progressive politics in New York and an illustration of precisely where La Guardia's commitments lay at that time that the Little Flower, a reform-minded Republican enamored of science and expertise, frequently aligned with Mayor Hylan, the anti-expert machine Democrat. La Guardia shared Hylan's democratic style; he also shared the mayor's concern about the impact of the postwar inflation on family budgets. La Guardia supported the construction of the Bronx Terminal Market and developed a pilot project of his own that involved the installation of vegetable departments in department stores to be used for direct farmer-to-consumer sales. Feeling his way toward the position that multifamily housing should be regulated as a public utility, he went to Albany to testify in support of rent control. And he joined Hylan in rejecting the private transit operating companies' request to raise the five-cent subway fare. He also supported Hylan's efforts to reinitiate a vigorous public investment program following a period of municipal austerity that had begun with the fiscal crisis of 1914 and lasted through the war, becoming heavily involved in Hylan's scheme to build a massive new port facility in Jamaica Bay.[35]

La Guardia sided with the Democratic mayor so consistently that, nearly a decade later, the good-government Citizens Union remem-

bered him unfavorably as a Hylanite and a Hearstian. Yet the Little
Flower's populist instincts coexisted with a commitment to municipal reform. Temperamentally suited to the role of budgetary watchdog, he garnered headlines by exposing cost overruns on a Tammany
courthouse project; the publicity led to two investigations which
killed the project and ultimately produced sixty-nine indictments. In
1921, prompted by a budget squeeze, La Guardia began preaching the
efficiency gospel. Employing the analogy of private business—"No
business could possibly survive if it were to operate in the same manner that the city government is forced to operate today"—he called
for revision of the city charter to eliminate duplication in bureaus
and departments and permit the removal of unproductive workers.[36]

La Guardia believed he had been promised the 1921 Republican
mayoral nomination as a condition of his leaving Congress—and he
may well have been. But then, in the fall of 1920, the GOP seized
power in New York State. As the party moved to implement its program, tensions developed between its upstate core and its fledgling downstate wing, leaving La Guardia isolated within the party
and turning this staunch organization man into a party insurgent.
Shortly after taking office, Republican governor Nathan Miller—a
man the ever acerbic Robert Moses later described as possessing
"the uncompromising and inflexible honesty, the financial vision,
and the range of sympathies of an upstate comptroller"—proposed
both to repeal the state's direct primary law (and hence to return
control of nominations to party leaders, insulating them from popular passions) and to take the question of New York City's subway
fare "out of politics" by vesting complete authority over transit policy in a three-person commission to be appointed by the governor.
La Guardia considered both proposals anti-democratic—the former
because it impinged on the people's right to choose their own representatives, the latter because it flew in the face of New Yorkers'
evident support for the five-cent fare. He also believed that their

enactment would ruin the Republican Party downstate. He lashed
out at direct-primary repeal and hinted that he would bolt the party
and run for mayor as an independent if it went through. Convinced
that the transit corporations' financial difficulties owed more to mis-
management and excessive dividends than to the low user fee, he
made a speaking campaign in defense of the five-cent fare—even,
brazenly, holding joint rallies with Hylan. He was soon being treated
as an apostate by the party.

Convinced that his preferment within the party was being
blocked by a few powerful corporate interests and their political
henchmen, La Guardia resolved to fight for the party's nomination in
the primary—a major transgression of party discipline. Manhattan
chairman Samuel Koenig, who had a close working relationship with
the upstate party leaders, took La Guardia to lunch to try to talk him
out of it. "Don't do it, Fiorello," he urged. "The town isn't ready for
an Italian mayor. You'll lose and won't be able to make a living." To
which La Guardia replied: "Sam, I'll run. So long as I have five dollars in my pocket I'll be all right, and if I can't earn that, I've always
got my service revolver."

Forced to find votes beyond the party base, La Guardia began to
envision a coalition grounded in independent-minded and underrepresented groups. "Progressives who believe in progress in government
as well as in science and industry will vote for me," the Little Flower
boasted to a newspaperman. "Taxpayers who are overburdened with
their taxes will vote for me. Rent payers who . . . know who their
friends are will vote for me. . . . Women who up to date have been
used to deliver the votes but have not been taken into the confidence
of officials . . . will vote for me." Like many municipal reformers, La
Guardia believed that women—who had been enfranchised only a
few years earlier—held the power to usher in a new era of good government. "Women in politics are the hope of American politics," he
said. "They are either going to break the control of the bosses or put

the political parties out of business." (Throughout his career, La Guardia would remain convinced that women held the key to progressive
municipal government, believing that women were more attuned
to the provision of public goods and services and less likely to view
politics through the lens of partisan loyalty. When his friend Maury
Maverick, a progressive Texas congressman, decided to run for mayor
of San Antonio and wrote La Guardia for advice on how to election-
eer effectively at the municipal level, the Little Flower replied: "Get
the women interested in your campaign. Municipal administration is
nothing but housekeeping and [women's] concern[s]—public health,
clean streets, good policing, good schools, proper marketing systems—[are] all matters which affect the home. Form as many various
groups of women as you can and get them enthusiastic so they will
take an active aggressive part in the campaign.")

It was not to be: in a four-way primary, Manhattan Borough president Henry Curran, the party organization's choice, garnered an
overwhelming 59 percent of the vote; La Guardia followed with 22
percent. Hylan defeated Curran easily in the general election, unit-
ing a working-class vote previously fractured by ethnicity and ideology under the Democratic banner. This local alignment would last
until the Great Depression broke it apart.[37]

These events played out against the background of horrific personal tragedy. In December 1920, La Guardia learned that his wife
and infant daughter—Fioretta, born in June—had contracted tuberculosis. On a doctor's advice, he borrowed money to move them to
progressively more bucolic settings, first to a stucco house on University Avenue in the Bronx, then to Long Island, and finally to a
sanitarium in the Adirondacks. Both continued to deteriorate; by the
time Fioretta died in May 1921, Thea was so sick that Fiorello had to
go to the graveyard alone to bury his little daughter. Thea followed
six months later, on November 29. In the days after Thea's death,
several of La Guardia's close Italian friends moved in with him to

cook and keep him company; one recalled seeing La Guardia, all but broken, walk to where the casket was sitting, "bend over the corpse, kiss her, and then break into the most pitiful sobbing." Two days later, Thea was buried in Woodlawn Cemetery alongside Fioretta.

La Guardia himself had been consigned to the hospital in early October, undergoing an operation to treat a chronic back injury sustained during a crash landing at Fiume. Henry Curran paused his mayoral campaign long enough to visit La Guardia's room at Roosevelt Hospital with an armful of flowers. "Fiorello is game," Curran remarked. "He always had all kinds of grit. . . . He is having more than his share of hardships. We all will be glad when he is back on his feet." La Guardia repaid the favor by campaigning for Curran in the Italian colonies as soon as he was able. "Forget the vendetta!" he demanded of a Brooklyn audience. "If you feel you are helping me by knifing the [Republican] ticket, forget it. You will do me a big favor by voting the Coalition ticket from top to bottom. Don't worry about me, boys. I'll take care of myself when the proper time comes. When I strike, I'll strike hard. . . ." But for now he was defeated. On December 19, with two weeks of his term on the Board of Estimate left to serve, he obeyed the orders of his physician and sailed for Havana with his friend Attilio Piccirilli, the sculptor, not to return until New Year's Day.[38]

V

Once, when he was president, Roosevelt found himself pressed by a young reporter to summarize his "philosophy." Was he a Communist? A capitalist? A Socialist? "Philosophy?" Roosevelt replied. "I am a Christian and a Democrat—that's all." As such a reply suggested, Roosevelt's ideological commitments were capacious, even amorphous. But by the early 1920s he had at least arrived at a characteristic sense of where social problems sprang from and what role government should play in meeting them. Western politics, he believed, had been committed largely to achieving the end goal of "liberty of the individual." And yet "[c]onditions of civilization that come with individual freedom," he argued, were "inevitably bound to bring up many questions that mere individual liberty cannot solve." To progress, he believed, modern societies—characterized above all by the interdependence of "individuals, of businesses, of industries, of towns, of villages, of cities, of states, of nations"—needed to develop new modes of cooperation, ways of constraining individual freedom in the interest of what he called "liberty of the community." He used the example of conservation to illustrate the point: rampant individualism, he noted, produced deforestation, spoliation of the water supply, and exhaustion of natural resources; active conservation measures were thus "necessary to the health and happiness of the whole people of the State."

"The State," to Roosevelt, was simply "the people as a whole": it was an organizational means by which the community could act to pursue its objectives. The proper end of government, he believed, was the "greatest good for the greatest number"—good, in his usage, encompassing preeminently "health and happiness." The "role of government" was not something to be strictly delimited on the basis of relatively immutable principles; rather, the functions of government would change as society developed and new impediments to the health and happiness of the people arose. Roosevelt was not yet especially closely associated with any particular set of policies; during the 1920s, when the Democratic Party was sharply divided, he would sometimes make concerted efforts to avoid becoming so. But already by 1919 he supported an extension of the federal farm loan program inaugurated under Wilson, a more progressive tax code, "guarantees of labor's right to organize," and "the use of public works programs during times of unemployment."[39]

La Guardia, too, had arrived by the early 1920s at certain fundamental beliefs about the nature and purposes of government. Several days after the 1921 elections, the Little Flower encountered Governor Nathan Miller when they were both speakers at the opening of a health center in the tenement neighborhood of East Harlem—a place which was to be, though La Guardia did not yet know it, the seedbed of his political rebirth. Miller, speaking first, suggested in his address that "paternalistic tendencies" were "dangerous to the progress of people. . . . I think it is a very unfortunate thing to the individual," he said, "if he is educated to lean too much upon the State. . . ." When it was his turn to speak, La Guardia practically exploded. "I don't care what the Governor says," he replied. "I am going to try to correct and change these conditions. . . . What an individual may receive from the State or community is only that to which he contributed and part of that which is rightfully his."[40]

The exchange neatly captured La Guardia's fundamental ideas about the role of government as they had evolved through the Progressive Era and the war. People had a right to a certain standard of living, he believed, because they had contributed to the wealth of the community. In exchange for enriching the community through productive labor (then and always, he believed adults had a responsibility to work), men and women had a right to expect a standard of living that reflected the advances made by modern technology and modern forms of organization. Government, in La Guardia's view, was not a special entity whose relation to society and the economy had to be tightly circumscribed, as Miller suggested, but rather an extension of the community, an instrument of social cooperation whose activities would be dictated not by doctrine but by the needs of society and the will of the people.

Like many progressives, La Guardia believed that the integration of professional training and expert knowledge into municipal bureaucracies held the key to the delivery of adequate public services. In the years ahead, once he had fully digested the precepts of the efficiency movement, he would come to view social maladies as a product of the failure of government to keep up with the advances of science and technology. The "science of government," he grew fond of saying, lagged decades behind engineering, medicine, chemistry, and agriculture. But as the battle over the five-cent fare had demonstrated, La Guardia never really believed, as many progressive reformers did, that expertise could displace political contestation by resolving interests and popular passions into a technocratic search for the best policy. A democratic politician to his core, he was acutely attuned to public opinion, and embraced expertise in the belief that to do so would ultimately win him public approval and political advantage.

When it came to specific proposals, La Guardia drew heavily on the prescriptions of Progressive Era social reformers. A few days before he left for Havana, he explained to a reporter what he would do if he could run New York City for a day:

> [F]irst, I would tear out about five square miles of filthy tenements, so that fewer would be infected with tuberculosis like that beautiful girl of mine, my wife, who died—and my baby. . . . Then I would establish "lungs" in crowded neighborhoods—a breathing park here, another there, based on the density of population. . . . Milk stations next. One wherever needed, where pure, cheap milk can be bought for babies. . . . After that the schools! I would keep every child in school, to the eighth grade at least, well-fed and in health. Then we could provide widows [with] pensions and support enough schools for every child in New York on what we saved from reformatories and penal institutions. . . . I would provide more music and beauty for the people, more parks and more light and air and all the things the framers of the constitution [sic] meant . . . when they put in that phrase "life, liberty, and the pursuit of happiness."

In the summer of 1922, La Guardia, then preparing to run for Congress, issued a personal platform, "Proposed Planks for the Republican State Platform." It called for permanent rent control laws; a strong Department of Markets to "check on the quality of food and merchandise sold in the city and post a list of fair prices"; creation of state-owned electric companies; municipal ice and steam works; municipally owned apartment buildings; free school lunches; infant care centers; municipal milk stations; public terminal markets; more parks and playgrounds; more schoolhouses; municipal open-air concerts; and a city music and arts center. It made a proposal, then much in vogue and later to see enactment during the New Deal, that plans for "parks, parkways, municipal farms, stadiums, boulevards, memorials, bridges, tunnels and all works of embellishment and construction . . . be provided for" in advance of recessions, "so as to absorb unemployment" when it occurred. The platform went so heavy on public sector provision that the New York Times asked sardonically why La Guardia had not included municipal ice cream sherbet stands.[41]

This was the first fully recognizable appearance of the La Guardia of the 1930s. He had translated the concept of a proper American standard of living that had guided his actions in Congress into the domain of municipal politics, and he had channeled the democratic impulse evident in his battles with the Republican old guard into a more specific and constructive program. His knowledge of government had grown, and he had developed a far more capacious view of what government could do. But for now his future, like Roosevelt's, was deeply uncertain. On the first day of 1922, he sailed back into New York Harbor, his family gone and his career in tatters.

2

A Season in the Wilderness

On New Year's Day, 1921, La Guardia had been at the midpoint of his short term as president of the Board of Aldermen—a position from which John Purroy Mitchel had launched his campaign for the mayoralty and Al Smith his bid for the governorship. Roosevelt, his political stature lifted by his vice-presidential candidacy, had stood in line for nomination as the Democratic candidate for governor or U.S. senator. Each had been a rising star in his party. Twelve months later, as La Guardia returned to New York, Roosevelt convalesced at his town house on East 65th Street, the worst of his illness behind him but many more uncertain months of recovery ahead.

The 1920s were to be difficult years for those who considered themselves progressives in politics. For Roosevelt and La Guardia, these would be years of frustration and relative powerlessness. But they would also be years of learning and rebuilding. Making effective use of the goodwill of others and taking advantage of the opportunities open to them, both men mustered the resolve and ingenuity to restart their careers. They became mutually admiring acquaintances, but their party affiliations kept them at cross purposes. At the decade's end they would finally encounter each other in the political arena.

I

As he studied the returns on primary night in September 1921, La Guardia could hardly have failed to note which neighborhoods had broken in his favor: Greenwich Village, East Harlem, Bushwick, South Brooklyn, Williamsburg, Tremont. Each possessed large enclaves of Italian immigrants and their children. He already understood that his ancestry represented his single greatest political resource: with 14 percent of the city's population either born in Italy or having one parent born there, "the Italian vote" provided him a personal following and a source of leverage with party leaders (especially given the Democratic Party's stubborn unwillingness to develop Italian candidates of its own). Some of La Guardia's first public acts following Thea's death had consisted of efforts to organize Italian voters: the Kings County League of Italian-American Republican Clubs in Bushwick had made him an honorary president, and within a few months he had helped launch a chapter in the Bronx. He had also begun speaking to Italian American conventions upstate.

The upstate appearances were interpreted as evidence that the Little Flower was planning an independent run for governor in 1922. William Randolph Hearst, still powerful in New York politics, proclaimed La Guardia the "logical" progressive candidate on the Republican ticket and gave him a regular column in the *Evening Journal*. La Guardia, however, had his eye not on Albany but on Washington. His friend and fellow Republican Isaac Siegel had vacated the congressional seat in New York's 20th district, covering East Harlem, in order to accept a judiciary appointment. Manhattan

GOP chairman Samuel Koenig relented and agreed to nominate La Guardia for the open seat.

New York's 20th, which stretched from 99th Street to 120th Street and from Fifth Avenue to the East River, was, like La Guardia's old 14th Congressional District, a polyglot, working-class immigrant neighborhood. One count found twenty-seven different nationality groups in East Harlem, with sizable enclaves of Greeks, Finns, Irish, and Germans. But unlike the 14th, two groups predominated—Eastern European Jews, concentrated in the western part of the district, and Italians, fanning out from the area around Thomas Jefferson Park in the east. By the early 1920s, East Harlem's Jewish population had begun to migrate, primarily to the Bronx; the Italian colony was ascendant, and by the time La Guardia returned to Congress, East Harlem possessed by far the largest "little Italy" in the city.

The Republican politician and community leader Edward Corsi evoked the neighborhood's sights and sounds in a 1925 essay:

> Picturesque markets, tenor-voiced venders, Vesuvio restaurants, candle-shops, statuette dealers, religious and patriotic societies, dark-eyed signorine and buoyant men. . . . We are a community of workers, and our life is proletarian. But we have our cafes, rathskellers, spaghetti houses, cabarets, dancehalls. . . . Yiddish theaters and Italian marionette shows. . . . Were it not for the stifling tenements and the necessity of having to "keep going," we would have great poets, great artists, great musicians.

With as many as 5,000 residents to a single block, East Harlem was second only to the Lower East Side as the densest neighborhood in America. Though primarily a dormitory community, it was pocked with "grimy factories amidst junkyards, warehouses, and repair shops"; the smells wafting from "coal yards and oil depots" and from the untreated sewage flowing into the East River intermixed with the scent of fermenting grapes and fresh tomato sauce produced from windowsill and alleyway gardens with which the daughters and sons of the Mezzogiorno ornamented their homes. A 1929 survey found residents employed as "milkmen, vegetable vendors, street cleaners, truck drivers, dock hands, factory hands, building plumbers, plasterers, stone masons, painters, and auto mechanics," along with a much smaller group of professionals and white-collar workers. Unemployment and seasonal employment were high, income was low, and the housing stock was outdated: as late as 1939, fewer than half the apartments in the district had private bathrooms.[1]

A hotbed of anarchism before the war and a Socialist stronghold during it, East Harlem had a tradition of radical politics. But this was mostly the work of the neighborhood's now-dwindling Jewish population. Notwithstanding a few party organizers and political appointees and a small but lively and dedicated band of immigrant radicals, the Italians, among the major New York ethnic groups, were almost uniquely politically apathetic. "The Italian," Corsi wrote, "prefers loftier pastimes. While the Irishman is organizing the ward and the Jew listens attentively to . . . the soapbox orator on 'Trotsky Square' . . . the Italian is at home, enjoying the rapturous strains of 'O Sole Mio.'" Politics was not ingrained in community social and economic life, as it was with the Irish; nor was it a central part of moral and intellectual life, as among the Eastern European Jews; nor was it central to the group's understanding of its place in American society as it was for the growing African American population of neighboring central Harlem. As late as 1925, only about one in ten Italian immigrants was enrolled to vote.

Scholars have found multiple explanations for Italian New York's relatively weak public engagement: "a lack of familiarity with the political system"; a "traditional distrust of government"; "the presumed temporary nature of their stay in New York"; and the all but total emphasis on the domestic and familial spheres in community ideology. But by the 1920s, all but the last of these factors had begun to dissipate. And as the historian Robert Orsi has argued, Italian Harlem's emphasis on the home could be mobilized in support of progressive politics. "The good life," Orsi writes, "meant the condition in which the domus could function well and happily: the family, old and young, gathered around the fireplace after a day of work, the older people on chairs, the children on mats on the floor talking over the events of that day in the cold evening. This was as fine a prelude as any to political action," and it was an ideology consonant with efforts to improve working conditions, strengthen the position of wage earners, restrain the cost of living, and improve housing conditions.

La Guardia's political appeal in Italian Harlem would be fortified by a national pride and desire for group advancement which was stoked by the events of the 1920s, a decade when American attitudes toward Italian immigrants were exemplified by quota restrictions and the Sacco and Vanzetti case. As one editorial endorsement from the 1922 campaign proclaimed: "For a long time the Italian soul has been misunderstood in the United States, resulting in a lack of sympathy for the vast body of Italian-American citizens. What better opportunity to create more favorable relations between the sons of the New World and the adopted children of Italian origin than to have La Guardia in Congress as an exponent of Italian psychology and tradition?" This politics of cultural ambassadorship began as a phenomenon of Italian Harlem's community leadership, which possessed a stronger sense of *Italianità* than their first-generation working-class counterparts (who tended to identify as natives of particular villages and regions). But ethnonational pride quickly became a crucial element of La Guardia's relationship with his working-class Italian American constituents as well.[2]

La Guardia won reelection to Congress in 1922 by a mere 168 ballots. He carried more than 60 percent of the vote in the most heavily Italian part of the district. In the predominantly Jewish quarters, which had given the Socialist Morris Hillquit majorities in 1920, he ran between 21 and 27 percent—some of them won over by the famous challenge La Guardia issued to his Democratic opponent, whose campaign had accused him of anti-Semitism, to debate the issues of the campaign in the Yiddish language. With the exception of the unusual campaign of 1924, this would be the basic makeup of La Guardia's East Harlem coalition. He never polled less than 55 percent in the most heavily Italian area; and as the Socialist Party went into decline and his own brand of progressive politics became more familiar to Jewish voters, his share of the vote in the western part of the district rose, reaching nearly 40 percent by the election of 1928.

Socially and culturally, La Guardia was always something of an outsider in East Harlem. Unlike his protégé and successor Vito Marcantonio, who was born on 112th Street and First Avenue, passed time in the coffeehouses, and attended religious services, La Guardia possessed no organic connection to the Italian community, and still less to the Jewish community. He did not even live in the district until 1929, preferring to remain in the West Bronx house he had purchased during Thea's illness. Nevertheless, he became a neighborhood fixture. Always proud of his ability both to stay abreast of public opinion and to "educate" his constituents, he delivered yearly "reports" at the Star Casino on East 107th Street. Every two years he converted his district office into what he called a "political museum," filled with exhibits, copies of speeches, platforms, and sample ballots. He also developed an effective personal political organization. A small band of Italian Americans did year-round work handling constituent matters, which ranged from assistance with citizenship applications and veterans' benefits claims to help solving rent problems and finding jobs. During campaign seasons, a larger group of a couple hundred volunteers under Marcantonio's direction "rang doorbells, distributed leaflets, and cheered [La Guardia] when he spoke." Local businessmen contributed campaign funds, and a team of amateur prizefighters—with a few professionals mixed in—guarded meetings and polling places. Evidence suggests that La Guardia knowingly countenanced the stuffing of ballot boxes in the name of fighting Tammany "on [its] own grounds."[3]

II

La Guardia's election in 1922 ushered in the second of three periods in his congressional career, and the most challenging to assess. During the wartime Congresses he had been a young man finding his footing—indeed, his most significant action in the 65th Congress had been the spectacular way in which he left it. And in the early 1930s, his third period in Congress, he would emerge as a leader of two overlapping groups, the first a bipartisan coalition seeking an alternative to President Herbert Hoover's response to the Great Depression, the second a bloc of progressive Republicans (and a few Democrats) who sought to play balance-of-power politics in the closely divided 72nd Congress. For a season he would hold a position of real influence, and he would be active in pushing for measures that would soon be incorporated into Roosevelt's New Deal: unemployment insurance, federal public works and relief, deposit insurance, and low-rent housing, among others.

Between 1923 and 1930, La Guardia was not a powerful member of Congress. He held no committee chairmanship, sponsored no major legislation, and occupied a strategic voting position only briefly. And yet neither was he a figure of minor importance as he had been in the 65th and 66th Congresses. His actions in the 1920s were widely discussed, and he gained (sometimes grudgingly) the admiration of other members, who would remember him in later years as a man of integrity and competence who had given great service in the House. One of the difficulties in making sense of La Guardia's career in this period, then, is the peculiar role he played in the Congresses of the 1920s. Another is the sheer diversity of his interests and activities. These ranged from the effort to illegalize war to the defense of the court-martialed Billy Mitchell, from trust-busting crusades launched with New York consumers' advocates to campaigns to call attention to the living and working conditions of Appalachian mineworkers. The self-appointed watchdog of the Wednesday consent calendar, he involved himself in many small, local projects. "La Guardia has affected more bills in the House than any other member," one journalist wrote. "There is not a branch of the government, from the Shipping Board to the Department of State, that he has not attempted to reform."[4]

The defining characteristic of La Guardia's politics in the 1920s, if there was one, was the way in which he sought to bridge the interests of those who toiled in the production of America's wealth in the cities and those who did so in the country and in the small towns. "His one slogan when he first went to Congress," Marie La Guardia later recalled, "was that there was no reason why the farmer, the farm Congressman, and the city Congressman couldn't get together. . . . Fiorello thought it was very important that they were friendly." He was convinced that there existed a community of interests between rural agricultural producers and urban consumers and between those who built machinery and clothing in the cities and those who used it on the farms.[5]

On some issues he clearly represented the values of his East Harlem constituents. Shortly after he took office, when Congress sought to make permanent the general restrictions on European immigration it had enacted in 1921, La Guardia naturally joined the opposition. To practically all of his constituents, immigration reform was an insult. To many of them, it was a personal catastrophe: they had labored long hours at mean jobs and denied themselves the barest diversions in the hope of bringing spouses, parents, and other family members to join them in America. La Guardia himself thought the Johnson-Reed bill "the creation of a narrow mind, nurtured by a hating heart." The crux of his argument was a deracialization of the concept of "Americanism." Against those who deemed the new immigrants incapable of assimilation by reason of their supposedly innate qualities, La Guardia argued that they had already exhibited proper "American" values and behavior—the desire to improve oneself and one's community, the aspiration to give one's children access to greater opportunity, the willingness to contribute to the development of one's community through productive labor and to fight for one's country if called to service. On these grounds, he reasoned, the tenement dwellers of East Harlem had shown themselves to be as American as anyone. Immigration restriction possessed such overwhelming support that its opponents could do little more than expose its ugly assumptions and puncture its proponents' arguments during the floor debate. After the bill passed both chambers by wide margins and became law with Coolidge's signature, La Guardia introduced an amendment to broaden exemptions in the quota system to facilitate family reunions. It died in committee.[6]

La Guardia also opposed Prohibition—another issue that tended to divide the country along urban–small town, "new stock"–"old stock" lines. He was not ideologically opposed to state proscription of ostensibly destructive personal behavior, as he was to racialist immigration restriction: this would become clear during his mayoralty, when he launched crusades against bingo and gambling that closely echoed Prohibitionist arguments, emphasizing the harm male intemperance could do to working-class families. But he did think national Prohibition was bad policy—impossible to enforce and certain to breed "contempt and disregard for law all over the country." When, in 1924, the supporters of Robert La Follette's third-party presidential bid were punished by the Republican House leadership with undesirable committee assignments, La Guardia was sent to the Committee on Alcoholic Liquor Traffic, where, as the only "wet" member, he would presumably be without influence. He was indeed too greatly outnumbered to have any real effect on policy, but the assignment provided him with a soapbox. As the anti-Prohibitionists' man in Congress, he received tips on official neglect, ineffectual enforcement efforts, collusion between investigators and bootleggers, questionable entrapment efforts, and rampant violation. These he aired, occasionally recklessly, but usually with sound documentation.[7]

On these cultural issues, La Guardia generally lined up with other urban representatives. On economic issues, he found his firmest allies among a group of midwestern and western congressmen who described themselves as "progressive" Republicans, nearly all of whom had voted for immigration restriction and some of whom were dedicated Prohibitionists. The leading figures in this group, especially Senators Robert La Follette of Wisconsin and George Norris of Nebraska, became La Guardia's mentors and role models, and for the rest of his career he thought of himself as a follower in the La Follette–Norris tradition.

So many congressmen with such diverging ideologies and conflicting voting records described themselves as "progressives" in the postwar years that contemporaries despaired of finding a single set of principles by which to define the term. However, the core group of senators that clustered around La Follette—Norris, Smith W. Brookhart of Iowa, Henrik Shipstead of Minnesota—did display a semblance of coherence. The House progressives actually formed an organization; numbering between twenty and thirty members (more than half of whom hailed from Wisconsin or Minnesota), the "progressive group" met regularly, announced a program, and sometimes sought to act as a bloc—a potential balance of power between the Republican and Democratic caucuses. La Guardia joined this group shortly before the opening of the 68th Congress and was immediately chosen as one of the three members who represented it in negotiations with the Republican leadership.[8]

The congressional progressives shared a characteristic style: they displayed discomfort with party discipline and control, a flair for making direct appeals to mass gatherings and through the mass media, a knack for using issues to build popular support, and a belief that it was their function to realize a latent public opinion stifled by elite domination—to "restore government to the people," as La Follette put it. The Little Flower identified these men as his natural allies in part because their style mirrored his own. But he also shared with them key commitments on issues of policy. They were concerned above all that the bounties of the American economy be spread more widely; and they believed that government should act to secure for the "producing classes" a larger share of the products of their labor. Against the exemplars of Republican orthodoxy, President Calvin Coolidge and Treasury Secretary Andrew Mellon, who believed that capital reinvestment, rising productivity, and innovations in private management would raise the standard of living and increase real wages—that wealth would, in one of the phrases of the day, "percolate down"—the congressional progressives argued that the government should act to promote a broader distribution of purchasing power.[9]

The policies congressional progressives sought fell into several categories. First, they supported the redistribution of wealth through taxation and spending policy. They opposed Mellon's efforts to roll back the progressive tax code implemented to finance the war. They supported the payment of a bonus to veterans of the world war, which they regarded as a more just and productive use of government money than Mellon's tax reductions. And they generally favored government spending to aid distressed classes—especially farmers, who suffered from depressionlike conditions for much of the decade. (Although some, including La Guardia, raised objections to the decade's most important agricultural bill, the McNary-Haugen Act, on the grounds that it did too little in the way of structural reform and that higher farm profits would therefore be reflected in higher prices to consumers. La Guardia did eventually vote for the bill, he explained, "for the simple reason that there was nothing else before us that promised any relief at all.")

Second, they supported government regulation, competition, or operation of particular parts of the distribution process—railroads, storage facilities, stockyards, terminal markets—with the objective of closing the gap between what producers earned and consumers paid. Toward the same end, they supported governmentalization of industries that used natural resources (such as hydroelectric power). Third, they sought to regulate labor markets through protective legislation with both social and economic objectives: child labor laws, for instance, which served both to remove children from the workplace and to eliminate downward pressure on wages. (Many progressives supported immigration restriction for similar reasons.) And fourth, they encouraged the development of countervailing powers to act on behalf of producers and consumers in private market exchanges: above all, they fought for the right of workers to form unions and to strike free from judicial interference.

The early years of the 1920s were heady ones for the congressional progressives. They rewrote the Mellon tax plan, providing for a more progressive federal income tax than the Treasury secretary envisioned, stymieing Mellon's calls for abolition of the federal estate and excess profits taxes, adding a gift tax, and mandating the public disclosure of federal tax returns. They helped to override Coolidge's veto of the soldiers' bonus bill and to send a federal child labor amendment to the states for ratification. Norris and Brookhart, to La Guardia's delight, used their strategic place on the Senate Agriculture Committee to block Henry Ford's bid to lease the unfinished federally built dam at Muscle Shoals, Alabama, leaving open the possibility that the facility might be used for the public development of hydropower to light the Tennessee River Valley. And Senate progressives began a series of investigations of the Harding administration that exposed corruption on a scale unseen since the presidency of Ulysses S. Grant.

At the same time, a variety of producer- and consumer-oriented groups and movements began to form and to coalesce into a broader movement. Political unions of farmers, laborers, and progressive reformers sprang up at the state level—in the prairie states (particularly La Follette's Wisconsin and Minnesota, where the Farmer-Labor Party grew rapidly after the war) and in the Pacific Northwest. New institutions were founded: in 1921, the Farm Bloc, the People's Reconstruction League, and the People's Legislative Service; and in 1922, the Conference of Progressive Political Action (CPPA), which aimed to provide the many disparate groups dissatisfied with the major parties a basis for collective action. Expectations crested in the fall of 1922 when self-identified progressive candidates swept many congressional and gubernatorial elections—a result Oswald Garrison Villard, publisher of The Nation (and a champion of La Guardia's) described as "a magnificent beginning" to a larger project of independent progressivism.[10]

In 1924, the CPPA nominated Senator La Follette, a revered figure among many progressive, labor, libertarian, and leftist groups, to run for president on a third-party ticket; it chose as his running mate the Montana Democrat Burton Wheeler, and it christened their campaign vehicle the Progressive Party. La Guardia, who had addressed the nominating convention, announced in an open letter that ran on the front page of the New York Times that he intended to bolt the Republican Party and endorse La Follette. Citing the Johnson-Reed Act, the Mellon tax plan, and Coolidge's veto of the soldiers' bonus, he explained that the Republican platform made "no appeal to the hope of the people whom I represent." Duly denied renomination by the GOP, he was given a ballot line by the Socialist Party, which had embraced independent progressivism in the hope that it might evolve into an American analog to the British Labour Party. He coasted to the largest margin of victory he would ever capture in East Harlem.

La Follette's campaign generated great enthusiasm in the Midwest and in the eastern cities alike; but it fell victim to poor organization, inadequate financing, and, not least, to the Republicans' charge that extensive reform of the capitalist economy would plunge the nation back into the economic chaos of 1919–22. "Fighting Bob" took 17 percent of the popular vote—not an unimpressive performance—but progressives reacted to his defeat with despondency, and thereafter independent progressivism disintegrated with astonishing speed. The CPPA dissolved in February 1925. State level radicalism went into crisis or died altogether. And some of the unions—which had already taken large hits in membership as a result of open-shop campaigns, an unfavorable legal climate, and the recession of 1921–22—fell into factional conflict. La Follette himself, sixty-nine years old and in precarious health when he accepted the Progressive nomination, died in June 1925.[11]

As the progressives' key institutions succumbed, the economic successes of mid-decade produced something of a philosophical crisis among them. "Big business in America," Lincoln Steffens wrote, "is producing what the Socialists held up as their goal; food, shelter and clothing for all." To be sure, the benefits of higher productivity were far from equally distributed, and industrial workers in particular saw little real wage growth and persistent high seasonal unemployment. But national prosperity changed the climate within which progressives worked. "I tell you," La Guardia remarked to a reporter, "it's damned discouraging trying to be a reformer in the wealthiest land in the world."

Convinced that only a broad shift in public opinion would make the policies he advocated politically possible, La Guardia devoted more and more energy to publicizing the issues he cared about. Seeking new ways of reaching voters, he began writing regular pieces for one of the tabloid papers that were then exploding in circulation in New York, the *Evening Graphic*, where he shared the editorial page with Walter Winchell and Ed Sullivan. He also honed his innate talent for publicity into a mastery of the more specialized art of communicating political ideas through headlines and news coverage. He developed a remarkable ability not only to make news—despite his middling influence in the House, he "garner[ed] more notices in the *New York Times* than any other member"—but also (as one New York politician later put it) to "dictate his own headline. . . . He'd think of a phrase to use that he was sure would catch the eye of the press."

After threatening to run as an independent in 1926, La Guardia rejoined the Republican Party on mutually advantageous terms. The House leadership finally granted him a seat on the Judiciary Committee, from which he could launch investigations into antitrust violations in the food industries and elsewhere; in return, he agreed not to campaign against Hoover in 1928. The rise of Al Smith and Jimmy Walker and the national Republicans' support for immigration restriction and Prohibition had secured the Democratic Party's dominance in New York City, rendering La Guardia—by 1927, the last remaining Republican in the New York congressional delegation—a precious resource. La Guardia happily obliged the party leaders, digging up "several hundred" patronage jobs for the Manhattan organization and steering through the House a bill to create additional judgeships in the Southern District of New York. By 1929 he was on sufficiently good terms with the Republican organization that had twice read him out of the party to be nominated for the mayoralty.[12]

III

For seven years following the polio attack in August 1921, Roosevelt remained largely out of the public spotlight. Though he retained his primary residence on East 65th Street and continued to supervise the New York office of the Fidelity & Deposit (forming, additionally, a new law partnership, Roosevelt & O'Connor), he spent more time out of New York than in it: Gotham was much more Eleanor Roosevelt's city during these years than it was Franklin's. FDR passed much of his time living as a "gentleman dilettante"—sailing, fishing, engaging in "interminable conversation," pursuing hobbies such as model shipbuilding, and making occasional efforts at writing antiquarian history. He devoted tremendous effort, in the end futilely, to recovering the use of his legs. Beginning in 1925 he spent much of his time in Warm Springs, Georgia, the location of a natural spring whose buoyant waters were thought to aid polio victims in their recuperation. Roosevelt invested much of his fortune to purchase the facility; he renovated and staffed it, and opened it as a treatment center, establishing in 1927 the non-profit Warm Springs Foundation.[13]

Though there was an unmistakable air of frivolity to much of what Roosevelt did during this time, the 1920s were in fact a period of intellectual growth for him. These were the years when Eleanor began a practice of leaving books out for her husband to read; when one of them engaged his interest, "she would then bring around the author to talk to him." Eleanor brought other people to talk with her husband, too, including the garment union leaders Rose Schneiderman and Maud Schwartz, who by Frances Perkins's account transformed FDR's favorable predisposition toward the trade union movement into a deeper appreciation for its purposes and objectives. Roosevelt himself sometimes sought out people from different backgrounds whose lives he wanted to know more about. An acquaintance who encountered one of these guests while meeting Roosevelt for tea recorded in her diary:

> After he had gone—Franklin told me that he was an East Side Jew—a tailor—from New York. He . . . had been over once before to spend the day. Franklin said he had a chance in this way to learn a great deal about conditions in [the young man's] life—his clubs and other organizations—at first hand. He felt he got to the bottom of situations that could and should be remedied—the scandalous housing conditions—labour—schools— churches and family life. He said the patience of people under unbearable tenement living—the lack of decent provisions for sanitary purposes—sometimes one water faucet in the whole house—and that in some cases the properties were owned by wealthy people who left the care to agents who had no interest but to extract rent.

Through encounters like these, the journalist John Gunther writes, Roosevelt "met a whole new world of men and women—teachers, social workers, research students, editors, intellectuals, and plain simple people. . . . [G]radually . . . he developed a new circle of acquaintances and interests, and new sources of information began to irrigate his mind."[14]

During the 1920s Roosevelt, with the essential support of his devoted political adviser and operative Louis Howe, remained active in a large number of associational, philanthropic, and civic activities. He took on occasional public work, including a turn as the president of the American Construction Council, a Hooverian effort at voluntary self-regulation of the construction industry; and he adopted several pet legislative projects. It was through this legislative advocacy work that Roosevelt first began to form a relationship with La Guardia. Marie La Guardia, then Fiorello's Washington secretary, recalled: "Roosevelt was getting interested in various pieces of legislation, and Louis Howe tried to keep his interest in things going. . . . There was one bill that they [La Guardia, Roosevelt, and Howe] had a great many conferences and a great deal of correspondence about. That was when they first became very friendly. Roosevelt would come down to Washington and stay at the Continental Hotel. Fiorello was living there at the time and would often confer with them when they would come to Washington." La Guardia also formed a relationship with Eleanor Roosevelt, with whom he corresponded about issues such as child labor; and there is ample evidence that the admiration he developed for her reinforced his esteem for her husband.[15]

The vehicle for Roosevelt's astonishing and improbable return to public life was the Democratic Party, and the story of how Roosevelt restarted his political career after 1921 is inextricably related to the stormy history of that party in the 1920s. After springing back to life in the 1922 midterms, the national Democracy fell into disarray. Tensions that had surfaced during the world war were exacerbated by the pace of urbanization and by the enactment of divisive measures like Prohibition and immigration restriction; by 1924, the party consisted of a hopelessly contradictory collection of "immigrants and Klansmen, Catholics and Protestant fundamentalists, rednecks and shanty Irish, bosses and antibosses, wets and dries." It was equally (if less spectacularly) divided on issues of political economy and social legislation—the descendants of Bourbonism squaring off against the followers of William Jennings Bryan. The Democratic divisions were most wrenchingly displayed at the 1924 National Convention in which New York governor Al Smith, representing the eastern, urban, Catholic, anti-Prohibitionist wing of the party, and former Treasury Secretary William G. McAdoo, champion of the southern and western, dry, Bryanite wing, battled for 103 ballots in the wilting summer heat. Finally, the delegates settled on a compromise candidate, the distinguished but uninspiring corporate lawyer John W. Davis, who was paired with Nebraska governor Charles W. Bryan, younger sibling of the Great Commoner, for reasons of sectional and ideological balance. It was, La Guardia quipped, a ticket "not even a brother can support."[16]

It was one of the unanticipated benefits of Roosevelt's paralysis that he was able to escape these internecine battles, remaining above the fray, warding off unwanted obligations by indicating his desire to concentrate on making a full physical recovery, and positioning himself as something of a bridge between North and South, East and West, urban and rural, wet and dry, internationalist and isolationist. Partly through astute maneuvering, partly because of personal advantages such as his upstate New York residency and his second home in Georgia, and in large measure because he was not forced to commit himself on the controversial issues of the day, FDR remained more acceptable to a wider range of party factions than any other major Democratic figure. Philosophically committed to ideals and purposes which were sufficiently broad that they could not in themselves be controversial—the continuation of free enterprise, the physical improvement of the country, the correcting of obvious injustices—he was vague and platitudinous when speaking on current issues. His statements on immigration, Prohibition, taxation, America's relation to international institutions, and other such subjects concealed more than they revealed, and they were carefully calculated not to alienate any faction of the party; when pressed, he demonstrated an impressive facility for "easy compromises" and evasions.[17]

Though unwilling to be pinned to any specific set of policies, Roosevelt did have a vision—if a somewhat vague one—of what the Democratic Party should be, and of how it could reattain national power. The party, if it were to have any hope of success, must be "unequivocally the party of progress and liberal thought": it had to become, somehow, the antithesis of a Republican Party that represented an ethic of "materialism" and cronyism which operated the agencies of government for the benefit of a few private interests rather than the public as a whole. At times, Roosevelt ascribed the Democrats' losses in 1920 and 1924 to the "complacency" of an electorate satisfied with the GOP's "gross materialism" in light of economic expansion: only when the bubble burst, he predicted, could the Democrats next elect a president. At other times, he maintained that the majority of voters continued to favor progressive policies and could be won over if the party learned to appeal to them. In an oft-noted review of his friend Claude Bowers's 1926 book, *Jefferson and Hamilton: The Struggle for Democracy in America*, he deployed Jeffersonian party-building efforts as a kind of analogy for the challenge facing the Democrats of the 1920s:

> Jefferson, eclipsed in the Cabinet by Hamilton . . . began the mobilization of the masses against the aristocracy of the few. It was a colossal task. With Hamilton were the organized compact forces of wealth, of birth, of commerce, of the press. . . . Jefferson could count only on the scattered raw material of the working masses, difficult to reach, more difficult to organize. So began a warfare of press and pamphlet . . . every new reader a step toward the goal of Jefferson. A true public opinion was being made possible.

Like the congressional progressives, Roosevelt was puzzling through the question of how to mobilize, organize, and give voice to the latent popular desires he believed had been muted by the most powerful forces in American public life—the national administration, the wealthy, the courts, the professional classes, the newspapers.[18]

In sharp contrast to the national Democracy, the Democratic Party of New York State was enjoying something of a golden age under the leadership of Governor Alfred E. Smith. First elected in 1918, narrowly defeated in the national landslide of 1920, and returned to office thrice in 1922–26, Smith, the first governor of New York raised in the immigrant tenement districts and promoted at every step of his career by Tammany Hall, had attained what seemed to be a lock on the executive mansion. Though frustrated for much of his first three terms by what he called the state's "constitutionally Republican" legislature, he assembled a record that led many progressives to consider him the greatest governor in the state's history, presiding over a vast expansion of the state parks system, passage and extension of the postwar emergency rent laws, a sharp increase in state spending on public education, stricter regulation of the working hours for women and children, a strengthening of the state's workers' compensation program, and enactment of a limited-dividend housing law that provided tax exemptions for development corporations that accepted a cap on their annual profit. So extensive was Smith's social reform record that Roosevelt later remarked that "practically all" the projects his own administration undertook in Washington were "like things Al Smith did as Governor of New York." Smith had also made the Democratic Party an instrument for institutional reform and good government in New York State, pushing through a landmark reorganization of the state bureaucracy and securing enactment of the executive budget, an efficiency reform measure which aimed to substitute a rationalized budget-making process for the logic of legislative logrolling.

Smith's governorship caused some influential progressives, social reformers, and opinion makers (though hardly all) to rethink the character of Tammany Hall. During the 1920s, the rampant corruption of Tweed and Croker's Tammany Hall seemed to abate. The columnist Walter Lippmann, a devoted Smith admirer, wrote of a "New Tammany," no longer particularly avaricious and corrupt, now graced by "men of high personal integrity who are really interested in the art of government, liberal in their sympathies, and extraordinarily deft in their understanding of human nature." Old progressive reformers such as Robert Moses and Belle Moskowitz (the two preeminent figures in Smith's circle) found not only that Smith was open to their ideas, but also that his practical knowledge of government and political power gave them a degree of efficacy they had not enjoyed in their alliances with good-government reformers.[19]

Unable to transcend the vast differences in their personal backgrounds, Roosevelt and Smith formed a relationship that was never more than cordial, sometimes distrusting, and sometimes prickly. "In many ways," Eleanor Roosevelt later wrote, "Governor Smith did not know my husband." Smith, though he liked Roosevelt, "took him at face value as a crippled millionaire playboy permanently out of politics." For his part, FDR had the "greatest admiration" for Smith's "knowledge of government," Eleanor Roosevelt recalled. He also respected Smith's ability as an educator of the public, which Roosevelt always believed was the primary function of a political executive: because Smith was so capable at presenting ideas to the public, Roosevelt suggested, "the men and women voters [of New York] have acquired a greater knowledge of their government than ever before, a greater interest, a nicer discrimination." Still, Roosevelt could hardly fail to resent the air of condescension with which Smith and his top advisers seemed to treat him.[20]

And yet Smith's mastery of New York and his rise within the national Democracy were to prove of incalculable value to Roosevelt—indeed, FDR rebuilt his own political career primarily through his relationship with Smith. Because Smith's record was so strong, Roosevelt felt few reservations about allying with Tammany Hall to support Smith's campaigns for the governorship and the presidency. These campaigns in turn allowed FDR to maintain and expand his relations with party leaders in New York State and across the nation. Roosevelt reentered the public eye in the summer of 1922 by issuing a public call for Smith to stand for reelection. Two years later, Smith asked Roosevelt to help him round up delegates in advance of the 1924 convention; Roosevelt undertook the work actively— perhaps more actively than Smith and his Tammany associates had expected—and emerged from the ill-fated Madison Square Garden convention as one of the few men whose reputation had been enhanced.

Roosevelt made three major speeches between August 1921 and his nomination for governor in 1928. Each time he had been chosen, as an upstate Democrat and a Protestant, to place Smith's name in nomination—first for the presidency in 1924, then for the governorship in 1926, then for the presidency again in 1928. Nothing did more to keep Roosevelt's name alive among Democrats, journalists, and the general public during his convalescence than these speeches, each a carefully staged performance meant to exhibit FDR's captivating personality, progressive principles, loyalty to the party, and improving health. The 1924 convention speech, Roosevelt's first public appearance as a paraplegic, represented one of the turning points of his career. Culminating with his famous line proclaiming Smith the "Happy Warrior" of American politics, it caused a sensation; and Roosevelt came away having impressed figures as diverse as Walter Lippmann and Kansas City boss Tom Pendergast (who wrote to an acquaintance that FDR had "the most magnetic personality of any individual" he had ever met and predicted Roosevelt would be the party's presidential nominee in 1928). Four years later, when the Democrats convened in Houston, Roosevelt once again put Smith's name in nomination. His speech, notable this time because it was the first major address Roosevelt composed (as he told Lippmann) "wholly for the benefit of the radio audience and the press," was again greeted rapturously.[21]

In 1928, Smith secured the Democratic nomination on the first ballot. Roosevelt expected to become a close adviser to the campaign; instead Smith, who had no path to the White House that did not include New York's 45 electoral votes, chose Roosevelt as the party's gubernatorial nominee. Prominent Democrats began to pressure Roosevelt (who had gone to Warm Springs after the national convention) to accept the nomination. Roosevelt was initially reluctant. He believed that with a few years of focused rehabilitation he might regain limited use of his legs. He also believed the timing was wrong. Defeat in 1928, which appeared likely, might set his career back several election cycles—or, should the New York Democrats draw from it the lesson that a physically handicapped man could not be elected, end it altogether. Moreover, he was already planning his next steps after Albany. He expected Herbert Hoover, who entered the 1928 campaign with great prestige, to defeat Smith and then to win reelection in 1932. Were he to run and win in 1928, he might be forced into a difficult presidential contest against a popular incumbent in 1932; were he to wait four years and run in 1932, he calculated, he would be well positioned for a shot at the White House in 1936.

Smith and his allies continued to press Roosevelt. The governor's financial angel (and soon-to-be DNC chairman) John J. Raskob promised to secure the future of the Warm Springs Foundation, and the New York investment banker Herbert Lehman, of whom Roosevelt thought highly, agreed to run for lieutenant governor and, if elected, to attend to administrative duties during Roosevelt's rehabilitation trips to Warm Springs. Finally, Smith himself appealed to Roosevelt: "Frank," he said, "I told you I wasn't going to put this on a personal basis, but I've got to." To decline, Smith intimated, would be counted as an act of disloyalty and would be weighed against Roosevelt when the party leaders decided future nominations. At last FDR relented. "[W]hen you're in politics," he is said to have remarked after getting off the telephone with Smith, "you've got to play the game."[22]

Roosevelt stood for election on Smith's record. He inherited from Smith the as-yet unsettled issue of the public development of hydroelectric power to bring down electricity rates; he added his own emphasis on the need for an affirmative farm policy. Rumors about his health—which was in fact excellent, notwithstanding his paralysis—necessitated a short but intensive campaign tour. At first "really kind of scared" (as Frances Perkins remembered) by the prospect of a rigorous physical campaign (for he and his campaign team had as yet little experience in handling the logistics and public relations challenges presented by his handicap), Roosevelt, once reimmersed in the excitement of electoral politics, "threw himself into running for office with total fervor." "If I could campaign another six months," he exclaimed to his mother, "I could throw away these canes." The tour carried him 1,300 miles around the state and saw him speak as many as seven times a day.

Smith never had a chance against Hoover; he lost overwhelmingly, beaten even in New York State, the national landslide obscuring a realignment and mobilization of new immigrant voters in the big cities that would later be described as the "Al Smith revolution." Roosevelt went to bed believing he too had been defeated, but after midnight he pulled ahead of his Republican opponent, the state attorney general Albert Ottinger, and eventually won by a thin margin of 25,000 votes out of a total of 4.25 million.[23]

Notwithstanding his response to the Great Depression (which will be discussed in the following chapter), Roosevelt is not remembered as a particularly effective governor. He suffered from the same legislative opposition that had stalled Smith's program, and the final year of his second term was consumed by his quest for the presidency and by an investigation into corruption in New York City's judiciary and municipal government. Yet he did score some notable victories. He prevailed in a protracted, bitter battle with the Republican-dominated legislature on the budget-making process, demonstrating an expansive view of the jurisdiction of the executive branch which would characterize his presidency. Of greatest interest to La Guardia and other congressional progressives was Roosevelt's policy on public electrical power. Enough Republicans were eager to shed the party's "power baron" image that Roosevelt was able to secure the creation of a New York State Power Authority, which was authorized to produce hydroelectric power and to build its own transmission lines if the private utilities corporations refused to contract at a specified rate. Public development of hydroelectric power on the St. Lawrence River was bottled up by the Hoover administration, but by the time he left Albany, Roosevelt had embraced the idea of a public "yardstick" against which to measure the service and rates provided by private companies—a position that earned him the support of those fighting in Congress for public development of the Muscle Shoals complex, La Guardia among them.[24]

Still, the primary significance of Roosevelt's governorship is that it prepared him for the greater challenges awaiting him when he ascended to the presidency. In Albany, he learned how to communicate through the mass media, how to bring the weight of public opinion to bear on the policy-making process, and how to manage relations with the legislators, parties, and interest groups. It was in Albany that Roosevelt first honed his exquisite sense of political timing. And it was in the governor's office that Roosevelt established the "working techniques" he would employ in Washington. "[H]ow he arranged his appointments and so on in the White House," John Gunther noted, "exactly duplicated the system he set up in Albany. The later Fireside Chats grew naturally out of his innovation of direct radio talks to the New York electorate. In Albany he customarily held a press conference twice a day; so it was no great burden, in Washington, to do the same thing twice a week."

And it was in Albany that Roosevelt first encountered men and women who would become important members of the 1932 campaign team and later cabinet members or close White House advisers: Samuel Rosenman, who served as an adviser and a speechwriter and continued in the same capacity until the end of Roosevelt's life; Frances Perkins, first chairwoman of the New York State Department of Labor and later secretary of labor for the entirety of Roosevelt's presidency; Henry Morgenthau, Jr., who served in Albany as the chairman of the Agriculture Advisory Commission and later became secretary of the Treasury; and Democratic State Committee chairman James A. Farley, a talented, tireless, and ambitious political organizer who oversaw Roosevelt's reelection campaign in 1930, managed Roosevelt's bid for the Democratic presidential nomination, and became postmaster general and chairman of the DNC.[25]

Roosevelt's first term marked the apogee of his relations with Tammany Hall. His loyal service to Smith and the physical courage he displayed during the 1928 campaign, Frances Perkins has written, "made it possible for many of the old politicians to forgive old scores." Once in office, Roosevelt retained most of Smith's appointees, replacing only the outgoing governor's top advisers (who were not partisan Democrats in any event). He filled the post of secretary of state, usually occupied by the governor's top political operative, with the young Democratic county chairman of the Bronx, Edward J. Flynn. Time would reveal this to have been a canny move; but in 1929, Flynn was known as a Charles Murphy protégé who had sided with Tammany over the Brooklyn organization in a 1925 primary fight, and his appointment suggested that Roosevelt was prepared to recognize the party's prerogatives. Once in office, FDR consulted the district leaders on appointments; in exchange, the party leaders and the Democrats in the legislature staunchly supported a policy agenda that concentrated largely on "upstate voters and issues."[26]

Events would soon destroy this comfortable arrangement, leading ultimately to the fracturing and reconstruction of the New York Democracy and to La Guardia's rise to power in the city. But first we turn our attention to the city itself—to its distinguishing character-

istics at the end of the 1920s and to the social and cultural changes
that were subtly reshaping the landscape within which its politics
would be conducted.

IV

To look at New York in 1929 was to see, as the scribes of the WPA
Writers Project would later put it, "the fortunate giant in his
youth." Gotham was unquestionably in the ascent, its global position strengthened by America's transformation from a debtor to a
creditor nation during the First World War, its place as a national
capital reinforced by the early development of the radio networks
and by the growth of the tourism business. "[I]mmense and prodi-
giously busy," New York was the nation's financial capital, its largest manufacturing center, its biggest internal consumer market, its
greatest port, and the headquarters of the rapidly growing corporate
management and services sectors. And to a degree that may surprise
many twenty-first-century readers, it was both demographically and
politically central. About 5.6 percent of the American population
lived in the five boroughs in 1930 (today about the same share lives
in the entire New York metropolitan area), and on a clear day one
could gaze out from the top of a Manhattan skyscraper upon the
residences of one in every ten Americans. And the national party
alignment amplified New York's political importance. For the rest
of Roosevelt's life, neither party would possess a sure-fire path to
the presidency that did not include victory in the Empire State, the
largest prize in the electoral college. In New York, as in other large
industrial swing states (such as Illinois, Ohio, and Pennsylvania), the
Democratic Party would have strategic incentives to build upon its
urban majorities by appealing to new ethnic voters, industrial workers, working-class women, and African Americans, and the GOP

would seek to win enough middle-class votes in the metropolitan areas to prevail on the strength of its upstate majorities.[27]

The social and economic diversity of the city was written into its physical profile: "a vast array of skyscrapers, department stores, and hotels juxtaposed with residential quarters both lavish and squalid, warehouses and port facilities, factories and sweatshops." Looking at this jumble of incongruities, one contemporary dubbed interwar New York "the City of Violent Contrasts." Still, in the aggregate, New York in 1929 was an extraordinarily rich and productive city with an unusually broad middle class. That year, the five boroughs contributed 9.5 percent of the value added by manufacture in the United States; a decade later, when the first federal census of business was conducted, New York City businesses paid their wage earners 43 percent more than the national average. Just under one third of the city's workers labored in manufacturing and mechanical jobs; the great majority of them worked in small shops that bore little resemblance to the sprawling factories of Chicago, Pittsburgh, Cleveland, and Detroit. Though New York's manufacturing sector was relatively small (and becoming ever more so), it nevertheless lay at the heart of the city's economy; upon it rested a large share of the city's white-collar proletariat and its entrepreneurial class. The sociologist Daniel Bell has aptly described the interwar city as "the New York of the small enterpriser"—a city characterized by "small, fast-moving, risk-taking, and highly competitive [manufacturing] firms" that prospered because they could respond to consumer demand quickly. Because New York shops tended to be small, capital requirements for entry were low and entrepreneurial opportunity high. This, Bell has surmised, "made for an extraordinarily large middle class . . . probably . . . the largest middle class aggregate of any urban center in this country."[28]

Between 1910 and 1929, the city had grown tremendously— upward, in the form of iconic skyscrapers and apartment buildings in midtown and downtown Manhattan, but also outward. Encouraged by the construction of new rapid transit lines and automotive thoroughfares, the massification of the automobile, and tax exemptions on new residential construction, investors plowed a vast amount of capital into housing construction in the New York market: fully 20 percent of new residential housing begun in America in the 1920s was built within the five boroughs. The New York populace flowed rapidly out of Manhattan onto Long Island and into the Bronx, making the metropolis, for the first time, roughly coextensive with the city's political boundaries. Row upon row of semi-detached houses and modern apartment buildings went up on the outwash plain that stretched south and east from Prospect Park to the Atlantic Ocean, transforming Brooklyn from the "borough of churches and bedrooms" ringing a core of older industrial waterfront neighborhoods into a polyglot metropolis in its own right. Queens, previously a collection of "scattered clustered settlements" grouped around industrial hubs, became an affluent residential borough. Manhattan experienced a net loss of population but was not altogether starved for new residential construction, undergoing a boom in luxury apartment housing on Central Park West, Park Avenue, and along the Hudson and East rivers.[29]

New York in 1929 was a city of staggering ethnonational diversity. Seventy-three percent of New Yorkers enumerated in the 1930 census had at least one parent born abroad—a much larger proportion than any other large city save Boston (71 percent). Gotham was home to 43,833 Greeks, 41,927 Latin Americans, 22,501 Spaniards, 24,678 Turks, 47,978 French, 77,497 Canadians, 71,187 Scots, 115,098 Hungarians, and 150,093 Scandinavians. By far the two largest "new immigrant" groups were Eastern European Jews, who made up about 26 percent of the population in 1930, and southern Italians, about 14 percent. Third and fourth, respectively, were the Germans and the Irish at 8 and 6 percent, though these communities were actually significantly larger than those figures suggest, for the census did not count as "ethnic" the grandchildren of the migrants of the 1840s and 1850s.[30]

The interwar years were a period of transition for the city's ethnic communities—a critical passage in the transition from the "immigrant city" of the *fin-de-siècle* to the "ethnic metropolis" of midcentury. The raising of new barriers to entry had curtailed the flow of new immigrants from abroad while also making it more difficult for people to shuttle back and forth across the Atlantic. As a result, ties between the city's neighborhoods and old country communities had weakened, and the character of ethnic communities in America had begun to change. The percentage of adult New Yorkers who were unnaturalized immigrants declined from about 36 percent in 1910 to 22 percent in 1930; the percentage of first- and second-generation New Yorkers who were American citizens increased correspondingly. As the size of the first generation shrank, and as the average length of an immigrant's time in America grew, the individual and social effects of transition from one economy and society to another dissipated: illiteracy declined; the median number of school years completed rose. In this sense, the great population of immigrants that had included La Guardia's parents were "assimilating" to American life.[31]

But "assimilation" did not mean that ethnicity was disappearing or withering away. Rather, this period saw the rise of what historians of urban ethnicity call (with some uneasiness) a "second generation." The sociologist Nathan Glazer's description remains apt: "[A]s the groups were transformed by influences in American society, stripped of their original attributes, they were recreated as something new, but still identifiable groups." In other cities, outward migration "produced ethnically mixed class-specific neighborhoods"; in New York, the development of distinctively ethnic housing industries meant that the second-generation neighborhoods in the boroughs would actually be *more* homogenous than the central-city immigrant communities had been. During the same period, New York's ethnic communities, long segmented into occupational niches, developed diversified, relatively autonomous ethnic economies. In 1929, many New Yorkers could—and did—shop at ethnic retailers (for instance, there were 10,000 Italian grocery stores in mid-1930s New York doing exclusively Italian trade), deposit savings at ethnic banks, do business with ethnic firms, retain ethnic legal counsel, and visit ethnic doctors and dentists. As second-generation neighborhoods and economies had developed, ethnicity had become embedded in social institutions, practices, and associations spatially situated in the new urban geography of the 1920s. Thus did ethnicity persist even as it was being remade.[32]

One "first-generation" community did develop in New York during the interwar period: central Harlem, which grew into the largest and most prominent African American and Afro-Caribbean community in the nation. After 1914, gaining access to jobs because of the restriction of European immigration, African Americans from the rural and urban South (primarily from the eastern seaboard) and immigrants from the islands of the West Indies "flocked to Harlem" in a migration of such dimensions, one minister remarked, that it seemed to be "inspired by Almighty God." New York's so-called non-white population grew by 66 percent in the 1910s and by 115 percent in the 1920s. (It was an indication of Gotham's sheer size that the nation's largest black community represented less than one twentieth of the city's population, a much smaller share than in practically any other northern industrial city.) The extraordinary density of interwar Harlem produced intense pressure on the local housing stock, a saturated job market, a high incidence of communicable disease, and other such conditions common to first-generation communities—but exacerbated in this instance by a regime of racial exclusion different in kind from what European immigrants had experienced. It also helped sustain vibrant movements for equal rights and self-reliance.[33]

New York in 1929, then, differed markedly from the city Roosevelt and La Guardia had encountered a quarter century earlier when they had arrived to begin their careers—and more to the point, it differed in ways that could become politically salient. Exceptional wealth and growing property values—still concentrated within the city's political boundaries—underpinned a growing public economy, making possible new public investments and amenities. The closing of the golden door, together with the rapid economic growth and relatively steady employment of the 1920s, had reduced the social stresses associated with the transition of individuals and families from one society, economy, and language to another (though, as La Guardia well knew, such stresses had hardly disappeared). The changing residential pattern elevated particular issues to greater importance— the construction of a metropolitan transportation infrastructure, for instance. The rise of the outer boroughs also promised to alter the balance of power between Greater New York's five Democratic county organizations, making intraparty conflict all but inevitable— awaiting, it would turn out, only the destabilizing effect of the Roosevelt revolution. More indeterminate was the development of second-generation ethnic communities and Harlem, the political incorporation of which promised to expand the electoral universe dramatically and to introduce a profoundly new mix of elements into the city's politics.

These changes in the city's economy and social geography and in the communities that made up its social fiber would form the context for New York's politics in the 1930s and 1940s. But social change does not produce specific political outcomes. There was nothing about the development of New York's economic and social landscape in the 1920s that necessarily pointed toward municipal reform—as La Guardia discovered when he finally commandeered the Republican mayoral nomination in 1929.

V

La Guardia's opponent that fall was the dazzling Democratic incumbent Jimmy Walker. Seven months Roosevelt's elder and eighteen months La Guardia's, Walker was a child of old New York, born and raised in gaslit Greenwich Village. His father, an Irish immigrant, had been welcomed with open arms by a Tammany district club (a fact his son never forgot) and had worked his way up through the political ranks, becoming an alderman, a state assemblyman, and eventually the leader of the old Ninth Ward. Jimmy, after flirting with a career in show business, followed his father into politics. He was only twenty-eight when Murphy tapped him for the state assembly; five years later he joined the state senate, where he would eventually rise to the position of Democratic floor leader. He owed the mayoralty to Al Smith—who, at odds with Hylan and his sponsor Hearst, had thrown his support behind a movement to oust the incumbent in the Democratic primary. Walker had won that contest and had gone on to carry the general election in a landslide.[34]

By the time he stood for reelection, Walker had become one of the most beloved public figures in the city's history: no other mayor, including La Guardia, has equaled the affection he inspired among New Yorkers from all walks of life. Witty, liberal, casual yet competent, he represented what New Yorkers loved best about their city at a time when the cosmopolitan ideal New York embodied was under attack. "The reason for his vast popularity," the columnist Ed Sullivan wrote, "was that Jimmy Walker somehow or other seemed to be New York brought to life in one person." He was also exceptionally intelligent: Bronx County Democratic chairman Edward J. Flynn later wrote that Walker possessed an unequaled ability to "absorb knowledge and present it to the public" and a "supreme capacity to present political ideas pertinently and attractively." And he plainly profited from the rising tide of urban prosperity—one group of unionists actually lauded him during the 1929 campaign for "solving" the "unemployment problem."[35]

Walker's mayoralty represented the pinnacle of the interwar Democratic regime. That regime had come to power when the collapse of the Mitchel coalition and the Socialist Party, in the context of intense class stress and urban-rural divisions in state and national politics, had left the Democratic Party with firm command over the loyalties of working-class voters. Hylan and Walker's administrations had consolidated working-class support partly through patronage. The metropolis was growing rapidly and the municipal workforce was expanding concomitantly. The electorate, however, was growing much more slowly, as many new residents were not registering to vote (and their children remained too young to do so); this meant that a growing share of voters owed their jobs to the Democratic administration, or knew someone who did. Tammany's was thus a coalition of direct stakeholders, backed by people dependent upon the party's continuity in office. The party clubhouses provided a second institutional means for consolidating working-class support. Because they could handle matters too small and local to merit the attention of the local state, and because they could work outside the bounds of legal procedure and finance, the clubhouses gave the Democratic regime a kind of local knowledge and governmental capacity considerably greater than the local state itself. When a family lost a wage earner or suffered an apartment fire, the district leader could provide relief; when a worker sought a job, the clubhouse could call upon a friendly contractor who needed labor. District clubs provided lawyers to represent tenants in eviction hearings and give legal aid to those who ran afoul of the law. On occasion the district clubs made life difficult for those who violated neighborhood norms of tolerance and respect. The clubhouse became part of the local community, and the district leader and his election district captains were the face of local government to many New Yorkers.[36]

Walker's primary spending commitment was to the construction of public works: public construction grew faster than any other sector of city spending during the 1920s. "I don't care what the budget amounts to in dollars and cents," Walker remarked. "If we're going to improve New York we've got to pay for it." By the time he stood for reelection, he had begun work on the Triborough Bridge and had promised billions in subway extensions, vehicular tunnels, schools, hospitals, parks, playgrounds, as well as a comprehensive plan to remake the West Side of Manhattan by covering the New York Central railroad tracks. In a city which fancied itself the very embodiment of urban modernity, a program of this sort carried major ideological appeal. Walker, his supporters claimed, was building a "wonder city," one equipped with "every modern improvement to make it worthy of the great people who live here," a city fit for the "richest individuals and corporations" and "the poorest immigrants and toilers" alike. But public construction also served to build the party's support among business and middle-class interests. This was the second decade of the great outer borough housing boom, and there was money to be made if the city government was willing to aid private resource development by building "roads, sewers, utilities, schools," and other improvements which would increase the value of realty and draw new residents. The city let contracts to firms which could be relied upon to kick some of the profit back into party coffers, enriching developers, contractors, and officeholders alike.[37]

Though Walker did extend some of Hylan's policies—attempting to enact a city rent control ordinance and successfully defending the five-cent subway fare—his administration largely turned away from the "social" reform agenda that had been so much a part of the city's politics in the Progressive Era. Walker's administration did little to develop the city's spaces for *public* use: at the end of the Democratic reign, New York ranked last in park acreage among both the ten largest cities in the United States and the ten largest cities in the world. In some instances, private charity and philanthropy replaced the local state as the most energetic force in urban social provision. Such was the case, for instance, in the area of public health. New York City's expenditures on public health in the late 1920s ran between 87 cents and 91 cents per capita, as against $1.29 in Chicago and $1.53 in Boston, with Gotham's private health and welfare organizations carrying much of the burden for health education, health screenings, and other such functions.[38]

Although Walker gave greater credence to expertise than had Hylan, he continued the Democratic practice of filling the city agencies with loyal party workers who, in comparison to the trained bureaucrats of the Mitchel years, lacked the expertise and knowledge to plan and implement expansions of state power. In some instances, this practice actually made the city bureaucracy more flexible, accountable, and even efficient, for non-professional bureaucrats tended to look lightly on violations of procedure and were quick to respond to party leaders, which provided a centralization of power (and hence of accountability). For these reasons, some social reformers actually found it easier to work with Democratic administrations: the public health pioneer Sara Josephine Baker, who directed the Division of Child Hygiene during both Democratic and reform administrations, believed that the Tammany appointees' "casual regard for regulations and bureaucratic procedures" rendered them quicker to act on her requests (though she noted, too, that the machine politicos had a habit of imploring her to take their "cast-off sweethearts" into her highly professional agency). But the practice of using the bureaucracy to reward party service also made it more difficult for the departments to innovate. The fate of the Bronx Terminal Market was a case in point: initiated during Hylan's first administration, it remained a white elephant until La Guardia came to power, primarily because no one in the Department of Public Markets, Weights and Measures knew enough about wholesale marketing to get it into operation.[39]

Municipal reform, the historian Clifton Yearley has noted, "really implied that the middle classes were distressed with the way money was being spent." Applied to interwar New York, this formulation is a bit too neat: plenty of middle-class people were happy enough with the way Walker's administration was spending money, and many working-class people (and their middle-class allies) would join the reform cause because they believed machine politics served the middle classes at the expense of laboring people. But the broader point is correct: opposition to the interwar Democratic regime sprung from dissatisfaction with how it used money. Through webs of graft, kickbacks, and personal influence, Walker's regime redistributed money—from taxpayers, contractors, small businessmen, labor unions, and the informal sector to politicians, contractors, city employees, and those who relied on clubhouse beneficence. As such, Tammany "corruption" represented a gigantic parallel system of quasi-public financing that paid for everything from Christmas turkeys for the denizens of the East Side to additional salary increments for public employees to Charles F. Murphy's Long Island estate and its private golf course. As of 1929, public discussion of Democratic corruption remained relatively muted; a series of scandals—involving sewer construction and the granting of a bus franchise to a company of dubious qualification—had captured headlines, but none inflicted any real damage on Walker. Eventually, though, corruption would become the defining characteristic of Walker's government.[40]

La Guardia, who had spurned encouragement that he run for mayor as an independent progressive in 1925, believed Tammany corruption would provide an issue on which to run in 1929. With strong support from party leaders and Italian American organizations, he held off his leading challenger, Upper East Side congresswoman Ruth Pratt, to claim the Republican nomination. Inevitably,

he failed to win the united and enthusiastic support of Republican
voters. Most of the famous names in the Party of Lincoln endorsed
him—Theodore Roosevelt, Jr., Charles Evans Hughes, Henry L.
Stimson, Ogden Mills, and Nicholas Murray Butler. But the Republican newspapers denounced him: the most esteemed, the *Herald
Tribune*, judged him a man of "unstable convictions and poor judgment." The pro-Volstead and pro-Mellon wings of the party both
roundly disapproved of his nomination. He scarcely did better with
the anti-partisan good-government reformers, many of whom overlooked his efficiency-directed platform and recalled his close political relationship with Hylan. Many reformers favored Norman
Thomas, who came across as more responsible, less demagogic, and
even somehow less radical—a Socialist, but a Princeton Socialist.[41]

"That does not worry me," La Guardia replied when told that
Thomas was making inroads among the "better class" of Republicans. "For every one of that type of Republican that Mr. Thomas gets
I will get ten needleworkers, ten bakers, ten hackmen and ten subway laborers to vote for me." But La Guardia's aspiration to broaden
the Republican Party's social base confronted insurmountable barriers: the weakness of organized independent progressivism in New
York, the Socialist orientation of the garment unions, and, paramount, the Democratic Party's continuing prestige in working-class
neighborhoods. More than a decade after the collapse of John Purroy
Mitchel's coalition, the laboring masses of New York—those who
voted—remained solidly Democratic.[42]

La Guardia's "one chance at election," Republican leaders frankly
admitted, rested in a major exposure of Tammany graft and corruption. As the active campaign season opened, close observers of New
York politics waited with interest to see what particulars the Little
Flower possessed on the Walker administration. La Guardia latched
on to an issue "over which tabloid editors had already whipped up
the public appetite": the unsolved murder of the bookmaker, gam-

bling house entrepreneur, and bootlegger Arnold Rothstein, who had been shot in the Park Central Hotel on November 4, 1928, and had died two days later. Over the following months, the NYPD and the Manhattan district attorney's office had fouled up a seemingly promising investigation so badly that New York newspapers had begun to suggest that the DA and the police had dragged their feet on the investigation lest it reveal Tammany's "intimate, close, personal, and pecuniary connections" with the city's criminal element. La Guardia and the other anti-Tammany candidates (along with the editors of the *New York World*) began to push Roosevelt for a state investigation of the Rothstein case.

Roosevelt had known for several years that scandal might flare up downstate; as early as 1927, Howe and Flynn had warned him that "wine, women and song" were playing "the very devil" with Walker. Now, the mayoral candidates' public pressure put him in an uncomfortable position: too far in one direction, and he risked alienating the downstate Democrats, whose support was essential to his legislative agenda and his reelection bid; too far in the other, and he might damage his reputation for independence from machine control. When pressed to investigate Tammany corruption, Roosevelt replied that he could do so only where specific instances of wrongdoing were alleged and indisputable evidence presented, and he invited the mayoral candidates to appear before him in Albany to make those allegations. "If they have the facts," he wrote Howe, "I will start an investigation; if not they will look silly."

The Little Flower pursued the Rothstein thread as far as he could, but he found only one concrete item (to which he was alerted by a sympathetic assistant U.S. attorney): Rothstein had "loaned" nearly $20,000 to a magistrate named Albert H. Vitale who was running Walker's campaign in the Italian sections of the Bronx. When La Guardia failed to produce more evidence, public pressure on Roosevelt dissipated. Without action from Albany, or more substantial coverage from the New York newspapers, La Guardia could not make the general corruption charges he was now leveling at Walker and Tammany Hall stick. "[H]e didn't have the proof," the Manhattan Republican Stanley Isaacs recalled. "What he said was probably true, but it didn't get under people's skin. They didn't believe him. They thought he was a little wild and reckless with his charges."[43]

Walker won reelection by the greatest margin to that point in the city's history. La Guardia carried only 26 percent of the ballots, to Walker's 62 percent and Thomas's 12 percent. Walker swept each of New York's sixty-two assembly districts—even those with majority Italian populations. Republicans seeking to explain the disastrous result were quick to note that the party had nominated a candidate it could not unite behind. It was true that parts of the Republican electorate had run out on La Guardia.[44] But this made the difference, not between victory and defeat, but between defeat and a Walker landslide. Neither did La Guardia lose, as Arthur Mann has concluded, primarily because the city was not yet ready for an Italian mayor: an Irishman or an Anglo-Saxon could no more have beaten Walker in 1929 than a Protestant could have beaten Hoover in 1928. As the Times put it, "The stars in their courses fought for Mr. WALKER."[45]

La Guardia spent election night with a large group of friends and supporters at the Hotel Cadillac in Times Square. Just after 8:30 pm, he emerged from a private office where he and Marie had been receiving the returns, "cheerful but undemonstrative" until one Italian American supporter ran over and kissed him on the cheek while another shouted out, "He is our fighting Congressman still!" "For a moment," a reporter wrote, "Mr. La Guardia's eyes glistened and a tear fell down his cheek."[46]

The following morning a New York Times editorial speculated about the election's political fallout. "Will Mr. LA GUARDIA now consider himself titular Republican leader in New York, and seek to control the party organization here, after remolding it to his heart's

desire? Does the Democratic triumph in this city make certain
the renomination of Governor ROOSEVELT next year, with a possible
Presidential boom for him in 1932?" The first question was plainly
fanciful: if anything, La Guardia now appeared to be finished as
a citywide candidate. The second was closer to the mark. Herbert
Hoover's White House was reportedly troubled by the outcome,
which they believed "endangered Republican success" in the 1930
state races and might even put New York State in play in the 1932
presidential election. La Guardia's inability to make his campaign
charges stick saved Roosevelt from suffering any significant political damage, and the governor did not lose the equilibrium in his
upstate-downstate, urban-rural balancing act. And the Democratic
successes—Walker's victory had produced a coattails pickup of three
seats in the state assembly—impressed Democrats west of the Hudson River who were searching for signs of hope after the elections
of 1928. Watching from afar, they had every reason to believe, as
the historian Frank Freidel has written, that Roosevelt was "working
political magic in New York State."[47]

3

The Deluge

The Great Depression came later to New York than it did to the industrial cities of the heartland. Though charity officials and the New York Urban League had noticed a rise in unemployment as early as 1927, it took more than two years before public officials began to pay sustained attention to the problem of joblessness. Even the stock market's sudden collapse in October 1929 registered only faintly on the city's civic and political life; in the heat of the mayoral campaign, neither La Guardia nor Walker made any real mention of it. The final months of 1929 saw the first widespread decline in employment, but Roosevelt did not discuss business conditions or unemployment in his January 1930 message to the state legislature. By the spring, however, conditions had deteriorated perceptibly, and breadlines had begun to form in the city.[1]

The months that followed offered fleeting moments of hope amidst an otherwise unrelenting contraction, punctuated, beginning in the fall of 1930, by terrifying bank runs. Within two years of the 1929 stock market crash, it was evident to all that the nation was facing its greatest domestic crisis since the Civil War. At the end of 1931, La Guardia described the economic collapse as a threat "to the very safety of the Republic," and by the following spring he (and many others) viewed the government's efforts to bring recovery as tantamount to a battle to save the very idea of liberal democracy. "Are we going to admit that Mussolini is right, that Republics and parliamentary forms of government are failures?" he asked.[2]

The effects of the great crash touched upon practically every area of American life. The depression shaped where people lived and with whom they lived and in whom they placed their trust. It changed how they related to their families and to God, how they envisioned their life prospects, whether or not they chose to bring children into the world, whether or not they were happy—and, for some, whether they thought life worth living at all. Ironically, perhaps, a decade which was to see vast changes in the role of government, radical visions and mass mobilizations, a "socialization of concern," began with millions of Americans longing to be able to fulfill their private obligations and harboring the essentially conservative wish that they be free to live as if there had been no depression.

The economic collapse also altered the course of American politics. The Great Depression destabilized existing arrangements, raised new issues, and cast doubt upon established truths about the role of government and the relation of America's governments to each other. It brought the national Democratic Party back to life in a revival as sudden and as stunning as the party's collapse had been a decade earlier. At the same time, by putting unbearable strain on municipal governments, it destabilized New York's Democratic regime, magnifying existing discontents and throwing into question Tammany's ability to govern. Four years after the stock market crash, Roosevelt was entrenched in the White House, having already presided over one of the most remarkable periods of reform in American history; La Guardia had managed an astonishing political comeback and stood ready to claim the mayoralty of New York City. As a new kind of national progressivism came into existence, forged in the fire of the depression, Roosevelt and La Guardia finally recognized each other as allies—even as party affiliations continued to hold them apart.

I

The Great Depression struck first and most forcefully at the nation's manufacturing and construction industries. Tracing the curve of industrial employment in New York through the late 1920s, one sees a series of gradually ascending M-shapes, rising in April and October and falling in the summer and winter months (their peaks and troughs corresponding with the busy and slack seasons in the garment and construction industries). The first deviation from this pattern came in the closing months of 1929: employment peaked in October and then fell off much more sharply than usual during the November and December slack season; it recovered slightly in the first quarter of 1930, and then collapsed, against the seasonal pattern; it rallied in the third quarter before falling again at the year's end. That winter, the winter of 1930–31, social workers discovered a group they called the "new poor"—first-time charity recipients who had held what were usually considered good jobs. Prominent among them were "able-bodied men of skill and good standing in well-paid seasonal occupations (the needle trades and the building trades, notably). They were used to periods of idleness, but ordinarily they earn[ed] enough in the good season to carry them through the slack time. Last year [1930] the preceding good season had been poor and brief, while the slack period was longer and slacker."[3]

As the crisis deepened, the ranks of the "new poor" grew more diverse. Many office workers—"accountants, stock-and-bond salesmen, high-grade clerical workers," and the like, which had been among the fastest-growing occupational categories in Jazz Age New

York—lost their jobs or saw their compensation reduced; others were forced into early retirement. By November 1932, white-collar workers constituted more than a quarter of the unemployed in New York. The spreading of the depression into the middle classes, in turn, dealt a hard blow to service sector workers and their families.[4]

As the months passed, and particularly as people who had achieved a measure of economic security lost their jobs, the recession became a psychological event as well as a social and economic one. Social workers enumerated the effects of unemployment: discouragement, desperation, bewilderment, confusion, loss of initiative, apathy, lethargy, obsessiveness, bitterness, cynicism, resentment, restlessness, irritability, loss of pride, and "constant fear." Many of those who lost their jobs struggled with these emotions as well as with the immediate challenges of getting bills paid and groceries purchased. One unemployed man, a former bank employee, wrote to a social worker at a private charity organization that had provided him with a work relief job:

> You have asked me to let you know how I am getting along. Today I have been able to gather my thoughts sufficiently to write you.
>
> As you know, I was lately reduced to the five days work, in alternate weeks, which still provides food for my family. I am grateful for that. But, since the five days pay has to be spread over a period of fourteen days, there is nothing left to pay rent, or gas. Personally I allow myself a meagre breakfast and then nothing to eat again until the night, just so my children may have three meals a day.
>
> In my search for steady employment, I have answered every possible ad in the papers, tried selling, canvassing, without any result. I have written nearly two hundred letters of application to various companies, banks, finance houses, in fact, every-

where, at any salary, just so it is steady, but without result. Out
of the five days pay, I squeezed out for postage. I pound the
streets, making cold applications from office door to office door.
I am wearing out shoes, and wearing out myself physically and
only God knows when or what the end will be. I am almost
losing faith in mankind, religion and everything. I try to keep
smiling when after a job, which isn't easy when your heart,
soul and mind are torn to pieces and your stomach empty at
times. I am doing my utmost to prevent going to pieces and
when I think of my unpaid rent, I get frantic thoughts, prejudice, hatred and everything else, but then I must pull myself
together for the sake of my family. Night after night I go to
bed, my mind in a whirl, wondering if I will ever get a job, get
some money to pay rent, etc. Nothing but restless nights and
troubled mind. What to do more than I have, I don't know, but
I hope to get a break soon.[5]

Some New Yorkers fell into complete destitution: shantytown
encampments housing some 2,000 people developed in Central
Park, near the garbage dump alongside the Hudson River, and
amidst factories and warehouses on the East River and in Red Hook.
Jobless men and women took to hawking "everything from pencils to
cheap neckties to apples" on Manhattan street corners. Some tenants
joined in neighborhood action to fight evictions; more relied on the
leniency of landlords, who were under informal pressure from City
Hall not to evict delinquent tenants and who in turn began referring
their tenants to relief agencies. The more fortunate deferred vacations and regular consumer purchases. A large internal migration
occurred as families that had moved into affluent neighborhoods
in the 1920s retraced their steps—from Queens back to Yorkville,
from the West Bronx back to the East Bronx. Eventually savings ran
out and real poverty set in. By 1934, according to one estimate, 20

percent of New York public school students suffered from malnutrition. Between 1930 and 1932, many families found that the material resources and the sense of security they had struggled to attain over the previous decades had vanished. "In general," a 1931 study concluded, "families accustomed to living at the margin dropped below it; families who had never before been dependent were reduced to the level of the usual run of cases under the care of the agencies; foreign-born families who by years of industry and effort raised themselves to a much better position were obliged to drop back to the level at which they started in America, or even lower." The city and the nation were submerged by the depression, and as the effects of individual material deprivation and psychic trauma rippled outward into relations with spouses, children, friends, and communities, the very foundations of everyday life were shaken.[6]

Dire as these conditions were, New York entered the depression in a relatively advantageous position. Because of the diversity of its economy and the size of its white-collar workforce, joblessness was nowhere near as catastrophic in the five boroughs as it was in the industrial cities of the Midwest.[7] Moreover, New York possessed not only great wealth but also well-established and highly professionalized charity organizations, a large population of social work professionals, and dense networks of ethnic and neighborhood social provision institutions such as churches, party clubhouses, ethnic societies, and even wealthy individuals such as William Randolph Hearst (whose breadlines and soup kitchens were soon serving 85,000 meals a day). These characteristics allowed the city to respond to the unemployment crisis more quickly, more generously, more professionally, and more creatively than any other large area of the country. By mid-1930, however, it was evident to city officials and private welfare officials alike that extraordinary measures were required. In October 1930, Walker created an Official Committee for Relief of the Unemployed and Needy which solicited contributions from municipal employees and distributed aid via the police precincts in the form of food baskets, grocery tickets, and rent money. (The Board of Education established a similar system that provided hot lunches in schools to children whose parents were without work.)[8]

What ultimately proved most distinctive about the civic response to the unemployment crisis of the 1930s, first in New York and then in the United States as a whole, was the degree to which it focused on providing work rather than the simple necessities of life. Recent studies of the New Deal works programs have tended to ascribe the federal government's turn to public employment as a product of changes in expert opinion—the conviction of policy thinkers during and after the Great War that public construction could be used as a tool for the management of business cycles on the one hand and the belief of social work professionals in the moral and social superiority of work over "direct relief" on the other. But the idea that the government should serve as an employer of last resort in times when work was scarce was of popular provenance. As the wage-labor economy had developed, many urban workers had come to believe that the opportunity to earn a reward was a right embedded in social life—for remunerative work held the key to self-respect, to public esteem, and, not least, to the ability to discharge one's obligations. For more than a century, New Yorkers, like workers in other cities, had responded to recessions by demanding jobs so that they could pay their debts and sustain their families until businesses began hiring again. "Relief" workers had dug the foundation for City Hall during the recession brought on by Jefferson's Embargo; they had started work on Central Park in the late 1850s. Charter reforms following the Tweed Ring scandals of the 1870s forced the city government out of its role as employer of last resort. But a coalition of unionists had won state authorization for some modest spending on public construction during the "Great Depression" of the 1890s. And when the national economy fell into recession in 1914–15, union leaders, social workers, and clergymen had asked city officials for a public program to assist the unemployed. The Women's Trade Union League had demanded "immediate relief for the unemployed women by establishing workrooms and recreational piers"; socialists had suggested that the unemployed be put to work collecting data on public health and, later, urged that city workshops employ the jobless in their own vocations. "Work relief" seemed a natural response to the unemployment crisis of the 1930s, in short, because a long tradition of working-class demands that the local government serve as the employer of last resort had made it seem so.[9]

In 1931, after a year of effort, labor leaders convinced the city to appropriate about $10 million to finance emergency public works projects—mostly parks maintenance, street repairs, and the like (but not subway construction and low-cost housing, as the union leaders had hoped). And in September 1930, the city's established private charity organizations—including the Association for Improving the Condition of the Poor (AICP), the Charity Organization Society, the Children's Aid Society, and the federations of religious charities—banded together to create an Emergency Employment Committee to coordinate their own emergency relief efforts. Known as the Prosser Committee after its head, Bankers' Trust chairman Seward Prosser, it operated for about ten months before it ran out of money; at that time another, similar group was formed under the chairmanship of Manufacturers Trust Company president Harvey Gibson (this one dubbed the Gibson Committee). About 600,000 people made donations to the two committees, which was sufficient to provide between twenty-one and twenty-four hours of work for $12 to $15 per week to about 81,000 men and women (a third of those who applied), most of them heads of families, representing "at least 420,000 people."

There developed between the city and the private charity organizations a rough division of labor in the administration of relief: the former took responsibility for most of the unemployed blue-collar workers and the latter for white-collar types, professionals, artists, and working women. The city put men to work planting trees and repairing playgrounds in the city parks and patching up streets under the supervision of the borough presidents. The Prosser and Gibson committees developed a number of innovative projects: garment workers sewed clothing for charity; unemployed artists painted murals, restored church statuary, and gave art lessons to children; out-of-work secretaries taught night classes in stenography and clerical work; musicians gave free public performances in the parks. More than a thousand people were furnished to the Port Authority to make a study of freight and vehicle movement in the metropolitan area. Others were loaned to NYU and City College to work on market analyses and translations of foreign works. The Gibson Committee even had a project for cobblers and barbers, who were paid to set up stands in the parks. But with a peak employment of 32,312, these committees, like the city government itself, did not come close to fully meeting the unemployment situation; and by 1931, despite the middling scale of their relief efforts, both the municipal government and the Gibson Committee were approaching insolvency. Eighteen months after the stock market crash, New York, like every other American community, possessed nothing approaching an adequate response to this unemployment crisis.[10]

III

It is often argued that the coming of the Great Depression, by shifting the center of American politics, moved La Guardia from the margins to the mainstream. This was true in a way, but La Guardia and other progressives were not simply waiting in the wings with solutions when the crisis struck. They had spent the 1920s engaged in issues such as taxation, farm aid, and the outlawing of war; they did not, by and large, possess a ready-made program for dealing with problems such as unemployment. What they did possess was a critical perspective on the American economy, and this enabled them to adapt relatively quickly to the new economic context. When the deepening of the depression discredited the Hoover administration's response, they found themselves exercising an outsized influence on the national policy agenda.

Like many Americans, La Guardia sought to grasp the causes of the Great Depression by puzzling through the basic paradox of want in the midst of plenty: why were people going undernourished in the cities while farmers lived in poverty because of overproduction? Though he saw irresponsible finance as the immediate cause (and issued some of the starkest anti-banker rhetoric of the era), he believed the roots of the depression were deeper and more structural. The mechanization of production, he believed, had initiated a vicious cycle: by displacing workers, it had reduced mass purchasing power; as mass purchasing power fell, consumers were removed from the marketplace; and as consumer markets shrank, more workers were thrown out of work. The fundamental cause of the economic crisis, La Guardia (and many other progressives) believed, was not the advance of technology or greater production in itself; rather it was the fact that the benefits of labor-saving machinery had gone almost entirely to the wealthy. Recovery would come only when the economy was adjusted such that the benefits of mechanized production went to all—not only to those who owned the machinery. "[W]e will never come out of the present condition," he said, "unless we change existing conditions and customs to meet the new methods of production. . . . We cannot stop progress; but the trouble is that legislation has not kept abreast of progress in the sciences, in chemistry, in electricity, in mechanics, in transportation, and in other modern methods of production." According to this view, the depression, the onset of which seemed so sudden, had been in the

works for fifty years or more. The nation had come out of other economic crises "because of the natural vigor of a growing country";
it had profited from an artificial boom after the world war because
the United States "had the entire world as our market. . . ." But now
the frontier was closed and there were no promising foreign markets. "Our situation is not temporary," La Guardia urged the House,
"and, gentlemen, you will be making a great mistake in your legislative enactments if you consider unemployment as merely something
temporary or spasmodic." There could be no "return" to prosperity;
only a new prosperity built on what La Guardia called an "economic
readjustment," which reformed the wage-price-profit ratio to spread
the benefits of mechanical production more broadly.[11]

La Guardia moved from diagnosis to prescription in a manner that
was simultaneously homespun and cosmopolitan. He renewed his
call for the development of public power (to drive down utilities rates
and destroy what he believed was a powerful conservative lobby) and
progressive taxation (to "break up the accumulated wealth of this
country," as he put it). After studying the British system of unemployment insurance, he introduced a bill that aimed to "make the
dread of starvation and poverty impossible in every American home"
by creating an American equivalent. The core of La Guardia's "economic readjustment," however, was the reduction of working hours
(and the retention of existing wage levels) to create what he called a
"spread of employment." "How are we going to extend the enjoyment
of machinery to the whole country?" he asked. "There is only one
answer. A reduction of the daily hours of work and a reduction of the
weekly hours of work. Perhaps six hours a day, five days a week. Less
profits, more work, more consumption, better times, happiness." In
addition to enlarging consumer markets by spreading employment,
he believed greater leisure time would create new industries: "It
will create an opportunity for education, for recreation, for travel,
for enjoyment of life. Of course it will. But it all creates work for

others—theaters, clothes, transportation, books, libraries, schools—all important in our modern life. . . ." This program of unemployment insurance, regulation of working hours, child labor laws, and progressive taxation would remain the heart of La Guardia's economic policy agenda for the rest of his life.[12]

La Guardia also joined a group of senators, led by Robert Wagner of New York, Robert La Follette, Jr., of Wisconsin, and Edward Costigan of Colorado, who supported the creation of a large federal public works program and federal grants to the states for the provision of relief—the nationalization, in other words, of the program that working-class movements had so often urged on city governments during times of high joblessness. In his opening speech to the 72nd Congress, in December 1931, La Guardia advocated immediate and "substantial" appropriation for relief to be administered through the states and localities. Advocating for a public works program, he suggested that money be used to build airports and affordable housing, and he wrote into the House's 1932 relief and public works bill a clause permitting loans for limited-dividend housing projects.[13]

By the time the 72nd Congress opened in December 1931, many progressives and leftists had coalesced around a common set of policy objectives: public works, federal relief, progressive taxation, public power, unemployment insurance, shorter working hours (in many cases), economic planning through a national economic council (in some cases), and some form of parity-price program for farmers. This activist, purchasing-power agenda was defined in opposition to Hoover's voluntarist approach to recovery, and, later, to the investment-side approach embodied in the Reconstruction Finance Administration and Hoover's emphasis on balancing the federal budget.[14]

Hoover notwithstanding, the Congress that convened in December 1931 was more conducive to progressive action than the 71st Congress had been. The Democratic Party had made large gains in the midterm elections, leaving the parties divided about equally in the

House and thus allowing a bloc of progressive Republicans and Farm-er-Laborites to act as a balance of power on votes that followed party lines. La Guardia, by 1931 a senior member of the House progressive group, called a meeting of the like-minded at the opening of the ses-sion. On December 4, he announced the formation of the "Allied Progressives," a group of nineteen members, mostly Republicans and mostly midwesterners. The group was divided on some issues (most notably Prohibition) but acted together on the most important eco-nomic policy measures considered by the 72nd Congress: Hoover's Reconstruction Finance Corporation (RFC), taxation, and federal spending on public works and relief.[15]

The progressives lost their fight against the RFC, a government corporation capitalized at $500 million and authorized to borrow $1.5 billion more designed to boost industry by creating liquidity, using tax dollars to make a pool of credit available to key financial institutions—banks, insurance companies, mortgage companies, building and loans, and railroad corporations. La Guardia, who believed the primary effect of the RFC would be to strengthen the position of the capitalist class in relation to producers—"I do not want my country to come out of this crisis with just two classes of people," he said, "one a small property-owning class, and the other an impoverished mass of workers and tenant peasants at the mercy of the other class"—dubbed the RFC a "millionaire's dole" and voted against it. But the measure passed the House by a vote of 335 to 56, the Allied Progressives joined in opposition only by a group of south-ern Democrats. It became law in January 1932.[16]

The progressives had more success on taxation. For the first two years of the depression, Hoover had avoided addressing the budget deficit that had opened as tax receipts fell. By the end of 1931, how-ever, he had become convinced that a balanced budget was neces-sary to stabilize the banking system and encourage investment. The administration proposed a revenue bill designed to close the deficit, the centerpiece of which was a 2.25 percent national sales tax. The administration's Revenue bill obtained broad bipartisan support (and the backing of the Democratic Speaker of the House, John Nance Garner) and was reported by the House Ways and Means Committee with only one dissenting vote.[17]

Within two weeks of the time the measure reached the floor, La Guardia and his allies had killed the sales tax, rewritten the Revenue bill, and ignited what the *New York Herald Tribune* called the "worst party revolt in thirty years." For days at a time La Guardia sat at his desk in the House chamber cracking peanut shells and directing a steady stream of rhetorical fire at the regressive sales tax, which he judged an attempt "to make the already exploited people who are compelled to work for a living . . . pay for the blunders of their exploiters." Gleefully shouting "soak the rich!" the Little Flower (who was, at least in theory, as firmly committed to the idea of a balanced budget as Hoover and Garner) counterproposed raising $475 million by increasing income, inheritance, and gift taxes, and $100 million by enacting a stock transfer tax. His dogged resistance gave opposition time to form; soon the sales tax got into the headlines and congressional offices started receiving mailbags full of anti–sales tax letters from their constituents. La Guardia struck an alliance with the Democratic representative Robert Doughton of North Carolina, who rallied a group of southern and western Democrats against the proposal. As the movement gathered steam, it broadened into a revolt against Hoover's investment-oriented recovery program and Garner's willingness to go along with it. In a series of votes in March, progressive Republicans and southern and western Democrats combined to kill the sales tax and hike income taxes, surtaxes, and inheritance taxes. "[W]hat had started as a wail of Little La Guardia of New York against both parties," Senator Hiram Johnson of California concluded, "ended in a roar that drowned both." Columnists and Republicans now referred to the Little Flower sardonically as "the new Democratic leader of the House"; the *St. Louis Post-Dispatch* wrote that La Guardia appeared in the chaos to be "the only member who still exerted an effective influence on both sides of the chamber. . . ."[18]

For the first time in his congressional career, La Guardia was scoring major victories. In March 1932, amidst the controversy over the Revenue bill, both houses passed, and Hoover signed, the Norris–La Guardia Anti-Injunction Act. A landmark piece of labor legislation, the bill rendered unenforceable in federal courts contracts stipulating that the worker could not join a union, limited the issuance of federal injunctions in labor disputes, and made it the policy of the U.S. government that workers be free to form unions without employer interference. La Guardia's involvement with the actual drafting of the bill was limited; a group of progressive lawyers and policy experts, including Felix Frankfurter, Donald Richberg, and Edwin Witte (all soon to be involved with the Roosevelt administration), drafted the bill. But for La Guardia, who had introduced anti-injunction bills in every session of Congress since 1924, it was a vindication and a sign that times were changing.[19]

After the revised Revenue Bill and Norris–La Guardia passed, progressives devoted much of the rest of the session to wringing federal relief and public works programs from Hoover. In May, La Guardia formed a bipartisan committee which vowed to keep Congress in session until a relief bill was passed. By the summer, Hoover conceded the need for more direct federal measures to address the unemployment crisis; it was now a question of how far-reaching the program would be. The crux of the issue was what types of projects would be included. The president supported a program of self-liquidating public works projects—structures such as waterworks and toll bridges which would produce revenue (and hence would not add to the tax burden or to the federal deficit). Speaker Garner's bill permitted the construction of smaller non-revenue-producing projects such as post offices and schools, which meant it could be put into operation more quickly and create more jobs, at the cost of adding to the deficit. Hoover considered the Garner program "the most gigantic pork barrel bill ever proposed to the American Congress" and believed, along with Treasury Secretary Ogden Mills, that federal deficit spending would harm recovery by undermining business confidence. In June, the Allied Progressives were instrumental in passing Garner's bill, which appropriated more than $2 billion for public works expenditures and loans to cities, states, and individuals. A less bold, more politically practical measure sponsored by New York senator Robert F. Wagner passed the Senate, and the two bills were reconciled in conference. After Hoover vetoed the measure, the exhausted Congress passed a more budget-neutral version—this one providing $300 million in loans to states for relief and $322 million for self-liquidating public works—and then adjourned. La Guardia stayed in Washington through July, observing that summer's Bonus Army disaster, and then went back to New York to stand for reelection.[20]

IV

Though he quickly became a leading critic of Hoover's economic policies, Roosevelt's initial efforts in New York mirrored the Republican president's in their emphasis upon voluntary cooperation by business. In the spring of 1931 he created a Commission on Industrial Employment Stabilization to conceive of ways for industry to alleviate seasonal unemployment (which at this stage he considered one of the major factors in the downturn) by spreading work on a voluntary basis, without government coercion. The principal difference between Roosevelt and Hoover in the early months was one of tone. Hoover projected optimism because he thought public confidence the key to recovery; Roosevelt, critical of the statements emanating from the White House, insisted on facing conditions as they were. "The situation is serious," he said in March, "and the time has come for us to face this unpleasant fact dispassionately and constructively as a scientist faces a test tube of deadly germs. . . ."[21]

More than La Guardia, Roosevelt ascribed the depression to a regular, periodic trough in the business cycle—exacerbated, he believed, because it had coincided with a period of technological displacement. As the depression deepened, he began to view it in more basic terms as a failure in the economic system to match production with consumption. If this was in essence the same problem La Guardia (and many others) identified as the core of the economic crisis, FDR approached it differently—though he eventually arrived at some of the same policy prescriptions. Whereas La Guardia focused on ways of building mass purchasing power, Roosevelt emphasized planning: deliberate efforts to arrange society and economic production so as to make more efficient use of resources. He was, however, vague in suggesting how planning could address the failure of production to create its own markets.

Roosevelt's one concrete planning initiative entailed the resettlement of the urban masses to rural areas. FDR believed cities were the epicenters of boom-and-bust cycles, "hothouses of growth that feel the chill winds of depression first"; and he thought they were overpopulated "in the sense that there are too many people in them to maintain a decent living for all." High urban land values, tax levels, and living costs, he claimed, disrupted the channels of economic distribution, contributing to the systemic breakdown in distribution that led to want amidst plenty. "[T]he proper distribution of the products of industry cannot be solved," he thought, "until we do something to solve the proper distribution of the population who will use the products."

Roosevelt envisioned a government-assisted back-to-the-land movement which would solve the problem of "sociological imbalance" while making available to urban families the moral satisfactions he had known as a son of the Hudson Valley aristocracy. Pastoral though it was, this was in a sense a quite modern vision. Roosevelt believed that a host of technological advances—including modern transportation, electrical lighting and refrigeration, the extension and improvement of telephones and the advent of the radio, the parcel post—had closed the gap in comfort and quality of life between rural and urban living. This, in turn, had made it possible to enjoy the advantages of rural life without sacrificing the material comforts of the city. "There is contact with the earth and nature and the restful privilege of getting away from the pavements and from noise" in the country, he suggested. "There is an opportunity for permanency of abode, a chance to establish a home in the traditional American sense."[22]

To these moral and social considerations were now added economic ones. Resettlement would carry urban workers away from the "places where it is most inconvenient and expensive for society to help them," and, with a bit of assistance, establish them in places where they could help themselves. (Though he could not admit it because of the adamant opposition of farmers, already awash in surplus production, he plainly expected the resettled workers to engage in subsistence farming.) And it would place working families where they could "live far more cheaply and with a greater deal of security." Resettlement appealed in the early years of the Great Depression, then, because it seemed to serve the ends of relief, recovery, and reform simultaneously. In 1930, FDR created a Commission on Rural Homes and charged it with "canvassing means for relocating people in the country." By May 1932, he was trying to "place as many families as possible on subsistence farms," the state providing money for rent, tools, and seed. A fair number of city dwellers wrote Roosevelt in excitement to inquire about the program, but the plan foundered because of its practical difficulty and high initial cost.[23]

Beyond his resettlement schemes, however, Roosevelt's program for meeting the depression looked much like the program La Guardia and the congressional progressives were pushing. As soon as the recessionary trend had became evident, he had moved to increase state public works spending. If Hoover had done the same, Roosevelt suggested in one 1930 campaign speech, the depression might not have become so severe. In a speech to the 1930 Governors' Conference, he advocated a five-day workweek. He also became the nation's most prominent proponent of unemployment insurance—albeit a cautious one. Claiming experience in the insurance field from his time at the Fidelity & Deposit (much as he claimed experience in the field of agriculture as a Hudson Valley gentleman farmer), he argued that unemployment insurance could be made actuarially sound, envisioning a public-private partnership in which a governmental program would be financed through private life insurance companies. If this vision was less statist than La Guardia's (which borrowed more frankly from the British model), it pointed in the same general direction. Like La Guardia, Roosevelt became a student of European programs, absorbing information given him by Frances Perkins and Paul Douglas, a professor of economics at the University of Chicago who was duly summoned to Albany for further discussion. In January 1931, briefed by Douglas, he spoke about unemployment insurance to a conference of northeastern governors he had convened to discuss state-level and interstate responses to the unemployment problem. In March, he asked the state legislature to create a commission to study unemployment insurance.

The key symmetry, at least in the near term, was in the area of relief. Like the congressional progressives, Roosevelt believed that the inadequacy of existing relief efforts should be addressed by utilizing the spending resources of higher levels of government. Though Roosevelt was more articulate than La Guardia in explaining exactly why he believed this, their thinking ran more or less parallel. Like

La Guardia, FDR understood governments as parts of a continuity of social organization, with responsibilities derived from the interdependence of modern society. "The State," Roosevelt suggested in his message urging creation of a state relief program, was "but the machinery through which . . . mutual aid and protection is achieved." Its responsibilities had been enlarged as society had "grown to a better understanding of government functions" and had come to recognize that there existed no such thing as a "self-supporting man"—"without the help of thousands of others, every one of us would die, naked and starved." In an age of mutual interdependence, "Modern society, acting through government," owed a "definite obligation to prevent starvation or the dire want of any of its fellows who try to maintain themselves but cannot . . . not as a matter of charity but as a matter of social duty."

This essentially Progressive conception of the state raised questions about the role of governments within the American federal system. What functions properly belonged to local governments? To the states? To the national government? What was and was not the function of government? Roosevelt sought to answer these questions by invoking the principle of subsidiarity: social obligations, he suggested, should be discharged at the most local level capable of discharging them. If the family or neighborhood could not meet these obligations, they became a responsibility of community organizations; if these should fail, responsibility passed to the local governments. And if local governments should prove unequal to the task, the states should step in. The state government was thus obligated to enter into what had previously been the field of private charity and local government simply because it had been conclusively demonstrated that local institutions alone could not discharge this social duty: state aid came "by a process of elimination, if by nothing else." Extending this principle during the 1932 presidential campaign, Roosevelt suggested that the federal government should act when it became evident that the states and communities could not meet the burden adequately. That point, he believed, had been reached; in January 1932 he cabled Senator Wagner in support of the La Follette–Costigan relief bill, adding that he believed federal relief should not be permanent policy.[24]

In early August 1931, Roosevelt sent a letter to the mayors of each New York city above 25,000 in population asking them to recommend a state relief program so that he "could make plans for it," thereby pioneering a technique he would use during the New Deal of using mayors to validate and support his relief policies. When the state legislature convened in August 1931, he sent a message recommending a comprehensive state relief program. By the end of August the legislature had passed Roosevelt's program, establishing the Temporary Emergency Relief Administration (TERA) and appropriating $20 million to reimburse local relief agencies 40 percent of their expenditures. With this action, New York became the first state in the nation to provide directly for the victims of the depression.[25]

Easily Roosevelt's greatest achievement as governor of New York, the TERA, in its first year, helped finance work relief for about 48,000 families in New York City and home relief (in the form of food tickets and rent and clothing vouchers) for about 90,000 more. These relatively modest numbers suggest that relief provision remained inadequate prior to the New Deal. But to those laboring in Congress to enact a federal relief program, Roosevelt's accomplishment was notable; and moreover, despite the fact that it was wholly consistent with Hoover's proposition that the localities and states should take the lead on providing relief, Roosevelt's willingness to take action stood out as a counterpoint to Hoover's reluctance to do so. CONGRATULATIONS ON PASSAGE RELIEF MEASURE, he cabled Roosevelt upon the TERA's enactment. YOUR CONSTRUCTIVE PROGRAM IS FIRST GOVERNMENTAL STEP IN RIGHT DIRECTION.[26]

Relief, public works, unemployment insurance, working hours,

official support for the right to bargain collectively, public power—
on each of these issues Roosevelt's record in New York was in accord
with the congressional progressives' agenda. And if progressives posited a clear distinction between those policymakers who favored an
investment-side approach and those who proposed to dig out of the
depression by increasing mass purchasing power, Roosevelt left little
doubt where he stood. "[T]here are two theories of prosperity and of
well-being," he remarked during the 1932 campaign (echoing William Jennings Bryan): "The first theory is that if we make the rich
richer, somehow they will let a part of their prosperity trickle down
to the rest of us. The second theory [holds] that if we make the average of mankind comfortable and secure, their prosperity will rise
upward, just as yeast rises up, through the ranks."

The depression and Hoover's response to it had put Roosevelt and
La Guardia on the same side of the most basic questions of their day—
indeed, had made them allies, albeit, for the moment, tacit ones.
Before FDR entered the presidency, he told his speechwriter, Adolf
Berle, Jr., that he considered the Little Flower "one of us, emotionally and ideologically." But the party difference would prove powerful
enough to keep them apart in the elections of 1932 and 1933.[27]

V

Across the world, the historian Daniel Rodgers notes, "political parties unlucky enough to preside over the early phases of the Depression . . . suffered dramatic losses of credibility." In America, the
multifarious pressures generated by the economic contraction led
to the collapse of one local regime after another. In the municipal
elections of 1931 and 1933 incumbents were turned out at an astonishing rate, with some northern and midwestern cities going to the
Democrats for the first time since the Civil War. Jimmy Walker and

the New York Democracy entered the Great Depression in stronger political position than most incumbents, and for a while they weathered the storm comparatively well. But ultimately New York's Democratic regime, tossed by the waves of the economic catastrophe, was to crash in spectacular fashion.[28]

The breadth of Walker's coalition had always depended on the steady growth of the city's tax base, and thus in turn upon the expansion of the local economy. When the depression removed this essential condition, Walker was forced into a negative-sum politics that was bound to produce powerful enemies. In 1930 and 1931, declining tax receipts produced a budget shortfall. Walker refused to cut salaries or institute furloughs, instead issuing short-term tax receipt notes; when in turn the anticipated tax revenue failed to materialize, he rolled those short-term notes over into long-term debt. At the end of 1931, the market for municipal bonds collapsed, and the city was left teetering on the edge of insolvency. New York's financial, business, and real estate communities mobilized to press Walker for budget cuts which he could not meet without alienating Tammany's core constituencies of municipal officeholders and contractors.[29]

Amidst this climate of anxiety, corruption, long a central feature of Walker's administration, moved to the forefront of New York's civic life. Late in the summer of 1930, Roosevelt, in an effort to preempt what he anticipated to be the Republicans' principal line of attack in the fall campaign, requested that the Appellate Division of the State Supreme Court begin an investigation into New York City's magistrate courts, which had come under scrutiny in the wake of a Bar Association inquiry earlier that year. The court chose as counsel the respected attorney Samuel Seabury, an independent Democrat who was to become the scourge of Tammany Hall and the leading force in the construction of an anti-machine fusion movement. Descended from a long and distinguished line of Episcopalian ministers, dignified in his bearing, and bombastic in his moral righteousness, Seabury could come off as a caricature of a patrician. In truth, there was more to Seabury than met the eye. Raised in an atmosphere of "genteel poverty" by a family that had experienced the kind of status decline so often associated with famous old families in the late nineteenth century, he had entered politics not as a Mugwump but as a follower of Henry George, the great social theorist, single-tax advocate, and aspirant to the New York mayoralty. Following George's death, Seabury had become a leading figure in Hearst's Municipal Ownership League and a populist-turned-Wilson Democrat. A talented politician in his own right, he had gotten himself elected to the State Supreme Court and the Court of Appeals, and in 1916 he had run as the Democratic candidate for governor. Thereafter he had retired from public life and had turned to corporation law. The investigation of the magistrate courts and eventually of the entire city government was to awaken in him both simmering, long-frustrated political ambitions, and a deep-set belief that machine politics was a curse not merely upon the taxpayers of the city but upon the people as a whole.[30]

Seabury's personal biography and appearance—"his great ability, his white hair and his dignity, his reputation"—enabled him to come across as something more than a spokesman for the propertied and the financial community. As a former politician, he understood the art of publicity better than most civic reformers. And he possessed sufficient ability to run away with the investigation. Beginning with the inquiry into the magistrate courts, Seabury became a kind of anti-corruption entrepreneur. He assembled a team of young and capable attorneys (many of whom would later serve in the La Guardia administration) and began tearing through testimony and bank accounts to document sordid practices within New York's criminal justice system.[31]

Much as La Guardia had turned to the politics of exposure when the mayoral campaign of 1929 seemed hopelessly lost, Tammany's opponents now seized on Seabury's investigations as the best available means of overturning the Democratic regime. Roosevelt would soon come to view the reformers as sanctimonious and publicity-mad, but he found it politically difficult to yield the high ground on the good-government issue. In March 1931, he enlisted Seabury to investigate allegations of incompetence in the Manhattan district attorney's office. A few weeks later, with the governor's consent, the state legislature created a Joint Legislative Committee to Investigate the Affairs of the City of New York, with Seabury as its counsel. La Guardia cheered the development, predicting that the investigation would reveal "a shocking system of large, middling and petty graft," adding that they would show "the absolute disconnection of Governor Franklin D. Roosevelt and Lieutenant Governor Herbert Lehman with the New York City scandal" and "make impossible the casting of any slurs or suspicions against Governor Roosevelt by partisans to the uninformed."

In the months that followed, evidence of corruption played out in spectacular fashion in hearing rooms and on the front pages of the New York newspapers, drawing ever greater public attention. Given the crucial power of subpoena, Seabury verified unsavory practices that had previously been all but documented and discovered others that were almost too wild to have been imagined. Among the men he charged were: several district leaders who had amassed half-million-dollar fortunes on municipal salaries; a county leader who commanded jobholders and city agencies alike to purchase their automobiles from his son-in-law's dealership; a district leader whose sinecure job as city marriage clerk had allowed him to collect hundreds of thousands of dollars in bribes ("tips") doled out by bridegrooms; and a well-connected veterinarian who had made nearly a quarter million dollars in a single year fixing applications for building and zoning regulation variances. In February 1932, Roosevelt established precedent by removing from office the man who

would become the most famous of the offenders: Manhattan sheriff
Thomas Farley, possessor of a "wonderful tin box," which he claimed
to be the origin of bank deposits totaling $310,000 in excess of his
salary earnings.[32]

Seabury put Jimmy Walker on the stand in May. Walker showed
up to the "duel at Foley Square" unprepared and tried to survive by
the grace of his wit. Seabury called attention to $300,000 the mayor
had accepted from people who sought to do business with the city
and to a safe deposit box jointly owned by Walker and his financial
adviser into which the latter (who had subsequently fled to Mexico) "had made deposits totaling nearly one million dollars." Walker
met Seabury's questions with "evasion, amnesia, cheap theatrics,
and shallow, unbelievable rationalizations," denying knowledge of
the safe deposit box and describing the $300,000 as mere "benefi-
cences" bestowed upon him by generous friends. Walker could not
refute Seabury's charges; but neither could Seabury present more
than circumstantial evidence that Walker had been personally
guilty of conduct requiring his removal for malfeasance. Still, the
Seabury hearings had demonstrated amply that Walker either could
not or would not enforce basic standards of honesty and competency
within his administration, leaving room for Roosevelt to remove him
on the grounds of nonfeasance.[33]

On August 5, after an exchange of public correspondence, Roosevelt summoned Walker to appear before him in the Executive
Chamber in Albany to answer charges. Hearings began on August
11 (the date, coincidentally, of Hoover's speech accepting the Republican nomination) and lasted for two weeks, with Roosevelt adding
evening sessions in order that the ordeal might be concluded before
the active phase of the campaign. The hearings served Roosevelt well
politically; he prepared diligently and used the occasion to display an
intellectual capacity and seriousness of purpose some still doubted
he possessed. However, he produced no better case for Walker's

removal than Seabury had, and as the campaign season neared, he was torn as to which course to follow. He was abruptly relieved of the burden of decision when Walker, personally exhausted and under pressure from Al Smith to resign "for the good of the party," stepped down from the mayoralty on September 1, 1932.[34]

The mayoralty passed to the president of the Board of Aldermen, a pious and competent Bronx Democrat named Joseph ("Holy Joe") McKee. Though he became popular as an interim mayor, display-ing a diligence and probity absent in the Walker years, Tammany refused to slate McKee as the nominee in the emergency election to fill Walker's seat in 1932; with Roosevelt apparently on his way to the White House, the Tammany chieftains feared Flynn's power was on the rise and wanted a Manhattanite in City Hall. Flynn, unwilling to risk dividing the party with Roosevelt and Herbert Lehman up for election, swallowed his objections and went along with Tammany's choice, a surrogate court judge named John O'Brien. Notwithstand-ing an unprecedented number of write-in votes for McKee (the result of a campaign by the *World-Telegram*) and the largest Socialist vote in the city's history, O'Brien was elected overwhelmingly, by more or less the same voters who pulled the lever for Roosevelt.[35]

By the time O'Brien took office, New York's creditors had essen-tially seized control of its spending policy. The fear of default finally shook Tammany free from its unwillingness to cut municipal salaries—smaller paychecks were better than no paychecks—and in early 1933 the Board of Estimate voted through a retrenchment program aimed partly at satisfying the bankers and partly at staving off a reform challenge in the fall municipal elections. That summer, O'Brien pro-posed to widen the city's revenue base by adding a slew of new taxes; interested groups mobilized to defeat each one, leaving only a higher water rate and a tax on cab fare, which in turn were soon invalidated by the courts. O'Brien was to bear the burden of this unpopular effort for the rest of his short political career.[36]

Finally, in September 1933, Governor Herbert Lehman brokered a deal between the city government and five of the largest investment banks, subsequently known as the Bankers' Agreement, which imposed strict conditions on the city in exchange for additional loans to meet current expenditures and relief costs. By agreeing to segregate tax receipts into a fund for repaying short-term notes, the city made repayment of debts its foremost priority; it likewise satisfied the real estate community by imposing a four-year cap on the property tax rate. In exchange, the bankers' consortium agreed to provide more operating loans and a $70 million serial bond issue expressly for unemployment relief. The Democratic regime of the 1920s was now dead; it had been replaced, temporarily, by a crisis regime whose policies were dominated by the city's creditors and property owners and whose social imagination ranged not much further than an appreciation of the social upheaval that might ensue should relief be shut off entirely.[37]

VI

Roosevelt's 1932 campaign is usually remembered as a conservative affair, full of "sunny generalities" and little substance. But the congressional progressives, already drawn to Roosevelt's record on relief, public power, and unemployment insurance, heard what they needed to hear. For his part, Roosevelt—whose willingness to reach out to members of the other party was rooted in his admiration for Republicans he had known as a young man, such as Theodore Roosevelt, Charles Evans Hughes, and Oliver Wendell Holmes—made conspicuous overtures to the progressive Republicans. A number of self-identified progressives from both parties—including the progressive Republicans George Norris, Henry A. Wallace, Amos Pinchot, and Donald Richberg, and the La Follette campaign veterans

Harold Ickes and David K. Niles—joined the Roosevelt campaign by way of the National Progressive League. La Guardia chose not to follow them, evidently making the calculation that alienating the Republican organization would cost him more in his own reelection effort than endorsing the popular Democratic governor would gain him. But his own platform—which called for national unemployment insurance, a five-day, thirty-hour workweek, and repeal of Prohibition—left little doubt as to where his sympathies lay. Accounts of La Guardia's East Harlem campaign rallies make it clear that both he and his supporters held Roosevelt in high esteem: crowds "roared their approval" when Roosevelt's name was mentioned.[38]

On election day, Roosevelt carried the city easily (winning 64.5 percent of the ballots) with a vote that looked very much like Al Smith's of 1928: he had inherited Smith's coalition of working- and middle-class non-Protestants and anti-Prohibitionists, though he also ran slightly better than Smith had among working-class Jews and notably better among African Americans. But if the electoral alignment remained more or less static, voter participation soared—and for La Guardia, this spelled trouble. The election of 1932 brought to the polls many men and women who had recently migrated to East Harlem from Puerto Rico; these new residents had not, for the most part, been integrated into La Guardia's organization, and they tended to be less familiar than long-term East Harlemites with the Little Flower's record in Congress. The Democrats ran a strong challenger, a young Columbia-trained engineer named James Lanzetta, and defeated La Guardia by about 1,200 ballots out of 31,000.

Instead of returning to Congress as a leader of a progressive coalition prepared to work with a progressive Democratic president, La Guardia was out of office for the first time since 1922. The timing seemed particularly cruel. "I so wanted to serve in the next Congress," he wrote a friend, "for I feel that many of the changes for which we have been preparing will have come up for decision then."

He served as one of the most active members in the lame duck session, working with Roosevelt's speechwriter and policy adviser Adolf Berle, Jr., on several notable measures—an early indication of his desire to cooperate with the new administration.[39]

Berle would soon be instrumental in helping La Guardia secure the fusion nomination for mayor of New York; later, he would serve as the primary intellectual figure in La Guardia's first administration, a kind of theorist of La Guardia's brand of progressive reform, and a key link between City Hall and the White House. But in the meantime, La Guardia's long and distinguished time in Congress, and his brief moment of power, had come to an end. Roosevelt contemplated appointing the Little Flower to one bipartisan federal commission or another, but decided that such an appointment would draw fire from regulars in both parties and might create too much of a distraction early in his presidency. On the day Roosevelt was sworn in as the thirty-second president of the United States, La Guardia left Washington to return home to New York.[40]

The next few months would witness one of the most remarkable bursts of lawmaking in American history. Suggesting in his inaugural address the necessity of "broad Executive power to wage a war against the emergency," Roosevelt acted unilaterally to shore up public support in the American banking system. Thereafter major legislation poured forth from the Democratic Congress in an unyielding torrent: the Emergency Banking Act on March 9; the Economy Act on March 13; the Federal Emergency Relief Act, the Agricultural Adjustment Act, and the Tennessee Valley Authority Act in mid-May; the Securities Act of 1933 (creating the Securities Exchange Commission) on May 27; and finally the Glass-Steagall Act of 1933 (establishing the Federal Deposit Insurance Corporation) and the National Industrial Recovery Act, both on June 16.

Beginning with the Hundred Days and stretching through Roosevelt's first term, the American national government would muster a capacity for large-scale innovation it had not displayed since the Civil War, and would match, perhaps, only in the mid-1960s. Several developments had converged to make this extraordinary passage possible. First, the Democratic Party, which had for a generation been more inclined than its counterpart to champion vigorous federal initiatives of the sort the New Dealers would put into operation, had attained tremendous majorities in both houses of Congress—owing partly to the depression and partly to the massive entry of first- and second-generation Americans into the electorate. (The Democratic Party had largely represented the interests of farmers and miners, but the continued growth of the metropolitan areas, the reapportionment of Congress following the 1930 Census, and not least the rise of an urban Democracy in the late 1920s and early 1930s helped to ensure that the interests of urban workers would be represented in Congress.) Second, the relative underdevelopment of the national state had given Roosevelt and the New Dealers an unusual freedom to be creative, as they felt little pressure to utilize preexisting national institutions to meet the unemployment crisis, rendering their choices relatively unconstrained by well-organized interests within the national bureaucracy. (The weakness of national state capacities also constrained New Deal policy making, as we shall see shortly.) Third, the presidency had become a powerful tool for active governance. Under conditions of emergency, Roosevelt had brought to culmination patterns of development in the American presidency that had been underway since the early twentieth century, combining the functions of chief executive, prime minister, party leader, and mass leader. (The development of the radio played an important role in this process, as did Roosevelt's own conception of the office: like TR and Wilson, he envisioned the presidency "not as an administrative job, primarily, but as a place of high *political leadership*. . . . He [believed] he must look personally to [the people's] needs and desires—and keep in his own hands the power of decision on vital matters.") The fourth and final factor was sheer lucky timing: the depression's nadir coincided almost exactly with Roosevelt's ascent to the presidency, leaving the Republican Party thoroughly discredited and the Democrats extremely well positioned to claim credit for the ensuing recovery.[41]

The new president was, beyond any doubt, the focal point of the Hundred Days. And yet much of the substance of the legislation was familiar, for it derived from the progressive agenda of the 72nd Congress. At Roosevelt's request, the legislators held off on unemployment insurance, which would be enacted by the Social Security Act of 1935. But within the Hundred Days, Congress created the Public Works Administration (PWA), a $3.3 billion program ($25 million of it earmarked for Roosevelt's pet project of resettling urban workers), and a Federal Emergency Relief Administration (FERA) authorized to distribute $500 million to states and localities. Federal deposit insurance, which La Guardia had urged as an alternative to the Reconstruction Finance Corporation, saw enactment under the Glass-Steagall Act. Senator Norris's long effort to bring public electrical power to the Tennessee Valley came to fruition with the creation of the Tennessee Valley Authority. And the centerpiece of Roosevelt's industrial recovery program, the National Recovery Administration (NRA), provided a guarantee of labor's right to organize, provisions forbidding child labor, and industry wages and hours codes that embodied the progressives' (and the AFL's) idea of spreading employment by shortening the workweek (though many progressives rued its suspension of antitrust laws). "Some of us have been working on this for years, and it is now enacted into law," La Guardia remarked.[42]

VII

If La Guardia saw the first Hundred Days as a fulfillment of his own vision of how to meet the depression, the weeks after Roosevelt's inauguration were personally difficult for him. Frustrated, unsure what to do with the hours he had previously committed to affairs of state, he told friends that he planned to retire to Arizona, teach government at a university, and raise chickens. Admirers in Iowa urged him to move to the Corn Belt and run for the Senate, an invitation La Guardia declined on the ground that the state had no symphony orchestra. After flirting with the idea of publishing a book manuscript he had written while in Congress, he took a job as a labor mediator in the garment industry. But already new political horizons beckoned.[43]

From the turn of the century there had been three paths to City Hall. Most of New York's mayors had been independent Democrats, selected by the party leaders because they commanded wide public respect or influential backing—attributes that would help keep City Hall in Democratic hands and shore up the machine candidates down ticket. Beginning with Walker, it had become possible for life-long organization Democrats to work their way to City Hall by serving effectively in lower offices. And twice since consolidation, in 1901 and again in 1913, anti-machine elements had formed temporary coalitions to oust the regular Democrats from office. As a rule, such "fusion" candidacies were preceded by fusion movements, in which "extraordinary conglomeration[s] of incompatibles united by a common hatred of Tammany"—the Republican Party; dissident Democrats; the financial, business, and property owner communities; good-government organizations and civic watchdog groups; editors; social workers; university faculty; clergy; the Bar Association; women's groups—sought out a candidate acceptable to a broad range of anti-machine elements.[44]

By the time La Guardia returned to New York in March, a fusion movement was brewing. In December 1932, Republican state chairman Kingsland Macy, an insurgent Long Islander who was seeking to build a power base in the city from which to challenge the upstate old guard, had appointed a committee to seek fusion with other anti-Tammany groups. A new political party, the City Party (later renamed the City Fusion Party), was formed. And a self-appointed committee consisting of a conservative Republican ex-governor, a member of the state chamber of commerce, a representative of a good-government civic group, and the head of still another third party began approaching potential fusion candidates—who, one by one, took themselves out of consideration.[45]

It still seemed highly unlikely that La Guardia would even be considered. Four years earlier, he had lost by the largest margin in the city's history; thousands of usually loyal Republicans had defected or stayed home on election day, and the party leaders had come under withering criticism following the election for their choice of nominee. He could claim real accomplishments since 1929 and could boast of a secondary role in exposing the corruption that had undone Walker. But he had also stood on the floor of the House shouting "soak the rich!"—a posture unlikely to win him favor among the prim, proper, and propertied men so heavily represented in fusion committee proceedings. Yet La Guardia did possess some advantages, and he made use of them with characteristic ingenuity and doggedness. He knew the efficiency program and he had perfected the rhetoric of anti-bossism, which enabled him to talk to reform-minded Republicans who might otherwise have been skeptical of him; as the year progressed, he made several well-received appearances before wellborn audiences, demonstrating a sobriety that surprised many in the crowd. He also had a personal following no other potential candidate possessed. His political manager Vito Marcantonio launched a petition-writing campaign in Italian neighborhoods and sent them "by the wheelbarrow" to Judge Seabury. And he threatened to challenge the fusionists' candidate in the Republican primary. "He would send for me every once in a while and say . . . 'Well, who's your latest mayor?'" the chairman of the City Fusion Party recalled, "and I would tell him. He would jump around and shake his fist and he'd say, 'Well, there's only one man going to be the candidate, and I'm the man. I'm going to run. I want to be mayor.'"[46]

Gradually La Guardia won the support of key fusionists. New York County Republican chairman Kingsland Macy, recognizing that FDR's emergence as the dominant figure in American politics had likely shut his party out of state and national office for the near future, came to view La Guardia as the Republicans' best opportunity to hold on to at least one major source of patronage. Adolf Berle, who sat on the "harmony committee" that ultimately selected a fusion candidate, gave his strong support to La Guardia. And most important of all, Samuel Seabury, whose status as the public face of the anti-Tammany movement gave him immense power in the fusion proceedings, set his heart on the Little Flower's candidacy. Berle, the first to approach Seabury on La Guardia's behalf, had satisfied the judge that La Guardia was not in fact a "noisy, cheap, self-promoting politician" by recounting the Little Flower's diligence and ability during the lame duck session. Seabury soon came to believe La Guardia combined the qualities he most wished to see in a reform candidate: "he's absolutely honest, he's a man of great courage, and he can win." By the time the harmony committee convened in early August 1933, Seabury would accept no one else. He used his influence to block all other candidates, and after a stormy backroom session on the evening of August 3, the committee chose La Guardia.[47]

After more than a decade in national politics, La Guardia now moved back to the municipal sphere. Even the most ambitious big-city mayor could not hope to effect the kind of economic "readjustment" for which La Guardia had worked in Washington—to spread the benefits of mechanical production more broadly, to boost mass purchasing power. These national concerns would guide La Guardia's local efforts in unexpected ways. But by and large, La Guardia's return to municipal politics meant a turn away from these issues of national political economy and toward the concerns of urban standard of living, quality of life, and public investment that had motivated the reform movements of the Progressive Era.

There was only one issue in New York's local politics, La Guardia told his fusion running mates at one September meeting, "and that issue is the Tammany Hall of [New York County chairman] John F. Curry." But if the politics of anti-bossism inevitably dominated the 1933 campaign, La Guardia himself had integrated good-government institutional reform into the vision of progressive municipal government he had developed a decade earlier; the two were now thoroughly intertwined, and though he devoted most of his words on the campaign trail to denouncing Tammany plunder and theft, he had little difficulty explaining how a government of "brokers and fixers" (as Seabury put it) impeded the realization of his own vision of civic progress. The city's collective advancement, he believed, had been blocked by politics conducted for private gain; the paternalistic, advantage-driven character of machine government had stymied the development of a local government that could make true social progress. "Too often life in New York is merely a squalid succession of days," he said in one campaign speech (later reworked as an op-ed), "whereas in fact it can be a great, living, thrilling adventure."

The reason, I think, is plain. . . . We need imagination in City Hall—imagination for the other fellow; and hitherto all we have had has been astuteness to find personal advantage. . . .

First and foremost, I want justice on the broadest scale. By this I do not mean the justice that is handed out in police courts. I mean the justice that gives to everyone some chance for the beauty and the better things of life. . . .

From Bowling Green to the south boundaries of Yonkers, from the Hudson River to Queens and Coney Island, there are great areas of the people who regard city government either as a natural enemy or as a devouring monster to be propitiated with offerings before their rights of citizenship can be secured.[48]

A sagacious Democratic leader in the Murphy mold, encountering the circumstances that confronted Tammany in 1933, would have nominated a respected outsider unbesmirched by the challenges involved in governing during the fiscal crisis and acceptable to the city's business community, which wanted reform but remained leery of La Guardia. But Tammany Hall did not possess sagacious leadership. "It is a fiction, the New Tammany," John F. Curry had proclaimed upon assuming the New York County chairmanship in 1929. "I will carry out the policies in which I grew up." The Seabury hearings and the rise of Roosevelt had only intensified Tammany's insistence on guarding the organization's prerogatives, and Curry now renominated O'Brien, one of the Manhattan machine's own. Almost immediately upon O'Brien's victory in the Democratic primary, a boom began among anti-Tammany, anti–La Guardia businessmen for a third ticket, the candidate to be the former acting mayor Joseph McKee. News soon broke that President Roosevelt's two top political operatives in New York, Flynn of the Bronx and New York State leader (now also DNC chair and postmaster general) Jim Farley, had agreed that McKee's candidacy on an independent Democratic ticket would be desirable. McKee, who did not really want to reenter public life, dithered for a few days before succumbing to pressure from the national administration and announcing his candidacy. The independent Democrats dubbed their invention the Recovery Party, evoking the most prominent of the New Deal alphabet agencies.[49]

It was widely believed at the time that McKee would not have entered the race without the White House's approval. Only years later would it become known just how active a role Roosevelt had in fact played. According to Farley's diary—the fullest, most contemporary, and most credible account—McKee's candidacy originated with the pro-Roosevelt forces within the New York Democracy: Farley, Flynn, and State Democratic Committee lieutenant Vincent Dailey had been planning it for some time prior to the Democratic primaries, spurred by poll data supplied by the *Literary Digest*, which showed O'Brien could not win in a two-man race with La Guardia. Once the primary ballots had been counted, the Democratic Party chieftains joined the president and presidential secretary Missy LeHand for dinner in the White House, where it was unanimously decided that McKee would enter the race. "The President is delighted," Farley wrote, "and while he will not actively take part the plan has his sanction and approval." Roosevelt personally helped to draft the statement announcing Farley's intention to vote for McKee and used his personal influence to secure at least one of McKee's ticket mates—Ferdinand Pecora, who had received great acclaim as the high-profile counsel of the Senate Banking and Currency Committee's investigation of Wall Street business practices and their connection to the Great Crash, and who now agreed to run for Manhattan district attorney.[50]

Roosevelt had intervened "so adroitly and indirectly," his biographer James MacGregor Burns later wrote, that "politicians were arguing years later as to which Democratic faction he had aided, or whether he was intent mainly on electing La Guardia." He definitely did not intervene with the intention of helping La Guardia get elected—for the decision was made based on polling evidence that La Guardia's victory in a two-way race with O'Brien was all but certain. It does not necessarily follow, of course, that Roosevelt was actually antagonistic toward the prospect of a La Guardia mayoralty. It seems most likely that the president was relatively indifferent to the outcome as between McKee and La Guardia; and that he saw in the 1933 municipal elections an opportunity to reorganize the Democratic Party in the city, building up the pro–New Deal factions in the Bronx and Brooklyn and marginalizing the incumbent leadership of Tammany Hall. (He and Farley would continue with this project during La Guardia's first term.)[51]

October saw a rough-and-tumble campaign in which La Guardia worked assiduously to keep bossism at the center of the election and McKee sought to make the race a referendum on the national administration. The campaign culminated in mid-October when the fusionists published selected parts of a quarter-century-old article penned by McKee which, when read out of context, suggested anti-Semitism. This incident, Flynn later claimed, prevented Roosevelt from making the open endorsement he had promised when he urged McKee to enter the race.[52]

La Guardia won with 40 percent of the total vote to McKee's 28 percent and O'Brien's 27 percent; fusion took the comptrollership and the presidency of the Board of Aldermen, along with the borough presidencies of Queens, Brooklyn, and Staten Island, giving it control of the Board of Estimate. Five factors stand out as essential to La Guardia's triumph. First, Italian Americans, who voted overwhelmingly for La Guardia, had provided fusion with a firm base of support. Second, the fiscal crisis and the political theater of the Seabury hearings together had produced a soaring turnout in affluent, Republican-leaning neighborhoods: in the two most staunchly Republican districts in Manhattan, voting had increased by 69 and 74 percent, respectively, and La Guardia's share of the vote had climbed by 21 and 16 percent. (The extraordinary jump in voter participation between 1929 and 1933, when the number of ballots cast grew by more than 50 percent, was disproportionately a mobilization of the affluent.) Third, a minority of independent Democrats—perhaps a third of those who were in play between La Guardia and McKee—had crossed party lines to vote for the Little Flower. Fourth, the Socialist Party, which had seemingly revived between 1929 and 1932, had suddenly and unexpectedly declined, with La Guardia apparently the main beneficiary. Fifth, and not least, McKee had been unable to convince habitual Democratic voters to abandon the star (the traditional Democratic ballot symbol) and vote Recovery: had he won even half of O'Brien's ballots, he, not La Guardia, would have been mayor of New York and the New Deal would have come to Gotham via a reformed Democratic machine.[53]

Roosevelt and La Guardia had come to power on the basis of quite different electoral coalitions. Roosevelt had garnered a traditional Democratic vote in New York, grounded in reinforcing cleavages of class and ethnicity. If Roosevelt's voters came disproportionately from the tenement districts, La Guardia (his Italian supporters notwithstanding) did best among the wealthy and the middle classes. But La Guardia's vote was not simply the inverse of Roosevelt's. The basic fact, which McKee discovered when he tried to make political advantage of his relation to the New Deal, was that in 1933, national and local politics were to a large degree *unrelated*. The traditional relation between national and local elections rested in the party connection; the fusion movement, the Democratic split, and the salience of the machine-reform cleavage had weakened that connection. And except insofar as they were organized by political parties, New Yorkers' preferences in national politics had little bearing on their preferences in local politics. The issues in question in the 1933 mayoral campaign were corruption, machine rule, solvency, and social order—issues largely unconnected to the divisions between workers and managers, wets and dries that animated voting in national elections. It was not that there was no set of problems common to both national and local politics—by 1933, unemployment was the dominant issue at all levels of politics—but rather that few policies or institutions (beyond the parties) were in place to link the two levels of government. In 1933, municipal and national politics still operated in different spheres.

The socialist muckraker Paul Blanshard, writing in *The Nation* several weeks before the 1933 election, predicted that a triumphant

La Guardia could "make out of New York a gigantic laboratory for civic reconstruction." But most progressives and leftists, appreciative of the constraints which would confront the new administration, harbored no such optimism. "Certainly there is nothing in the outcome of the election which makes it unlikely that Tammany will come back in 1937," *The New Republic*'s editorialists offered, "and when we consider the financial difficulties with which La Guardia will be confronted, the continuing and perhaps increasing burden of relief for the unemployed, the iron dictatorship of the bankers to which the city has pledged itself far into the future, it is hard to see how he can go out of office as popular as he enters it."[54]

VIII

Three days after his election, seeking some rest after the campaign, La Guardia left New York for a ten-day vacation—the last he would enjoy for six years. Accompanied by Marie, two family friends, and six newspaper reporters, the mayor-elect boarded a steamship bound first for Havana and then the Panama Canal Zone. Each day the newspapermen sent dispatches back to New York via wireless, recounting the day's recreation and relating La Guardia's pronouncements on what he expected to do once he took office. En route to Cuba, La Guardia suggested an approach to cutting the city's expenditures and bringing its budget into balance; from Panama, he promised to seek unification of the rapid transit system and revision of the city charter. A few days later, he issued a plan for municipal beer gardens along the Harlem River, modeled on Vienna's, to provide "wholesome recreation, based on a liberal, constructive and intelligent attitude" with the aim of giving jobs to the unemployed. On the last day of the trip, after speaking with Adolf Berle and Robert Moses in New York, La Guardia announced that he had made appointments in Washington with Public Works Administration director Harold Ickes and "minister of relief" Harry Hopkins to discuss public works and work relief projects for the city. The party then set out for Washington, not by ship, but aboard a fourteen-passenger Curtiss Condor biplane.

La Guardia emerged from the meetings with Ickes and Hopkins visibly elated. To more than twenty Washington reporters who crowded into his hotel suite for an afternoon press conference—the meeting "took on for a time the aspects of a college reunion," the *New York Times* reported—he announced that the conferences had been "very satisfactory. I am certain not only of full cooperation but a sympathetic understanding of our problems just as we understand their problems." Several weeks later, a second visit to Washington, and his first meeting with Roosevelt, resulted in assurance of a PWA grant to complete the outer borough segments of the Eighth Avenue Independent subway line, a project that had been written off as dead only days before La Guardia's White House visit.[55]

By the time of La Guardia's election, it was no longer as unusual as it would have been only a few years earlier to see a big-city mayor beat a path to Washington. Before 1933, one had to look hard to find direct federal-municipal contacts outside of wartime; "the great majority of federal-city relations," one study concluded, "were casual and incidental, if not extralegal," pertaining mostly to rivers and harbors, the construction of courthouses and post offices, and party patronage appointments. But as one city after another reached the edge of bankruptcy in the early 1930s, local officials, having quickly given up on rural-dominated state governments unsympathetic to urban issues (particularly unemployment relief, frequently denounced as a "dole"), had begun to reach out to the federal government. In mid-1932, Detroit mayor Frank Murphy, whose city had been hit harder than practically any other as a result of the centrality of heavy manufacturing to its economy (and whose admirable record on local relief gave him a good deal of moral standing), had assembled many big-city mayors, including Jimmy Walker, to discuss collective measures for easing the relief burden and addressing the financial dilemma. Six months later, the United States Conference of Mayors was founded so that America's big cities could petition the federal government collectively for a national unemployment program and municipal debt refinancing. "Mayors are a familiar sight in Washington these days," T. Semmes Walmsley of New Orleans would remark the following autumn. "Whether we like it or not, the destinies of our cities are clearly tied in with national politics."

Still, that La Guardia made a visit to Washington one of his first official acts, and that he did it in such spectacular fashion—for air travel in the early 1930s still represented the pinnacle of modernity, La Guardia's flight to Washington being a kind of counterpart to Roosevelt's own dramatic flight to Chicago to accept in person the 1932 Democratic nomination—broke all precedent. And if nascent federal-municipal relations derived from the prostrate condition of America's big cities, La Guardia had a more expansive vision of what the federal government and the cities, acting in concert, could achieve. After he took office, he sent some of his commissioners to Washington to make the acquaintance of federal department secretaries and undersecretaries. "It is part of my program to establish very close relations between your Department and the City of New York," he wrote to Secretary of Agriculture Henry A. Wallace in a letter introducing Markets Commissioner William Fellowes Morgan, Jr. "The possibilities are tremendous. The surface has not even been scratched."[56]

PART II
THE NEW DEAL

4

"Jobs Is the Cry"

"It's more than a New Deal," Harold Ickes remarked of Roosevelt's Hundred Days. "It's a new world." As La Guardia took office, many New Yorkers believed a new era had likewise dawned in Gotham. The *Herald Tribune* put it this way on the first day of 1934: "It is a new year so singular for this community as to be somewhat difficult to take it all in at once; its implications may prove so far-reaching in the lives of all residents of the city that no one would attempt to foresee them."

La Guardia took office with a blaze of activity and publicity, moving quickly and spectacularly to end the Walker-era practices of political preferment, graft, and low municipal productivity. "Perhaps never before," the *New York Times* wrote, "did a mayor of New York begin his term with such an air of getting down to business and enforcing industry and honesty on the part of every city employee." He rushed to fires; he conducted unannounced inspections of city hospitals, relief offices, and job sites; and as soon as the courts permitted him, he confiscated slot machines, smashed them with a sledgehammer (as the newsreel cameras rolled), and sunk them in the Long Island Sound. One New Yorker recalled that it was as though a hundred short men in black Stetsons had been loosed upon the city.

The dynamism with which La Guardia began his administration, the sense of urgency he displayed, and above all the force with which he broke from the old regime prompted countless comparisons to Roosevelt's first days in office. Their styles were different—Roosevelt the patrician who reassured the public with his jaunty confidence, La Guardia the scowling defender of the public interest. But each brought vigorous action after an interlude in which government had seemed impotent; each offered a firm hand on the wheel and promised bold experimentation; and each, coming to power in the context of fear, confusion, and desperation, stood forthrightly in opposition to the received order. In this sense, New York had a New Deal of its own.[1]

The power to create a new political order, as the political scientist Stephen Skowronek has brilliantly elucidated, hinges on the authority to repudiate the old order. La Guardia, like Roosevelt, possessed extraordinary authority of this sort. But the political freedom of action and the authority such a position implied would, it appeared, be tightly constrained by a poverty of governmental resources. La Guardia assumed command of a government limited by the shrinking of its revenue base, whose finances would presumably be subject, for the duration of his term, to the conditions imposed in the Bankers' Agreement. Under such circumstances, Norman Thomas had forecast, the mayor of New York would be "scarcely more than a receiver in bankruptcy under a broken-down political and economic system." Indeed, most signs indicated that La Guardia would preside over an era of austerity and public disinvestment, and would do so without strong party support or even much of an electoral mandate.[2]

Yet already the events and processes that would liberate La Guardia from the logic of negative-sum politics were underway—in Washington, where Roosevelt was grasping for a means by which to address the problem of unemployment. Joblessness had been the nation's paramount political and moral problem when Roosevelt took office; it remained such two years later. But in the interim the problem of "unemployment" had been redefined, and Roosevelt's own ideas and preferences for how to address it had changed. Initially, he had viewed reemployment as an objective to be attained through a broader intervention in market economies: when a rationalized and harmonious economy produced greater purchasing power for the "consuming classes," he believed, reemployment would naturally follow. But the persistent failure of reemployment to match the rapid economic expansion of Roosevelt's first term forced the president to search for a program specifically to provide jobs. From numerous alternatives, he chose to employ jobless workers, under the auspices of municipal governments, in the production of public goods and services—in the process altering the very possibilities of urban government.

I

Like his reform predecessors, La Guardia drew his top-level appointees from the worlds of professional philanthropy and charity, private business, and the academy. He also retained several members of Walker's administration, enlisted the most prominent alumnus of Al Smith's cabinet, and conducted national searches—a novelty—to find commissioners of Health and Corrections. A few owed their appointments primarily to service rendered during the 1933 campaign. Sworn in to much fanfare, La Guardia's commissioners assumed the work of ending the abuses of the Walker era and moved to institute administrative practices (such as centralized purchasing) that had their origins in the Progressive Era efficiency program. They also assumed the vital task of choosing able deputy commissioners to oversee particular programs and departmental initiatives.

If the upper, appointive reaches of La Guardia's government were filled primarily according to professional qualification and secondarily in recognition of service in the fusion cause, meritocratization was the theme in staffing the rest of the Civil Service. Tammany had filled the most desirable midlevel positions with party workers and had distributed other municipal jobs through the clubhouses: this was where New Yorkers could most easily learn about job openings, and a recommendation from a party leader was usually enough to see an applicant through the Civil Service examination procedure. Conversely, La Guardia's Civil Service Commission began the practice of publicizing job openings and replaced the essay exams the Democrats had used to give their examiners maximum discretion with multiple-choice tests. The commission also increased the number of municipal jobs that required a competitive Civil Service examination: the percentage of jobs in the "competitive" class rose from 54.5 in the last year of O'Brien's mayoralty to 74.3 at the midway point of La Guardia's.

Meritocratization, combined with the weak private job market of the 1930s and the relatively great prestige the city's public sector now enjoyed, caused Civil Service applications to soar—from 6,327 in 1933 to 252,084 in 1939. The La Guardia administration, drawing from a much broader and deeper pool than had its Democratic predecessors, reaped a windfall of talent; the extraordinary cohort that entered the structurally powerful *mezzo* level of the Civil Service during these years, later known as the "Depression geniuses," would run the day-to-day operations of Gotham's municipal government until they began to retire in the 1960s. (There were, of course, exceptions to these general trends of professionalization and meritocratization. People who had served effectively in La Guardia's campaigns were more likely to be selected for preferment, and La Guardia used the powers of appointment to fortify his own political organization and those of the parties that supported him, as well as to satisfy powerful civic, religious, and ethnic groups. Sometimes he made patronage appointments simply on personal whim. Manhattan Borough president Stanley Isaacs recalled one instance when La Guardia sent over names for two paving inspection positions that required neither expertise nor a full day's work. One was "the nephew of a very important cleric in the Catholic Church"; the other was the mayor's "favorite drunkard.")[3]

La Guardia's first priority upon taking office was to shore up the city's balance sheet and, by so doing, regain access to the credit markets. Like Roosevelt, who had used his powers of appointment to herd reluctant Democratic congressmen into line behind his own Economy Act, La Guardia considered it politically and financially essential to begin his administration from a strong fiscal position. Restoring the value of municipal bonds offered the mayor a way of pulling the investor class more securely into his coalition (and winning over that part of it which had backed McKee in the 1933 election). The city's credit rating also had symbolic power: at a time when creditworthiness had strong moral overtones, bond ratings and balanced budgets became for La Guardia a touchstone by which to contrast fusion with the "immoral" Tammany regime that had preceded it. Most important, poor municipal credit impeded the new administration's ability to undertake other parts of its agenda. "[U]nder the present economic system," La Guardia remarked, "a city simply cannot do the things it would like to do unless financially able."

By the time La Guardia took office, New York was no longer threatened by default, thanks to the Bankers' Agreement. But neither could it sell its bonds on the open market: this, La Guardia and his advisers believed, would necessitate closing an inherited budget deficit of some $30 million. With little sympathy for the Tammany-appointed public employees—many of whom he considered incapable of providing the kind of productive labor progressive city government required—La Guardia was prepared to slash jobs from the city and county governments and reduce salaries in order to close the budget deficit. On his first day in office, he submitted to the Board of Estimate a piece of legislation which proposed to close the deficit by allowing the mayor to override charter provisions and Civil Service laws to reorganize city and county offices (and abolish those deemed unnecessary), impose new salaries, compel month-long pay-less furloughs, and cut up to 10,000 jobs—all by executive order. The provisions of the proposal (which was dubbed the Economy Bill) were to last for two years; the Board of Estimate quickly amended this to nine months. Despite some opposition, the city legislatures passed the bill, and Governor Herbert Lehman gave his approval after persuading La Guardia to vest the powers in the Board of Estimate (which fusion controlled) rather than in the mayor's office. The real test took place in Albany, where the bill required a two-thirds majority in each chamber, allowing for concerted opposition from the Democratic organizations and public employees.

When the measure came up for a vote in late January 1934, the state assembly voted it down. "I would be against this bill even if the City of New York went bankrupt or the United States went bankrupt," one Manhattan assemblyman remarked. For more than two months, La Guardia shuttled back and forth between New York and Albany, working the State House assiduously; downstate civic groups and newspapers, particularly those that had supported McKee in the election, began to rally around him. Powerful Democrats came out in support of the measure—first Postmaster General and DNC chairman James A. Farley and Bronx County chairman Edward J. Flynn, then Roosevelt himself. FDR, who was sufficiently worried about New York's financial management that he had specifically instructed Public Works administration director Harold Ickes to withhold federal loans to the city until it demonstrated a balanced budget, had discussed the outlines of the legislation when the two first met following La Guardia's election in December 1933. (La Guardia later hinted that Roosevelt had given him advice on how to get it through the state legislature.) After the bill stalled in the assembly, Roosevelt called the two ranking Democrats, assembly minority leader Irwin Steingut and Senate president *pro tempore* John J. Dunnigan, to the White House, presumably to indicate his own support for the measure; when the Albany Democrats voted it down for a second time, Roosevelt brought Steingut and Dunnigan back to Washington. "I told the Majority Leader in the Senate and the Minority Leader in the Assembly [the Democratic leaders in each chamber] that the quicker the City of New York was put into a proper financial status, the quicker they would get federal funds," he explained afterward, "and that we could not wait all year, that some other city might balance its budget and be entitled to it." La Guardia's representatives in Albany made additional concessions, and the bill passed the assembly on April 5; a few days later, after heaping abuse and epithets on La Guardia, the state senate followed suit.

The final bill left fusion hardly any authority to reorganize the city and county governments: this would await the voters' enactment of a new city charter in 1936 and reform of the county governments by petition and referendum in 1941. In the meantime, La Guardia was able to use its provisions for salary reductions and month-long payless furloughs to cut about $13.5 million from the city budget. The rest of the $30 million deficit was made up by restoring O'Brien's utility taxes and levying a very small tax on business and professional income. Together, these measures had the desired effect on the financial markets. A few months after the Economy Bill finally passed, La Guardia, Comptroller Joseph McGoldrick, and Chase National Bank chairman Winthrop Aldrich, with Reconstruction Finance Corporation chairman Jesse Jones mediating, negotiated a refinancing of the city's long-term debt, dropping the interest rate from 5.75 to 3.8 percent. For the first time in several years, municipal bonds were selling at above par; by the midpoint of La Guardia's first term, new bond issues were carrying the lowest interest rates in the city's history. "So ends another cycle in New York City financing," Adolf Berle wrote to Roosevelt, "and, incidentally, finishes what I set out to do in this New York adventure. Now all we have to do is to govern the town."[4]

The Economy Bill represented an important early victory for La Guardia, for it not only won him the admiration of many good-government reformers and municipal bondholders but also permitted him to establish a reputation as a skilled and resourceful political fighter. Roosevelt's involvement had demonstrated to Farley, Flynn, Kings County Democratic chairman Frank Kelly, and Governor Lehman (with whom La Guardia thenceforth would have a stormy but productive relationship) that they would not simply be able to take the president's support for granted in their contests with New York's fusion mayor.[5]

Still, the fact remained that La Guardia had begun his administration by cutting further into departments that had already been pared close to the bone. La Guardia's commissioners discovered upon taking office that the mayor expected them to reduce their expenditures: he required this of every department except Hospitals and Welfare. They found, too, that there was insufficient money in the city coffers for even the smallest and most advantageous of local projects. Under these conditions, an ambitious social program appeared out of the question. But programmatic innovations already enacted at the national level would soon alter this calculus, loosening the constraints that operated upon New York's municipal government.[6]

II

"Our greatest primary task," Roosevelt had proclaimed at his inauguration the previous March, "is to put people to work." That those words were followed almost immediately by an appeal to recognize frankly "the overbalance of the population in our industrial centers" indicated that FDR had not at all abandoned his desire to move workers out of the cities and into the countryside. A full resettlement program would come later; in the interim, the new administration produced as its first substantial jobs effort a scheme to employ a quarter of a million young men in rural conservation and flood control work for terms ranging from six months to two years. Thousands of city youths soon found themselves planting saplings, clearing undergrowth, building watchtowers, restoring battlefields, fighting forest fires, or battling insects under the auspices of the Civilian Conservation Corps (CCC).[7]

Yet unemployment per se remained a secondary consideration for much of Roosevelt's first two months in office. During that time, the president signed into law (or enacted by executive order) a series of measures intended to achieve general economic recovery. First was the Emergency Banking Act, which suspended transactions in gold, enabled Roosevelt to appoint receivers to reorganize banks that could not meet government stability tests, and authorized the Reconstruction Finance Corporation to buy preferred stock in American banks in order to recapitalize them. Next came the Economy Act, which gave the president broad authority to cut federal salaries and trim veterans' pensions in order to reduce the federal deficit (and thereby, Roosevelt believed, encourage private investment). Soon, the president would depart from the gold standard, take various measures to reflate the dollar, and sign into law several programs to facilitate the refinancing of mortgage debt.

Legislation of this sort, Roosevelt suggested, represented "foundation stones," intended to halt a deflationary cycle that was destroying assets and national confidence and causing myriad economic and personal dislocations. By mid-May 1933, Roosevelt and the Democratic Congress had moved on to measures the president claimed would go "much more fundamentally into our economic problems."

The common objective of these measures was to raise the level of purchasing power among "the consuming classes" and, in so doing, to build markets for the products of American industry and agriculture. "If all our people have work and fair wages and fair profits, they can buy the products of their neighbors and business is good," Roosevelt told his audience in a July "fireside chat." "But if you take away the wages and the profits of half of them, business is only half as good. It doesn't help much if the fortunate half is very prosperous— the best way is for everybody to be reasonably prosperous." His approach, as he explained it, was to use the power of government to enable (in some instances to force) producers to take collective action for the collective good, which they could not do on their own in a competitive economy. "Partnership," "coordination," and "planning" became the key words of this phase of the New Deal.

In May, Roosevelt signed into law the Agricultural Adjustment Act, a measure which aimed to raise the prices of agricultural commodities (and hence rural purchasing power) by limiting farm production. The following month, Congress created the National Recovery Administration, an agency which attempted to do for the industrial economy some of the things the Agricultural Act sought to do for farmers. The NRA was the product of many hands and combined elements of many different agendas and approaches, but its provisions served two main purposes. First, its authors hoped that by suspending antitrust laws and providing "government sponsorship for industry-by-industry cooperation to coordinate prices and regulate production levels and conditions of employment," they could halt the recession-driven "cutthroat competition" which placed powerful downward pressure on prices, profit margins, labor costs, and working standards. In other words, they sought to use government coordination to stabilize the industrial sector as a whole. Second, by using the carrot of legal sanction for "business self-government," they sought to induce industries to accept voluntarily some of the objectives for which congressional progressives had been fighting—"reasonable wages," "reasonable hours," an end to child labor, and a guarantee of the right of workers to bargain collectively. Like the congressional progressives, Roosevelt argued that the limitation of working hours would serve to "spread" employment more broadly and thereby to address the maldistribution of purchasing power.[8]

Throughout the Hundred Days, and notwithstanding the Civilian Conservation Corps, Roosevelt had viewed efforts to create jobs directly by government spending with considerable skepticism. He had little faith in the concept of a "multiplier" effect that underpinned arguments for countercyclical government spending—i.e., that the respending of government payments by workers and businesses would stimulate additional private sector employment and production. "It is the habit of the unthinking," he had remarked during the 1932 campaign, "to turn in times like this to the illusions of economic magic. People suggest that a huge expenditure of public funds by the Federal government and by State and local governments will completely solve the unemployment problem. . . . Let us admit frankly that it would be only a stopgap." Absent a larger economic rationale, a spending approach to job creation promised only to undermine the reputation for sound finance he had worked so hard to earn with his Economy Act.

Yet Roosevelt was not prepared to resist the powerful movement for a federal public works program that had developed in Congress, among unionists, and within the broader progressive community. Pressed both by the pro-spending group in Congress—Senators La Follette, Costigan, Wagner, and others—and by some of his own advisers and cabinet members, he agreed to a $3.3 billion appropriation for the construction of public works projects, non-self-liquidating as well as self-liquidating. Roosevelt remained so concerned with sound finance that he committed nearly half his message to Congress recommending passage of the National Industrial Recovery

Act to ways of raising adequate revenue to pay interest and amortization on the debt the government would incur. But by agreeing
to include non-self-liquidating projects, he had gone well beyond
Hoover's reluctant public works program. The $3.3 billion was appro-
priated under Title II of the National Industrial Recovery Act, which
also authorized Roosevelt to create a Public Works Administration
(PWA) to allocate and administer the funds.[9]

Much of the appropriation was earmarked for one purpose or
another: $450 million for roads, $238 million for shipbuilding, and
$25 million for resettlement. But to spend the larger share, some
$2.2 billion, federal policymakers turned to local officials: the money
was distributed in the form of grants and loans (at first, 30 percent
grant and 70 percent loan) to local and state governments whose
project applications the PWA had approved. This intergovernmental approach was partly dictated by the limits of the federal government's jurisdiction, as many of the projects would be built on state
and local property. But it was also a practical solution to the underdevelopment of the American central state. Seeking a means by
which to attain the national objectives of job creation and the stimulation of heavy industry through purchase orders, federal officials
had enlisted the planning, operational, and fiscal resources of local
governments by offering to help them solve pressing problems of
their own—joblessness and the inadequacy of local infrastructure.[10]

This early New Deal venture in intergovernmental collaboration
was not a success. Even as they sought to draw upon the strengths
of local governments, the New Dealers had designed a program
that bumped up against their weaknesses, for the exhaustion of
local finances and the constraints of municipal debt ceilings all but
ensured that local governments would choose not to invest in public
works, even on the comparatively favorable terms the PWA offered.
(Federal officials had exacerbated this flaw by making federal loans
contingent on the sound credit of recipient governments.) New York

was representative: before the Bankers' Agreement, Mayor O'Brien did not apply for a single PWA grant; the PWA was able to funnel money into Gotham only through public authorities such as the Port Authority and the Triborough Bridge Authority, which were not encumbered by state borrowing limits and could pledge future toll revenues as security for their bonds. (The Port Authority received $17 million from the PWA for the construction of the Lincoln Tunnel; the Triborough Bridge Authority received $44.2 million for the massive three-span complex it was building to connect Manhattan, the Bronx, and Queens via Wards and Randall's islands.) Thus constrained, the PWA directed much of its early spending toward federal agencies, particularly the military; it could show little in the way of job creation "in the field," and by the end of the summer of 1933, journalists had begun to chide the agency for not showing concrete results. PWA administrator Harold Ickes, in turn, blamed the delays on state and municipal governments.[11]

As the PWA spun its wheels, the industrial economy as a whole, having recovered rapidly in the months following Roosevelt's inauguration, turned sour. Relieved of the crippling fear that had gripped the American economy during the interregnum, business had expanded rapidly in the second quarter, with indices such as factory output and industrial stock prices shooting up from their March lows. But in July, this expansion came to a sudden halt. At first, Roosevelt viewed the slowdown as a "healthy reaction to speculation," but by the fall he was expressing privately his worries about the direction of the American economy. This, the first of several economic contractions to occur on Roosevelt's watch, prompted the administration to undertake a new round of policy initiatives, utilizing authority delegated by Congress during the Hundred Days. National Recovery Administration director Hugh Johnson issued a "blanket code" providing for uniform wages and hours standards in industry and launched the massive "Blue Eagle" propaganda campaign to persuade businesses to comply with it. (On the second Wednesday of September, some 1.5 million New Yorkers turned out to watch the city's employers and employees affirm their support for the president's recovery program by marching down Fifth Avenue in one of the greatest parades in the city's history.) Roosevelt created the Commodity Credit Corporation, an effort to raise agricultural prices by purchasing surplus goods (which were distributed to relief families), and began buying gold at above-market prices—another effort to reflate commodity prices. And that fall, he launched a new jobs program that utilized the direct employment approach pioneered by the Civilian Conservation Corps—but which was centered not in the American wilderness but in the great cities.[12]

III

During the rapid expansion of the second quarter of 1933, private industry had begun to reemploy the most productive workers thrown out of work at the depth of the depression. Yet as summer turned to fall, unemployment remained widespread, touching members of all classes and professions. Lorena Hickok, the garrulous and acute journalist employed as a roving reporter by federal relief administrator Harry Hopkins, wrote after visiting New York:

> One city block will contain almost 200 families on the relief rolls. Those 1,250,000 human beings [the city total] represent a complete cross-section of the population, the best and the worst—the most intelligent, and the most highly educated, and the most helpless and the most ignorant. Among them are represented more than 30 nationalities. . . . And among them are business and professional men whose incomes five years ago ran into many thousands of dollars. There they are, all thrown

together into a vast pit of human misery, from which a city, dazed, still only half awake to the situation, is trying to extricate them.[13]

Twelve thousand of the 15,000 members of the New York City musicians' local were unemployed, and paid memberships in the Actors Equity Association had declined by 70 percent, two thirds of New York's "legitimate" (non-burlesque) theaters having been closed for most of that season. Many advertising agencies had reduced their staffs by half or more. No one could tell precisely how many doctors were out of work, but the head of the Kings County Medical Society reported that 30 percent of Brooklyn doctors had taken the telephones out of their offices; the figure for Manhattan was even higher. With construction all but stopped, *The Nation* estimated that one half of engineers and six of every seven architects were out of work. In some of the building trades, unemployment was estimated at 90 percent.[14]

Many of these unemployed men and women, having exhausted personal, family, and community resources, now relied on public relief. The responsibility for administering unemployment relief in New York City belonged primarily to the city's Home Relief Bureau and the New York State TERA, which continued to reimburse local governments a share of their relief expenditures. Since March 1933, the Federal Emergency Relief Administration had given essential support to state and local relief efforts, dispensing grants-in-aid to state relief agencies (half on a matching basis—one federal dollar for every three local dollars—and half at the director's discretion). Though the FERA did seek to assert a measure of control—building up a staff of welfare professionals to combat "local incompetence, miserliness, fiscal conservatism, and outright corruption" and in a few instances actually nationalizing inadequate state-level relief setups—the federal presence was generally limited to channeling federal money to state and local relief administrations. This was especially true in places like New York where state and local relief institutions were relatively strong.

The FERA's establishment had, however, provided an institutional base from which social welfare professionals could seek to expand the federal presence in the field of social provision. Preeminent among those who pushed for a greater federal role was the agency's director, Harry Hopkins, the Iowa-born social worker whom Roosevelt had previously made the operational head of the TERA. Educated in the Christian social reform milieu of Grinnell College, Hopkins had gone to New York and found work at the Christadora settlement house; in the next two decades he had moved through the city's charity organizations, serving first as a supervisor for the Association for Improving the Conditions of the Poor (where, during the recession of 1914–15, he had overseen a survey of the city's unemployed and a small work relief project for the Bronx Zoo), then as executive secretary of the Board of Child Welfare, and later as director of the New York Tuberculosis and Health Society. An associate in the New York social work world remembered him this way:

> He was intense, seeming to be in a perpetual nervous ferment—a chain smoker and black coffee drinker. . . . Most of the time he would show up in the office looking as though he had spent the previous night sleeping in a hay loft. . . . While other executives . . . would say, "We have this amount of money available—and this is how much we can spend," Hopkins, by contrast, never worried about the cost until later . . . and then he would scramble around to get the money.

Politically, Hopkins had followed a fairly common path for a left-leaning New York social worker: a registered but relatively uncommitted Socialist, he had voted for John Purroy Mitchel in

1913 (and had seen Mitchel appoint his mentor, AICP director John Kingsbury, commissioner of Charities); in 1917, having soured on municipal reform, he had voted for Morris Hillquit; thereafter he had supported Al Smith, and by the early 1930s he was a liberal Democrat. But he owed his appointment to the TERA more to his professional reputation within the New York social work world than to his party affiliation.[15]

Like many New York social workers, Hopkins was acutely attentive to the social, moral, and psychological dimensions of the unemployment crisis. And like many of his former colleagues, he had come to believe that idleness exacted a toll far beyond lost wages: humiliating and destructive, it created a sense of failure and uselessness that ate away at a worker's social status, sapped people of their "self-respect," "ambition," and "pride," and weakened families. He also believed that so-called home relief, meaning relief without the requirement of work, exacerbated these costs, depriving people of "their sense of independence and strength and their sense of individual destiny." Hopkins favored work relief—a form of social provision, he believed, that mitigated rather than reinforced the social and psychological damage of unemployment and that would, moreover, conserve the job skills and work habits of the unemployed such that they would be employable when private industry recovered. Through the summer of 1933, Hopkins pushed state administrators both to expand their work relief programs and to improve the quality of the projects (which varied widely in social utility); the FERA also established some limited projects of its own. By the end of the summer, Hopkins and his aides were making plans to nationalize the function of work relief by creating a public employment program over which the federal government would have direct control.[16]

It was Hopkins's good fortune to be pushing a program with strong expert support (and potentially strong popular support) at a moment when Roosevelt considered it politically desirable to expand his administration's efforts on behalf of the jobless. "We are not going through another winter like the last," FDR had promised the nation in July. "I doubt if ever any people so bravely and cheerfully endured a season half so bitter." As the first winter of the New Deal approached, Roosevelt knew that he bore the weight of popular expectations to make good on this promise (not least because of the extraordinary connection with the public he had forged during the Hundred Days). This was the first time—it would not be the last— that Roosevelt's search for a politically advantageous way of treating the unemployment crisis created an opening for Hopkins's vision for American social policy.

Hopkins took his plan to Roosevelt in late October; Roosevelt agreed to divert money from the Recovery Act appropriation for several months to launch a program of small-scale, capital-light public improvements. On November 8, 1933, the day La Guardia was elected mayor, Roosevelt announced a "fundamental change" in his administration's approach to the problem of unemployment: within three weeks, the federal government would hire 4 million men and women directly. The objective, he explained, was to remove everyone capable of working from the relief rolls and "place them on regular employment" at prevailing wages, with enough jobs left over to give work to those who were unemployed but were muddling through without having registered for government assistance. The following day he created by executive order a new—and explicitly temporary— agency, the Civil Works Administration (CWA), to undertake the work, with Hopkins named director.[17]

"Now this work is really and truly a partnership," Roosevelt remarked of the new agency. America's governments, working collaboratively with each level "do[ing] its share," "ha[d] in [their] hands to accomplish something that no nation has ever before done." Like the PWA, the CWA was premised on intergovernmental collaboration— on the idea that the compatibility of interests between the national and the local governments could be utilized to form a relationship that would permit an exercise of power neither level would be capable of on its own. But the CWA envisioned a more intensive relationship than the simple grants-in-aid administered by the PWA and the FERA (and by pre-Depression-era programs that had provided federal aid to education, highway construction, and maternal and infant health). The PWA had helped local governments hire private construction contractors, who in turn hired workers; under the CWA, the federal government itself would hire workers, paying them wages for their work on useful public projects devised, planned, and carried out (with some federal and state supervision) by municipal and county officials. Thus the CWA marked the apotheosis of the Progressive Era idea of "cooperation" between governments "in pursuit of shared social ideals."[18]

Unlike the Public Works Administration, the CWA utilized the capabilities of America's local governments very effectively. It required little of the state and local governments in the way of expenditures (standing out in this regard from both the PWA and the federal matching programs created by the Social Security Act), which meant that the program would be less likely to suffer from underfunding or from a reluctance on the part of local officials to participate. And it took full advantage of the planning and operational capacities of local governments. The synthetic pairing of federal legal and fiscal resources and local operational capacities enabled the federal government to meet its objective of employing some 4 million men and women quickly and usefully while also permitting local officials to undertake projects that might otherwise have been deemed unaffordable even during flush times. The new program, New York City CWA administrator Travis H. Whitney rightly said, offered "a challenge and an opportunity to this city to have done those things which make our city more beautiful and useful, and which the city on its own behalf would hardly ever be financially able to do."

Only days after his election, La Guardia assembled groups of architects, engineers, and other experts to develop proposals for everything from a city airport to park improvements, from subway extensions to public art projects, public housing to municipal beer gardens, promising Hopkins that they would be put into operation on the first day of his administration. There followed a brief three months in which New Yorkers attained a glimpse of the difference such an infusion of federal resources could make, not only in meeting the unemployment crisis but also in urban social policy and public investment more broadly.[19]

No city agency benefited more from the CWA than the Parks Department, newly consolidated into a single citywide agency and placed by La Guardia under the driving leadership of Commissioner Robert Moses. A Yale-, Oxford-, and Columbia-educated career civil servant, Moses had begun what would be a remarkably long and eventful life in public service with the Bureau of Municipal Research; following John Purroy Mitchel's defeat, he had received, unexpectedly, an invitation to join Al Smith's state administration— an opportunity which was to change his life profoundly. Without Smith, Moses later wrote, "I would have been just another academic researcher." As secretary of state and chairman of Smith's Council of Parks and Long Island State Parks Commission, Moses had garnered enough public acclaim to be seriously considered for the fusion nomination in 1933. Imperious and blunt, Moses brought to the city parks job a tremendous energy, a knowledge of the byways of political power in New York acquired in his service to Smith, brilliance in the fields of administration and public relations, and—not least—an exceptional network of landscape architects, engineers, designers, superintendents, and contractors.[20]

Moses and his deputies, commanding the army of laborers the CWA had made available to him, set about restoring a recreational plant that had fallen into disrepair during the fiscal crisis years.

CWA workers repainted and repaired vandalized benches, restored crumbling statues, exterminated rats, reseeded barren lawns, resurfaced pathways and tennis courts, and planted new trees; they also opened scores of new parks and playgrounds. By the end of April, every lawn in the park system had been reseeded, every park bench repainted, and every drinking fountain, trash can, and comfort station repaired or refurbished. The Central Park menagerie, America's oldest zoo, had been reborn as the Central Park Zoo, "a cluster of charming, small-scale red-brick buildings" intended to serve not as a full-scale zoo but rather as "a delightful place for children." Work had begun on Sara Delano Roosevelt Park on the Lower East Side and the 79th Street Boat Basin. September would see the reopening of Bryant Park, a priceless midtown green space which had been used in the early 1930s as a storage yard for the Board of Transportation (coming to resemble the site of an oil strike, Lewis Mumford wrote) and which would reemerge as one of the stateliest parks in the city.

Many New Yorkers were astonished at what had been accomplished. "Even with the aid of Federal funds," the *New York Times* noted, these achievements "seem little short of miraculous." The vast expansion of resources provided to local officials by the advent of federal work relief had enabled Moses and La Guardia to accomplish feats that had seemed to many New Yorkers to be beyond the reach of city government; in so doing, it allowed both men to establish reputations as charismatic public servants able to do the impossible.[21]

Besides the Parks Department, which commanded about 35 percent of the CWA's expenditures in New York City, the principal beneficiaries of the CWA were the borough presidents, who used the money for long-deferred street repavings, sewer repairs, and the like. Other projects, following in the Gibson Committee's footsteps, employed professionals, clerical workers, and artists. To publicize La Guardia's anti–slot machine crusade and his "Fish Tuesday" campaign (an effort to help the fishing industry by promoting fish consumption), the city created, in conjunction with the CWA, a Mayor's Poster Commission—the germ of what would later become the WPA Poster Division. Under the leadership of Whitney Museum director Juliana Force, the CWA employed hundreds of artists and sculptors. Other CWA workers staffed libraries, worked in fire stations, and opened a nursery school. By February 1934, the Civil Works Service (the white-collar division of the CWA) employed 21 cartographers, 12 botanists, 59 doctors, 531 nurses, 135 dentists and 38 dental hygienists, 1,841 teachers, 210 librarians, 167 architects, 7 geologists, 28 linguists, and thousands of researchers, statisticians, stenographers, secretaries, bookkeepers, and accountants.[22]

In some instances, CWA workers effectively replaced furloughed civil servants. In others, federal relief workers became a constituent part of local state building, allowing the municipal government to launch new programs and services which were to become a permanent part of the municipal landscape. Moses's parks projects offered one example of the second phenomenon; the creation of the Department of Markets' Consumers Service Division offered another. The latter, launched by Deputy Commissioner Frances Foley Gannon, sought to help housewives take advantage of market gluts which periodically reduced the price of consumer goods and brought luxury items—strawberries, for instance—within the range of working-class budgets. Each morning, the department sent supervisors to the warehouses and docks where the city's food supply was being unloaded to collect data; this information was then broadcast at 8:25 am over most of the city's major radio stations, providing consumers with valuable and otherwise unavailable information. Within a year, estimates found that more than 1 million people were listening to the broadcasts and that the Consumers Service's notices and informational campaigns had increased the sale of particular items by as much as 20 percent. New York's pioneering program became the basis for a portable model developed by the federal Agricultural

Adjustment Administration, which was eventually instituted in more than thirty American cities. None of this could have been done without the infusion of manpower supplied by the CWA (and, later, the Works Progress Administration). In its first year, the Consumers Service Division had a municipal appropriation of all of $200; as late as 1936, it had six Civil Service workers and seventy-five federal work relief employees.[23]

The arrival of federal work relief also shaped local social politics in indirect ways. Perhaps most important, it allowed New York City to raise the standards of its own relief program. By removing many employable people from the city relief rolls, the CWA had raised the ratio of resources to recipients. (Additional funds had also been made available by loan under the Bankers' Agreement.) The Board of Estimate was able to appropriate $1 million more in January 1934 than it had in December, and an additional million in February; this in turn permitted municipal relief authorities to regularize payments, extend relief to unmarried adults, and raise monthly allowances. Around the same time, an act of the state legislature enabled the city to distribute cash instead of food tickets, which restored to unemployed families the normal human activity of handling money and likewise restored to housewives that part of their work which brought them into contact with the commercial economy. (Cash relief was justified by one welfare association on the grounds that it "tend[ed] to preserve the ingenuity and energy of the housewife," and several unemployed men interviewed in one study "remarked with pride as to the managing ability of their wives.") Unemployed families used the flexibility provided by cash relief, studies found, to buy according to ethnic dietary customs and to follow doctors' dietary recommendations, to cover expenditures such as haircuts, household purchases, and subway fare, and in some cases to hide their unemployed status from neighbors.[24]

In the third week of January 1934, despite public clamoring for a continuation of the program beyond its scheduled termination date, Hopkins announced that the CWA would be phased out by the end of March. Roosevelt had always intended the program to be temporary, a makeshift measure to buy time for industrial recovery and for the launch of the Public Works Administration's heavy construction program. Still deeply committed to the idea of economy and the principle of fiscal discipline, he now seemed to realize that, if allowed to continue, the "spending solution" implicitly presented by the CWA might inadvertently become a permanent part of the New Deal. "We must not take the position that we are going to have a permanent depression in this country," he remarked at a meeting of the National Emergency Council, "and it is very important that we have somebody to say that quite forcefully to these people." Telegrams of protest flooded into the White House from cities across the country—from CWA workers, mayors, and chambers of commerce. Congressional progressives, led by Senators Bronson Cutting and Robert La Follette, Jr., registered strong objections.[25]

In New York, the announcement touched off protests that were aimed as much at La Guardia as at Roosevelt and Hopkins—an example of how new national programs could create greater demands on local officials. La Guardia sent Hopkins a public telegram, lauding the federal government for its "vision" in creating the CWA. "Surely all this good work should not be destroyed . . . ," he wrote, "thus precipitating a real crisis." He announced publicly that he hoped to see Roosevelt to protest the termination but withdrew his request after a long talk with Hopkins. On April 1, the CWA went out of operation, and the cities returned to the system of state and local administration and local, state, and federal funding in place before.[26]

But if the intergovernmental administrative and fiscal aspects of work relief returned to something like the *status quo ante*, the politics of work relief did not. Policy made politics: mayors, the unemployed, local merchants, and elements within the labor movement had acquired a stake in the CWA's continuation, and the ill-fated fight to continue it brought them into an informal alliance that would be fortified in the years ahead. And although reports of point-less "leaf-raking" projects and "political interference" had abounded, impartial audits convinced Roosevelt that the agency had largely succeeded at the task of creating useful work for 4 million unem-ployed Americans in nearly every locality in the nation. The CWA had shown that a national public employment program, though com-plex and costly, was at least possible; and thus this brief experiment had established new boundaries and expectations in the realm of federal employment policy.[27]

IV

It is practically axiomatic that the New Deal did not "end" the Great Depression; but by some measures, the American economy in Roo-sevelt's first years in office was a remarkable success. After stabiliz-ing in the spring of 1933, the industrial economy, with some fits and starts, had recovered rapidly. Real GDP had grown by 10.9 percent in 1934; with the exception of the war production years of 1941–43, the American economy has never expanded so rapidly since. Although some economic indicators continued to lag, by 1937 real GDP had matched its 1929 level. And for those with steady employment, real wages were higher than they had been in the Roaring Twenties. The problem was that job creation did not keep pace with the rise in out-put. Mass unemployment had allowed managers "to be very selective in hiring and retaining workers, and they made the most of their opportunity"; as a result, productivity and real wages had soared (at the time GDP reached its 1928 level, "output per worker-hour was 22 per cent higher" and "[hourly] real wages averaged 36 per cent higher") while reemployment had lagged. Whereas GDP returned to its pre-Depression level in the mid-1930s, it would be 1943 before unemployment did the same.[28]

Amidst what would now be called a "jobless recovery," unmistakable public pressure for a government jobs program began to build. The dispatches from Hopkins's field reporter in New York, the journalist Wayne Parrish, convey nothing more clearly than the intensity of popular sentiment for government action to create jobs. Young people, Parrish found, were " 'bored' with relief" and "want[ed] something to do"; older people had begun to realize they were "out for good" in the new, more productive economic order and yearned for work to assuage the sense of futility they felt. "Jobs is the cry everywhere, and I can't over-emphasize this point. All agree that this is the one solution, and with no jobs in private business, they must be created by the government." "Clients have no ideas about what the government should do except that it should provide jobs. Among the supervisors and administrators, they are at a loss to predict what is to come and have only one suggestion to solve the problem. That is jobs."[29]

That these public expectations were directed so squarely at the White House was a product both of the evolution of the presidency and the changes in American political culture produced by the early New Deal programs. Beginning in his first inaugural address, the political scientist Samuel H. Beer has written, "Roosevelt called not only for a centralization of government, but also for a nationalization of politics. He not only said that the federal government would take the lead; he also . . . exhorted voters and citizens to turn to Washington as the center of power on which to exert their pressures and project their expectations." Though some New Dealers continued to feel constrained by the localistic tendencies that operated in American public life, there was no question that many unemployed Americans expected the national government to find a solution to the jobs crisis. As a Pennsylvania miner told another of Hopkins's field investigators: "If he doesn't make a go of this, a lot of people are going to be surprised, that's all."

Moreover, the earlier New Deal social programs had wrought, with astonishing speed, a virtual revolution in popular ideas of the mutual obligations of citizens and the national state. Shown that it was possible for the national government to serve as the employer of last resort, many Americans had begun to insist that they had a "right" to a job—or at least to a subsistence living. New York City Deputy Commissioner of Welfare Stanley Howe told Parrish that many New Yorkers were "now look[ing] on relief as a right equivalent to a Spanish-American War veteran's pension or a rural mail carrier's pension. . . ." New Deal pronouncements about economic security and a higher standard of living were driving popular expectations for government policy, and programs such as the FERA and the CWA appeared to validate these expectations. The new medium of radio did much to facilitate this nationalization of popular political demand. "The relief client not only reads newspapers for relief and works news announcements," Parrish wrote, "but listens to all the radio stuff out of Washington."[30]

The termination of the CWA and the concomitant decline in standards as work relief was returned to the localities touched off a series of public demonstrations in America's large cities—the largest of which, in New York, pitted six hundred unemployed workers and their advocates in a fistfight with one hundred policemen outside the Department of Welfare. In the context of rising popular protest and organizational gains by the Communist Party, many urban officials voiced fears of social upheaval. One New York City relief administrator, stationed in East Harlem, told Parrish that she felt like she was "sitting on a volcano"; Commissioner of Welfare William Hodson remarked that if reemployment "doesn't come, and come pretty quickly, there is trouble ahead." There is little evidence to suggest that radical protest "forced" the Roosevelt administration to respond

with a new policy; nor is the administration's search for a jobs program best understood as an effort to head off social upheaval. But
radical protest played an important role during these months, for it
articulated broader public opinion and kept in front of public officials the plain fact that the status quo was unacceptable to much of
the public.[31]

By the end of the summer of 1934, Roosevelt was convinced that
joblessness represented the primary economic and political problem facing his administration. He defined his immediate task not
as reviving the industrial economy as a whole—for this was already
occurring—but rather as finding work for those who remained
unemployed. The intensity of public pressure for some kind of jobs
program made it clear that there was a political profit to be won by
programmatic innovation and, likely, a cost to be incurred by maintaining the status quo. Yet if the political necessity for some kind of
action was clear, public opinion provided few real cues as to what
form it should take: a wide variety of programs could have satisfied
the same popular demand. And many different policy alternatives
existed, each with strong advocates and at least some claim of expert
support. Roosevelt remarked in a mid-September press conference
that he had received "150 or 200" different plans for dealing with
the unemployment problem. Over the course of several months, the
president, guiding the policy-making process in the absence of an
established bureaucracy or a council of advisers for economic policy, narrowed them down until he arrived at a set of proposals that,
though still vague, could be submitted to the newly convened 74th
Congress.[32]

One alternative open to Roosevelt was to subsidize the creation
of jobs by private employers. Experience with subsidization was, at
the time, limited to a few experiments (perhaps most notably in
the dying days of the Weimar Republic). But this approach did have
influential support—above all from the eminent economist Irving

Fisher, who had first proposed the idea to Roosevelt shortly after the inauguration and believed FDR had "expressed special interest" in it. And it could offer some clear advantages over government-made work: private subsidies were less costly (because private employers would supply most of the overhead); they helped the unemployed retain the job skills required for work in private industry better than did employment on government public works; and they could likely be implemented more quickly and more efficiently.

One reason the idea of private subsidies made no headway was that it lacked champions within the administration's inner circles. Whereas Harry Hopkins and Harold Ickes had personal stakes in the creation of an expanded public employment program, there was no bureaucratic advocate of private subsidies. Yet Roosevelt himself entertained the idea, at least briefly. When Fisher urged the plan on him again during a private meeting at Hyde Park in September 1934, he found the president outwardly enthusiastic: Roosevelt read Fisher's memorandum out loud (Fisher wrote to his son) "with running comments. When he finished, he said 'Grand! Perfectly Grand!'" But Fisher found Roosevelt already thinking "in terms of employment by the Government rather than reemployment in private industry." Perhaps, as the historian Richard Jensen has speculated, Roosevelt recoiled at the idea of subsidizing "economic royalists." Perhaps he believed public works would be more powerful politically, for workers would know whom they had to thank for their jobs. Perhaps he thought subsidies unworkable, or considered public works more desirable than private production. Perhaps he was swayed by the opposition of the building trades to job training for the unemployed (which they feared would glut the market for skilled labor). Whatever his reasons, Roosevelt never seriously considered creating jobs by paying private businesses to hire unemployed workers.[33]

Other groups, also envisioning a program that would put the unemployed to work manufacturing goods for private consumption, proposed that the federal government finance "production-for-use" by leasing underused factories and idle land, making them available to the unemployed, and establishing a system by which the items produced by unemployed workers could be exchanged outside the commercial system. The most famous champion of this idea was the novelist and muckraker Upton Sinclair, who was then campaigning for governor of California (having swept the Democratic primary in August) on his "End Poverty in California" (EPIC) plan. Some limited "self-help production" programs were already underway at the state level, with FERA funding. The State Relief Commission of Ohio had established a program in which workers, by laboring beyond the hours required to draw their work relief checks, earned credits which could be redeemed for "dresses, overalls, furniture," and other manufactured items.

Roosevelt was enthusiastic about the experiment of the "Ohio Plan," and Sinclair's candidacy earned him meetings with Hopkins, Ickes, Treasury Secretary Henry Morgenthau, Jr., and RFC chairman Jesse Jones, as well as with the president himself. But FDR did not consider production-for-use feasible even on a statewide basis, as Sinclair had proposed: it was "impossible, absolutely impossible, on a scale anything like that," he remarked in a press conference. "[I]f Sinclair has any sense in him," he concluded, "he will modify at least in practice this perfectly wild-eyed scheme of his and carry it on as a community experiment. It will do a lot of good work that way." Roosevelt and Hopkins were sufficiently committed to the ideas embodied in the Ohio Plan to see that some production-for-use projects were undertaken by the Works Progress Administration (which would employ workers to make garments, toys, and other objects for relief families). But Roosevelt did not seek to make production-for-use the centerpiece of his national employment program.[34]

The search for a jobs program also gave renewed impetus to Roosevelt's dream of balancing the population by resettling urban workers in the countryside. The president still saw massive unemployment as a symptom of social imbalance, and the old talk of decentralization picked up again as Roosevelt and Hopkins began discussing plans for meeting the unemployment crisis. "There are a million people too many [in New York]," FDR remarked at a press conference. "Suppose we could come back to the 1929 level of industry? Wouldn't we still have a million people on relief in the City of New York?" From this sociological perspective, a program designed to achieve "decentralization of population" by subsidizing the creation of subsistence homesteads and model industrial towns promised to get at the root causes of unemployment in a way other government spending programs could not. The FERA drew up plans for rural-industrial "relief towns" housing between 150 and 700 families each, 80 percent self-sufficient, and Roosevelt talked about them enthusiastically.

FDR discussed this subject with La Guardia from time to time. "Mayor," he once said, "I think you have two million more people than you ought to have in your city." La Guardia answered cheerfully, "Mr. President, I don't agree with you. We have four million more than we ought to have." On another occasion, when Secretary of Agriculture Henry A. Wallace asked Roosevelt to boost funding for rural work projects "in order to result in a slight movement of the city workers to places where they can be put to work more economically," La Guardia drew laughter from high-level administration officials by offering a counterproposal: "I would pay $100 for each man you could drag out of the city to your rural districts." La Guardia himself sometimes lamented that New York was too big; still, he was wary of the decentralization schemes. They struck him as transparent attempts by industry to secure cheaper labor. "[I]t will bring our whole standard down," he cautioned, "and no city can afford to meet that kind of competition."[35]

Roosevelt's back-to-the-land schemes were simply too expensive and too socially disruptive to serve as a way of meeting mass unemployment. FDR never surrendered his decentralization hopes, but he did learn to set them aside. "[Employment] is our first task," he told the advisers. "That, in turn, means that we have got to know certain facts: Where these unemployed are located, and we have got to give these projects insofar as is possible to those localities where these unemployed on the relief rolls actually live. That means also that a lot of us will have to give up a lot of 'pet' projects of our own." Roosevelt hoped to move 1 million families to subsistence farms; in the end, the Resettlement Administration placed only 11,000 families, and only three out of sixty proposed "Greenbelt Town" model suburbs were built.[36]

By ruling out subsidization of private industry, production-for-use, and resettlement, Roosevelt had decided that unemployed workers would be deployed to produce non-commodified goods in the locales where they resided. It was a short step to ground the new program in the kind of public investment projects sponsored by the PWA and undertaken by the CWA. The search for a program now narrowed: policy making became a question of how to re-form previous federal programs, and of how to reconcile the conflicting visions of public employment and public works embodied in these agencies. Historians have tended to depict this process as a struggle between Hopkins and his proto-Keynesian economic rationale for a program of relatively light work relief projects spreading broadly among the unemployed population and Ickes, the champion of heavier, more capital-intensive public works projects. But many of those who participated in top-level policy-making discussions in the fall of 1934 were pulled in conflicting directions. Hopkins, for instance, returned from a tour of Europe in August 1934 "much impressed by the public construction he had observed, especially in the Scandinavian countries. Why [he asked] should not the United States, with its vast resources, embark upon a grand scheme for building public housing, dams, and electric transmission lines, which would add appreciably to our national wealth?" For a while, he seemed to support a program of large-scale, self-liquidating public works projects such as those associated with Ickes's Public Works Administration.[37]

It was at this juncture that mayors, and La Guardia in particular, became heavily involved in the policy-making process. On September 5, the day after he met with Fisher and the day before his highly publicized meeting with Sinclair, Roosevelt chatted with La Guardia in the small, book-lined study he used as his office when he was in Hyde Park. La Guardia told reporters afterward that the two men had gone "into some detail concerning conditions and many plans for meeting the [unemployment] situation" and conditions in the cities more generally. Apparently La Guardia already had a fairly detailed set of proposals, for when he cabled the White House a few days later to arrange an appointment for the entire executive committee of the U.S. Conference of Mayors, he noted that Roosevelt was already "familiar with [the mayors'] program."[38]

Basing their suggestions upon the premise that the nation had reached a "new normal" level of unemployment (seemingly borne out by the lag between rising production and reemployment), the mayors proposed "a long-term program which will meet what is called the 'unemployment problem.'" Their program had five features: "(1) It would include workers of all types; (2) The governments, Federal, state and municipal, should draw upon those benefited from the fund for work on public work relief projects; (3) Such benefited persons should be paid prevailing wage rates up to the amount of determined benefits; (4) The United States should be divided into regions for the purpose of fixing weekly benefits in accordance with the regional costs and standards of living; (5) General administration and supervision of the plan and fund should be the responsibility of the Federal Government." The mayors urged specifically the construction of low-cost housing and new schoolhouses, and suggested that the program be financed out of current revenue, as La Guardia was attempting to do in New York.

The mayors' proposals looked more like what eventually became the Works Progress Administration than did the memos Hopkins and Ickes were submitting to the president, which still envisioned a large program of self-liquidating public works. That this was true said less about the intellectual or political influence exercised by the mayors' lobby than it did about the congruence of objectives between national and local officials. Both shared the basic goal of moving authority in relief policy from the states to the national government. (FERA officials were concerned with the question of how to operate work relief programs in cities where state governors and legislatures favored less expensive home relief and were "generally more resistant to New Deal policies" than were big-city mayors.) Most of all, both Roosevelt and the mayors wanted to employ people quickly. In this context, the mayors' proposals indicated to Roosevelt that he would have administrative and political allies for a program that would look something like the CWA.[39]

In one respect, the mayors' plan *was* intellectually influential. As a way of justifying the creation of a federal work program, the mayors proposed a division of labor between the national and the state and local governments, the former to take responsibility for the "employable" unemployed and the latter for "unemployables"—"those mentally, physically or otherwise unfit for regular gainful employment." They repurposed the old distinction between "employables" and "unemployables," used since the early nineteenth century to distinguish between the "worthy" and "unworthy" poor, in order to provide Roosevelt a justification for a vast expansion of the federal government into what had traditionally been the functional domain of the localities.[40]

It would be a year before Roosevelt had settled the questions the New Dealers wrestled with in the fall of 1934—the ratio of capital to labor, the share of projects that should produce new revenue, and so on. But by Christmastime of 1934, he knew what he wanted to ask of Congress. In the interim, the last political barrier had been surmounted: the electorate had returned a huge Democratic majority in the midterm elections, meaning that Roosevelt would retain the quasi-parliamentary relation he had enjoyed with the legislature for much of the 73rd Congress. "Boys—this is our hour," Harry Hopkins famously remarked. "We've got to get everything we want—a works program, social security, wages and hours, everything—now or never."

Roosevelt's proposal of a major new works program in his annual message to Congress on January 4, 1935, broke, one reporter wrote, "with bombshell suddenness." Proclaiming that the New Deal had "undertaken a new order of things . . . through tested liberal traditions," Roosevelt used the address to broadcast and amplify the New Deal's commitment to security—"the security of a livelihood," "security against the major hazards and vicissitudes of life," and "the security of decent homes." The centerpiece of the speech was the work program proposal. "We have here a human as well as an economic problem," Roosevelt said. "When humane considerations are concerned, Americans give them precedence"—and that, according to the president, meant providing jobs to those employable people currently on public relief. "The Federal Government must and shall quit this business of relief," he declared. He adopted the mayors' distinction between employables and unemployables, remanding the latter to the care of local welfare programs. For the 3.5 million employable people on relief, Roosevelt said, "the problem is different and the responsibility is different. This group was the victim of a nation-wide depression caused by conditions which were not local but national. The federal government is the only government agency with sufficient power and credit to meet this situation." He proposed a new program of emergency public employment. All the work, he stipulated, should be useful; it should not compete with private industry; and it should be designed to provide the greatest ratio of labor to material costs. In order to make work relief less desirable than private employment, workers would be paid in the form of "security wages"— larger than home relief benefits but less than the prevailing wage for private industry. In his annual budget message, submitted the following day, Roosevelt requested $4 billion to start the works program; it was the largest peacetime appropriation to that point in U.S. history.[41]

By this time, New York had put its own relief program on permanent footing. Around the time the Civil Works Administration was liquidated, it had become evident that the $70 million bond issue which had funded municipal relief since the Bankers' Agreement would be exhausted by the end of the summer. Rather than negotiate another loan with the city's financial community, La Guardia and the fusionists pursued new taxes, to be earmarked specifically for the city relief program, the mayor arguing with conviction that this "pay-as-you-go" policy was morally correct—that his generation had no right to expect its children and grandchildren to pay for its "blunders." Beginning in midsummer, La Guardia had cast about for politically acceptable sources of revenue; each of his proposals elicited vehement protest. The matter was finally resolved in November, when, having exhausted all other options, the mayor agreed to a 2 percent sales tax on all items excluding food and medicine—duly assailed in the New York press as a "soak the poor tax"—along with lower-yielding taxes on public utility corporations and inheritances.

These taxes would provide a firm fiscal basis for New York's local relief program for the duration of the Great Depression before being absorbed into the city's general revenues in 1941. In the interim, the extraordinary expenditure of political capital La Guardia had made to attain their enactment gave the Little Flower strong moral authority when he asked for additional federal spending; pleas for federal money were invariably accompanied by the reminder that New York City was "doing its part" in the "partnership" of which Roosevelt spoke.[42]

———

ROOSEVELT'S PROGRAM WENT to Congress in the form of an extremely vague joint resolution that aimed above all to give the president as much control as possible over how the appropriated funds would be spent and what machinery would be established to spend them. The group that drafted the resolution, supervised by the acting director of the budget, spent much of its time devising "inclusive phrases that would invest the President with ample discretion"; the finished product—which ran to all of two pages—was so broad that its authors feared it would run afoul of the delegation of powers clause. The objective was to leave the administration room for "adjustment," "flexibility," and "ingenuity." The House passed the resolution almost exactly as the administration had submitted it; the Senate added only a few broad directives on how the money was to be spent. Roosevelt signed the bill into law in April 1935.[43]

Given immense discretion by the Congress, Roosevelt went about establishing the machinery by which the billions appropriated under the Emergency Relief Appropriation Act would be dispensed. The central question remained whether the new program would emphasize direct public employment or capital-intensive projects and indirect employment—whether the new program would look more like the CWA or the PWA. Roosevelt was not prepared simply to jettison the idea of large-scale, monumental public works projects. He chose to continue the PWA, and at the urging of La Guardia (who operated during the summer of 1935 as a kind of informal adviser on urban affairs), he improved the terms it offered its applicants, raising the grant-to-loan ratio from 30:70 to 45:55 and dropping the interest rate of the loan by 1 percent.[44] But he remained skeptical of economists' claims that capital-intensive public works projects created jobs indirectly through a "multiplier" effect; and he "could not get over the fact," the economist Herbert Stein writes, "that, per dollar, [work relief] put about four times as many people to work *directly* as did the public works program." The purpose of the new bill, he told one administrative committee, was to "use as much of it as possible for the purpose of employing people now on the relief roll—and nobody else—directly." And so he leaned toward a program of labor-intensive, small-scale public projects.

At the end of the summer, Roosevelt gave about 20 percent of the unexpended works money to the Public Works Administration, which also drew upon a revolving fund made available by the repayment of loans and the sale of municipal securities. The other 80 percent he directed to a new agency, the Works Progress Administration, which he had created by executive order, placed under Hopkins's direction, and tasked with carrying out "small and useful projects." The new agency would pay the workers on projects "planned and sponsored" by local units (like the CWA) rather than making grants-in-aid (like the PWA). To ensure that the jobs went to those who most needed the income, the WPA would draw its workers almost entirely from local relief rolls—meaning that those who wished to apply for jobs with the agency would be required first to apply for relief, and hence to submit to a "means test," the invasive (many felt degrading) procedure local authorities used to ensure that relief recipients did not possess other means of support. Launched "with no considered plan for either its duration or its scale," this dual public employment and public investment program would lie at the heart of the New Deal until the coming of the Second World War.[45]

V

We tend to remember the New Deal as a response to the Great Depression. The historian Daniel Rodgers has rightly issued a corrective: Roosevelt and the Democratic Congress, he notes, moved into space created not only by the economic collapse but also by the "inability of the Hoover administration to stem the economy's ever-downward slide and the attendant devaluation of the idea of the market's self-adjusting capacity." But we would do well to remember, too, that key parts of the New Deal were a response to the failure of Roosevelt's own program. The failure of the recovery measures enacted in the first year of Roosevelt's presidency to reduce unemployment to a politically acceptable level created a political space into which temporary public employment, until 1935 a purely emergency measure, was to spread out into something like a program for meeting the problem of joblessness.[46]

The New Dealers forged many kinds of states: with the NRA and AAA, they built a microeconomic management state; Roosevelt's devaluation of the dollar and experiments with gold (and later, his experiments in fiscal policy) embodied a macroeconomic management state; the FERA and the Social Security Act of 1935 created a safety net state; and, less prominently, the resettlement programs and the National Resources Planning Board pioneered a social and economic planning state. To these was now added an intergovernmental public investment state that relied heavily on the labor of the unemployed and the initiative of local officials—channeling underutilized manpower to produce goods and services for the public wealth. Until the coming of the Second World War, the federal government would commit about a quarter of its annual expenditure to public investment via the WPA and the PWA—about 2.3 percent of annual GDP (see Table 4.1).

By the answer it developed to the paramount moral, economic, and political problem of unemployment, the federal government had shifted the balance of American production away from goods and services for private use and toward the production of public goods for the common wealth. The great majority of this production would come in the form of of projects designed, proposed, and supervised

Table 4.1: *Federal spending devoted to intergovernmental public works and work relief programs, July 1935–June 1939 (dollar amounts in millions)*

	Total Fed. Expend.	GDP (1937 Dollars)	Work Relief and Public Works	(% of Fed. Expend.)	(% of GDP)
FY 1936	9,069	86,005	1,298.3	14.30	1.5
FY 1937	8,281	91,900	2,079.9	25.10	2.3
FY 1938	7,304	87,218	1,570.2	21.50	1.8
FY 1939	8,765	94,626	2,569.6	29.30	2.7

Calculated from *Annual Report of the Secretary of the Treasury on the State of the Finances for the Fiscal Year Ended June 30, 1940* (Washington, DC, 1941), 24, 26, 28, and U.S. Bureau of Economic Analysis, *National Income and Product Accounts*, Table 1.1.5. Excludes FERA money, some of which was used by state and local relief administrations for work relief. Fiscal years ended on June 30 (e.g., "FY 1935" ran from July 1, 1934–June 30, 1935).

by local officials. The New Dealers had been able to create a public investment state without parallel in the democratic world because they had learned to utilize the operational capacity of the local governments effectively. In turn, they had made it possible for local officials to extend the reach of the city government and to undertake more creative local programs than fiscal and personnel constraints would otherwise have allowed. It is to the effect of these federal innovations upon New York City's public sector that we now turn.[47]

5

The New Deal's "Lost Legacy"

S hortly before the election of 1940, La Guardia, deeply involved
in Roosevelt's bid for a third term, participated in a question-
and-answer session with a group of Roosevelt campaign workers. A woman asked him how she and her fellow volunteers should
respond to the charge that WPA workers did nothing but "[lean] on
their shovels and so forth"—evoking the stereotype of lazy, unproductive workers and useless projects that had plagued the agency
since its inception. In response, La Guardia ran through some of
the standard arguments the New Dealers used to defend their most
controversial program: federal work relief had allowed Americans to
retain their dignity and self-respect; the circulation of dollars first
paid as work relief wages had stabilized the American economy and
contributed to recovery; calls for the abolition of work relief made
in the name of fiscal probity and personal self-reliance were in fact
nothing more than a cloaked attempt to saturate the job market and
bring down the price of labor. He also made a telling admission. "I
get credit and take the bows for parks and playgrounds and swimming pools and buildings and firehouses and airports," La Guardia
said, "but it was through the medium of WPA that all of that was

possible. . . . Reputations have been built on what the WPA made possible for New York City."[1]

Indeed, not only political reputations but also key parts of the city's infrastructure and of its public sector were built by and through the New Deal works programs. By the decisions they made as they pursued their own objectives, the New Dealers had pushed the federal government into functionary realms that previously belonged primarily to local governments. The New Deal, wrote Roy Rosenzweig and Elizabeth Blackmar in their history of Central Park, "added parks to the national political agenda"; it did the same for community health, adult education, mosquito control, recreation, and low-cost housing. Yet these would not cease to be municipal activities simply because the national state assumed some responsibility for them. Rather, by injecting the resources of the national state into local governance, the New Deal works programs had created an unprecedented degree of functional overlap between the national and the local governments; they had also made possible a remarkable expansion of government activity at the local level. Before the conservative congressional resurgence and the shifting of national resources to war production curtailed their efforts, the federal government and the city of New York, acting collaboratively, built highways, tunnels, bridges, subway extensions, and a major world airport; they also opened and staffed neighborhood health clinics, launched a program of working-class public housing, staged high-quality music and dance performances at affordable prices, gave new life to the city's public radio station, WNYC, built campuses for Brooklyn and Hunter colleges, and opened new schoolhouses across the city.[2]

Central to the public investment impulse was a broad understanding of "wealth" and a belief that government shared in the responsibility for creating it, particularly by filling lacunae in a system of economic production that cleaved hard toward the private and com-modifiable. Adolf Berle, the great theorist of the La Guardia regime as well as one of its leading policy intellects, explained:

> We are wrong in thinking that wealth is only that sort of goods which produce other goods and result in a mercantile profit. Central Park, for instance, is one of the great resources of New York City. It does not produce a profit, and never will. It pro-duces enjoyment, instead. Yet enjoyment satisfies a human need just as much as a plate of pork and beans. It is justifiable, accordingly, for a municipality to incur a long term bonded debt for assets which steadily supply a human necessity, as, for instance, parks, schools, playgrounds, hospitals, bridges, roads.

Projects of this sort were not really antagonistic to private enter-prise. If public sector provision challenged private industry for land, labor, and market share, it also contained the promise of future pri-vate wealth; advocates of public health clinics and public housing could and did argue that such services would render the workforce more efficient, would produce cost savings to employers and property taxpayers by reducing illness and disorder. (And *pace* Berle, Central Park did, and does, produce private profits by its effect on the value of surrounding property.) Still, this was public investment in a capa-cious sense: with the aid of the national government, New Yorkers undertook not only to fashion an infrastructure which would permit commerce in the city to flourish and develop, but also to provide goods and services that would increase the common wealth of the city and the happiness and freedom of opportunity of its citizens, families, and communities. Now a "lost legacy" of the New Deal, public investment became the cornerstone of the local state Roos-evelt's national program made possible in New York.[3]

I

The Public Works Administration, as we have seen, operated on a straightforward principle: in order to meet national objectives—the provision of jobs, the stimulation of heavy industry—it sought to encourage local governments to expand their activities in the traditional municipal area of public works construction by relieving them of a large part of the cost. By utilizing the operational capacities of local governments, the PWA allowed the national government to extend its own infrastructural power beyond what would otherwise have been jurisdictionally and operationally feasible. But it also ensured that its efforts would be constrained by local conditions—especially by local state capacity and local political forces.

Municipal resources were a major constraint on the PWA, for the success of this federal program depended on both the ability of local governments to plan desirable projects and the ability and willingness of those governments to shoulder a majority of the cost. These constraints, which had prevented the PWA from making a quick launch in 1933, proved manageable enough that the agency was eventually able to build in all but three American counties. Even so, local institutional factors contributed to wide variations in PWA spending from one jurisdiction to another.

Political opposition, in theory, should have been less troublesome. Public works projects generally enjoyed the support of a broad coalition of well-organized and politically powerful groups—construction firms, the building trades, merchant associations, civic organizations, financial institutions (which handled the associated bond issues), newspapers, and public officials and party leaders eager to claim credit for them. In the absence of the kinds of neighborhood, preservationist, and environmental checks on the public construction process that developed in earnest beginning in the 1960s, the only reliable set of opponents were those directly inconvenienced by their construction. Yet in some cities, the PWA did encounter stiff political opposition. Sometimes this was of a partisan nature: the most famous case was Philadelphia, where the local Republican administration eschewed the PWA's offer to finance a badly needed water filtration system, it was said, for fear that the project would redound to the favor of Roosevelt and the local Democrats. In other localities, economy- and solvency-minded forces worked to restrain public spending.[4]

New York was comparatively free of both institutional and political constraints on public works spending. Because they had expanded so rapidly in the preceding decades, most American cities possessed relatively great capacity to plan new public construction projects. New York stood out in this respect even among the big cities: the Port of New York Authority, Robert Moses's public construction empire, the municipal departments' own engineering bureaus, and a loose network of entrepreneurs who moved easily between the realms of planning, engineering, finance, and government gave it a capacity to plan public improvements that no other American locality could match. Organizations such as the Regional Plan Association and the Mayor's Committee on Plan and Survey (created by Jimmy Walker in 1926) had assembled inventories of desirable public works projects such that, when the PWA arrived, New York could draw upon a great number of already-developed plans (some of which had actually been started, only to be halted by the depression). Yet the city was not, from an economic point of view, "overbuilt": its population still growing and the assessed valuation of its property declining only modestly, it possessed a relatively great ability to spend on capital improvements. Only in the late 1930s would it begin to bump up against its constitutional debt ceiling; in the interim, the development of the new instrumentality of the public authority, authorized to issue revenue bonds outside the limits imposed on municipal debt by the state, had created additional local spending capacity.[5]

Political conditions in New York also favored heavy public capital investment. Natural public works constituencies—contractors, building trades workers, merchants, bond investors—were all strong and well organized. Property- and solvency-minded "economic elites" whose counterparts in other cities formed the core of anti-spending coalitions were not, generally speaking, particularly averse to taking on additional debt for capital improvements—which they considered essential to the continued commercial development of the city. They also tended to trust La Guardia's appointees, men such as Robert Moses (whom the city's well-to-do held in particularly high esteem), to invest municipal appropriations wisely. More puzzling, perhaps, is why the New York Democracy, which regained control of the Board of Estimate from 1935 to 1937 and was thus able, if it so desired, to obstruct La Guardia's local spending program, offered little opposition.

Several potential explanations stand out. First, the rise of the pro-Roosevelt wing of the New York Democracy, centered in Brooklyn and the Bronx, made it less likely that the opposition party would seek to obstruct federal programs created by a popular Democratic president (while also marginalizing the Manhattan organization, which was quickly developing into a bastion of conservatism both within the city and in the U.S. Congress and might otherwise have made the party as a whole into a vehicle for fiscal retrenchment). Second, the Democrats did not realize until it was too late that they would not be able to translate credit for the New Deal programs into support for local Democratic candidates; instead, they would engage La Guardia in a credit-claiming contest, urging New Yorkers to indicate their approval of "economic and social plans that were Democratic in conception and Democratic in execution" by "preserv[ing] that instrument of progress," the Democratic Party. And third, many Democrats simply shared La Guardia's vision of what was good for their constituents and good for the city. Whatever their disagreements on issues such as charter reform and the abolition of county offices, they would not stand in the way of new schools, roads and bridges, and recreational and health facilities. Thus Peter J. McGuinness, the legendary "Duke of Greenpernt" whose Brooklyn ward was the single most regular Democratic district in the city, remarked at the dedication of a new building at Greenpoint Hospital: "Thanks be to God we had such a Mayor and such a Commissioner of Hospitals to help us. They will take care of our poor people from now on, irrespectless of what befalls. They have done it honest and done it good." Several years later, McGuinness wrote in a letter to La Guardia:

> By the way . . . I know the President thinks the world of you. He told me so himself. . . . He said to me, "Peter, he is a great man and my pal." And the President said he was very happy to give you whatever monies he could at that time to help out our City, and he did not make any mistake when he said that because he has given you plenty and thanks be to God, you were there to get it.

Flynn himself later wrote that he was willing to work with La Guardia because he considered much of the mayor's program to be "in the best interests of the city." At least as pertains to public spending, there is little in the historical record to contradict him. And for his part, La Guardia, for all his anti-political rhetoric, was willing to meet cooperative Democrats halfway; he allowed Democratic leaders like McGuinness to share credit for projects in their districts, and he developed a close working relationship with Flynn, which, by the 1940s, involved significant collusion on appointments.[6]

La Guardia, then, enjoyed both the opportunity and the ability to spend heavily on PWA-financed projects. Like many politicians of his generation—a generation that had seen the advent of electrical lighting, the spanning of the Hudson River, the rise of skyscrapers and of

automotive and air transport—he considered it one of the responsibilities of a progressive public leader to leave his dominion in better
physical condition than he had found it. He shared the civic booster
mentality which had long underpinned municipal public investment;
but more than this, he viewed himself as a shaper of the metropolis.
"You know, I am in the position of an artist or a sculptor," he once
remarked; ". . . I can see New York as it should be and as it can be if
we all work together."[7]

From the moment they were able, La Guardia and his fusion colleagues invested heavily in PWA-financed public works projects. As
soon as the city had closed its budget deficit in April 1934, La Guardia hastened to Washington with City Chamberlain Adolf Berle and
Comptroller Joseph McGoldrick to persuade PWA administrator
Harold Ickes to release more than $37 million in grants and loans
for the completion of the Eighth Avenue Independent subway line
and the construction of new schools, hospital buildings, and incin-
erators. Ten months later, with Roosevelt's works bill before Congress, he traveled to Washington to present Ickes with a new pile
of blueprints—this one including more than $1 billion in spending
for highways, subways (including a long-stalled line from Brooklyn
to Staten Island), schools, hospitals, sewage treatment and disposal
plants, playgrounds, parks, housing projects, a tunnel beneath Manhattan linking New Jersey and Queens, and a viaduct that would
double the city's water supply, all ready to start at once.[8]

As New York's engineering bureaus turned out "an endless
stream" of detailed plans with complete blueprints, cost estimates,
and amortization schedules, La Guardia assumed responsibility for
expediting the city's grant applications. He formed a close (if frequently contentious) relationship with Harold Ickes, an old Chicago
political reformer whose emphasis on honest and "clean" public
administration mirrored La Guardia's own. ("We talk the same language," La Guardia said after their first meeting.) In his efforts to

protect the federal Treasury from graft-inflated construction costs, Ickes had overstaffed his agency's legal and investigation divisions and had wound the application process in red tape; La Guardia more than once saw fit to denounce the agency's "semi-colon boys," but he usually managed to surmount bureaucratic impediments to his own projects by working directly with Ickes—and sometimes with Roosevelt himself. When procedural barriers in his own jurisdiction threatened to stall construction, he cleared those, too. Of one PWA project he later claimed that "We fussed around with it for months and finally [Secretary Ickes] said, 'Now look here, if you can get title to the land in 30 days I will give you the money for the first project.' . . . Well, you don't pick that much money up every day, so we went out and condemned the land. Now that it is over and the buildings [are] there, I can tell you about it. If something had happened to Mr. Ickes or if something had gone wrong with that appropriation, I don't know what the Mayor would have done with that land or who could have paid for it. But we got away with it!"[9]

New York ultimately claimed some $58 per capita in PWA grants and loans—considerably more than the national mean (about $33). In total, Ickes's agency helped finance 107 projects in New York City. In so doing, it made an immense investment in the physical infrastructure of the city and the region. As Table 5.1 suggests, there was a striking variety in how America's largest cities chose to utilize PWA financing. Mayor Kelly of Chicago used PWA funds to build the Loop section of the Windy City's mass transit system. Los Angeles spent its PWA money primarily on educational facilities. Philadelphia and Detroit chose to spend significantly less than the national mean, and less still than the other large cities. New York utilized the PWA above all to construct a new automotive transportation infrastructure: the PWA financed the Lincoln and Queens-Midtown tunnels, the Triborough Bridge, the Belt Parkway ("the greatest municipal highway venture ever attempted in an urban setting," the *Times* claimed),

Table 5.1: *Per capita spending on PWA non-federal projects of the five largest U.S. cities by facility type*

	New York	Chicago	Philadelphia	Detroit	Los Angeles
Transportation	$36	$26	$5	$1	$9
Automobile	$32	$9	$0	$1	$9
Highways	$4	$3	$0	$0	$4
Bridges and tunnels	$25	$4	$0	$0	$0
Streets	$3	$2	$0	$1	$5
Rail	$4	$17	$5	$0	$0
Education	$7	$6	$11	$2	$31
Health and hospitals	$7	$19	$0	$14	$4
Other	$8	$9	$2	$2	$6
Total	$58	$59	$18	$19	$50

"List of Allotted Non-Federal Projects as of May 30, 1942," RG 135, Entry 59, Box 1, NA II. Figures include both federal grants and municipal spending for projects sponsored by municipalities, counties, and public authorities, excluding limited-dividend housing loans and Housing Division projects. They may not add up, due to rounding. Among the most common facilities in the "Other" category were government office buildings, courthouses, firehouses, dispensary plants, sewage facilities, and waterworks.

and a number of smaller bridge, tunnel, and grade-crossing removal projects.

The building of a specifically automotive infrastructure, though it introduced a radically new element to urban life, represented but the latest phase in a longer project to forge a transportation infrastructure adequate to support an interconnected, interdependent metropolitan area and region. Since the early twentieth century, if not before, New York's engineers, bureaucrats, and civic leaders had sought to link the central business areas more securely to the metropolitan region (and to New England and the mid-Atlantic beyond); reduce the inefficiencies associated with an outmoded, chaotic, sclerotic transportation system; and open up new areas for development—which they hoped would relieve the intense crowding of the central city. They had built hundreds of miles of rapid transit lines and scores of bridges. Now, the growth of automotive transport left them with the challenge of building automotive crossings and arterial highways. In particular, they faced the challenge of adapting a primarily insular city "shaped and in large measure completed before the age of the automobile" to the new technology of the combustion engine. This they accomplished, relying on the new bases of state infrastructural power developed by Moses and the Port Authority and the fiscal aid of the national government.[10]

Though roads, bridges, and tunnels dominated New York's PWA-financed expenditures, Ickes's agency also spent generously on educational and health facilities—expenditures which helped to build the infrastructure upon which expanding city services would depend. The construction of Brooklyn College's Midwood campus and a new administrative facility at Hunter College's midtown east site (presently known as the North Buiding) allowed the city to extend its singular system of municipal higher education. The construction of fifteen neighborhood health centers facilitated the most important institutional innovation the Department of Health made during La Guardia's mayoralty: the creation of a system of district health centers that allowed the department to target resources where they were most needed, build local knowledge, and work closely with community institutions like churches, schools, and labor unions, respond more rapidly to outbreaks of communicable disease, and "bring health" (as Commissioner John Rice put it) "to the doorstep of all."[11]

The PWA also helped to launch public housing in New York. What was true of municipal social politics in general was particularly true of public housing: local aspirations would have foundered on the shoals of austerity had it not been for innovations at the national level. The New York City Housing Authority (NYCHA), created by the state legislature in early 1934 at La Guardia and Lehman's urging, did not even have an appropriation; it met its bills by selling scrap from work relief demolitions of old-law tenements and got by in large part with the clerical and research assistance of CWA workers. And in the absence of a convincing display of its financial soundness, it had difficulty establishing the marketability of its bonds.

Crucial support came from the PWA Housing Division, written into the National Industrial Recovery Act by Senator Wagner, which financed the construction of two public housing projects in New York: the Williamsburg Houses and the Harlem River Houses, both low-rise complexes with on-site laundries, social rooms, playgrounds, child care and public health facilities, and public art. The Williamsburg project came first. After months of jousting over bureaucratic procedure and the division of labor between the PWA and local authorities, Ickes and La Guardia, after Roosevelt's personal intervention, arrived in September 1934 at a working accord which allowed the city to begin assembling property titles; fifteen months later, the two men clambered into the cabin of a steam shovel and jointly broke ground on the project. In the autumn of 1937, the first residents moved in. Assuming that public housing would not acquire broad public legitimacy should it flout Depression-era racialist attitudes, NYCHA filled the Williamsburg Houses with white tenants; "We don't want to act in such a way . . . that it will deter white people from going into projects," NYCHA board member Mary Simkhovitch told a group of Harlem advocates in 1939. "You may say it is up to the white population to receive the colored people in equal numbers everywhere because that is justice. But . . . [we] have to think first of housing." Adhering to this philosophy of separate-but-equal (and pressed hard by Harlem community leaders after riots engulfed the neighborhood in March 1935), NYCHA and the PWA undertook a second project at the northern terminus of Seventh Avenue. Both complexes drew about thirty applicants for each available unit, which allowed NYCHA to conduct a highly intensive selection process. These fortunate tenants enjoyed a living environment that had practically no equal at the price: the Harlem River Houses in particular provided an example of "what New York might be," Lewis Mumford wrote, "if we wanted to make it rival the richer suburbs as a place to live and bring up children." Too expensive to serve as a reproducible model for public housing within the market-pricing paradigm, they stand today as monuments to a fleeting moment when the federal government built housing of exceptional quality for the "submerged middle class."[12]

The PWA Housing Division would be succeeded in 1937 by the United States Housing Authority (USHA), authorized to allocate $1 billion over four years for slum clearance and public housing. Senator Wagner, the program's chief sponsor, would be forced to make such considerable compromises to get the bill through Congress that the final act amounted almost to a Greek gift from a Congress in which the antagonists of New Deal urban policy were starting to gain the upper hand. Limits on per room and per unit construction costs, inserted to guarantee non-competition with the private sector, would ensure that the new buildings were of much lower quality than the PWA projects (and, additionally, that federal public housing would never gain a working-class or middle-class constituency). The USHA would spend 50 percent less per room on its Queensbridge and Red Hook projects than the PWA had spent on the Williamsburg Houses and the Harlem River Houses, making necessary such cost-cutting measures as doorless closets, concrete-slab floors, and an architectural style Mumford dubbed "Leningrad formalism." The national government would now help to build housing for the poor—which the PWA Housing Division had not—but it would no longer build for the "submerged middle class."

Yet as the federal government withdrew from an area it had pioneered in collaboration with local authorities, the city and state would move to fill the vacancy. The year after the USHA's creation, New York State voters would approve a constitutional amendment creating state and municipal housing programs, which would serve a considerably larger sector of the housing market. The state and city projects, the first of which opened during and shortly after the Second World War, would occupy the space ceded by the termination of the PWA Housing Division; as the historian Nicholas Dagen Bloom writes, their creation would allow New York to continue to build working-class housing and thus to reject the premise of federal policymakers that public housing should be "only for the poorest families."[13]

II

Like the PWA, the Works Progress Administration operated on the principle of collaborative federalism: it utilized the planning and operational capacities of the local governments to meet the national objective of creating some 3 million public sector jobs, paying particularly needy unemployed men and women (whom it selected from among those certified by local relief officials) for their work on projects planned, operated, and partly funded by local governments. It left local officials broad discretion to determine how this labor would be deployed, requiring only that they comply with a few directives: work should be useful, should be done on public property, and should neither compete with private industry nor displace the "normal" operations of state and local governments; and the unemployed should be placed, as far as possible, in positions that utilized their existing skills. Though designed primarily as a way of making the federal government an employer of last resort, the WPA also routed the labor of millions of Americans through municipal and county governments for the purposes of producing public wealth—not only infrastructure (as with the PWA) but also other public goods and services.

From the point of view of the municipalities, the WPA was essentially a gift of manpower. Just how valuable a gift this was depended largely on a particular locality's structural position within the American economy—for the WPA could be most productive where it could allocate to municipal governments workers whose abilities, training, and experience were compatible with the manpower requirements of public-sector production. As Table 5.2 suggests, New York (like

Table 5.2: *Number of workers in select WPA-compatible occupations per thousand residents, 1930*

	New York City	United States
Construction		
Building trades	317.1	219.0
Builders and building contractors	14.0	13.6
Architects	4.2	1.8
Technical engineers	24.6	18.4
Operatives, laborers and helpers	70.7	35.7
White-Collar, Professional, and Arts		
Actors and showmen	22.9	6.1
Artists, sculptors, and art teachers	16.8	4.7
Authors, editors, and reporters	13.5	5.2
Dentists	9.0	5.8
Musicians and teachers of music	30.7	13.4
Physicians and surgeons	18.1	12.5
Trained nurses	32.3	24.0
Librarians	3.2	2.4
Social and welfare workers	5.2	2.5
Technicians and lab assistants	2.8	1.3
Total Population	6,930,446	122,775,046

U.S. Department of Commerce, *Fifteenth Census of the United States: 1930, Population: Vol. 4* (Washington, DC, 1933), 7–15, 1088–1100. "Building trades" includes brick- and stone-masons and tile-layers; carpenters; electricians; stationary engineers, cranemen, hoistmen; painters, glaziers, varnishers, enamelers; plasterers and cement finishers; plumbers and gas- and steamfitters; roofers and slaters; and structural ironworkers. "Operatives, laborers, and helpers" includes those working in the construction and building industries only.

most large cities) was far richer than the nation as a whole (and the agricultural and mining regions in particular) in workers whose occupational experience rendered them well suited to public sector and public construction work. New York City WPA administrators and local officials did face the challenge of employing waiters, garment workers, skilled artisans, and the like, and a fair number of them ended up in unsuitable construction jobs. But the New York City WPA could also draw upon many skilled tile-layers and carpenters, nurses and dentists, researchers and engineers—people whose skills and experience made them valuable as auxiliary municipal workers.[14]

The federal policymakers created an additional set of constraints on the value of WPA-sponsored manpower to municipal governments. In order to provide first for relief-eligible breadwinners, they stipulated that 90 percent of WPA workers be drawn from local relief rolls and that only one person per family be permitted to hold a WPA job—rules which ensured that its pool of manpower would be less skilled, older, more male, and more destitute than the unemployed labor force as a whole. Whatever the other significances of these policies, they rendered the WPA workforce less productive than it might otherwise have been. So did Hopkins and Roosevelt's decision to restrict the use of labor-saving machinery on WPA jobs in order to keep the labor-to-capital ratio as high as possible. (Rexford Tugwell, then undersecretary of agriculture, has recalled encountering Roosevelt and La Guardia in the presidential study in March 1935 talking through early plans for what would become La Guardia Airport. Tugwell realized to his horror that they were in happy agreement that power machinery should not be used in construction—only hand tools, so more men would be employed. After listening with mounting exasperation, he finally interjected that the government's effort might better be directed to building a number of airports rather than a "single hand-crafted one in New York.") And when forced by the building trades to pay union wages, the administration's stubborn insistence that WPA work pay less than private employment resulted in a compromise under which prevailing wages were paid and working hours restricted, producing constant turnover and discontinuity on job sites, particularly among supervisors and skilled workers.[15]

Within these bounds, the WPA's potential to produce public wealth varied a great deal depending on how the program was administered by local officials and WPA administrators. Some urban regimes saw the agency primarily as a means of building or fortifying party organizations: more concerned with rewarding supporters than using the manpower constructively, they placed ward and precinct workers in important (and desirable) supervisory positions for which they were frequently unqualified. La Guardia and his appointees, on the other hand, wished to maximize the WPA's productivity, and they received important assistance from Roosevelt and Hopkins. The president and his "minister of relief" acceded to La Guardia's pleas that New York City be given its own administrative unit rather than being subsumed in the New York State setup; Gotham thus became the WPA's "49th State," preventing an extra layer of administrative procedure and permitting city officials to retain a relatively high degree of command over its operations. They also favored La Guardia with their appointments to the position of New York City WPA administrator. The first, former NRA director Hugh Johnson, was mutually agreed upon by Hopkins and La Guardia; he essentially federalized the city's existing work relief program, which had been run by professional engineers under the leadership of William J. Wilgus (of Grand Central Terminal fame). Johnson was succeeded in September 1935 by the German American editor and publisher Victor Ridder, a longtime La Guardia supporter; Ridder was followed by Colonel Brehon Somervell, a career Army officer chosen by Hopkins apparently without consulting any New York politician. Each of the three directors filled the agency's administrative and supervisory positions with non-partisan professionals, especially engineers and Army officers.[16]

A professional, non-partisan local WPA administration helped to provide equal access to WPA jobs. But it also enabled New York to maximize the WPA's potential to produce public wealth. New York City was far more successful than most administrative units in providing WPA workers with jobs roughly in line with their previous occupations—two thirds met that standard in New York, studies found, compared to 39 percent in Pennsylvania. The quality of job site supervision provided in New York was also extraordinarily high. Whereas political machines in some cities filled desirable supervisory positions with loyal party workers, the New York City WPA and city officials, with La Guardia's blessing, requisitioned experienced foremen and subforemen and gave them wide latitude to discipline sluggish workers, which mitigated substantially the WPA's tendency toward low productivity. Lorena Hickok wrote to Hopkins after touring work sites in the city:

Mister, we're getting some very, very fine work out of these men, work that makes jobs done by contractors look silly! . . . This is due entirely, I think, to the kind of supervision they have in that New York City show. It's so far above the average that there just isn't any comparison! [Not a single subforeman was] sent in by some ward-heeler! These men actually knew their jobs, the great majority of them—even down to the little fellows in charge of gangs of 10 or 15 men! It simply knocked me cold to find the New York City show so clean, so free of political manipulation. Gosh, if you could just see for yourself the contrast between New York City and—Camden, where today I was told about one supposed "engineer" in charge of a project who didn't even know what a culvert was!

Studies showed that WPA construction was inefficient even under such favorable circumstances: Robert Moses thought the same work could have been done by private contractors for about 50 percent of the cost; La Guardia and Somervell placed the figure at 60 percent. But impartial audits also found that the work done in New York was, by and large, of notably high quality: in fact, it was less likely to be deemed substandard by city inspectors than that performed by contractors. La Guardia's commissioners turned in mixed reviews of the white-collar and professional WPA workers who labored in their departments: some were extremely valuable additions, they reported; others, qualified for the jobs they held, dragged their feet because they resented doing the same work as Civil Service workers for lower wages; others simply were not fit for the work that was being asked of them. In nearly all cases, commissioners would have preferred regular Civil Service workers to WPA workers. Still, thousands of WPA workers became so fully integrated into the departments' activities that, as WPA appropriations fell, municipal agencies found it difficult to operate without them.[17]

Table 5.3 provides a snapshot view of how New York used the manpower afforded it by the WPA. As under the CWA, the primary beneficiaries were the Parks Department, the Board of Education, and the borough presidents' offices—the agencies responsible for maintaining the city's physical property. As this would suggest, a great deal of the WPA's labor went toward patching and repairing the city's public face and the physical plant upon which urban life depended. Consequently, a decade that had begun with typical recession-era disinvestment—the kind of public squalor we associate with the 1970s—ended with the public property of the city in perhaps the best physical condition in its history. But the WPA also did much more. WPA workers under Moses's direction not only refurbished the city's public spaces and recreational facilities but also

Table 5.3: *WPA expenditures on behalf of New York City agencies as a percentage of departmental appropriations in the 1937 municipal budget*

	Annual WPA Expend. on Behalf of NYC Agencies, 1935–37	1937 Municipal Budget	WPA Expend. as % of 1937 Budget
Dept. of Parks	$59,215,903	$7,165,468	826.4
Board of Education	$23,369,707	$145,539,953	16.1
Boro. Pres. of Brooklyn	$13,520,092	$4,858,686	278.3
Boro. Pres. of Queens	$12,806,428	$5,288,007	242.2
Boro. Pres. of Manhattan	$11,978,980	$6,573,506	182.2
Boro. Pres. of the Bronx	$10,831,189	$3,310,617	327.2
Boro. Pres. of Richmond, SI	$8,628,822	$1,610,311	535.8
Dept. of Public Welfare	$9,672,730	$23,616,045	41.0
Dept. of Hospitals	$8,804,721	$24,331,254	36.2
Dept. of Health	$6,102,240	$4,855,564	125.7
Dept. of Water Supply, Gas, and Electricity	$5,218,889	$17,282,616	30.2
Dept. of Docks	$5,011,736	$1,193,565	419.9
Dept. of Plants and Structures	$3,802,774	$6,638,438	57.3
Tenement House Dept.	$2,629,590	$901,803	291.6
Board of Higher Education	$1,964,165	$7,929,907	24.8
Police Dept.	$1,962,832	$56,948,485	3.4
Armory Board	$1,776,579	$156,397	1135.9
Dept. of Purchase	$1,741,823	$1,452,404	119.9
New York Public Library	$1,665,392	$1,427,326	116.7
Dept. of Markets	$1,663,091	$701,976	236.9
Fire Dept.	$1,560,829	$25,043,205	6.2
Dept. of Sanitation	$1,457,269	$28,982,142	5.0
Dept. of Correction	$1,015,391	$3,394,322	29.9
Queens Public Library	$922,382	$659,814	139.8
Brooklyn Public Library	$353,152	$865,536	40.8
Metropolitan and City Museums	$221,125	$1,079,357	20.5
Total	$201,303,352	$640,492,281	31.4

John D. Millett, *The Works Progress Administration in New York City*, 206 (Chicago, 1938), and text of Mayor's Message Submitting 1938 Executive Budget to Estimate Board, *NYT*, Oct. 3, 1937. Annual WPA expenditure is a twelve-month average for the period Aug. 1, 1935–June 30, 1937.

greatly expanded them. The WPA, like the PWA, enabled the city to build crucial new infrastructure, some of it serving to connect the city physically, some of it facilitating the expansion of municipal services. And by injecting additional manpower into municipal departments, the WPA, like the CWA before it, served to catalyze new innovations in public sector provision.

Relieved by the WPA of a good share of its labor costs and able to commit its resources to the acquisition of land (which could be had in the 1930s at favorable prices) and the purchase of materials, Moses and his Parks Department deputies expanded park acreage by nearly 24 percent—pushing New York from a laggard position to the front of the pack of America's large cities in the share of its territory given to parks—and produced a staggering number of new recreational facilities. Utilizing WPA labor, the Parks Department built the grounds of the 1939 World's Fair, Randall's Island Stadium, and Orchard and Jacob Riis beaches. It also built nearly two hundred playgrounds, some in the dense central-city neighborhoods and some in the older parks, as well as eleven spectacular swimming pools spread throughout working-class neighborhoods—Astoria, Morrisania, Red Hook, Greenpoint, Harlem, Sunset Park, Brownsville, Tompkinsville. It added golf courses, tennis courts, baseball diamonds, football and soccer fields, bocce courts, bridlepaths, and even a polo field to the public recreational plant. And it produced stunning renovations in many of the city's older, more formal and pastoral parks (adding, among other elements, Central Park's Conservatory Garden, a stunning triptych awash with lilacs, hollyhocks, and flowering crabapple trees).[18]

Perhaps more than most New Yorkers realized, the expansion of recreational space during the 1930s was one aspect of a conscious *rearranging* of city space. New Yorkers had long used the city's streets for urban commerce, social contact, political life, and recreation; as the urbanist Daniel Bluestone has detailed, La Guardia's administration attempted to claim them for "traffic," and, in so doing, displaced "earlier social uses of the street" in the name of the "broader specialization of urban space. . . ." New playgrounds, neighborhood parks, and swimming pools aimed explicitly to move people (particularly children) from the congested and often dangerous streets to discrete recreational spaces; the Parks Department filled its official publications with statistics on declining traffic accidents.[19] But as they sought to untangle the functions of urban space and to rearrange the geography of city life, La Guardia and Moses also provided access to a world of recreation many city dwellers had previously been denied.

Moses, who was smitten by the British Civil Service system while a graduate student at Oxford University, saw it as his task to translate European-style public provision to the context of America's democratic, polyglot megalopolis. "We must recognize that we have a different kind of population here," he wrote to a friend who had compared New York's parks with those in European cities, "and not just one with lower standards, and we must also realize that New York conditions are peculiar because of our huge, mixed population, over crowding, high land values and other factors which do not by any means involve bad character, deficiencies in education or plain cussedness." He was at heart (as the historian Jerald Podair puts it) a "middle-class moralist"; if a city such as New York was to have a world-class recreational plant, he believed, it would have to construct facilities that were "obviously suitable, adequate, durable, and perhaps even a little imposing." He scorned the "sideshows [and] shooting galleries" of Coney Island; instead, he built the sparer, more elegant beaches at Pelham Bay and Jacob Riis parks. He forbade "amusements" in the city parks, filling them, rather, with active recreational facilities "intended to promote good health and good behavior as well as to make living conditions more pleasant."[20]

Still, if Moses's parks conveyed a touch of the bourgeois paternalism of their nineteenth-century predecessors, they also threw open the doors to a kind of leisure previously denied to many New Yorkers. "Suddenly," note Roy Rosenzweig and Elizabeth Blackmar, "the city's working-class communities had full entry into a recreational world previously reserved for the middle and upper classes. Access to recreation was undergoing its most dramatic 'democratization' of the past hundred years." People who could not afford to go away on the weekends now had access to "an afternoon's tennis or a Sunday at the beach"—or, despite Moses's preference for active recreation over the pastoral vision of Olmsted and Vaux, to "quiet and a broad prospect and tranquility" in the sort of ordered natural setting that brought a touch of grace to the cacophonous city. Projects such as the pools and beaches, which had no counterparts in Depression-era urban America, bear out the urbanist Marshall Berman's characterization of Moses as "a true creator of new material and social possibilities." But even the renovations of old parks—which, after all, had been a part of the cityscape for decades—struck some New Yorkers as unlike anything they had imagined possible in the United States. "I really thought I was in another Country," a Yorkville woman wrote to Moses following the renovation of Central Park. She had grown "so sick and tired" of the scenery in the old undermaintained space; now she likened the renovated masterpiece to "the beautiful parks in Scotland + England."[21]

Despite its relatively light use of capital, the WPA made a considerable contribution to the city's economic development—above all in the construction of La Guardia Airport, which connected New York not simply to the metropolitan area and to surrounding regions but to other world cities. La Guardia, a booster of American aviation during his time in Congress, foresaw clearly a day when airports would be as important in the economic life of cities as waterfronts and train depots, and he aspired to have New York claim a dominant position as the region's air hub. "When our program is completed," he promised, "New York City will have a ring of airports within a few minutes distance of the business and commercial center." First, he had tried to claim from the War Department part of Governors Island, the Inner Harbor outpost. As they sailed up the East River during a fleet review in the spring of 1934, he had plied Roosevelt and Secretary of War George Dern with his vision for an airfield only minutes from downtown Manhattan. But slowly, his focus shifted to a 105-acre marsh on the south shore of Flushing Bay. Though some believed the site impractical, La Guardia saw its advantages: favorable weather conditions, low-rise surroundings, proximity to midtown via the newly opened Triborough Bridge and the Queens-Midtown Tunnel (a PWA project begun in 1936), and sheltered waters which offered outstanding facilities for the marine clippers that made the majority of international flights in the 1930s. (It also allowed for the possibility of seaplane taxi service to Wall Street and midtown, an early plan for transporting travelers to the airport.)

In August 1937, the city exercised its option to buy the property and appropriated $12 million for improvements. A few weeks later, Roosevelt, perhaps seeing a chance to bury the myth that WPA workers did little more than rake leaves, gave his full support to the project; eventually the cost would rise to $40 million, of which the WPA contributed $27 million. The airfield opened in 1939 and was immediately christened La Guardia Airport in an act of magnanimity by the Democrats on the Board of Estimate. "It is the greatest, the best, the most up to date, and the most perfect airport in the United States," La Guardia wrote to Roosevelt when the project was finished. "It is 'the' airport of the New World." The major airlines signed hangar leases, and New York became, as La Guardia had hoped, one of the world's air traffic centers. (Meanwhile, air travel was expanding so rapidly that only a few years after it opened, the new airport was considered inadequate in size, and the city began work on a second, far larger airport near Jamaica Bay—what would become Idlewild, now known as JFK.)[22]

The WPA's blue-collar workforce also built twenty-five school-houses, eighteen new hospital buildings, Hunter College's Bronx campus (currently the home of Lehman Honors College), single-story baby health stations in "dozens of neighborhoods"—and scores of other such facilities. Much like the district health centers and college campuses constructed by the PWA, these projects enabled the city to expand the range and quality of its public services. The fate of WNYC, New York's municipal radio station, offers a case in point. During the 1933 mayoral campaign (and again at intervals during the first six months of his mayoralty), La Guardia had actually pledged to abolish the station, weak in signal and programming alike, in the name of municipal frugality. But he had reversed course when a committee headed by CBS chairman William S. Paley returned a recommendation that the station receive a larger appropriation and new facilities. The WPA helped build ample new studios in the Municipal Building and, at the foot of Greenpoint Avenue in Brooklyn, a technical facility that housed a new transmitter, antennae, and motor. With the station made technically viable by the WPA, La Guardia's appointees, programming director Seymour Siegel and (beginning in 1938) station director Morris Novik, set about transforming it into something more than an "inept imitation of commercial radio." Soon it would provide not only quality entertainment and cultural fare but also civic news, educational programming, and "information to help [New Yorkers] thrive in an increasingly complex world." It became a kind of prototype for public radio in America.[23]

About 30 percent of New York City WPA workers labored on projects especially designed to employ professionals, clerical workers, and artists. Like the CWA workers who had preceded them, many of these workers essentially became adjuncts in the city departments and in city-supported non-governmental institutions. Their labor enabled these agencies to expand their operations at a time when they would otherwise have been forced to cut back, and in some cases to initiate new programs. The availability of WPA workers allowed the New York Public Library not only to extend its hours but also to create an "Open Air Reading Room" in Bryant Park. By 1937, the Department of Hospitals was using 4,000 WPA workers as "doctors, nurses, pharmacists, dentists, clerks, typists, kitchen help, orderlies, . . . laboratory technicians" and even barbers in the twenty-six city hospitals. The Department of Health sponsored 2,000 WPA workers; some were engaged in a large mosquito eradication project, while others worked on the department's anti-venereal disease campaign, administered chest X-rays to check for tuberculosis, or staffed dental clinics, child health stations, or school health services. WPA researchers undertook studies that were foundational to the initiation of municipal projects: the Mayor's Committee on City Planning, operated as a WPA project, laid the groundwork for the City Planning Commission by making surveys, maps, and models; another set of WPA studies aided in the establishment of America's first free port in Staten Island (a project that La Guardia had devised to salvage a group of white-elephant piers built during the Hylan administration). Workers on the WPA Radio Project, "skilled in programming, writing scripts and continuity, and undertaking research" (many of them having been previously employed in broadcasting, cinema, and public relations), provided the critically understaffed WNYC with essential manpower.

If some WPA projects augmented or extended the activities of municipal departments, others introduced altogether new functions. Some WPA workers set up community playgrounds and operated them in conjunction with local institutions (such as the settlement houses); others provided domestic work and home visits for the elderly and infirm. The WPA also paid unemployed teachers and experts—many of them young City College, Brooklyn College, and Hunter College graduates who had the misfortune of entering the job market in the mid-1930s, others older people who could find no market for their expertise—to teach free classes on everything from philology to astronomy to dance to such vocational subjects as "homemaking, sewing, typing, bookkeeping, accounting, and business management."[24]

III

The Works Progress Administration is today perhaps best remembered for a set of projects that took up only a sliver of its budget: the "Federal One" arts, music, and theater projects. Roosevelt had initially conceived them simply as a way to create jobs for a set of particularly hard-hit occupational groups: artists "have to live," he remarked; "I guess the only thing they can do is paint and surely there must be some public place where paintings are wanted." From these origins grew a program of remarkable social imagination. As the historian Sharon Musher has documented, other federal officials saw government sponsorship of the arts as a means to broader ends— as a way of strengthening national, regional, and local identities and cultural bonds and a means of fostering good government. Under the sponsorship of the WPA, painters, sculptors, writers, actors, musicians, and researchers of all varieties produced works ranging from some of the most celebrated books and plays of the decade to neighborhood theater productions and phenomenally popular Saturday night dances and park concerts. They produced murals and sculptures to grace America's public spaces, gave free music lessons and opened excellent art schools, staged famous "Living Newspaper" productions, and performed high-quality musical works (some of them newly commissioned from emerging American composers) in free or inexpensive concerts, making the fine arts available to a much broader audience.[25]

Unlike the blue-collar and white-collar/professional projects, the

WPA arts projects were not co-administered by the city government; run directly by Washington, they required no local sponsorship, and as a result they were not formally interlaced with the activities of the municipal government. Yet they, too, stimulated the development of the city's public sector. La Guardia, the bandleader's son, harbored the conviction, then highly unorthodox in the United States (though not in continental Europe or Britain), that "high art" was intrinsically a proper concern of government, not only because it was a mark of civic achievement but also because it represented a means of happiness and fulfillment of which working-class people were being unjustly deprived. From the beginning of his mayoralty, La Guardia, who loved classical (especially Romantic) music deeply, entertained two related but distinct visions: first, to create a municipal arts center that would include an opera house, a symphonic concert hall, an auditorium, art galleries, and perhaps a campus for the high school of music and art which he was to create in 1936; and second, to provide public venues where working-class families could have access to the fine arts. "The industrial worker has a monotonous job," he once remarked. "He sews on buttons, say, all day long, stitch after stitch after stitch after stitch. But when the worker's day is over, he can find his spirit refreshed and uplifted through—yes—through music, through art."[26]

Eventually these two impulses merged in the creation of the City Center of Music and Drama. As with so many of La Guardia's initiatives, the birth of City Center was midwifed by the federal works programs. In 1939, City Council president Newbold Morris, acting as the administration's liaison to the Federal One arts projects, arranged for the best of the city's three WPA orchestras to perform a series of concerts—Wagner and Tchaikovsky—at the new Center Theater at Rockefeller Center. Morris filled the subway with advertisements that read: "Mayor La Guardia presents the New York City Symphony," with the identification "WPA Project" in small script at the bottom. The series sold out on the first night and later moved to the Metropolitan Opera House; it continued for three years, first at the Metropolitan, then at Carnegie Hall. Thus was it demonstrated, the *Times* music critic Olin Downes later wrote, "that there was a large music public for . . . symphony concerts . . . when these concerts were made accessible in price."

In 1942, the city came into possession (through tax delinquency) of the neo-Moorish Mecca Temple, a "massive masterpiece of Turkish-bath rococo" located on 56th Street between Sixth and Seventh Avenues, built by the Shriners and equipped with a large auditorium. It was Morris, in the wake of his experience with the WPA orchestra series, who convinced La Guardia to convert the building into a performance venue. He and La Guardia organized a non-profit corporation to run the enterprise and enlisted a group of subscribers consisting mostly of labor unions and philanthropists to meet the initial costs. Persuaded of the project's viability in part by the popularity of the WPA concerts, they reacted with enthusiasm. The city repaired the building and agreed to lease it to the non-profit on the condition that the maximum pre-tax ticket price be set at $2 (about a third the price of an orchestra seat at the Metropolitan Opera).[27] By then the WPA had been liquidated and the Federal One music project along with it, but Morris and La Guardia persuaded top performers to work for free or at the lowest union rate to launch the enterprise—effectively replacing the federal subsidy of Morris's WPA concerts with subsidization by the performers, who were willing to donate their talent out of enthusiasm for the project and appreciation for City Center's engaged and enthusiastic audience. City Center scheduled its maiden performance for December 11, 1943, in honor of La Guardia's sixty-first birthday, and produced its first opera, a ragged-but-right *Carmen* cheered lustily by "Dubinsky's garment workers and Curran's seamen," the following March. La Guardia dubbed it "the Cosmopolitan Opera house"; it would flourish for more than a decade as an alternative to the higher-priced performing arts venues that surrounded it.[28]

IV

The New Deal works programs, in brief, had allowed New York City to extend a public works program that had flourished under the old Democratic regime, now shifting its focus to the ascendant technologies of the automobile and the airplane. They had helped to capitalize new and expanded social programs—the district health center system, the public housing program, the city schools and colleges, the municipal radio station. And they had supplied auxiliary labor which had enabled the city to undertake a range of new initiatives—from public health screening to adult education.

Many of these new public programs were smash successes from the standpoint of use. More than 1.7 million New Yorkers attended a WPA concert in the first four months alone; about the same number pushed through the turnstiles at the WPA-built swimming pools in the summer of 1936 (with usage at the largest, McCarren Pool in Greenpoint, often topping 14,000 swimmers per day). Orchard and Jacob Riis beaches registered nearly 4 million admissions during the summer of 1937. Millions tuned in to the Department of Markets' morning broadcasts. More than 200,000 New Yorkers attended a WPA adult education class. When La Guardia and Moses opened local parks and playgrounds, entire communities turned out, and the occasions became something of a civic pageant; the openings of larger projects were genuine mass events, with the largest, the dedication of La Guardia Airport, drawing some 325,000 people. Those numbers indicated the constituencies these new public goods and services would enjoy. They also signaled public approval of the role government was now playing in the city. Indeed, many New Yorkers came to view the goods and services now provided by the public sector as "rights" of urban citizenship.[29]

But the New Deal also did something more. By linking citizens to the government in new ways, by enabling citizens to "see" government differently, it helped alter the political culture of New York. Social provision turns on power, but also on imagination: "What people do about the government," the political scientist E. E. Schattschneider has written, "depends on what they think the government is able to do." Much of what La Guardia's government did in the mid-1930s had been on the urban agenda since the reform socialist and the municipal populist movements of the early twentieth century, if not before. But mass popular support for this conception of government and the elements of which it consisted grew rapidly once the New Deal, with its dramatic demonstrations of state competency, had shown these things to be actually attainable. The New Deal had made possible a new standard of municipal government; it had also catalyzed a rapid and far-reaching change in popular expectations for public sector production. This phenomenon would continue to shape the city's public life long after the New Deal works programs had passed out of existence.[30]

V

The New Deal works programs lifted most cities; if New York was exceptional, it was in the effectiveness with which its municipal officials had deployed the resources made available by the New Deal—not simply in the quantity of federal money it pulled in. La Guardia worked hard to maximize New York's share of federal aid, and, as we have seen, he and his colleagues on the Board of Estimate were willing to put the city's own resources on the table in order to do so. But except for a few brief periods, New York did not receive more federal money than other large cities. WPA jobs were allocated by formula;

under La Guardia and Hugh Johnson's initiative, the New York City WPA administrative unit got up and working several months before any other, but by the end of the year the disparity had been reduced. And while New York invested heavily in PWA projects, so did several other large cities; over the life of the program, Chicago and Los Angeles both pulled in more PWA grant money per capita than did New York (though New York's combined grant and loan share exceeded that of Los Angeles). Several western states, too, garnered outsized shares of federal spending.[31]

And yet in spite of this, many Americans came to believe that New York was the New Deal's favored city. La Guardia, the story went, used his personal good graces with the White House to secure a disproportionate share of federal money for his city. And Roosevelt seemed to confirm this. "Our Mayor is the most appealing man I know," he said on one occasion. "He comes to Washington and tells me a sad story. The tears run down my cheeks and the tears run down his cheeks and the next thing I know, he has wangled another $50 million out of me." By the latter half of the 1930s, the myth of a special relationship between New York's City Hall and the White House had become so pervasive that Republican mayoral candidates in other cities made reference to it to undermine their opponents' claims that they, as Democrats, could bring home a greater share of federal largesse.[32]

This "special relationship" myth had a certain basis in fact: New York, for reasons we have noted, tended to do unusually well in the very early stages of the New Deal programs, when perceptions were being formed. But the myth developed primarily because Roosevelt and La Guardia cultivated it, independently, for political purposes. For Roosevelt, emphasizing his close relations with La Guardia was a way of showing the federal government's responsiveness to local officials and local conditions and its willingness to work with members of the opposing party, while assuring the strategically crucial voters of New York that the New Deal was looking after their city. For his

Above: Franklin Roosevelt with his parents at the family's Hyde Park estate, 1891. Roosevelt's privileged country upbringing fostered in him a deep sense of personal confidence and security as well as a conviction in the moral superiority of rural living. *Below*: Prescott, Arizona, ca. 1908, a decade after La Guardia left it. La Guardia's western upbringing informed his progressive Republicanism and his conception of a "proper American standard of living."

Above left: La Guardia at the time of his graduation from New York University School of Law, 1910. *Above right*: Roosevelt in a formal photo taken during his final year at Harvard, 1904. *Below left*: Major La Guardia poses with the airplane designer Gianni Caproni in Milan shortly before returning from service, 1918. *Below right*: The newly inaugurated Governor Roosevelt greets his predecessor, Al Smith.

Above: La Guardia (right) and Parks Commissioner Robert Moses (left) inspect a blueprint at the groundbreaking for the 1939 World's Fair. (World's Fair Corporation chairman Grover Whalen stands between them.) *Below*: The Roosevelts join La Guardia and his most powerful political adversary, Bronx County Democratic chairman Edward J. Flynn, en route to the World's Fair, 1939.

Above: The Triborough Bridge shortly after it opened to traffic in 1936. *Below*: La Guardia Airport in its inaugural year, 1936. "Mega-projects" such as these helped tie the five boroughs together and link New York to the greater metropolis, the surrounding regions, and the world beyond.

Above: Brooklyn College ca. 1940. *Below*: La Guardia, New York City WPA director Brehon Somervell, and Health Commissioner John Rice at the opening of a child health station in Jamaica, Queens, 1938. By financing projects such as these, the New Deal works agencies helped create an infrastructure within which the city's own public services could be expanded.

Two views of the Harlem River Houses. *Above*: a scene from the on-site nursery school, one of many social spaces incorporated in the project's design. *Below*: two tenants pose for a photo in their living room. The New Dealers' commitment to public housing helped establish the New York City Housing Authority on sound footing.

The New Deal works agencies helped carve out new facilities for rest, play, and social interaction while also improving the quality of many existing ones. *Above*: The New York Public Library's Open-Air Reading Room, staffed by WPA workers and located in newly restored Bryant Park. *Below*: The municipal swimming pool at Astoria Park, one of eleven opened by the Parks Department in the summer of 1936.

Iconography of the New York–Washington connection. *Above*: La Guardia looks on as PWA director Harold Ickes signs an allocation order for a project in his city. *Right*: The conservative cartoonist Rube Goldberg depicts La Guardia as Roosevelt's line cook, an essential element of the New Deal's "tax, spend, and elect" mode of politics.

(*Left to right*): Mayor Edward J. Kelly of Chicago, La Guardia, and Mayor Garnet Coulter of Winnipeg lay a wreath on Roosevelt's grave at Hyde Park, 1945.

part, La Guardia went to great lengths to tie his own administration to the New Deal political project, making ingenious use of the mass media—newspapers, newsreels, and the radio—to publicize his relationship with the White House. Rather than send commissioners to do the city's business in Washington, he went himself—the better to establish the New York–Washington connection in the public mind. He replaced train travel with air travel, another means of garnering publicity, and he became known, as the *New York Times* wrote in May 1935, as "the first air-commuter in the grand manner between New York and Washington." He also sought to involve federal officials in dedication ceremonies and ribbon-cuttings, knowing that their participation provided further evidence of the connection between the city government and the New Deal. Whether or not federal officials were in attendance, La Guardia almost always mentioned Roosevelt in his remarks, usually lauding FDR's "vision." Sometimes he credited the president as the inspiration for the projects, as in this account of the origins of the East River Drive (which appeared in the *Times*):

> Let me tell you just how it happened that WPA funds were made available for this project. I was driving down the West Side Highway with President Roosevelt . . . and he was admiring the highway. I told him about our plans to revise and rebuild Riverside Drive, covering the tracks and extending that thoroughfare down to the Battery. President Roosevelt, who knows his New York, said: "How about the East Side; are you ready with a drive there?" I said, "Sure we are." I didn't know at the time whether we were or not. "Can you start right away?" the President asked. I said, "Sure."[33]

The myth of a special relationship was, finally, underpinned by the real ideological similarities between Roosevelt's politics and La

Guardia's. Roosevelt and La Guardia told similar "stories"—similar accounts of the innovations in governmental activity over which they had presided, and of the objectives toward which those innovations reached. One of those objectives was the improvement of the national estate: both men, and both regimes, sought to leave the physical condition of the nation and the city better than they had found it. But their purposes went beyond the simple renovation and augmentation of the common wealth. They sought, too, to elevate people, families, and communities by using the power of government to meet "needs" private production could not—with the ultimate aim of promoting happiness (a key word which ran through both men's rhetoric like a blue thread). American society and its component parts were basically sound, they believed; but they had been submerged by conditions more or less outside their control, most of which involved deprivation of access or opportunity—to the earned reward and moral satisfaction of work, to adequate housing and recreation, to decent health care, to education, et cetera. Private industry having proven incapable of removing these constraints, it fell to government to do so. La Guardia's argument for public housing illustrates the point well: "Take a family from an old, long tenement house railroad apartment—middle room, no windows, a kitchen dark and drab, crowded, insufficient light. That family is depressed. Children are running around unkempt. The poor mother just bedraggled. . . . You take that same family and you put them into one of our low-cost housing, and you have really created new human beings. There is a new family." This was what Roosevelt had in mind when he remarked in 1934 that America was "definitely in an era of building, the best kind of building—the building of great projects for the benefit of the public, and with the definite objective of building human happiness."

These stories were, finally, inscribed in narratives of civic virtue and national difference. The New Dealers lauded the WPA as the

"American way" of meeting the depression, contrasting American public investment to the British "dole" and German military production. (The United States, Roosevelt noted in his famous "quarantine speech" of October 1937, was putting its resources into "bridges and boulevards, dams and reforestation, the conservation of our soil and many other kinds of useful works rather than into huge standing armies and vast supplies of implements of war.") La Guardia's admirers, particularly in the late thirties and early forties, described their city as a showcase for American democracy, a place where the sons and daughters of all nations lived together in peace and contributed to social progress.[34]

Some conservatives, too, thought that Roosevelt and La Guardia stood for many of the same things. Heavy public spending, they believed, violated the rights of property and hence impinged on basic American liberties. If the New Dealers used the idea of work as the basis for social solidarity, some anti–New Dealers grounded their opposition to public spending in concepts of difference: the New Deal works programs, they charged, favored the foreign over the native, the parasitic over the productive. Some came to view public spending as a means of political control. La Guardia, they became convinced, was an essential cog in the New Deal's "tax-spend-and-elect" machine, a mode of politics that purchased the support of new voters with public money. Particularly in the second half of the thirties, these themes of otherness and political control ran together. The columnist Arthur Krock said of Hopkins and the WPA:

> Hopkins was able to show Roosevelt the combination that would be made by . . . favoritism of the government, the administration, and the court to labor—the Negroes, the Jews, racial groups of certain kinds. . . . They held the majority, when together. Hopkins showed him that the binding element was the New Deal program of federal spending, and Hopkins of

course was in charge of the largest spending that we've ever known outside of war itself.

The rise of the New Deal spending state fed into the images of Roosevelt and La Guardia as demagogues, and detractors assailed both men as slick, unprincipled, power-hungry politicians who were "ruthless and unscrupulous" in their political means, who played on public passions, and who were brilliantly devious at knowing "what would influence voters and what would get votes." And by 1937, they seemed eager to storm the last bastions of conservative freedom—the principle of judicial review and the U.S. Supreme Court itself.[35]

Especially as Roosevelt grew more closely associated with La Guardia's municipal reform project, many local Democrats came to believe that the president was complicit in the destruction of the old party clubhouse system and its hallmarks of local knowledge and control—a mode of governance which, not surprisingly, they believed possessed real value. When Roosevelt endorsed La Guardia's reelection bid in 1941, a Bronx party worker wrote him in anguish:

Mayor La Guardia may revel in the parks and playgrounds and road [sic] and bridges with which he has beautified this City with the money obtained from the Federal Government but he hasn't done one thing for what may be termed the soul of the City. . . . Where do the Democratic Clubs fit into this picture? They are the haven—sometimes the last resort—for the citizens of the community whose cases are not spectacular enough for this Mayor! They give free legal aid for the unfortunates who run into the law. The lawyers of the club houses know their communities, the background of their people, their families and the circumstances which brought them to this end and can plead their cases with a personal appeal! They work in cooperation with the churches of all denominations in the community in the recommendation of material or social aid. In other words they work to live up to the standard of their civic and political beliefs!

To these exemplars of the old pre–New Deal Democratic regime, too, Roosevelt and La Guardia had come to stand for the same things.[36]

By 1936, La Guardia and Roosevelt were more closely associated in the public mind than any mayor and president had ever been. "He has a confidential relationship with Mr. Roosevelt enjoyed by no Democrat," the *Brooklyn Times Union* political columnist John A. Heffernan wrote of La Guardia. "The doors of the White House open at his radiant approach, and the President is never too busy to sit down and have a chat with him." And New York City had become a kind of laboratory for New Deal reform. But it remained to be seen how the newly forged ties between the White House and City Hall would play out in the electoral arena.[37]

6

From Fusion to Confusion

A warm May evening in Fond du Lac, Wisconsin, 1935. Nearly 10,000 people crowded in the square facing the red-brick courthouse, the surrounding buildings draped in red, white, and blue bunting and American flags. The city was host to the first anniversary celebration of Wisconsin's Progressive Party, a third party co-founded in 1934 by the La Follette brothers, Senator Robert, Jr., and Governor Phil, and their allies after they had lost control of the state Republican Party in 1932. La Guardia, detained in New York by city business, arranged to pipe in his address via radio.

Though he had pledged upon his election in 1933 that he would "stay out of politics" for four years, La Guardia had kept in close communication with his erstwhile congressional allies. In 1934, he had endorsed Senator Bronson Cutting of New Mexico and had traveled to Wisconsin to campaign for Robert La Follette, Jr., who was running for reelection on the new Progressive Party line. "It may seem strange that a Mayor from an Eastern town should come to the great state of Wisconsin," he had admitted. But the prairie state crowds had received him with an enthusiasm that must have lifted La Guardia's hopes for a political alliance between the producing classes of the great cities and their rural and small-town counterparts. Wisconsin congressman Tom Amlie had written the Little Flower after La Follette's reelection that La Guardia's appearance had done "more to swing over public sentiment than any other thing."[1]

Now, at 6:15 pm, La Guardia's high-pitched voice rang out over the loudspeakers on the shores of Lake Winnebago. "We are living in a critical period," he began. Rapid changes were occurring as America entered "a new economic system"; progressives in government shouldered the responsibility for managing these changes in order to create "an equal enjoyment of progress in science, machinery, transportation and the natural resources of the country" and to bring "economic security and uniform happiness [to] all of the people of the country." The conservatives in both parties, he charged, talked "with a parrot-like monotony of constitutional rights, of rugged individualism, of government interference, and seem to accept and consider themselves the anointed and chosen few to exploit the land, and seem to believe that the Constitution was written for no other purpose than to guarantee continued exploitation of the many by the chosen few." In the face of these challenges, progressives could no longer allow themselves to be separated by party affiliations. "This is no time for political fence building," he said. "The conditions are such that division along old-time party lines barely seems possible." The 1936 presidential election would place a greater responsibility on progressives of all parties, he claimed, "than ever before in the history of this country."[2]

The following eighteen months would give La Guardia cause for great optimism. Labor, progressive, and dissident organizations would flourish, coalescing to form a broad movement that looked beyond the Democratic Party toward fuller reform of the American political economy. In 1936, when those groups joined together behind the New Deal banner, La Guardia would speak of his joy at seeing for "the first time . . . the American working men and women . . . all

united on one big subject." As he made his first foray into presidential politics since the La Follette campaign, the progressive dreams of
1924 seemed to be coming to fruition.³

If 1936 augured a "great shuffling about" (as the Little Flower
had predicted in mid-1934), the following year's municipal elections
evinced a similar state of flux. Galvanized by the political upheaval
that had swept the nation, political time in the city seemed to be
running at warp speed: Tammany Hall collapsed; a new political
party emerged; and tens of thousands of new voters continued to
enter the electorate. La Guardia was to win reelection by an unprecedented margin on the strength of a coalition unlike any New York
had seen before. Visible in the election returns was the architecture
of a new age in the city's politics—one made possible, in large measure, by Roosevelt's New Deal.⁴

I

"The spring and summer of 1935," the historian Alan Brinkley writes,
"were heady times for those awaiting a major political upheaval in
America." The national economic recovery that was ultimately to
carry Roosevelt to reelection had momentarily stalled, the Republican Party remained "weak and demoralized," and "[d]issident
movements were springing to life and gaining remarkable strength
in virtually every region of the country." By 1935, Wisconsin's Progressive Party and the Minnesota Farmer-Labor Party had both won
notable electoral victories, and insurgent groups working within the
major parties had demonstrated electoral strength in several western states. Movements of small farmers remained alive in the Farm
Holiday Association and the National Farmers' Union. Intellectuals
led by the philosopher John Dewey and the economist Paul Douglas,
among others, had organized the League for Independent Political

Action (LIPA)—La Guardia had signed its 1929 founding statement—
which had as its ultimate aim a planned economy that operated on
the production-for-use model. And the Communist Party, newly liberated from the "extreme leftist sectarianism" of the Third Period by
Comintern's popular front policy, began to emerge as an important
political force in a handful of states.[5]

Most significant of all, perhaps, was the rise of industrial unionism. Periods of high unemployment had usually been disastrous for
the American labor movement. But the favorable legal and political
environment provided by the National Industrial Recovery Act—
with its guarantee of the right to collective bargaining, its wages and
hours codes, and not least the propaganda tools it had made available
to union leaders (embodied in John L. Lewis's slogan, "The President
wants you to join the union")—had given invaluable support and
resources to an aggressive and skilled cohort of labor leaders. Organizing by plant and industry rather than by craft, these unions, many
of them soon to affiliate with the Committee on Industrial Organization (later the Congress of Industrial Organizations, or CIO),
were sweeping into labor's ranks many first- and second-generation
urban semi-skilled and unskilled workers. New York City's largest
union, the International Ladies Garment Workers (ILGWU), had
been on the brink of collapse in the early 1930s, reduced to 40,000
members and "bankrupt in every respect, financially, morally, and
organizationally." In 1933, it had added 125,000 members—"NRA
babies," they were called, mostly immigrant women and their daughters. The Amalgamated Clothing Workers of America (ACWA) had
fared better than the ILGWU in the 1920s, but it too had doubled in
membership following the NRA's enactment. Concurrently, industrial unionism was restoring a radical edge to the American labor
movement. "This new unionism does not stop at the formal lodge
meeting," one CIO leader wrote. "It sees the union as a way of life
which involves the whole community"—and thus inevitably became

wrapped up in political questions beyond those directly affecting the unions' ability to bargain with employers.[6]

La Guardia had observed these developments with great interest. His own vision for the American economy, with its emphasis on "readjustment" of the existing system of wages, prices, and profits rather than a full shift to production-for-use, was a few shades to the right of that embraced by many mid-thirties dissidents. But he shared their basic belief that the existing system had failed, as the socialist editor Alfred Bingham wrote, "because it [could not] take advantage of the country's immense wealth producing capacity." He also shared their conviction that progressive politics depended, as Congressman Tom Amlie put it, on "a political alignment that will place the exploiting reactionary on one side and the producer, consumer, independent business and professional interests on the other." "[T]here is in course of formation," La Guardia wrote as the 1936 party conventions approached, "a new group of experienced students of political and economic conditions such as Eastern liberals, the miners, the printing trades, needleworkers' groups, railroad workers, and not a few farm organizations"; among these groups there existed "considerable potential leadership. They refuse to follow the old school of politics and a party emblem no longer impresses them. Nothing short of a brand-new start, a new standard of political ethics, and an entirely new line-up will meet their demands."[7]

Nineteen thirty-six, the Little Flower ventured, might see the "last contest between the two great existing parties." Thereafter, he believed, the interaction between Roosevelt and his party would determine the alignment of American politics. "If the President is swept into office and takes complete control of his party, modernizes the political machine, he will then rebuild out of the old party a real cohesive, united Progressive Party, and the line-up after that will be between Progressives and Republicans. If—again assuming the President's re-election—the machine takes control, refuses to take all of the Roosevelt program, temporizes with social and economic legislation, then there will be found a Labor Party in this country the likes of which is way beyond the hopes of its sponsors and the fear of its opponents."[8]

The rapid growth of independent progressive, leftist, and labor politics caused Roosevelt considerable anxiety. The greatest threat to his reelection prospects, he believed, was a third-party challenge which might strip him of enough votes in a handful of key states to swing the election to his Republican challenger; at one sour moment he claimed to a Democratic associate that the progressive Republicans intended to sabotage his reelection in order to swing the nation "far to the left" in 1940. He feared the progressives, he told a group of top Democratic politicos in the spring of 1935, more than he feared the clear-and-present threat posed by Louisiana senator Huey Long.[9]

Beginning about the same time as La Guardia's Fond du Lac speech, Roosevelt moved to incorporate these movements into the New Deal coalition. The spring and summer of 1935 (the "Second Hundred Days") saw the enactment of the Emergency Recovery Appropriation Act, the National Labor Relations Act, the Social Security Act, the "soak-the-rich" tax bill, and the "death sentence" on public utilities holding companies. It saw, too, the development of a potentially powerful and highly visible conservative opposition, embodied in the Supreme Court (which had already invalidated several New Deal measures) and the American Liberty League, a well-funded and vocal group which proclaimed itself "the spokesman for a business civilization." By the fall of 1935, many of those who might otherwise have been inclined to challenge Roosevelt from the left had come to see themselves as stakeholders in the New Deal project. Of all the groups that had been contemplating a third-party candidacy in 1936, only Father Charles E. Coughlin, Dr. Francis Townsend, and the remains of the late Huey Long's organization took the plunge, forming a National Union ticket with the midwestern populist William Lemke at the top.[10]

As the election of 1936 approached, the forces of labor and independent progressivism rallied to the defense of Roosevelt and the New Deal. Yet they were not simply "co-opted" or "absorbed," as some accounts would have it; the reality was a good deal more complicated. For a time, the desire to return Roosevelt to the White House and the pursuit of a realignment of national politics along progressive-conservative lines merged into a single project. These would be the grounds on which La Guardia would join the Roosevelt campaign.

The unenviable task of herding the various progressive factions into a campaign organization of Progressives-for-Roosevelt fell to Senator La Follette, who issued a call for a conference of progressives to be held in Chicago in early September.[11] As the historian Drew McCoy has written, the conference's "tactical goals" were to undercut the claims of both the Republican candidate Alf Landon and Lemke and Coughlin's National Unity ticket to progressive support and to trumpet Roosevelt's own progressive record. But the group convened in Chicago with larger purposes: they sought to strengthen and to bring coherence to the progressive movement at a moment when its future possibilities seemed promising, and to claim the New Deal for independent progressivism rather than permit the Democratic Party to absorb the progressive movement. Its broader purposes were evident in a "statement of principles" drafted at the convention (under La Guardia's chairmanship) that represented, as the New York Times put it, a kind of "platform of the new Liberal-Progressive movement."[12]

Union leaders, also torn between a desire to build their own independent movement and a wish to aid in Roosevelt's reelection, adopted a broadly similar course of action. This was particularly true of the old socialists so heavily represented in New York's garment unions. "The position of our organization is known: that we are for a labor party," ACWA president Sidney Hillman explained. "We are

today bound . . . to help bring about a labor or farmer-labor party."
But, he continued, "We have participated in making the labor policy
of this Administration. . . . We know that the defeat of the Roosevelt
Administration means no labor legislation for decades to come." In
April 1936, Hillman, along with United Mine Workers president John
L. Lewis and George L. Berry of the AFL-affiliated International
Pressmen's Union, formed a national group, Labor's Non-Partisan
League (LNPL), to assist in the Democratic campaign. Yet the LNPL,
too, had broader objectives. In seeking Roosevelt's reelection, it aimed
to fortify the development of industrial unionism—what Hillman
called "the beginning of creating a real labor movement" in America—which in turn would act as an organizational basis for the mat-
uration of New Deal liberalism into labor-based social democracy.[13]

In New York State this course of action bore immediate institutional fruit. Because state ballot laws permitted candidates to run
on more than one party line, New York labor leaders could nominate Roosevelt on a third-party ticket. At Hillman's suggestion, the
leaders of the needle trades unions, which had a combined membership of approximately 395,000 (221,000 of whom lived in Gotham),
together with the representatives of the pro-Roosevelt wing of the
Yiddish socialist movement—the "old guard" of the Socialist Party,
the *Forverts*, the Yiddish radio station WEVD, the Workmen's
Circle decided to form a statewide labor party.

Ladies Garment Workers president David Dubinsky later
explained the decision as a practical means of obviating the effects of
the needle trades unions' decades-long educational campaign against
Tammany Hall. "[O]ur people are all Socialists . . . ," he told Frances
Perkins. "We've been warning them for years to never vote for Tammany Hall. 'Never vote for Tammany Hall. Tammany Hall is against
the working man. Never vote under the star [the Democratic ballot
emblem].' Now I can't teach them to vote under the star all of a sud-

den. I've got to have them vote under something that's got labor in
it." But the third-party option also offered a way of resolving, at least
locally, the tension between "desire for a genuine third party . . .
and the vision of a 'realignment' whereby the New Deal Democratic
Party created by Roosevelt might contain within it the seeds of a
social democratic labor party. . . ." The labor party was to Jewish
labor socialism what the Progressive National Committee was to the
broader progressive movement—simultaneously an attempt to channel independent votes for Roosevelt and an effort to use the political
upheaval wrought by the New Deal to advance the enduring dream
of an independent labor politics which predated the New Deal and
did not entirely align with Roosevelt's own objectives.[14]

It remains unclear when exactly La Guardia became involved in
the labor party project. Adolf Berle, present at some of the earliest
discussions, recalled that La Guardia entered only later; Steve Fraser, Sidney Hillman's painstaking biographer, has found that Hillman talked through the labor party idea with La Guardia (and with
Berle and Eleanor Roosevelt) before proposing it to the leaders of the
needle trades unions and the old guard Socialists. What is certain is
that La Guardia, recognizing how important a labor party might be
to his own reelection prospects, took to the idea immediately. Along
with Hillman and the first lady, he presented the plan to FDR, arguing that it would bring 75,000 new voters to the polls in New York
and would swing part of the Socialist vote to Roosevelt. Jim Farley
(who subsequently blamed La Guardia entirely for selling Roosevelt
on the plan) and Edward Flynn both opposed it: a labor party, they
feared, would introduce an element of irregularity into New York
City politics and destabilize a political alignment that was working
well for the Democrats. Despite the Democratic leaders' objections,
Roosevelt encouraged Hillman to go ahead with the plan, and on
July 16, 1936, the New York chapter of Labor's Non-Partisan League
formed the American Labor Party (ALP).[15]

II

Roosevelt campaigned in 1936, one historian has written, "as the leader of a liberal crusade which knew no party lines." He gave much of the speechmaking burden to the administration's leading Republicans, Ickes and Wallace. And although Republican leaders invoked La Guardia in the hope of driving a wedge between the administration and the New York Democratic organizations, Roosevelt involved the Little Flower heavily in his campaign. In late September, he invited La Guardia to Hyde Park for a high-profile visit. A few days later he went to New York to lift the first shovel of dirt in the construction of the PWA-sponsored Queens-Midtown Tunnel. "Every now and then," he told the crowd, "I would hear that your Mayor had slipped off to Washington, and each time I said to myself, 'There goes another $5,000,000 or $10,000,000.' But I was proud to help because everything that was initiated was a useful project. There were years when the interest rates were so high and there was such a noticeable lack of teamwork that we fell behind in carrying forward these needed public works."[16]

La Guardia himself seemed somewhat reluctant to engage in the active phase of the campaign. "I'm not mad at anybody," he said on several occasions—a remark partially directed, one imagines, at Al Smith, now a vocal Liberty Leaguer, but also expressive of the discomfort he felt at taking an action that had once gotten him read out of the Republican Party. "Some of us are burning all our bridges ahead of us," he wrote a friend from the Chicago progressive convention, "and we do so with our eyes wide open." But once he had committed himself, he had little difficulty enumerating his reasons for doing so. "[T]his new cooperation [between the federal government and the municipalities] is so refreshing and novel," he told one Bronx audience. "The understanding and sympathy of the administration in Washington has resulted in an improvement in public conditions throughout the city, and also in almost every other city in the country." The election, he suggested, posed a "clean-cut issue" between laissez-faire on the one hand and, on the other, a philosophy that "after surveying the situation . . . says, 'This is something beyond industry and business. It now becomes the function of government to step in, and it is the duty of government to establish conditions by meeting the machine age.'"[17]

A week before the election, La Guardia joined Governor Lehman (whom he had endorsed), Senator Wagner, John L. Lewis, David Dubinsky, and a host of other labor leaders in a rally at Madison Square Garden; there he announced that he would vote for Roosevelt and Lehman on the American Labor Party ticket. The following day he accompanied Roosevelt on a thirty-mile automobile tour of the city; and that evening he spoke for the Democratic ticket alongside Ickes and the businessman/philanthropist Edward Filene at Carnegie Hall. Then, leaving the fusionists to fight out the city races, he went off to Rochester and Gary, Indiana, to shore up Italian and labor support for FDR, then to Nebraska to stump for George Norris. He returned in time to make a final radio talk for Roosevelt over WABC on election eve—a quiet, unadorned reflection on the local improvements brought about by the New Deal, which he claimed would be "lasting monuments to the vision and energy of President Roosevelt. . . ."[18]

The following day, New Yorkers voted 3 to 1 for Roosevelt, doubling his 1932 plurality and giving him by far the largest total to that time in the city's history. They also ratified, against the opposition of all five Democratic county chairmen, two major municipal reform measures that had been put on the ballot as referenda: a new city charter and proportional representation. The fruits of the labor of the second of two charter revision commissions La Guardia had assembled, the new charter reorganized several departments, created a new City Planning Commission with theoretically broad powers over land use and capital budgeting, and replaced the Board of Aldermen with a new, smaller City Council. The proportional representation law, long championed by civic reformers (and quietly favored by Roosevelt when he was governor), created a complicated rank-order voting system organized by borough rather than by district which was designed to give minor parties (i.e., the city's anti-machine elements) representation on the City Council in proportion to their share of the total vote. Proportional representation was designed to break the Democratic stranglehold on the city legislature, and it did: in the last aldermanic election, the Democrats won 66 percent of the vote and garnered 95 percent of the seats; in the first City Council election, organization Democrats won 47 percent of the vote and took 50 percent of the seats. But instead of simply elevating traditional anti-machine elements, as reformers had expected, proportional representation also empowered the left—allowing parties that stressed the relation between labor and capital, including the ALP and the Communist Party, far greater representation than they had enjoyed at any previous time in the city's history.[19]

Here was one more paradox in a season of political confusion: New Yorkers had voted overwhelmingly to reelect Roosevelt while simultaneously dealing a powerful blow to the local Democratic Party. Like so much else that fall, the success of La Guardia's ballot measures served to highlight an as-yet-unresolved question: what would be the relation of the Roosevelt coalition to the Democratic Party? In time, the election of 1936 would come to be viewed as the culmination of a party realignment that had begun in 1928 and which drew some of the most dynamic constituencies in Depression-era American politics—urban workers and housewives, progressives and ethno-racial minorities—into a Democratic coalition the basic contours of which would endure for three decades. But many contemporaries, at all points on the political spectrum, saw the election of 1936 not as the fanfare for a new Democratic majority but rather as a landmark in a long process of realignment which might well result in the obsolescence of the Democratic Party. The *New York Times* reflected after the election: "Even now it is predicted that Democrats throughout the nation who gave their endorsement of President Roosevelt's re-election may, incidentally and unconsciously, have signed the death warrant of traditional political Democracy in this country and the traditional two-party setup dominant in the politics of the nation from the start and prepared the way for a political realignment with sharp dividing lines among radicals, liberals, and conservatives. . . ." "It is to men the stripe of Dubinsky, Antonini, La Guardia, Norris, and [Minnesota Farmer-Labor senator-elect Ernest] Lundeen . . . that Mr. Roosevelt will turn for counsel," wrote the archconservative *Chicago Tribune*. "They are now the dominant forces in the New Deal party. The old leaders, particularly the organization men in the metropolitan cities, do not know it yet, but they are already on the way out."[20]

As the new year dawned, it remained unclear what would emerge from the upheaval. The first electoral test would come the following year in New York City as La Guardia, having turned down vague offers of a cabinet position, tested the flexibility of party lines by tapping some of the political forces Roosevelt had successfully channeled in 1936. Before then, there remained the pageantry of the first January inauguration. La Guardia inadvertently caused a stir when, in a Board of Estimate meeting, he scheduled a public hearing for inauguration day. Wouldn't he be at the inauguration? a colleague asked. Joking with one of the Democratic borough presidents, La Guardia replied that he had not been invited. The dry quip went over everyone's heads and the room fell into an awkward silence. Word reached Roosevelt, who fired a memo to a White House secretary: "Make sure he did get invited." As it happened, La Guardia caught an illness shortly before the inauguration and spent the day at home. He listened to Roosevelt's address on the radio—"I see one third of a nation ill-housed, ill-clad, ill-nourished"—and sent a congratulatory note: "My Dear President: Speech—Magnifico!"[21]

III

As New Yorkers surveyed their city in advance of the 1937 municipal elections, they saw a political landscape that had been thoroughly reworked by the Roosevelt revolution. The realignment of national politics and the policy innovations of the New Deal had fractured preexisting coalitions and had given rise to new ones, strengthening some groups and weakening others. In so doing, it had altered the organizational calculus of municipal electoral politics, making new combinations possible.

Nowhere was the Roosevelt revolution felt more acutely than in the inner sanctum of Tammany Hall. After the 1933 party split, Roosevelt and Farley had moved to oust Bosses Curry of Manhattan and McCooey of Brooklyn and replace the traditional process of brokering between outer borough leaders and a dominant Manhattan organization with a "council of five" in which each county leader would be represented. By the summer of 1934, McCooey had died and Curry had been subjected to the first formal removal of a county leader in Tammany's history. McCooey's replacement in Brooklyn, Frank Kelly, had satisfied the White House in nearly every regard and had joined Flynn as the co-leader of the pro–New Deal wing of the New York Democracy. In Manhattan, a compromise between the pro-Roosevelt forces and the Tammany district leaders had made James J. Dooling the county leader. But Dooling had developed close ties to the now ardently anti–New Deal Al Smith, and from 1935 through the spring of 1937, Farley was maneuvering to replace him without an open break.[22]

As the 1937 election approached, it was clear that Tammany's hegemony in New York Democratic politics had been destroyed; the pro-Roosevelt combination of Brooklyn and the Bronx reigned supreme everywhere except the Board of Aldermen, and that Tammany bastion would soon pass out of existence when the new charter and proportional representation went into effect on the first day of 1938. But it was still not evident exactly what had replaced it. As the primary season neared, the warring Democratic chieftains tried to draft the one man acceptable to all factions: Senator Robert Wagner. Strongly urged by the party leaders—and evidently still deeply committed to the idea of a reformed Democracy in New York—Roosevelt personally asked Wagner to consider running. But New York labor leaders were vehemently opposed to the removal of their great champion from the Senate; and Wagner, who treasured his Senate seat, refused the invitation. A split between Tammany and the Flynn-Kelly combination now became unavoidable. Farley pushed for the State Supreme Court judge Jeremiah Mahoney, a former law partner of Wagner's and a longtime advocate of reform within Tammany's councils of power who had come out for Roosevelt's nomination before the 1932 Chicago convention; and Mahoney was accepted by Flynn, Kelly, and the less powerful party chairmen of Queens and Staten Island. Dooling, however, announced that the Manhattan organization would contest the Democratic primary, running as its candidate Wagner's Senate colleague Royal S. Copeland, a Hearst protégé and Tammany loyalist who had come out in opposition to Roosevelt's proposals to reorganize the federal court system and bureaucracy. For the second consecutive election, the New Deal had split the New York Democracy.[23]

The New Deal had also reshaped New York City's Republican Party. Many New York Republicans detested Roosevelt and stood in unwavering opposition to his policies. But others, especially the members of a rising generation of party leaders and public officials concentrated in Manhattan, appreciated the depth of popular support the New Deal commanded and concluded that their party would never be capable of challenging the Democracy's hold on moderates, independents, and organized labor so long as it adhered to the policies and philosophy of old guard Republicanism. The New York GOP should emulate the British Conservative Party, one prominent Republican suggested, and appropriate all the good ideas of their liberal and labor counterparts, emphasizing their own ability to "administer them so that they work."[24]

La Guardia's anti-partisanship had so frustrated the Republican clubhouse element that three of the county chairmen had come out against his renomination. But the rise of the moderate faction, attuned to the party's standing with independent voters, gave him a group within the party with which he could negotiate; and it was one of these young moderate Republicans, New York County chairman Kenneth Simpson, who prepared the way for La Guardia's renomination on the Republican line. Even as he chided La Guardia publicly for espousing a "new political alignment" and a "collectivist state," Simpson opened negotiations with the Little Flower over drinks in the well-appointed library of his East 91st Street house. A few days later, following a conclave at the Yale Club, Simpson made it known that he would support La Guardia in the party primary. Subsequent negotiations with the Republican leader of Brooklyn ensured that La Guardia would not be overwhelmed by the organization vote.

The conservative wing of the party could not be won over so easily. Conservative Republicans objected to La Guardia's local spending program and even-handed treatment of labor-management disputes; and his public support of Roosevelt fed these discontents. The staunchest anti-Rooseveltians were prepared to make common cause with Senator Copeland, whose anti–New Deal bona fides they thought more than sufficient to counterbalance his Tammany affiliation. Copeland entered the Republican primary, making La Guardia's New Dealism his primary issue. Copeland's supporters identified La

Guardia as "one of the most aggressive and militant supporters of the New Deal" and "Republican Public Enemy No. 2," and in the days before the primary, his campaign manager claimed that eight U.S. senators had written him expressing concern over the impetus La Guardia's reelection would give to the New Deal in Congress.[25]

The New Deal had also produced in New York a potentially formidable new political party: the American Labor Party. Hillman, the original force in the ALP's creation, had apparently expected it to go out of operation following the 1936 presidential campaign; instead, its leaders, under the direction of Alex Rose of the Hat, Cap, and Millinery Workers, had moved to establish it on permanent footing, hoping that it would grow into the "New Deal Party of our country" and a balance of power between the two major parties in New York State. La Guardia, David Dubinsky has recalled, became "terribly interested" in the ALP's prospects and development. Recognizing that it might represent a "personal ace in the hole" (as one New York Republican later put it), he cultivated its leaders and helped to strengthen the fledgling party by supplying it with patronage and publicity.

La Guardia's record in his first term was almost entirely satisfactory to the labor movement's leaders. Declaring it his intention to make New York a 100 percent union city, the Little Flower had written unionization clauses into city contracts, had required city printing jobs to bear the union label, and had at times used the tactics of an old-time political boss—selective pursuit of back taxes, for instance—to force business owners to comply with NRA wages and hours codes. He had assisted the CIO with its unionization drives; on the eve of the 1937 primaries (at the risk of losing Republican voters) he had traveled to Lawrence, Massachusetts, to urge the Italian American textile workers there to support the CIO's Textile Workers Organizing Committee in an upcoming National Labor Relations Board election. He had spoken out, prominently, in support of state and federal policies organized labor favored: prohibition of child labor, wages and hours regulations, social insurance, and a guaranteed right to collective bargaining. Under his leadership the city had invested heavily in public works, a boon to construction workers; and it had used the New Deal programs to create recreational facilities and activities that workers and their families could use and afford.

La Guardia himself had mediated countless labor-management disputes, often in an informal fashion which allowed him to claim the personal gratitude of the union leaders; and in 1937, he created a City Industrial Relations Board staffed with some of the best labor mediators in the country to adjudicate intrastate labor disputes outside the National Labor Relations Board's jurisdiction (a task soon taken over when the state legislature created the New York State Board of Mediation, which possessed greater legal powers). With a few exceptions the NYPD had been notably even-handed during industrial disputes. The issue of closed-shop public employee unionism, later to drive a wedge between La Guardia and a considerable part of the New York labor movement, would not become a major one until the city completed its buyout of the transit corporations in 1940. This record left La Guardia well positioned to claim the ALP nomination; with the Little Flower awaiting his Republican primary contest with Copeland, the ALP chieftains put him on the November ballot, issuing a platform calling for the extension of New Deal public investment—the provision of adequate relief and low-cost milk, the construction of more parks and playgrounds, a yardstick municipal power plant, and adequate sewage disposal plants, slum clearance and public housing, and "a frank attack on social diseases."[26]

The rise of the ALP also had the unexpected side benefit of helping La Guardia to consolidate support among the heavily Irish Catholic craft unions, previously tied at both the leadership and the membership levels to the Democratic Party. As late as 1933, State Federation of Labor president George Meany later explained, the craft unions had "looked upon La Guardia . . . with some suspicion; we looked upon him as a Socialist who was a gadfly. We didn't take him seriously." The AFL union leadership was won over primarily by La Guardia's record on labor issues and his close working relationship with Meany. But they were also eager to ensure that the popular mayor not be viewed as a "CIO" candidate. Thus did the dynamic of competition between the AFL and the CIO, often a great bane to state and local labor-based coalitions, work to La Guardia's advantage. Meany, claiming (with exaggeration) to control an "AFL vote" of 1.5 million—600,000 union members, family, and friends—organized a large steering committee and set the business agent from practically every AFL union in the city to work for La Guardia's reelection.[27]

By altering both the strength and the behavior of key groups in New York City's local politics, the New Deal had presented La Guardia with challenges and opportunities. It had exacerbated a division between the mayor and the conservative wing of his own party that could only partially be bridged by the appeal of "good government"; and in laying the groundwork for a liberalized, post-Tammany Democracy it had helped to create a potentially powerful adversary in municipal politics. But it had also helped La Guardia to expand the organizational bases of his coalition beyond the fusion movement that had lifted him to power with a 40 percent plurality in 1933. It had allowed him to solve the basic problem in New York's reform politics: the fusion coalition's inherent instability. Each time reform had come to the city, writes the political scientist Theodore J. Lowi, "its onset was widespread, energetic, irresistible. But once there was a partial redress of the Democratic imbalance of power, the components dispersed. There has been no club core; no central bureaucracy; thus, reform has not been institutionalized." But shifts in national politics and policy had altered the reform calculus. Working within the favorable circumstances created by the Roosevelt revolution, and utilizing the resources made available by the New Deal works programs, he had met a challenge that had evaded every other reform administration in the city's history: he had remade his original fusion coalition into something more stable and more durable.[28]

IV

If the New Deal reordered the constellation of forces contending for political power in New York City, destabilizing old organizational patterns and making combinations possible, it also shook up the behavior of the city's voters. Highly visible, easily understood, and quickly traced to the regimes that had put them into effect and the charismatic political leaders at the front of those regimes, New Deal policies—work relief above all—proved remarkably potent. By making possible a new kind of urban government, the New Deal produced a novel electoral coalition in New York.[29]

The municipal electorate might have been expected to contract in 1937, following the extraordinary surge of 1933. But it did not. Rather, it grew by 3.6 percent above the already high mark of 1933— and this figure masked double-digit jumps in central Harlem and working-class outer borough neighborhoods such as Brownsville, Stuyvesant, Hunts Point, and Tremont, offset by drops in suburban Queens and elsewhere. Other New Yorkers shifted their voting loyalties: many of those who had voted for McKee on the Recovery Party line in 1933 now pulled the lever for La Guardia, as did many of those who had previously voted the Socialist ticket.

An analysis of the 1937 election returns reveals three findings of particular interest. First, the voters who entered La Guardia's coalition in 1937 were likely to have entered Roosevelt's in 1936: the Republican mayor's vote was converging with the Democratic president's, not because each man was winning over part of the other's base, but because they were gaining ground with the same groups

of voters—many of whom had not previously voted, or had voted
for third-party candidates. Second, most of those voters were Jewish or African American. Italian Americans voted heavily for Roosevelt and La Guardia, too, but they had done so previously, and in
similar numbers. La Guardia's share of the "Irish Catholic vote" rose
significantly—a consequence, most likely, of the AFL unions' support
and of the restoration in 1937 of municipal salaries to their pre-1934
levels. But the rate of increase was only half that of Jewish and black
voters; and it entailed little entry of new voters into the electorate (see
Table 6.1). Third, black and Jewish women played an especially pronounced role in the growth of the urban electorate, and likely made
up a disproportionate share of the newly mobilized constituencies
Roosevelt and La Guardia had won over. The rise in voter participation between 1928–29 and 1932–33 had been predominantly male: 70
percent of those who had joined the registered presidential electorate
in New York between 1928 and 1932 were men; the figure for municipal elections was 55 percent. Conversely, the jump in voting between
Roosevelt and La Guardia's first elections and their reelection cam-

Table 6.1: *Estimates of voting by ethnic group, New York presidential and
mayoral elections, 1932–1937*

	FDR 1932	FHL 1933	FDR 1936	(Change)	FHL 1937	(Change)
Jewish	72.2%	36.3%	87.5%	15.3%	68.6%	32.3%
Italian	80.5%	62.2%	78.7%	-1.8%	62.6%	0.4%
Irish	75.7%	21.8%	72.8%	-2.9%	36.8%	15.0%
Black	48.8%	36.7%	79.5%	30.7%	69.8%	33.1%
City	64.6%	40.4%	72.5%	7.9%	60.1%	19.7%

Jewish, Italian, and Irish estimates are compiled from Ronald Bayor's ecological analysis in
Neighbors in Conflict: The Irish, Germans, Jews, and Italians of New York City, 1929–1941, 2nd
ed. (Urbana, IL, 1988), 130, 137, 147. The estimated "Black vote" is based upon a simple
ecological analysis: the cumulative vote of every election district wholly contained within
a health area with a "non-white" population of 90 percent or greater in 1930.

paigns was predominantly female: the rise in registration was 58 percent female in the presidential electorate and 72 percent female in the
mayoral electorate. The New Deal mobilization of women was strongest in working-class ethnic neighborhoods and in Harlem, a pattern
which reflects the relative slowness with which working-class women
had entered the electorate before the New Deal while also raising
intriguing questions about the relation between women's "interests"
and the contours of the New Deal public investment state: it was,
after all, mostly women who listened to WNYC's market information
broadcasts, took their children to Moses's parks and swimming pools,
and utilized the new infant health clinics.

It was, in short, primarily Jews and African Americans, with
newly mobilized women playing an especially important role, who
extended Roosevelt's New York coalition beyond the old Al Smith
vote, and it was primarily they who turned La Guardia's 40 percent
plurality into a 60 percent majority. Of course, there were many
reasons why Jewish and black New Yorkers might break from their
previous voting patterns to cast ballots for La Guardia in 1937. Particular segments of each group had benefited from Civil Service
reform, which opened up comparatively desirable public sector jobs
to those who possessed education but not political connections. La
Guardia wooed both groups with symbolic appeals to equality and
tolerance. Like Roosevelt, he appointed an unprecedented number
of black men and women to positions of authority and visibility. New
York's version of Roosevelt's "Black Cabinet" included Tax Commissioner Hubert T. Delaney, Magistrate Myles Paige, Industrial Relations Board member T. Arnold Hill, and Jane Bolin, the first black
woman ever to sit on the American bench. To a group that had long
been deemed incapable of contributing to civic life, appointments
like these could be symbolically powerful. ("Have a colored man
sit in judgment on the taxes upon 18 billion dollars in property?"
Roy Wilkins wrote after Delaney's appointment, as though the very

thought of full civic participation were audacious.) And like national
figures such as Eleanor Roosevelt and Harold Ickes, the Little Flower
partook of what the historian David Levering Lewis has called a
"New Deal propaganda of racial equality," making small, symbolic
gestures intended to signal the full and equal worth of African
Americans as part of the American community. He invited Joe Louis
to City Hall before his first title fight and gave the boxer "one of the
most cordial welcomes ever accorded an athlete in New York City,"
the *Pittsburgh Courier* wrote. Early in his second term, he insisted on
taking the son of his family's African American cook, whom he considered part of his extended family, to visit the Roosevelts at Hyde
Park—an action which was considered uncouth in certain quarters
but which delighted the first lady.[30]

But these electoral realignments were also largely motivated by
the ways in which New Yorkers responded to the intergovernmental state the Roosevelt and La Guardia administrations had forged
during their first terms. Ethnicity proved the primary determinant
of voting behavior not because New Yorkers were especially tribal
(though they sometimes were, and the city's politicians knew them
to be). Rather, the power of ethnicity resided in the fact that it was an
aggregative concept, encompassing a great many politically salient
social and economic characteristics: what neighborhood one lived
in; what job one worked; whether or not one were on relief, owned
a home, belonged to a union, paid income taxes, held municipal
bonds; whether or not one had a strong commitment to a particular
political party. Ethnicity also tended to correlate with membership
in particular communities of opinion. For this reason, ethnic group
membership tended to overlap with immersion in distinctive political cultures. What the historian Deborah Dash Moore has written of
second-generation Jewish New Yorkers is equally apt for many of the
city's ethnic groups: through their encounters with the city and its
politics, they "evolved a . . . political style, affiliation, and program

that was distinctively Jewish," rooted in the neighborhoods and responsive to the urban experience and to perceived group interest. These ethnic political cultures, reproduced and developed through a host of neighborhood- and city-based institutions, fostered common ways of interpreting the political world which guided the voting decisions of members of the group. The New Deal shook up electoral politics in New York because it intersected with these social structures and political cultures in powerful ways.[31]

Unlike their Italian neighbors, solidly Democratic in national elections and just as resolutely behind La Guardia in municipal elections, Jewish New Yorkers collectively entered the New Deal years without a strong commitment to either major party. Though Tammany's ward politicians did have some success organizing first-generation Jewish immigrants, Democratic candidates for mayor and president, aside from Woodrow Wilson, had never garnered majorities in the most heavily Jewish precincts of Harlem and the Lower East Side. They did better following the collapse of the Socialist Party in the early 1920s, especially once the emergence of Al Smith, Herbert Lehman, Franklin Roosevelt, Robert Wagner, and Jimmy Walker gave credence to the idea that the Democratic Party was the party of progressive social legislation and ethno-religious tolerance. Concurrently, some second-generation Jewish lawyers had begun joining the Democratic clubs of the outer boroughs as a means of professional advancement. Yet at the end of the 1920s, Democratic strength among Jews was concentrated in the inner-city tenement neighborhoods that had been organized by effective district organizations. In 1932, Roosevelt polled an overwhelming percentage in older Jewish neighborhoods like the Lower East Side and Williamsburg, from which the more radical and upwardly mobile had already migrated; in working-class outer borough districts he lost as much as 10 percent of the vote to Norman Thomas, and in more affluent areas like Eastern Parkway he lost a similar share to Hoover. In the municipal election of 1933, the "Jewish vote" had split about the same as the electorate as a whole. There was, additionally, widespread non-participation: as late as 1925, the historian Thomas Kessner has estimated, only 20 percent of first-generation Russian Jews were registered to vote.[32]

Many Jewish New Yorkers still labored in the garment industry, where they were very likely to be union members. Others were unemployed: tenement neighborhoods such as the Lower East Side, Williamsburg, and Brownsville had a density of relief cases as high as anywhere in New York save Harlem. Many more had moved into managerial, proprietary, and professional positions. One contemporary study found that Jews owned two thirds of New York's industrial factories and were the proprietors of two thirds of its wholesale and retail establishments; another found that 34 percent of Jewish heads of family were employed as proprietors or managers, compared to 15 percent of non-Jews (and that only 3 percent were employed as unskilled or service workers, compared to 19 percent of non-Jews). Many members of the second generation had earned undergraduate and professional degrees.[33]

Despite their rapid ascent out of the industrial workforce, New York Jews partook of the labor politics of the 1930s with great gusto—an indication of the way ethnic political culture continued to influence voting decisions after the social context within which that culture had been constructed had begun to change. Ethnic political values formed by New York's tradition of Jewish socialism and Jewish unionism gave rise to a collective affinity for New Deal liberalism and municipal labor party reform. Jewish socialism (or Yiddish socialism, in its prewar, Yiddish-language variant) was an organic creation of the first-generation Jews of the Lower East Side—a product of the mingling of Jewish intellectuals with German socialists; of turn-of-the-century experience of class conflict, particularly in the garment industry; of the persistence of religious emphasis upon learning and a belief in charity and "social justice" as matters of right; and of a collective emphasis on individual enlightenment. Not a doctrine or a program, it was, rather, "a whole climate of opinion that cemented, both socially and intellectually, a Jewish world in turmoil." Simultaneously a youth movement (later augmented by the influx of Eastern European radicals after the failed revolution of 1905) and an enlightenment project through which "individuals could make themselves into better human beings—*mentschn*—as they struggled to improve society," Yiddish socialism aimed to build a new, more moral society "freed from poverty and bigotry." It took much of its energy from the conditions that met the immigrants in New York: the long hours, low pay, and poor working conditions of the garment lofts, the squalid tenements. "In the socialist movement," one garment union leader recalled, "you heard for the first time language which meant to us that we were regarded as human beings with human rights." Though Yiddish socialism developed for the most part outside the bounds of electoral politics, by the end of the First World War New York's Jewish neighborhoods had elected Socialists to Congress, to the state assembly, and to the Board of Aldermen. More enduringly, the first-generation Yiddish socialists had created a network of social institutions—newspapers, unions, the Workmen's Circle, the Young People's Socialist League, various public forums and lectures—which reinforced each other, forming a distinctive rights oriented political culture at odds with both Tammany paternalism and New Era Republicanism.[34]

Jewish socialists "retained their ideals but slowly shed their militancy" as they entered the New Deal coalition, often by way of the ALP. "Abandoning formal socialism," Irving Howe writes, "they seemed to feel they were preserving something of its original moral intent." The trajectory from Yiddish Socialism to New Deal liberalism was most visible in the conversions of men and women of the first generation like Abraham Cahan, the longtime editor of the *Forverts*, the socialist daily which became the nation's most read

foreign-language publication and a key institution of Yiddish socialism. La Guardia and Cahan were friends of long standing, but in
spite of that, Cahan had denounced La Guardia during the 1933 campaign as an agent of "the rich and the landlords." But already in the
fall of 1933, Cahan was lauding Roosevelt (whom the *Forverts* had
likewise spurned in 1932) as having "earned the gratitude of every
thinking man in the country. He should be a Socialist[;] if anybody
is entitled to membership in our party he is." In 1936, the *Forverts*
endorsed Roosevelt, and the following year it endorsed La Guardia.

For those who had followed Cahan on the arc from immigrant
radicalism to labor socialism to what seemed the incipient social
democracy of the New Deal, the historian Beth Wenger aptly writes,
Roosevelt's policies "marked their coming of age as legitimate par-
ticipants in mainstream American political culture." Perhaps Cahan
preferred to see it from the other perspective: if the Wagner Act and
the creation of the welfare state in the nation and the blossoming of
urban progressivism in the city constituted the trading of revolution
for reform, it also marked a triumph of the values, if not the full
transformative vision, of Yiddish socialism. La Guardia remarked
pitch-perfectly to Cahan during a 1941 campaign event:

> You and I have grown together in this city. We started to make
> this a better city, to improve the condition of the workers,
> to have better homes, to educate our children, to have our
> rights recognized, to gain the respect of our fellow citizens.
> We started all this 25 and 30 years ago. We were pioneers—
> you and I, Mr. Cahan. I am sure you are as gratified as I am,
> notwithstanding the many heartaches and sometimes peri-
> ods of discouragement, that what we set out to do has been
> accomplished. Today your people have acquired their place
> in this community. They do not need to be patronized by any
> stranger. They do not care to hear that some candidate now

tolerates them. They are entitled to the rights that they have acquired. Today your people are respected in this community. They are part of this community. They are part of the very life of the city itself.[35]

Black New Yorkers, who comprised a much smaller share of the city's population, embraced Roosevelt and La Guardia with even greater enthusiasm. Roosevelt's share of central Harlem's vote climbed by more than 30 percent between 1932 and 1936 (compared to 8 percent citywide); La Guardia's shot up by 33 percent (against a little under 20 percent citywide). And nowhere else in the city did the mobilizing effects of New Deal policy prove more powerful. The number of ballots cast in New York's two predominantly African American assembly districts (Manhattan's 19th and 21st) grew by 42 percent between 1932 and 1936, against 25 percent in the city as a whole; between 1933 and 1937, voting rose by 18 percent, against 3.6 percent citywide. All of this occurred despite the fact that neither Roosevelt nor La Guardia could boast of any significant civil rights achievements, beyond the simple and painless act of appointing highly qualified men and women to public office; despite the fact that both the White House and City Hall had avoided specifically racial questions on the pretense that to do otherwise would be a distraction from the more immediate problems of economic recovery and municipal reform; and despite the fact that the dominant discourse in Harlem about both Roosevelt and La Guardia, especially among community leaders, had been one of protest, not approval.

Like Jewish New Yorkers, black New Yorkers were in but not of the local Democratic Party. Mayors Hylan and Walker were gracious toward the rapidly growing black populace, making regular visits to Harlem and undertaking symbolic acts of courtesy—for instance, demanding the excision of the most objectionable scenes from D. W. Griffith's *The Birth of a Nation* as a condition of its being shown in

New York. Appointments to the municipal workforce expanded significantly, particularly under Walker. But black Democrats were also
confined to a parallel party organization, the United Colored Democracy, a "powerless segregated institution whose primary tasks were
winning votes for Tammany and isolating blacks from positions of
real political influence." As a result, the Democrats tended to carry
Harlem in mayoral elections without integrating Harlemites into the
Democratic Party in any substantive way. At the national level, black
New Yorkers tended to vote Republican, though the Party of Lincoln
had so nearly defaulted on its historic goodwill that the predominantly African American precincts in Harlem had nearly given Roosevelt a majority in 1932.[36]

A very small number of black New Yorkers had attained significant
wealth; a larger but still modest group had achieved stable prosperity
and could be called a "middle class." A small entrepreneurial class
was concentrated in a relatively narrow range of enterprise (mostly
storekeepers, ice and coal dealers, restaurateurs, undertakers, pharmacists, and proprietors of pool rooms and cabarets). But most black
New Yorkers were workers. A significant number possessed the job
skills and in some instances the professional or technical training of
a "middle class" but were consigned to working-class occupations, or
worse, by discrimination in employment markets and in the unions:
they constituted a kind of black middle class-in-waiting, the presence
of which was one of the outstanding (but often ignored) features of
interwar Harlem. (The size of this group might be gauged by noting
that the average number of school years completed by Harlem residents, in 1940, was generally well above that attained in the older
immigrant neighborhoods; in the more prosperous parts of Harlem,
the figure was considerably higher than the city average. An under-
standably bitter dictum rang true: "Turn a machine gun on a crowd
of red caps . . . and you would slaughter a score of Bachelors of Arts,
Doctors of Laws, Doctors of Medicine, Doctors of Dental Surgery.")

Others survived on low-paying domestic work, menial labor, and other undesirable jobs, or on government relief. Because African Americans were overrepresented in the occupations hardest hit by the Great Depression, and because they faced discrimination when hiring resumed (as well as competition from displaced white workers being pushed down the occupational ladder), black New Yorkers suffered catastrophic levels of unemployment. By the New York Urban League's estimate, 60 percent of Harlem was unemployed in 1935.[37]

In this context, the advent of government relief was of tremendous importance. The historian Nancy Weiss has presented convincing evidence that the New Deal relief programs were the primary contributing factor to the realignment of the "black vote" at the presidential level. Likewise Roy Wilkins of the NAACP wrote after the 1937 mayoral election: "Thousands of Negroes voted for Mayor La Guardia because they thought he and his entourage were responsible for the continuation of relief. They did not know or care about Mr. La Guardia's alleged 'good government.'" The local administration of relief was hardly unimpeachable: if the kind of wholesale discrimination present in many local relief offices was notably uncommon in Gotham (though not altogether absent), unequal treatment did result from relief officials' initial failure to account for conditions caused by racial discrimination. African Americans, for instance, were more likely to have difficulty proving their residency and their past income, which made it harder for them to qualify for relief; their cost of living was likely to be higher because their rents included what amounted to a tax on dark skin, a fact relief authorities did not account for when calculating family budgets. And yet federal employment and city relief kept families together and rent paid, and WPA and relief checks "constitute[d] a considerable part of the community life-blood," rescuing small business owners as well as the unemployed.[38]

These were not inconsiderable accomplishments. But in some instances, work relief meant much more. For many black workers,

accustomed to exploitation by private employers, WPA jobs represented a distinct step up in terms of pay, hours, working conditions,
job security, and dignity. Despite the stinginess of government relief,
WPA wages and even home relief payments often amounted to more
than black workers (particularly black women) could earn in the dis-
criminatory private job market: the Bureau of Labor Statistics found
that the average unskilled black worker earned $630 per year com-
pared to the WPA's minimum rate of $720; the story was similar for
semi-skilled and skilled workers. And if the WPA too often placed
black New Yorkers in menial jobs, whatever their skill level and previous occupation, it at least *attempted* to do what private employers
rarely had: provide black New Yorkers with something like "a white
man's chance" in the workplace. A Harlem woman named Norma
Mair recalled how her husband, an engineer, had had trouble finding a job in his profession.

> In the meantime he drove a cab. It was no living at all as a
> taxi driver. . . . Those things I did resent, because he had more
> to offer. He met so many people on the cab line. . . . He met
> professors who were driving cabs and couldn't get a job. First
> it was color. Then it was color and Depression. . . . When the
> WPA came in, that was the first time he got to work in his pro-
> fession. He worked on theaters, schools. They did everything,
> and it meant a lot that he was finally able to work in his field.

The *Amsterdam News* reported in 1939 that many educated black
men and women had enjoyed "the best jobs they've ever had in their
lives. Thousands of Negro clerks and other white collar relief workers found the kind of employment they were trained for." In this
fashion, public employment lifted a portion of Harlem's submerged
middle class to a position more commensurate with their education
and abilities.[39]

In voting for Roosevelt and La Guardia, black New Yorkers were also responding to what the New Deal public investment programs had produced in Harlem. Inadequate though it was in quantity, the PWA had constructed the best housing for its price in the city in central Harlem. The WPA had built new school buildings, had opened a massive state-of-the-art swimming pool in Colonial Park, had doubled the physical capacity of Harlem Hospital, had staffed health centers, recreational facilities, and nurseries, and had assigned trained personnel to church and community centers. The WPA adult education programs had offered free courses on forty-five subjects in Harlem; 30,000 people had participated regularly in at least one "arts or education program." The Federal Theater Project had been responsible for reopening Harlem's only legitimate theater, the Lafayette. Harlem artists employed by the Federal One arts projects had produced work of enduring value—the Federal Theater Project's "Voodoo *Macbeth*," the sketches of black life in New York in the *WPA Guide to New York City* and *New York Panorama*, and the seminal Harlem Hospital murals, among many others. All told, no section of New York, WPA officials believed, had given "greater support to the [WPA's] culture, recreational and vocational projects than . . . upper Manhattan." Community advocates such as the Reverend Adam Clayton Powell, Jr. (the future congressman and son of a staunch and influential La Guardia supporter), pushed La Guardia to direct more New Deal money to predominantly black neighborhoods. But by the fall of 1937 what had been accomplished in Harlem was not inconsiderable.[40]

V

"There were two gods in my house in the '30s and '40s: F.D.R. and La Guardia," one son of Depression-era New York has recalled. This was how many New Yorkers came to view their political leaders: they were men of singular powers, uniquely capable of guiding the city and the nation through crisis and, in the process, rendering them more just. It seemed a blessing of providence that they should appear when they could be most useful, and when they were needed most.[41]

Roosevelt and La Guardia did possess outstanding personal qualities. But this does not fully account for how they came to loom so large in the public life of the nation and the city. We are accustomed to thinking about political leadership in personal terms—as something that inheres in an individual's character, or ability, or capacity to learn. But leadership is also a social phenomenon, and its quality depends largely on structural features outside the individual's control. As we have seen, Roosevelt and La Guardia acquired charisma because events rendered them capable of accomplishing governmental feats that seemed beyond the ability of ordinary mortals. Their emergence as mass leaders was facilitated by patterns of communication: they were able to forge close relations with the public in part because they could speak to their constituents through the mass circulation newspapers, the newsreels, and particularly the radio.

And crucially, when they spoke, they did so to mobilized and relatively informed publics. In New York, as elsewhere, the 1930s were a period of unusually high popular political mobilization. This was distinctly true of New York's Jewish and African American communities, which were extensively organized by unions, political clubs, consumer and tenant groups, civil rights organizations, uplift organizations, churches and synagogues, and highly local community groups, to name but a very few. These organizations varied widely in the scale on which they organized, the identities they sought to mobilize, the political ideologies they espoused, and the objectives they pursued. But each, in one way or another, articulated commonly held values; and the discourses they fostered were reproduced as their members read the newspaper, listened to the radio and to street corner debaters, and talked politics with their neighbors. As a result, many New York neighborhoods were rich in social capital of a specifically political sort: "organizational memberships, networks, structural positions, and attitudes that explicitly build opportunities and capacities to participate in politics," and which provided a social basis for robust political action.[42]

Roosevelt and La Guardia were able to garner much electoral support by winning the support of the leaders of these organizations, some of which—like the ALP, which had a ballot line and a campaign organization, and the Communist Party, which commanded a significant bloc of votes—had real electoral clout. But community organizations also played a less obvious, but equally crucial, role in the electoral politics of Depression-era New York. As the historian Cheryl Greenberg has emphasized in her study of 1930s Harlem, organization leaders often followed broader community sentiment at least as much as they shaped it. In doing so, they converted powerful but amorphous community aspirations into political demands that were recognizably in tune with community values. Collective mobilization around a set of demands provided a social basis for community engagement with the state.[43]

In 1945, after La Guardia announced he would not seek a fourth term, notes of gratitude started arriving at City Hall. One of those moved to write was C. T. Nesbitt, an African American from Jamaica, Queens, who headed a community organization with the motto "A Job for Every Citizen." Nesbitt wrote to La Guardia:

> Kindly take this letter as a way of giving you thanks for every-thing that your office has ment to my people since you taken office in City Hall. (I mean colored people) My race has made greater progress while you was in City Hall then we have in all the History of this great City. and I wants to tell you while you are [y]et in office that there are colored people that do give thanks to you for the wounderful fight that you has put up for

the under dog ([c]olored people) And my organization wants to know that we thank you.

You and the Hon. F. D. Roosevelt ment more to my people then all the Presidents, and all the Mayors that held office before you. And we wants you to know that we are not a sleep, for it was my organization that went to you and beged you to clean up our schools. and I went back and beged for a park for our children to play, I went back to you and beged you to give my people a chance to work among our own people on releif, by making them investgatores, Clerks, and case workers. It was my organization that asked you for a releif station in Herlem. My organization asked you to [put] milk stations in Harlem. . . .

These or just a few of the things that we asked you for, and did get them and more than we ask you for. . . . But what we wants you to know is there are colored men and women in my race that can,t forget you and F. D. Roosevelt.[44]

Nesbitt's letter is full of revealing bits: its premise that a good government was one which permitted "the race" to make progress; the inextricable link between race and class embodied in his equation of "the under dog" and "colored people"; and the close association many New Yorkers made between Roosevelt and La Guardia. But it also illustrates the role community leaders and community organizers played in the development of leader-follower relationships at the time. Some community leaders, like Nesbitt, perceived themselves to be actively working with the president and the mayor on a shared project, each with responsibilities to the other—"we wants you to know that we are not a sleep." Other activists, particularly the more radical ones, thought of elected officials in more adversarial terms. But each served the same function. By defining a goal and mobilizing their members in pursuit of it, they helped to make possible the leader-follower relation that played so large a role in Depression-era New York politics. When matched to the extraordinary governmental capacities made possible by the New Deal, it proved a potent mix.

VI

The campaign itself was mostly uneventful. Neither Mahoney nor La Guardia had much difficulty in their respective primaries. Thenceforth, La Guardia, his own election all but certain, spent much of his time "mumbling statistics" (as one reporter put it) about the money saved and efficiency achieved by the city departments and pleading for the election of a pro-reform Board of Estimate. La Guardia's campaign rhetoric revolved primarily around the merits of good government against odious Tammany corruption; Mahoney's speeches seemed to yearn for the lost paradise of Irish New York, a city without Communists where law and order had reigned. The only moment of real tension was manufactured by the German American Bund, an organization of Nazi partisans, which requested a permit to march through Yorkville several days before the election. La Guardia, whose anti-Nazism was by then well known, took the side of free speech and free assembly and allowed the permit to be granted; the Democratic Yiddish newspaper *Der Tog* argued in response that a Democratic mayor would have "stood firm against anything that might arouse race hatred in the city."[45]

On the eve of New York's municipal elections, La Guardia, clad in a well-worn dark gray overcoat, stood at the intersection of Lexington and 116th—the "lucky corner" on which he had closed his campaigns since the early twenties—and addressed a crowd of some 8,000 supporters. The mood was buoyant, and La Guardia was ready to proclaim victory. "Never mind what the opposition has told you," he said. "The campaign is over and the election is won." The following day, New Yorkers gave him the largest mayoral vote in the city's history (though in percentage terms his victory did not match Walker's 1929 landslide). His running mates nearly ran the board, winning the comptrollership, the presidency of the City Council, four of five borough presidencies (losing only the Bronx), and the Manhattan district attorney's office—the last a crucial defeat for Tammany Hall, which had held the post for twenty-eight years and stood ill-suited to lose either the jobs or the favorable prosecutorial treatment. All told, the Republican ballot line supplied 50 percent of La Guardia's total and the ALP some 36 percent—482,459 votes—with the remainder coming from the Fusion and Progressive parties. He had become the first reform mayor ever to win reelection in New York City.[46]

Adolf Berle, who spent the night of La Guardia's reelection at ALP headquarters, called the Little Flower around ten o'clock that night and found him on the phone with Roosevelt. "[T]he President apparently wasted no time on congratulations," Berle wrote in his diary; "he proposes to annex this if he can—and he is right." In the days following the election, the New Dealers and the GOP each jostled to claim La Guardia's smashing victory as a triumph for their own cause. Two days after the election, Roosevelt, returning to Washington from a vacation at Hyde Park, stopped off in New York City to see La Guardia. Despite the mayor's protestations that it was "merely a social call," the visit was interpreted by the press as an indication that Roosevelt was well pleased with the election's outcome and wished to claim La Guardia's victory for the New Deal. La Guardia arrived promptly at 2:40 pm at Roosevelt's town house; he, Farley, and Harry Hopkins talked amiably with Roosevelt about the election and particularly the ALP. Then Farley and Hopkins left, so that Roosevelt and La Guardia could talk alone for ten or fifteen minutes off the record. "There is no doubt in my mind that the President was quite satisfied with the La Guardia victory," Farley wrote in his diary afterward. "While he did not say so I am sure he likes La Guardia personally and that he has been extremely dissatisfied with Tammany's attitude."[47]

To the extent that FDR could claim La Guardia's triumph as a victory for the New Deal, it came as a relief in a year of political setbacks. In the months since his own reelection, Roosevelt had encountered a tempest partly of his own making. His proposal to augment the membership of the Supreme Court had split the Democratic Party, damaged his relations with Congress, and—for practically the first time—allowed his conservative adversaries to stake out a popular position against him. A wave of sit-down strikes, centered in the auto production industry, had raised temperatures, and Roosevelt's "plague on both your houses" response had satisfied virtually no one. Most important, the industrial economy had stalled in the summer and then, suddenly, collapsed. Within a few days of La Guardia's reelection it had become clear that Roosevelt was facing a dire situation, an economic crisis matched in American history only by the worst days of 1932–33—and one which had occurred on his watch. As La Guardia, in the wake of his triumphant reelection, turned his own eyes toward the national political scene, he would find that the upheaval of the mid-thirties had taken an unexpected turn.

7

New Dealer for the Duration

L a Guardia's stunning victory, wrote *The Nation's* editors, "marks the high point of his tumultuous political career. He now joins President Roosevelt and Senator La Follette as one of the three major national figures, looking toward 1940. . . ." A few months earlier, La Guardia had hardly registered among the contenders for national office; now public opinion polls showed him as the third choice among Republicans and the fifth choice among Roosevelt voters when asked who they would like to see as their party's next nominee for the presidency. An outpouring of profiles—in *Time*, *Newsweek*, the *Atlantic*, *The New Yorker*, and later *Collier's*—and a *March of Time* newsreel feature introduced him to a broader section of the public.[1]

Roosevelt watched La Guardia's ascent with a mixture of respect and wariness. He had long regarded the Little Flower as an extraordinarily skilled administrator; now he took note of his abilities as a popular politician. "That little wop has something," he told Attorney General Homer Cummings after observing La Guardia's commanding performance at the cornerstone-laying ceremony for the 1939 World's Fair. He told Adolf Berle that "so far as all personal reasons

were concerned, [he would] support Fiorello 100% as a first-rate liberal President who was easily the ablest of the lot." But if Roosevelt
welcomed La Guardia's emergence as a dynamic progressive force in
national politics, this also introduced a complicating element into
their relationship. "The difficulty with Fiorello vis-à-vis Franklin was
that of any potential successor," Rexford Tugwell later wrote. "He
[Roosevelt] wanted the progressives as allies, but those who might
be rivals had to be kept at a distance." Increasingly conscious of the
political ambitions of others, Roosevelt went "out of his way at various times," James Farley later recalled, "to tax . . . La Guardia . . .
with nursing plans to redecorate the White House."[2]

But even as this dynamic of competition created a certain tension
between the two men, other, larger forces were sweeping over American politics—and these would pull La Guardia ever more firmly into
the New Deal political orbit. The closing years of the 1930s would
see the growth of a conservative coalition centered on opposition to
the very programs that were driving progressive politics in the big
cities; the birth pangs of realignment in the Democratic Party, the
revival of the Republican Party, and the fracturing of independent
progressivism; and the emergence of foreign policy as a preeminent
issue in American politics. Within this context, what had been a
working collaboration grounded in mutual self-interest and ideological affinity, tempered by partisan distrust, became, by 1940, a political partnership.

I

As Roosevelt and his cabinet had anticipated, the Works Progress
Administration quickly became an extremely polarizing agency. "In
the memory of American workers," the historian David Montgomery
writes, "no act of the New Deal evokes a warmer response than the

massive scale of its relief effort." And yet few New Deal measures stirred up as much angry opposition—opposition so intense that even mainstream political commentators raised for public consideration the prospect of disenfranchising all public sector workers lest the WPA become the basis for a huge New Deal political machine. When, in 1939, George Gallup's pollsters asked men and women from every state and all walks of life to name the New Deal's "greatest accomplishment" and "the worst thing the Roosevelt administration has done," the WPA topped both lists by wide margins.[3]

La Guardia, his own administration deeply implicated in the WPA's operations, became heavily involved in the New Dealers' efforts to defend the agency from its critics and political adversaries. Trading on his reputation as an honest and efficient administrator, he spoke on the WPA's behalf in venues across the country, emphasizing, in turn, the "chaos" that would wrack the big cities if relief were returned to the states and the "right" of American citizens to work "so that they can support their families decently and properly." He pleaded the WPA's cause so forcefully that he sometimes felt he was doing more for the New Deal than were the New Dealers themselves. Once, after trips to New Orleans and Boston, he chided Hopkins for not helping him adequately in his efforts to sell Hopkins's own program: "Now listen, Harry," he said, "I can't carry the ball alone. I have to have a team." (La Guardia did similar publicity work for the far less controversial Public Works Administration. During one of his periodic dust-ups with Harold Ickes, who on this occasion had referred to the mayor as a "publicity seeker," a wounded La Guardia wrote: "I might have been guilty of getting publicity in the last few months, but it was publicity in favor of your program. No one in this country has more favorably advertised and explained the PWA program than I have. . . . I am sure the President knows about it, because we have discussed it many times.")[4]

The United States Conference of Mayors, which elected La Guardia its president in 1935, would serve as the primary organizational vehicle by which America's mayors worked in defense of the New Deal's intergovernmental programs. Founded in 1932 to foster federal-municipal relations by giving the political leaders of the big cities an "effective organizational base" for lobbying Congress and the executive branch, the Conference of Mayors was a structurally powerful participant in the federal policy-making process. Though its members represented exclusively urban areas, they were otherwise an extraordinarily diverse lot: they represented cities in every region of the country; and they were the creatures of all different types of political regimes. And as an organization of local officials, the mayors' conference could speak with authority on some of the most contentious questions of the 1930s: whether or not federal spending was efficacious and desirable; whether or not the national programs initiated by the New Deal impinged upon the autonomy and freedom of smaller political communities.[5]

La Guardia had become a major voice within the mayors' conference even before he took office, when, in December 1933, the mayors lobbied for the expansion of the Civil Works Administration to include all unemployed persons. By the following year he was the group's spokesman and de facto leader (as was evident in the September 1934 lobbying trips to Hyde Park); he was elected its president in 1935, a one year term that the mayors chose to extend in 1936 and again in the years that followed; he would continue to hold the presidency until he left office in 1946. "[W]e sort of broke the rules," Mayor Kelly of Chicago recalled, "because of his closeness to Washington, not only as to distance, but of the powers that be. . . ." Under La Guardia's direction (and that of executive secretary Paul Betters), the Conference of Mayors would emerge as one of the primary sources of organized support for the WPA.[6]

One aspect of the mayors' work involved publicizing the WPA's contributions to local communities. Especially in a large and diverse nation such as the United States, federal spending programs may suffer from deficits in public understanding: citizens may be unaware of what those programs do; or they may assume money is being spent in sections of the country other than their own, or for the benefit of people unlike themselves. The WPA was far less vulnerable to the "invisibility" problem than most government spending programs; indeed, it was one of the most visible national spending programs in American history. But its advocates were acutely concerned about public comprehension of what the agency was doing—particularly the dissonance between the popular conviction that the WPA was doing useful work in local communities and the lurking suspicion that, as a national undertaking, it was wasting taxpayer money on useless "boondoggle" projects. "There is a great deal of misrepresentation concerning the W.P.A., resulting in misunderstanding on the part of many well meaning people," La Guardia wrote to a state administrator nine months into the program's existence. "The projects themselves and work given to the unemployed will in the long run fully answer the criticism." To help translate local support for WPA-sponsored public investment into support for national work relief policy, he and Betters produced a series of reports which publicized the benefits accruing to communities as a result of the WPA, and, most importantly, showed a striking consensus in support of the program that crossed regions and party lines, and included machine and reform administrations—Democrats, Republicans, Socialists, and non-partisan city managers alike. Though the reports were presented as the work of a disinterested and non-partisan organization of local officials, La Guardia discussed them with Hopkins, and he corresponded with Roosevelt as to how they could be most effectively released.[7]

The Conference of Mayors also emerged as a key participant in the lobbying process that determined how much was appropriated for the federal works programs and what rules would guide the spending of that money. In requesting WPA appropriations from Congress (which were adopted without alteration until 1939), Roosevelt was subjected to two strong, antithetical popular pressures: first, the demand for adequate relief and public employment; second, a broad and powerful public sentiment for economy in government and a balanced budget. Popular support for "economy," strong even in the mid-1930s (when it consistently polled second after joblessness in surveys that asked respondents to identify the most important problem facing the nation), picked up after the election of 1936, particularly among congressional Democrats who represented districts that had, by 1937, returned to something like pre–Depression-era conditions and who feared another economic collapse should rampant budget deficits continue and inflation, default, or a sharp hike in taxes follow. In the spring of 1937, some of these Democrats joined Republicans to form an "economy bloc" committed to reducing the federal budget by cutting appropriations for the works programs. The Conference of Mayors, along with the Workers' Alliance (a union of WPA workers) and the WPA itself, acted as a countervailing force, articulating popular support for an adequate public employment program.

Roosevelt himself sought to steer a course between these two forces—reducing work relief spending, but more gradually than the economizers wished. To counterbalance the well-organized and structurally powerful congressional economy group, he fostered the development of the Conference of Mayors, frequently bringing La Guardia to the White House to discuss WPA appropriations, which ensured that the mayors' requests would make the newspapers nationwide. With the economizers establishing the lower bound of mainstream public discussion and the Conference of Mayors' requests indicating what would be sufficient to continue the WPA at its existing levels, Roosevelt could make middle-of-the-road requests that protected the WPA from draconian cuts while

satisfying centrists that he accepted the need to make progress
toward a balanced budget.[8]

The politics of work relief entered a new phase in the spring of
1937 when, in the first rumblings of what would ultimately prove
a seismic shift, southern congressmen began to look at the WPA
more critically. Some focused on the program's pro-urban character. By soaking up the excess of labor in the cities, they now suggested, the agency was subsidizing an unsustainable (and perhaps
undesirable) social arrangement. "What are we going to do with the
folks in the cities?" one rural congressman asked. "The answer is
that we continue on with this relief business and permit people to
go to the cities and live there." If work relief spending were curtailed
and labor markets allowed to take their course, these congressmen
suggested, decentralization of the kind Roosevelt claimed to support
would be the natural result. As it was, rural tax dollars were being
funneled into the Northeast and Midwest to maintain people in the
overgrown cities. Other southern Democrats fixed upon the WPA's
regional wage differentials, a policy they had previously supported
but now came to see as a threat to the separateness of the southern
labor market—in some ways the very foundation of southern society. Senator James Byrnes of South Carolina cited a much-publicized
case of a Georgia man who, faced with the choice between a $21 a
week WPA wage in Georgia and a $61 wage in New York, had packed
up and moved to the city. WPA work, some had concluded, "constitute[d] a tempting alternative to tenant farming and agricultural
work"; as such, it seemed to threaten basic elements of the southern
social order.[9]

Southern congressmen responded to these mounting concerns by
seeking to reclaim policy-making authority they had ceded to the
administration in the Emergency Relief Appropriation Act of 1935.
WPA policy thus became enmeshed in a larger struggle between
Congress and the executive branch, and, by extension, between

the traditional elements of the Democratic Party and the New Deal forces. This institutional tension between Congress and the administration, exacerbated by Roosevelt's recently introduced court reform and executive reorganization measures, first boiled over in a contest between the administration and southern Democrats in Congress over the "sponsor's share" demanded of local governments by the WPA. Unlike the Public Works Administration, which had a fixed ratio of federal to local expenditures, Harry Hopkins had exercised broad discretion in determining how much a local government would be required to pay for a particular project. He had used this discretion to promote local government spending on PWA projects and home relief—in other words, to encourage local governments to provide work or income maintenance for those "employables" the perennially underfunded WPA could not employ. In the summer of 1935, he had struck what Secretary Morgenthau described as a "deal" with La Guardia. Under this informal understanding, the WPA had required New York to put up an unusually small "sponsor's share" in recognition of its heavy investment in PWA projects and its generous provision of home relief to the "employable" people the WPA could not put to work (and, later, in exchange for occasional extraordinary city contributions to WPA projects, such as those required to build La Guardia Airport). On this understanding, La Guardia later wrote to Hopkins, the mayor "proceeded to the very limit" with the city's public construction program.[10]

When Senator Byrnes looked over the WPA's spending figures, he saw that his state of South Carolina was paying 23.6 percent of the cost of its WPA projects and New York City was paying 0.5 percent—a detail he promptly made public. Byrnes's revelation became one more bit of evidence that the WPA was funneling money into the urban North. But his complaint was not exclusively about inequity; he also charged that, through such arrangements, Roosevelt had ceded to mayors broad authority to determine what consti-

tuted relief—powers Byrnes believed should belong to Congress. The
position Hopkins, Roosevelt, and La Guardia had agreed to, he said,

> is that you should take into consideration the amount spent by
> the mayor of New York for what he terms relief, and that when
> you take that into consideration it is not unfair to ask that they
> contribute only one-half of 1 percent, and I submit that if that
> is to be the test, then the Congress must determine what shall
> be included, what definition that shall be of the word relief,
> instead of leaving it to the mayor of a city. For instance it should
> be determined whether free hospitalization in Denver or Mem-
> phis or Charleston shall be included in the expenditures which
> a State makes for relief.

Byrnes proposed a rider requiring the sponsor to pay 40 percent of
the cost of a project or else specify in writing its inability to pay—a
"pauper's oath"—in which case the president could proceed as under
existing law after investigating the local government's taxes and
credit facilities to see if it could not in fact pay more. A list of cases in
which exceptions were made would be furnished to the Congress.[11]

   "I cannot understand some of my old friends," La Guardia said
ruefully as he prepared to fight the measure. "I stood up for aid in
their districts for fifteen years and it seems to me the Senators are
not serving the best interests of their constituents lining up the farmers against the cities." The onus for defending the existing arrangement fell to Roosevelt, who first took Byrnes on directly. Hopkins
provided the totals of what the state and local governments of New
York and South Carolina had spent on direct relief, work relief, and
public works combined and found that New York, with its robust
state and local social welfare and public investment programs, had
spent on a per capita basis $56 to South Carolina's $8. "It occurs to
me," FDR wrote to Byrnes, "that due publicity should be given to

this comparison when you speak on the floor of the Senate. What do you think? Or do you want me to do it?!" Byrnes's rider made it through the Senate Appropriations Committee over Hopkins's objections and gathered the support of the majority leader Joe Robinson, president *pro tempore* Key Pittman, and Appropriations Committee chair Pat Harrison—the first time the Democratic leadership in the Senate had lined up unanimously against Roosevelt. When the question of sponsor contributions reached the Senate floor, the administration pulled enough strings to defeat it by 15 votes. "It was beaten by a combination of the President, Mr. Harry Hopkins, and his lobby of big city mayors, largely manipulated by Mr. La Guardia of New York," the conservative syndicated columnist Frank Kent wrote.[12]

But for La Guardia, the victory was not complete. Having successfully defended executive discretion, Roosevelt quietly moved to mollify the congressional conservatives, urging Hopkins to raise the sponsors' shares wherever it was feasible. Worse, the ideas voiced during the 1937 debates signaled a turn against the very lineaments of the New Deal work relief state—national executive authority, the intergovernmental "cash nexus," and generous treatment of the cities—by an absolutely crucial group of congressmen. Thus did New York's local New Deal find its first powerful set of adversaries, not within the city but in the legislative chambers of Washington.[13]

The politics of the WPA reversed direction momentarily in 1938. The American economy had collapsed suddenly the previous fall, driving employment and industrial activity down to levels comparable to early 1933. The coming of the "Roosevelt recession" had shocked the administration and had touched off a months-long search for a policy response. Gradually, Roosevelt was won over to what became known as the "spending solution"—an approach, favored by an influential group of White House advisers (including Hopkins, Lauchlin Currie, Leon Henderson, and Marriner Eccles), which embraced countercyclical government spending, until then

a more or less unintended by-product of the New Deal relief and
works programs, as a positive tool of national macroeconomic
management. "From 1934 to 1936," Currie argued in an influential
memorandum, "the largest single factor in the steady recovery movement was the excess of Federal activity-creating expenditures over
activity-decreasing receipts"; the logical response, then, was "a very
substantial increase in the Government's contribution to national
buying power." The works programs represented the natural vehicle
for injecting purchasing power into the American economy through
deficit spending.[14]

In mid-April 1938, Roosevelt requested of Congress more than $4
billion in new spending, including a new appropriation for the PWA
and an increase in WPA spending. La Guardia and the Conference
of Mayors again moved swiftly into action. After meeting with FDR,
Adolf Berle "asked [La Guardia] to stand by to offer to put some of
the public works money to work." La Guardia hastened to Washington with a program intended to demonstrate that there would be no
repeat of the PWA's plodding start in 1933 and 1934—that a "spending solution" grounded in local public investment projects was feasible from the standpoint of implementation. While Ickes put the onus
on "our cities . . . to produce faster than ever before," La Guardia
went before Congress to testify that he could "have the dirt flying
within 15 days of the time Secretary Ickes and the President approve
the projects. . . ." The Conference of Mayors undertook an extensive
lobbying effort, their appeals aided by the congressmen's attention to
the coming midterm elections and the economy group's willingness
to accept that the rationale they had deployed the previous year—
that conditions had returned to "normal"—had been shattered by
the recession. When Roosevelt's program passed in mid-June, blueprints, long since prepared, were pulled off the shelf. The New York
City WPA expanded its operations; and although New York was
prevented from investing as heavily in large public works projects

as it had in the mid-1930s by the fact that it was now bumping up against its constitutional debt ceiling, the third incarnation of the PWA funded the construction of schools, piers, public buildings, and the pioneering Belt Parkway.[15]

Nineteen thirty-eight was to be the Indian summer of the New Deal intergovernmental public investment state. That fall, the Republican Party, whose members had always been the most steadfast opponents of federal work relief, swept the midterm congressional elections, enabling congressional conservatives finally to claim a measure of control over the WPA. The anti-spending movement, moreover, had acquired a new edge following Roosevelt's effort to "purge" selected conservative Democrats in the 1938 party primaries—which had exacerbated congressional conservatives' discomfort with the immense discretion and unrestrained spending power the Congress had yielded to Roosevelt, leading them to view the WPA as a kind of national New Deal political machine that could be deployed to control state and local elections. When Roosevelt brought La Guardia to the White House at the end of December 1938 to discuss strategy for the WPA deficiency appropriation, La Guardia recommended that Roosevelt make it large and then allow the economy-minded Congress to cut it freely. If all went to plan, the "economizing congressmen would soon hear from their districts, which would strengthen the President's control over the law-makers" when the regular fiscal year appropriation came up in the spring. The economy group in the House, openly orchestrated by Vice President Garner, took the bait, slicing $150 million off Roosevelt's request of $875 million (itself a more modest figure than La Guardia's recommended $915 million) and writing into the bill a provision forbidding political activity by WPA workers—the seed of what would become the Hatch Act ("An Act to Prevent Pernicious Political Activities").[16]

Senators Glass and Hatch had scarcely announced that they planned to trim the appropriation further when the WPA lobby went

into motion. La Guardia, AFL president William Green, and John
L. Lewis of the CIO beseeched members of both chambers not to
wreak havoc on the cities, claiming that the House bill would dis-
miss upwards of a million WPA workers. The Workers' Alliance, a
union of WPA workers, threatened a hunger march. The WPA itself
released a study which showed where its wages went: out of $1 mil-
lion of WPA money in a typical city, relief workers "immediately paid
$335,000 to the butcher, grocer and baker, $23,000 to the landlord,
and $145,000 to the clothier, druggist and shoe store. . . ." All told,
"small business got 75 per cent of the $1,000,000." WPA officials
supplied Labor's Non-Partisan League with a copy of the study; the
unionists circulated it, and small businessmen in many cities joined
the letter-writing and telegraphing campaign. The Senate economizers did not waver. Taking the pro-administration forces by surprise,
the Senate economy group passed the House measure by a single
vote. The leader of the House economizers, Representative Clifton
Woodrum of Virginia, applauded the vote as a demonstration that
Congress "can legislate and that it does not have to delegate those
powers to the Workers' Alliance or to the Mayors' Conference."[17]

By the time the fiscal year appropriation came up in June 1939,
all factions were prepared to ask for an extensive reorganization of
the works programs. La Guardia—by now viewed by conservatives
as something of an accomplice in the New Deal machine-making
project (and by WPA workers across the country as one of their
greatest champions)—had been called as a witness before the House
committee investigating relief and, in the course of a long hearing
that touched upon nearly every facet of the question, had recommended more or less in total the English system of integrating the
administration of social insurance and work relief with a national
employment service. Roosevelt proposed that the WPA be renamed
(it became the Work Projects Administration) and consolidated,
along with the PWA, the U.S. Housing Authority, the Bureau of

Public Roads, and the procurement bureau of the Treasury Department, into a new agency, the Federal Works Agency. Conservatives in Congress, if they did not seek to end the WPA altogether, wanted "a more equitable distribution of relief fund quotas among the states" and a means of preventing WPA workers from believing they had a "right" to a public job.

The House bill, passed that June, reduced the regional wage disparity, forced a 25 percent contribution by local governments, ordered furloughs for all those under forty-five years of age who had been on WPA for longer than eighteen months, capped the cost of WPA projects at $25,000, mandated loyalty oaths, excluded aliens, abolished the supposedly subversive Federal Theater Project, and struck $125 million from Roosevelt's request (already substantially reduced from the previous year). La Guardia, testifying before the Senate, decried the limit on project costs and called for the Congress to "leave the limitation as to the manner in which it is to be spent in each district, and what should be done in each district, to the discretion and judgment of the Administrator and local sponsorship." He attempted to logroll votes by sending a telegram to the president of the Farm Bureau Federation endorsing a $365 million hike in farm aid, widely circulated by the farm bloc as their request sat in conference committee. The Senate work relief bill did away with the furloughs and raised the cap on project costs to $75,000. The conference report, however, more closely resembled the House bill. Passed the day before the new fiscal year began, Roosevelt had no choice but to sign a bill he believed would "work definite hardship and inequality on more than two million American citizens—about eight million if we count in their families . . . who through no fault of their own are in dire need."[18]

This marked the beginning of the end of the intergovernmental relief and public investment state first incarnated by the CWA in late 1933. The WPA itself, leaner, less socially imaginative, more efficient, and increasingly devoted to the new tasks of building the national defense infrastructure and training the long-term unemployed for work in defense industry jobs, would live on until 1943, when Roosevelt, consumed with war and its attendant domestic pressures and unwilling to expend the political capital necessary to salvage the agency following the Republican gains in the 1942 midterms, ordered its liquidation. To the consternation of the New York left—the CIO unions in particular—La Guardia registered no strong objection. Both men were by then planning a postwar intergovernmental spending program free of the WPA's political baggage.[20]

It had been evident as early as 1934 that the federal work relief programs were stimulating the development of municipal agencies in ways that would not easily be curtailed once those emergency programs had been liquidated. "The record of accomplishment in one single year has been so great," Markets Commissioner William Fellowes Morgan had written La Guardia in early 1935, "that I do not believe it can be overlooked in future administrations when economic conditions have improved to the extent that this so-called free labor will no longer be available." Now, federal cutbacks created stresses in practically every part of the local government; even the Domestic Relations Court—which hosted a tiny fraction of the city's WPA workers—found itself in a "very grave situation" (as its presiding judge wrote) as a consequence of the shift in federal policy. Commissioners who had once denigrated the contributions of relief workers came increasingly to understand that their agencies depended upon them. Robert Moses, who had earlier described the WPA workers in his parks as "vagrants," by the spring of 1937 thought it "decidedly worth trying as an experiment . . . to recruit a small force from home relief, add a few foremen and some material out of the $100,000 fund they promised us and see how much we can do with this gang. . . . There must be quite a few people on home relief who are willing and able to work."

Beginning especially in 1937, the city responded to federal cuts by assuming financial responsibility for projects that had previously been operated with WPA labor, and by absorbing into the Civil Service many WPA workers who had become essential to the functioning of the municipal departments. Somervell's announcement in June 1937, for instance, that 34,000 local WPA jobs would be cut was met by an announcement that some 2,800 WPA workers in the Department of Public Welfare and the Emergency Relief Bureau and another 1,000 in the Department of Hospitals would receive permanent positions as soon as they qualified for the Civil Service.[19]

As Table 7.1 suggests, this process of incorporation produced higher municipal spending in areas where the WPA had been particularly active, such as recreation and public health. As the municipal government picked up a larger share of the costs of the public investment state the New Deal had helped forge, debates about public

Table 7.1: *New York City municipal spending on selected functions, fiscal years 1936 and 1939–1940 (in 1937 dollars)*

	FY 1936	FY 1939–40	(% Change)
Municipal admin.	$13,150,151	$14,690,105	11.7%
Court admin.	$12,875,261	$13,771,369	7.0%
Borough and county govts.	$28,850,037	$22,899,150	-20.6%
Parks, libraries, museums, etc.	$9,559,853	$15,336,449	60.4%
Police, fire, and corrections	$82,202,416	$98,420,604	19.7%
Health, sanitation, water, housing	$51,401,533	$61,151,569	19.0%
Welfare, hospitals, etc.	$59,519,610	$89,393,321	50.2%
Public property, public works, etc.	$12,954,263	$18,726,140	44.6%
Total budget (excl. education)	$487,508,133	$534,763,918	9.7%

Citizens Budget Commission, *Fiscal Facts Concerning the City of New York: Vols. 1–2* (New York, 1940, 1947).

sector provision—previously focused squarely upon Washington—shifted back into the municipal arena. Property taxes began to rise: from 2.64 percent when La Guardia stood for reelection in 1937 to 2.84 percent in fiscal year 1940–41. For the first time during La Guardia's mayoralty, high taxation became a major issue in city politics; organizations such as the Citizens Budget Commission were demanding a moratorium on all but the most essential municipal construction and grousing that the La Guardia administration's "record for competency" excelled its "record for economy." Soon, La Guardia and the Board of Estimate would pull back sharply on spending in the interest of conserving resources for the war effort, and many city workers were to take leaves of absence to join the armed services or the federal war bureaucracy. But already the pattern was evident: as the New Deal public investment state withered at the national level, its initiatives were picked up by the city.

II

Shortly after his reelection, La Guardia, in Washington for the annual meeting of the Conference of Mayors, joined Harold Ickes for lunch at Harvey's Restaurant. After chatting about the New York campaign (in which Ickes, during a visit to the city, had all but endorsed La Guardia), the two men turned to the presidential election of 1940, discussing at length the scenarios that might elevate another progressive to the White House. La Guardia believed Roosevelt would not be able to control the Democratic Convention, and he expected the Democrats to nominate a conservative; he took seriously the possibility that liberals might capture the Republican Party, though Harold Ickes's war stories from the 1912 convention now gave him second thoughts. Perhaps, he suggested, it would be necessary for progressives to organize a third party. The people were liberal, La Guardia remarked; they needed a "crusader" to bear the standard. "[N]aturally," Ickes wrote, "the thought occurred to me that La Guardia regarded himself as the possible crusader that would be required."[21]

Roosevelt, surveying La Guardia's prospects after the 1937 election, believed the Little Flower would be undone by his ethnicity. Berle recorded the president's thoughts in his diary: "As a practical matter . . . although he [La Guardia] had been brought up in the west and was a Mason and a Protestant, the country was not ready to elect an Italian whose mother was partly Jewish as President of the United States, and his language and accent were those of New York." In the following years, as his dreams of the national office slipped away, La Guardia would reach the same conclusion. "[The] son of a wop who lives in a tenement," he said, "doesn't get nominated for vice-president." But 1938 was a season of hope; and for a while it even looked as though La Guardia might succeed at bridging the cultural divide between the immigrant cities and the small-town interior. In January 1938, the Little Flower traveled to downstate Illinois to berate the middlemen in the food industry and introduce the broad strokes of his own "farm plan." In April, he made a national radio broadcast over NBC's Blue Network, calling for a subsidized government export monopoly to recapture South American consumer markets from Germany and Japan. (He forwarded a copy of the speech to FDR with a note to White House secretary Missy LeHand: "Here is my bed-time story for the President.") Later that month he journeyed to Oklahoma and Texas. In September, he undertook a second, more extensive western trip, stopping in Little Rock, Shreveport, northern Texas, and Prescott, Arizona, en route to the annual American Legion convention in Los Angeles, then returning through St. Louis and Indianapolis, adding Detroit to the itinerary when Michigan governor Frank Murphy beseeched him to make a campaign appearance to aid him in a close election. He was received with great enthusiasm across the South and Southwest.[22]

Party, not ethnicity, posed the greatest immediate challenge to La Guardia's national ambitions. Despite his popularity among Democratic voters and his close relation with the Democratic president, it was difficult to imagine any future for La Guardia in the Party of Jackson. The Republican picture, for the moment, looked somewhat better, if only because La Guardia had been one of the few well-known Republicans to survive the electoral gauntlet of the 1930s. After his reelection, political observers as far apart as William Allen White and Heywood Broun suggested that the discrediting of the incumbent Republican leaders and the need to appeal to the constituencies mobilized by the New Deal might create an opening for La Guardia in the Republican Party. Finally, there remained the possibility of a third party. As La Guardia's star rose, his name was increasingly linked to the leading practitioners of third-party politics, the La Follette brothers.[23]

Roosevelt had invited the La Follettes aboard the presidential yacht in the summer of 1937 and, to Governor Phil La Follette's hearing, had given them the go-ahead to try to "get a movement going in other states as had been done in Wisconsin and Minnesota." "I got the impression," Phil wrote in his memoirs, "that Roosevelt had given up hope of liberalizing the Democratic party and was ready to go along with realignment." Mindful of the lessons of his father's effort in 1924, Phil was prepared to move slowly and do the painstaking work of building state organizations before going national. But then the political setbacks dealt the New Deal in 1937 and the coming of the Roosevelt recession had caused him to rethink his course. "Doubtless realizing that the recession had badly eroded Roosevelt's prestige and power and sensing that liberals might welcome a new leader and a new party," the historian Patrick Maney has written, La Follette "decided to launch the third-party movement ahead of schedule in the spring of 1938." At the end of April, he declared from the livestock pavilion at the University of Wisconsin the formation of "*the* party of our time," the National Progressives of America.

La Guardia, like most eastern progressives and pro–New Deal social democrats, was convinced La Follette had lit the third-party fuse too soon. "There was very great interest," wrote Berle, who attended the first organizational meeting of the party as La Guardia's representative, "but a very distinct feeling that the result of this ought not to divide the liberal forces especially under the leadership of President Roosevelt. . . ." The appropriate moment for a third-party movement would come "if and when the Democratic Party repudiated the Roosevelt leadership"; until then, La Guardia and Berle believed, the development of a formidable conservative opposition made it essential that liberals and progressives circle the wagons. Acting on La Guardia's behalf, Berle declined to sign the certificate incorporating the new party; La Guardia himself issued a statement indicating his sympathy for the new party and stating his belief that a national alignment was underway, but maintaining that he viewed Roosevelt as the leader of the liberal forces. As it turned out, he did well to keep his distance. The NPA was a fiasco from its inception; bereft of powerful allies, it would be wiped out in the 1938 elections.[24]

And yet if the third-party movement had fizzled, many progressives, as they pondered their tactics and their strategies in the spring and summer of 1938, were more convinced than ever that a realignment of the two major parties was underway. The tensions between longtime Democrats and those brought into the party (or at least into its orbit) by the New Deal that had been evident in the 1936 campaign had, as early as the spring of 1937, broken into the open. The great policy battles between the White House and Congress over court reform, work relief, the regulation of working hours and wages, and the reorganization of the federal bureaucracy had been, among other things, skirmishes in a war for control of the party. As the midterm season approached, the former White House speech-writer Stanley High's assessment appeared more and more prescient: "The issue . . . is to determine whether the Democratic Party is to be the Democratic party as it has always been or whether it is now to become the liberal party."[25]

Roosevelt's deteriorating relations with the conservative Demo-crats in Congress led him to consider intervening in party affairs to strengthen the party's commitment to New Deal measures. In May 1938, with the wages and hours bill still stuck in the House Rules Committee, FDR threw his support to Florida senator Claude Pep-per, a staunch New Dealer, in his primary fight against a conser-vative challenger, Congressman Mark Wilcox. Pepper's easy victory convinced southern Democrats of the popularity of the wages and hours bill, which Congress passed and Roosevelt signed into law in June as the Fair Labor Standards Act. It also convinced the White House that such interventions could be effective. At the end of June, Roosevelt announced in a fireside chat that he would openly par-ticipate in Democratic primaries where there was a "clear issue" between the candidates involving the "definitely liberal" principles set forth in the party platform on which he had run in 1936.[26]

Roosevelt's "purge" of the Democratic Party was to prove a disor-ganized, even haphazard affair. But it was motivated by a coherent vision—of a party system composed of "two effective and respon-sible political parties, one liberal, the other conservative." He had arrived, in other words, at much the same position La Guardia had championed more than three years earlier to the meeting at Fond du Lac. There was, of course, the crucial difference that Roosevelt had chosen as his vehicle the Democratic Party—the political organiza-tion least conducive to La Guardia's ambitions. Yet La Guardia was delighted by the upheaval. Looking back on his earlier statements, he noted with pride "how smart I was to prognosticate a political situation a couple of years in advance"; now, he predicted that "the realignment that is taking place . . . will, in all likelihood, be general in 1940. . . ."²⁷

And he was eager to help push that realignment along. After failing in its efforts to "purge" conservative Democratic senators in party primaries in Georgia, Maryland, and South Carolina, the White House turned to the more favorable climes of Manhattan. It set its sights on Representative John O'Connor of New York's 15th Congressional District (stretching from the Gaslight District to Yorkville), a Tammany conservative in the Copeland mold who, as chairman of the House Rules Committee, had bottled up both the wages and hours bill and the executive reorganization bill. La Guardia gave the venture his enthusiastic support; indeed, as the historian Richard Polenberg has written, he took a more active role in the "purge of O'Connor" than did Roosevelt himself. He campaigned on behalf of the New Dealers' candidate, a war hero named James Fay. He lent his secretary James Kieran to the Fay campaign and gave leave to one of his own political operatives, the adept Major William J. Walsh, to serve as Fay's campaign manager. There is evidence that La Guardia's office, like the White House, promised Fay a cache of patronage jobs to help him peel off key Democratic workers and thereby split the district organization.²⁸

More important, La Guardia's administration had prepared the political ground in the city, making Manhattan into a far more favorable environment for the purge effort than what Roosevelt encountered when he attempted to do battle with the entrenched courthouse gangs of Maryland and Georgia. La Guardia's hold on the city government had deprived O'Connor's congressional office of patronage jobs: except in census years, congressional offices did not usually control many jobs, and with Tammany shut out of the patronage-rich municipal posts, O'Connor's access to patronage was severed. "Following the defeat in 1933 and the crushing defeat of last November," his campaign manager wrote, "we do not have 10%

of our captains on the payroll. Some of these fellows are desperate and we are at the end of our wits trying to devise ways and means to help them." This dissatisfaction within O'Connor's organization, and the strong ideological popularity of the New Deal in New York Democratic circles, made it possible for Fay and his political sponsor, Flynn of the Bronx, to foment insurgency by winning over disgruntled regular Democratic workers, splitting the regular Democratic organization in a way the other purge efforts never succeeded in doing. Beleaguered Tammany could not sustain the organizational strength mustered by the targets of Roosevelt's party purge in Maryland and Georgia, and Fay defeated O'Connor in the primary. In this sense, the purge succeeded in New York because it took place within the context of the city's own political reorganization.[29]

Much as Royal Copeland had done the previous year, O'Connor accepted an invitation from conservative Republicans to run on their ticket; unlike Copeland, he carried the Republican primary over the moderate Wall Street lawyer Allen Dulles. O'Connor filled the general election campaign with the rhetoric of Democratic congressional conservatism. He denounced "self-styled liberals" for "fanning the flames of class hatred" and imposing "barriers" to commerce in the form of high taxes and interference by "countless bureaus." He accused his adversaries of instructing WPA workers on how to vote (and leveled the same charge at city relief officials).[30] Above all, he tried to define the contest as one between representative democracy and executive authoritarianism. All to no avail: Fay won the general election with 53 percent of the vote. "Well," said Roosevelt, putting on his best face, "we won the Yale game."[31]

The other New York election of national importance that fall, and for La Guardia a much more vexing one, pitted Herbert Lehman, running for governor for the fourth (and final) time, against Thomas Dewey—who had run on La Guardia's ticket the previous year as fusion's candidate for Manhattan district attorney. Dewey, short and neatly mustachioed, had burst onto the scene a few years earlier when, as assistant prosecutor to investigate racketeering in New York, he had scored a series of stunning successes—culminating in 1936 with the conviction of the Mafia empire builder "Lucky" Luciano on the charge of running a prostitution ring. A young man with an undeniable record of accomplishment, Dewey was a fresh face in a tired political party, "a live figure," the columnist Raymond Clapper wrote, "in a party of snoozing stuffed-shirts." Ideologically and politically, Dewey was in line with the younger generation of New York Republicans who had supported La Guardia for renomination in 1937. He drew no sharp contrasts with Lehman over substantive issues, instead assailing machine politics and accusing the Democrats of a "weak, sloppy, and lazy" administration of the state government.[32]

La Guardia and his supporters had been eyeing Dewey with suspicion from the time they drafted him to run on the fusion tickets in 1937. Now, his ascent came at a terribly inopportune moment. For not only did it create a potentially troublesome rival; it also threatened to force La Guardia to choose between the White House and the New York State GOP, which badly wanted to recapture the governor's mansion and would be indispensable should La Guardia pursue the Republican presidential or vice-presidential nomination. Faced with this dilemma, the Little Flower had tried to dissuade Dewey from running, asking him to consider what would happen to his political career if he lost to the politically formidable Lehman. It was a thin pretext, and Dewey had brushed it aside. To make matters more difficult, the Republican state leaders had taken care to court La Guardia by slating one of his closest political allies, the Italian Harlem Republican and Home Relief Bureau head Edward Corsi, as their candidate for U.S. Senate. As the campaign season approached, well-wishers both in New York and elsewhere urged La Guardia to solidify his standing in the party by backing Dewey. "More and more attention is turning to you as the best man to nominate for the presidency," one Ohioan wrote. "As one of your multitude of friends I am persuaded that if you can see your way clear to get behind Dewey and place him in the gubernatorial chair in New York it will multiply your admirers many fold." These pressures, according to several sources, had been sufficient to elicit from La Guardia a promise not to campaign against Dewey.[33]

But now pressure came from the White House as well. Farley urged Roosevelt to "be a little rough with" La Guardia and "positively bear down on him" to solicit an endorsement of Lehman. Roosevelt invited La Guardia to Hyde Park on October 22; whatever transpired between them face-to-face, La Guardia announced after the meeting that he would "endorse and support every candidate for the Senate and House who can be depended upon to support the present National Administration"—a statement which not only prepared the way for an endorsement of Lehman but also pushed Lehman (who had split with the administration over the court reform plan) to state explicitly his allegiance to Roosevelt. Lehman consented the next day, asking the voters to "strengthen the hands of President Roosevelt in his humane legislation" by electing the Democrats' adamantly pro–New Deal Senate candidates, Wagner and Representative James Mead of Buffalo. This was enough for the president, who endorsed Lehman and spoke for him in a radio broadcast the night before the election. La Guardia never explicitly endorsed Lehman, but he did make a public appearance with Lehman shortly before the election and praised Roosevelt's radio talk on Lehman's behalf as "a very splendid statement on behalf of a progressive governor." (When a reporter asked him whether that statement constituted an endorsement, La Guardia, plainly uneasy, replied, "What do you want me to do? Draw you a picture?") The *New York Times* estimated that La Guardia's tacit support would bring Lehman 200,000 votes. If that figure was even close to accurate, it swung the election, which was decided by less than 70,000 ballots.[34]

Lehman had, by a hairsbreadth, avoided being swept up in a national Republican tide that saw the GOP take eight Senate seats, twelve governorships, and eighty-one House seats, and oust from office such prominent progressives as Frank Murphy and Minnesota governor Elmer Benson (whom La Guardia had also endorsed). La Guardia conceded that the election represented a "black eye for the New Deal." "It is becoming increasingly apparent . . . ," he wrote to the historian Charles Beard shortly after the election, "that forces are at work which endanger progress." The lesson was plain: "There has been too much cacophony among our own ranks." Proclaiming that "the progressive forces of this country have got to get together," he announced his intention to organize a series of conferences with leading progressives—George Norris, the La Follettes, and Frank Murphy. Liberals, punch-drunk after the election, met the call with enthusiasm; Paul Y. Anderson of *The Nation* wrote that the conferences would push the country closer to "that political realignment which is the indispensable prerequisite of intelligent voting and responsible government." By that standard or any other, however, the project was a disappointment. The first and only conference took place at City Hall in mid-November, when La Guardia hosted Murphy and the recently defeated Senator Robert Bulkley of Ohio. The trio talked for several hours about the possibility of forming a third party if the New Dealers lost control of the Democratic Party; Murphy proceeded hence to Washington to meet with FDR and emerged afterward convinced that "Progressivism can and must go forward, but . . . it must be carried forward through the Democratic party."[35]

If La Guardia was at something of a loss for how to proceed, he had unmistakably committed himself by his actions in the elections of 1938. La Guardia's stance in the gubernatorial campaign, Joseph Alsop and Robert Kintner wrote in their syndicated "Capital Parade" column, was "unusually interesting as a revelation of one of the smartest politicians in the country. It can only mean that La Guardia thinks his own best bet is a firm, unqualified alliance with the liberal progressive forces. . . . For, by slighting Tom Dewey, La Guardia has cut himself off forever from his former friends among New York Republicans. . . ." La Guardia had broken from party orthodoxy to endorse Roosevelt in 1936. But then the stakes had been relatively low; he had done so as part of a broad progressive movement, and local party leaders had not held his activity too much against him. His tacit endorsement of Lehman was different. And the purge of O'Connor marked the first time the Little Flower had put not only his personal prestige but also the resources of his own political organization behind a Roosevelt electoral cause. At the same time, the rise of a new generation of Republicans had begun to crowd him out of the party. Only a year earlier, the GOP had been so damaged that knowledgeable observers (including La Guardia himself) had taken seriously the possibility of a progressive capture. In twelve months, everything had changed. The Roosevelt recession and the court-packing imbroglio had created space for a Republican revival along ideological lines starkly different from La Guardia's brand of farmer-labor progressivism. Dewey's campaign had not put forward a compelling alternative to New Deal Democracy, but the outlines of a new Republican Party ideology—emphasizing law and order and opposition to professional politics, labor politics, and heavy public spending—was gaining definition.[36]

The development of a powerful conservative opposition, the continuing realignment of national politics, the Republican revival— each of these had forced La Guardia to declare his allegiances, and each had tied him more closely to Roosevelt. As the troubled decade came to a close, another consideration would bind him tighter still to the Democratic president—and ultimately bring him into Roosevelt's administration. This was foreign policy.

III

On the third day of March 1937, La Guardia made a brief address to what should have been a humdrum luncheon of the women's division of the American Jewish Congress. The preceding speaker, Michael Williams, editor of the Catholic magazine *Commonweal*, had proposed the erection of a "temple of tolerance" at the upcoming World's Fair and, as an aside, had asked the mayor to support the project. La Guardia cheerfully agreed. Then, giving every indication that he was speaking off the cuff, he added: "But with that temple dedicated to the progress of world religious freedom, I'd have a chamber of horrors, and as a climax I'd have in it a figure of that brown-shirted fanatic who is now menacing the peace of the world. I'd give them an exhibit they would look at and learn."[37]

These remarks, neither the first nor the most critical La Guardia had directed at Adolf Hitler and the Nazi regime, garnered only passing notice in the New York newspapers. Then, the next day, Americans saw the vile slurs the German press had directed at La Guardia in response: "procurer," "well-poisoner," "Jewish ruffian," "scoundrel super-Jew," "New York gangster-in-chief." (La Guardia's Jewish ancestry was not yet widely known, especially outside of New York; when out-of-town newspapermen queried City Hall, La Guardia's secretary told them that he was mostly Italian but that his mother did have some Jewish blood.) What had barely been news the day before quickly grew into an international contretemps. The German Embassy demanded an apology for La Guardia's remarks; and although the standard response would have been to make an informal expression of regret, Secretary of State Cordell Hull instead issued a formal statement to the effect that La Guardia's comments did not reflect the attitude of the U.S. government toward the German government. Round one of "La Guardia v. Hitler" (as *Time* styled it) drew national newspaper coverage. Within a few days of Hull's apology, more than seven hundred letters and telegrams arrived at City Hall, postmarked from forty-one states and sixteen countries. Scores of people wrote to commend La Guardia for his courage in saying "what every decent man thinks," for speaking out against "the practices of the Dark Ages," and for taking "an upright American stand."[38]

A few days after the outburst, Roosevelt began a cabinet meeting by turning to Hull and asking, with an impish grin on his face, whether there was any more news on the La Guardia front. Before Hull could answer, he added: "What would you say if I should say that I agree completely with La Guardia?" Hull replied that the affair would have ended quickly had La Guardia desisted after his initial remarks (which the Little Flower had not). Roosevelt, still smiling, gave himself a light slap on the wrist. "We shall chastise him like that," he said. "It was plain," the adamantly anti-fascist Harold Ickes wrote, barely restraining his elation, "that he would like to see a gold medal pinned on La Guardia's lapel for what he had done." The president told Henry Morgenthau after the meeting that he thought La Guardia's remarks were fine, except he would have made them stronger.[39]

Nine days after Hull's formal apology, La Guardia made a surprise appearance at a Madison Square Garden anti-fascism rally staged by the American Jewish Congress and featuring United Mine Workers leader John L. Lewis and former NRA director Hugh Johnson. As Johnson finished his speech, the hour nearing 11:15 pm, the audience began to stamp and call for the mayor. La Guardia stood up and tried to shout out a few words; drowned out, he made his way down to the speakers' platform. "Whatever Mr. Hitler may say pay no attention to it," he shouted, "because public opinion of the world has decreed that Mr. Hitler is not personally or diplomatically *satisfaktionsfaehig*." He left the microphone as German-speaking audience members explained the last term—"worthy of satisfaction"—to the crowd. La

Guardia had suggested that Hitler was of such low social standing that a gentleman impugned by him would feel no obligation to challenge him to a duel.[40]

The German ambassador lodged another protest, explaining to Hull that the word La Guardia had used was "unimaginably offensive in Germany," and the American press raised the question of whether President Roosevelt's "personal intervention" would be required "to check the Mayor." By happenstance, La Guardia had scheduled an appointment with Roosevelt for several days later. He went into the Oval Office fearing a reprimand, but instead Roosevelt greeted him with a smile and extended his right arm in a mock Nazi salute: *"Heil,* Fiorello!" La Guardia snapped to attention and replied, *"Heil,* Franklin!" and the matter passed with no further mention. It was, La Guardia recalled after Roosevelt's death, the only time he called the president by his first name.[41]

The New York newspapers were practically unanimous in adjudging La Guardia's rhetorical assaults on Hitler and the Nazi regime a cynical bid for Jewish votes in the fall election—a "smart piece of petty politics," the *Herald Tribune* wrote, which would appeal to "some elements" of the electorate. Perhaps they were; but this was not their primary significance. La Guardia's views on foreign policy were evolving, and as the storm clouds darkened over Europe, the Little Flower, already envisioning himself as a national figure in domestic politics, attempted to transcend the bounds of his local office to become a national spokesman for the anti-Nazi cause.[42]

Since the end of the Great War, La Guardia, like many Americans, had been guided in his foreign policy thinking by a profound fear of war. Always well attuned to technological innovation, he understood how destructive another major war would be: the development of "long-distance guns, aerial bombardments, and poisonous gases," he had forecast in 1930, all but ensured that the "civilian population in large and industrial centers . . . will suffer more than

the military forces in actual combat." This horrific vision of technological destruction, together with a progressive conviction that
war redounded against the interests of working people, demanding
of them unbearable sacrifices as profits accumulated to financiers
and industrialists, had led him to declare himself a proud pacifist.
He had joined with the western progressives who were his allies in
domestic policy in their efforts to reduce dramatically the size of the
U.S. military (casting a vote he later considered one of the worst of
his career) and to outlaw war.[43]

In the mid-1930s, as he observed the domestic policies and mili-
tarism of the Nazi regime, La Guardia—like Roosevelt—had come
to believe that international peace could not be ensured unless the
contagion of Nazi "lawlessness" were somehow contained. "The
psychology, the arrogance and the cruelty of the present German
Government are the same that brought about and caused the World
War," he claimed. "If we learned one lesson, it was that the peace
of Europe concerns us most vitally. We can't stand idly by and permit Hitler and his kind to imperil peace." His rhetorical strategy
of name-calling—leaning heavily on the language of insanity and
anarchy—is best understood as an attempt to impress upon a public concerned above all with avoiding entry into another major war
the danger he believed Hitler posed to international peace. Though
more colorful, it was philosophically of a piece with Roosevelt's calls
for an international "quarantine" action to contain "an epidemic of
world lawlessness" which threatened to plunge "the whole world
into war. . . ."[44]

Soon, as the democracies pursued their strategy of appeasement,
this rhetorical approach was taken off the table. (After *Kristallnacht*, the Conference of Mayors had considered issuing a statement
denouncing German violence but instead decided, as local officials,
to pledge their neutrality with respect to affairs of state. When La
Guardia read the declaration at the White House with an air of

solemnity, Roosevelt began shaking with suppressed laughter and then interjected, "Of course, Fiorello, that resolution applies to you, too." "Yep," the mayor responded, "and I'm taking the pledge right now. No more dirty cracks at Hitler.") La Guardia found an outlet for his international convictions by way of a new interest in Latin America. Like most pan-Americanists, La Guardia was driven by a fear of Nazi incursions into South America and Mexico—the logical staging ground for an attack on the United States—but also by a belief that the republics of the western hemisphere shared a common destiny, apart from the warring Old World. He began practicing Spanish; in September 1939 he approached the White House regarding the feasibility of a goodwill tour of South America. That plan never materialized, but he did make several major speeches on the subject of pan-American cooperation, including one at the Commonwealth Club in San Francisco that attracted substantial attention, and helped to establish a scholarship program for Latin American exchange students to attend college in New York.[45]

It was also in the context of German influence in Latin America that La Guardia presented his export subsidization plan. To increase domestic employment and to counteract German barter agreements that were hurting U.S. trade in Latin America, he proposed that the federal government purchase $1.5 billion worth of "shoes, typewriters, clothing, agricultural machinery, automobiles, tobacco products, and cotton products" from U.S. firms that agreed to hire new workers and then sell these products in Latin American markets for a sum of $1 billion. (The difference would be paid from the WPA appropriation on the theory that the purchases would create enough jobs to make that money superfluous.) The idea was to undercut "dictator countries" by "destroy[ing] the balance of trade and [thereby] prevent[ing] them from buying war material for munitions." Some Americans thought the plan visionary. It would deliver "the final blow to Germany's hopes of dominating the world," Bernard Baruch wrote the mayor. The "La Guardia plan" went nowhere, but this was perhaps less notable than the mere fact that a local official would even think to propose so elaborate a scheme.[46]

When general war finally came to Europe in September 1939, La Guardia parted ways with progressives such as Robert La Follette, Jr., and Henrik Shipstead who, fearing to take "the first fatal step that will lead to our being drawn into war," marshaled the forces opposing revision of the Neutrality Acts, which inhibited American aid to non-aggressor nations. The Little Flower not only supported revision, but also, while the matter was still before Congress, presented Roosevelt with a scheme to circumvent the acts by selling war materials and supplies to still-neutral Canada. ("What happened to such shipments after that would not be our concern," he added. "No doubt you have thought of it long since [Roosevelt in fact had], but in these anxious moments, one wants to do everything to shorten and end the terrible situation.") Like the western progressives, he dreaded the thought of American involvement in the war; but like Roosevelt, he could not imagine a peaceful coexistence with a Nazi-dominated Europe.[47]

IV

Late in 1938, Rexford Tugwell, who had left the Department of Agriculture to become the chairman of New York's new City Planning Commission and had replaced Berle as La Guardia's sounding board on matters pertaining to the Roosevelt administration, found himself unexpectedly summoned to the mayor's office. Upon arriving he was given "unshirted hell" for publicly advocating Roosevelt's nomination for a third term. La Guardia, visions of the White House in his mind, still saw Roosevelt as an impediment to his own ambitions.

Roosevelt himself had seemingly gone out of his way to suggest to La Guardia that he intended to retire rather than seek reelection.

When, in August 1938, the La Guardia family had visited the Roosevelts at Hyde Park, FDR gave the Little Flower a tour of the hilltop stone cottage he was building on the eastern end of his estate in anticipation of his return to private life. Then, at the end of that year, he had told La Guardia explicitly that he would not be a candidate in 1940.[48]

"I feel very certain that Roosevelt considered prayerfully whether Mayor La Guardia might not succeed him in 1940," Tugwell later wrote. In the opening months of 1940, as a lull settled over Europe and it remained uncertain whether Germany would move against France and England, Roosevelt began inviting congressmen to his office, jotting down possible combinations for the Democratic ticket, asking for reactions, and tearing them up. By the end of January, La Guardia's name had begun to appear more and more frequently; one presidential visitor, Ed O'Neal of the Farm Bureau Federation, told a cabinet member that Roosevelt had "tackled La Guardia to run with [Cordell] Hull." Drew Pearson and Robert Allen, of the popular syndicated column "Washington Merry-Go-Round," reported in March 1940 that Roosevelt had told La Guardia, "I'm for you, not only because I'm for you personally, but because you know so much about government." To a friend who observed that Roosevelt had likely been saying the same thing to the other presidential aspirants, La Guardia was said to have replied, "Maybe, but it sounds good anyway."[49]

In February, La Guardia found himself unexpectedly entered in the Illinois Republican primary. Though he feigned surprise before the newspapermen, his candidacy had its origins in a luncheon meeting in Secretary Ickes's office. The two men were discussing Thomas Dewey's campaign for the Republican nomination (upon which neither looked with any fondness) when La Guardia remarked in jest that he was planning to enter the Illinois primary: the Chicago vote and his popularity among downstate farmers, he calculated, would make it possible for him to defeat the upstart Dewey without even campaigning. Ickes, evidently intrigued, phoned one of his old Chicago associates and asked her to collect the signatures required to put La Guardia's name on the ballot. The effort was so hasty that the signature collectors were forced to set up headquarters in Italian neighborhoods in Chicago "and quite literally shout out the windows for La Guardia admirers to come in and sign up."[50]

News of the filing of La Guardia's petition, Ickes wrote in his diary, went off like a "loudly detonating bomb" in Illinois and within a few weeks sent the Dewey campaign into a panic. Roosevelt was "delighted" by the maneuver, Ickes wrote, and phoned La Guardia in New York to discuss strategy. But sometime over the course of the next week, La Guardia changed his mind and withdrew. Perhaps, as Pearson and Allen wrote, he did not want to "stamp himself definitely as a Republican" while he still thought he had an outside shot at the Democratic vice-presidential nomination. Perhaps he simply underestimated his popularity in Illinois—Ickes didn't get reports on the strength of La Guardia's candidacy until after the mayor had sent his withdrawal—and removed his name from the ballot so as not to risk a humiliating loss to Dewey. Whatever the reason, he announced that he did not want to split the progressive vote, and he advised those who might have voted for him to cast their ballots in the Democratic primary for Roosevelt (who was listed on the ballot, though he had yet to announce his intention to seek a third term).[51]

By April, La Guardia had surrendered his presidential aspirations and devoted himself to the pursuit of the vice presidency. Odd alliances were struck: John Nance Garner, one of the leaders of the economy bloc, was described as a "straight shooter" whom La Guardia held in personal high regard; Berle cultivated Jim Farley while La Guardia made friendly gestures toward the New York Democratic organizations (which might have welcomed the chance to help La Guardia at the convention in order to get him out of New York).

Meantime, the Little Flower had become "picturesquely profane" in his comments about the Department of Agriculture, believing Secretary Henry A. Wallace to be a competitor should the Democratic Convention seek a progressive Republican for the second position on the ticket. A national committeeman from the Little Flower's home state of Arizona was engaged to present La Guardia's name for the vice presidency at the Democratic Convention.

Then, at the end of April, during one of his regular political talks with Tugwell, La Guardia divulged that he had "information" indicating Roosevelt would run for a third term—which would preclude him from consideration for the second line on the Democratic ticket (since he and Roosevelt hailed from the same state). His demeanor took Tugwell by surprise. "He seemed pleased" by the news of Roosevelt's candidacy, Tugwell noted, whereas "always before [he] has been indignant at the suggestion. . . . He must think now that he can see some advantage for himself, but I can't imagine what." On May 13, at a New York convention of the Amalgamated Clothing Workers, La Guardia announced his support for Roosevelt's renomination.[52]

PART III
WAR AND POSTWAR

8

The Local Politics of
Foreign Policy

A month after La Guardia came out for a third term, Italy declared war on France and Britain. The news sent shock-waves through New York's Italian American communities. Reporters who staked out interviews in East Harlem and on Mulberry Street found unhappy and bewildered people worried about family and property in Italy and citizenship applications in America. Young men proclaimed their willingness to fight for the United States should they be called. Some recent arrivals, blaming England for Italy's entry, claimed that Mussolini "knew what he was doing" and would win quickly; immigrants who had been in America longer were "cynical and sad." The informal canvasses conducted by the *Times* and *Herald Tribune* found opinion in Italian American communities evenly divided between those who believed the Axis would win quickly and those who believed Mussolini had "done much for Italy" but had now "made a big mistake."[1]

Roosevelt, speaking that afternoon at the graduation exercises of the University of Virginia, used the occasion to deliver his most forceful statement to date in support of the Allied cause. Describing the fight against fascism as a rare moment that forced the Amer-

ican people to ask themselves "what is to become of the country
we know," he conjured a future in which America remained "a
lone island in a world dominated by the philosophy of force . . . [a]
nightmare of a people lodged in prison, handcuffed, hungry, and fed
through the bars from day to day by the contemptuous, unpitying
masters of other continents." Then, after reviewing his efforts to
keep Italy out of the war, he delivered the searing line for which the
speech would long be remembered: "On this tenth day of June, 1940,
the hand that held the dagger has struck it into the back of its neighbor." The final part of the speech called for the extension of "the
material resources of this Nation" to "the opponents of force" and for
accelerated defense production and training. This was the rhetorical
beginning of the policy of all-out aid to the democracies.

Few men must have savored Roosevelt's words more than Winston
Churchill. Yet even he, listening from the War Admiralty Room in
London, stopped to ponder the effect the speech might have upon
"the Italian vote" in the coming elections. Italian entry had introduced one more perilous crosscurrent into American politics—
one that threatened La Guardia even more than it did Roosevelt.
Pro-Fascist sentiment remained strong in New York, in part because
the Italian government had diligently cultivated it; consequently, La
Guardia, even as he excoriated Hitler, had been reluctant to speak ill
of Mussolini. His supporters were sharply divided in their attitudes
toward the European conflict, and Italian entry (and Roosevelt's
response to it) threatened to push the issue to the breaking point.[2]

Just as Roosevelt went on the air from Charlottesville, La Guardia
arrived in Ottawa, where he was to address a conference of Canadian mayors. As a motorcade shuttled him from the airport to the
Château Laurier, he "bent forward, listening intently" to the broadcast. "I have never heard anything as wonderful as the President's
speech," he told the Canadian press upon arriving. Before Roo-

sevelt's talk, he said, he had been wondering how far he could go in his own address. "Now I will be able to open my mouth and say just what I want to." La Guardia's speech the following day was among the most effective of his career. Before a crowd that included most of the Canadian government—"perhaps as enthusiastic a crowd as had ever been seen in Ottawa," the *Ottawa Journal* wrote—La Guardia "categorically endorsed" FDR's Charlottesville speech. Punctuated by bursts of applause, he proclaimed his confidence that "the tank hasn't been made or the bomb yet devised that can destroy or crush the democracies of the world" and voiced his belief that the United States would have a "complete understanding" of Canada's position—and, by implication, Britain's.[3]

The months between Mussolini's declaration of war in June 1940 and American entry in December 1941 represent a kind of interlude in New York's political history. Before and after, Gotham's politics revolved around rapid changes in the role of government. But in the eighteen months before the attack on Pearl Harbor, foreign policy dominated the city's political life. Because international affairs mattered so deeply to so many people, and because La Guardia was to become so closely associated with Roosevelt's interventionist course, foreign policy became, for a time, the central issue of local politics, producing political and electoral shifts on a scale similar to those produced by the New Deal. And it was foreign policy that finally cemented the Roosevelt–La Guardia partnership. La Guardia, a tepid campaigner four years before, would marshal the forces of progressivism and social democracy behind Roosevelt's third-term bid; the following year he would enter Roosevelt's administration and secure a third term of his own—with Roosevelt's endorsement, but bearing the burden of his support for FDR's foreign policy.

I

As he watched the Wehrmacht engulf Europe, the Little Flower grew consumed with securing a role in the defense effort. "What shall we do?" he lamented to Tugwell. "I can't stay here with the world falling to pieces." He was now mentioned as a possible secretary of the Navy or of labor, or as an "American Beaverbrook"—the industrial czar in charge of airplane production in Great Britain. And he was being considered seriously for the position he desired most—secretary of war. Roosevelt, who had once reportedly called La Guardia the "greatest red tape cutter" he had ever seen, remarked to Tugwell repeatedly that La Guardia was "just what he needed" as the emergency developed. In June 1940, FDR appointed another New Yorker with firmer Republican credentials: the august Henry Stimson, a conservative Wall Street lawyer who had served in the cabinets of both Taft and Hoover. But believing Stimson too short of stamina (and spurning the warnings of Ickes, Bernard Baruch, Sam Rosenman, and Felix Frankfurter, each of whom suggested in one way or another that La Guardia was, in Frankfurter's phrase, a "mad genius" who was too mercurial for the position), Roosevelt continued to contemplate La Guardia for the position. In August he finally delivered a firm promise, informing La Guardia through two intermediaries that he would be made secretary of war immediately after the election.[4]

This was to be the first of several broken promises that would, by the war's end, do great damage to Roosevelt and La Guardia's personal relationship. Stimson would serve for the duration of the war, leaving Tugwell to wonder how war contracts might have been handled differently had La Guardia been in charge of the War Department. (Stimson would also oversee the removal of Japanese and Japanese Americans to inland internment camps and the decision not to divert American military resources to disrupt the operation of

Nazi concentration camps. One may safely assume that La Guardia, who as his biographer Thomas Kessner notes not only defended the policy of Japanese internment but also objected when, at the war's end, the U.S. government began to release non-threatening American citizens from custody, would have handled internment much as Stimson did. It is less clear how La Guardia might have approached the concentration camps. His own sister, who was married to a Hungarian Jew, spent the last year of the war imprisoned by Nazi authorities before being liberated by the Soviet army. By 1943, he, like many Americans, was aware of the Nazi extermination program, and he asked Congress to create a commission to "save the Jewish people of Europe from extinction at the hands of Nazi Germany." But he never fully utilized his powers of publicity to call for American military action against the concentration camps or the railroads that led to them, and there is no evidence that he took the matter up with Roosevelt. In any case, ultimate responsibility rested with the president. "If Roosevelt had wanted to divert the planes, we would have," recalled Assistant Secretary of War John J. McCloy.)[5]

But Roosevelt was prepared in August 1940 to give La Guardia his first official role in the defense effort. The president had proposed to Canadian prime minister Mackenzie King the formation of a U.S.-Canada joint board on hemispheric defense. Such an agency, Roosevelt believed, would strengthen the defense of Newfoundland and the Canadian coast, potential jumping-off points for a German attack on the United States, and would encourage the Royal Navy to withdraw to Canada rather than surrender to the Germans should Hitler succeed in subjugating the British Isles. The proposal had the additional benefit of being uncontroversial: polls indicated that the American public supported it overwhelmingly. Prime Minister King, who was attempting to balance aid to Britain with the necessity of preparing Canada's own defenses, immediately agreed to the proposal. The ten-member Permanent Joint Board on Defense was created and composed in late August, with La Guardia as the chair of the American section.

The board set to work immediately on the strategically important question of the defense of Newfoundland as well as contingency plans for continental invasion. La Guardia clashed with his Canadian counterparts over the issue of strategic direction: La Guardia, like the U.S. military brass, wanted unified command under the direction of the commanding officer of the largest force (i.e., the United States); the Canadians sought to retain Canadian direction of Canadian forces. But despite this sticking point, and despite Prime Minister King's distaste for La Guardia's "unfortunate craze for publicity," the initial meetings went very well. Though it was not the War Department, La Guardia enjoyed the work—he told his wife that he had never worked with a better group.[6]

Until mid-August, when Roosevelt appointed the Little Flower to the Permanent Joint Board on Defense, Republicans held out hope that they could induce La Guardia to back their candidate for the presidency, the Indiana-born president of the Commonwealth & Southern utilities holding company, Wendell Willkie. Bruce Barton, a famed Madison Avenue executive and new-model Manhattan Republican who had won election to Congress three years earlier with La Guardia's support, approached the party leaders with a plan to offer La Guardia the Republican Senate nomination in exchange for his support of the national ticket. (According to Washington gossip, Willkie had hoped before the convention that La Guardia would run as the vice-presidential candidate on the Republican ticket.) But La Guardia had been planning Roosevelt's quadrennial campaign tour in the city since mid-July, and by the time of the Permanent Joint Board on Defense appointment he was already poised to accept one of the leadership positions in Roosevelt's campaign. Edward Flynn (who had succeeded James A. Farley as chairman of the Democratic National Committee) and Harold Ickes (with Henry Wallace, still the leading progressive Republican in Roosevelt's cabinet) had selected the Little Flower to direct a committee of independent progressives for Roosevelt, akin to the National Progressive League of 1932 and the Progressive National Committee of 1936. La Guardia became, in his own words, the committee's "working chairman"; Senator Norris, who stood out among the western congressional progressives as a supporter of Roosevelt's foreign policy, served as honorary chairman. The committee, named the National Committee of Independent Voters for Roosevelt and Wallace (NCIV), was formally launched the third week of September.[7]

Though it shared much of its leadership—Norris, La Guardia, David Niles, Sidney Hillman, James Causcy—with the Progressive National Committee of 1936, the NCIV differed from its predecessor in important ways. The PNC had been formed at the insistence of the White House for campaign purposes, but it was at heart the organizational manifestation of a loose independent movement that looked forward beyond Roosevelt's cause toward a national realignment and perhaps a third party. The NCIV, in comparison, was more clearly an instrument for Roosevelt's reelection, mobilized at a transitional moment when independent liberals had no shared program more elaborate than the retention of the New Deal and the political defeat of the titans of industry. Though the NCIV considered itself "completely independent," raised its own funds, and refused to make its financial information available to the DNC, the two organizations exchanged advice, corresponded on where to send speakers, and printed and distributed each other's campaign literature. Tellingly, the NCIV, unlike the PNC, issued no independent platform or statement of principles.

The NCIV was also much larger than its predecessors; accordingly, it played a more extensive role in the campaign. Raising money from unions (especially the Ladies Garment Workers and the Amalgamated Clothing Workers) and small individual contributions, the NCIV spent four and a half times what the PNC had spent in

1936. It established regional offices in five cities which in turn organized state- and local-level activity; the organizations in some places
reached down to the precinct level. The national office produced and
distributed 2.5 million pieces of literature and devised imaginative
radio spots in which scripted testimonials targeted groups of voters
regarded as political independents: first-time voters, college women,
widows, housewives, professional women, and immigrants.

Much as he had during the purge of John O'Connor, La Guardia
put his own political operatives to work on the Roosevelt campaign.
Perhaps the most notable of these was J. Roland Sala, a former leader
of the Fusion Party and organizer of the American Labor Party who
worked in La Guardia's Department of Investigations and directed
the NCIV's Foreign Language Division. Sala's organization employed
journalists, field workers, organizers, speakers, and clerical workers
to undertake both publicity and organizing work among twenty-three
different language groups. Working closely with local fraternal and
benevolent societies and especially with the Amalgamated Clothing
Workers, which put its offices at the command of the NCIV, the Foreign Language Division established a campaign organization that in
some neighborhoods rivaled the Democratic Party in its reach.[8]

La Guardia himself spent much of the fall of 1940 on the campaign trail. He announced his support for Roosevelt on September
12 in a radio broadcast that aired nationally over NBC's Red Network. In the face of world conditions, he said, he preferred Roosevelt
with his "known faults" to Willkie with his "unknown virtues." After
reviewing the New Deal record and essaying a few sharp words
about Willkie's background as a utilities executive and his lack of
experience in government, La Guardia ended with a reflection on
the alterations to the American state wrought by the New Deal:

President Roosevelt during the past seven years has brought
about a great change in our Uncle Sam. He is no longer the

stern old Uncle[,] interested only in diplomacy, rivers and harbors, and interstate commerce. We now have a rejuvenated
Uncle Sam[,] smiling and friendly, concerned with the welfare and happiness of every home in the land. He is no longer
a distant, strange figure in Washington. He is in every State,
county, city and town. . . . Roosevelt has regenerated our country. Roosevelt has made America the hope of the world. That is
why I am for President Roosevelt.

Thereafter La Guardia's campaign rhetoric took a turn toward
the confrontational. He was later to discover that there was much to
admire in Willkie, who, before dying tragically early in 1944, would
become a champion of one-world internationalism and anti-imperi-
alism, a civil rights hero, a defender of the rights of Communists, and
a pariah of the Republican Party. But in 1940, La Guardia seemed
personally piqued by Willkie's nomination. Passed over for serious
consideration despite his own unexcelled record as a public administrator, he was annoyed to see the Republican nomination go to a
man untrained in the handling of "large governmental problems."
Willkie, he believed, was a mere public relations man, enlisted by
the corporate interests and financiers to put a pleasant face on their
efforts to restore the economic policies of the 1920s.[9]

"It was simply incredible how he spoke against Willkie—personally
vituperative," former New York City Corporation Counsel Paul Windels recalled. La Guardia's spirited campaign talks—he traveled to
Newark, Pittsburgh, Boston, Providence, Philadelphia, New Haven,
Chicago, Cincinnati, and St. Louis—led one conservative columnist to declare him "by all odds the most brutal and dishonest campaigner" in the Roosevelt camp. Many of his personal references to
Willkie were dismissive, insulting, and rude, and he was at times
plainly dishonest: in one national radio talk entitled "Willkie-vs.-
Willkie," La Guardia spliced together out-of-context quotations to

depict Willkie as inconsistent; in several other speeches he misleadingly compared U.S. bond quotes with the price of Commonwealth & Southern stock.[10]

La Guardia's campaigning in 1940 has been viewed as erratic—an instance of a loss of self-control that marked his final years in City Hall—and it certainly affected his stature among independents and liberal Republicans. In the context of the campaign, however, it was effective. By raising doubts about Willkie's background in however spurious a manner, La Guardia's speeches struck at Willkie's Achilles' heel: a widespread fear of transferring power to an unknown entity at a moment of crisis. Above all, La Guardia's class language capitalized upon workers' fears that a Roosevelt defeat would mean the repeal of New Deal legislation and the reappearance of a Republican regime intent on giving government sanction to business exploitation. For if the 1940 campaign was conducted in the shadow of the European war, it was also one of the most intensely class-conscious campaigns in American history; sensitized by the ferocious industrial conflict of the late 1930s, many Americans believed, despite Willkie's professed acceptance of basic New Deal reforms, that the continuation of the New Deal depended on the election's outcome. Garment workers of the Amalgamated Clothing Workers, the historian Steve Fraser writes, were "ready to attribute the same world-historic significance to the contest of 1940 that they had once reserved for the 'final conflict' between Labor and Capital."

Depicting Willkie as an agent for the domination of corporate capital became part of the New Dealers' campaign strategy. Roosevelt had told Ickes shortly after the Republican Convention that he "was going to try to tie Willkie in with the idea of the 'corporate state' . . . corporate, entrenched wealth against the great mass of the people." This became the Little Flower's primary line of attack. The campaign had brought "a wholesome division," La Guardia said, opposing a man versed in "the field of cold, sordid business" with one who came from "the field of government, of humanity." Words like "predatory interests," "materialistic," and "cheap labor" peppered his speeches. "Tell the boss you're for Willkie," he told a crowd, "but remember the ballot is secret." Letters from local politicians and organizers testified to La Guardia's ability to rouse the electorate. The response to his speech in New Haven, a local organizer wrote, was, "to put it mildly, sensational. . . . [The] talk not only made votes but made enthusiastic and energetic workers for the cause."[11]

La Guardia's endorsement of Roosevelt, and his class-based appeals, alienated many of the good-government reformers who had been so crucial to the original fusion coalition—not least Samuel Seabury, who accused La Guardia of "stepp[ing] down from his position of leadership among those who are striving for decent municipal government" by allying with the Democratic bosses who had masterminded the third-term drive. It also elicited a popular reaction of striking depth. Willkie's support was strongest, writes the historian Robert Burke, among "middle-class business and professional people who did not normally engage in political activity and who were generally suspicious of those who did so"—people who might have been drawn to La Guardia's brand of municipal anti-partisanship. Most of those moved to write La Guardia during the campaign accused him of surrendering the good-government banner by making irresponsible appeals to "the ignorant, uninformed and illiterate portion of our population." During the campaign, La Guardia's mailbag was full of letters accusing him of running out on the cause of good government, of being corrupted by Roosevelt and the New Deal, of becoming a "politician," all of them testifying to the fact that La Guardia had violated an impalpable but deeply held sensibility that underlay his support among reformers, Republicans, and others who had soured on the New Deal during Roosevelt's second term. A substantial number of them vowed that they would not support La Guardia again.[12]

As the heated campaign moved toward its climax, these political tensions seemed to exact a psychic toll. During one campaign event in Detroit, the Little Flower was making his way down the steps of City Hall when a man who had been trailing him shouted out, "Are you still taking orders from Boss Flynn?" La Guardia wheeled and grabbed the man by the collar of his shirt, shook him, and ordered, "Take that back." Police pulled the two apart, and the man, a local bus company employee, went on his way with a torn collar and a twisted necktie. After the campaign had ended, La Guardia unburdened himself in a letter to the most esteemed of the reformers for Willkie, accusing them of "betraying the cause of good government" by backing the candidate of the utility corporations. Quoting self-righteously from II Timothy 4:7 ("I have fought a good fight"), he vowed he would not stand for reelection.[13]

La Guardia, who had served as a spokesman for the administration's foreign policy in Italian communities since June, spent the last week of the campaign attempting to convince Italian Americans not to leave the New Deal coalition. The language Roosevelt had directed at Mussolini's government in his Charlottesville speech, with its overtones of the old stiletto-wielding Black Hand stereotype that had plagued southern Italian immigrant communities in the early twentieth century, still rang in Italian ears (and, FDR's partisans were convinced, seemed to run in every campaign newsreel). Still, Roosevelt's domestic policies enjoyed deep support in the Italian American community. In a series of broadcasts over the Italian-language stations WOV and WHOM, La Guardia portrayed Willkie as a stranger who could not be vouched for and a businessman unsympathetic to working people: "I never heard of Mr. Wendell Willkie," he claimed, "except when . . . he was fighting against the Government helping poor people to get cheap light and cheap heat."

Roosevelt carried New York City with 59.9 percent of the vote—a sharp decline from his 1932 and 1936 totals. The returns illustrated nothing as much as the political whirlwind unleashed by the president's foreign policy. Irish Catholic New Yorkers, about 56 percent of whom voted for Roosevelt (down from 73 percent in 1936 and 76 percent in 1932), had additional reasons for leaving the Roosevelt coalition: the nomination of Hugo Black, a former Klansman, to serve on the Supreme Court; the administration's support for child labor laws (which the Catholic clergy opposed) and its tendency toward the "deification of the state" (a theological anathema); and its supposedly lax opposition to communism. But among German and Italian New Yorkers, foreign policy and the status issues that accompanied it were incontestably paramount. However they might have felt about Hitler, New York's German Americans, fearful that American entry would be accompanied by anti-German hysteria akin to that of the First World War, tended to vote for Willkie; about 42 percent voted for Roosevelt, down from 66 percent in 1936.

Among Italian Americans, conflicted in their feelings toward Mussolini's actions but widely opposed to aid to the Allies, Roosevelt's share of the vote dropped from some 78 percent in 1936 to 42 percent in 1940. So fearful were the Roosevelt forces of massive defections within this part of their coalition that they greeted the returns with relief. "Truthfully, we worked very hard but most of the German and Irish vote went against us and it comprises about 70 percent of the total vote," Queens County Democratic leader James Roe wrote La Guardia after the election; the Italian vote "was fine, thanks to your help. . . ."[14]

Roosevelt was sworn in for the third time on January 20, 1941. His inaugural address, a hymn to democracy in the form of American nationalism, made up the third and most philosophical of a triad of addresses, beginning with the "arsenal of democracy" fireside chat just after Christmas and continuing with the "four freedoms" message to Congress in early January, in which FDR made his case for aiding the Allies and sought to build public support for his Lend-

Lease plan (for which La Guardia would testify, alongside Willkie). La Guardia missed the inauguration once again, this time because the Permanent Joint Board on Defense had scheduled a meeting for that afternoon. "Naturally the Canadians did not have the date in mind," he wrote to Eleanor Roosevelt afterward; "our army and navy officers did not think of it, and I was so dumb and stupid as to have forgotten it. The Canadians however did appreciate the compliment, when I told them that the President would sooner have us on the job in Canada, than attending the festivities in Washington."[15]

II

Though he had begun to grapple with the fact that no successor had emerged in New York—and that, consequently, he could not leave the mayoralty without returning power to the Democrats—La Guardia still yearned to go to Washington. Roosevelt now owed him a substantial campaign debt, and with White House aides noting that La Guardia had been "making a lot of unhappy noises since the election," the administration sought to find a suitable job for him.[16]

Many top administration officials still considered the Little Flower too spectacular, mercurial, and attention-seeking for a cabinet job. Ickes, who had ample regard for La Guardia's ability, nonetheless believed care should be exercised "not to put him in a position where his dramatic qualities would have too great an opportunity to feed themselves." But Roosevelt thought he saw a useful outlet for those talents. The president and his aides were then in the process of creating an office of home defense, an agency that would weave together a number of different plans to mobilize the home front for the national defense effort (and, not coincidentally, in support of the administration's foreign policy). Roosevelt wanted "a big name to head the organization," he told his aides, someone "who would attract public attention as a good ballyhoo artist and speechmaker" and who could make inroads in a task the president considered "of the utmost difficulty"—namely, "mak[ing] people realize what the effect of a German victory would be. . . ." The Little Flower seemed a natural choice.[17]

La Guardia was intrigued by the public relations facet of the job, but he was more interested in another aspect of the agency's mission. As the European war progressed, La Guardia, certain that cities would be targeted in a modern war, had become fixated on the possibility that New York might be subjected to aerial attack. Gotham, of course, enjoyed geographic advantages London and the German cities did not; but in the war's early years, before the Allies gained firm control of the Atlantic, it would have been possible for German pilots to subject the east coast cities to hit-and-run bombardment. (Shortly after Pearl Harbor, Secretary of War Henry Stimson wrote in his diary that he thought it "very likely" some of America's big cities would be bombed "in the immediate future.") La Guardia had begun air-raid preparation in New York City in the fall of 1939, surveying building types and identifying the city's vulnerable spots. In January 1941, he had convened a City Defense Council to begin drafting contingency plans in the event of an attack. By mid-January, the city had produced a series of pamphlets and posters, entitled "If It Comes," which provided instructions on what to do in the event of an air raid; a month later, plans were under study for local trial blackouts, a step toward the technically difficult task of blacking out the entire city. Concurrently, the Conference of Mayors had begun to press for a federal agency to subsidize the purchase of equipment, pool useful information, provide training to key personnel, and otherwise "coordinate and standardize" the efforts of state and local defense councils. That same January, La Guardia submitted to Roosevelt on the conference's behalf a memorandum on urban air-raid defense, based on a body of English technical literature, which urged the creation of a national coordinating board to supervise and advise localities and share costs.[18]

Roosevelt called La Guardia to the White House on April 22 and offered him the directorship of the new agency. Knowing the Little Flower would be hesitant to leave the mayoralty for anything other than a cabinet-level position, FDR told La Guardia he could do both jobs concurrently (and encouraged him to stand for reelection in November). He also invited La Guardia to attend cabinet meetings. La Guardia accepted, and on May 20, 1941, Roosevelt created the Office of Civilian Defense (OCD) by executive order. The new agency would serve as a center for the coordination of federal, state, and local civilian defense activities; assist state and local governments in forming defense councils and provide a clearinghouse of information for those councils; study and plan measures to safeguard life and property in the event of attack; and "consider proposals, suggest plans, and promote activities designed to sustain the national morale and provide opportunities for constructive civilian participation."[19]

La Guardia, visions of the Battle of Britain in his mind, directed most of the agency's efforts toward "civilian protection"—the many tasks involved in defending against and responding to air raids. The OCD established special committees composed of governmental departments and agencies (at the national, state, and local levels), universities, hospitals, peak organizations, and private corporations to study the problems involved in an air-raid scenario: protecting facilities, evacuating target areas, maintaining communications, fighting fires, controlling traffic, and so on. This knowledge was disseminated in the form of training booklets—more than 5 million were produced and distributed through state and local defense councils. The OCD also worked on securing firefighting gear and gas masks for local governments, and it established a training program for local first responders (and, later, for local air defense corps, who in turn trained volunteer air wardens). By the end of November, some 750,000 men and women had volunteered—still a far cry from the 6 million the agency deemed necessary, but about as much as could be expected in a pre–Pearl Harbor environment. La Guardia himself traveled the length and breadth of the country, meeting hundreds of local officials and expounding on the need for firefighting preparedness in as many as fifty speeches per month.[20]

Because the OCD lacked the authority to establish its own organizations at the state and local levels (or even to disseminate its own publications), it depended on the active cooperation of state and local home defense councils—much as the New Deal works programs had once used local governments as auxiliary administrative units. La Guardia predictably sowed seeds of discontent in state houses and executive mansions by attempting to bypass the state defense councils and deal directly with municipalities. Motivated by the belief that civilian protection was a "uniquely urban problem," he staffed the OCD with former mayors and fostered the direct federal-municipal relations he had been instrumental in developing in the 1930s. But if federal-city relations were desirable in the case of the largest cities, in less populous areas the states proved the only realistic and immediately available organizing entities. La Guardia's efforts to circumvent them not only created a backlash from governors and other state officials but also ensured that the development of local defense councils outside a handful of large cities would fall far behind.[21]

Still, the OCD's civilian protection efforts were a comparative success. The agency's other programs, mired in confusion and neglect, developed much more slowly. The German government, John J. McCloy noted, had developed "instruments to mold public opinion in Germany and outside, and in modern warfare these instruments have become almost as important as guns." He and other administration officials (most notably Harold Ickes and Henry Wallace) had pushed for the creation of a strong, independent "propaganda" bureau to give the United States the same capacities. Roosevelt chose to house the bureau in the OCD—over the objections of Ickes, who argued that a civilian defense agency would be too overloaded with its other duties to give propaganda the attention it required.

La Guardia seemed flummoxed by this highly technical field. "If I continue much longer talking to these people," he wrote to Roosevelt after a meeting with some psychologists, "I will be 'nuts' too." Preoccupied with air-raid defense, he took several months to settle on an organizational structure; thereafter, the office of "facts and figures" La Guardia established stalled due to lack of organizational leadership. Roosevelt soon came to view this component of La Guardia's operation as ineffectual. Complaints from Chief of Staff George Marshall of low morale among draftees and the near defeat of his effort to extend the Selective Training and Service Act reinforced his belief that his foreign policy had not yet obtained (as he told Stimson) the support of the "little man of America." In October, the president removed the Office of Facts and Figures from the OCD, eventually folding it into the Office of War Information (which he established in mid-1942).[22]

The OCD's volunteer division likewise made little headway. Advocates of a robust volunteer program believed the energies of those eager to contribute to the defense effort could be put to the service of WPA-style community improvement projects, ranging from child nutrition initiatives to physical fitness programs. La Guardia, whom some liberals thought would be attentive to this aspect of the agency's mission, proved entirely uninterested—he even denied, on one occasion, that his agency had any responsibility for it. At the end of July, at Eleanor Roosevelt's suggestion, FDR brought the OCD's Volunteer Participation Committee to the White House and administered a pep talk, remarking that he considered the volunteer and morale aspects of civilian defense more important than the agency's "quasi-military" activities. This jolted

La Guardia, but only temporarily. The OCD's neglect of this facet of its mission was soon so egregious that the Bureau of the Budget threatened to withhold the agency's appropriation for non-compliance with the executive order.[23]

At the end of the summer, La Guardia managed simultaneously to assuage liberal advocates of a vigorous volunteer program and satisfy his own fondest wish for the program—namely, that he be relieved of immediate responsibility for it—by persuading Eleanor Roosevelt to serve as its director. La Guardia, who had known and admired the first lady since the 1920s (he thought her "the most marvelous woman in the whole world," their mutual friend Anna Rosenberg later recalled), had asked her to chair the women's division upon his appointment, and though she had turned him down, he had continued to consult her on issues relating to the volunteer program. Now he asked again, and this time she accepted. La Guardia knew the appointment carried risk, as Eleanor was a lightning rod for conservative criticism and was less heedful of political realities than were the professional politicians he had placed elsewhere in the agency. But the organization stood to benefit from the first lady's leadership, wide-ranging network of contacts, and ability to inspire service. Eleanor's presence also promised to raise the agency's public profile. She took the job and began the arduous work of building an organization ("there is none," she wrote), recruiting specialists, and finding activities for local volunteers. Before long she was greatly frustrated both with La Guardia's managerial failings and with her inability to get him to stand still "long enough for an important discussion."[24]

By the end of the summer, La Guardia was under fire both in official circles and in the print media. The Washington columnists Drew Pearson and Robert Allen reported "considerable underground grumbling" about La Guardia's performance, as did Newsweek (which published rumors that La Guardia planned to resign). Ernest Lindley, an early proponent of a national civilian defense program who had lauded La Guardia's appointment, published a searching critique of the agency in *The Washington Post*, writing that La Guardia had fallen "far short of expectations, alike as a morale arouser, administrator, and policymaker."

Inside the White House, Bernard Baruch told Ickes as early as July that La Guardia was "getting in the President's hair" and that FDR was glad, at least, that he had not made the Little Flower secretary of war. By October, Roosevelt and Hopkins were cracking jokes over dinner about La Guardia's preoccupation with air defense—an extension, Hopkins thought, of his well-known proclivity for racing to three-alarm fires. The White House tasked Anna Rosenberg to "stick close to the Mayor, and, above all, keep him away from the President." The appointment of Eleanor Roosevelt as assistant director helped quell some of the discontent but did not address its underlying causes. The criticism would break out again after Pearl Harbor with a much greater urgency, augmented by attacks on the first lady's newly assertive volunteer participation program.[25]

III

The most far-reaching national matter with which La Guardia became involved during his months at OCD had nothing to do with the specter of air raids or the organization of local volunteer activities. At Roosevelt's insistence, he played a minor role in the creation of the Fair Employment Practices Committee (FEPC), the first federal agency devoted expressly to equal rights since the Freedmen's Bureau, and an opening wedge for a politics of equal opportunity in the job market that would make up a major part of civil rights politics in the following decades.

Beginning in late 1940, war production began to pull industrial America out of the Great Depression. Because the national govern-

ment was committed to rapid production, war industry jobs paid
well and regularly; to many Americans who had lived through the
depression, they represented the first opportunity in years for steady
work and decent wages. Indeed, war industry jobs were so appealing that they precipitated one of the largest internal migrations in
American history. But large groups of Americans found themselves
shut out of the war economy. Because the defense boom of 1940–41
occurred amidst an extreme labor surplus, employers were relatively
free to indulge racial and religious preferences. (At the same time,
advances in production processes meant that war industries jobs
were, by 1940, more likely to require skills which black workers in
particular were less likely to possess, due to historic discrimination
in employment, education, and union membership, and historic concentration in the agricultural sector.) As a result, many ethnic and
religious minorities and women found war industries work difficult
to come by. African Americans were the worst off, as employment
figures at the largest factories in the New York metropolitan area
testify. Two of the metropolitan area's largest manufacturing corporations, Bethlehem Steel and Sperry Gyroscope, employed African
Americans roughly in proportion to the general population; others lagged far behind. Black New Yorkers made up some 6 percent
of the city's population but only 4.5 percent of the workers at Ford
Instruments, 2.7 percent of those at Socony-Vacuum Oil, 1.6 percent
those at Brewster Aeronautical and American Airlines, and less than
1 percent of those at Bell Labs. Mergenthaler Linotype and American Machine & Foundry employed workforces of 2,200 and 1,783,
respectively, with not a single black man or woman on the payroll.

Because the U.S. government had let the contracts which produced all those war industries jobs, civil rights organizations had
strong grounds on which to demand redress. Many groups would
ultimately be involved in the movement for "fair employment practices," but African Americans took the lead: black workers were the

most fully shut out, and black communities could draw on a recent history of collective action to open labor markets as a basis for mobilizing mass support. In September 1940, NAACP head Walter White and Brotherhood of Sleeping Car Porters president A. Philip Randolph presented to Roosevelt a number of racial inequities, including discrimination in defense production and continuing segregation of the armed services. Finding the president charming but evasive, Randolph decided that continuing efforts to work with the administration were "not going to get us anywhere" and began contemplating a strategy of confrontation: a march on Washington. The idea captured the imagination of the broad civil rights movement, and over the winter months it "grew like Topsy" (as one black labor leader recalled). When Randolph made his plans known to the White House in late May 1941, Roosevelt and press secretary Steve Early, fearing embarrassment and perhaps violence, went to work trying to quash the march. La Guardia, the closest thing the administration had to an honest broker, was enlisted to conciliate the movement's leaders. "Get the Missus and Fiorello and Anna [Rosenberg]," Roosevelt insisted, "and get it stopped."[26]

La Guardia never really felt comfortable with the idea of government regulation of private employment practices. Like many New Deal liberals, he believed racial discrimination to be a matter of personal prejudice that could only truly be resolved by the evolution of individual attitudes; efforts to fight discrimination through the exercise of state power, he believed, were akin to "asking the wind to be still." He was, however, broadly sympathetic to the concerns White and Randolph had raised, sufficiently so that White, thinking the mayor a potential ally, had kept him briefed on his meetings with Roosevelt. La Guardia also possessed a deep respect for Randolph, whom he considered the greatest progressive labor leader of his generation and a personal friend. When White and Randolph met with the mayor, Eleanor Roosevelt, Anna Rosenberg, and National Youth

Administration director Aubrey Williams at City Hall on the second Friday in June, they found the Little Flower opposed to the march but understanding of the basic problem. For his part, La Guardia quickly grasped that the civil rights leaders held the trump cards: once they had decided on a direct action strategy, the administration had no choice but to make an accommodation. He recommended to FDR that the president convene a meeting of Randolph, White, Secretaries Stimson and Knox, and William Knudsen and Sidney Hillman of the Office of Production Management, "and thresh it out right then and there." Randolph cabled the president to ask that La Guardia attend.[27]

Roosevelt arranged a White House meeting for Friday of that week. Randolph brought with him a list of demands: executive orders banning discrimination on account of race, creed, or color by all federal agencies and forbidding the awarding of contracts to any firms that so discriminated, with the government taking control of repeat offenders; an executive order abolishing segregation in the armed forces; and presidential backing for a law withholding the benefits of the Wagner Act from Jim Crow unions. In the bargaining that followed, Randolph and White set desegregation of the military and the unions aside and made jobs the first priority. The meeting grew tense as Roosevelt rebuked the two civil rights leaders for using the threat of a march on Washington as a bargaining chip, saying coldly that it was not the policy of the president of the United States to rule with a gun at his head. At that point La Guardia interjected. "Gentlemen," he said, "it is clear that Mr. Randolph is not going to call off the march and I suggest we all begin to seek a formula." Roosevelt yielded, and a committee headed by La Guardia trooped off to the Cabinet Room to draft the order.[28]

Five days later, after several more drafts had shuttled back and forth between Randolph, La Guardia, the Department of Justice, and the White House, the final product was ready for Roosevelt's signature. Executive Order 8802, issued on June 25, 1941, forbade discrimination by federal agencies and defense contractors, created the Fair Employment Practices Committee, and authorized the committee to investigate violations and issue cease-and-desist orders to enforce compliance. White and Randolph both requested that La Guardia be made chairman of the new committee—White wanted La Guardia appointed, he said, because he believed no one would try "to pull anything" on a board headed by the pugnacious mayor— but Roosevelt decided that the mayoralty, the OCD post, and the co-chairmanship of the Joint Defense Board was enough work for one man. The committee formed with Louisville newspaperman Mark Ethridge at the helm. From that point, La Guardia's involvement with the agency was mostly limited to forwarding complaints lodged by New Yorkers (many of which came from Jewish and Italian job applicants).[29]

The FEPC lived a "short and troubled existence," beset by institutional difficulties that prevented it from meeting the high expectations black workers and civil rights leaders had placed in it. Its primary tools consisted of cease-and-desist orders and public hearings, a case-by-case approach that the civil rights advocate and New Deal administrator Robert C. Weaver (then working in the War Manpower Commission) believed was better suited to garnering public support and publicity than to securing greater access to employment. In fact, scholars are skeptical as to whether the agency had any impact at all in "opening up any job opportunities beyond the ones generated by tight wartime labor markets."[30]

But this was not the full measure of the FEPC's significance. By forcing Roosevelt to create a federal agency devoted to fair employment practices, Randolph and his allies had put the problem on the national agenda. The effort to establish a permanent FEPC at war's end would bring together a broader coalition of groups than had fought for racial justice at any time since Reconstruction. And when that campaign bogged down at the national level, it would move to the states. In January 1945, New York State assemblyman Irving Ives would introduce a bill to prohibit discrimination on the basis of race, creed, color, or religion. The measure would garner strong support from civil rights organizations, practically all of the unions, the American Jewish Congress, the New York Federation of Churches, the YMCA, and the Democratic, American Labor, and Liberal parties. It would be opposed most vigorously by the railroad brotherhoods and the business community. The most effective spokesman for the latter group would turn out to be none other than Robert Moses, who argued that a maximal interpretation of the law would require employers to hire in strict proportion to the religious and racial makeup of their localities. Such, Moses suggested, would spell "the end of honest competition . . . the death knell of selection and advancement on the basis of talent," and, he added with characteristic literary verve, the imposition of a "Hitlerian rule of quotas." La Guardia dispatched his aide Reuben Lazarus to remind the legislators that the proposed measure simply forbade discrimination—no less and no more. Backed strongly by Thomas Dewey, the Ives-Quinn bill passed with a broad bipartisan majority, and New York became the first of twenty-five states to outlaw employment discrimination on the grounds of race, religion, or national origin.[31]

IV

As the mayoral election of 1941 approached, the realignment that had swept American politics in the second half of the 1930s nearly pulled La Guardia fully into the Democratic Party. Adolf Berle, strongly averse to the growing Communist influence in the American Labor Party, began working through a Depression-born group called the Affiliated Young Democrats, which claimed a member-

ship (likely inflated) of 65,000, to stage a hostile takeover of the
New York Democracy. The day after La Guardia accepted the OCD
job, Berle called on the group to enter La Guardia into the primary
and "let the Democratic leaders find out what leadership the mass
of New York City Democrats follow." Evidence suggests that Roosevelt himself pushed Flynn to take La Guardia as the head of the
Democratic ticket. La Guardia and Flynn's working relationship had
been strengthened in the course of the 1940 presidential campaign,
and in March 1941 Flynn, speaking at the University of North Carolina, had called the Little Flower "perhaps one of the best mayors
New York City has had." (Paul O'Dwyer, the brother of the man who
would challenge La Guardia on the Democratic ticket in 1941, later
remarked that "there was a very close relationship between Flynn
and La Guardia. We could never quite pin it down. . . ." After the
election it would come out that La Guardia had been making patronage appointments at Flynn's request.)

Ultimately, national political forces proved insufficient to effect a
full fusion of the New Deal Democracy and La Guardia's progressive
coalition. Flynn later claimed that when Roosevelt suggested that
he and La Guardia should "get together" and "run things as [they]
liked," he balked because he believed La Guardia's stance on political
parties to be "intellectually dishonest." But the idea of bestowing the
Democratic nomination upon La Guardia died because of politics as
well as principle. The Democratic district leaders, who feared that
full integration of the New Dealers into the Democratic Party would
subject them to leadership fights "which some of them would be sure
to lose," opposed it; and La Guardia himself, always unwilling to
suffer constraints on his personal power, wanted ticket mates who
owed their primary loyalty to him. Instead, the Democrats nominated Kings County District Attorney William O'Dwyer, a native of
Ireland's County Mayo who had worked his way up from a waterfront police beat before exploiting the Democratic fissures of the

early 1930s to win appointment as a city magistrate. After serving two years in that capacity, he had resigned to run for Kings County DA, had won, and had quickly amassed an eye-catching record prosecuting the group of killers for hire known as Murder, Inc.—though, it was noted, he had put away only the hit men, not the higher-ups.[32]

Ironically, the Republican resurgence that had closed off La Guardia's chances within the party at the state and national levels helped make it possible for him to retain the party's nomination at the municipal level. Particularly in the outer boroughs, the rank and file were eager to dump La Guardia for a "true Republican" who would build the party and reward its workers. The respected old guard Republican John R. Davies entered the GOP primary, declaring baldly that if good government were the only issue, he would not be in the race. Charging that La Guardia was "the perfect symbol of the New Deal," he claimed that the New York City municipal election represented the "last chance" to protest against "reckless waste at Washington, which threatens national bankruptcy, inflation and repudiation. . . ."[33]

The crucial intercession came from Dewey, who as much as anyone now controlled the Republican county organizations. The party's presumptive nominee for governor in 1942, Dewey had come under pressure from leading Republicans to oppose La Guardia in the interest of defeating Roosevelt in 1944. He also harbored personal resentments toward La Guardia: the Little Flower's last-minute intervention in the 1938 gubernatorial race, he told Judge Seabury, represented an "unparalleled act of betrayal." But, Dewey decided, "I would rather have one SOB in City Hall and know where he is than to have a whole lot of them scattered all over the city, with the enormous patronage of the Mayor, his Commissioners and the New York Police"—as he would if O'Dwyer won the general election. The Republican organizations in Manhattan and Brooklyn turned out the primary vote for La Guardia, who prevailed with 56 percent of the ballots.[34]

If tensions within the major parties had been resolved according to local- and state-level imperatives, the American Labor Party's tortured course forecast the role international affairs would play in the general election. The party was, by 1941, divided into "right-wing" and "left-wing" factions, the former composed of inveterate opponents of Communist involvement, the latter consisting of most everyone else. The socialists who had launched the ALP in 1936 had formally forbidden Communist membership, but Communists had enrolled en masse anyway, and by the late 1930s they had become a significant presence in the party (as they had in many left-progressive organizations).

The deep antipathy between anti-Communist and Communist forces, which dated back at least to the factional conflicts that had wracked the garment unions in the 1920s, would have produced struggles for party control in any event. As it happened, the coming of the European war and particularly the signing of the German-Soviet non-aggression pact in 1939 fanned the flames of discord. Beginning in earnest at the end of 1940, the left-wingers turned against Roosevelt—whom they now denounced as an imperialist "warmonger"—and bitterly denounced aid to Great Britain, "the very cornerstone of the world capitalist system" and "the main enemy of everything progressive. . . ." The right-wingers supported Roosevelt and considered themselves anti-fascist in foreign policy.[35]

La Guardia had compromised his extraordinarily broad labor support by his opposition to public sector unionism, which had become a major issue when the city took over operation of the IRT and BMT lines in 1940. With the Roosevelt administration's support, La Guardia resisted the Transport Workers Union's efforts to secure collective bargaining rights, arguing that public employees already possessed "full and complete protection as to employment, rights, and privileges" through the Civil Service system, and that public officials must be free to act without "threat of disorder, discontinuance of service, or disregard of existing law." The city's CIO-affiliated unions lined up in support of the TWU, with the Greater New York Industrial Union Council assailing "the Mayor's union-busting game." La Guardia's support for aid to the Allies exacerbated the division. The Little Flower, wrote the CP leader Simon Gerson voicing the left-wing attitude, had transformed New York's "government and politics" into "adjuncts of the Roosevelt war machine." As the nominating season approached, there was speculation that the left-wingers would impose upon Vito Marcantonio to run against La Guardia on an "anti-imperialist" platform. Then, in June 1941, the German army invaded the Soviet Union, abrogating the non-aggression pact, and overnight the CPUSA became a strong proponent of Roosevelt's foreign policy. By November the left-wingers were urging New Yorkers to reelect the city's anti-fascist mayor by voting the "Smash-Hitler Ticket." The Greater New York Industrial Union Council gave La Guardia its endorsement—"This is necessary to defeat reactionaries and guarantee that [an] effective fight against fascism at home and abroad will be carried on"—though La Guardia's opposition to municipal unionism created enough dissatisfaction among the rank-and-file that O'Dwyer was able to secure the support of some union locals.[36]

With the nominations determined, Roosevelt's foreign policy—and La Guardia's relation to it—became the focus of the campaign. The editorial board of the New York daily *PM* expressed the sentiments of many pro-Roosevelt liberals when it urged New Yorkers to support La Guardia because he had made the right enemies: "the Christian Fronters, the Bundists, the Fascists and the appeasers. . . ." Jewish opinion makers endorsed La Guardia on the same grounds. The editors of the Yiddish daily *Der Tog*, usually a Democratic paper, wrote: "New York possesses the role of leader in the present crucial hour in the history of American people. . . . Thanks to La Guardia, it became the greatest center for anti-Hitlerism in America." La

Guardia's supporters viewed him as "one of democracy's great leaders" and lauded him for making New York City "a living example of democracy at a time when democracy everywhere is in the gravest peril"; they urged his reelection as "a hopeful sign to those who share our belief in the ultimate triumph of all those things which the United States of America represents." Such rhetoric contained an element of irony, for much of what these people admired in La Guardia's mayoralty—his efficiency as an executive, his strong leadership, his emphasis on civic purpose, his ability at mitigating conflict between labor and management, his achievement of large public works projects—overlapped with what Americans had admired in fascism (particularly Italian Fascism) in the 1920s and 1930s. The crucial difference, of course, was that La Guardia operated within a framework of liberal democracy in a city that celebrated diversity and dissent.[37]

There was never any doubt that Roosevelt would endorse La Guardia's reelection bid. Although O'Dwyer had stated publicly his support of Roosevelt's foreign policy, the president recognized that a La Guardia defeat would be widely interpreted as a repudiation. At a press conference on Friday, October 24, he read a prepared statement, copies of which were handed out to reporters. "I have lived and worked in the City of New York off and on since 1904," he said. "I have known and observed New York's mayors since that time. I am not taking part in the New York election, but"—laughter broke out among the reporters as the sentence turned—"*but*, because the City of New York contains about half the population of my State, I do not hesitate to express the opinion that Mayor La Guardia and his Administration have given the City the most honest and, I believe, the most efficient municipal government within my recollection." "The President knows his New York City," La Guardia said when word reached him, flashing a thumbs-up gesture. Then he dispatched a brief telegram to Roosevelt: "*Merci*—Fiorello."[38]

The full effect of the foreign policy issue became evident only once the ballots had been counted. Election day saw the closest mayoral contest since the Democrats' ill-won 1905 victory over William Randolph Hearst. La Guardia won with 52.5 percent of the total, down from 60.1 percent in 1937. His vote declined in suburban areas, particularly in Queens, where rising property taxes (resulting in part from the demobilization of the New Deal's intergovernmental spending programs) were a major issue. But the voters who nearly turned La Guardia out of office in 1941 were, by and large, the same ones who had sent Roosevelt's share of the New York vote tumbling the previous year. His total among Irish New Yorkers fell by 13 percent; among German New Yorkers, it dropped by 18 percent. Most significant was the erosion of La Guardia's Italian base. The Little Flower won an estimated 46 percent of Italian American votes, down from 63 percent in 1937. He lost Manhattan's 2nd Assembly District, which contained the Little Italy neighborhood along Mulberry and Elizabeth streets; he lost in East Harlem; and he slumped in other districts with large Italian populations. By 1941, there were "rumblings" in the Italian colonies that La Guardia had "neglected his own people," especially with regard to appointments, and that he had taken "the Italian vote" for granted as he rebuilt his political coalition to include other traditionally underrepresented ethnic groups. But foreign policy was the foremost grievance in Italian American neighborhoods, and moreover it fed into the sense that the mayor was ethnically disloyal: on the issue that mattered most to New York's Italian American communities, he stood in opposition.[39]

By 1940–41, Roosevelt's and La Guardia's electoral coalitions were strikingly similar for major politicians from different parties. A June 1941 Gallup Poll found that 71 percent of those who had voted for Roosevelt the previous November planned to vote for La Guardia, compared to only 43 percent of those who had voted for Willkie; only 16 percent of those who had voted for Roosevelt planned to vote

against La Guardia, compared to 40 percent of those who had voted
for Willkie. By the simplest statistical measure, La Guardia's vote
resembled Roosevelt's from 1940 about as much as Roosevelt's in
1936 had resembled Al Smith's in 1928. Only two sizable groups had
resisted the realignment that took place in New York between 1932
and 1941: partisan Democrats (many, but not all, Irish Catholic), who
tended to reside in areas such as Hell's Kitchen and Greenpoint that
had (or had once had) strong district party organizations; and affluent Protestants, concentrated on the Upper East Side, in Gramercy
and Washington Square North, and to a lesser degree in Flatbush—
communities in which Republican identification was as much a part
of group identity as Irish Catholic Democracy was in Hell's Kitchen
and the old industrial neighborhoods of the Brooklyn waterfront.[40]

V

The day after the 1941 election, *The Times* of London, in its lead editorial, applauded the people of New York for their "thoughtfulness"
in returning La Guardia to office; the Italian Fascist editor Virginio
Gayda issued a statement in *Il Giornale D'Italia* that the New York
election offered proof that "a good half of the American people do
not want to hear of the policy of their President." The mayor himself
was back at work the next day. "No, my friends, I am not going to
take a vacation," he said in a post-election broadcast. "I can't take a
vacation when there is so much to do here, and when the country
needs the efforts and the toil and the work and the sweat of every
one of its sons."

Managing the city under extraordinary circumstances and
attempting to direct the OCD at the same time, La Guardia was
working himself to the bone. Emotion impinged on his thinking
more often, and fatigue clouded his judgment; decisions were made

too fast and without a proper sense of perspective. The OCD was operating without balance, without proportion, without control. La Guardia handled the mounting criticism of his work extremely poorly. He insisted on taking even well-meaning criticism (as the *Herald Tribune* wrote) "as a reflection on his own ability, integrity and good intentions." Unwilling or unable to see the organizational problems in the OCD, he dodged responsibility for them, shouting down criticism and firing those who pressed the point.[41]

The events that would finally lead to La Guardia's ouster from the OCD, and also put an end to the agony of neutrality, were in the making—halfway around the globe. During a White House visit three days after the election, Roosevelt briefed La Guardia on the rapidly deteriorating situation in the Far East, where the administration's efforts to halt imperial expansion by freezing Japanese assets were, in Churchill's words, "steadily forcing the Japanese to decisions for peace or war," leading seemingly inexorably to a confrontation between the Japanese and the Americans, British, and Dutch in the South Pacific. "Our country is faced with real danger in this very moment," La Guardia cautioned at the end of November. "There is no telling what may happen in a few days in the Far East."[42]

La Guardia was at home in his East Harlem apartment when word came that Japan had bombed the American naval base at Pearl Harbor. Speeding downtown in a police cruiser, he summoned his commissioners and instructed them to put into operation plans to safeguard the city's bridges, tunnels, railroads, docks, reservoirs, and power plants. A telephone operator worked torridly patching through La Guardia's calls to a host of local, federal, and military officials and to the regional directors of the OCD. Guards were sent to the Japanese consulate. Air-raid wardens and volunteer aircraft spotters went on duty. The 62nd Coast Artillery set up antiaircraft machine-gun nests in Prospect Park. FBI agents and local alien and sabotage squads rounded up between one hundred and two hundred Japanese "enemy aliens" and transported them through station houses and the federal courthouse to Ellis Island, where they were held awaiting word from federal authorities on their status. The mayor ordered all Japanese subjects to remain in their homes until their status was determined by the federal government and closed local Japanese clubs and restaurants—the first manifestation of a malignant racism La Guardia would display toward people of Japanese ancestry, foreign nationals and American citizens alike, during the war. The following day, La Guardia went to the White House to talk with Roosevelt before setting off to meet with officials on the west coast.[43]

The attack at Pearl Harbor and American entry into the war removed any chance that La Guardia could retain both the mayoralty and the OCD directorship. Columnists (led by Lippmann), editorial boards, and congressmen called rashly for the OCD to be handed over to the War Department despite Secretary Stimson's protestations that he did not want jurisdiction over it. New York's newspapers and civic leaders demanded loudly and nearly unanimously that the city receive the service of a full-time mayor—noting, additionally, that the days after Pearl Habor had revealed a striking level of disorganization in the city's own civilian protection program. And if this public reaction was insufficient to force Roosevelt's hand—before long, critics would accuse the president of "criminal negligence" for failing to establish a more effective civil defense program—there were also those within the administration who knew firsthand of the OCD's organizational deficiencies. On December 13, special assistant to the president Wayne Coy and budget director Harold Smith, who had been warning Roosevelt of the agency's disorganization since the fall, delivered a memo suggesting bluntly that the president could no longer turn a blind eye to the matter. Eleanor Roosevelt, who had found La Guardia difficult to work with and ineffective as an administrator, agreed.

On December 19, Roosevelt called La Guardia to the White House and told him that he could not handle both the mayoralty and the OCD at the same time; it was too much for anyone, he said, and he recommended that La Guardia find an assistant to handle the administrative work. The president was plainly looking for a solution short of firing La Guardia, but the mayor gave him little help. As soon as Roosevelt concluded, La Guardia launched into a long defense of his work. The newspaper criticism was unfair, he said, and other attacks on the agency were politically motivated. He finished by saying that "the civilian protection side of the picture should never have been mixed in the Executive Order in the first place." Roosevelt reiterated his initial suggestion and then instructed La Guardia and Harold Smith to consider whether the OCD could be reorganized so that La Guardia could handle civilian protection only. Then, on January 2, 1942, Roosevelt pulled La Guardia aside after a cabinet meeting and told him he was going to elevate New England regional director (and Harvard Law School dean) James M. Landis to the position of executive to run the agency's day-to-day operations. Out of options, La Guardia agreed to surrender his own position.[44]

As Warren Moscow, the *New York Times* political correspondent, was to suggest shortly after La Guardia's death, the Little Flower's standing never recovered from the OCD misadventure. After eight months of non-stop work, the mayor had been forced to resign, having done permanent damage to his reputation and strained his relationship to the White House. His record in New York had fostered the belief that he was a brilliant administrator; but his failure to establish a functioning, self-sustaining organization had left him, for the first time in his career, open to the charge of incompetence. Liberals had accused him of neglecting the social potential of volunteer programs to focus on the air-raid threat, thus squandering an opportunity to extend New Deal–style social welfare and community improvement activities. And La Guardia himself, having used his talents for publicity indiscriminately, had become an object of derision—his newsreel appearances, one New York daily wrote, drew "more raucous laughter than Abbott and Costello." The enduring memory of his tenure at the OCD would be that of the mayor, racing around post–Pearl Harbor Washington in a police cruiser with siren blaring, shrieking into a loudspeaker: "Calm! Calm! Calm!"[45]

9

The Battle of New York

entlemen: This is a war budget!" So began La Guardia's April 1942 message to the Board of Estimate, transmitting his yearly requests for the city's departments, agencies, commissions, courts, and cultural institutions. Police, fire, and hospitals—on call should the Axis powers breach the five boroughs—were spared deep cuts; but the agencies that had expanded their output most rapidly during the New Deal years—and had seen their municipal appropriations grow quickly as the WPA was rolled back in the late thirties—were forced to make do with less in the interest of conserving national resources for the war effort. Together with the ongoing withdrawal of WPA manpower from the city departments, these cutbacks reflected a larger shift in American public sector spending away from the production of public goods and services and toward the production of the implements of war. New Deal–style public investment would be suspended for the duration.

The Second World War would see the rise of a new cluster of national state activities—a "warfare state" that contracted for the production of military supplies, raised vast amounts of revenue through taxation and borrowing, managed the allocation of national resources and manpower, and sought to minimize the economic and social dislocations produced by national mobilization. Local governments would be enlisted as partners in some of these undertakings. But because the state-building project of the 1940s entailed the expansion of governmental functions in which municipalities had never been much involved—and because nationalization enjoyed a legitimacy in war that it had not done in peace—the "sweeping transformation in the foundations of national government" that occurred during the war years did not implicate local governments to nearly the same degree as had the New Deal state-making efforts of the mid-thirties. The collaborative federalism upon which the New Deal's public investment and employment programs had been built withered as corporate contractors replaced municipal governments as Washington's primary partners in production. The New Dealers had built a federal state; wartime officials would build a national one.[1]

Even so, policy innovation at the national level continued to stimulate local governmental action. In order to supply the armaments and materiel needed to fight the war, Washington created a vast centralized procurement bureaucracy—the first incarnation of the military-industrial complex that would be such a vital component of the American economy for the remainder of the twentieth century and beyond. In so doing, it encouraged localities to develop means of competing effectively in the political economy of war and defense production.

The Roosevelt administration's efforts to limit inflation and provide for the equitable distribution of wartime sacrifice on the home front had even farther-reaching effects. By galvanizing a grassroots- and labor-led movement for "fair prices," these national policies helped to produce a vibrant cost-of-living politics which fed back into the municipal arena. La Guardia would mobilize the city government to address these popular concerns—using his own offices to enforce federal price regulations, provide valuable market information to the city's purchasers, lead consumers in informal boycotts of expensive goods, push the national Office of Price Administration to extend its policies, and orchestrate the campaign that would bring rent control to New York City.

La Guardia's third term is almost universally regarded as his worst, and not without ample reason. Physically and emotionally worn down and increasingly irritable, he cut corners more frequently, asserted power arbitrarily and unfairly, made more bad appointments, and generally lost interest in the day-to-day challenges of municipal government. Yet his efforts to bring wartime employment to the city and to stabilize the cost of living—neglected episodes in his career—stand among his most creative work. Even so, La Guardia was never content to fight the battle of New York; he never reconciled himself to what he believed was a secondary role in the struggle for the future of civilization. For him, the war years were ones of frustration and disappointment—and the bitterest disappointment of all was to come at Roosevelt's hands.[2]

I

Beginning in mid-1940, when the federal government started to spend heavily on defense, industrial America emerged at long last from the Great Depression. But New York missed out on this economic revival. As late as mid-1942, with the American economy growing more rapidly than at any other time in its history, 50,000 more men and women were registered as unemployed in New York than had been in the depression year of 1939.[3]

One source of New York's wartime economic blues was an infestation of German U-boats, which had settled in the Lower New York Bay and were sinking American vessels by sighting them against the illuminated skyline. As a result, shipping had been temporarily diverted from the New York port, depriving work to stevedores, truck drivers, and others whose jobs depended on port activity—about 100,000 people in all. But more important, the city was getting passed over for government war production contracts. New York was left far behind the big industrial metropolitan areas of the Midwest and the burgeoning cities of the Sun Belt (see Table 9.1); it was also faring poorly compared with the other dense, highly unionized cities of the eastern seaboard. The New York metropolitan area had garnered $136 per capita in war supplies contracts compared with $286 in Boston, $350 in Philadelphia, $650 in Newark–Jersey City, $700 in Cleveland, $715 in Buffalo, and $952 in Baltimore.[4]

These disparities were rooted in the structural characteristics of New York's manufacturing economy. New York's manufacturers, far more than those of other northern industrial cities, specialized in non-durable consumer goods—items that were intended to last three years or less, like clothing, newspapers and other printed items, and food products. They lacked the durable goods facilities readily adaptable to the mass production of implements of war. (By one analy-

Table 9.1: *War supplies and war facilities construction contracts per capita in selected metropolitan areas, June 1940–February 1942*

	NYC	Chicago	Detroit	LA	SF-Oak.	Seattle-Tacoma, WA	Hart-ford, CT
Supplies contracts	$136	$143	$806	$703	$617	$1,199	$1,829
Facilities contracts	$30	$101	$169	$65	$168	$177	$188

Compiled from M. P. Catherwood and Meredith B. Givens, "The Problem of War Production and Surplus Labor in New York City," May 13, 1942, RG 211, Entry 94, Box 2, NA. New York City figure includes Westchester and Nassau counties.

sis, only 23.5 percent of New York City manufacturing employees worked in industries "closely allied" to war production, compared with 57 percent in upstate New York.) Second, the practices of the military procurement bureaucracy worked against small manufacturers; and the city's manufacturing sector had long been populated primarily by small-scale, highly specialized plants, not by the large assembly-line factories that characterized cities such as Detroit. New York's manufacturing sector averaged 20 workers per factory, compared to 43 in the nation as a whole and 113 in the Motor City.

Some defenders of small business, including La Guardia, were convinced that the large corporations' hold on war contracts— by one count, 73 percent of contracts let in the two years following the invasion of France went to the nation's one hundred largest corporations—was the work of the dollar-a-year men those corporations had loaned to the War Production Board. No doubt, personal influence of this sort did play a role. But small producers also faced formidable structural obstacles, for they often lacked the engineering staff required to convert their equipment, the legal personnel needed to handle complicated contracts and subcontracts, and the accountants and expeditors required to pursue government contracts. For its part, the military procurement bureaucracy lacked the capacity to seek out smaller firms and was reluctant to depart from the practice of giving "contracts to big companies with a reputation for performance" for fear that a newspaper or congressional committee would reveal that they had overpaid. As a result of this mismatch between the military procurement process and the structure of New York's manufacturing sector, an acute unemployment problem persisted within the five boroughs even in the midst of national labor shortages. Hundreds of thousands of New Yorkers had been drafted for service, and yet there remained more than 368,000 registered job seekers and probably as many as 400,000 unemployed altogether. With curbs on civilian production, high wartime taxes, and bond

savings drives in the offing, some analysts predicted joblessness in
New York would rise as high as 600,000.[5]

The *Herald Tribune* ran a series of long articles urging optimism
and predicting that what the city lost in industry and blue-collar
workers it would gain in corporate headquarters and cultured, middle-class managers. But this perspective, though it anticipated the
attitude assumed by politicians, business people, real estate owners,
and newspapers after the war (when unemployment was low and
property values more stable), was a distinctly minority one in 1942.
La Guardia's own statement captured the sense that war production was rearranging America's industrial geography to New York's
detriment:

> The factories . . . that can keep going and can keep their per-
> sonnel intact because they are working on war orders will be
> the ones who will be able to resume peacetime production
> without interruption. Unless we can get more war contracts in
> this city the result may well be, that a large proportion of the
> manufacturing that we normally do in New York will be per-
> manently diverted. . . .

The *New York Post* noted with alarm that federal money was going to
capitalize non-union factories in Southern "cow pastures and cotton
fields"—"rank union busting," its editors cried—which would continue
to undercut New York industry after the war. Some New York newspapers raised the specter that Gotham might become a "ghost town."[6]

One of the reasons New York had been so successful in its implementation of the New Deal works programs was that, at the time
those programs were created, it had already possessed strong organizational bases in the fields of social welfare and public works: the
charity organizations and the social work profession, the machinery
established by the Gibson and Prosser committees, the local relief

bureaucracy that had developed after Roosevelt created the Temporary Emergency Relief Administration, the municipal departments and their engineering staffs, and Robert Moses's network of engineers, architects, landscape architects, and managers. In comparison, there existed very little organizational capacity and little knowledge upon which the city could draw to improve the competitiveness of its private manufacturers. There had existed no local equivalent of the "associational state" Secretary of Commerce Herbert Hoover had pioneered at the national level in the 1920s; New York's Department of Commerce dated to late 1939 and consisted of a small staff on loan from other city agencies working out of donated Rockefeller Center offices, a large share of its "shoestring" budget paid out of pocket by the commissioner. And both the city government and New York's business and manufacturing elites possessed remarkably little policy-relevant knowledge. "In discussions with leading business men during recent weeks," a 1943 study initiated by Governor Dewey concluded, "the committee has found that the representatives of a particular industry were aware of the problems of their own industry, but that in very few cases was there adequate understanding of the total problems of all business and industry in the community." The same study judged that New York City was "far behind" other localities in its efforts "to attract business and to safeguard the interests of existing enterprises" in large measure, one concludes, because its industrialists and public officials had long been able to take the city's prosperity for granted.

To create a means of aiding New York's private manufacturers, La Guardia assembled his own group of dollar-a-year men, led by George A. Sloan, a director of U.S. Steel and Goodyear Tire & Rubber, to serve as the Mayor's Advisory Committee on Business. (Sloan also became the commissioner of the recently born Department of Commerce.) Neither was a particularly strong agency—it would be decades before New York's municipal government developed any real capacity in the realm of economic development policy—but their creation did ensure that at least one high-ranking figure was working full time to bring war contracts to the city and had responsibility for assembling a picture of the overall industrial situation in New York. Sloan's office went to work playing matchmaker between corporate prime contractors and small New York shops, and attempting to create pools of smaller plants that could engage the engineering consultants they so desperately needed to convert their machinery for war production.

La Guardia and Sloan also hoped to persuade federal officials to intervene in the contracting process on behalf of small businesses. They made an alliance with rural and small-town congressmen, who were pushing for the creation of a federal agency tasked with helping small enterprises secure government contracts. These efforts bore fruit in June 1942, when Congress created the Smaller War Plants Corporation (SWPC), tasked with taking prime contracts and subcontracting them to small plants. La Guardia began to take the city's concerns to leading Washington war bureaucrats: War Production Board chairman Donald Nelson, War Manpower Commission director Paul McNutt, and Office of Price Administration head Leon Henderson. Until June 1942 he received sympathy but relatively little in the way of cooperative action. "It is most discouraging," he wrote to Roosevelt in March, "to keep on writing and phoning, appealing, begging and pleading to use existing facilities in New York City for war production. This is only a small part of what we can do here. We [have] hundreds of thousands of skilled people out of work."[7]

In early June, La Guardia and Governor Lehman asked Roosevelt to convene a conference to discuss what could be done to alleviate unemployment in New York City. They found the president receptive. The underutilization of Gotham's manpower, manufacturing facilities, housing stock, and transportation system (during a period of gasoline and rubber rationing) represented a significant waste of resources. Moreover, Thomas Dewey stood poised to make political capital of the unemployment problem in the fall gubernatorial election. Roosevelt agreed to convene a high-level conference at Lehman and La Guardia's request. McNutt, Nelson, Henderson, Henry Morgenthau, Jesse Jones, Undersecretary of War Robert Patterson, Undersecretary of the Navy James Forrestal, and Vice Admiral Emory S. Land of the Maritime Commission attended.[8]

The conferences ultimately produced a series of agency-based efforts directed at particular sectors of the New York workforce. In order to provide jobs for beleaguered construction workers, whose skills were readily adaptable to shipyard work, Navy Secretary Frank Knox and Undersecretary Forrestal agreed to expand work at the Brooklyn Navy Yard—the city's largest manufacturing establishment. The Maritime Commission gave more construction contracts to New York shipyards; construction workers were soon being hired at a net clip of 600 per week. Employment at the yard peaked in 1944 at 71,000 men and women; from Pearl Harbor through the end of the war, they built seventeen ships, including two large battleships (a third, the USS *North Carolina*, had been commissioned in April 1941) and five aircraft carriers.[9]

Other policies were aimed at New York's largest industry, the garment industry. New York, the center of American clothing production, might have seemed a natural supplier of Army uniforms. But the city's garment shops, producing mostly higher-end clothing of superior styling and workmanship, employed relatively highly skilled and well-paid workers. It was often less costly for the procurement agencies to capitalize new factories in low-wage states than it was to meet the cost of New York's skilled, unionized labor. New York manufacturers, the garment unions determined, produced 40 percent of the nation's men's pants, yet by the spring of 1942 they had received only 3 percent of the contracts let for woolen Army trousers. La Guardia, pushed by the unions, petitioned for higher minimum wages on war contracts to cut the advantage of low-wage producers. The War Production Board responded with a directive allowing the procurement agencies to negotiate contracts at prices above the lowest competitive bid, permitting bid differentials of up to 15 percent; this was raised to 25 percent as a result of the summer conferences.[10]

To La Guardia's consternation, the garment companies still did not submit bids: profit margins on government contracts were too small to entice garment firms so long as the civilian market remained open. In response, La Guardia used his personal power to arrange a kind of informal corporatism; under mayoral suasion, the unions and the garment manufacturers each made concessions in the interest of the broader aim of defending New York's share of the garment industry. La Guardia asked the unions to reduce their wage scales as a way of inducing the manufacturers to enter more bids; the unions agreed, viewing this as a way of providing steadier employment for their members. La Guardia then put pressure on the manufacturers to bid for less than attractive contracts. "We are both seeking the same objective," he wrote the head of the New York Clothing Manufactures Exchange; "that is we do not want to have the clothing industry taken away from New York after the war. . . . Now I can't perform miracles nor can I go down to the shops and sew these pants but I do expect cooperation especially when I am being used as the shock troop in this matter." When Sloan notified La Guardia that the Quartermaster Depot was seeking bids for more than 3 million pairs of cotton khaki trousers and that the ACWA and the manufactures had told him they could not meet the government asking price without negotiating a special rate, he got this response: "By all means, New York City is to bid. . . . They must bid. Tell them I said so." And they did.[11]

The effort to boost war production in New York never quite came together as Gotham's advocates wished. New Yorkers were particularly disappointed in the performance of the Smaller War Plants

Corporation, the failure of which left the city without an effective means of aiding its small metal- and woodworking shops. Even so, the New York economy recovered rapidly in the second half of 1942 and into 1943. The value of war contracts let to New York manufacturers grew from a little over $77 million in the month before Roosevelt's intervention to nearly $222 million three months later; the total between July and December of 1942 was more than $1.5 billion. War Manpower Commission regional director Anna Rosenberg estimated that half of the 400,000 unemployed at the beginning of the summer were placed in jobs between July and the end of September, and by spring of 1943 the Department of Commerce declared that, with the exception of woodworking and metalworking shops, unemployment in the city had reached an "irreducible minimum." These numbers were bolstered by seasonal employment in the garment industry, by outmigration, and perhaps most of all by the steady removal of workers into the armed services; but a net gain of three hundred manufacturing plants in the first quarter of 1943 indicated that industry was also reviving. As early as November 1942, Roosevelt believed enough had been accomplished to declare political victory. When Dewey, newly elected as governor, appointed a commission to study industrial conditions in New York, FDR sent a note to his administrative assistant David Niles: "Please check supervision over unemployment in New York City. . . . Between Fiorello and the U.S. Government we have decreased unemployment from 400,000 to 280,000 and we are progressing rapidly. I think we can show Dewey up in this first attempt of his to make political Kudos."[12]

Tens of thousands of New Yorkers owed their wartime employment to this extraordinary intervention into the political economy of war production. But the very singularity of the episode portended trouble: New York's public officials had been able to capitalize upon the city's demographic and economic centrality, the relative weakness of a military-industrial complex still in the early stages of its development, and the sympathy and responsiveness of key federal officials. (If ever there was a time when reality matched Roosevelt's image of La Guardia "wangling" millions of dollars out of the federal government through a skillful presentation of his city's problems, this was it.) In later years, when these conditions were attenuated or absent, New York would be all but shut out of the defense economy—and thereby precluded from one of the most important sources of local economic growth in postwar America. But in 1942, New Yorkers had marshaled their ample political resources effectively; and thus did the Great Depression finally come to an end in New York, more than two years after prosperity had returned to the rest of urban America.[13]

II

As New York's economy recovered, the cost of living replaced joblessness and economic decline at the center of the city's politics. Government spending enabled the American economy to operate at full capacity, which raised the cost of labor and other factors of production; the curtailment of consumer production and the disruption of international trade on the one hand and growing consumer purchasing power on the other opened up an inflationary gap between the supply of consumer goods and civilian demand for them. Beginning in 1942 and 1943, the Second World War arrived in New York in the form of shortages, rising prices, black markets, rationing, lease termination notices, and lower-quality consumer goods.[14]

Both the range of actions open to local officials to meet these conditions and the incentives for them to do so would be shaped by the development of the national government's anti-inflation program. Roosevelt and his policy advisers did not build their own program upon the capacities of local governments, as they had done with the New Deal works programs in the thirties; in fact, they made a reasoned decision to avoid doing so. But as conditions forced them toward a more interventionist policy, and as congressional opposition narrowed the range of approaches available to them, they developed a program the features of which gave local officials an informal role in its enforcement, and which stimulated the development of a vital, neighborhood-based consumer movement—in turn providing local constituencies for vigorous municipal action in defense of "fair prices." La Guardia, his own activities deriving from and responding to the national government's anti-inflation efforts, would engage in a kitchen-table politics with few parallels in modern American political history, insinuating the city government still further into New Yorkers' daily lives in visible and traceable ways. "People who used to think of the mayor as a colorful fellow who rushed around to fires and meetings kicking up a fuss about this and that," one wartime essayist wrote, "now know him much more intimately as someone who can and will help them solve their everyday problems."[15]

Roosevelt, leaning on the experience of the First World War, feared the tendency of inflation to deharmonize the national economy. Once prices were out of joint, resources would be misallocated and social groups rendered discontent; if costs became unpredictable, businesses would be shy to enter into war production contracts and speculators would be tempted to withhold "essential raw materials." "Economic chaos," as Roosevelt called it, would threaten to disrupt war production, to increase the cost of the war, and to demoralize the home front by the depreciation of wages, savings, and pensions. The experience of the Great War, he believed, had illustrated both the necessity of a vigorous anti-inflation policy and the incapacity of the federal government to pursue such a policy. "Most of us went through the World War period and we [saw] a very vicious upward spiral," he told reporters two weeks after the invasion of France. "Well, it was caused by a lack of knowledge of how to do things on a big scale. We, none of us, knew. We were completely inexperienced during 1917 and 1918." In May 1940, he enlisted the New Deal economist Leon Henderson and the consumer advocate Harriet Elliott to monitor wholesale and retail prices, respectively. This was, in Roosevelt's eyes, primarily an effort to build knowledge—Henderson and Elliott would be doing "more a statistical job than anything else for the time being." But as inflationary pressures continued to build, Henderson's agency obtained operational powers.[16]

From the fall of France until shortly after Pearl Harbor, Roosevelt's anti-inflation program entailed selective administration of wholesale prices. Henderson's Office of Price Administration and Civilian Supply (OPACS, later simply OPA) focused more on ensuring "smooth production" than on restraining the cost of living. Because the OPA lacked statutory authority, compliance with its price schedules was voluntary, attained by moral suasion, the prospect of bad publicity, and the threat of withholding government business. The agency's lack of enforcement mechanisms "limited the field of enforceable price control to those basic commodities which were dealt in by a relatively few buyers or sellers" (most notably steel); the OPA exercised as yet no direct control over consumer goods. Henderson and his top aides, primarily economists, resisted the idea of a general freeze—proposed most prominently by the financier Bernard Baruch—because they thought it overly "simplistic" for their task: they were reluctant to surrender the use of market pricing as a means of matching supply and demand, and they believed discretionary price increases were useful for boosting output. Fiscal policy aimed at curbing consumer demand, Henderson believed, should do the heavy lifting in the anti-inflation effort.[17]

After Pearl Harbor, the OPA gained statutory enforcement powers, consumer goods came under its purview, and the idea of a general price freeze gained popularity. Prices had risen steadily from the fall of France through Pearl Harbor and continued rising in the early months of 1942, and they promised to climb faster as America went on total war footing and the remaining Depression-era slack was taken out of the industrial economy. In January 1942, passage of the Emergency Price Control Act (proposed by Roosevelt the previous July) gave the OPA legal authority to control prices and rents, ending the period of voluntarism, consultation, and persuasion. Shortly thereafter the agency initiated its first rationing program, encompassing mostly goods rendered scarce by the disruption of international shipping and justified as a way of ensuring the "equitable distribution of commodities in short supply." Two months later, Roosevelt held a series of interdepartmental meetings "in order to map out a full scale Administration program against inflation." The results were made public in April, when the president asked in a message to Congress and a fireside chat for a broad anti-inflation program, which would include general price and wage stabilization as well as fiscal measures such as high taxes, restrictions on credit and installment buying, and an aggressive (but voluntary) savings program to curb civilian demand.

The OPA responded immediately, placing price ceilings on many consumer goods: under its General Maximum Price Regulation ("General Max"), retailers were to take the highest price they had charged for an item in March 1942 as the ceiling price for that item. The National War Labor Board followed suit several months later, when it issued its "Little Steel" decision, which made it federal policy to prevent industrial wages from rising more than 15 percent above their January 1941 levels. But the fiscal measures Roosevelt requested of the Congress would not materialize; it was October before Congress passed the Revenue Act of 1942, and even then it provided for less than half of the $7.6 billion in new taxes Roosevelt had deemed necessary. The political failure of Roosevelt's tax program forced the administration to rely more heavily than it had wished upon price and wage controls; in turn, the system of controls developed after

Roosevelt's April 1942 messages proved inadequate to the task. With many farm products effectively exempted from price control, food prices continued to rise. So did wages—for the National War Labor Board had jurisdiction only in cases where wages were disputed. The Stabilization Act of 1942, passed at Roosevelt's insistence in October, addressed these problems by extending price controls to 90 percent of food products and giving the president the authority to stabilize all wages. And yet prices continued to climb—at least in part because shoppers, not knowing exactly what a particular retailer had charged for a given item in March 1942, did not know when they were being asked to pay above-ceiling prices.

In early 1943, key White House allies made it clear to Roosevelt and his administrators that General Max was not meeting the standards they sought in a price control program. The War Labor Board's "Little Steel" policy had made the cost of living an issue of primary importance to the labor movement: with the pay envelope practically fixed, increases in the cost of living steadily ate away at the wage gains workers had made in the first two years of the defense production boom. In March 1943, AFL president William Green and CIO president Philip Murray visited Roosevelt at the White House and asked him to abandon the Little Steel policy, citing "protests from their members in all parts of the country covering complaints of high prices, the presence of black markets and the apparent lack of action by Federal authorities to prevent the sale at high prices of bootleg items." ILGWU president David Dubinsky did likewise. And it was the failure of General Max that first focused La Guardia's attention on federal price control policy. At the end of 1942, New York experienced an acute meat shortage, with black markets springing up across the city. La Guardia formed a committee (which he chaired) to "ascertain the facts from the time the animal arrives in New York . . . right through to the moment it is sold to the consumer." The committee found that violation of OPA regulations was "the rule and not the exception" and that, as a result, consumers were practically defenseless against high wartime prices. La Guardia sent the findings to the OPA and the Department of Agriculture and hastened to Washington to confer in person with their principals.[18]

The accumulation of pressure forced Roosevelt to revise the federal price control program once more. On April 8, 1943, the president issued what became known as his "Hold-the-Line" order, severely limiting the authority of both the OPA and the War Labor Board to grant further price and wage increases. "The practical consequence," the OPA's official historian writes, "was to strengthen the hands of stabilization officials, especially in OPA and NWLB, by reducing their discretion. . . . The 'Hold-the-Line' Order marked a turning point in OPA operations, legally, psychologically, and administratively." The Hold-the-Line order coincided with two other major changes in OPA policy. First, the agency introduced rationing for many domestically produced food products by concocting a system of "point rationing." Under this system, each person received forty-eight ration "points" each month to spend however he or she liked on goods that were assigned point values based on their scarcity—essentially demonetarizing the purchase of many basic consumer goods. Second, the OPA established standardized, dollar-and-cent community ceiling prices for each item. Under dollar-and-cent ceilings (for which La Guardia had been pushing since the meat inquiry), there would no longer be any confusion as to what the legal price was: armed with ceiling-price charts—posted in stores and distributed to individual shoppers by consumer councils and later by the OPA itself—consumers could more easily enforce the ceilings by simply refusing to pay more than the legal price.[19]

By April 1943, Roosevelt's anti-inflation program looked very different from what had been in place at the time of Pearl Harbor. The combination of fiscal management and technocratic price administration Henderson had envisioned had been replaced by a regime that froze market prices and wages as they reflected supply and demand at particular moments in the past and used ration coupons rather than private purchasing power to apportion many consumer items. Hold-the-Line proved remarkably successful at preventing inflation—prices remained essentially flat from mid-1943 through the end of the war—but by suspending market mechanisms in order to hold down the cost of living and allocate goods more equitably, it created new problems. How would ceiling prices actually be enforced? What could be done to help consumers live with the dislocations and frustrations that would result? Could the agency sustain popular support for a program predicated on sacrifice?

Unlike the New Deal works programs, the OPA was not intergovernmental by design; in fact, OPA officials, fearing that subnational governments would be "drawn into a competition in leniency when supply shortages grew acute," had sought to minimize reliance on states and localities for enforcement. And yet the Hold-the-Line regime was designed in such a way as to open up a broad terrain for local governmental action. Two of the OPA's most pressing tasks under Hold-the-Line, enforcement and what might be called consumer empowerment, were tasks the local governments were singularly equipped to carry out, as even a national state builder like Leon Henderson recognized. ("It is only cooperation such as you have furnished," he admitted to La Guardia in May 1942, "that makes price regulation a living thing.") By assuming local functions without displacing them, Hold-the-Line enabled local officials to tinker with, articulate, and elaborate upon the basic structure the national government had put in place.[20]

The Hold-the-Line regime also helped to mobilize a powerful constituency for local governmental action—grassroots consumer organizations. The simple fact that the federal government had finally created a strong price control system served to organize grassroots activism that had previously been unorganized and diffuse: by making effective collective action seem possible, the Hold-the-Line regime provided consumers with incentives to organize. An official in a Bronx consumers group explained to reporters how her club had sprung to life as she and her neighbors were sitting in a local park with their baby carriages: "The main topic of conversation was the high cost of living and how our food dealers were failing to observe ceiling prices. We got so mad we decided to do something about it, and the Mosholu Consumers Group was the result." At the end of 1943, Brooklyn boasted thirty-five neighborhood consumers' councils, "not one of which was in existence two years ago," the chairman of the Crown Heights Consumer Council noted. Similar sentiments impelled housewives to join one of the 135 consumer interest committees organized by New York's Civil Defense Volunteer Organization. This grassroots mobilization elevated the cost of living to the center of urban politics and created a constituency not only for the OPA but for anyone who would work effectively on these issues. Parallel to this, the War Labor Board's wage stabilization policy had made the cost of living a key issue for organized labor. The social democratic and Second Popular Front labor unions aligned with the CIO especially made "the control of living costs" their top priority. Union workers and the broader labor left joined housewives to form a strong alliance in support of cost-of-living politics.[21]

It was "not the function of the City of New York" to enforce federal price control regulations, La Guardia admitted; but he resolved to do so anyway. In the aftermath of the meat inquiry, the Little Flower wrote the OPA and the Department of Agriculture offering to have his Department of Markets enforce price ceilings in New York. Federal officials, who did not yet have a viable enforcement system of their own, did nothing to dissuade him. In the early months of the Hold-the-Line regime, local enforcement required a degree of ingenuity. The city did not yet possess the legal authority to enforce ceiling prices, but it did have a law protecting consumers against short weighting and short measuring. La Guardia explained over the radio that shoppers could lodge complaints with the Bureau of Weights and Measures against merchants for selling too little at a given price rather than overcharging for a given quantity. Complaints started coming in, and the city began issuing summonses—1,370 on a particularly busy Saturday—and collecting fines; a group of Bronx merchants promptly subjected the city to an injunction action. Shortly, the State War Council (which had an enabling grant from the legislature to enact emergency war measures) rescued the city from legal limbo by giving OPA regulations the force of state law, which permitted the city to use the magistrates' courts for cases involving retailers. The city adopted a three-strike policy: the Department of Markets first issued a warning, then sought a fine, and finally pursued a jail sentence. (Cases involving wholesalers were referred to the OPA.) Later, La Guardia posted the names and addresses of three-time offenders in the Department of Markets and invited civic organizations to come and copy them down. By the end of 1944, the city was placing market inspectors on the premises of repeat offenders, just as it stationed police officers in hotels suspected of being houses of ill repute. All things considered, New York's commissioner of Markets claimed proudly that Gotham "was the foundation on which OPA modeled its enforcement throughout the country," though in fact few cities came close to matching New York's enforcement effort.[22]

La Guardia also encouraged the consumers groups that provided the first line of enforcement (and that were later enlisted en masse by the OPA to serve as volunteer price wardens). Like most liberals with sensitive political antennae, he was wary of allying with the more militant groups, which had been stigmatized, in blatantly misogynistic fashion, as "snoopers." (OPA deputy administrator John Kenneth Galbraith, who favored paid inspectors, once remarked that he hoped price regulation would not be enforced by a "Gestapo of volunteer housewives.") But by 1944, La Guardia was encouraging the neighborhood consumer councils by publicizing their successes at getting repeat offenders punished. To the councils, which devoted great effort to showing their neighbors that price control could be effective (staging parades and other such events to celebrate victories in the magistrates' courts), garnering mention during La Guardia's weekly radio broadcast was both a source of validation and a powerful recruiting tool.[23]

La Guardia also mobilized the local government and his own informal political power to help New Yorkers negotiate consumer goods markets. In so doing, he took advantage of the rise in price-consciousness the OPA had helped to create. This price-consciousness was in part a direct byproduct of the design of the Hold-the-Line policy—what political scientists refer to as an "informational" policy feedback effect. It was also fostered by the OPA's efforts, particularly under Chester Bowles (who had a considerably better understanding than did his predecessors of "the ability of the average citizens to help him carry out his program"), to involve, educate, and empower housewives, workers, and the salariat—its natural constituencies. Beginning in late 1943, the OPA recruited hundreds of thousands of housewives to serve as volunteer price-checkers in their communities. High-profile figures, beginning with Eleanor Roosevelt, lent visibility to the anti-inflation effort by signing pledges to pay no more than ceiling prices. The OPA's Division of Information distributed pamphlets, brochures, and public programs ("Economics on the Home Front," "Home Maker's Course in Wartime Food Buying"), which aimed to help families live under Hold-the-Line and to convert people into what the historian Lizabeth Cohen has termed "citizen consumers"—consumers who understood the impact of their purchasing decisions and who bore in mind larger social objectives when making their purchases.[24]

As in the 1930s, grassroots mobilization and local state expansion worked symbiotically. Searching for ways to deal with wartime dislocations, consumers looked to the government for information of use in their everyday lives. La Guardia directed his commissioner of Markets to have "all of [his] personnel devote all of their time to aid the consumer in the war food situation." With civilian defense volunteers replacing the WPA workers who had collected market data in the 1930s, the New York City Department of Markets continued to broadcast market information daily over WNYC and now augmented its reports with "rationing news and recipes for plentiful and seasonable foods," information on OPA regulations, and, on Tuesdays, advice from nutrition experts on how to cook healthy meals using what was available and affordable. The New York Civilian Defense Volunteer Organization, in conjunction with several of the labor unions, held courses in consumer education so that neighborhood leaders might "pass the knowledge along to the community." The Department of Markets also distributed recipe booklets and gave free cooking classes in which housewives were "advised on the use of their ration points . . . and the substitution of plentiful, reasonable foods in place of scarce and expensive ones." In advance of the Jewish high holidays in 1943, department workers created an exhibition in the Essex Street municipal market to demonstrate to Lower East Side housewives how less expensive saltwater fish could be used in place of the usual freshwater yellow pike and carp to prepare gefilte fish.[25]

Above all, La Guardia used the radio to communicate directly with the city's purchasers. Following his ouster from the OCD, frustrated by the editorial abuse he had taken, he had stopped speaking to print reporters (sometimes for months at a time) and, in a Rooseveltian attempt to go over the heads of the newspapers, had begun a series of thirty-minute broadcasts that aired on Sunday afternoons over the municipal radio station. He called them "Talks to the People," and he opened and closed each broadcast with a phrase he had apparently picked up during a meeting of the Permanent Joint Board on Defense: "Patience and Fortitude."

Unlike Roosevelt, La Guardia was not a natural radio talent. His high-pitched voice could become shrill when he grew animated; when he tried to restrain himself, he tended to speak at a laboriously slow tempo and with a herky-jerky rhythm. The format and setting of the Sunday WNYC broadcasts, however, helped him find his own distinctive radio style: he was peppery, melodramatic, ebullient, and theatrical, and his talks were both informative and highly entertaining. The broadcasts seemed to satisfy a desire for a common civic culture in wartime, and to the dismay of New York Democrats—who tried to cut off funding for WNYC because it had become so effective a political tool for the mayor—as well as some prim-and-proper fusionists (one of whom lamented the Little Flower's "radio exhibitionism"), La Guardia won a large and unusually responsive radio audience. (One Tammany district leader glumly reported that his own mother was a devoted listener.) By the spring of 1945, his broadcasts were drawing audiences of 2 million each Sunday afternoon.[26]

Along with news from the war fronts and his eternal crusade against vice and gambling, food became a fixture of La Guardia's broadcasts. Only when he devoted the entire broadcast to a particular subject—the municipal budget, his city health insurance plan, the Atlantic Charter—did he not spend at least a few minutes discussing the price and supply of food in the city. Especially in the early days of point rationing, New Yorkers wrote in with questions about OPA procedures, and La Guardia answered them on air. He provided his audience with information on what was plentiful, what the ceilings were for various products, and what constituted good ration-point values. He collected recipes using ingredients that were low in cost and point value—*pasta e fagioli*, mutton pie—to read over the air. He was soon influencing kitchen-table fare across the New York metropolitan area.

The size and loyalty of La Guardia's "following of consumers" (as the New Jersey state secretary of agriculture described the Little

Flower's regular audience) enabled him to intervene in markets in ways few other local officials could. In March 1944, for instance, he decided the OPA's price ceilings for eggs were too high and enlisted the help of New York's housewives to bring them down:

> I told you about butter and eggs. Eggs should be selling about 7 c. below ceiling prices. By the way, do you see how we brought those egg prices down[?] That shows that you and I can work together. If we just hold off from buying, it will bring the prices down.

His radio following also provided a means of increasing the flow of food into the New York market—a way of offsetting the disadvantage he believed New York's strenuous enforcement efforts created. In 1945, he dispatched a telegram to the South Carolina Peach Growers' Association: HOPE CROP IS BIG AND THAT YOU WILL SEE TO IT THAT YOUR REPRESENTATIVES, JOBBERS AND WHOLESALERS IN NEW YORK CITY WILL SELL AT LAWFUL OPA WHOLESALE PRICES. IF YOU DO THAT I WILL PLUG AND BOOST YOUR PEACHES AND CAN ASSURE YOU OF A GOOD MARKET.[27]

As he had during the New Deal, La Guardia frequently pressed the national administrators of the OPA to amend their policies to make the program function more smoothly and to relieve pressures in New York and the other big cities. Much as he had once written to Hopkins that he could not "carry the ball" for the WPA by himself, he now wrote to OPA director Prentiss Brown, "I am doing all I can but need help." He was compelled to intervene, too, because the OPA created local political pressures and because New Yorkers had come to believe he could address problems which were by any reasonable calculation beyond the function of local government. ("Well, of course, the mayor is blamed for everything," La Guardia quipped during a beef shortage. "I suppose I will have to go out West and start a social bureau and introduce some of the bulls to the mamma cows, if it keeps up at this rate.")

He typically committed a minute or two of his Sunday broadcasts, usually following his market reports, to riffing on OPA policy and making minor recommendations to federal OPA officials. ("Here, Mr. OPA, is something for you, and we have the facts.") "It takes them about a year and a half . . . to follow [my] suggestions," he chirped on one broadcast. In telegrams, letters, and personal conferences with the heads of the OPA, the Department of Agriculture, and the Office of Economic Stabilization, he made a number of more far-reaching suggestions: allocate food supplies by district; expand the subsidy program; allow the value of ration coupons to fluctuate according to market conditions; permit custom slaughtering so that meat retailers could bypass middlemen. Some of these larger suggestions were adopted, but they were more often found unworkable, for they were frequently conceived from the parochial vantagepoint of the city or else required disruptions to the standard channels of distribution in excess of what the OPA would tolerate.[28]

III

Officially, the OPA was an emergency program tasked with preventing economic dislocation and ensuring equitable wartime sacrifice that was intended to last for the duration of the inflationary period—the war and reconversion. But because many Americans viewed price control as a recognition by the government of their "right" to quality goods at fair prices, it also sparked popular claims on the state that imbued it with a more expansive purpose. From the beginning, many sympathetic liberal policymakers viewed the OPA as a means to work toward long-desired interventions in the market economy. As conservatives well recognized, what was officially a wartime economic stabilization program jumped the tracks to become a species of New Deal reform.

Seldom was this political aspect of the OPA on more vivid display than in the enactment of what would prove the agency's most enduring legacy in New York: rent control. In most American cities, the OPA imposed rent control (capping rents at March 1942 levels) in order to meet the genuine housing crises that followed the inundation of war boom cities by industrial workers. Labor unions and tenants' organizations often pushed hard for the institution of OPA rent control (and property owners' associations often fought it bitterly), but it was beyond question that the severe pressure on housing markets in the big cities put inflationary pressure on the national economy: whatever local passions it had stirred up, rent control could in most instances be justified in purely economic terms. This was not the case in New York.

The five boroughs had experienced a modest housing shortage since the mid-1930s, the result of slow construction during the depression and the WPA's demolition of old-law tenements. But because New York was not a war boom city, the vacancy rate remained relatively high during the early forties and rents rose very little above their prewar levels. Had the restraint of inflation been the only consideration, the OPA would not have been justified in extending rent control to New York—at least not when it did. The imposition of rent control in New York was essentially a *political* event; it occurred because local officials responded to the desire of their constituents for the protecting hand of government in their relations with property owners.[29]

Like the OPA's retail price ceilings, the mere existence of a national rent control program served to generate popular demands upon local officials: because a potential solution existed, tenants and their supporters had something concrete to ask for. Most working-class New Yorkers had not actually been much affected by the war rental market; rather, they seized upon the OPA as an instrument for addressing longtime grievances. Few neighborhoods embraced the idea of rent control as fully as Harlem, which possessed strong traditions of both tenant activism and landlord dereliction. The best studies at the time suggested that federal rent control would have no real effect on Harlem, where rents had always been high but had not risen substantially during the war and hence would not be affected by a program that capped rents at 1942 or 1943 levels. "[T]o urge such control as a 'cure' or even as a palliative," the housing reformer Charles Abrams suggested, "would simply be another extension of the type of measure that promises rather than performs and which, in the end, leaves the problem where it was before, or worse." Even so, Harlem organizations such as Adam Clayton Powell, Jr.'s, People's Committee, the Consolidated Tenants League, and the National Negro Congress demanded rent control, moved by the sense that something good would ultimately come of government intervention in the landlord-tenant relationship. They were joined by union leaders (especially those affiliated with the CIO), by the American Labor Party, and by tenant groups in other working-class neighborhoods.[30]

They were also joined by middle-income tenants, the only segment of the local housing market actually affected by the war mobilization. As unemployment dried up, as high wartime taxes prompted the affluent to relocate to more modest apartments, and as Army and Navy men and war bureaucrats moved into the city, housing became very difficult to find in middle-class areas such as the West Bronx, Bay Ridge, Flatbush, and much of Queens. Some small property owners, faced with rising property taxes and operating costs (and in many cases eager to make a return on investments which had taken a hit during the depression), declined to adhere to the policy of voluntary rent control the real estate community had put in place to ward off government rent regulation. Increasingly, they deferred repairs, turned off boilers, raised rents, or issued eviction notices. Letters addressed to La Guardia's office evinced a growing anti-landlord sentiment. Placed in a position of power, the writers charged, landlords had become "arrogant and arbitrary"; they held "a virtual sway of life and death over their tenants" and demanded higher rents for the continuation of basic services. "When in the name of Heaven is this dirty business going to stop[?]" one Brooklyn Navy Yard worker demanded to know.[31]

By mid-July 1943, the idea of rent control had attained broad popular support. In the months that followed, La Guardia said little to indicate that he aimed finally to make good on his long-held belief that housing should be regulated as a public utility; property owners, then up in arms over high property taxes, might have been pushed into open opposition by a landlord-baiting campaign. But he was nevertheless orchestrating public opinion in order to convince the OPA to extend rent control to New York. On July 15, he formally petitioned the OPA to do so. OPA officials denied the request, citing Bureau of Labor Statistics data that plainly showed no general rise in rents to justify it.

But the issue would not go away. On August 1, the shooting of an African American serviceman by a New York City police officer in Harlem precipitated a wave of destruction, looting, and violence which ultimately cost six lives and some $5 million in property damage. Most leftists and many liberals pointed to the high cost of living as a root cause of community dissatisfaction and proposed rent control as a countermeasure. Two weeks later, with the city's traditional "moving day" of October 1 approaching and two thirds of the leases in the city due for renewal, La Guardia told the listeners of his radio broadcast:

> [A]ll tenants who are receiving notices of termination of lease
> [so the apartments could be rented to new tenants at higher
> rents] or who have received notice of increased rent, please

inform the Mayor's Committee on Rent, Department of Housing and Buildings, or if you cannot remember that address, just write me a letter giving me the facts. . . . I want to keep all the records up to September 1st, when I've arranged for another conference with the OPA in Washington on the subject of rent. It costs so much to move. . . . That is something I fear our friends in Washington do not quite understand.[32]

At the end of September, following another round of meetings and the completion of two more surveys, the OPA announced that it would extend federal rent control to New York effective November 1. Landlords and renters alike understood that the decision did not entail simply a neutral effort to restrict national inflation. "The whole things smacks of a political pay-off—the New Deal owes the Mayor a few favors," claimed the Taxpayers Association of Greater New York's monthly magazine. One Brooklyn renter wrote: "I hope that you will not leave City Hall in 1945, as you are the only person to whom the plain people can look for guidance and protection." This was how most of those moved to write La Guardia viewed the new federal policy the city government had secured: as a salutary source of government protection in the relationship between renters and owners.[33]

Unlike price control, which would be phased out in 1946 and 1947 following a concerted attack by business and agricultural interests and the conservative coalition that ruled the 79th Congress, rent control would live on in New York after the war. In the context of a severe postwar housing shortage, Congress would enact the Federal Housing and Rent Act of 1947, continuing rent control for buildings constructed before February 1, 1947; two years later, it would pass another measure giving states the authority "to assume administrative control" of the existing rent regulation program—thus devolving the function of rent regulation to the states. Under heavy pressure from downstate politicians and tenant, consumer, and labor advocates (and amidst a housing shortage considerably more acute than what had existed in 1943), the New York State legislature would enact a rent regulation program that closely followed the OPA's. By the time the postwar shortage finally abated, rent regulation had become "politically sacrosanct." It has been a feature of the New York City housing market ever since, though its original universalism has long since eroded.[34]

III

Beginning in late 1942, La Guardia resolved to cash in his remaining credits with Roosevelt for a part in the war effort. He now yearned to be sent to Europe or the Pacific with a military commission—he was, as the columnist for *PM* Max Lerner put it, practically sprouting epaulets. Whenever anyone asked why he would trade the political leadership of New York for a secondary military position, La Guardia replied that he considered the war all-important. He had limited patience with the argument, advanced in the press, by his friends, and by people close to the White House, that he could make a greater contribution to the war effort in New York than he could in uniform. The idea of military valor retained a strong hold on the old Army brat, and he could not stand the thought that the fate of civilization was being decided in Europe and the Pacific while he attended to municipal housekeeping in New York.[35]

He was also ready to leave the mayoralty. The contraction of resources produced by the demobilization of the New Deal works programs and the ever-continuing decline of property tax yields (and by La Guardia's shortsighted and transparently political request, shortly before the 1941 election, that the city sales tax be cut from

2 percent to 1 percent) had rendered the annual budget-making process utter agony. And the remarkable assemblage of talent that had populated La Guardia's first two administrations had been depleted. La Guardia's ever-worsening lack of self-restraint had caused the city to lose the services of Clendenin Ryan and James Kieran of the Mayor's Office and Commissioner of Markets William Fellowes Morgan, Jr., among others. The war had claimed others: more than one in ten municipal employees had taken military leave, as had many top officials—among them, Brehon Somervell of the New York City WPA, Gerard Swope of the Housing Authority, budget director Kenneth Dayton, and corporation counsel William Chanler. La Guardia wrote to a friend that he was surprised anything was getting done at all, with "so many of the more brilliant members of my official family . . . in the service."[36]

La Guardia started talking with Roosevelt about an Army position a little over a week after Allied troops landed in French North Africa in November 1942. When La Guardia remarked that he "just could not stand it if he didn't get into uniform," the president replied (so he later told Harold Ickes) that the mayor was "too old and too fat; that he could not possibly fly an airplane as he had done during the last war." Apparently this was merely an ice-breaker, for La Guardia found the subsequent discussion "very satisfactory" and believed that he and the president were "thinking along the same lines." Roosevelt proposed that La Guardia be made a brigadier general and sent to North Africa, "where he will be engaged constantly in sending propaganda to Italy," thereafter to follow the Allied invasion into Italy behind the lines.[37]

His military commission awaiting Allied progress in North Africa, La Guardia's anticipation grew intense. On February 3, 1943, he sent the following note, in longhand, to the president, who had recently returned from his Casablanca conference with Churchill:

My dear Chief:—

Welcome home! It was great—even the most chronic anti-newdealers here are admitting the trip did a tremendous amount of good and are expressing admiration for your great contribution.

You had us all guessing and worrying for several days.

I still believe General Eisenhower—can not get along without me and am awaiting your order (but as a soldier)—

Food, man-power, prices & wages are still our big troubles & headaches.—

Let me know how & when I can help.

I hope to see you soon.—in the meantime

Con Amore,
Fiorello[38]

On March 14, 1943, Stephen Early told the White House press corps that "all indications point[ed] to service in the Army for the Mayor." La Guardia was "bantering with the City Hall press corps about his imminent departure"; he announced the selection of three aides and was said to have decided on several others. Scores of people began writing City Hall asking to accompany the mayor to Italy, and longtime advisers sent other names to be considered. On March 15, the day after Early's statement, La Guardia met with Roosevelt in the White House to go over the assignment, since broadened from exclusively propaganda work to include administration of civil affairs in conquered areas of Italy. "I saw the Chief yesterday and I am so happy I can be of service to my country—besides cleaning the streets of New York City," he wrote to Harry Hopkins after the meeting. "I expect to get my medical exam next week. The Chief indicated that I should be commissioned right after I finish the executive budget in April." La Guardia even got measured for a uniform.[39]

Prominent civic figures inveighed against the appointment. "I can-

not hurrah for F.H.'s warlike spirit," C. C. Burlingham wrote to Judge
Seabury. "It is infantile and shows no true sense of proportion." But
it was Secretary of War Henry Stimson who fought the appointment
the hardest. News of La Guardia's imminent appointment had gotten
out while Stimson was on vacation, and though Stimson considered
La Guardia less objectionable than other "political generals"—the
Little Flower was "a very good citizen in spite of his defects of manner and speech," Stimson believed, and would "play the game as a
soldier pretty well"—he chose the La Guardia case to draw the line
against Roosevelt's "confounded happy-go-luckiness" in promising
generalships "without having any consultation with those of us who
are responsible for all those matters. . . ."[40]

The question of La Guardia's service was still undecided when, at
General Marshall's request, Stimson scheduled a meeting with La
Guardia for the morning of April 6. Stimson's memorandum to Roosevelt describes the content of the meeting: "As a friend I strongly
advised him to remain in his present pulpit of the mayoralty and to
use his influence with Italians from there; that his words would carry
much further if he was a civilian soldier rather than a make-believe
general." If he "insisted on being a soldier," he could accept a colonelcy and enter officer training school at Charlottesville, Virginia. La
Guardia told Stimson that he understood General Eisenhower had
asked for him personally. Stimson replied that "he was mistaken:
that I had looked into it personally and that Eisenhower didn't want
him in Africa until the fighting was over." Crestfallen, La Guardia
concluded that "that ended it[,] for he wouldn't dream of going if he
was not wanted by Eisenhower."[41]

As Stimson expected, La Guardia tried to go over his head. Roosevelt phoned Marshall late that night "much perturbed" by a telephone talk he had had with New York's Little Flower. A few days
later he pulled Stimson aside after a cabinet meeting and told the
secretary that he had been too hard on La Guardia. "I think from

what he said that he gave himself away as having promised the man something beforehand," Stimson speculated. The next afternoon, Stimson returned from a horseback ride to find a stinging letter from Roosevelt answering point by point his memorandum relating the content of Stimson's meeting with La Guardia and defending the Little Flower's motives in seeking a commission:

> Frankly, I think you have this La Guardia business all wrong. . . .
>
> I do not like your second paragraph where in you suggested that he ought not to be a make-believe General. In the strict sense of the word, you have a great many make-believe Generals.
>
> I do not like your telling him about "insisting on being a soldier." You have taken in many people who felt they ought to serve in the Army in this war. La Guardia never insisted on being a soldier any more than they did. . . .
>
> In regards to Eisenhower wanting him, I don't think La Guardia had any thought that this meant going to Africa while the Tunis project is in operation. Eisenhower told me himself that he did want La Guardia for the next operation—not for the Tunis operation—and I think La Guardia understood this thoroughly. . . .
>
> I do not think that La Guardia wants "adventure." I think that is imputing a motive to him which is not strictly fair to him. Like most people with red blood, he does hope he can get war service.[42]

Stimson spent the better part of three days composing a conciliatory but unyielding response. It was largely for the record; beneath the stiff language of Roosevelt's letter lay the concession that La Guardia would not be made a general. The president did not wish to submit La Guardia's name to the Senate for confirmation, as gen-

eralships required, in defiance of the wishes of the secretary of war
and the chairman of the Joint Chiefs. La Guardia's only option was to
take the colonelcy and go to officer training school without a specific
assignment. Even he realized the absurdity of resigning as the wartime leader of America's largest city to become a common colonel.[43]

Embarrassed to concede defeat, La Guardia continued in a
pathetic manner. This to Roosevelt on June 6, again handwritten:

> *Dear Chief:—*
>   *Soldier La Guardia reports to the C. in C. that he awaits*
> *orders.—*
>   *He believes General Eisenhower needs him now more than ever.*
>   *F. H. La Guardia*
>   *Major U.S. Air Service, 1st W.W.*

Even those who had supported Stimson's effort to keep La Guardia
out of the Army found the mayor's humiliation difficult to watch. "I
really feel sorry about La Guardia," Harold Ickes wrote in his diary.
"I agree that he should not be sent into the Army as a general to
do propaganda, but he has been hurt on several occasions now by
an administration that owes him a good deal. . . . [The] succession
of these episodes must be hurting Fiorello tremendously." Stimson
himself found the work "very difficult and trying . . . because I had
to hurt the Mayor's feelings very deeply and he was very broken up.
I felt very sorry for him. . . ." "All of this trouble and sorrow," the
secretary thought, "was brought on by the weakness, nothing but the
weakness and happy-go-luckiness of the President."[44]

The next time the matter came up, in the fall of 1944, La Guardia
had better prospects. In the intervening months he had undertaken
a series of propaganda broadcasts beamed into Italy by the Office
of War Information and had become perhaps the most prominent
American advocate for recognition of the new Italian government

as an ally, both of which made him widely popular in Italy. Word of La Guardia's popularity was reaching America through letters from servicemen, which in turn built public support for the idea of sending the mayor to serve as a liaison between the Allied forces and the Italian government. Senator Ernest McFarland of Arizona, the recipient of one such serviceman's letter in November 1943, forwarded it to James Byrnes (now director of the Office of War Mobilization) with the suggestion that Roosevelt appoint La Guardia as an Allied administrator in Italy when the moment came. Byrnes wrote back that he would pass the information along to the president, appending a note: "The President regards Fiorella [sic] as one of his best friends and frequently sees him." The timing was also favorable: the Republican presidential candidate Thomas Dewey was then seeking to capitalize upon Italian American dissatisfaction with the administration's policy toward Italy, claiming that a vote for Dewey meant "helping reinstate Italy to the position she deserves." Thus, from a political perspective, the idea of appointing La Guardia to implement "a New Deal for Italy" had great appeal.[45]

With the end of the war approaching, Roosevelt wrote to Stimson, "I do not think that you and I can still say that he must remain as Mayor of New York." The Department of War still believed La Guardia's appointment would roil its relations with Congress, but the secretary decided he would no longer stand between La Guardia and a generalship. News broke via Drew Pearson's radio program in late September that Roosevelt and Churchill had agreed at their Quebec conference to commission La Guardia a brigadier general and place him as the top U.S. adviser to the Italian civilian government. Roosevelt did in fact intend to make La Guardia a brigadier general, although his assignment had not been pinned down with anything like the specificity Pearson's report indicated. On October 17, Roosevelt invited the Little Flower to the White House for a "long talk" that ended up running two and a half hours. The following day, La Guardia sent Roosevelt a letter saying that he did not want to go to Italy unless he would have full authority and "the President's complete backing and support and equal say with the British." La Guardia rejected the job, apparently because he believed it was not endowed with sufficient authority. "Either you're allowed to do something or you're not," he explained. "And I'm not going to Italy to sit on my fanny." This time, La Guardia at least had the satisfaction of declining the offer. But once again his ardent hope to play a meaningful part in the European theater had been dashed in full view of the public. "[O]ne wonders," Oswald Garrison Villard wrote sharply, "what has become of the Mayor's self-respect."[46]

Relations between the president and the mayor cooled palpably during the generalship saga. Once a more frequent visitor to the White House than many congressmen and some high-ranking administration officials, La Guardia set foot in the presidential office only once in 1944. The era of active collaboration that had begun during La Guardia's first year in office was all but over. But as the war came to a close, La Guardia would attempt to shape national policy in other ways. He would appear much more frequently before congressional committees, taking part in a robust discussion of how the government should prepare for the postwar period. Perhaps most notably, he would develop local programs that he hoped would serve as "examples" to other cities and even to the federal government. In the midst of the war, amid the quotidian details in which he had long since lost interest, La Guardia would lay plans to carry the New Deal era of urban reform into the postwar decades.

10

"I Hope Others Will Follow New York's Example"

eginning in earnest in mid-1943, when mobilization was far along and the war had begun to turn in the Allies' favor, Americans engaged in a long, multi-phased debate about what should be done with the governmental legacies of the New Deal and the Second World War. Policies such as work relief and price control had been undertaken on an emergency basis; and yet many citizens had come to value them. Should they be continued once the emergency had passed? Should the government's role as an employer of last resort, a producer of public wealth, a socializer of risk, and a protecting presence in the marketplace be extended into the postwar period? These questions were at the heart of the national discussion that began in 1943 and 1944 under the guise of "postwar planning," and continued through the fevered debates over the fate of the Office of Price Administration and the consideration of a group of progressive legislative initiatives which aimed, in effect, to extend the legacy of the New Deal.[1]

It was a notable feature of La Guardia's third term that he framed his municipal agenda with the intention of intervening in these national debates. He believed that if New York City, acting on the municipal scale, could demonstrate the feasibility and desirability of elements of the postwar liberal policy agenda, it could serve as an "example" to other political communities—including the nation itself. Encouraged by Roosevelt and other leading national progressives, he planned a slate of postwar public works projects meant to soak up unemployment during the reconversion period while laying down the physical infrastructure he believed necessary to the city's future as a global capital. He also initiated a local health insurance program intended to give New Yorkers access to comprehensive health care and protection from devastating medical expenses. Through these municipal undertakings, he sought not only to shape the contours of the postwar national state but also to carve out a role for subnational governments within the postwar liberal project. In short, he envisioned a progressive federal polity built upon the intergovernmental cooperation of the New Deal era.

The political contests of the 1940s and 1950s would preserve some essential features of the New Deal political order while rolling back others. The social insurance and categorical relief programs created by the Social Security Act would, for the time being, be accepted by the political mainstream. Congress would make only a modest frontal attack on the trade union movement where it already existed—though the sanctioning of state "right to work" laws would render the unionization of previously unorganized regions all but impossible. Stewardship of the national economy would become an accepted function of government, and the national state would continue to make massive investments in transportation infrastructure and the development of human capital (above all through the provisions of the Servicemen's Readjustment Act of 1944, commonly known as the

G.I. Bill). But other uses of national state power would not outlive the emergency period—including those which had been most central to the formation of New York City's local politics and government during the Roosevelt years, namely, intergovernmental public spending and national price control.[2]

One of the consequences of the postwar adjudication of the New Deal legacy was a withdrawal of federal resources from local public sectors. The postwar national state, like its New Deal predecessor would spend vigorously in pursuit of domestic social objectives, but quite differently: it would direct resources to different geographic areas, through different channels, and toward different ends. In an important sense, the urban New Deal would die just as the suburban New Deal—with its complex of subsidies and middle-class entitlements, divvied out with far less visibility—was poised to take off. National social spending would go increasingly to the supply of private goods (such as private housing, family insurance plans, and the like), provided not by governments but by private and quasi-public organizations.[3]

The New Deal had transformed New York City's local polity in ways that left it stronger yet also vulnerable. In the short term, the withdrawal of federal resources stimulated the development of the city's local state: as the national government ceased to build public markets, to renovate parks, to staff health clinics and public libraries, and to regulate rents, local and state officials would move to fill the vacancy. The rise and fall of the New Deal intergovernmental state had thus prepared the way for a robust local social politics which, sustained by the political forces the New Deal had brought into being and underwritten by the city's immense postwar affluence, would continue to shape New York's public life for decades after Roosevelt and La Guardia passed from the scene.

I

Christmastime of 1940 saw the dedication of the Fort Greene Health Center, one of the last PWA-financed public buildings opened in New York before the war. Addressing the city officials, borough notables, and curious neighborhood residents gathered for the occasion in the building's auditorium, La Guardia made note of the fact that the ribbon-cuttings and cornerstone-layings which had been so much a part of the city's civic life in the thirties would soon be stopped on account of the war. It was "a pity," the mayor said, that the progress of the nation and indeed of the world had been halted by the "rash, unnecessary and irresponsible acts of just a few individuals." But already he was thinking of ways in which the march of progress might be jump-started following the war.

> [W]hile we have no illusions as to the possibility of continuing the vast public works program in this or other cities, we have learned a lesson from the last war and plans should be made now as to what exactly we must do after the national defense program is completed . . . so that when this unhappy period is over all that will be necessary will be to reach out and go to work. At no time must the growth and the development of progress end in our country.[4]

From the time the war turned in the Allies' favor in 1943, few subjects engaged the attention of the American home front as fully as "postwar planning"—the ubiquitous term for making all manner of preparations for the reconversion period. Some who urged national planning, including La Guardia, were moved by the memory of the end of the First World War, which had been followed by a period of economic dislocation and, several years later, by a deep recession; some feared that a demobilized economy would simply return to its

prewar doldrums. But the planning impulse also drew energy from
the nearly universal conviction that the postwar world, whatever it
would look like, would be very different. With so much seemingly
up for grabs, groups ranging from the National Association of Manufacturers to the CIO viewed the postwar planning moment as an
opportunity to present the best arguments for their own visions of
how American society should be organized: what kind of economy
would best ensure prosperity, security, and freedom and what kind
of society would best reflect and conform with American values.[5]

The idea of postwar planning appealed deeply to La Guardia's
sense of himself as a visionary. The exercise of postwar planning
satisfied his urge to participate in the solving of great national problems despite being shut out of the war effort while also affording
him an opportunity to extend his legacy. After Pearl Harbor, the
Little Flower formed a blue-ribbon study group to survey the entire
question of postwar reconstruction, including under that rubric
a wide variety of subjects: employment, infrastructure, tax policy,
transportation, housing, immigration, education, health care, and
problems relating specifically to industry, manufacturing, and small
business. He aspired, he said, to prepare a postwar program which
would furnish his successors for two or three administrations with
"a complete, well studied, well-rounded planned public improvement program covering every civic, social, health, traffic and safety
requirement insofar as intelligent planning and predictable funds
make it possible."[6]

New Deal–style public investment came to dominate La Guardia's
postwar program, for several reasons. First, he feared that demobilization would see the return of mass unemployment. "I tell you now,"
he wrote Florida senator Claude Pepper in mid-1942, "that unless we
are ready and know exactly what to do after the war, all the effort,
all the sacrifice, all the loss of life will not have been worth while.
Hell will break loose in such a way that it will take generations to

recover." These were widely held concerns, particularly in the early years of the war, before deferred purchasing power had accumulated. "When war contracts are withdrawn, the danger is that the entire edifice will topple over," a Senate committee under the chairmanship of Harry Truman concluded. "Unless an economic substitute is found for war contracts, mass unemployment will become a serious threat, and the number of unemployed men and women . . . could easily surpass anything that was dreamed of during the last depression." Wartime morale studies found that workers expected demobilization to plunge the nation back into economic stagnation. They believe everything "is going to be worse after the war," one study reported. "There won't be any work, people will be crippled, and in hospitals, and on welfare. Factories will close up, there'll be nothing to produce."[7]

Second, the idea of public investment continued to hold strong appeal. As the major world city least stricken by the war and the largest city in the nation that was already beginning to organize the postwar world, New York stood poised to emerge as a truly global metropolis—the capital of the nascent "American century." The city crackled with energy and anticipation as perhaps at no other point in its history, and New Yorkers were quick to conceive of ways to take advantage of the opportunities that lay at their doorstep. "What we are going to build will be vital to the continuance of the largest and most dynamic city in the world," La Guardia suggested.

> We want to make it an even better City than we have now. We want the workers and their children, the mothers and old people to live more healthful, wholesome lives, and to enjoy more advantages than the present generation. And we want business and industry to operate more efficiently and economically. . . . We have a big program, but it is not too big for the New York which is going to emerge from this war.

La Guardia's program divided the city's civic and economic elite. The Citizens Budget Commission fought it tooth-and-nail, arguing that La Guardia's "grandiose" proposals "threatened the City with financial chaos." The *New York Times*, on the other hand, lauded the mayor for "look[ing] forward confidently to great days coming for the community and for America." For ordinary New Yorkers, the program represented a way of investing in communities at the neighborhood level, much as the New Deal had done. Once the city began publicizing the program, many New Yorkers learned that the plans included schools within walking distance of their homes and other such contributions to neighborhood life—now presented as community-level rewards in recognition of wartime sacrifice.[8]

Finally, and not least importantly, the idea of a New Deal revival held out a solution to a local problem which seemed all but insoluble: the inadequacy of municipal revenues. In 1941, the Federal Works Agency (into which the PWA and other federal public works agencies had been consolidated) had begun financing the development by local governments of blueprints and working plans which could be activated at the first sign of a postwar downturn to provide jobs and PWA-style stimulus to heavy construction industries. This particular initiative had proven short-lived; Congress defunded it in July 1942 in the interest of devoting more resources to the war effort. Even so, it had seemed to signal the administration's commitment to the financing of postwar public works. Though he never quite said as much, La Guardia clearly viewed a postwar works program as a way of reinitiating the fiscal relations between the federal government and the municipalities that had existed during the 1930s. He became so committed to the idea of federal spending that he assumed its inevitability when formulating the city's own budget, despite the fact that the national government had supplied funds only for the preparation of blueprints—as an act of prudence, not as a promise. The city's 1945 capital budget would anticipate federal grants-in-aid nearly equal in many cases to what the city itself planned to spend: 97 percent of the amount allocated by the city for the Board of Higher Education, 92 percent for the Department of Health, 91 percent for the Department of Hospitals, and so forth.[9]

Some observers have viewed this grasp for intergovernmental revenues as an indication that New York had become "addicted" to federal funding during La Guardia's first two terms. And yet it is also the case that intergovernmental aid offered a solution to a vexing structural problem whose development long predated La Guardia's mayoralty. The inadequacy of municipal revenues was a product of forces more fundamental than municipal budgetary policy or the exigencies of the Great Depression; its sources belonged to the *longue durée* of American urban political development. Until the early twentieth century, the expansion of municipal governments had been financed primarily from the growth of property tax receipts—which is to say, the growth in government was paid for by increases in urban land values. In the early twentieth century, two developments had combined to produce a divergence between urban land values and municipal spending commitments. First, new transportation technologies and capital investment patterns had allowed city dwellers to escape the crowded tenement districts and industry to locate outside the city core, producing a downward pressure on central city property values that would become evident as soon as the hothouse metropolitan development of the early twentieth century had ceased. At the same time, the scope of municipal government had expanded rapidly during the Progressive Era and beyond; the revolution in how people conceived of the functions of government had pushed municipal spending higher even as the course of urban development ate away at what the inherited revenue structure could supply.[10]

Rapid economic and population growth within the big cities' political boundaries had obscured the extent of this problem in the teens and twenties; then the depression had laid it bare. Once the immediate threat of default had passed, city officials had begun to ask more philosophically how they could govern their cities under modern conditions. City dwellers, remarked New Orleans mayor T. Semmes Walmsley in his presidential address to the 1934 meeting of the U.S. Conference of Mayors, demanded "well lighted streets, proper electric traffic regulation, libraries, adequate parks and playgrounds and swimming pools and even zoos" as well as public welfare and public health programs and many other services and amenities besides. And yet the very basis upon which those services would be provided was deteriorating. "The crying need of the hour," Walmsley proclaimed, "is *stable revenues* for municipal governments"—a source of financing that would enable cities to meet the demands imposed upon them by the modern social conception of city government in the face of the decline of urban property values.

The New Deal work relief and public works programs had acted as a surrogate for urban fiscal reform. By channeling resources through municipal departments, they had enabled local governments to continue to grow as they had in the pre-Depression decades—had allowed some departments to grow much *more* quickly—despite the stabilization or decline of urban populations and the attenuation of municipal revenue bases. Once those programs were phased out, it became evident how dire New York City's fiscal situation was. The strong economic recoveries of the mid-1930s and the 1940s did not spell relief for New York; the assessed valuation of the city's real estate continued to fall, declining every year of La Guardia's mayoralty but one, and dropping by a cumulative total of nearly 38 percent during his twelve years in office.[11]

Given this reality, how was a modern city government to be financed? La Guardia, and the mayors of many other older northeastern and midwestern cities facing similar conditions, could choose from among three options: they could reduce expenditures to fit with declining revenues; they could raise new revenues by increasing local taxes or creating new ones; and they could seek to bring in more revenue from state and federal governments. Beginning in fiscal year 1942–43, his first budget after Pearl Harbor, La Guardia did reduce municipal spending sharply. Leaves of absence taken by Civil Service workers to join the war effort and rapidly falling expenditures on relief, capital improvements (curtailed because of war priorities on building materials), and education (a product of the remarkably low birthrate during the worst years of the Great Depression) allowed La Guardia to cut deeply into the budget. As a result of this wartime economization, New York's first budget in the postwar era was more than 9 percent smaller in real terms than La Guardia's first budget.[12] But in a larger sense, La Guardia did not really seek to restrain municipal spending. Though his was not a high-spending administration by latter-day standards—indeed, the low cost of labor in the Depression decade enabled him to provide progressive government on the cheap—he did not jettison municipal functions; rather, he added to them. It was simply antithetical to La Guardia's vision of progressive municipal government to cut too deeply into the functions and activities of city government.

The Little Flower had only mixed success convincing the state legislature to bestow new taxing powers upon the city. In 1941, the state permitted New York City to use surplus funds gathered from the emergency relief taxes for welfare functions other than relief, such as hospitals, old-age assistance, child welfare, and veterans' pensions. But La Guardia promptly squandered this new revenue source, requesting in advance of the 1941 municipal election that the sales tax be cut in half, from 2 percent to 1 percent (a suggestion which prompted one Democratic assemblyman to remark that he did not trust the Little Flower "as far as I can throw a piano"). In 1943, when La Guardia went back to Albany to plead for the restoration of the 2 percent sales tax and additional taxing powers, "[a]ssertions were made to the effect that the Mayor had . . . repeatedly hoodwinked the legislature," and the request was denied. Thereafter, local taxes became enmeshed with the question of the subway fare. Full municipalization of the subway system in 1941 bequeathed the city an annual deficit that by the mid-1940s had reached $40 million. Liberals and leftists argued that the subway should be fully socialized, financed out of the property values it did so much to improve rather than operated from user fees; conservatives, among whose ranks were numbered many of the original fusionists, argued that the system should be placed on a self-sustaining "business" basis. La Guardia refused to advocate for a higher fare, noting that the vast majority of city residents opposed it. But his alternative, an elaborate package which included a controversial commuter tax (in the form of a payroll tax on workers who lived outside the city), got nowhere. "It is easier to exchange prisoners of war with an enemy country," the mayor lamented to a congressional committee on postwar planning, than it was to negotiate revenue reform in Albany. Only after the war, during the mayoralties of William O'Dwyer, Robert F. Wagner, Jr., and John Lindsay, would the state legislature authorize extensive new local taxation.[13]

This left the alternative of intergovernmental revenue—La Guardia's preferred alternative, not only because it was politically the easiest, but also because he preferred it as a matter of policy. He believed that the social problems that drove the cost of modern government were national in origin and local in effect, and that it was therefore the duty of the national government to protect what he called the "enlightened" states and localities from the risk of capital disinvestment that came with heavy state and local taxation. Beginning in the early 1940s, he called for the federal government to collect all taxes and "then proceed to allow due credit to each State"—a policy of centralized collection which faced insurmountable political barriers. There remained the compelling memory of the New Deal, and this was what guided La Guardia as he made his plans for the postwar city. The New Deal had permitted La Guardia to realize his own vision of progressive city government, and he could not in the end imagine any viable alternative.[14]

In September 1941, La Guardia tasked the City Planning Commission (under Moses's direction) with assembling a shelf of blueprints and working drawings. The city prepared plans so vigorously that it was accused of "hoarding" technicians needed in the war effort. By mid-1942, the commission had collected plans for $628 million in construction projects. The program included ninety-four playgrounds, 6,600 acres of park land, sixty new elementary and secondary schools (as well as additions to many existing ones), ten new health centers and nine substations, three new hospitals and several laboratories, a new science building for Queens College and a new student center and auditorium for Brooklyn College, a large wholesale produce market to be located on the Lower West Side of Manhattan, six Hudson River piers and a new terminal facility at the foot of Atlantic Avenue, thirteen public housing projects (to be financed by the state's housing program), the completion of the Brooklyn-Battery Tunnel (which had been started in 1940 but stalled by the war), and an assortment of highways, including early plans for Robert Moses's Cross-Bronx, Midtown Manhattan, and Lower Manhattan expressways. (The largest public works project La Guardia launched during the war, Idlewild Airport, proceeded independent of the City Planning Commission's oversight.) La Guardia and Moses rushed the plans along, paying little heed to urban planners who urged them to relate the program to a comprehensive plan for the city's future growth. By V-J Day, more projects had been added and the cost of the program had grown to $1.25 billion.[15]

By that time, La Guardia had become the leading voice in the nation for a postwar public works program. In mid-1942, he had told those he invited to serve on his postwar planning committee that he "plan[ned] to have committees in other cities organized, taking up the same problems. . . ." This, of course, was beyond his power, but the Little Flower could and did use the U.S. Conference of Mayors and his own contacts with other mayors (a great many of whom shared his worries about postwar unemployment) to form a strong lobby in support of federal financing for a postwar public works program. Roosevelt, who was committed to domestic postwar planning but did not wish to devote much time or political capital to it, used La Guardia as a spokesman—much as he once had done with the New Deal works programs. When the city circulated an illustrated magazine in early 1943 depicting the new schools, public health facilities, parks, and highways it expected to build in the postwar years, Roosevelt wrote La Guardia expressing his hope that other cities and states would "follow New York's example," and that "upon the basis of the pioneering done in New York in this field, the Congress will be more inclined" to supply federal aid for detailed plan preparation. La Guardia read out the letter on his Sunday radio broadcast, printed it in city publications, quoted it in correspondence with congressmen, and espoused its contents before numerous congressional hearings.[16]

As victory in the war began to appear imminent, La Guardia testified repeatedly (and increasingly stridently) in favor of federal appropriations, not only for blueprints but also for construction. Before Pearl Harbor, he had told a Senate subcommittee: "Ask me who is going to finance these public works afterwards—I am probably as well informed as anyone in this country, and the answer is, 'I don't know.' Nobody knows, gentlemen; nobody knows." By the last year of the war, his position was that the federal government would have to pay 75 percent of the cost of working plans and 50 percent of the cost of construction.[17]

These arguments proved less than compelling to the majority of the 79th Congress. Some members of the congressional conservative coalition that exercised an effective veto on taxation and spending policy during the war years doubted that postwar public works would be necessary (and some believed that public construction would compete with private construction for scarce building materials). Others believed that cities and states would emerge from the war "in better fiscal shape than the federal government," which would bear the burden of paying down the war debt. But above all, they, like La Guardia, saw a postwar works program as an opening wedge for a restoration of the New Deal intergovernmental spending state they had fought so resolutely to dismantle.

As it happened, mass unemployment did not materialize after the war; inflation rather than unemployment emerged as the central problem of the reconversion period, removing the basic premise upon which Roosevelt, La Guardia, and others had pitched their appeals for a federal public works program. Ultimately, Congress provided only categorical grants for the construction of particular types of local public works projects—highways, hospitals, public health facilities, water treatment plants. When federal urban spending did return in the 1950s, it would be directed at "urban renewal" projects meant to assist local officials in their efforts to create facilities and institutions capable of anchoring the middle classes in their cities. The New Deal works programs had increased the public wealth, operating outside the sphere of private capital; prior to Lyndon Johnson's Great Society, postwar federal urban policy would seek to employ private capital as a partner to produce both private goods (e.g., private housing) and quasi-public ones (facilities for "third sector" institutions such as private hospitals, universities, and performing arts venues). But as New Deal–style public investment dwindled, state and local officials would be prepared to move into the vacancy.[18]

II

The same desire to kindle national policy innovation was evident in what was perhaps the most novel undertaking of La Guardia's final term: his establishment of a quasi-public system of prepaid medical care. National health insurance, tabled during the deliberations of Roosevelt's Committee on Economic Security in 1934–35, emerged during the war years as a major front in the progressive fight for social and economic security, in no small measure because medical costs were climbing so rapidly that serious illness now threatened middle-class as well as working-class family budgets. Health care appeared prominently in Roosevelt's famous 1944 message to Congress, which articulated a "second bill of rights," and there is good evidence that the president was "ready to go on health insurance," as Hopkins wrote an acquaintance, as soon as the exigencies of war permitted. In the interim, Senator Wagner had introduced a national, comprehensive, government-directed program of prepaid medical care as one part of the Wagner-Murray-Dingell social security bill of 1943. Pending national action, state and local officials launched health insurance experiments of their own—notable among them, California governor Earl Warren's proposal for a compulsory program of prepaid health coverage for families of workers making $2,500 or less (about two thirds of California families).[19]

La Guardia had been thinking about public health insurance since at least 1928, when, during a meeting of the Interparliamentary Union, he had made a personal study of the German system. In April 1943, two months before Wagner introduced his bill in the U.S. Senate, La Guardia appointed a committee of city officials, health policy experts, unionists, businessmen, doctors, and industry representatives to develop recommendations for the city's own health care program. As with Wagner-Murray-Dingell, the primary motive was economic security: a serious illness or a major operation, La Guardia

explained in the radio talk announcing the formation of the committee, "sets the average family's budget back not only months but sometimes for years." Estimating that the cost of medical care had gone
up between 350 and 400 percent during his tenure in office, he cited
studies which showed that 30 percent of small, high-interest loans
in the city went toward medical bills and another which estimated
that 60 percent of families that went into debt did so for health-
related reasons. But La Guardia also made a rights-based argument
for a public health care program. Everyone, he said, was entitled to
the best medical care available; he believed it was a function of government to develop a "sufficiently economical distribution" of care
such that everyone could have access to it.[20]

La Guardia's committee designed a program of voluntary prepaid
comprehensive coverage on the group practice model, to be administered by a non-profit organization: in exchange for 4 percent of the
enrollee's annual wages or salary, at least 2 percent of which would
be contributed by the employer, subscribers and their families could
seek whatever medical treatment they required (with a few exceptions) from any group of participating physicians. The program's
contours reflected both its designers' preferences and the many
constraints they faced. La Guardia liked the idea of comprehensive
coverage, and health policy experts liked the fact that prepayment
encouraged preventive medicine, because subscribers did not have to
pay an extra charge for physicals and routine checkups. The mayor
would have preferred an "open-panel" system, perhaps sensing that
people wished to visit whatever physician they liked; but the opposition of the county medical societies to government health insurance
precluded the possibility. Making a virtue of necessity, La Guardia
embraced what he called "teamwork medicine": group practice on
the model of the innovative Mayo Clinic, organized not around individual providers but around teams of general practitioners and specialists (akin to modern health maintenance organizations). These

groups of physicians were compensated according to the "capitation" model: their pay was based on the number of patients in their care, rather than the number of services they provided—a payment structure that tended to contain costs. Individuals were required to join as part of a group—a union, a fraternal lodge—in order to ensure that high-risk people did not flood the pool.[21]

Health insurance was a new frontier for municipal government. But as La Guardia presented it, the plan represented a logical extension of the New Deal public investment state. Now, rather than investing public money, the city was establishing machinery which would enable families to invest in their own health. "[A] man earning $2,500 to $3,000 a year," La Guardia explained, "would pay $4 or $5 a month and would know that his whole family could get, whenever needed, the services of a general practitioner either in the home, office, or hospital; all specialist services, X-rays, laboratory tests, and other diagnostic procedures; major and minor surgery; maternity care, pediatrics; hospitalization; and, perhaps most important of all, continuing *preventive* medicine to keep the family healthy." As it had in the 1930s, the government was making available a useful service that private industry had failed to provide.[22]

The plan had only one group of opponents, but they would turn out to be an important one: the county medical societies. These organized providers opposed the plan in part because it proposed to vest operational control in a board of directors, among whom laymen would outnumber physicians, and in part because they opposed any challenge to traditional fee-for-service medicine. They also feared the plan would make their compensation subject to political pressure. Because La Guardia's plan had no precedent, no data existed to establish the actuarial tables; the 4 percent deduction figure La Guardia had proposed was in this sense arbitrary, and with that number already fixed, physicians feared their income would become "the unknown x in the equation," as one New York practitioner put it.

In the short term, La Guardia had little difficulty surmounting the opposition of organized providers. When the county medical societies attempted to limit participation in the program to those earning $2,500 a year or less, which would have restricted enrollment to the working classes, La Guardia went public with his own figure of $5,000—which permitted the program to reach well into the middle classes. He unveiled the plan in April 1944, in a brilliant radio talk; it quickly gained strong public support as well as backing from newspapers, big businessmen, financiers, most of the unions, medical schools, and the public health profession. Albany approved the charter, and the Health Insurance Plan of Greater New York (HIP) was incorporated in September 1944 by an assemblage of labor leaders, civic reformers, liberal businessmen, and financiers, joined by the Catholic prelates, by Henry J. Kaiser (whose own prepaid group practice plan, Kaiser Permanente, was something of an analogue to HIP), and by leading politicians (including Wendell Willkie and Al Smith, neither of whom would live to see it in operation).[23]

La Guardia conceived of HIP as a stopgap until national compulsory health insurance was passed: in this sense, the program represented an instance of what scholars have recently taken to calling "compensatory federalism"—a scenario in which subnational officials dissatisfied with national policy are able to "step into the broach." But he also intended HIP to be a demonstration of how government-sponsored health insurance could work. Thus the program also embodied a Progressive Era conception of subnational units as "laboratories" whose experiments could provide information to other governments. New York City could do for health insurance, La Guardia seemed to suggest, what Wisconsin had done for unemployment insurance and what New York State had done for work relief: it could demonstrate the feasibility and the desirability of comprehensive, government-sponsored health insurance, perhaps insulating federal officials from the claim that government health insurance was impractical, radical, or unwanted. "Everything must have a begin-ning," he explained; "I am perfectly willing to be guinea-pigged if only we can get it started in this country."[24]

Though quick in many instances to note that local voluntary health insurance was not the same as national compulsory health insurance, proponents of national health insurance, especially lib-erals and unionists, understood La Guardia's plan the same way the mayor did. Brooklyn congressman Emanuel Celler wrote that he hoped HIP would "needle" the federal government into "responding more quickly to the demands of the people. . . ." HIP accorded with the national CIO's policy of encouraging local medical cooperatives and non-profit insurance plans, and so trade unionists and Ameri-can Labor Party leaders were quick to speak of La Guardia's program as "the beginning of a nationwide movement," a "stepping stone" to national health insurance, and the "stimulus that will make the Wagner-Murray-Dingell Social Security Bill the law of the land." The *American Journal of Public Health* wrote that La Guardia's plan represented "the first large-scale attempt to work out in detail the local machinery which is essential to the success of any state or fed-eral program of prepaid care." Both organized labor and the medical societies took to referring to HIP as "the 'baby Wagner bill.'"[25]

In retrospect, one is struck by the distance between these state-ments and the reality of what La Guardia had proposed. HIP never was a "baby Wagner bill"; it differed in kind from the national com-pulsory health insurance envisioned in Wagner-Murray-Dingell, not least because a voluntary program of its type could do relatively little to socialize the cost of medical care. And even had HIP gotten under-way smoothly, which it did not, one might just as easily have viewed it as an alternative to the Wagner bill rather than a stepping stone to national compulsory insurance—as an illustration of the adequacy of voluntary non-profit prepaid insurance. In fact, HIP more closely resembled the compromise proposals put forward by liberal Republicans (including a young Richard Nixon) in 1947 and 1948, which would have created "a locally controlled, government-subsidized, private nonprofit insurance system, with premiums scaled to subscribers' incomes," than it did Wagner and Truman's proposals for a full national health insurance program.

And yet if HIP was not, strictly speaking, a government program, it was decidedly *public*: its goals and structure had been established by an elected official, who created an organizational framework which gave public interests precedence over those of organized providers and private insurance corporations. As such, it represented one of the most ambitious of the many labor- and community-based efforts in the 1930s and 1940s to "remove health care from the realm of corporations, insular elite professional control, and private markets." This public character stood out in the 1940s, when medical societies and private insurance companies were hastily creating voluntary, private insurance plans to head off a governmental program. Together with the city's singular system of municipal hospitals and its new network of community health centers, HIP gave New York a remarkably broad (quasi-) public health provision system.[26]

III

In September 1944, about the time HIP was incorporated, Roosevelt, deeply committed to winning the war and beginning the construction of a new international order, began his campaign for a fourth term. He faced Thomas Dewey, who had unified the Republican Party with seeming ease, fending off Willkie's quixotic liberal challenge and an untidy movement to draft General Douglas MacArthur, and prevailing at the convention over the conservative wing's candidate, Ohio governor John W. Bricker. Forty-two years old and twenty months into a governorship rendered significantly easier by the war boom–derived revenue pouring into the state's coffers, Dewey campaigned for president much as he had run for governor of New York: he accepted basic New Deal reforms, chided the Democrats for their various failings, and promised a more efficient and more business-friendly government devoid of the "regimentation" and "centralization" he ascribed to the New Deal.[27]

La Guardia was conspicuously reluctant to participate in the campaign. He took little part in the activities of the National Citizens' Political Action Committee (NCPAC) or the Independent Voters' Committee of the Arts and Sciences (IVCAS), organizations that filled in 1944 roughly the role the National Committee of Independent Voters had four years earlier. Though he did accept Mayor Kelly's invitation to speak on Roosevelt's behalf in Chicago, he spurned pleas from other urban Democrats who asked him to speak to Italian American and black voters in their cities, and he likewise parried requests to address rallies of the IVCAS and Mary McLeod Bethune's National Non-Partisan Committee for the Re-election of Roosevelt, excusing himself on the grounds that the campaign had "not reached a point where the real issues [had] been formulated." His reticence had partly to do with the Republicans' choice of candidate: La Guardia had little personal affection for Dewey, but the former crime-buster was now the dominant figure in the New York GOP, and La Guardia needed to maintain a working relationship with him. The Little Flower's measured distance from Roosevelt's campaign also reflected his feeling that he had been badly treated by the Roosevelt administration.[28]

It was not until mid-October that La Guardia agreed to make a speaking tour in support of Roosevelt and the Democratic ticket. He traveled to Pittsburgh, Boston, Philadelphia, Paterson, and Buffalo—where, so Mayor Joe Kelly informed the White House, the Little Flower's pro-Roosevelt rally drew thousands more than had Dewey himself. He gave talks over Italian and Polish radio stations, and on the Thursday night before the election he chaired a Madison Square Garden rally that featured Ickes, Wagner, and Frank Sinatra, and went out nationally over the NBC network. Gone was the sharp class rhetoric of 1940. Instead, he emphasized Roosevelt's record, especially in war production, and spoke of the need to advance the fight for economic security after the war, asking voters to elect a Congress that would work with the president toward that end. Most of all, he argued that Roosevelt should represent the United States at the peace table: "At the conference table to protect the interests of our country and to insure [sic] peace for the world, I am choosing the man who has lived through it all, who has seen the horrors and cost in human lives of the war, who has gained not only the admiration but the respect and confidence of the oppressed people of the world. I am choosing this man to finish the job." La Guardia was not as central to the Roosevelt campaign as he had been four years earlier, but for two weeks he was an effective and energetic worker, and he came out of the election season with the gratitude and admiration of future Democratic Party chairman Robert Hannegan, who apparently approached Flynn and Kelly to run the Little Flower as the Democratic candidate for Senate in 1946.[29]

The bitterness of the generalship saga was set aside long enough for La Guardia to help stage what would be the climactic event of Roosevelt's 1944 campaign, his quadrennial automobile tour through New York. The 1936 and 1940 tours had been triumphal celebrations of Roosevelt's political mastery of the city; the 1944 tour was an exercise in deception, intended to demonstrate to the public the physical well-being of a man whose health had, in fact, sharply declined. Roosevelt met with La Guardia at the White House on Tuesday, October 17, and evidently asked him to arrange the tour on four days' notice. Whether La Guardia helped sell FDR on the idea is not known. However it was initiated, La Guardia began sketching out an itinerary the next morning.

The day of the New York motorcar parade dawned "cold, rainy, bone-chilling." The president's physician advised him to cancel his outdoor appearances and save himself for his evening speech at the Waldorf-Astoria, but Roosevelt wrapped himself in his Navy admiral's cape and braved the elements in the backseat of an open car. The procession started at the Army Supply Base in Brooklyn, lined with tanks and jeeps waiting to be shipped to Europe, then moved to the Navy Yard and on to Ebbets Field where Roosevelt spoke, standing and hatless, "facing a lashing rain," at a rally for the reelection of Senator Wagner. The party wound through Queens, to Hunter College in the Bronx, south through Harlem, then Times Square and the Garment District—fifty-one miles in all—to Eleanor Roosevelt's apartment north of Washington Square. Unbeknownst to the press and public, the parade route was lined with garages where Secret Service agents gave Roosevelt rubdowns, redressed him, and supplied him with sips of brandy. Through it all, the president remained "cheerful, animated, conversing, and waving. . . . The pictures and press coverage were stunning."

The crowd was thinner in places and the cheering less boisterous than it had been four and eight years earlier, but even so about a million New Yorkers turned out, mostly women and children, waiting for the motorcade and cheering as their teeth chattered from exposure to the rain and the raw wind. La Guardia, watching the passing faces from alongside Roosevelt in the presidential car, predicted a plurality of "exactly 762,347." Roosevelt, with a look of mock suspicion, demanded to know how La Guardia could be so precise. "I counted them," La Guardia replied. He turned out to be 9,000 short of the mark.[30]

The tour was, Warren Moscow of the *Times* later wrote, Roosevelt's greatest personal triumph in New York. "You could see it," La Guardia said afterwards of the response the city had given FDR; "he was touched by it." Upon his return to Washington, Roosevelt, plainly satisfied with the way the trip had gone, sent La Guardia a cable expressing his gratitude and conveying his hope that the mayor had suffered no ill effects from the exposure to the elements. La Guardia had spent the following morning sick and in bed.[31]

IV

By the time Roosevelt was sworn in for the fourth and final time, New York was aflutter with speculation about La Guardia's intentions to seek a fourth term of his own. La Guardia pronounced himself bemused by the newspapers' earnest analyses of the cryptic signals the impish mayor was feeding them. "[If] I say I must repair my glasses since they are getting loose, and I am going to need them for a long time, the next day they say, 'Mayor indicates he is going to run for office,'" he quipped. "Or, if I reach over and say I do not have much tobacco but it will do, they say, 'Mayor indicates he may not run for office.'"[32]

In fact, La Guardia's prospects for a fourth term were dimming: his coalition was falling apart. By the end of March it was clear that he could not win the Republican nomination. Dewey might have been willing to run La Guardia again in order to help the party maintain control of the state in 1946, but local party leaders believed that even the governor's endorsement could not get the Little Flower through the Republican primary. After surveying his assembly district leaders, New York County chairman Thomas J. Curran, a Dewey ally, explained that his organization could not hold the lines well enough in a primary to offset the likely deficit in vehemently anti–La Guardia Queens. Thus did La Guardia's stormy career as a Republican finally come to an end, not because the organization had rejected him, but because he could not survive a Republican primary—the very institution he had first broken with the party to defend.[33]

La Guardia might still have launched a third-party bid but for the scission of the American Labor Party. The divisions between anti-Communist and Popular Frontist elements that had racked the party since the late 1930s exploded in 1944 when Sidney Hillman, who had not been heavily involved in the party's affairs since 1936, proposed to reform the ALP's institutional structure with the objective of broadening its membership. Hillman proposed that all trade unions in New York State be invited to affiliate with the party "and to pay it a per capita tax based upon their membership within the State. All matters of party policy [would] be determined by the vote of representatives of the participating trade unions, based upon their per capita tax payments to the party." By increasing the representation of the CIO unions in the state party machinery, the "Hillman plan" would have elevated some Communists and fellow travelers to positions of power, for these elements were powerful within the Greater New York CIO and its member unions. Right-wing union leaders understood the Hillman plan as a threat to non-Communist control of the party. Convinced that the ALP would lose both its independence and its broader liberal appeal were it to "merge" with the Communist Party, they rejected the Hillman plan—which in turn prompted the left-wingers to declare their intention to oust the anti-Communists from control of the state committee in a March 1944 party primary.[34]

Both the White House and City Hall were alarmed at the prospect of a split, and both sought to arrange a compromise. A week before the primary, La Guardia announced his own plan "for restoring peace within the American Labor Party," the core of which was a repudiation of "any [form] of organization based on numerical membership," and a compromise slate of non-Communists for the state executive committee, to which all candidates running in the primary for election to the state committee would be pledged. Despite this repudiation of his own plan, Hillman accepted the compromise unconditionally; the right-wing leaders David Dubinsky and Alex Rose, considering it an evasion of the paramount issue of Communist infiltration of the state committee, rejected it. The left-wingers scored a smashing primary victory, carrying 80 percent of the state committee seats and securing control of the Bronx County organization, the anti-Communists' last stronghold within the five boroughs. Dubinsky fumed that La Guardia was "in large measure responsible."

The next day, the right-wingers withdrew from the ALP. They soon formed their own party, the Liberal Party, taking with them a disproportionately Jewish, disproportionately middle-class section of the ALP. The scission of the ALP would certainly cost La Guardia thousands of votes; barring a dramatic about-face, the Liberal Party and the Ladies Garment Workers would align against him. But it also had a broader impact on the organizational landscape of city politics. By splitting the needle trades unions' organizational strength, it made a labor-based coalition (difficult to begin with) practically impossible. And it provided crucial organizational support to the Democratic Party. And by making it possible for the Democracy to claim *some* labor party support, it allowed a party which had topped out at about 45 percent of the city vote to forge a majority coalition, thereby changing the basic arithmetic of electoral competition in the city.[35]

La Guardia, then, had been cut off from the Republican Party and the Liberal Party. He had only the ALP, the remnants of the deteriorated fusion movement, and his own personal popularity with which to confront a Democratic opposition rendered far more potent by the Labor Party split. This was the situation when Roosevelt died on April 12, 1945, struck by a massive brain hemorrhage as he was sitting for a portrait in Warm Springs. News of the president's death reached New York just before six o'clock in the evening, as the city was on its way home from work; many people learned of it as they ascended the stairs of the subway. Disbelief was followed by an outpouring of public grief and a period of bereavement and eulogizing. La Guardia delivered a short extemporaneous tribute over WNYC; during his Sunday broadcast, he spoke movingly of his own relationship with Roosevelt: their first meeting in Turin, their conferences at the Hotel Continental in the mid-twenties, the laugh they had exchanged during La Guardia's imbroglio with the German ambassador. The nation bore a responsibility to Roosevelt's memory, the Little Flower concluded, "to work for the better world that he planned; to make war impossible in the future; to make life better and happier for all the peoples of the world." Three weeks later, La Guardia, aware of the odds against him, tired of the mayoralty, and increasingly worried about his health—he was suffering constant pain in his lower back and now kept a bottle of pain pills on his desk at City Hall—announced over WNYC, to the city's surprise, that he would not seek a fourth term. The announcement, the *Herald Tribune* wrote, epitomized La Guardia's time in office—"it was annoying, it was gracious, it was entertaining and courageous."[36]

La Guardia's coalition split three ways in the 1945 campaign. The "New Deal" component—most of the unions, the ALP, the CIO-PAC and its sister organization the NCPAC, the *New York Post*, and national figures like Henry Wallace, Henry Morgenthau, and Eleanor Roosevelt—endorsed the Democratic candidate, William O'Dwyer, who had emerged in the months before Roosevelt's death as something of a presidential favorite. (Some, like Sidney Hillman, saw in O'Dwyer "a fitting successor to Mayor La Guardia"; others, like Eleanor Roosevelt, viewed the 1945 mayoral election as "a fight for control by the people as against control by certain powerful groups.") The Republican Party and the Liberal Party nominated the reputable and popular Court of General Sessions Judge Jonah Goldstein, an Al Smith protégé and a Walker appointee, thus finally consummating the nearly decade-long flirtation between Tammany and the GOP— though Goldstein's nomination evidently owed less to the ideological conservatism that had underpinned the GOP-Tammany link in the late thirties than it did to Dewey's desire to make a gesture to Jewish voters before the 1946 state campaign.[37]

La Guardia considered endorsing O'Dwyer but instead encouraged City Council president Newbold Morris, a moderate silk stocking Republican who had served frequently as acting mayor during La Guardia's absences from the city and had emerged as something of a fusion heir apparent, to run on a third-party ticket—dubbed by a less than inspired Little Flower the "No Deal" ticket. La Guardia made several stirring radio broadcasts on Morris's behalf, conjuring up the city as he had found it in 1933: "hospitals without supplies, blackboards without chalk; judgments for millions against the city for land sold by politicians; assessments high and services low; incompetency in office, political clubs assessing payrolls, hungry people in lines before political clubs for an okay in order to obtain food stamps that could be cashed only at politically selected grocery stores at ten to fifteen per cent discount. . . ."[38]

O'Dwyer triumphed with 57 percent of the vote (44 percent on the Democratic line and 13 percent on the ALP line) to Goldstein's 22 percent (15 percent Republican, 6 percent Liberal, and 1 percent City Fusion) and Morris's 21 percent. Morris ran strongest in midtown Manhattan, on the Upper East Side, and in Flatbush, his support coming overwhelmingly from the affluent good-government element of La Guardia's coalition. O'Dwyer's vote was an amalgam of Roosevelt's from 1932 and 1940, resembling the former more than the latter. He ran strongest in the working-class Irish and Italian neighborhoods that had been the backbone of the Democratic Party before the New Deal, but which by the 1940s had begun to leave the Roosevelt coalition—Greenwich Village, East Harlem, the South Brooklyn waterfront, and Mott Haven. He ran twenty or thirty points behind Roosevelt's 1944 vote on the Upper West Side and the Lower East Side, in Coney Island and Bensonhurst, Midwood, Brownsville, East New York, the Grand Concourse, Hunts Point,

Morrisania, and Tremont—all strongly pro-Roosevelt, pro–La Guardia neighborhoods, where large minorities cast their ballots for the
(Jewish) Liberal Party candidate, Judge Goldstein, or, in the case of
the more affluent Upper West Side, for Newbold Morris.

V

On New Year's Day, 1946, control of City Hall passed into Democratic hands for the first time in a dozen years. There it would remain
for the next twenty. The depth of institutional and political change
enabled by the New Deal ensured that there would be no simple
restoration of the old Democratic regime; instead, O'Dwyer and his
successors would move to accommodate many of the political forces
which had been central to La Guardia's coalition: organized labor,
professional civil servants, reform-minded liberals. (Democrats
would also take advantage of the postwar anti-Communism hysteria
to marginalize the most powerful independent leftist forces in city
politics, including the ALP and the Communist Party.) Though rid-
dled with fault lines and plagued by defections, this postwar Democratic coalition would hold together until the sixties, serving as the
primary vessel for what came to be called "New York liberalism."[39]

There would be no postwar revival of the New Deal intergovernmental public investment state. Direct federal-municipal relations of the sort pioneered in the early thirties would endure; and
co-functionality across the federal system would remain a basic feature of American governance. But notwithstanding a few targeted
grant-in-aid programs, the national government would withdraw
its fiscal resources from local governments. At the peak of the New
Deal, federal spending on projects sponsored by New York's municipal departments had totaled more than 30 percent of the city's
annual budget. In the postwar decade, that figure fell dramatically;

as late as fiscal year 1965–66, federal contributions would make up only 6.8 percent of the city's annual expenditures.[40]

Probably never again would New York's elected officials command as large a share of the city's resources at they had in the thirties. Figure 10.1 illustrates the municipality's control of one basic resource: labor. During the heyday of the New Deal, more than one in eleven New York City workers had worked for the city—either directly, or on a WPA project. By the mid-fifties, that number would be about one in seventeen. This reallocation of manpower from the public sector to the private sector would impoverish the former even as the latter flourished; it was surely with the baseline of the thirties in mind that the economist John Kenneth Galbraith, in one of the signal works of the postwar era, pointed to the decay of New York's municipal services as a conspicuous symbol of "public squalor" amidst "private opulence." Even at the height of postwar prosperity, the passing of the New Deal would be evident in the shabbiness of New York's parks, in the cracks proliferating in its sidewalks, and in the languishing of the social and cultural community improvement projects which had been as central to the urban New Deal as La Guardia Airport and the Triborough Bridge. Many New Yorkers might have shared the Italian American educator Leonard Covello's 1958 lament: "It is ironical but true that the years of the great depression and immediately following were the most productive in our Benjamin Franklin [High School] experiment. Because of the unemployment situation, many capable WPA workers worked without cost to us on our numerous community programs. Bitter irony indeed! Workers in a depression made possible what today is practically out of the question."[41]

And yet, even as the alphabet agencies of the 1930s faded into memory, New York's local New Deal would seem to continue. Forced to build alliances with organized labor and the third parties and to appeal to an electorate whose conceptions of the local state had been

Figure 10.1: *Total municipal workers (including WPA workers) in New York City per 1,000 residents, 1937–56.*

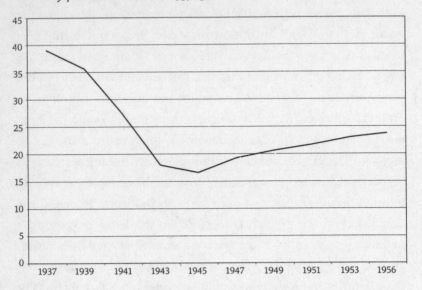

Municipal personnel data, which exclude teachers, can be found in Clarence Ridley, Orin Nolting, et al., eds., *The Municipal Yearbook* (published annually). WPA data can be found in Federal Works Administration, Work Projects Administration, *Report on the Progress of the WPA Program, June 30, 1939* (Washington, DC, 1939), 158–59, and FWA, *Report on the Progress . . . , June 30, 1941,* 103.

shaped by the experiences of the 1930s and 1940s, the Democrats who governed postwar New York would continue to extend the city's public sector, following the blueprint drawn by Roosevelt and La Guardia. During his 1949 reelection campaign, O'Dwyer would point to the number of new schools, housing units, hospitals, day care centers, health stations, parks, and playgrounds his administration had built. Four years later, when Vincent Impellitteri sought the Democratic nomination, he would emphasize his public construction record and his efforts to eradicate social diseases and limit water pollution. Wagner, whom the Democrats chose over Impellitteri that year, would build his campaign around the cost of rental housing, accusing the Republican Party of being too lax in its administration of rent control. Drawing upon the wealth that accrued in the city as the postwar "headquarters economy" developed—per capita personal income (in 1967 dollars) would grow from $2,422 in 1940 to $3,722 in 1965—the city and state would construct and open new schools, hospitals, middle-class and low-rent housing units, day care centers, health stations, and parks and playgrounds; expand the city's public health programs and extend its municipal broadcasting system; and protect rent control. In so doing, they would fill, at least in part, the social-political vacancy left by the withdrawal of federal resources in the late thirties and early forties, sustaining in New York a public sector which stood apart in the American experience, the very symbol of American urban liberalism.[42]

The institutional, political, and cultural legacies of the New Deal had left a profound tension at the heart of the city's politics. In the postwar decades, as New Yorkers utilized the city's immense wealth to extend the public sector the New Deal had helped build, the conviction that no important problem was outside the sphere of municipal government helped sustain as ambitious a social politics as urban America has ever seen. But it also ensured that New York's political leaders would overextend themselves, making promises they could not keep. New Yorkers had learned to love a kind of government that had come into creation under the extraordinary conditions of the New Deal and that had developed under the singular conditions of midcentury—when New York was, as never before or since, an exceptionally wealthy city possessing a thriving port and manufacturing sector, high land values, a remarkably broad middle class, and a residential population roughly coextensive with its political boundaries. Even in the postwar decades, the tension between "endless ambitions" and "finite resources" had been evident in the annual agony of the budget-making process, in the fact that highways and sidewalks went unrepaired even as new schoolhouses and public apartments proliferated. When the conditions of affluence that had sustained New York's local public sector through the 1960s yielded to the painful restructuring of the 1970s, much of the remaining political legacy of the New Deal would be undone. In the decades to come, New York's civic leaders would seek an alternate model for public investment, enlisting private partners to fill the role the federal government had abdicated and in some instances to displace the municipal government itself.[43]

VI

The period between William O'Dwyer's election and his swearing-in offered an opportunity for those whose lives and work had been touched by La Guardia's mayoralty to pay tribute to the outgoing mayor. Among those who did so were the members of the U.S. Conference of Mayors, which held its annual meeting in New York in December. At the close of the conference the incoming executive officers presented La Guardia with a new Packard automobile to replace his official city coupe and passed a resolution expressing their gratitude to their outgoing president, whose "matchless knowledge of all levels of government," "immense prestige in the nation's capital," and "willingness to pioneer new modes of government administration" had, they believed, helped America's big cities weather "a period of incomparable trials and difficulties." After adjourning, the group made a pilgrimage to Roosevelt's Hyde Park estate, where La Guardia, Chicago mayor Edward Kelly, and Winnipeg mayor Garnet Coulter placed a wreath on Roosevelt's grave.[44]

EPILOGUE

La Guardia was to live only twenty months after leaving the mayoralty. These were months of bustling activity and profound disappointment, as liberals reeled in the aftermath of Roosevelt's death and the New Deal coalition was fractured by the coming of the Cold War. La Guardia would spend the last months of his life engaged in a contest to preserve what he regarded as Roosevelt's proper legacy; he would die believing it had been all but lost.

After leaving office, La Guardia carved out a role as a radio and newspaper commentator—the self-described "unauthorized spokesman of unorganized Americans." Finding himself a soapbox and a bit of money at the same time, he signed deals with *PM*, June Dairy, *Liberty* magazine (for a broadcast series over the national ABC network), and Sachs Furniture (which printed his opinion pieces adjacent to its advertisements). He also began work on his memoirs, the first volume of which would be published posthumously in truncated form. He enjoyed real wealth for the first time in his life—the memoirs paid a $10,000 advance, the local broadcasts more than $50,000 per year and the national ones $2,500 per week—but the work gave him no rest; he set up an office on the fiftieth floor of the

RCA Building at Rockefeller Center and hired six secretaries to help keep his affairs in order. It took him hardly any time to run afoul of the controversy-shy sponsors, two of which dropped him within the first six months.[1]

He devoted some attention to municipal issues, denouncing Robert Moses's plan to lease the municipal airports to a new airport authority and then Moses himself, whom he now referred to as "oberburgermeister," a dictator who considered New York "his exclusive and personal domain. . . ." ("Yes," the ex-mayor admitted when someone pointed out that he had given Moses much of his power, "but I could control him. Now nobody will be able to control him.") As the weeks passed, La Guardia spent less time on local matters and more on national issues, especially questions of economic policy. Still believing that a sound social and economic system could only be created through a more equitable distribution of purchasing power, he advocated the use of federal income taxes and excess-profit taxes to encourage employers to raise wages; he presented his own tax plan to counter the GOP's proposal for a 20 percent "across the board" reduction of wartime taxes. He campaigned for the continuation of price and rent controls, taking up the chairmanship of the National Fair Rent Committee. He spoke in support of the Wagner-Murray-Dingell health care and social security bill; the Wagner-Ellender-Taft housing bill; and Representative Matthew Neely's bill to fund a national cancer research program. He joined the campaign for a permanent Fair Employment Practices Committee and an anti–poll tax law; he pushed a plan of his own devising to create a federal industrial court for semi-compulsory arbitration of labor-management disputes; and he advocated a guaranteed annual wage, though he was never able to demonstrate how it might work.[2]

La Guardia was, in short, an avowed champion of the liberal program that had emerged during the war years and would form the basis of Harry Truman's Fair Deal. That program ran aground in the

79th Congress, which was dominated by a bipartisan coalition of conservatives. Of the three measures La Guardia most wanted to see passed—the Wagner-Murray-Dingell national health insurance bill (which he considered the most important single piece of legislation ever to come before the Congress), the Wagner-Ellender-Taft housing bill, and the Full Employment bill—the first was ultimately defeated, the second passed only after his death, and the third became so watered down that La Guardia believed it no longer represented Roosevelt's vision for a full employment economy. The Congress's record in 1946 consisted of "bickering and face-making and disagreements," La Guardia said, with little "looking to the future" and not enough "contribution[s] to making life better and happier in this world."[3]

Many liberals looked at the difference between what Roosevelt had wrung from Congress and what Truman had managed, deciding the difference resided in Truman's unwillingness or inability to exercise effective leadership. La Guardia, too, considered Truman "unpardonably weak" in his leadership on domestic issues, but he did not consider Truman primarily culpable for the demise of the liberal postwar program.[4] Blame properly lay with Congress, he believed, and consequently a New Deal revival would require not only more effective presidential leadership but also a broad progressive movement. The midterm elections of 1946, in which congressional Democrats suffered heavy losses, only strengthened these convictions. "[W]ith Franklin D. Roosevelt no longer here," he wrote, "the [Democratic] party leadership did not know how or did not want to defend what the New Deal has done for the American people. They tried to go conservative, if not reactionary. When the National Democratic Party goes conservative, it is out of role. If people want a reactionary, conservative government, they are justified in voting for the Republicans, who are experts at it." Liberals and progressives, he suggested, should present a "solution for every problem"; he proposed the creation of a legislative drafting bureau and issued his own "program

for progressives." And he began to contemplate, more seriously than
at any point since the mid-thirties, the necessity of a third party.[5]

II

In March 1946, at the urging of Secretary of State James Byrnes, La
Guardia accepted the directorship of the United Nations Relief and
Rehabilitation Administration (UNRRA), an organization founded
by the Allies during the war to provide relief to war-stricken people
and assist in repatriation efforts and the running of displaced persons camps. UNRRA was, *Life* wrote, "the most ambitious humanitarian effort ever undertaken by mankind." The assignment fit La
Guardia's interests perfectly. The Little Flower had been thinking
and speaking about the issues involved since early 1943; now he was
able to play a leading part in the provision of humanitarian aid while
also helping to breathe life into one of the international institutions
he considered the world's best hope for peace. "It is all so hopeful, as
never before in the whole history of the world," he remarked upon
accepting the directorship; "forty-eight nations coming together to
save lives. We are united to preserve life, to build, not to kill, not to
destroy. . . ." Following Herbert Lehman, who had overseen the organization since its creation, he left in July on a tour through Yugoslavia, Italy, Poland, Russia, Czechoslovakia, Morocco, Egypt, Greece,
Austria, and Germany, places where the devastation of war almost
defied imagination, making allocation decisions and reports on local
conditions.[6]

La Guardia's tenure at the UNRRA, which lasted until the agency's scheduled termination at the end of December 1946, coincided
with the escalation of tensions between the United States and the
Soviet Union and the emergence within the Truman administration
of an approach to postwar foreign policy fundamentally at odds with

La Guardia's own. The first point of contention stemmed from La Guardia's belief that humanitarian aid should be totally separated from diplomacy and foreign policy. "People are crying for bread, not advice," he remarked upon taking the UNRRA post; refusing to ask difficult questions about the regimes that governed nations receiving UNRRA aid, he likened efforts to tie relief funds to the internal affairs of the recipient nation to the old-time Tammany method of trading coal for votes. La Guardia's desire to build a wall between aid and what he called "politics," driven in part by the extent of the devastation he had witnessed on his tour, led him to set aside questions of geopolitics and the responsibilities of regimes receiving UNRRA aid. Dean Acheson, speaking for the State Department, responded that UNRRA aid was shielding from popular discontent regimes which, "instead of centering their efforts on recovery and reconstruction . . . have impaired the production of Europe's agricultural surplus areas . . . [through] nationalization, economic control and currency inflation, coupled with a liquidation of the former managerial class. . . ."

La Guardia came to believe, too, that the Truman administration was drifting away from the commitment to international institutions he considered essential to the preservation of world peace. Only strong international institutions, he maintained, could prevent a return of "plain, ordinary, old-time power politics" which had produced "war after war." La Guardia bemoaned what he saw as an American and British drift toward nation- and bloc-based foreign policy. He pleaded for a UN Emergency Food Fund to succeed the UNRRA, and protested when American objections to providing aid to "countries that were rearming or using food as a political weapon" killed the proposal. In March 1947, when Truman requested $400 million in aid to stabilize the governments of Greece and Turkey (the former faced a strong communist insurgency), La Guardia called for the effort to be made through the United Nations, fearing that the decision to bypass it would destroy the young organization's credibility as a mechanism for the resolution of international disputes.[7]

The Little Flower's conviction that the Truman administration was drifting away from Roosevelt's vision for the postwar world brought him into an alliance with America's preeminent champion of "peace" through international cooperation: Henry Wallace. The two men had not always seen eye-to-eye; in the thirties, La Guardia had probably directed more verbal shots toward Wallace than he had toward any other member of Roosevelt's cabinet save Farley. But now they shared a sense that the world was drifting toward another war and were united in the belief that the Truman administration's foreign policy had strayed from the principles that had guided Roosevelt's wartime diplomacy. When Wallace gave the famous speech at Madison Square Garden which sealed his break with the administration, La Guardia phoned him to say (as Wallace recalled) that "he thought I had done the right thing"; when Truman forced Wallace's resignation shortly thereafter, La Guardia praised him as "a casualty of peace" and a "true Christian," who was "bigger than any man in his party." As the 1948 elections approached, it was widely speculated that La Guardia might serve as Wallace's running mate on a third-party presidential ticket; and even after it became clear that his rapidly deteriorating health would not allow it, La Guardia told Wallace through mutual friends that he hoped the two could "stump the country together in the fight for peace" as soon as he was well enough.[8]

III

"[The] trouble with us liberals and progressives," La Guardia remarked at the end of 1946, "is that we're not united. Let's not fool ourselves—we have more than fifty-seven varieties." Within

a few months, those factions were sorted into two relatively distinct camps, organized by the question of communism, foreign and
domestic. The leading organizations of the pro-Roosevelt left, the
National Citizens' Political Action Committee and the Independent
Citizens' Committee of Artists, Scientists, and Professionals—both
of which had come out of the 1944 campaign—merged, creating a
new group, the Progressive Citizens of America (PCA). The formation of the PCA, a progressive organization which took a Wallace-like
stand on foreign policy and welcomed to its ranks all progressives
(which in practice meant that it accepted Communists as members),
stimulated the development of a relatively small wartime group, the
Union for Democratic Action, into a much larger and more powerful
organization of anti-Communist liberals, Americans for Democratic
Action (ADA)—in essence replicating the scission of the American
Labor Party. The unified progressive movement to which La Guardia
staked his hopes was not to be; there emerged instead two separate
groups, each aiming "to be a potent force in perpetuating and realizing the ideals of the late President Roosevelt," which seemed to
regard each other with more contempt than either expressed for the
conservative majority in Congress.[9]

La Guardia, who had dealt as extensively with Communists as
any major officeholder of the time, viewed the issue of Communism
much as he had viewed Bolshevism after the First World War: he
thought it was a slogan employed by the privileged and their political
allies to discredit efforts aimed at economic justice. He pronounced
the presence of Communists within progressive organizations a
non-issue: "No one with the faintest knowledge of the history of our
country and the present situation," he claimed in his *PM* column,
"gives a hoot about the Communists." This was perhaps less than
fully candid: La Guardia knew well what Communist organizers
had contributed to the CIO unionization drives of the mid- and late
1930s, he knew their fervor and their organizing abilities, he knew

the votes they had given him in 1937 and 1941, and he knew their capacity for ruthlessness and subversion. But La Guardia was basically sincere in his belief that progressives and liberals could only lose by allowing themselves to echo the anti-Communist language of their conservative opponents. Viewed in relation to the conservative ascendancy, Communism looked to him to be a trivial matter—a distraction from the issues at stake as the postwar era dawned and a bogeyman conservatives could use to fracture the liberal-progressive forces and hoodwink unorganized progressive groups.[10]

In early April 1945, La Guardia sent Eleanor Roosevelt a long and distressed letter about the state of New Deal liberalism. Claiming to see a "shattering and a distortion and a weakening of New Deal principles at every turn" within the Democratic Party, he decried the tendency of the ADA (with which the former first lady was associated) to seek Democratic regularity. A great many progressives, he noted, were "not dyed-in-the-wool members of any party. We have, during the past twenty-five years, because of our independent attitude, been able to force good legislation as well as to improve the calibre of candidates." Independent progressives could not agree to work within a party, he argued—especially one which was trending toward "ultra-conservatism." "It may be necessary to have a third party," he decided. "I don't know. I hope not."

The ADA liberals' decision to work within the Democratic Party was only one deviation from his ideal of unity that worried La Guardia. "The technique and even the nomenclature of selfish, conservative, money-minded groups seem to have been adopted recently by your group [the ADA]," he wrote Eleanor Roosevelt.

> The brand of Communism is hurled indiscriminately. Do you think that is fair? What is the test of excluding any one from a progressive group? How is a sympathizer or fellow traveler . . . to be identified? . . .

Do you consider Henry Wallace a Communist? I do not.
Neither would our late President consider him a Communist.
I know, for on several occasions he resented the abuse of Mr.
Wallace along those lines. . . .

It has gotten so now that anyone who has a difference of
opinion or is not in agreement is charged with being a Communist or a friend of a Communist. My dear Mrs. Roosevelt,
where will all this end? . . .

We are getting away from the New Deal. Much of it has
already been destroyed. . . .

The only way to safeguard what remained, and to begin again to
obtain "the objectives of the New Deal—a better, a fuller, a happier
life, and economic security"—was to force the major parties to the
left through the organization of a "strong, independent and progressive movement," incorporating those the ADA sought to exclude.[11]

The course of American politics in the following months only con-
firmed, to La Guardia's mind, the veracity of what he had written to
Mrs. Roosevelt. At the end of May, 1947, Congress sent to Truman
the Taft-Hartley labor bill, which among other provisions enabled
states to pass "right to work" laws outlawing union shops, radically
curtailing the prospects of unionization in all but the industrial
Northeast, Midwest and the Far West. Together with the termination
of the OPA, the failure of the Full Employment bill, and the weakening of the Fair Labor Standards Act by the Portal-to-Portal Act of
1947, Taft-Hartley signified to La Guardia the piece-by-piece disman-
tling of the New Deal. "The social welfare and economic reforms of
the New Deal are being shattered to pieces," he wrote. "We [are] back
not only to where we started in 1933 but to the old days of the '90s.
Liberals and progressives are too busy calling each other names . . .
and making faces at each other . . . to prevent a throwback to the
days of special privilege and exploitation of the masses." The fact

that more House Democrats voted for Taft-Hartley than against it indicated to La Guardia that the ADA's strategy of working within the Democratic Party had failed; only the external threat of a third party could force it to move to the left, and such an external threat would be impotent so long as the progressive-liberal-labor forces were divided.

On June 23, 1947, Congress overrode Truman's veto to pass Taft-Hartley. "The New Deal initiated by Franklin D. Roosevelt is for the moment dead," La Guardia wrote. "Nothing short of a sudden awakening of the American people and smashing of the present political partnership between the leadership of the two parties can prevent a period of frenzied finance, legalized exploitation and return to power of concentrated wealth." This was how he envisioned post–New Deal America, three months before his death:

> There will be no rough stuff. . . . Foreign countries will be kept in line—they have no choice. . . . There will be great solicitude for the individual. For some time yet there will be full freedom of speech. . . . There will be free and open elections as usual— . . . two parties with a single thought. There will not be the slightest interference or even remote attempt to interfere with religious freedom. There will be plenty of organized sports for the recreation of the workers—and plenty of good, wholesome literature for their edification, and to keep the mind off such subversive and crazy ideas as a better and fuller and happier life. There will be no ruthlessness or shoving around—just a gradual and systematic reduction in the pay envelope. A plutocracy within a democracy.[12]

La Guardia, like Roosevelt, did not live to confront the difficult choices New Deal liberals faced in the early Cold War years. During the summer of 1947, he went into a sharp decline; George Baehr, his personal physician and longtime friend, suspected a malignancy but decided La Guardia would prefer to continue his work and chose not to tell him. Fiorello kept up his radio broadcasts when he could but was soon confined to bed in the large English cottage–style house in Riverdale he had purchased shortly before leaving Gracie Mansion. By the end of the summer, he had nearly wasted away; visitors left with tears in their eyes at the sight of so vital a man so thoroughly drained of life. "He should have died splendidly in battle," the journalist I. F. Stone would write, "not shrinking into skin and bone on a sick bed. . . ." But the mixture of righteous pugnacity and egotism that had driven La Guardia throughout his life remained unabated until the end. "I've got to live," he told a close friend when he was very near death; "the people need me." Henry Wallace recounted the last time he saw the Little Flower: "In leaving I said, 'Fiorello, we all think you have fought the good fight.' He turned his face and wept. . . . He knew how terribly the world needed him, but his strength was gone."[13]

La Guardia succumbed to pancreatic cancer on September 20, 1947. He died on the cusp of a new chapter in American national life and in the history of his native city—a city that might have seemed strange to him, though it was, in many small ways and in a few big ones, of his creation. President Truman paid tribute, as did George Marshall, Harold Ickes, Thomas Dewey, Herbert Lehman, David Dubinsky, Edward Flynn, Clement Attlee, and Eamon de Valera. But perhaps the most powerful eulogy came from Henry Wallace, three months away from the beginning of his ill-fated presidential candidacy. "The people of the world have lost a friend when they needed him most," Wallace said. "He was the most colorful, most beloved figure in American politics and his loss is our greatest tragedy since April 12, 1945. First Roosevelt, now Fiorello—the fighters are taken from us when we need them most, but the fight continues."[14]

ACKNOWLEDGMENTS

Like all students of broadly familiar subjects, I owe my primary debt to other scholars who have worked on related topics. In some instances, I have drawn upon their interpretations (because I agree with them); in others, their work has made it possible for me to provide a deep context to the story I have told here. I am grateful to them all. I should like to say thank you especially to Thomas Kessner, author of what is presently the outstanding biography of Fiorello La Guardia, for his generosity and encouragement when I approached him out of the blue several years ago to ask if he thought this project worthwhile. He assured me that it was, and he pointed me toward some of the puzzles I have attempted to address.

This work has been made possible by the efforts of archivists, librarians, and staff at many institutions: among others, Firestone Library at Princeton University, Butler and Lehman Libraries and the Oral History Research Office at Columbia University, the New York Public Library's Manuscripts and Maps Divisions, the National Archives at College Park, Maryland, the Library of Congress Manuscripts Division, the La Guardia and Wagner Archives at La Guardia Community College in Queens, Sterling Library at Yale University, the Robert F. Wagner Labor Archives at New York University, and the Municipal Reference Library, New York. Above all, I am grateful to the staff at the Franklin D. Roosevelt Library, whose friendliness, professionalism, and good cheer were as much a source of pleasure as were the early morning and early evening train rides along the Hudson; to the staff of the New York Municipal Archives, who lived with this project nearly as long as I did; and to the custodians of the Allen Room at the New York Public Library, overseen during the period in which this book was written by the estimable David Smith and Jay Barksdale. My research in Hyde Park was assisted by a grant from the Franklin and Eleanor Roosevelt Institute's Levy-Beekman Fund. The generous subvention attached to Columbia's Bancroft Dissertation Prize has assisted in the publication of the book.

Tony Grafton and Dan Rodgers (whose own scholarly insights run through this book) began what I imagine was the thankless task of introducing me to the professional study of history. Betsy Blackmar, Alan Brinkley, Eric Foner, Ira Katznelson, and Sarah Phillips picked up where they left off. To recount here their contributions to this book and to my scholarly development more generally would be tedious, but I want them to know how greatly I appreciate the time and energy they have invested in me. They should, of course, be excused from responsibility for the rough edges that remain.

Ken Jackson was a friend to this project in many different ways. He taught me to view the subject from an urban historian's perspective. He offered appropriate criticism when I needed to hear it and support when he thought I was on to something. Mike Wallace allowed me to participate in a seminar he was giving on twentieth-century New York at the City University of New York Graduate Center; I learned a great deal—how could one not?—from reading a partial draft of the forthcoming second volume of his *Gotham* project, and the seminar more generally. Joshua Freeman generously served as outside reader on my dissertation committee; his interest in the research meant a great deal to me.

I owe a particular debt of gratitude to my graduate school colleagues at Columbia, several of whom would be within their rights to view this project as a personal affliction. A special thanks to Justin Jackson, Thai Jones, Keith Orejel, Ezra Tessler, Tamara Mann Tweel, and Michael Woodsworth, each of whom read through (at least) several chapters of the manuscript. Erik Linstrum, now a postdoctoral fellow at the University of Michigan, has been with this project since the beginning, and I am happy to have the opportunity to thank him again now for his friendship and support. Mary Jo Bane, Brent Cebul, Jack Epstein, Archong Fung, Jennifer Hochschild, Alex Keyssar, Stephen Macekura, Andrew Meade McGee, Guian McKee, and Moshik Temkin each helped me to think more deeply about the research presented here. Brian Balogh's unusual conception of how to treat "someone else's graduate student" resulted first in my acquisition of a fridge full of Chinese food, then in my introduction to a remarkable community of scholars of American political history.

Sean Wilentz got me started writing history, and it was his belief that I was on to something important that first gave this study life beyond the walls of Mudd Manuscript Library. He brought the project to the attention of Steve Forman and Drake McFeely at W. W. Norton & Company, who decided to take a chance on it and watched with good cheer as it grew from a one-off book project into a doctoral dissertation. Steve and his extraordinarily sharp assistant, Justin Cahill, treated the manuscript with great care and improved it in many ways. Ann Adelman did a marvelous job copyediting the finished text.

I was blessed to grow up surrounded by people who value knowledge for its own sake, and who encouraged my own curiosity at every stage. For that, and for so much else, I can never thank my family enough—Shawn, Walter, Charlie, James, Eugenia, and the late Richard Williams, and Bill and Mickey Reilly. I hope they will not mind if I say a special thank you to James, who gave his time to assemble a great deal of election return data underpinning parts of chapters 3, 6, and 8. Dona, Keith, and Brian Schaitkin have been wonderful additions. (It was Dona's insistence that I see the Whitney Museum's exhibit of Edward Hopper's interwar paintings which serendipitously yielded the book's title.)

Alexis Schaitkin has done so much work on this book that it is really hers as well. What remains mine I give to her in gratitude for the life we have begun and in happy anticipation of what is to come.

NOTES

Abbreviations

CCOHC	Columbia Center for Oral History Collection
FDR	Franklin Delano Roosevelt
FDRL	Franklin D. Roosevelt Library (Hyde Park, NY)
FHL	Fiorello H. La Guardia
LC	Manuscripts Division, Library of Congress
MRL	New York City Department of Records, Municipal Reference Library
NA	National Archives II (College Park, MD)
NYMA	New York Municipal Archives
NYPL	Manuscripts and Archive Division, New York Public Library
OF	Franklin D. Roosevelt Presidential Papers, Official File
PPF	Franklin D. Roosevelt Presidential Papers, President's Personal File
PSF	Franklin D. Roosevelt Presidential Papers, President's Secretary's File
SF	Fiorello H. La Guardia Mayoral Papers, Subject Files
SWLAC-CU	Social Work Library Agency Collection, Lehman Library, Columbia University

AHR	*American Historical Review*
APSR	*American Political Science Review*
JAH	*Journal of American History*
NYHT	*New York Herald Tribune*
NYP	*New York Post*
NYT	*New York Times*

NYWT	*New York World-Telegram*
SAPD	*Studies in American Political Development*
TNR	*The New Republic*
WP	*Washington Post*
CPPC	*Complete Presidential Press Conferences of Franklin D. Roosevelt*, 25 vols. (New York, 1972)
CR	*Congressional Record*
PL	Elliott Roosevelt, ed., *F.D.R.: His Personal Letters. Vol. 2: 1928–1945* (New York, 1947–50)
PPA	Samuel I. Rosenman, ed., *The Public Papers and Addresses of Franklin D. Roosevelt*, 13 vols. (New York, 1938–50)
SB	*Text of Mayor F. H. La Guardia's Sunday Broadcasts to the People of New York . . . Over WNYC* (New York Public Library)

An Additional Note on Sources: Unless otherwise indicated, all election return data has been compiled from the *Annual Report of the Board of Elections of the City of New York* and the annual volume of the *City Record* entitled *Official Canvass of the Votes Cast . . .* The New York Public Library and the Municipal Reference Library hold maps of each assembly district, showing election district boundaries; Arthur Mann, *La Guardia Comes to Power: 1933* (Philadelphia, 1965), appendix, contains borough maps showing assembly district boundaries. Budgetary data are drawn from Citizens Budget Commission, *Fiscal Facts Concerning the City of New York: A Statistical Summary of the City's Finances, Vols. 1–2* (New York, 1940, 1947). Citations for Drew Pearson and Robert Allen's "Washington Merry-Go-Round" columns may be found at the Washington Research Library Consortium's online archive: http://www.aladin0.wrlc.org/gsdl/ collect/pearson/pearson.shtml. For constant dollar calculations, I have used Robert C. Sahr's conversion factor table: http://oregonstate.edu/cla/polisci/individual-year -conversion-factor-tables. A bibliography and fuller notes may be found in Mason B. Williams, "City of Ambition: Franklin Roosevelt, Fiorello La Guardia, and the Making of New Deal New York," PhD diss., Columbia University, 2012.

Epigraphs: Adolf A. Berle, Jr., "New York Today and Tomorrow" (address over WEVD, Aug. 25, 1937), Berle Papers, Box 141, FDRL; Reminiscences of Reuben Lazarus, CCOHC, 199.

Introduction

1 Though there exists no general history of New York City's "little New Deal," a large and generally excellent biographical literature, much of it deeply informed by history, treats Fiorello La Guardia's mayoralty. In addition to the works cited in note 12, see esp. Jerold S. Auerbach, "A New Deal in New York City: Fiorello

La Guardia, 1934–1937," MA thesis, Columbia University, 1959; Arthur Mann, *La Guardia Comes to Power: 1933* (Philadelphia, 1965); William Manners, *Patience and Fortitude: Fiorello La Guardia, a Biography* (New York, 1976); August Heckscher with Phyllis Robinson, *When La Guardia Was Mayor: New York's Legendary Years* (New York, 1978); Lawrence Elliott, *Little Flower: The Life and Times of Fiorello La Guardia* (New York, 1983); Thomas Kessner, *Fiorello H. La Guardia and the Making of Modern New York* (New York, 1989); Ronald H. Bayor, *Fiorello La Guardia: Ethnicity and Reform* (Arlington Heights, IL, 1993); and the relevant passages of Robert A. Caro, *The Power Broker: Robert Moses and the Fall of New York* (New York, 1974). The study which most closely anticipates the findings presented here is Martin Shefter, "Economic Crises, Social Coalitions, and Political Institutions: New York City's Little New Deal," American Political Science Association paper, 1981.

2 Arthur Mann, *La Guardia: A Fighter Against His Times* (Philadelphia, 1959), 143, 326. Part of the phrasing of the final sentence of this paragraph, and the idea embodied in it, are borrowed from Samuel Grafton, "I'd Rather Be Right," *NYP*, Apr. 13, 1945.

3 Daniel T. Rodgers, "'Moocher Class' Warfare," *Democracy* (Spring 2012), 85.

4 Nathan Glazer, *From a Cause to a Style: Modernist Architecture's Encounter with the American City* (Princeton, 2007), 224.

5 William J. Novak, "Public-Private Governance: A Historical Introduction," in Jody Freedman and Martha Minow, eds., *Government by Contract: Outsourcing and American Democracy* (Cambridge, MA, 2009), 23–40.

6 Samuel H. Beer, "In Search of a New Public Philosophy," in Anthony King, ed., *The New American Political System* (Washington, DC, 1978), 8. Cf. Christopher Capozzola, *Uncle Sam Wants You: World War I and the Making of the Modern American Citizen* (New York, 2008), a very rich study of the relation between localism and national citizenship during the First World War.

7 Frederic C. Howe, *The City: The Hope of Democracy* (New York, 1906), 302. On the strength of local government, see, e.g., Martha Derthick, *Keeping the Compound Republic: Essays on American Federalism* (Washington, DC, 2001), chap. 1, William J. Novak, "The Myth of the 'Weak' American State," *AHR*, vol. 113, no. 3 (June, 2008), 752–72 (esp. 765–67). Brian Balogh, *A Government Out of Sight: The Mystery of National Authority in Nineteenth-Century America* (Princeton, 2009), offers the best general analysis of the pre–New Deal national state.

8 The classic model of "cooperative federalism" is Morton Grodzins, *The American System: A New View of Government in the United States*, ed. Daniel J. Elazar (Chicago, 1966); Elazar, "Cooperative Federalism," in Daphne A. Kenyon and John Kincaid, eds., *Competition Among States and Local Governments: Efficiency and Equity in American Federalism* (Washington, DC, 1991), chap. 4, offers a useful review; and Paul E. Peterson, Barry G. Rabe, and Kenneth K. Wong, *When Federalism Works* (Washington, DC, 1986), an incisive qualification. Still worth

reading is Edward S. Corwin, "The Passing of Dual Federalism," *Virginia Law Review*, vol. 36, no. 1 (1950).

9 Richard Valelly, *Radicalism in the States: The Minnesota Farmer-Labor Party and the American Political Economy* (Chicago, 1989), in addition to offering a terrific case study, provides a useful framework for conceptualizing the ways in which the New Deal shaped politics at the subnational level.

10 Eric Monkkonen, *The Local State: Public Money and American Cities* (Stanford, CA, 1995), 108. Related is the tendency to equate localism with anti-statism; see, e.g., Meg Jacobs and Julian Zelizer, "Introduction," in Jacobs et al., eds., *The Democratic Experiment: New Directions in American Political History* (Princeton, 2003), 1–2.

11 See Peterson et al., *When Federalism Works*, 6.

12 Scholars should read this book as an intervention in the literatures on municipal reform and political incorporation in interwar New York. Relevant works include Charles Garrett, *The La Guardia Years: Machine and Reform Politics in New York City* (New Brunswick, NJ, 1961); Richard C. Wade, "The Withering Away of the Party System," in Jewell Bellush and Dick Netzer, eds., *Urban Politics, New York Style* (Armonk, NY, 1990); Theodore J. Lowi, "Machine Politics: Old and New," *Public Interest* 9 (1967); Martin Shefter, *Political Crisis/Fiscal Crisis: The Collapse and Revival of New York City* (New York, 1985); Kenneth Finegold, *Experts and Politicians: Reform Challenges to Machine Politics in New York, Cleveland, and Chicago* (Princeton, 1995); Chris McNickle, *To Be Mayor of New York: Ethnic Politics in the City* (New York, 1993), chaps. 2–3; Ronald Bayor, *Neighbors in Conflict: The Irish, Germans, Jews, and Italians of New York City, 1929–1941*, 2nd ed. (Urbana, IL, 1988), chaps. 3, 7; David C. Hammack, "Political Participation and Municipal Policy: New York City, 1870–1940," in Thomas Bender and Carl Schorske, eds., *Budapest and New York: Studies in Metropolitan Transformation, 1870–1930* (New York, 1994); Martin Shefter, "Political Incorporation and the Extrusion of the Left: Party Politics and Social Forces in New York City," *SAPD* 1 (1986), 50–90; and Steven P. Erie, *The Rainbow's End: Irish-Americans and the Dilemmas of Urban Machine Politics, 1840–1985* (Berkeley, CA, 1988), chaps. 4–5.

13 Joshua B. Freeman, *Working-Class New York: Life and Labor in the City Since World War II* (New York, 2000). Freeman points to the comparative strength of the city's labor and leftist movements, the relative political weakness of its homeowner class, and the receptivity of its "majority minority" population to "dissent and struggle" and to "ideas and movements outside the mainstream." Other scholars have emphasized the city's sheer wealth. Cf. Paul Peterson and Margaret Weir, "Is New York a Deviant Case?" in Peterson, *City Limits* (Chicago, 1981), chap. 10.

14   Stephen Berger, "Breaking the Governmental Habit: Proposals for the Mayor," *City Journal* (Winter 1993), 21.

Part I: Foundations

Chapter 1: Beginnings

1   *SB*, Apr. 15, 1945; Newbold Morris, *Let the Chips Fall: My Battles Against Corruption* (New York, 1955), 199; Frank Freidel, *Franklin D. Roosevelt: The Apprenticeship* (Boston, 1952), 361–63.

2   Freidel, *The Apprenticeship*, 5–6; Elliott Roosevelt, ed., *F.D.R.: His Personal Letters, Vol. I: The Early Years* (New York, 1947), 443, 464–65; "The Roosevelt Family in New Amsterdam Before the Revolution," Sophomore thesis, Harvard University, 1901, Roosevelt Family and Business Papers, Box 36, FDRL, quoted in Arthur M. Schlesinger, Jr., *The Crisis of the Old Order, 1919 1933* (Boston, 1957), 323–24.

3   Patrick J. Maney, *The Roosevelt Presence: A Biography of Franklin Delano Roosevelt* (New York, 1992), 1; Raymond Moley, *27 Masters of Politics, in a Personal Perspective* (New York, 1949), 31; Frank Freidel, *Franklin D. Roosevelt: A Rendezvous with Destiny* (Boston, 1990), 3–4; Alan Brinkley, "Hoover and Roosevelt: Two Approaches to Leadership," in Walter Isaacson, ed., *Profiles in Leadership: Historians on the Elusive Quality of Greatness* (New York, 2010), 194.

4   Freidel, *The Apprenticeship*, 13–14, 20–34 (quote at 14); Rexford G. Tugwell, *The Democratic Roosevelt: A Biography of Franklin D. Roosevelt* (Garden City, NY, 1957), 46; Geoffrey C. Ward, *Before the Trumpet: Young Franklin Roosevelt, 1882–1905* (New York, 1985), chaps. 3–4.

5   Eleanor Roosevelt, *This I Remember* (New York, 1949), 69–70; Thomas H. Greer, *What Roosevelt Thought: The Social and Political Ideas of Franklin D. Roosevelt* (East Lansing, MI, 1958), 3–9.

6   Freidel, *The Apprenticeship*, 57; Tugwell, *The Democratic Roosevelt*, 33–34, 36, 41, Joseph Alsop, *FDR, 1882–1945: A Centenary Remembrance* (New York, 1982), 37.

7   See esp. Ward, *Before the Trumpet*, chaps. 7–8.

8   Howard Zavin, "Forward to the Land: Franklin D. Roosevelt and the City, 1882–1933," PhD diss., New York University, 1972, 1–5, 8, 10–11, 14; Roosevelt, ed., *Personal Letters: Vol. I*, 77, 453–54; Tugwell, *The Democratic Roosevelt*, 24; Eleanor Roosevelt, *This Is My Story* (New York, 1937), 27; Ward, *Before the Trumpet*, 319n3 (emphasis added by Ward).

9   Freidel, *The Apprenticeship*, 87.

10   Robert F. Wesser, *A Response to Progressivism: The Democratic Party and New York Politics, 1902–1918* (New York, 1986), 30–31. See esp. Martin Shefter, "The Elec-

toral Foundations of the Political Machine: New York City, 1884–1897," in Joel Silbey et al., eds., *The History of American Electoral Behavior* (Princeton, 1978), esp. 263–266, 290–96. General histories of Tammany Hall include Gustavus Myers, *The History of Tammany Hall* (New York, 1971 [1901]), and M. R. Werner, *Tammany Hall* (New York, 1968 [1932]). See also David C. Hammack, *Power and Society: Greater New York at the Turn of the Century* (New York, 1987), 159–72.

11 Wesser, *A Response to Progressivism*, 21–22 and passim; Ernest K. Lindley, *Franklin D. Roosevelt: A Career in Progressive Democracy* (New York, 1931), 72.

12 Freidel, *The Apprenticeship*, 99; Lindley, *A Career in Progressive Democracy*, 77–101.

13 Geoffrey C. Ward, *A First-Class Temperament: The Emergence of Franklin Roosevelt* (New York, 1989), 137–39, 154, 498.

14 Freidel, *The Apprenticeship*, 122–26, 174–89; J. Joseph Huthmacher, "Urban Liberalism and the Age of Reform," *Mississippi Valley Historical Review*, vol. 49, no. 2 (September, 1962), 231–41; John D. Buenker, *Urban Liberalism and Progressive Reform*, 2nd ed. (New York, 1978).

15 Freidel, *The Apprenticeship*, 338–39; Freidel, *The Ordeal*, 51–91; *NYT*, July 31, 1926.

16 Frances Perkins, *The Roosevelt I Knew* (New York, 1946), 29; David M. Kennedy, *Freedom from Fear: The American People in Depression and War, 1929–1945* (New York, 1999), 96.

17 See esp. Hugh Gregory Gallagher, *FDR's Splendid Deception* (New York, 1985), 14–33, 63–66, and passim; Ward, *A First-Class Temperament*, chaps. 14–17.

18 Duff Gilfond, "Americans We Like: Congressman La Guardia," *The Nation*, Mar. 21, 1928, 320; Arthur Mann, *La Guardia: A Fighter Against His Times, 1882–1933* (Philadelphia, 1959), 21; FHL, *The Making of an Insurgent: An Autobiography, 1882–1919* (Philadelphia, 1948), 17–19; Thomas Kessner, *Fiorello H. La Guardia and the Making of Modern New York* (New York, 1989), 23.

19 Mann, *A Fighter Against His Times*, 25–35; Kessner, *Fiorello H. La Guardia*, 9–17; Lawrence Elliott, *Little Flower: The Life and Times of Fiorello La Guardia* (New York, 1983), 26–33; FHL, *The Making of an Insurgent*, 22–38, 33; Joseph Lilly, "La Guardia," *The Nation*, Oct. 4, 1947, 336.

20 Mann, *A Fighter Against His Times*, 39–41, 68; FHL, *The Making of an Insurgent*, 60–61.

21 Lilly, "La Guardia," 336; Arthur Mann, *La Guardia Comes to Power: 1933* (Philadelphia, 1965), 31; Kessner, *Fiorello H. La Guardia*, 23–24.

22 Mann, *A Fighter Against His Times*, 47–49, 54–60; FHL, *The Making of an Insurgent*, 96–97; Kessner, *Fiorello H. La Guardia*, 37, 59–60.

23 FHL, *The Making of an Insurgent*, 30–31, 102, 123–27; Mann, *A Fighter Against His Times*, 49–54, 61–71; Kessner, *Fiorello H. La Guardia*, 34; Elliott, *Little Flower*, 66; Reminiscences of Frederick Tanner, CCOHC, 15, 18–19, 40; Reminiscences of

Francis Stoddard, CCOHC, 29, 50–51. On the integration of Italian Americans into the Democratic Party, see Thomas M. Henderson, *Tammany Hall and the New Immigrants: The Progressive Years* (New York, 1976), esp. chap. 3. For district boundaries, see *Brooklyn Eagle* Library, *Reapportionment of 1906 . . .* (New York, 1906), 17–18, 22.

24 Mann, *A Fighter Against His Times*, 75–81, 100–08; Howard Zinn, *La Guardia in Congress* (Ithaca, NY, 1959), 13–47; FHL, *The Making of an Insurgent*, chap. 6; Dana Frank, "Housewives, Socialists, and the Politics of Food: The 1917 New York Cost of Living Protests," *Feminist Studies*, vol. 11, no. 2 (Summer 1985), 255–83; William Frieburger, "War Prosperity and Hunger: The New York Food Riots of 1917," *Labor History*, vol. 25, no. 2 (Spring 1984), 217–39; CR, 65th Cong., 1st Sess., 1700, 4014–4016; "La Guardia Sees Real Peril in Reactionaries, Not Reds," *NYT*, Feb. 29, 1920.

25 FHL, *The Making of an Insurgent*, 138–45; Zinn, *La Guardia in Congress*, 14–15n30; Lowell M. Limpus and Burr W. Leyson, *This Man La Guardia* (New York, 1938), 42–43.

26 Mann, *A Fighter Against His Times*, 94–100; Zinn, *La Guardia in Congress*, 32; Kessner, *Fiorello H. La Guardia*, 57.

27 Alan Brinkley, *Franklin Delano Roosevelt* (New York, 2010), 14; Mann, *A Fighter Against His Times*, 79; Maney, *The Roosevelt Presence*, 23; Robert Wiebe, *The Search for Order, 1877–1920* (New York, 1967), 160–161; Saladin M. Ambar, *How Governors Built the Modern American Presidency* (Philadelphia, 2012).

28 Martin J. Schiesl, *The Politics of Efficiency: Municipal Administration and Reform in America, 1880–1920* (Berkeley, 1977), chaps. 5–8; Jane S. Dahlberg, *The New York Bureau of Municipal Research: Pioneer in Government Administration* (New York, 1966); Kenneth Finegold, *Experts and Politicians: Reform Challenges to Machine Politics in New York, Cleveland, and Chicago* (Princeton, 1995), 49–52; Henry Bruère et al., "Efficiency in City Government," *Annals of the American Academy of Political and Social Science* 41 (May 1912), quote at 3; Keith D. Revell, *Building Gotham: Civic Culture and Public Policy in New York City, 1898–1938* (Baltimore, 2003), esp. chap. 4.

29 Among many others, Daniel T. Rodgers, *Atlantic Crossings: Social Politics in a Progressive Age* (Cambridge, MA, 1998), esp. chaps. 4–5; Allen F. Davis, *Spearheads for Reform: The Social Settlements and the Progressive Movement, 1890–1914* (New Brunswick, NJ, 1984); Roy Lubove, *The Progressives and the Slums: Tenement House Reform in New York City, 1890–1917* (Pittsburgh, 1962); Daniel Eli Burnstein, *Next to Godliness: Confronting Dirt and Despair in Progressive Era New York City* (Urbana, IL, 2006); Harry P. Kraus, "The Settlement House Movement in New York City, 1886–1914," PhD diss., New York University, 1980; Marilyn Thornton Williams, "New York City's Public Baths: A Case Study in Urban Progressive Reform," *Journal of Urban History*, vol. 7, no. 1 (November 1980), 49–77;

John Duffy, *A History of Public Health in New York City, Vol. 2: 1866–1966* (New York, 1974), chaps. 10–11.

30 Irving Howe, *World of Our Fathers* (New York, 1976), 310–21; Morris Hillquit, *Socialism in Theory and Practice*, 2nd ed. (New York, 1919), 207–09, 214–15, 286–88, 315–19; Morris Hillquit, *Present-Day Socialism* (New York, 1920), 53, 66–71; Zosa Szajkowski, "The Jews and New York City's Mayoralty Election of 1917," *Jewish Social Studies*, vol. 32, no. 4 (October 1970), 287.

31 Finegold, *Experts and Politicians*, 45–49, 52; Federal Writers' Project, *New York Panorama: A Comprehensive View of the Metropolis* (New York, 1938), 306; David Nasaw, *The Chief: The Life of William Randolph Hearst* (Boston, 2000), 172–73, 189–90, 194–201; Roy Everett Littlefield III, *William Randolph Hearst: His Role in American Progressivism* (Lanham, MD, 1980), 63–76, 177–98; Harold C. Syrett, ed., *The Gentleman and the Tiger: The Autobiography of George B. McClellan, Jr.* (Philadelphia, 1956), 225–26.

32 Rodgers, *Atlantic Crossings*, 159; Morris Hillquit, *Socialism Summed Up* (New York, 1913), 83.

33 Lowell M. Limpus and Burr W. Leyson, *This Man La Guardia* (New York, 1938), 96; Mann, *A Fighter Against His Times*, 109–17; Kessner, *Fiorello H. La Guardia*, 67–70; Frederick Shaw, *The History of the New York City Legislature* (New York, 1954), chaps. 2–4; Henry Curran, *Pillar to Post* (New York, 1941), 126; Reminiscences of Marie La Guardia, CCOHC, 9; Leonard Covello, *The Heart Is the Teacher* (New York, 1958), 153.

34 W. A. Swanberg, *Citizen Hearst: A Biography of William Randolph Hearst* (New York, 1961), 307–20; John F. McClymer, "Of 'Mornin' Glories' and 'Fine Old Oaks': John Purroy Mitchel, Al Smith, and Reform as an Expression of Irish American Aspiration," in Ronald H. Bayor and Timothy J. Meagher, eds., *The New York Irish* (Baltimore, 1996), 388–89; John F. Hylan, *The Autobiography of John Francis Hylan, Mayor of New York* (New York, 1922); Clifton Hood, *722 Miles: The Building of the Subways and How They Transformed New York* (New York, 1993), chap. 8; John F. Hylan, *Seven Years of Progress . . .* (New York, 1925); *NYT*, Mar. 11, 1920; Walter Lippmann, *Men of Destiny* (New York, 1926), 6; "Hylan: A Symbol," *TNR*, Nov. 23, 1921, 364.

35 La Guardia's activities as president of the Board of Aldermen are well documented in the clippings scrapbook in the FHL Papers, NYPL. Here, see *NYT*, Jan. 30, Mar. 24, July 24, Aug. 1, 1920, Feb. 2, July 18, 1921; also FHL, "Congress and the Port," in *NYT*, May 27, 1921.

36 Mann, *A Fighter Against His Times*, 122–24; *NYT*, Jan. 4, 1921; *New York Tribune*, Apr. 21, 1921.

37 "La Guardia Thinks He Could Be Mayor," *New York Tribune*, July 31, 1919; Mann, *A Fighter Against His Times*, 127–36; Judith Stein, "The Birth of Liberal Republicanism in New York State, 1932–1938," PhD diss., Yale University, 1968, chap.

2; Robert Moses, *Public Works: A Dangerous Trade* (New York, 1970), 876; *NYT*, Jan. 4, 26–28, Feb. 2, 4, 7, 9, 27, Sept. 11, 1921; FHL to Maury Maverick, Mar. 27, 1939, SF, "General Correspondence—M," NYMA.

38   Mann, *A Fighter Against His Times*, 136–40; Kessner, *Fiorello H. La Guardia*, 76; *New York Tribune*, Oct. 5, 1921; *NYT*, Nov. 4, Dec. 18, 1921; Limpus and Leyson, *This Man La Guardia*, 127.

39   Frances Perkins, *The Roosevelt I Knew* (New York, 1946), 330; Daniel R. Fusfeld, *The Economic Thought of Franklin D. Roosevelt and the Origins of the New Deal* (New York, 1956), 49; FDR, *Looking Forward* (New York, 2009 [1933]), 210–11; Edgar B. Nixon, ed., *Franklin D. Roosevelt and Conservation, 1911–1945* (Hyde Park, NY, 1957), Douglas B. Craig, *After Wilson: The Struggle for Control of the Democratic Party, 1920–1934* (Chapel Hill, NC, 1992), 18, 19–20.

40   *NYT*, Nov. 11, 1921.

41   *NYT*, July 14, 1922; Kessner, *Fiorello H. La Guardia*, 82–84; Zinn, *La Guardia in Congress*, 51–52; Mann, *A Fighter Against His Times*, 147–149.

Chapter 2: A Season in the Wilderness

1   Arthur Mann, *La Guardia: A Fighter Against His Times, 1882–1933* (Philadelphia, 1959), 144, 149–51; Howard Zinn, *La Guardia in Congress* (Ithaca, NY, 1959), 60–62; Thomas Kessner, *Fiorello H. La Guardia and the Making of Modern New York* (New York, 1989), 134–35; Jeffrey S. Gurock, *When Harlem Was Jewish, 1870–1930* (New York, 1979), chap. 6; Edward Corsi, "My Neighborhood," *Outlook*, Sept. 16, 1925, 92; Gerald Meyer, "Italian Harlem: Portrait of a Community," in Philip V. Cannistraro, ed., *The Italians of New York: Five Centuries of Struggle and Achievement* (New York, 1999), 58; Robert A. Orsi, *The Madonna of 115th Street: Faith and Community in Italian Harlem, 1880–1950* (New Haven, CT, 1985), 14–31, 37.

2   Corsi, "My Neighborhood," 61; Thomas Kessner, "Jobs, Ghettoes, and the Urban Economy," *American Jewish History*, vol. 71, no. 2 (December, 1981), 232; Meyer, "Italian Harlem," 62–63; Samuel L. Baily, *Immigrants in the Lands of Promise: Italians in Buenos Aires and New York City* (Ithaca, NY, 1999), 209–11; Orsi, *The Madonna of 115th Street*, chap. 4 (esp. p. 96); Zinn, *La Guardia in Congress*, 68–69; *Il Pubilo*, Oct. 9, 1922, quoted in Mann, *A Fighter Against His Times*, 154. On first-generation Italian American radicalism, see esp. Philip V. Cannistraro and Gerald Meyer, eds., *The Lost World of Italian American Radicalism: Politics, Labor, and Culture* (Westport, CT, 2003), and Marcella Bencivenni, *Italian Immigrant Radical Culture: The Idealism of the Sonersini in the United States, 1890–1940* (New York, 2011).

3   Meyer, "Italian Harlem," 61–62; Mann, *A Fighter Against His Times*, 231–46.

4   Duff Gilfond, "Americans We Like: Congressman La Guardia," *The Nation*, Mar. 21, 1928, 319.

5   Reminiscences of Marie La Guardia, CCOHC, 17–18.

6   Mann, *A Fighter Against His Times*, 189–199; *CR*, 68th Cong., 1st Sess., 1896, 1902, 5886–5887. Orsi, *The Madonna of 115th Street*, 21–25, details the sacrifices some East Harlemites made in the hope of bringing family members to join them.

7   Mann, *A Fighter Against His Times*, 199–206; Arthur W. MacMahon, "First Session of the Sixty-Ninth Congress, December 7, 1925, to July 3, 1926," *APSR*, vol. 20, no. 3 (August, 1926), 613n17.

8   William Hard, "What Is Progressivism?," *The Nation*, Jan. 9, 1924, 27–28; Mann, *A Fighter Against His Times*, 166; *NYT*, Nov. 27–29, Dec. 1–2, 1923.

9   La Guardia articulated these positions most powerfully when discussing the McNary-Haugen legislation: see, e.g., *CR*, 68th Cong., 1st Sess., 9351.

10 David P. Thelen, *Robert M. La Follette and the Insurgent Spirit* (Boston, 1976), 167–76; David A. Horowitz, *Beyond Left and Right: Insurgency and the Establishment* (Urbana, IL, 1997), 43–57; Alan Dawley, *Changing the World: American Progressives in War and Revolution* (Princeton, 2003), 313–30; Richard Valelly, *Radicalism in the States: The Minnesota Farmer-Labor Party and the American Political Economy* (Chicago, 1989), 17–42; Mann, *A Fighter Against His Times*, 159–63, 166–68; Eugene Tobin, *Organize or Perish: America's Independent Progressives, 1913–1933* (Westport, CT, 1986), 132, 141.

11 *NYT*, June 16, Aug. 11–12, 1924; Mann, *A Fighter Against His Times*, 166–80; Thelen, *Robert M. La Follette*, chap. 9; Valelly, *Radicalism in the States*, 49–53; Tobin, *Organize or Perish*, 155–72; FHL to John M. Nelson, Sept. 6, 1924 (quote at 154).

12 William E. Leuchtenburg, *The Perils of Prosperity, 1914–1932* 2nd ed. (Chicago, 1993), 201; Lizabeth Cohen, *Making a New Deal: Industrial Workers in Chicago, 1919–1939* (New York, 1990), 102; Ray Tucker and Frederick R. Barkley, *Sons of the Wild Jackass* (Boston, 1932), 398; Mann, *A Fighter Against His Times*, 260–63, 266–68; Kessner, *Fiorello H. La Guardia*, 101; Reminiscences of Stanley Isaacs, CCOHC, 162–63; Zinn, *La Guardia in Congress*, 163–69; Kenneth C. Martis, *The Historical Atlas of United States Congressional Districts, 1789–1989* (New York, 1989), 181.

13 On Roosevelt's activities in the 1920s, see esp. Geoffrey C. Ward, *A First-Class Temperament: The Emergence of Franklin Roosevelt* (New York, 1989), 600–799; Kenneth S. Davis, *FDR: The Beckoning of Destiny, 1882–1928* (New York, 1972), 684–811; Frank Freidel, *Franklin D. Roosevelt: The Ordeal* (Boston, 1954), chaps. 7–14; and Alfred B. Rollins, Jr., *Roosevelt and Howe* (New York, 1962), chap. 13.

14 Frances Perkins, *The Roosevelt I Knew* (New York, 1946), 31–33; Annelise Orleck, *Common Sense and a Little Fire: Women and Working-Class Politics in the United States, 1900–1965* (Chapel Hill, NC, 1995), 146–47; Freidel, *The Ordeal*, 206; John Gunther, *Roosevelt in Retrospect: A Profile in History* (New York, 1950), 249.

15 Ernest K. Lindley, *Franklin D. Roosevelt: A Career in Progressive Democracy* (New

York, 1931), 226; Reminiscences of Marie La Guardia, CCOHC, 22–23; Mann, *A Fighter Against His Times*, 215.

16　Mann, *A Fighter Against His Times*, 170. On the national Democratic Party in the 1920s, see David Burner, *The Politics of Provincialism: The Democratic Party in Transition, 1918–1932* (New York, 1967), and Douglas B. Craig, *After Wilson: The Struggle for the Democratic Party, 1920–1934* (Chapel Hill, NC, 1992). Peter L. Peterson, "Stopping Al Smith," quoted in Craig, *After Wilson*, 1.

17　Freidel, *The Ordeal*, chaps. 12–13; Rollins, *Roosevelt and Howe*, 222. Many of Roosevelt's public writings from the 1920s are collected in Donald S. Carmichael, ed., *F.D.R., Columnist: The Uncollected Columns of Franklin D. Roosevelt* (Chicago, 1947).

18　Rollins, *Roosevelt and Howe*, 218; Freidel, *The Ordeal*, 205–06; Franklin D. Roosevelt, "Is There a Jefferson on the Horizon?" in Basil Rauch, ed., *The Roosevelt Reader: Selected Speeches, Messages, Press Conferences, and Letters* (New York, 1957), 46.

19　Perkins, *The Roosevelt I Knew*, 158; Walter Lippmann, "Tammany Hall and Al Smith," *Outlook*, Feb. 1, 1928, 163–65. On Smith's governorship, see esp. Craig, *After Wilson*, chap. 6; Christopher M. Finan, *Alfred E. Smith: The Happy Warrior* (New York, 2002), esp. 104–156; and Robert A. Slayton, *Empire Statesman: The Rise and Redemption of Al Smith* (New York, 2001), chaps. 8–12. "Constitutionally Republican" was Smith's characterization of New York's districting practices, quoted in Gerald Benjamin, "The Political Relationship," in Benjamin and Charles Brecher, eds., *The Two New Yorks: State-City Relations in the Changing Federal System* (New York, 1988), 129.

20　Eleanor Roosevelt, *This I Remember* (New York, 1949), 50–51; Freidel, *The Ordeal*, 218–19; Ward, *A First-Class Temperament*, 498–99, 692; Arthur M. Schlesinger, Jr., *The Coming of the New Deal, 1933–1935* (Boston, 1959), 558; "Text of Roosevelt's Democratic Keynote Speech," *NYT*, Sept. 28, 1926.

21　Freidel, *The Ordeal*, 169–80, 241–43; Ward, *A First-Class Temperament*, 693.

22　Rollins, *Roosevelt and Howe*, 227; Freidel, *The Ordeal*, 245–55; Warren Moscow, *Politics in the Empire State* (New York, 1948), 15; Ward, *A First-Class Temperament*, 793–94.

23　Freidel, *The Ordeal*, 257–66; Harold F. Gosnell, *Champion Campaigner: Franklin D. Roosevelt* (New York, 1952), 84–88; Gunther, *Roosevelt in Retrospect*, 253; Hugh Gregory Gallagher, *FDR's Splendid Deception* (New York, 1985), 73–74; James MacGregor Burns, *Roosevelt: The Lion and the Fox* (New York, 1956), 101–04; Ward, *A First-Class Temperament*, 794–99.

24　Among others, see Frank Freidel, *Franklin D. Roosevelt: The Triumph* (Boston, 1956), chaps. 1–12; Bernard Bellush, *Franklin D. Roosevelt as Governor of New York* (New York, 1955); and Kenneth S. Davis, *FDR: The New York Years, 1928–1933* (New York, 1985), 63–142.

25 Gunther, *Roosevelt in Retrospect*, 257, 260–61.
26 Perkins, *The Roosevelt I Knew*, 45; Lindley, *A Career in Progressive Democracy*, 262–64; Charles LaCerra, *Franklin Delano Roosevelt and Tammany Hall of New York* (Lanham, MD, 1997), 62; Freidel, *The Triumph*, 31–32, 91–92.
27 Federal Writers' Project, *New York Panorama: A Comprehensive View of the Metropolis* (New York, 1938), 13, 153, 161; Edwin G. Burrows and Mike Wallace, *Gotham: A History of New York City to 1898* (New York, 1999), viii.
28 David Ward and Olivier Zunz, "Between Rationalism and Pluralism," in Ward and Zunz, eds., *The Landscape of Modernity: Essays on New York City, 1900–1940* (New York, 1992), 3; Peter Marcus, *New York: The Nation's Metropolis* (New York, 1921), 9; Bureau of the Census, *Fifteenth Census of the United States: Manufactures, 1929* (Washington, DC, 1933), I–15, III–378; Bureau of the Census, *Sixteenth Census of the United States: Business, 1939* (Washington, DC, 1942), III–16, III–325; Daniel Bell, "The Three Faces of New York," *Dissent* (July 1961), 224–26.
29 Ric Burns and James Sanders, *New York: An Illustrated History* (New York, 2003), 399–400; Deborah Dash Moore, "On the Fringes of the City: Jewish Neighborhoods in Three Boroughs," in Ward and Zunz, eds., *The Landscape of Modernity*, 254; Moore, "Class and Ethnicity in the Creation of New York City Neighborhoods," in Thomas Bender and Carl Schorske, eds., *Budapest and New York: Studies in Metropolitan Transformation, 1870–1940* (New York, 1994), 143–44; Evelyn Gonzalez, *The Bronx* (New York, 2004), chaps. 4–6; Eleanora Schoenebaum, "Emerging Neighborhoods: The Development of Brooklyn's Fringe Areas, 1850–1930" PhD diss., Columbia University, 1977, chaps. 7–10; Robert A. M. Stern et al., *New York 1930: Architectural Urbanism Between the Two World Wars* (New York, 1987), 390–441; Marion R. Casey, "From the East Side to the Seaside: Irish Americans on the Move in New York City," in Ronald H. Bayor and Timothy J. Meagher, eds., *The New York Irish* (Baltimore, 1996), 396–97.
30 Walter Laidlaw et al., *Population of the City of New York, 1900–1930* (New York, 1932), 268; Joshua Zeitz, *White Ethnic New York: Jews, Catholics, and the Shaping of Postwar Politics* (Chapel Hill, NC, 2007), 12–14.
31 Bureau of the Census, *Thirteenth Census of the United States: Population, Vol. III, Pt. 2* (Washington, DC, 1913), 240; Bureau of the Census, *Fifteenth Census of the United States: Population, Vol. III, Pt. 2* (Washington, DC, 1932), 302–03. The idea of a transition from an "immigrant city" to an "ethnic metropolis" is Deborah Dash Moore's: see Moore, "On the Fringes of the City," 255.
32 Beth S. Wenger, *New York Jews and the Great Depression: Uncertain Promise* (New Haven, CT, 1996), 7; Nathan Glazer and Daniel Patrick Moynihan, *Beyond the Melting Pot: The Negroes, Puerto Ricans, Jews, Italians, and Irish of New York City* (Cambridge, MA, 1963), 13; Deborah Dash Moore, *At Home in America: Second Generation New York Jews* (New York, 1981), 33–58; Zeitz, *White Ethnic New York*, 15, 19, 22–23; Ronald Bayor, *Neighbors in Conflict: The Irish, Germans, Jews, and*

Italians of New York City, 1929–1941, 2nd ed. (Urbana, IL, 1988), 14–24; Federal Writers' Project, *The Italians of New York: A Survey* (New York, 1938), 170–206. See also Cohen, *Making a New Deal*, chaps. 2–3.

33 Gilbert Osofsky, *The Making of a Ghetto: Negro New York, 1890–1930* (New York, 1966), esp. 105–49; Cheryl Lynn Greenberg, *"Or Does It Explode?": Black Harlem in the Great Depression* (New York, 1991), 13–41.

34 Gene Fowler, *Beau James: The Life and Times of Jimmy Walker* (New York, 1949), 11–110; George Walsh, *Gentleman Jimmy Walker: Mayor of the Jazz Age* (New York, 1974), 12–57; Edward J. Flynn, *You're the Boss* (New York, 1947), 46–53.

35 Fowler, *Beau James*, 354; Flynn, *You're the Boss*, 52; *NYT*, Oct. 21, 1929.

36 Steven P. Erie, *Rainbow's End: Irish-Americans and the Dilemmas of Urban Machine Politics, 1840–1945* (Berkeley, 1988), esp. 91–100; Richard C. Wade, "The Withering Away of the Party System," in Jewell Bellush and Dick Netzer, eds., *Urban Politics, New York Style* (Armonk, NY, 1990), 272–73, provides a concise and lucid summary of the party clubhouses' functions.

37 Clifton K. Yearley, *The Money Machines: The Breakdown and Reform of Governmental and Party Finance in the North, 1860–1920* (Albany, NY, 1970), 260–64; Craig F. Thompson, "New York's Jimmie," *TNR*, Aug. 28, 1929, 217; *NYT*, July 19, Oct. 3–4, 1929. For a recent analysis of state expansion and metropolitan development in the 1920s, emphasizing the role of businessmen, see Daniel Amsterdam, "The Roaring Metropolis: Business, Civic Welfare, and State Expansion in 1920s America," PhD diss., University of Pennsylvania, 2009.

38 Joseph A. Spencer, "New York City Tenant Organizations and the Post–World War I Housing Crisis," in Ronald Lawson with Mark Naison, eds., *The Tenant Movement in New York City, 1904–1984* (New Brunswick, NJ, 1986), 86; *NYT*, July 13, 30, Sept. 14, 1926, Mar. 4, Apr. 11, 1929; Stern et al., *New York 1930*, 707; Michael M. Davis and Mary C. Jarrett, *A Health Inventory of New York City: A Study of the Volume and Distribution of Health Service in the Five Boroughs* (New York, 1929), 21–22.

39 John Duffy, *A History of Public Health in New York City, Vol. 2: 1866–1966* (New York, 1974), 261; Department of Public Markets, Weights and Measures of the City of New York, *Annual Report: 1934* (New York, 1935), 9–17; Department of Public Markets, *Annual Report: 1936*, 8–9.

40 For a similar formulation, see Yearley, *The Money Machines* (quote at 256). Walker's first term is best chronicled in Walsh, *Gentleman Jimmy Walker*, 60–208.

41 Mann, *A Fighter Against His Times*, 269–73; *NYT*, Aug. 3, Sept. 9, 23, Oct. 21, Nov. 6, 9, 1929.

42 *NYT*, Aug. 6, Oct. 21, 24, 26, Nov. 3, 1929; Mann, *A Fighter Against His Times*, 273–76.

43 *NYT*, Sept. 23, 1929; Freidel, *The Triumph*, 91–92; Kessner, *Fiorello H. La Guardia*, 162–63; "A Murdered Rothstein Is Political Dynamite," *Literary Digest*, Oct. 19, 1929, 68, 70; Lindley, *A Career in Progressive Democracy*, 264; M. R. Werner,

"Fiorello's Finest Hour," *American Heritage*, vol. 12, no. 6 (October, 1961), 107–10; Davis, *The New York Years*, 103; Rollins, *Roosevelt and Howe*, 273; *PL*, 75–77, 83–84; Reminiscences of Stanley Isaacs, CCOHC, 71. On Rothstein, see Michael Alexander, *Jazz Age Jews* (Princeton, 2001), 15–64.

44 La Guardia ran 17 percent behind the party's 1925 total in Manhattan's 15th Assembly District (the Upper East Side) and 15 percent behind in Manhattan's 10th (which encompassed Gramercy, part of Washington Square North, and the midtown hotels). The drop in the 10th was entirely attributable to the switch of 2,000-odd Republicans to Thomas; in the 15th it was due about equally to Thomas voters and abstentions.

45 Mann, *A Fighter Against His Times*, 279–80; *NYT*, Nov. 3, 6, 1929.

46 *NYT*, Nov. 6, 1929.

47 *NYT*, Nov. 6–7, 1929; Freidel, *The Triumph*, 94.

Chapter 3: The Deluge

1 Cheryl Lynn Greenberg, *"Or Does It Explode?": Black Harlem in the Great Depression* (New York, 1991), 39–40; Bernard Bellush, *Franklin D. Roosevelt as Governor of New York* (New York, 1955), 128.

2 *CR*, 71st Cong., 3rd Sess., 135; Arthur Mann, *Fiorello H. La Guardia: A Fighter Against His Times, 1882–1933* (Philadelphia, 1959), 288.

3 Emergency Employment Committee, *What About This Man?* (November, 1930), SWLAC-CU; Lilian Brandt, *An Impressionistic View of the Winter of 1930–31 in New York City . . . A Report Made to the Executive Committee of the Welfare Council's Coordinating Committee on Unemployment* (New York, 1932), 22.

4 Brandt, *An Impressionistic View*, 22–23.

5 Emergency Unemployment Relief Committee, *The Next Step on the Stair* (1932), SWLAC-CU, 4; Brandt, *An Impressionistic View*, 16–17; W. H. Matthews et al., *Report of the Emergency Work and Relief Bureau of the Emergency Unemployment Relief Committee, October 1, 1931–August 1, 1932*, SWLAC-CU, 25–26 (quote). See esp. Lizabeth Cohen, *Making a New Deal: Industrial Workers in Chicago, 1919–1939* (New York, 1990), chap. 5.

6 L.H.R., "Shacktown Pulls Through the Winter," *NYT Sunday Magazine*, Mar. 26, 1933; Patrick J. Maney, *The Roosevelt Presence: A Biography of Franklin Delano Roosevelt* (New York, 1992), 33; Beth S. Wenger, *New York Jews and the Great Depression: Uncertain Promise* (New Haven, CT, 1996), 108–14; Mark I. Naison, *Communists in Harlem During the Depression* (Urbana, IL, 1983), 41; Roy Rosenzweig, "Organizing the Unemployed: The Early Years of the Great Depression, 1929–1933," *Radical America* 10 (July–August 1976), 44–45, 58n33; Brandt, *An Impressionistic View*, 8–14; Jerold S. Auerbach, "A New Deal in New York City: Fiorello La Guardia, 1934–1937," MA thesis, Columbia University, 1959, 24.

7   A 1931 study, differentiated by race and gender, found that 19.4 percent of white
     men, 25.4 percent of black men, 11.2 percent of white women, and 28.5 percent
     of black women living in Manhattan were unemployed; the corresponding fig-
     ures for Chicago, were 29.7, 43.5, 19.4, and 58.5. In heavily industrial cities—
     Cleveland, Detroit, Pittsburgh, Buffalo, Akron—it was worse still; the figures in
     Detroit, e.g., were 32.4, 60.2, 17.4, and 75.0. Greenberg, *"Or Does It Explode?"* 44
     (table 2.1).

8   Maney, *The Roosevelt Presence*, 33; Greenberg, *"Or Does It Explode?"* 42–52.

9   Jason Scott Smith, *Building New Deal Liberalism: The Political Economy of Pub-
     lic Works, 1933–1956* (New York, 2006), 23–26; William W. Bremer, "Along the
     'American Way': The New Deal's Work Relief Policy for the Unemployed," *JAH*,
     vol. 62, no. 3 (December 1975), 236–52; Edwin G. Burrows and Mike Wallace,
     Gotham: A History of New York City to 1898 (New York, 1999), 624–25, 833, 1024–
     1029, 1186–1190; *New York Call*, Jan. 29, Feb. 3, 6, 1914; *NYT*, Jan. 30, 1914. On
     the Mitchel administration's response, see Donald A. Ritchie, "The Gary Com-
     mittee: Businessmen, Progressives and Unemployment in New York City, 1914–
     1915," *New-York Historical Society Quarterly*, vol. 57, no. 4 (October 1973), 327–47.

10   Greenberg, *"Or Does It Explode?"* 50–51; John D. Millett, *The Works Progress
     Administration in New York City* (Chicago, 1938), 1–7, 11; *NYT*, Mar. 7, 1930; Bar-
     bara Blumberg, *The New Deal and the Unemployed: The View from New York City*
     (Lewisburg, PA, 1979), 19–21; *Literary Digest*, June 24, 1933, 17–18; Charles W.
     Berry, *Program for Meeting New York City's Relief and Unemployment Problems:
     Recommendations for Expediting Public Improvements. . . . : Report to Honorable
     Joseph V. McKee* (1932), SWLAC-CU, 14; Blumberg, *The New Deal and the Unem-
     ployed*, 19–22; Emergency Unemployment Relief Committee, *The Next Step on
     the Stair* (1932), SWLAC-CU, 10–11; Matthews et al., *Report of the Emergency
     Work and Relief Bureau*, 16–19.

11   *Hearings Before the Committee on Labor . . . on H. R. 14105*, House, 72nd Cong.,
     2nd Sess., 241; *CR*, 71st Cong., 3rd Sess., 135, 137. See also a later speech along
     the same lines, *NYT*, Jan. 22, 1934. For La Guardia's attacks on bankers, see *CR*,
     72nd Cong., 1st Sess., 1035; Mann, *A Fighter Against His Times*, 286–87, 302, and
     Zinn, *La Guardia in Congress*, chap. 15; Thomas Kessner, *Fiorello H. La Guardia
     and the Making of Modern New York* (New York, 1989), 192; Ernest Cuneo, *Life
     with Fiorello: A Memoir* (New York, 1955), 39–40, 48–49.

12   *CR*, 71st Cong., 3rd Sess., 135, 136–38, 452; *CR*, 72nd Cong., 1st Sess., 1035, 14328;
     "Statement of Representative F. H. La Guardia in Favor of Unemployment Insur-
     ance . . . ," SF, "Unemployment," NYMA.

13   *CR*, 71st Cong., 3rd Sess., 910; *CR*, 72nd Cong., 1st Sess., 14326; *CR*, 72nd Cong.,
     1st Sess., 1034, 12242; *Hearings Before the Committee on Ways and Means . . . on
     H.R. 12353 . . .* , House, 72nd Cong., 1st Sess., 90, 93.

14   Patrick J. Maney, *"Young Bob" La Follette: A Biography of Robert M. La Follette, Jr.*,

1895–1953 (Columbia, MO, 1978), 85–87; Richard Lowitt, *George W. Norris: The Persistence of a Progressive, 1913–1933* (Urbana, IL, 1971), 509–11; Steven Fraser, *Labor Will Rule: Sidney Hillman and the Rise of American Labor* (New York, 1991), 280–81; Jordan A. Schwarz, "The Politics of Fear: Congress and the Depression During the Hoover Administration," PhD diss., Columbia University, 1967, 141.

15 James J. Lorence, *Gerald J. Boileau and the Progressive-Farmer-Labor Alliance: Politics of the New Deal* (Columbia, SC, 1994), 52–54.

16 Albert U. Romasco, *The Poverty of Abundance: Hoover, the Nation, and the Depression* (New York, 1965), 183–89; David M. Kennedy, *Freedom from Fear: The American People in Depression and War, 1929–1945* (New York, 1999), 82–85; Mann, *A Fighter Against His Times*, 309; CR, 72nd Cong., 1st Sess., 1033, 2081, 14692, 14803.

17 Kennedy, *Freedom from Fear*, 79–80; Jordan A. Schwarz, *Interregnum of Despair: Hoover, Congress, and the Depression* (Urbana, IL, 1970), 106–17; Mann, *A Fighter Against His Times*, 302–03; Zinn, *La Guardia in Congress*, 220.

18 Cuneo, *Life with Fiorello*, 42–46; Zinn, *La Guardia in Congress*, 220; NYT, Mar. 23, 1932; Mann, *A Fighter Against His Times*, 303–05; Schwarz, *Interregnum of Despair*, 118–41; Lorence, *Gerald J. Boileau*, 60; Henry Suydam, "La Guardia Bolt Is Protest at Favors for Rich," *Brooklyn Daily Eagle*, Mar. 22, 1932; Hiram Johnson to his sons, Mar. 26, 1932, in *The Diary Letters of Hiram Johnson, 1917–1945* (New York, 1983, unpaginated).

19 Mann, *A Fighter Against His Times*, 311–12; Irving Bernstein, *The Lean Years: A History of the American Worker, 1920–1933* (Boston, 1960), 393–414; CR, 72nd Cong., 1st Sess., 5468, 5474, 5478–5480, 5503–5504, 5508–5509.

20 NYT, May 15, 27, 1932; Zinn, *La Guardia in Congress*, 202–05.

21 Freidel, *The Triumph*, 133–39; Daniel R. Fusfeld, *The Economic Thought of Franklin D. Roosevelt and the Origins of the New Deal* (New York, 1956), 175–78.

22 Fusfeld, *The Economic Thought of Franklin D. Roosevelt*, 200–05; PPA: Vol. 1, 1928–1932, 116, 503–18.

23 Freidel, *The Triumph*, 225–26.

24 PPA: Vol. 1, 1928–1932, 457–68, 777, 788. See esp. Maney, *The Roosevelt Presence*, 34. For a normative treatment of subsidiarity with respect to social policy, see Mary Jo Bane and Lawrence W. Mead, *Lifting Up the Poor: A Dialogue on Religion, Poverty and Welfare Reform* (Washington, DC, 2003), 128.

25 Fusfeld, *The Economic Thought of Franklin D. Roosevelt*, 161–64; Freidel, *The Triumph*, 193–94; PPA: Vol. 1, 1928–1932, 456; Bellush, *Roosevelt as Governor of New York*, 136–37, 169, 173–74.

26 Mann, *A Fighter Against His Times*, 321; Zinn, *La Guardia in Congress*, 196.

27 PPA: Vol. 1, 1928–1932, 772; Mann, *A Fighter Against His Times*, 323.

28 Daniel T. Rodgers, *Atlantic Crossings: Social Politics in a Progressive Age* (Cambridge, MA, 1998), 413.

29 Ester R. Fuchs, *Mayors and Money: Fiscal Policy in New York and Chicago* (Chicago, 1992), 57–62; Cynthia Horan, "Agreeing with the Bankers: New York City's Depression Fiscal Crisis," in Paul Zerembka and Thomas Ferguson, eds., *Research in Political Economy*, Vol. 8 (1985), esp. 212–16; Martin Shefter, "Economic Crises, Social Coalitions, and Political Institutions: New York City's Little New Deal," American Political Science Association paper, 1981, 17–24.

30 Mann, *La Guardia Comes to Power*, 41–44; Herbert S. Mitgang, *The Man Who Rode the Tiger: The Life and Times of Judge Samuel Seabury* (Philadelphia, 1963), 7–156.

31 Reminiscences of Reuben Lazarus, CCOHC, 132–43. See esp. Shefter, "Economic Crises, Social Coalitions, and Political Institutions"; also Mann, *La Guardia Comes to Power*; Mitgang, *The Man Who Rode the Tiger*, 159–310; Kessner, *Fiorello H. La Guardia*; Freidel, *The Triumph*; Charles Garrett, *The La Guardia Years: Machine and Reform Politics in New York City* (New Brunswick, NJ, 1961); and Bellush, *Franklin D. Roosevelt as Governor of New York*.

32 NYT, Mar. 25, 1931. In emphasizing the reformers' political motivations, I follow Shefter, *op. cit.*

33 Mann, *La Guardia Comes to Power*, 61.

34 Freidel, *The Triumph*, 333–35; Gene Fowler, *Beau James: The Life and Times of Jimmy Walker* (New York, 1949), 325–27; George Walsh, *Gentleman Jimmy Walker: Mayor of the Jazz Age* (New York, 1974), 320–28.

35 Edward J. Flynn, *You're the Boss* (New York, 1947), 129–30.

36 Mann, *La Guardia Comes to Power*, 91; Garrett, *The La Guardia Years*, 93, 104; James A. Hagerty, "A New Deal for New York," *Current History*, vol. 39, no. 5 (February, 1934), 566. On anti-tax sentiment in the early 1930s, see David T. Beito, *Taxpayers in Revolt: Tax Resistance During the Great Depression* (Chapel Hill, NC, 1989).

37 Kessner, *Fiorello H. La Guardia*, 262–64; Horan, "Agreeing with the Bankers," 201, 218–24.

38 Alan Brinkley, *Franklin Delano Roosevelt* (New York, 2010), 24–25; FPA, Vol. 1, 1928–1932, 649; Ronald L. Feinman, *Twilight of Progressivism: The Western Republican Senators and the New Deal* (Baltimore, 1981), 41; Lowitt, *The Persistence of a Progressive*, 554–58; NYHT, Sept. 22, 1932; Lowell M. Limpus and Burr W. Leyson, *This Man La Guardia* (New York, 1938), 349–51.

39 Kessner, *Fiorello H. La Guardia*, 193–95; Mann, *A Fighter Against His Times*, 313–20, 323; FHL to Berle, May 13, 1932; FHL to Berle, Nov. 16, 1932; Berle to FDR, Dec. 2, 1932; all in Adolf A. Berle, Jr., Papers, Box 8, FDRL; Berle to Raymond Moley, Nov. 28, 1932, in Beatrice Bishop Berle and Travis Beal Jacobs, eds., *Navigating the Rapids, 1918–1971: From the Papers of Adolf A. Berle* (New York, 1973), 81. On Berle, see Jordan A. Schwarz, *Liberal: Adolf A. Berle and the Vision of an American Era* (New York, 1987), 1–91.

40 Rexford Tugwell, *The Art of Politics as Practiced by Three Great Americans: Franklin Delano Roosevelt, Luis Muñoz Marín, and Fiorello H. La Guardia* (Garden City, NY, 1958), 199; Mann, *A Fighter Against His Times*, 323–26.

41 Elizabeth Sanders, *The Roots of Reform: Farmers, Workers, and the American State, 1877–1917* (Chicago, 1999); Kristi Andersen, *The Creation of a Democratic Majority, 1928–1936* (Chicago, 1979); Gail Radford, *Modern Housing for America: Policy Struggles in the New Deal Era* (Chicago, 1996), 90; John H. Mollenkopf, *The Contested City* (Princeton, 1983), 52–59; Margaret Weir and Theda Skocpol, "State Structures and the Possibilities of a 'Keynesian' Response to the Great Depression in Sweden, Britain, and the United States," in Peter Evans et al., eds., *Bringing the State Back In* (New York, 1985), 121–23, 127–29, and passim; Jeffrey Tulis, *The Rhetorical Presidency* (Princeton, 1987); Sidney M. Milkis, *The President and the Parties: The Transformation of the American Party System Since the New Deal* (New York, 1993), 26–31; Fred Greenstein, "Continuity and Change in the Modern Presidency," in Anthony King, ed., *The New American Political System* (Washington, DC, 1979), 47–50; E. Pendleton Herring, "First Session of the Seventy-third Congress, March 9, 1933 to June 16, 1933," *APSR*, vol. 28, no. 1 (February 1934), 65–67, 80–83; Thomas Greer, *What Roosevelt Thought: The Social and Political Ideas of Franklin D. Roosevelt* (East Lansing, MI, 1958), 92–93 (quote; emphasis in the original).

42 *NYT*, Oct. 15, 1933. Maney, *The Roosevelt Presence*, 50–55, offers a similar interpretation. On progressives' response toward the NRA, see Ellis W. Hawley, *The New Deal and the Problem of Monopoly: A Study in Economic Ambivalence* (Princeton, 1966), 29–30; and Maney, *"Young Bob" La Follette*, 117–18. Anthony J. Badger, *FDR: The First Hundred Days* (New York, 2008), has joined Frank Freidel, *Franklin D. Roosevelt: Launching the New Deal* (Boston, 1973), as the outstanding general treatments of the First Hundred Days.

43 Kessner, *Fiorello H. La Guardia*, 107, 197, 238–39.

44 Oswald Garrison Villard, "Issues and Men: Norman Thomas and the New York Election," *The Nation*, Sept. 27, 1933, 343; Mann, *La Guardia Comes to Power*, 67. Martin Shefter, *Political Crisis/Fiscal Crisis: The Collapse and Revival of New York City* (New York, 1985), 21–26, offers a very useful theoretical treatment of fusion in New York. See also Francis Barry, *The Scandal of Reform: The Grand Failures of New York's Political Crusaders and the Death of Nonpartisanship* (New Brunswick, NJ, 2009), 227–30.

45 Judith Stein, "The Birth of Liberal Republicanism in New York State, 1932–1938," PhD diss., Yale University, 1968, 45; Garrett, *The La Guardia Years*, 95–98.

46 Mann, *La Guardia Comes to Power*, 79, 86.

47 Ibid., 73–74, 80–87; Reminiscences of William Jay Schieffelin, CCOHC, 42–43; Martin Shefter, "Political Incorporation and Political Extrusion: Party Politics and Social Forces in Postwar New York," in Shefter, *Political Parties and the State:*

The American Historical Experience (Princeton, 1994), 202; Stein, "The Birth of Liberal Republicanism," 54–55; *NYT*, Oct. 23, 1933.

48 Mann, *La Guardia Comes to Power*, 92; *NYT*, Oct. 3, Nov. 4, 1933; FHL, "New York as No. 1," *NYT*, Dec. 4, 1982 (a reprint of an edited version of the Bronx address printed in *Liberty* magazine shortly after La Guardia's inauguration).

49 Milton MacKaye, *The Tin Box Brigade: A Handbook for Larceny* (New York, 1934), 29; *NYT*, Sept. 22–23, 1933.

50 Flynn, *You're the Boss*, 133; James A. Farley diary, Aug. 28, Sept. 20–21, 1933, Farley Papers, Private File, LC; Reminiscences of Ferdinand Pecora, CCOHC, 793. The draft of Farley's statement and correspondence related to it is in the Farley Papers, Presidential File, "Roosevelt, Franklin D., 1929–1933," LC. For other accounts of the September 1933 meeting, see Adolf A. Berle, Jr., diary, Oct. 31, 1939, Berle Papers, Box 211, FDRL; *NYWT*, Nov. 2, 1940.

51 James MacGregor Burns, *Roosevelt: The Lion and the Fox* (New York, 1956), 377; Mann, *La Guardia Comes to Power*, 95–96.

52 Mann, *La Guardia Comes to Power*, 103–18; Flynn, *You're the Boss*, 136–38. Reminiscences of Paul Windels (1953 interview), CCOHC, 18, on La Guardia's fear that McKee would claim the mantle of the New Deal.

53 See esp. Mann, *La Guardia Comes to Power*, chap. 5, though Mann neglects the mobilization of affluent Republicans, the single greatest change in La Guardia's vote between 1929 and 1933.

54 Paul Blanshard, "La Guardia Versus McKee," *The Nation*, Oct. 25, 1933, 477; "Turning Out the Ins," *TNR*, Nov. 22, 1933, 33.

55 *NYT*, Nov. 11–15, 18–20, 22–24, Dec. 6–7, 9, 10–11, 13, 1933; Warren Moscow interview in *New Deal / New York*, Dante J. James, dir., PBS Home Video, 1993.

56 John Mollenkopf, *The Contested City* (Princeton, 1983), 47 (quoting a study by the National Resources Planning Board); Arthur Schlesinger, Jr., *The Crisis of the Old Order, 1919–1933* (Boston, 1957), 249–50; Richard Flanagan, "Roosevelt, Mayors and the New Deal Regime: The Origins of Intergovernmental Lobbying and Administration," *Polity*, vol. 31, no. 3 (Spring 1999), 415–16; Sidney Fine, *Frank Murphy: The Detroit Years* (Ann Arbor, MI, 1975), esp. chap. 13; Alex Gottfried, *Boss Cermak of Chicago: A Study of Political Leadership* (Seattle, 1962), 258, 278–79; Roger Biles, *Big City Boss in Depression and War: Mayor Edward J. Kelly of Chicago* (DeKalb, 1984), 23–24; Mark I. Gelfand, *A Nation of Cities: The Federal Government and Urban America, 1933–1965* (New York, 1975), 33–41, 66; John J. Gunther, *Federal-City Relations in the United States: The Role of Mayors in Federal Aid to Cities* (Newark, DE, 1990), chap. 3; T. Semmes Walmsley, "Presidential address," in Paul V. Betters, ed., *City Problems of 1934: The Annual Proceedings of the United States Conference of Mayors* (Washington, DC, 1934), 4; FHL to Wallace, Jan. 15, 1934, SF, "Correspondence with Federal Officials," NYMA.

Part II: The New Deal

Chapter 4: "Jobs Is the Cry"

1   Arthur M. Schlesinger, Jr., *The Coming of the New Deal, 1933–1935* (Boston, 1959), 23; *NYHT*, Jan. 1, 1934; Thomas Kessner, *Fiorello H. La Guardia and the Making of Modern New York* (New York, 1989), 259, 281, 351–53; *NYT*, Jan. 2–3, 30, Feb. 24, Oct. 14, 1934; Stephen Skowronek, *The Politics Presidents Make: Leadership from John Adams to Bill Clinton* 2nd ed. (Cambridge, MA, 1997), quote at 26–27.

2   Skowronek, *The Politics Presidents Make*, 27 and passim; "Issues and Men: Norman Thomas and the New York Election," *The Nation*, Sept. 27, 1933, 343.

3   Charles Garrett, *The La Guardia Years: Machine and Reform Politics in New York City* (New Brunswick, NJ, 1961), 127–41; Kessner, *Fiorello H. La Guardia*, 275–77, 287–89; William P. Brown, "The Political and Administrative Leadership of Fiorello H. La Guardia as Mayor of the City of New York, 1934–1941" PhD diss., New York University, 1960, esp. 18–123; *NYT*, Apr. 11, July 10, 1934, Jan. 11, 1935; Paul Blanshard, *Investigating City Government in the La Guardia Administration . . .* (New York, 1937); Charles Morris, *The Cost of Good Intentions: New York City and the Liberal Experiment, 1960–1975* (New York, 1980), 49; Reminiscences of Stanley Isaacs, CCOHC, 98. For one example of how Civil Service reform strengthened its *mezzo* level, see Reminiscences of William Jay Schieffelin, CCOHC, 45–46.

4   Leonard Chalmers, "The Crucial Test of La Guardia's First 100 Days: The Emergency Economy Bill," *The New-York Historical Society Quarterly*, vol. 57, no. 3 (July 1973), 246–51; Kessner, *Fiorello H. La Guardia*, 264–69; Harold Ickes to Louis Howe, Dec. 29, 1933; Frederick L. Cranford to Howe, Dec. 6, 1933, OF 88, FDRL; *NYHT*, Mar. 18, 1934; *CPPC*, Mar. 16, 1934; *Time*, Aug. 2, 1937, 14; *NYT*, Jan. 6, 8, 19, 20, 23, 25–26, Apr. 6, 10, 18, July 9–11, 13–14, 18–19, Aug. 1, 1934; Martin Shefter, "Economic Crises, Social Coalitions, and Political Institutions: New York City's Little New Deal," American Political Science Association paper, 1981, 54; Rebecca B. Rankin, ed., *New York Advancing: A Scientific Approach to Municipal Government . . . 1934–1935* (New York, 1936), 5; Berle to FDR, July 25, 1934, Berle Papers, Box 10, FDRL; Marvin McIntyre to FDR, July 20, 1934, OF 200-F Miscel., FDRL. On county reform, see Garrett, *The La Guardia Years*, 243–48.

5   On "reputation building," see Richard Neustadt, *Presidential Power and the Modern Presidents: The Politics of Leadership from Roosevelt to Reagan* (New York, 1990), chap. 4.

6   John Duffy, *A History of Public Health in New York City, Vol. 2: 1866–1966* (New York, 1974), 345; Robert Caro, *The Power Broker: Robert Moses and the Fall of New York* (New York, 1974), 374–78.

7   *PPA: Vol. 2, 1933*, 13; Neil Maher, *Nature's New Deal: The Civilian Conservation Corps and the Roots of the American Environmental Movement* (New York, 2008).

8   *PPA: Vol. 2, 1933*, 163–65, 297–300; Theda Skocpol and Kenneth Finegold, "State

Capacity and Economic Intervention in the Early New Deal," *Political Science Quarterly*, vol. 97, no. 2 (Summer 1982), 260. See esp. Anthony J. Badger, *FDR: The First Hundred Days* (New York, 2008), esp. chaps. 2–4; Herbert Stein, *The Fiscal Revolution in America* (Chicago, 1969), 47–49; Schlesinger, *The Coming of the New Deal*, chaps. 1–6; and Ellis W. Hawley, *The New Deal and the Problem of Monopoly: A Study in Economic Ambivalence* (Princeton, 1966), esp. chap. 1.

9   Stein, *The Fiscal Revolution in America*, 49–54; Badger, *The First Hundred Days*, 85–88; Frances Perkins, *The Roosevelt I Knew* (New York, 1946), 268–74; Raymond Moley, *After Seven Years* (New York, 1939), 173; Margaret Weir, *Politics and Jobs: The Boundaries of Employment Policy in the United States* (Princeton, 1992), 33; Thomas Janoski, *The Political Economy of Public Unemployment: Active Labor Market Policy in West Germany and the United States* (Berkeley, 1990), 69–70; *PPA: Vol. 1, 1928–1932*, 625; *PPA: Vol. 2, 1933*, 202–04.

10 Badger, *The First Hundred Days*, details very effectively the many instances in which a lack of central state capacity shaped and constrained the policy options available to the New Dealers; see also Skocpol and Finegold, "State Capacity and Economic Intervention in the Early New Deal."

11 Jason Scott Smith, *Building New Deal Liberalism: The Political Economy of Public Works, 1933–1956* (New York, 2006), 46–51.

12 Leuchtenburg, *Franklin D. Roosevelt and the New Deal*, chap. 4; Freidel, *Rendezvous with Destiny*, chap. 10; *NYT*, Sept. 14, 1933.

13 Richard Lowitt and Maurine Beasley, eds., *One Third of a Nation: Lorena Hickok Reports on the Great Depression* (Urbana, IL, 1981), 44.

14 The figures are from *The Nation*'s series, "The Professions and the Depression," Nov. 15, Sept. 27, Dec. 20, Sept. 13, and Aug. 9, 1933, respectively; Lorena Hickok to Hopkins, Dec. 19, 1933, Hopkins Papers, Box 59, FDRL; and Nicholas Dagen Bloom, *Public Housing That Worked: New York in the Twentieth Century* (Philadelphia, 2008), 15.

15 Badger, *The First Hundred Days*, 58–63; Robert Sherwood, *Roosevelt and Hopkins: An Intimate History* (New York, 1950), 14–37, 44–45 (quote at 30), George McJimsey, *Harry Hopkins: Ally of the Poor and Defender of Democracy* (Cambridge, MA, 1987), chaps. 1–3; *New York Call*, Feb. 3, 1914.

16 William W. Bremer, "Along the 'American Way': The New Deal's Work Relief Policy for the Unemployed," *JAH*, vol. 62, no. 3 (December 1975), 636–52; see also William W. Bremer, *Depression Winters: New York Social Workers and the New Deal* (Philadelphia, 1984).

17 Schlesinger, *The Coming of the New Deal*, 268–69; Joseph P. Lash, *Dealers and Dreamers: A New Look at the New Deal* (New York, 1988), 245; *PPA: Vol. 2, 1933*, 299–300, 454–57; Sherwood, *Roosevelt and Hopkins*, 51; "Address on Civil Works," *NYT*, Nov. 16, 1933.

18 "Roosevelt's Address on Civil Works"; Martha Derthick and John J. Dinan, "Pro-

gressivism and Federalism," in Derthick, *Keeping the Compound Republic: Essays on American Federalism* (Washington, DC, 2001), 106.

19 *NYT*, Sept. 16, Nov. 23–24, 30, Dec. 21, 1933; *New York American*, Nov. 26, 1933; *NYHT*, Nov. 29, 1933; *NYWT*, Nov. 23–24, 29, 1933; *New York Daily News*, Nov. 19, 29, 1933.

20 Robert Moses, *Public Works: A Dangerous Trade* (New York, 1970), 823.

21 *NYT*, Jan. 19, May 6, 1934; Caro, *The Power Broker*, 332–33, 368–85; Kessner, *Fiorello H. La Guardia*, 308–09; *NYT*, Mar. 28, Sept. 13, 15, 1934; Lewis Mumford, "The Sky Line," *New Yorker*, Dec. 1, 1934, 50; Robert A. M. Stern et al., *New York 1930: Architecture and Urbanism Between the Two World Wars* (New York, 1987), 707, 710–11. This paragraph employs the traditional Weberian conceptualization of charisma: see Max Weber, "The Nature of Charismatic Authority and Its Routinization," in *On Charisma and Institution Building*, trans. S. N. Eisenstadt (Chicago, 1968), chap. 6.

22 *NYT*, May 6, Feb. 4, July 20, 1934; Dec. 22, 1933; Christopher DeNoon, *The Posters of the WPA* (Los Angeles, 1987), 17–19; Michele H. Bogart, *Artists, Advertising, and the Borders of Art* (Chicago, 1995), 120; Hickok to Hopkins, Dec. 29, 1933, Hopkins Papers, Box 59, FDRL; Rankin, ed., *New York Advancing . . . 1934–1935*, 283–84. In fact, New York City did not receive a disproportionate share of money from the CWA: $7.03 per capita under the program, compared with Chicago's $10.50, Philadelphia's $1.77, Detroit's $11.09, Los Angeles's $12.60, and Cleveland's $14.28. See Clarence E. Ridley and Orin F. Nolting, eds., *The Municipal Yearbook: 1937* (Chicago, 1937), 430; cf. Kessner, *Fiorello H. La Guardia*, 296. The difference was presumably due to the fact that unemployment was more acute in the centers of heavy industry.

23 John J. McElligott to FHL, Feb. 13, 1934, SF, "Civil Works Administration," NYMA; Department of Public Markets, Weights and Measures of the City of New York, *Annual Report: 1934* (New York, 1935), 21–28, 59–60; Department of Public Markets, *Annual Report: 1936* (New York, 1937), 56.

24 Garrett, *The La Guardia Years*, 190–91; Rankin, ed., *New York Advancing . . . 1934–1935*, 345; *Final Report of the Emergency Relief Bureau of the City of New York to the Hon. F. H. La Guardia . . . June 6, 1934–December 31, 1937* (New York, 1938), esp. chaps. 2–3; Gladys Niebling and Ruth Hanauer, "A Study of the Use of Cash Relief in the Emergency Home Relief Bureau of New York City," New York School of Social Work, 1934, 22–43; William Hodson, transcript of Feb. 4, 1934 radio address, Hodson, Address to Women's City Club, Feb. 13, 1934, Hodson Papers, Box 10, NYPL.

25 Leuchtenburg, *Franklin D. Roosevelt and the New Deal*, 122–23; Forrest A. Walker, *The Civil Works Administration: An Experiment in Federal Work Relief, 1933–1934* (New York, 1979), 149. The protest telegrams are filed in OF 1892, FDRL. See also FHL to T. Semmes Walmsley, Jan. 22, 1934, SF, "Mayors—Correspondence," NYMA.

26 *NYT*, Mar. 13–14, 16, 30, 1934; FHL to Hopkins, Mar. 12, 1934, SF, "Correspondence with Federal Officials," NYMA; *PPA: Vol. 3, 1934*, 107–11; *CPPC*, Feb. 28, 1934; Arthur W. MacMahon, John D. Millett, and Gladys Ogden, *The Administration of Federal Work Relief* (Chicago, 1941), 19–20.

27 Richard M. Flanagan, "Roosevelt, Mayors and the New Deal Regime: The Origins of Intergovernmental Lobbying and Administration," *Polity*, vol. 31, no. 3 (Spring 1999), 428–29; John J. Gunther, *Federal-City Relations in the United States: The Role of Mayors in Federal Aid to Cities* (Newark, DE, 1990), 95–97; Sherwood, *Roosevelt and Hopkins*, 53–55. See also *Hearings Before a Subcommittee of the Committee on Education and Labor . . . on S. 3348 . . .* , Senate, 73rd Cong., 2nd Sess., esp. 161–77, 184–89.

28 U.S. Bureau of Economic Analysis, *National Income and Product Accounts*, Table 1.1.1; Eric Rauchway, *The Great Depression and the New Deal: A Very Short Introduction* (New York, 2008), 55; David Montgomery, "Labor and the Political Leadership of New Deal America," *International Review of Social History*, vol. 39, no. 3 (December 1994), 355; Richard J. Jensen, "The Causes and Cures of Unemployment in the Great Depression," *Journal of Interdisciplinary History*, vol. 19, no. 4 (Spring 1989), 553–83; U.S. Department of Commerce, Bureau of the Census, *Historical Statistics of the United States, Colonial Times to 1970* (Washington, DC, 1975), series D 85–86.

29 Wayne W. Parrish to Harry Hopkins, Nov. 11, 17, Dec. 8, 1934, Hopkins Papers, Boxes 65–66, FDRL.

30 Samuel H. Beer, "In Search of a New Public Philosophy," in Anthony King, ed., *The New American Political System* (Washington, DC, 1978), 8; Lorena Hickok to Harry Hopkins, Aug. 7–12, 1933, Hopkins Papers, Box 67, FDRL; Parrish to Hopkins, Dec. 8, 1934, Hopkins Papers, Box 66, FDRL. Linda Gordon, "Share-Holders in Relief: The Political Culture of the Public Sector," Russell Sage Foundation working paper, 1998, offers a very smart assessment of the New Deal relief programs' impact on what Gordon calls "political culture," including a discussion of grassroots "rights claiming."

31 Parrish to Hopkins, Nov. 11, 24, 1934, Hopkins Papers, Box 65, FDRL. Public demonstrations by the unemployed and their advocates are amply documented in the major daily newspapers; for New York, see e.g., *NYT*, Apr. 29, May 27, 29, June 5, July 1, Aug. 24, Sept. 23, 1934.

32 MacMahon et al., *The Administration of Federal Work Relief*, 25; *CPPC*, Nov. 7, 1934; Weir, *Politics and Jobs*, 32–33.

33 Irving Fisher to FDR, Oct. 22, 1934, PPF 431, FDRL; William R. Allen, "Irving Fisher, F.D.R., and the Great Depression," *History of Political Economy*, vol. 9, no. 4 (Winter 1977), 575–76; William Norton Fisher, *My Father, Irving Fisher* (New York, 1956), 283; Jensen, "The Causes and Cures of Unemployment in the Great Depression," 574–75.

34 Schlesinger, *The Coming of the New Deal*, 279; Raymond Gram Swing, "Epic and

the Ohio Plan," *The Nation*, Oct. 3, 1934, 379–81; Arthur M. Schlesinger, Jr., *The Politics of Upheaval, 1935–1936* (Boston, 1960), 113–17; *CPPC*, Sept. 7, 1934.

35 *CPPC*, Nov. 7, 28, 1934; *NYT*, Aug. 19, 24, Oct. 20, Dec. 2, 1934; Betters, ed., *City Problems of 1945–1946*, 47; "Proceedings of the Advisory Committee on Allotments," June 3, 1935, Hopkins Papers, Box 47, FDRL; William Seabrook, "The Wild Bull of Manhattan," in *Reader's Digest* (November 1937), 94; Betters, ed., *City Problems of 1935*, 13–14.

36 *Hearings Before the Subcommittee of the Committee on Appropriations on Work Relief and Relief for Fiscal Year 1940*, House, 76th Cong., 1st Sess., 370–71; "Proceedings of the Advisory Committee on Allotments," May 7, 1935, Hopkins Papers, Box 47, FDRL; John A. Garraty, "The New Deal, National Socialism, and the Great Depression," *AHR*, vol. 78, no. 4 (October 1973), 920.

37 MacMahon et al., *The Administration of Federal Work Relief*, 28–35; "Relief Administrator Predicts More Public Works, Less Dole," *American City* (October 1934), 35.

38 *NYT*, Sept. 6, 1934; FHL to Marvin McIntyre, Sept. 13, 1934, OF 1892, FDRL; Kathleen McLaughlin, "At Hyde Park: An Intimate Picture of the President at Home," *NYT Sunday Magazine*, Aug. 24, 1941 (Roosevelt's study).

39 *NYT*, Sept. 23, 1934; Paul Betters to FDR, Sept. 24, 1934, OF 1892, FDRL; Flanagan, "Roosevelt, Mayors, and the New Deal Regime," 419, 435; U.S. Work Projects Administration, *Final Report on the WPA, 1935–1943* (Washington, DC, 1946), 8. For state officials and the New Deal programs, see James T. Patterson, *The New Deal and the States: Federalism in Transition* (Princeton, 1969), esp. chaps. 3–4.

40 *NYT*, Sept. 23, 1934.

41 Schlesinger, *The Politics of Upheaval*, 265; Donald S. Howard, *The WPA and Federal Relief Policy* (New York, 1943), 776; *PPA: Vol. 4, 1935*, 15–25, 35–36; Gunther, *Federal-City Relations*, 102; *NYT*, Feb. 1, 1935.

42 *NYT*, Mar. 15, June 24, Aug. 23–26, 28–29, Sept. 5, 15, 19, 20–21, Dec. 6, 12, 1934; August Heckscher, *When La Guardia Was Mayor: New York's Legendary Years* (New York, 1978), 78–81; Kessner, *Fiorello H. La Guardia*, 269; Garrett, *The La Guardia Years*, 178; Berle to FDR, Oct. 23, 1934, PPF 1306, FDRL.

43 MacMahon et al., *The Administration of Federal Work Relief*, 44–45, 47. On the bill's legislative history, see ibid., and E. Pendleton Herring, "First Session of the Seventy-Fourth Congress, January 3, 1935 to August 26, 1935," *APSR*, vol. 29, no. 6 (December 1935), 991–93. It is frequently noted that congressional progressives called for a much larger appropriation than Roosevelt recommended; but Harrington's analysis suggests there was at least as much strength on the conservative side, not least on the Senate Appropriations Committee, which nearly converted the entire measure into a fund for the provision of direct relief.

44 La Guardia, sitting as the U.S. Conference of Mayors' representative on the Advisory Committee on Allotments, a short-lived board Roosevelt had established

to hash out allotment policy, argued that more favorable terms were required before cities would submit the volume of grant applications necessary for the PWA to serve as an effective stimulus mechanism. Producing a telegram from the mayor of Oklahoma City, he told the committee that a number of cities had projects ready to go as soon as the federal government improved the terms. He suggested a 50:50 grant-to-loan ratio with a 3.8 percent interest rate; after conferring with Treasury Secretary Henry Morgenthau, Roosevelt arrived at the terms of 45:55 and 3 percent interest—"Proceedings of the Advisory Committee on Allotments," Hopkins Papers, Box 47, FDRL; "Memorandum of Conference Held in Secretary's Office May 23, 1935," Henry Morgenthau, Jr., Papers, Box 65, FDRL; Henry Morgenthau, Jr., diary, May 23–24, 1935, FDRL.

45   Stein, *The Fiscal Revolution in America*, 57–58 (emphasis in original); Smith, *Building New Deal Liberalism*, 96–97; Schlesinger, *The Politics of Upheaval*, 345–51; Robert D. Leighninger, Jr., *Long-Range Public Investment: The Forgotten Legacy of the New Deal* (Columbia, SC, 2007), 63, 80; "Proceedings of the Advisory Committee on Allotments, May 7, 1935"; Bonnie Fox Schwartz, *The Civil Works Administration, 1933–1934: The Business of Emergency Employment in the New Deal* (Princeton, 1984), 253–54; MacMahon et al., *The Administration of Federal Work Relief*, 168.

46   Daniel T. Rodgers, *Atlantic Crossings: Social Politics in a Progressive Age* (Cambridge, MA, 1998), 413.

47   Edwin Amenta, *Bold Relief: Institutional Politics and the Origins of Modern American Social Policy* (Princeton, 1998), 3–12; Montgomery, "Labor and the Political Leadership of New Deal America," 351; John D. Millett, *The Works Progress Administration in New York City* (Chicago, 1938), 199–200. On different dimensions of New Deal state power, see Ira Katznelson and Bruce Pietrykowski "Rebuilding the American State: Evidence from the 1940s," *SAPD*, vol. 5, no. 2 (Fall 1991), 301–39, and Theodore J. Lowi, "The Roosevelt Revolution," in Peter Katzenstein et al., eds., *Comparative Theory and Political Experience: Mario Einaudi and the Liberal Tradition* (Ithaca, NY, 1990), 188 nn.

Chapter 5: The New Deal's "Lost Legacy"

1   Remarks to Roosevelt Campaign Volunteers at the Hotel Biltmore, Oct. 24, 1940, National Committee of Independent Voters for Roosevelt and Wallace Papers, Box 14, FDRL.

2   Roy Rosenzweig and Elizabeth Blackmar, *The Park and the People: A History of Central Park* (Ithaca, NY, 1992), 458.

3   Adolf A. Berle, Jr., "Taxation and Municipal Finance," speech delivered Nov. 19, 1937, Berle Papers, Box 141, FDRL; Alan Brinkley, "Liberals and Public Investment: Recovering a Lost Legacy," *American Prospect* 13 (Spring 1993), 81–86.

4   Jason Scott Smith, *Building New Deal Liberalism: The Political Economy of Public
    Works, 1933–1956* (New York, 2006), 88; Thomas P. O'Neil, "Philadelphia: Where
    Patience Is a Vice," in Robert S. Allen, ed., *Our Fair City* (New York, 1947), 62;
    Paul A. Stellhorn, "Depression and Decline: Newark, New Jersey, 1929–1941,"
    PhD diss., Rutgers University, 1982.

5   Keith D. Revell, *Building Gotham: Civic Culture and Public Policy in New York City,
    1898–1938* (Baltimore, 2003); Jameson W. Doig, *Empire on the Hudson: Entrepre-
    neurial Vision and Political Power at the Port of New York Authority* (New York,
    2001), chaps. 1–7; Robert Caro, *The Power Broker: Robert Moses and the Fall of
    New York* (New York, 1974), 360–65 and passim; Martin Shefter, "Economic
    Crises, Social Coalitions, and Political Institutions: New York City's Little New
    Deal," American Political Science Association paper, 1981, 78–79. On the devel-
    opment of Public authorities in the interwar period, see Gail Radford, "From
    Municipal Socialism to Public Authorities: Institutional Factors in the Shaping
    of American Public Enterprise," *JAH*, vol. 90, no. 3 (December 2003), 863–90;
    also Caro, *The Power Broker*, chap. 28 and passim.

    The rise to political independence of those public authorities operating
    entirely within the city limits was one of the great subterranean developments of
    the 1930s. La Guardia had assumed that the directors of these authorities would
    simply recognize the authority of elected officials; gradually, he came to appreci-
    ate the implications of the legal and fiscal powers the authorities possessed, and
    what these would mean in the absence of centralized party control. An exchange
    of correspondence with Triborough Bridge Authority chairman Robert Moses
    pertaining to the hiring of toll-takers is revelatory:

    Moses: "This may appear to be a small matter, but it goes to the heart of
    these business enterprises which depend on the proper collection of tolls for the
    integrity of their bonds. It is silly to force a court test on such a matter, but I shall
    have to take this up with attorneys for the bondholders and with the trustee
    unless the matter is adjusted."

    La Guardia: "Now, there is one matter I want to make perfectly clear. The
    Authority bondholders have absolutely nothing to say and have no control over
    purely administrative matters of the City of New York. . . . The Mayor estab-
    lishes the policy for the City as well as the selection of the Commissioners of
    the Authorities. . . . You are a City official and will take up matters with the
    Corporation Counsel of the City of New York and not with 'attorneys for the
    bondholders.'"

    Moses: "If, as you say, you can straighten this matter out . . . there is nothing
    further to argue about. As to your statements about the powers of the bondhold-
    ers, I think you had better read the agreements and contracts. You will find that
    the bondholders have very substantial powers, and that we are obligated to them

in a great many ways."—Moses to FHL, Apr. 7, FHL to Moses, Apr. 11, Moses to FHL, Apr. 12, 1938, in Moses Papers, Box 90, NYPL.

6   Shefter, "Economic Crises, Social Coalitions, and Political Institutions," passim; *NYT*, Oct. 8–9, 19, 27, 1937; *Bronx Home News*, Jan. 26, 1938; Peter J. McGuinness to FHL, Sept. 6, 1940, SF, "Walker, James J.," NYMA; Edward J. Flynn, *You're the Boss* (New York, 1947), 139; Reminiscences of Paul O'Dwyer, CCOHC, 200; August Heckscher with Phyllis Robinson, *When La Guardia Was Mayor: New York's Legendary Years* (New York, 1978), 323, 326.

7   Arthur M. Schlesinger, Jr., *The Politics of Upheaval, 1935–1936* (Boston, 1960), 131. La Guardia's early civic boosterism is best observed in his work on port development while president of the Board of Aldermen, documented in the newspaper clipping scrapbooks in FHL Papers, Series VI, NYPL.

8   *NYT*, May 17, 1934, Feb. 12, 1935; Joseph McGoldrick to Ickes, May 17, 1934, SF, "United States—Miscellaneous," NYMA.

9   Shefter, "Economic Crises, Social Coalitions, and Political Institutions," 79; *NYT*, Nov. 24, 1933, June 7, Nov. 19–20, 1935; FHL, "Postwar Era Offers a Challenge to Engineering," *Heating, Piping, and Air Conditioning* (April 1944), 240. On the overstaffing of the PWA's legal department, see Smith, *Building New Deal Liberalism*, chap. 3. For La Guardia's role as an expediter, see the correspondence between the Mayor's Office and the PWA in SF, "Federal Works," NYMA.

10 *NYT*, June 29, 1940; Hilary Ballon and Kenneth T. Jackson, eds., *Robert Moses and the Modern City: The Transformation of New York* (New York, 2007), esp. 86–93, 204–41; Robert A. M. Stern et al., *New York 1930: Architectural Urbanism Between the Two World Wars* (New York, 1987), 685–700; Revell, *Building Gotham*; Doig, *Empire on the Hudson*; Nathan Glazer, *From a Cause to a Style: Modernist Architecture's Encounter with the American City* (Princeton, 2007), 222. For a complete list of PWA projects, see "List of Allotted Non-Federal Projects as of May 30, 1942," RG 135, Entry 59, Box 1, NA II.

11 New York City Department of Health: *Program for the Construction of District Health Center Buildings and Bath Stations* (New York, 1936), *Your Health Center* (New York, 1940), and *Public Health Progress in New York City, 1934–1941* (New York, 1941); "The Social Front," *Survey Midmonthly* (September 1936), 277.

12 Bloom, *Public Housing That Worked*, 25–34; Reminiscences of Charles Abrams, CCOHC, 44–46; Daniel T. Rodgers, *Atlantic Crossings: Social Politics in a Progressive Age* (Cambridge, MA, 1998), 468; Peter Marcuse, "The Beginnings of Public Housing in New York," *Journal of Urban History*, vol. 12, no. 4 (August 1986), 365–75; Kessner, *Fiorello H. La Guardia*, 323–27, 331–33; *NYT*, Jan. 4, 1936, Oct. 1, 1937; Gail Radford, *Modern Housing for America: Policy Struggles in the New Deal Era* (Chicago, 1996), esp. chap. 6; Robert Wojtowicz, ed., *Sidewalk Critic: Lewis Mumford's Writings on New York* (Princeton, 1998), 212.

13 Rodgers, *Atlantic Crossings*, 473–78; Bloom, *Public Housing That Worked*, chaps. 2–3. Mumford quoted in Radford, *Modern Housing for America*, 192.

14 Barbara Blumberg, *The New Deal and the Unemployed: The View from New York City* (Lewisburg, PA, 1979), 62.

15 Bonnie Fox Schwartz, *The Civil Works Administration, 1933–1934: The Business of Emergency Employment in the New Deal* (Princeton, 1984), 255–58; Rexford Tugwell, *Roosevelt's Revolution: The First Year, a Personal Perspective* (New York 1977), 45; Michael Vincent Namorato, ed., *The Diary of Rexford G. Tugwell: The New Deal, 1932–1935* (New York, 1992), 229. See also Grace Adams, *Workers on Relief* (New Haven, CT, 1939), a skillfully done polemic which grounded its general indictment in these features of the program.

16 Bruce Stave, *The New Deal and the Last Hurrah: Pittsburgh Machine Politics* (Pittsburgh, 1970), chaps. 6–7; Steven P. Erie, *Rainbow's End: Irish-Americans and the Dilemmas of Urban Machine Politics, 1840–1985* (Berkeley, 1988), 128–35; John Kennedy Ohl, *Hugh S. Johnson and the New Deal* (DeKalb, IL, 1985), 269–70; FHL to Hopkins, Sept. 23, 1935, Hopkins Papers, Box 92, FDRL; FHL to Marguerite LeHand, Sept. 23, 1935, PPF 1376, FDRL; FDR to McIntyre, Sept. 24, 1935, PPF 1376, FDRL; *NYT*, June 19, June 26, Sept. 27, 1935; John D. Millett, *The Works Progress Administration in New York City* (Chicago, 1938), 23–24, 31, 46; James A. Farley diary, Sept. 25–26, 28, 30, Oct. 1–2, 1935; Farley Papers, Private File, LC.

17 Caro, *The Power Broker*, 369–71; Hickok to Hopkins, Mar. 2, 1936, Hopkins Papers, Box 67, FDRL; Carter Irving, "Parks for Seven Million: A Vision Realized," *NYT*, Aug. 16, 1936; Blumberg, *The New Deal and the Unemployed*, 136–37, 149, 152–53; William Hodson, Address to the League for Political Education, Mar. 11, 1936, Hodson Papers, Box 10, NYPL; *NYT*, June 26, 1937.

18 Judith Anne Davidson, "The Federal Government and the Democratization of Public Recreational Sport: New York City, 1933–1945," PhD diss., University of Massachusetts, 1983; New York City Department of Parks, *Six Years of Park Progress* (New York, 1939); Charles Garrett, *The La Guardia Years: Machine and Reform Politics in New York City* (New Brunswick, NJ, 1961), 187–88; Blumberg, *The New Deal and the Unemployed*, 127–29; Marta Gutman, "Equipping the Public Realm: Rethinking Robert Moses and Recreation," in Ballon and Jackson, eds., *Robert Moses and the Modern City*, 72–85; *NYT*, Aug. 17, Sept. 17–19, 1937.

19 Daniel Bluestone, "The Pushcart Evil," David Ward and Olivier Zunz, eds., *The Landscape of Modernity: Essays on New York, 1900–1940* (New York, 1992), chap. 13 (quote at 287).

20 Moses to Iphigene Ochs Sulzberger, Nov. 4, 1936, Box 97, Moses Papers, NYPL; Jerald Podair, *The Strike That Changed New York: Blacks, Whites, and the Ocean Hill–Brownsville Crisis* (New Haven, CT, 2002), 13; Moses, "You Can Trust the Public," *American Magazine* (July 1938); H. I. Brock, "Play Areas Expand," *NYT*, Nov. 17, 1935. This rationalizing impulse extended to the designation of space

within the parks. See, e.g., Moses's defense of his decision to lay out baseball diamonds within Central Park against those who desired a "formal treatment": "The North Meadow has been used for years for baseball in Summer and football and soccer in the Fall in a haphazard sort of way. All we're doing is to come out frankly and recognize that this is a play arena and lay it out as such. We couldn't go on in the old way. The North Meadow has got to be one thing or another"—*NYT*, May 18, 1934.

21 Rosenzweig and Blackmar, *The Park and the People*, 450–51, 458, 463; Catherine MacKinzie, "New York's Play Areas Expand," *NYT*, May 29, 1938; "Moses and the Park," *NYT*, May 6, 1936; Marshall Berman, *All That Is Solid Melts into Air: The Experience of Modernity* (New York, 1982), 308; Mrs. J. French to Robert Moses, Jan. 18, 1935, Robert Moses Papers, Box 91, NYPL; "a disgruntled democrat" to Al Smith, Mar. 3, 1935, ibid.

22 Blumberg, *The New Deal and the Unemployed*, 133–34; Henry Morgenthau, Jr., diary, Dec. 28, 1937, FDRL; Kessner, *Fiorello H. La Guardia*, 432–35; *New York Journal*, May 14, 1935; *Time*, Sept. 20, 1937, 37; *NYT*, Dec. 5, 9, 16, 1934, Jan. 6, Mar. 10, 1935, July 19, 1936, Apr. 22–23, Aug. 15, 21, 26, Sept. 10, 1937, Sept. 16, Oct. 16, 1937, Nov. 3, 1939, July 21, 1940, Nov. 9, 1941; FHL to FDR, July 23, 1935; Sept. 13, 1939, SF, "President," NYMA; Alastair Gordon, *Naked Airport: A Cultural History of the World's Most Revolutionary Structure* (New York, 2004), 112–17.

23 Rebecca Rankin, ed., *New York Advancing: A Scientific Approach to Government: World's Fair Edition* (New York, 1939), 41; FHL, *Community Improvement Appraisal* (New York, 1938), 3–8; Blumberg, *The New Deal and the Unemployed*, chap. 5; "Interview with Mr. Grover A. Whalen . . . 22 November, 1950 . . . ," Vertical File, "Radio and Television Broadcasting," MRL; Saul Nathaniel Scher, "Voice of the City: The History of WNYC, New York City's Municipal Radio Station, 1920–1962," PhD diss., New York University, 1965, chaps. 5–8; Irving Foulds Luscombe, "WNYC, 1922–1940: The Early History of a Twentieth-Century Urban Service," PhD diss., New York University, 1968, chap. 5 (quote at 153); Bruce Lenthall, *Radio's America: The Great Depression and the Rise of Modern Mass Culture* (Chicago, 2007), 101–02, 235–36n34.

24 Blumberg, *The New Deal and the Unemployed*, 165–73, 183–217; Department of Health, *Public Health Progress in New York City, 1934–1941*, 8, 12–13, 15; Luscombe, "WNYC, 1922–1940," 161–62; Somervell, *Brief Review of the Developments in New York City*, 7; Millett, *The WPA in New York City*, 122; *Current History* (May 1938), 58–59. New York's venereal disease program belongs to the long list of social programs the city borrowed from Europe: see John Duffy, *A History of Public Health in New York City, Vol. 2: 1866–1966* (New York, 1974), 352.

25 Frances Perkins, *The Roosevelt I Knew* (New York, 1946), 75–76; Sharon Musher, "A New Deal for Art," PhD diss. Columbia University, 2007; Blumberg, *The New Deal and the Unemployed*, 183–217.

26 Jerold S. Auerbach, "A New Deal in New York City: Fiorello La Guardia, 1934–1937," MA thesis, Columbia University, 1959, 76; Jay Franklin [John Franklin Carter] with Joseph C. Bailey, *La Guardia: A Biography* (New York, 1937), 162–64; Benjamin M. Steigman, *Accent on Talent: New York's High School of Music and Art* (Detroit, 1964), 15 (second quote); Murielle Vautrin, "Government and Culture: New York City and Its Cultural Institutions, 1870–1965," PhD diss., Brandeis University, 1997, chap. 4.

27 As the historian Murielle Vautrin has noted, City Center was not "public" in the sense that the European municipal theaters to which La Guardia looked for inspiration were public: it was operated by a non-profit organization rather than by a public agency, and it actually received less in the way of public subsidy than many privately founded, quasi-public institutions (such as the major art museums). City Center did, however, originate at the initiative of elected officials; its ticket prices were established by the city government; and, not insignificantly, credit for it accrued primarily to the city government.

28 Vautrin, "New York City and Its Cultural Institutions," chap. 5 (Downes quoted at 149); Newbold Morris, *Let the Chips Fall: My Battles Against Corruption* (New York, 1955), 156–82; *NYT*, Nov. 19, Dec. 18, 1939, Mar. 20, 1940; "Rhinestone Horseshoe," *Time*, Mar. 6, 1944, 55; Joshua Freeman, *Working-Class New York: Life and Labor Since World War II* (New York, 2000), 67.

29 Marta Gutman, "Pools," and Benjamin L. Marcus, "McCarren Pool," in Ballon and Jackson, eds., *Robert Moses and the Modern City*, 135, 147–48; Blumberg, *The New Deal and the Unemployed*, 168; Department of Public Markets, Weights and Measures of the City of New York, *Annual Report: 1935* (New York, 1936), 14; *NYT*, Sept. 26, 1935; Catherine MacKinzie, "New York's Play Areas Expand," *NYT*, May 29, 1938; *NYT*, Oct. 16, 1939. Caro, *The Power Broker*, 454–57, documents La Guardia's and Moses's efforts to stage civic pageantry.

30 Schattschneider quoted in Margaret Weir, *Politics and Jobs: The Boundaries of Employment Policy in the United States* (Princeton, 1992), xiii; cf. Richard M. Valelly, *Princeton Readings in American Politics* (Princeton, 2009), 51.

31 On New Deal spending in the West, see Leonard Arrington, "The New Deal in the West: A Preliminary Statistical Inquiry," *Pacific Historical Review*, vol. 38, no. 3 (August 1969), 311–16, and Gavin Wright, "The Political Economy of New Deal Spending: An Econometric Analysis," *Review of Economics and Statistics*, vol. 56, no. 1 (February 1974), 30–38.

32 *NYT*, Oct. 29, 1940; *St. Louis Post-Dispatch*, Apr. 4, 1937. For a contemporary version, see, e.g., William Fulton, "New York Gets Inside Track on U.S. Easy Money," *Chicago Tribune*, Sept. 12, 1937; for works of history and biography that incorporate or repeat elements of the myth, see among others Garrett, *The La Guardia Years*, 179–80; Ric Burns and Jim Sanders, *New York: An Illustrated History* (New York, 2003), 447; and Caro, *The Power Broker*, 453–54 (emphasizing

Robert Moses's role). The meme that New York received a disproportionate share of New Deal works money derives from Millett, *The WPA in New York City*, vii, which noted that New York, with 5.6 percent of the U.S. population, claimed 14 percent of the WPA's spending in its first eighteen months. In fact, nearly all of the discrepancy between the city's share of the national unemployed population and the amount it received from the WPA may be ascribed to the fact that it launched its operations three to four months more quickly than the other administrative units. Comparative figures can be found in Mason B. Williams, "City of Ambition: Franklin Roosevelt, Fiorello La Guardia, and the Making of New Deal New York," PhD diss., Columbia University, 2012, Tables. 3.4 and 3.5.

33 FHL to Hopkins, Oct. 28, 1935, Hopkins Papers, Box 92, FDRL; Caro, *The Power Broker*, 455–56; *NYT*, May 30–31, 1935, June 12, July 3, Aug. 9, 18, 1936, Oct. 16, 1939; "Roosevelt 'Built' East Drive Link," *NYT*, June 30, 1937. Plans for the East River Drive had in fact been in the works for many years.

34 *Hearings Before the Committee on Banking and Security . . . on S. 1592 . . .* , Senate, 79th Cong., 1st Sess., 137 (La Guardia quote); *PPA: Vol. 3, 1934*, 361; *PPA: Vol. 6, 1937*, 409–10. See also Lawrence Friedman's conceptualization of a "submerged middle class," originally in Friedman, *Government and Slum Housing* (Chicago, 1968), and his broader application in *American Law in the 20th Century* (New Haven, CT, 2002), 153–54.

35 Smith, *Building New Deal Liberalism*, chap. 6; Reminiscences of Arthur Krock, CCOHC, 64–65; Reminiscences of Francis Stoddard, CCOHC, 119–22.

36 Florence S. McDonough to FDR, Oct. 22, 1941, OF 300—New York, FDRL.

37 John A. Heffernan, "How New York's Mayor Boxed Political Compass," *Brooklyn Times-Union*, June 27, 1935.

Chapter 6: From Fusion to Confusion

1 FHL to Yolanda Matteucci, Oct. 26, 1934, SF, "Campaign Endorsements," NYMA; *NYT*, Nov. 24, 1933, Oct. 23, 1934, Tom Amlie to FHL, Nov. 30, 1934, FHL Mayoral Papers, 1941 Campaign Series, Box 4141, NYMA. The title of this chapter is borrowed from William P. Vogel, Jr., "What Did New York's Election Prove?" *Common Sense* (December 1937), 14.

2 *Chicago Tribune*, May 19, 1935; *NYT*, Nov. 24, 1933, May 20, 1935; *WP*, May 20, 1935.

3 *NYT*, Oct. 28, 1936.

4 Jay Franklin [John Franklin Carter] with Joseph C. Bailey, *La Guardia: A Biography* (New York, 1937), 145.

5 Alan Brinkley, *Voices of Protest: Huey Long, Father Coughlin, and the Great Depression* (New York, 1982), 226–41; Arthur M. Schlesinger, Jr., *The Politics of Upheaval, 1935–1936* (Boston, 1960), chaps. 6–7, 9–10; Donald R. McCoy, *Angry Voices: Left-of-Center Politics in the New Deal Era* (Lawrence, KS, 1958), 70–114;

Russel B. Nye, *Midwestern Progressive Politics: A Historical Study of Its Origins and Development, 1870–1950* (East Lansing, MI, 1951), 325–38; Alan Lawson, *The Failure of Independent Liberalism, 1930–1941* (New York, 1971), 39–46; Alfred M. Bingham, *Insurgent America: The Revolt of the Middle-Classes* (New York, 1935), esp. chap. 19; Seymour Martin Lipset, "Roosevelt and the Protest of the 1930s," 68 *Minnesota Law Review* 273 (1983–84), 274–79.

6   J. David Greenstone, *Labor in American Politics* (New York, 1969), 29–49 (quote at 44); Michael Denning, *The Cultural Front: The Laboring of American Politics in the Twentieth Century* (New York, 1996), 6–11; Steven Fraser, "The Labor Question," in Fraser and Gary Gerstle, eds., *The Rise and Fall of the New Deal Order, 1930–1980* (Princeton, 1989), 62–68; Robert D. Parmet, *The Master of Seventh Avenue: David Dubinsky and the American Labor Movement* (New York, 2005), 82–93, 113; Robert Zeiger, *The CIO, 1935–1955* (Chapel Hill, NC, 1995), 16–17; Irving Howe, *World of Our Fathers: The Journey of the East European Jews to America and the Life They Found and Made* (New York, 1976), 348–49.

7   Bingham, *Insurgent America*, 223–24; Nye, *Midwestern Progressive Politics*, 335; FHL, "What Will the Progressive Republicans Do?" *Liberty* (April 1936), 45.

8   FHL, "What Will the Progressive Republicans Do?" 46.

9   FDR to Col. E. M. House, Feb. 16, 1935, in *PL*, 452–53; James A. Farley diary, May 1, 1935, Farley Papers, Private File, LC.

10   McCoy, *Angry Voices*, 106; Lipset, "Roosevelt and the Protest of the 1930s," 283–89; Steve Fraser, *Labor Will Rule: Sidney Hillman and the Rise of American Labor* (New York, 1991), 355.

11   Among those who co-signed the call were Senators Norris, Elmer Benson, (Farmer-Labor, MN), and Homer T. Bone (Dem., WA), Minnesota Farmer-Labor governor Floyd Olson (who died before the convention), Adolf A. Berle, and La Guardia; prominent attendees included Philip La Follette, Senators Hugo Black (Dem., AL) and Lewis Schwellenbach (Dem., WA), labor leaders John L. Lewis and Sidney Hillman, and the labor lawyer and New York Power Commission head Frank P. Walsh—in all, four senators, two governors, twelve U.S. representatives, and twenty-seven labor leaders, Democrats as well as Republicans, Farmer-Laborites, Socialists, and independents.

12   *NYT*, Sept. 11, 12, 1936; Donald R. McCoy, "The Progressive National Committee of 1936," *Western Political Quarterly*, vol. 9, no. 2 (June 1956), 454–69. See also "Minutes of the Proceedings of the National Progressive Conference Held in Chicago on September 11, 1936," Robert La Follette, Jr., Papers, La Follette Family Papers, Box C: 436, "Progressive Conference 1936: Important Papers RML Wants," LC. An original copy of the resolutions as reported to the conference by La Guardia may be found in the Box C: 436 of the Robert La Follette, Jr., Papers.

13   Fraser, "The Labor Question," 67–71; Fraser, *Labor Will Rule*, 356–63; Greenstone, *Labor in American Politics*, 49.

14 Fraser, *Labor Will Rule*, 363–64; Reminiscences of Frances Perkins, Part II, CCOHC 511; Denning, *The Cultural Front*, 10.

15 Kenneth Waltzer, "The American Labor Party: Third Party Politics in New Deal—Cold War Era New York, 1936–1954," PhD diss., Harvard University, 1977, 112; Fraser, *Labor Will Rule*, 356, 363–65, 626n25; Thomas Kessner, *Fiorello H. La Guardia and the Making of Modern New York* (New York, 1989), 408–10; David Dubinsky and A. H. Rankin, *David Dubinsky: A Life with Labor* (New York, 1977), 267–69; Reminiscences of James A. Farley, CCOHC, 15; Reminiscences of Edward J. Flynn, CCOHC, 20–21; Reminiscences of Frances Perkins, Part VII, CCOHC, 224–25.

16 William Leuchtenburg, *Franklin D. Roosevelt and the New Deal, 1932–1940* (New York, 1963), 190; Farley diary, Dec. 20, 1934, Oct. 30, 1936; Schlesinger, *The Politics of Upheaval*, 587; Franklyn Waltman, Jr., "Tammany and FDR," *NYT*, Oct. 6, 1936; Frank R. Kent, "The Great Game of Politics," *Baltimore Sun*, Sept. 20, 1936; *Atlanta Constitution*, Sept. 27, 1936; *Chicago Tribune*, Sept. 26, 1936; *NYT*, Sept. 27, Oct. 3, 11, 18, 21–22, 1936.

17 August Heckscher with Phyllis Robinson, *When La Guardia Was Mayor: New York's Legendary Years* (New York, 1978), 138; *NYT*, Oct. 11, 18, 28–29, 1936; *Atlanta Constitution*, Nov. 3, 1936; *NYHT*, Oct. 30, 1936.

18 *NYT*, Nov. 3, 1936; "Budgets, Deficits, and Assets—Human Beings or Bank Balances," FHL speech draft, WABC, Nov. 2, 1936, SF, "Speeches—1936," NYMA. For La Guardia's campaign speeches, see FHL to Marguerite LeHand, Oct. 29, 1936, Stephen Early to FHL, Oct. 29, 1936, in PPF 1376, FDRL; *NYT*, Oct. 30, Nov. 1, 1936; and correspondence from Democratic candidates and party leaders, OF 1710, Box 1, FDRL.

19 Garrett, *The La Guardia Years*, 220–43; George H. McCaffrey, "Proportional Representation in New York City," *APSR*, vol. 33, no. 5 (October 1939), 841–52; Belle Zeller and Hugh A. Bone, "The Repeal of P.R. in New York City—Ten Years in Retrospect," *APSR*, vol. 42, no. 6 (December 1948), 1127–1148.

20 *NYT*, Nov. 4–5, Dec. 27, 1936; "The New New Deal, *Chicago Tribune*, Nov. 4, 1936; Beatrice Bishop Berle and Travis Beal Jacobs, eds., *Navigating the Rapids, 1918–1971: From the Papers of Adolf A. Berle* (New York, 1973), 121.

21 *NYT*, Jan. 16, 1937; FDR to McIntyre, Jan. 16, 1937, PPF 1376; FHL to FDR, Jan. 21, 1937, PPF 1376, FDRL.

22 Farley diary, Nov. 18, 1933, Jan. 7–9, 27–29, 1934, Dec. 6, 1935, Jan. 13, Dec. 24, 1936, Jan. 10, Mar. 13, 18, May 10, 17, June 14–15, 1937; *Brooklyn Citizen*, Nov. 9, 1933; *NYT*, Jan. 6, 9–10, 17–18, 21–22, 24, 28–30, Feb. 4, 7, 13, 16, 28, Mar. 19, 22–23, Apr. 21–24, 30, May 30, June 26, July 17, 1934.

23 Harold Ickes, *The Secret Diary of Harold Ickes, Vol. 2: The Inside Struggle, 1936–1939* (New York, 1954), 161–62; *NYT*, May 2, 1937; *NYWT*, Aug. 30–31, 1937; Reminiscences of Jeremiah T. Mahoney, CCOHC, passim. Smith, who was credited

with Copeland's nomination, later told James Farley that he had been hoping to retire from politics and had agreed to support Copeland only at Dooling's request. Dooling himself died before the primary (Farley diary, Oct. 31, 1938).

24 Judith Stein, "The Birth of Liberal Republicanism in New York State, 1932–1938," PhD diss., Yale University, 1968, 5, 151, 157–59, 167–73; Richard Polenberg, "Franklin Roosevelt and the Purge of John O'Connor: The Impact of Urban Change on Political Parties," *New York History*, vol. 48, no. 3 (July 1968), 315 (quoting Bruce Barton).

25 Kessner, *Fiorello H. La Guardia*, 410–11, 413–14; Heckscher, *When La Guardia Was Mayor*, 165, 169–71; *NYT*, Feb. 13, Mar. 9, Apr. 14, Aug. 17, 25, Sept. 10, 14–16, Oct. 29, 1937. Noel F. Busch, "Boss Without Cigar," *New Yorker*, Oct. 28, 1939, 21–27, offers a personality sketch of Simpson.

26 Dubinsky and Raskin, *A Life with Labor*, 268–69; Reminiscences of Paul Windels (1953 interview), CCOHC, 6; *NYT*, Sept. 8, 1937. See also the citations in note 15 of this chapter. On La Guardia's labor policy record, see George Kaplan, "The Labor View of Fiorello H. La Guardia," PhD diss., New York University, 1962, esp. chaps. 3–4, 6; Irving Bernstein, *Turbulent Years*, 620; Annelise Orleck, *Common Sense and a Little Fire: Women and Working-Class Politics in the United States, 1900–1965* (Chapel Hill, NC, 1995), 162; "Report to the Mayor from Elinore M. Herrick . . . Director, National Labor Relations Board, District 2," [n.d], FHL Mayoral Papers, 1937 Campaign Series, Box 4121, NYMA; Shefter, "Economic Crises, Social Coalitions, and Political Institutions," 69–70.

27 Archie Robinson, *George Meany and His Times: A Biography* (New York, 1981), 94; "Excerpts from Resolutions Adopted by the N.Y. State Federation of Labor, N.Y. Building Trades Council, Central Trades and Labor Council and N.Y. City Allied Printing Trades Council," [n.d.], FHL Mayoral Papers, 1937 Campaign Series, Box 4121, NYMA; Joseph C. Goulden, *Meany* (New York, 1972), 50, 60–62, 65–66; George Meany et al., "La Guardia Works for Labor and Labor Works for La Guardia," *New York Daily News*, Oct. 23, 1937; "Minutes, Executive Board Meeting, Building and Construction Trades Council of Greater New York," Sept. 13, 1937, microfilm reel R-7418/1, Robert F. Wagner Labor Archives, New York University. Additional union endorsements are in FHL Mayoral Papers, 1937 Campaign Series, Box 4114, NYMA.

28 Theodore J. Lowi, *At the Pleasure of the Mayor: Patronage and Power in New York City, 1898–1958* (Glencoe, IL, 1964), 186.

29 On "visibility" and "traceability," see R. Douglas Arnold, *The Logic of Congressional Action* (New Haven, CT, 1990), esp. 48–51, and Paul Pierson, "When Effect Becomes Cause: Policy Feedback and Political Change," *World Politics*, vol. 45, no. 4 (July 1993), 622.

30 Roy Wilkins, "Watchtower," *New York Amsterdam News*, Aug. 12, 1939; *Pittsburgh Courier*, Feb. 3, 17, 1934, May 15 1937; Floyd J. Calvin, "Calvin's Digest,"

Pittsburgh Courier, Feb. 24, 1934; David Levering Lewis, "The Appeal of the New Deal," *Reviews in American History*, vol. 12, no. 4 (December 1984), 558; Lawrence Elliott, *Little Flower: The Life and Times of Fiorello La Guardia* (New York, 1983), 228.

31 Michael Parenti, "Ethnic Politics and the Persistence of Ethnic Identification," *APSR*, vol. 61, no. 3 (September 1967), 718; Deborah Dash Moore, *At Home in America: Second Generation New York Jews* (New York, 1981), 201–02.

32 Moore, *At Home in America*, 19–58, 203–20; Henry L. Feingold, *A Time for Gathering: Entering the Mainstream, 1920–1945* (Baltimore, 1992), 194; Thomas M. Henderson, *Tammany Hall and the New Immigrants: The Progressive Years* (New York, 1976), 302–04, 308; Irving Howe, *World of Our Fathers*, 365–91; Thomas Kessner, "Jobs, Ghettoes, and the Urban Economy," *American Jewish History*, vol. 71, no. 2 (December 1981), 232–33 (Table IV). On Jewish votes in the 1933 election, see Arthur Mann, *La Guardia Comes to Power: 1933* (Philadelphia, 1965), 138–52.

33 Nettie P. McGill and Ellen N. Matthews, *The Youth of New York City* (New York, 1940), 45; Beth S. Wenger, *New York Jews and the Great Depression: Uncertain Promise* (New Haven, CT, 1996), 17–18; Dorothy Helen Goldstein, "The 'Disproportionate' Occupational Distribution of Jews and Their Individual and Organized Reaction," MA thesis, Columbia University, 1941, 20–25; Melvin M. Fagen, "The Status of Jewish Lawyers in New York City," *Jewish Social Studies* 1 (1939), 73–104; Kessner, "Jobs, Ghettoes, and the Urban Economy," 229–32; Ronald Bayor, *Neighbors in Conflict: The Irish, Germans, Jews, and Italians of New York City, 1929–1941*, 2nd ed. (Urbana, IL, 1988), 20. A confidential study conducted by the city in December 1933 found that only one sixth of home relief recipients were Jewish, or under 17 percent, compared to 27 percent of the general population—Mary Gibbons, Confidential memorandum, Dec. 8, 1933, William Hodson Papers, Box 5, NYPL.

34 Among many others, see Tony Michels, *A Fire in Their Hearts: Yiddish Socialists in New York* (Cambridge, MA, 2005); Arthur Liebman, The Ties That Bind. The Jewish Support for the Left in the United States," *American Jewish Historical Quarterly*, vol. 66, no. 2 (December 1976), 285–321; Moses Rischin, *The Promised City: New York's Jews, 1870–1914* (Cambridge, MA, 1962), 148–257; Howe, *World of Our Fathers*, 101–15, 235–49, 287–359; Lawrence H. Fuchs, *The Political Behavior of American Jews* (Glencoe, IL, 1956), 178–91; and Wenger, *New York Jews and the Great Depression*, 105–06. The quotations are from Michels, *A Fire in Their Hearts*, 71–72, 79.

35 Mann, *La Guardia Comes to Power*, 155; Michels, *A Fire in Their Hearts*, 255; Howe, *World of Our Fathers*, 351; Seymour Martin Lipset and Gary Marks, *It Didn't Happen Here: Why Socialism Failed in the United States* (New York, 2000), 210; Wenger, *New York Jews and the Great Depression*, 135; Transcript of radio broad-

cast, "Sunday, 11 a.m. through WVED," FHL Mayoral Papers, 1941 Campaign Series, Box 4142, NYMA.

36 Cheryl Greenberg, *"Or Does It Explode?": Black Harlem in the Great Depression* (New York, 1991), 95–96; Ralph J. Bunche, *The Political Status of the Negro in the Age of FDR* (Chicago, 1973), 606; Ira Katznelson, *Black Men, White Cities: Race, Politics, and Migration in the United States, 1900–1930 and Britain, 1948–1968* (New York, 1973), chap. 5 (quote at 69); Gilbert Osofsky, *Harlem, The Making of a Ghetto: Negro New York, 1890–1930* (New York, 1968), 169–70, 173; John C. Walter, *The Harlem Fox: J. Raymond Jones and Tammany, 1920–1970* (Albany, 1989), chaps. 2–3; Edwin Lewison, *Black Politics in New York City* (New York, 1974), 58–80; Nancy J. Weiss, *Farewell to the Party of Lincoln: Black Politics in the Age of FDR* (Princeton, 1983), 3–33.

37 U.S. Department of Commerce, Bureau of the Census, *Sixteenth Census of the United States: 1940: Population and Housing: Statistics for Health Areas, New York City* (Washington, DC, 1942), 6, 138–40; Greenberg, *"Or Does It Explode?"* 21.

38 See, among others, Osofsky, *Harlem: The Making of a Ghetto,* 136–37, 195; Greenberg, *"Or Does It Explode?"* chaps. 1–3 (quote at 21); E. Franklin Frazier, "Negro Harlem: An Ecological Study," *American Journal of Sociology,* vol. 43, no. 1 (July 1937), 72–88; Herbert Gutman, *The Black Family in Slavery and Freedom, 1750–1925* (New York, 1976), 453–55, 512–14. David Levering Lewis, *When Harlem Was in Vogue* (New York, 1981), offers glimpses of what people did to make a living in Harlem in the interwar period. Essential data may be found in Bureau of the Census, *Sixteenth Census of the United States: 1940: Population and Housing: Statistics for Health Areas, New York City* (Washington, DC, 1942), education data at pp. 138–40.

39 Greenberg, *"Or Does It Explode?"* 145–66; Weiss, *Farewell to the Party of Lincoln,* 210–16; Roy Wilkins, "Watchtower," *New York Amsterdam News,* Nov. 13, 1937; Federal Writers' Project, *New York Panorama* (New York, 1938), 142 ("community life-blood"); Jeff Kisseloff, *You Must Remember This: An Oral History of Manhattan from the 1890s to World War II* (New York, 1989), 326–27 (Norma Mair quote); Mark I. Naison, *Communists in Harlem During the Depression* (Urbana, IL, 1983), 194 ("reported in 1939"). Cf. Christopher G. Wye, "The New Deal and the Negro Community: Toward a Broader Conceptualization," *JAH,* vol. 59, no. 3 (December 1972), 621–39, a case study of Cleveland, which found that in that city, the New Deal public employment programs maintained or even exacerbated an inequitably occupational pattern "by employing Negroes in occupational categories below those which had been opened to them in the private sector of the economy."

40 James Weldon Johnson, "The Making of Harlem," *Survey Graphic* (March 1925), 635; Greenberg, *"Or Does It Explode?"* 13, 96, 152, 163–65; Federal Writers' Project, *New York Panorama,* 146; William M. Welty, "Black Shepherds: A Study of

the Leading Negro Clergymen in New York City, 1900–1940," PhD diss., New York University, 1970, 287–88. For critiques of La Guardia's public improvements record in Harlem, see Adam Clayton Powell, Jr., "Soap Box," *New York Amsterdam News*, Nov. 6, 1937, and "Claiming Credit," *New York Amsterdam News*, Oct. 23, 1937.

41 Robert Gottlieb quoted in Charles McGrath, "Robert Caro's Big Dig," *NYT Sunday Magazine*, Apr. 12, 2012.

42 Ester Fuchs et al., "Social Capital, Political Participation, and the Urban Community," in Susan Saegert et al., eds., *Social Capital and Poor Communities* (New York, 2001), 290–305 (quote at 305). See esp. Wenger, *New York Jews and the Great Depression*, chap. 5, and Greenberg, *"Or Does It Explode?"* chap. 4. In Harlem, the church was a particularly important source of political social capital, particularly among women. The Harlem ministry had mostly supported Hoover in 1932 and supported La Guardia only tepidly in 1933; in 1937, La Guardia received "overwhelming support" from Harlem ministers, many of whom had "led the campaign for Roosevelt" in Harlem the previous year—Welty, "Black Shepherds," 320–27.

43 Greenberg, *"Or Does It Explode?"* 94.

44 C. T. Nesbitt to FHL, Aug. 27, 1945, FHL Papers, Series II: Mayoral Correspondence, Reel 45, NYPL.

45 *NYP*, Oct. 29, 1937; *NYT*, Nov. 2, 1937. Transcripts of La Guardia's campaign speeches and broadcasts are in SF, "Municipal Government—Lessons on," NYMA. Mahoney's campaign statements are best documented in the daily press.

46 *NYT*, Nov. 2, 1937.

47 Berle and Bishop, eds., *Navigating the Rapids*, 145; *NYT*, Nov. 4–5, 1937; Farley diary, Nov. 3–4, 1937; Alex Rose to FDR, Nov. 3, 1937, PPF 3892, FDRL; *WP*, Nov. 5, 1937; *NYT*, Nov. 4–5, 1937.

Chapter 7: New Dealer for the Duration

1 "Mayor La Guardia and the Future," *The Nation*, Nov. 6, 1937, 492; Survey #103, Question #8a, and Survey #108, Question #7b, in George H. Gallup, *The Gallup Poll: Public Opinion, 1935–1971, Vol. 1* (New York, 1972), 77–78, 88–89; Thomas Kessner, *Fiorello H. La Guardia and the Making of Modern New York* (New York, 1989), 425–27; *NYT*, Sept. 30, 1937.

2 Homer S. Cummings diary, July 4, 1938, Reel 2, Small Special Collections Library, University of Virginia; Adolf A. Berle, Jr., diary, Dec. 10, 1937, Berle Papers, Box 210, FDRL; James A. Farley diary, Dec. 11, 1937, Farley Papers, Private File, LC; Rexford G. Tugwell, *The Democratic Roosevelt* (New York, 1957), 411–12; James A. Farley, *Jim Farley's Story: The Roosevelt Years* (New York, 1948), 123.

3 Harold L. Ickes, *The Secret Diary of Harold L. Ickes, Vol. 1: The First Thousand*

Days (New York, 1953), 351–52; Farley diary, May 10, 15, 1935; Linda Gordon, "Share-Holders in Relief: The Political Culture of the Public Sector," Russell Sage Foundation working paper, 1998; David Montgomery, "Labor and the Political Leadership of New Deal America," *International Review of Social History*, vol. 39, no. 3 (December 1994), 352; Walter Lippmann, "Today and Tomorrow," *WP*, Jan. 5, 1939.

4   *NYT*, May 16, 1937, Dec. 2, 1938; Hopkins and FHL, telephone transcript, Mar. 28, 1936, Hopkins Papers, Box 74–76, FDRL; FHL to Ickes, Nov. 23, 1935, SF, "Electric Street Lights," NYMA.

5   Richard M. Flanagan, "Roosevelt, Mayors, and the New Deal Regime: The Origins of Intergovernmental Lobbying and Administration," *Polity*, vol. 31, no. 3 (Spring 1999), 415–50; Mark I. Gelfand, *A Nation of Cities: The Federal Government and Urban America, 1933–1965* (New York, 1975), 23–70; John J. Gunther, *Federal-City Relations in the United States: The Role of Mayors in Federal Aid to Cities* (Newark, DE, 1990), 68–132.

6   *NYT*, Dec. 15, 1934, Dec. 16, 1933; Paul V. Betters, ed., *City Problems of 1945–1946: The Annual Proceedings of the United States Conference of Mayors* (Washington, DC, 1946), 160.

7   Donald S. Howard, *The WPA and Federal Relief Policy* (New York, 1943), 155; FHL to William Lynch, Apr. 13, 1936, SF, "Works Progress Administration," NYMA; Jason Scott Smith, *Building New Deal Liberalism: The Political Economy of Public Works, 1933–1956* (New York, 2006), 146–47; National Appraisal Committee, *U.S. Community Improvement Appraisal: A Report on the Work Program . . . by the National Appraisal Committee, April, 1939* (Washington, DC, 1939); "One Hundred American Cities . . ." and "A Report on the Existing Relief Situation Covering 100 Major American Cities . . . ," Hopkins Papers, Box 53, FDRL; FHL to FDR, Dec. 30, 1936, OF 1892, FDRL; "Appraisal of W.P.A. in Terms of Community Values," *Social Service Review*, vol. 12, no. 4 (December 1938), 331. See also Robert D. Leighninger, Jr., *Long-Range Public Investment: The Forgotten Legacy of the New Deal* (Columbia, SC, 2007), chap. 13.

8   James E. Sargent, "Woodrum's Economy Bloc: The Attack on Roosevelt's WPA, 1937–1939," *Virginia Magazine of History and Biography*, vol. 93, no. 2 (April 1985), 179; Flanagan, "Roosevelt, Mayors, and the New Deal Regime," 431–32; Alan Brinkley, *The End of Reform: New Deal Liberalism in Recession and War* (New York, 1995), 25–26; *NYT*, Jan. 14, 1936, Jan. 3, May 14, 1937; *Baltimore Sun*, Apr. 1, 1937. On popular support for economy in government, see, e.g., Survey #8, Question #3, and Survey #15, Question #3, in Gallup, ed., *The Gallup Poll*, Vol. 1: *1935–1948*, 5, 12.

9   *Hearings Before the Committee on Appropriations Pursuant to H.J. 361, Emergency Relief Appropriation*, Senate, 75th Cong., 1st Sess., 80–83, 85–86, 110–12; Richard D. McKinzie, *The New Deal for Artists* (Princeton, 1973), 161; Edwin Amenta et al., "Bring Back the WPA: Work, Relief, and the Origins of American Social Pol-

icy in Welfare Reform," *SAPD*, vol. 12, no. 1 (Spring 1998), 45; Gavin Wright, *Old South, New South: Revolutions in the Southern Economy Since the Civil War* (New York, 1986), 8 and passim. See also Ira Katznelson, Kim Geiger, and Daniel Kryder, "Limiting Liberalism: The Southern Veto and Congress, 1933–1950," *Political Science Quarterly*, vol. 108, no. 2 (Summer 1993), 283–306; Sean Farhang and Ira Katznelson, "The Southern Imposition: Congress and Labor in the New Deal and Fair Deal," *SAPD* 19 (Spring 2005), 1–30.

10　Henry Morgenthau, Jr., diary, Dec. 8, 1934, FDRL; FHL to Hopkins, Oct. 6, 1937, SF, "Federal Works," NYMA.

11　*Hearings Before the Committee on Appropriations Pursuant to H.J. 361, Emergency Relief Appropriation*, Senate, 75th Cong., 1st Sess., 259–65.

12　*NYT*, June 13, 16–18, 20, 22, 1937; FDR to Byrnes, June 9, 1937, OF 444-C, FDRL; Frank R. Kent, "The Great Game of Politics," *Baltimore Sun*, June 25, 1937; FDR to Hopkins, July 27, 1937, OF 444-C, FDRL. See also FDR to Byrnes, June 11, 1937, OF 444-C, FDRL.

13　Gelfand, *A Nation of Cities*, 398n57.

14　Brinkley, *The End of Reform*, chap. 5 (esp. 98–103); Margaret Weir, *Politics and Jobs: The Boundaries of Employment Policy in the United States* (Princeton, 1992), 34–41.

15　*NYT*, Apr. 10, 17, 1938; Beatrice Bishop Berle and Travis Beal Jacobs, eds., *Navigating the Rapids, 1918–1971: From the Papers of Adolf A. Berle* (New York, 1973), 172; PWA press release no. 3352 (July 4, 1938), copy at NYPL; *Hearings Before the Subcommittee of the Committee on Appropriations on the Emergency Relief Appropriation Act of 1938 and the Public Works Appropriation Act of 1938*, House, 75th Cong., 3rd Sess., 767; Sargent, "Woodrum's Economy Bloc," 179, 181–82.

16　Smith, *Building New Deal Liberalism*, chap. 6; Sidney M. Milkis, "Franklin D. Roosevelt and the Transcendence of Partisan Politics," *Political Science Quarterly*, vol. 100, no. 3 (Autumn 1985), 492–96; Arthur Krock, "Some Plans Affecting Relief and Its Politics," *NYT*, Nov. 3, 1937, Jan. 1, 5, 7, 9, 11–13, 15–23, 26–29, 1939; Alsop and Kintner, "The Capital Parade, *Atlanta Constitution*, Jan. 11, 1939; Blumberg, *The New Deal and the Unemployed*, 231–32.

17　Alsop and Kintner, "The Capital Parade," *Atlanta Constitution*, Jan. 11, 25, 1939; *NYT*, Jan. 28, 1939; Sargent, "Woodrum's Economy Bloc," 196.

18　*Hearings Before the Committee on Appropriations on H.J. Res. 326*, Senate, 76th Cong., 1st Sess., 256, 257, 259; Smith, *Building New Deal Liberalism*, 198; *NYT*, Jan. 10, June 22–23, 30, 1939; Blumberg, *The New Deal and the Unemployed*, 233–41; Arthur W. MacMahon et al., *The Administration of Federal Work Relief* (Chicago, 1941), 35; Sargent, "Woodrum's Economy Bloc," 200–01. For the esteem with which WPA workers in other cities viewed La Guardia, see, e.g., R. C. Edwards to FHL, May 19, 1939, SF, "Works Progress Administration," NYMA.

19　Department of Public Markets, Weights and Measures of the City of New York,

Annual Report: 1934 (New York, 1935), 59–60; Lawrence B. Dunham to Charles C. Burlingham, Jan. 31, 1938, copy in Thomas Kessner's Research Notes, Box 27D8, Folder 5, La Guardia and Wagner Archives, La Guardia Community College, Queens; Kessner, *Fiorello H. La Guardia*, 340; Robert Moses to Allyn R. Jennings, Apr. 28, 1937, Moses to FHL, Apr. 29, 1937 both in Moses Papers, Box 97, NYPL; *NYT*, June 26, 1937; Citizens Budget Commission, *Annual Report: 1938* (New York, 1938), 5, 21.

20   Blumberg, *The New Deal and the Unemployed*, 254–78; FHL, "Presidential Address," in Paul V. Betters, ed., *City Problems of 1940: The Annual Proceedings of the United States Conference of Mayors* (Washington, DC, 1940), 13; Minutes, Greater New York Industrial Union Council, Oct. 17, 1940, microfilm reel R-7419/1, Wagner Labor Archives, NYU. Amenta et al., "Bring Back the WPA," 46, presents a useful tabulation of key congressional votes on the WPA.

21   Harold Ickes, *The Secret Diary of Harold Ickes, Vol. 2: The Inside Struggle, 1936–1939* (New York, 1954), 252–53.

22   Berle and Jacobs, eds., *Navigating the Rapids*, 151–52; William Manners, *Patience and Fortitude: Fiorello La Guardia, a Biography* (New York, 1976), 246; *NYT*, Jan. 28, Apr. 12, 1938; FHL, "Balancing the—Population," *Survey Graphic* (January 1938), 15; Smith Brookhart to FHL, Dec. 26, 1937, SF, "Speeches—Subject—Farm Speech," NYMA; FHL to FDR, FHL to LeHand, Apr. 11, 1938, SF, "President," NYMA; August Heckscher with Phyllis Robinson, *When La Guardia Was Mayor: New York's Legendary Years* (New York, 1978), 202–03; Kessner, *Fiorello H. La Guardia*, 465–66; William Conklin, "La Guardia Gains from Tour," *NYT*, Sept. 25, 1938. See correspondence in SF, "Out-of-Town Trips," NYMA.

23   *Emporia Gazette*, July 19, 1937; *NYWT*, Nov. 8, 1937; Alsop and Kintner, "The Capital Parade," *Atlanta Constitution*, Dec. 6, 1937; Kent, "The Great Game of Politics," *Baltimore Sun*, Jan. 25, 1938.

24   Patrick J. Maney, *"Young Bob" La Follette: A Biography of Robert M. La Follette, Jr., 1895–1953* (Columbia, SC, 1978), 198, 204–06; Alsop and Kintner, "The Capital Parade," *Atlanta Constitution*, Dec. 6, 1937; Donald Young, ed., *Adventure in Politics: The Memoirs of Philip La Follette* (New York, 1970), 252; Berle and Jacobs, eds., *Navigating the Rapids*, 173–76; *NYT*, May 1, 1938.

25   Brinkley, *The End of Reform*, 21–22; Sidney M. Milkis, *The President and the Parties: The Transformation of the American Party System Since the New Deal* (New York, 1993), chap. 3; James T. Patterson, *Congressional Conservatism and the New Deal: The Growth of a Conservative Coalition in Congress, 1933–1939* (Lexington, KY, 1967), esp. chaps. 4–5; Stanley High, "Whose Party Is It?" *Saturday Evening Post*, Feb. 6, 1937, 10.

26   Milkis, *The President and the Parties*, 77–87.

27   Susan Dunn, *Roosevelt's Purge: How FDR Fought to Change the Democratic Party*

(Cambridge, MA, 2010), 6; FHL to Fulton Oursler, Sept. 2, 1938, SF, "Oursler, Fulton," NYMA.

28   *NYT*, Aug. 12, 21, 1938; Alsop and Kintner, "The Capital Parade," *Atlanta Constitution*, Sept. 25, 1938; Richard Polenberg, "Franklin Roosevelt and the Purge of John O'Connor: The Impact of Urban Change on Political Parties," *New York History*, vol. 48, no. 3 (July 1968), 318; Mrs. Charles E. Greenbough to FDR, Sept. 7, 1938, PPF 1330, FDRL. For a full history of the purge effort, see Dunn, *Roosevelt's Purge*; for an incisive analysis, see Anthony J. Badger, "Local Politics and Party Realignment in the Late Thirties: The Failure of the New Deal," *Storia Nordamericana*, vol. 6, nos. 1–2 (1989), 69–90.

29   Polenberg, "The Purge of John O'Connor," 309, 315–325; Alsop and Kintner, "The Capital Parade," *Atlanta Constitution*, Sept. 25, 1938.

30   Both the WPA's internal investigation and a Senate investigation into political interference in the WPA found O'Connor's charges to be unsubstantiated. There is more conclusive evidence that Hopkins sought to mobilize the IRS agents in the 15th CD to work for Fay, though he was stopped by Secretary Morgenthau. Conversely, one of La Guardia's secretaries complained to Hopkins during the campaign that the O'Connor forces within the WPA were playing "the crudest kind of politics" and that Colonel Somervell was doing nothing to halt it—See Amy D. Burke, "The Politics of Relief: The Impact of State Party Structure on the Works Progress Administration," PhD diss., Brandeis, 2003, 139–40; Joseph P. Lash, *Dealers and Dreamers: A New Look at the New Deal* (New York, 1988), 361; and James Kieran to Hopkins, Oct. 1, 1938, copy in OF 300—New York, FDRL.

31   *NYT*, Aug. 12, Oct. 22, Nov. 9, 1938; "Voters of the 16th Congressional District Should Support John J. O'Connor for Reelection . . . ," copy in SF, "Campaign of 1938," NYMA; Ernest Cuneo, "The Hero Assaults the High Priests," unpublished TS, Cuneo Papers, Box 112, FDRL, 9.

32   Richard Norton Smith, *Thomas E. Dewey and His Times* (New York, 1982), 161, 267–73 and passim; Judith Stein, "The Birth of Liberal Republicanism in New York State, 1932–1938," PhD diss., Yale University, 1968, chap. 10, places Dewey's ascent within the context of New York State's post–New Deal Republican politics.

33   M. Elwoollard to FHL , Oct. 7, SF, "Campaign (1938)," NYMA; John C. Bickel to FHL, Oct. 6, 1938, SF, "Politics—Campaign of 1938," NYMA; Berle diary, Feb. 8, 1939; Alsop and Kintner, "The Capital Parade," *Atlanta Constitution*, Nov. 8, 1938.

34   Frederick M. Davenport to FHL, Oct. 3, 1938, SF, "Campaign (1938)," NYMA; Farley diary, Oct. 14, 1938; *NYT*, Oct. 22, Nov. 6, 1938; J. C. Thomson to Edward J. Flynn, Nov. 4, 1938, SF, "Politics—Campaign of 1938," NYMA; Berle and Jacobs, eds., *Navigating the Rapids*, 190. See also Krock, "The Mayor Grabs the Horns of a Dilemma," *NYT*, Nov. 4, 1938; Kessner, *Fiorello H. La Guardia*, 465–66.

35   FHL to Charles Beard, Nov. 30, 1938, SF, "Philosophy—The Philosophical View,"

NYMA; Paul Y. Anderson, "What the Election Means," *The Nation*, Nov. 19, 1938, 528; *NYT*, Nov. 10, 13, 14, 1938.

36   Alsop and Kintner, "The Capital Parade," *Atlanta Constitution*, Nov. 8, 1938.

37   *NYHT*, Mar. 4, 1937; *NYT*, Mar. 4, 1937.

38   *NYT*, Mar. 4–8, 1937; *Chicago Tribune*, Mar. 5, 1937; *WP*, Mar. 7, 1937; "La Guardia v. Hitler," *Time*, Mar. 15, 1937, 18. See correspondence in SF, "Hitler—Correspondence Relating To," NYMA.

39   James V. Compton, *The Swastika and the Eagle: Hitler, the United States, and the Origins of World War II* (Boston, 1967), 73; Ickes, *The Secret Diary: Vol. 2*, 89; Morgenthau diary, Mar. 5, 10–11, 1937.

40   *NYT*, Mar. 16, 1937; *NYWT*, Mar. 16, 1937; *NYHT*, Mar. 16, 1937.

41   David M. Esposito and Jackie R. Esposito, "La Guardia and the Nazis, 1933–1938," *American Jewish History*, vol. 78, no. 1 (September 1988), 49; *NYT*, Mar. 16–18, 1937, Apr. 16, 1945.

42   *NYHT*, Mar. 4, 1937; *New York Daily News*, Mar. 5, 1937; *Bronx Home News*, Mar. 5, 1937; *Brooklyn Eagle*, Mar. 6, 1937; *NYWT*, Mar. 6, 1937; "La Guardia v. Hitler," *Time*, Mar. 15, 1937, 18.

43   Kessner, *Fiorello H. La Guardia*, 468; Arthur Mann, *La Guardia: A Fighter Against His Times, 1882–1933* (Philadelphia, 1959), 221–22.

44   *NYT*, Feb.15, 1935; *PPA: Vol. 6, 1937*, 410. See also James T. Sparrow, *Warfare State: World War II Americans and the Age of Big Government* (New York, 2011), 26–28.

45   Gunther, *Federal-City Relations in the United States*, 133; Pearson and Allen, "The Washington Merry-Go-Round," Sept. 28, 1939; *New York Daily Mirror*, Jan. 6, 1941; Jordan A. Schwarz, *Liberal: Adolf A. Berle and the Vision of an American Era* (New York, 1987), 130–31; *NYT*, Apr. 12, Nov. 20, 1938, Mar. 17, Nov. 8, 1939, May 26, 1940; FHL to Marguerite LeHand, Apr. 11, 1938; Edwin Watson office memo, Sept. 28, 1939, both in PPF 1376, FDRL; Irwin F. Gellman, *Good Neighbor Diplomacy: United States Policies in Latin America, 1933–1945* (Baltimore, 1979), 107–08; Robert Dallek, *Franklin D. Roosevelt and American Foreign Policy, 1932–1945* (New York, 1979), 175–77, 205–06.

46   *Hearings Before the Committee on Ways and Means . . . on Proposed Legislation Relating to Tax-Exempt Securities*, House, 76th Cong., 1st Sess., 322–23; David Green, *The Containment of Latin America: A History of the Myths and Realities of the Good Neighbor Policy* (Chicago, 1971), 34–35; Thomas H. Beck to FDR, Apr. 22, 1941, OF 81, FDRL.

47   David A. Horowitz, *Beyond Left and Right: Insurgency and the Establishment* (Urbana, IL, 1997), 169–70; FHL to Marguerite LeHand, Sept. 5, 1939, PPF 1376, FDRL; David M. Kennedy, *Freedom from Fear: The American People in Depression and War* (New York, 1999), 428.

48   George Britt, "The Fiery Little Flower," *Collier's*, Mar. 11, 1939, 45; Rexford G. Tugwell diary, Apr. 26, 1940, Tugwell Papers, Box 32, FDRL; Alsop and Kintner,

"The Capital Parade," *Atlanta Constitution*, Nov. 10, 1938; Manners, *Patience and Fortitude*, 246–47; *NYT*, Aug. 27, 28, 1938; Ickes, *The Secret Diary: Vol. 2*, 554–55.

49 Rexford G. Tugwell, *The Art of Politics as Practiced by Three Great Americans: Franklin Delano Roosevelt, Luis Muñoz Marín, and Fiorello H. La Guardia* (Garden City, NY, 1958), 199; *NYT*, Jan. 29, 1940; Henry A. Wallace diary, Jan. 18, 1940, in Reminiscences of Henry Wallace, CCOHC, 683; Arthur Krock, "In the Nation," *NYT*, Sept. 14, 1938; Alsop and Kintner, "Capital Parade," *Atlanta Constitution*, Apr. 27, 1939; Ickes, *The Secret Diary: Vol. 2*, 257–58; Pearson and Allen, "The Washington Merry-Go-Round," Mar. 4, 1940.

50 *NYT*, Feb. 10, 1940; Alsop and Kintner, "The Capital Parade," *Atlanta Constitution*, Feb. 26, 1940; Harold Ickes diary, Feb. 11, 1940, Ickes Papers, LC.

51 Tugwell diary, Feb. 28, Apr. 26, May 16, 1940; *NYT*, Feb. 24, 1940; Ickes diary, Feb. 11, 17, 24, 1940; Pearson and Allen, "The Washington Merry-Go-Round," Apr. 10, 1940.

52 Wallace diary, Nov. 18, 24, Dec. 9, 1939, Jan. 18, 1940, in Reminiscences, CCOHC, 580, 591, 605, 683; *NYT*, May 2, 14, 1940; Tugwell diary, Nov. 30, 1939, Mar. 25, Apr. 26, 1940.

Part III: War and Postwar

Chapter 8: The Local Politics of Foreign Policy

1 *NYT*, June 11–13, 1940; *NYHT*, June 11, 1940.

2 *PPA: Vol. 9, 1940*, 259–64; Robert Dallek, *Franklin D. Roosevelt and American Foreign Policy, 1932–1945* (New York, 1979), 228; Samuel I. Rosenman, *Working with Roosevelt* (New York, 1952), 198–99; Doris Kearns Goodwin, *No Ordinary Time: Franklin and Eleanor Roosevelt and the Home Front in World War II* (New York, 1994), 67–69.

3 *NYT*, July 12, 1940; *Ottawa Journal*, June 11–12, 1940; *Ottawa Citizen*, June 11–12, 1940.

4 William Manners, *Patience and Fortitude: Fiorello La Guardia, A Biography* (New York, 1976), 212; *NYT*, May 22, 30, 1940; Joseph Alsop and Robert Kintner, "The Capital Parade," *Atlanta Constitution*, May 30, 1940; Rexford G. Tugwell diary, June 10, July 30, Aug. 6, 1940, Tugwell Papers, Box 32, FDRL; Adolf A. Berle, Jr., diary, May 17, 1940, Berle Papers, Box 211, FDRL; *Pittsburgh Courier*, Sept. 30, 1939; Rexford G. Tugwell, *The Art of Politics As Practiced by Three Great Americans: Franklin Delano Roosevelt, Luis Muñoz Marín, and Fiorello H. La Guardia* (Garden City, NY, 1958), 91; Harold Ickes, *The Secret Diary of Harold Ickes, Vol. 3: The Lowering Clouds, 1939–1941* (New York, 1954), 180–81, 186–87; Joseph P. Lash, *Eleanor and Franklin: The Story of Their Relationship, Based on Eleanor Roosevelt's Private Papers* (New York, 1971), 640. For correspondence in support of La

Guardia's appointment, see OF 25-A, FDRL. See also Tugwell diary, May 16, 22, 1940, and Frankfurter to FHL, June 26, 1940, SF, "General Correspondence—Frankfurter, Felix," NYMA.

5 Tugwell, *The Art of Politics*, 111; Thomas Kessner, *Fiorello H. La Guardia and the Making of Modern New York* (New York, 1989), 524–26, 537; Walter Isaacson and Evan Thomas, *The Wise Men: Six Friends and the World They Made* (New York, 1986), 200–01.

6 Tugwell diary, Aug. 28, 1940; Nicholas Mansergh, *Survey of British Commonwealth Affairs: Problems of Wartime Co-operation and Post-War Change, 1939–1952* (New York, 1958), 51–53; Galen Roger Perras, *Franklin Roosevelt and the Origins of the Canadian-American Security Alliance, 1933–1945: Necessary, But Not Necessarily Enough* (Westport, CT, 1998), 66–85; W. A. B. Douglas, "Democratic Spirit and Purpose: Problems in Canadian-American Relations, 1939–1945," in Joel J. Sokolsky and Joseph T. Jockel, eds., *Fifty Years of Canada-United States Defense Cooperation: The Road from Ogdensburg* (Lewiston, ME, 1992), 35–37; Stanley W. Dziuban, *Military Relations Between the United States and Canada, 1939–1945* (Washington, DC, 1959), 86; Robert Bothwell, *Canada and the United States: The Politics of Partnership* (Toronto, 1992), 19; Reminiscences of Marie La Guardia, CCOHC, 43.

7 Alsop and Kintner, "The Capital Parade," *Atlanta Constitution*, Sept. 12, 1940; *NYT*, Aug. 18, 1937; Ickes, *The Secret Diary: Vol. 3*, 307, 321; FHL to FDR, July 20, 1940, SF, "President," NYMA; Joseph P. Lash diary, Aug. 7, 14, 1940, Lash Papers, Box 31, FDRL; Ronald L. Feinman, *The Twilight of Progressivism: The Western Republican Senators and the New Deal* (Baltimore, 1981), 174–75, 178–79, 182–86; Harold Ickes diary, Sept. 15, 1940, Ickes Papers, LC; *NYT*, Sept. 25, 1940.

8 *Hearings Before the Special Committee Investigating Campaign Expenditures, 1940, Vol. 4*, Senate, 76th Cong., 3rd Sess., 440; Sol Rosenblatt to David K. Niles, Oct. 18, 1940; Niles to Rosenblatt, Oct. 21, 1940, NCIV Papers, Box 3, FDRL; Paul C. Aiken to FHL, Sept. 24, SF, "Politics—Campaign of 1940," NYMA; Louis Overacker, "Campaign Finance in the Presidential Election of 1940," *APSR*, vol. 35, no. 4 (August 1941), 709; *NYT*, Sept. 29, Oct. 10, 26–27, 1940, Jan. 4, 1941; "Report of the Literature Department," [n.d.]; radio scripts, in NCIV Papers, Box 1, FDRL; J. Roland Sala, "Report of the Chairman of the Foreign Language Division of the National Committee of Independent Voters on the Political Activity, Submitted to Mr. Niles, Oct. 30, 1940," NCIV Papers, Box 4, FDRL; Arnold P. Johnson, "Report Covering Activities of the Negro State Division of the Independent Voters for the Re-election of Roosevelt and Wallace," in SF, "Politics—Campaign of 1940," NYMA, 4; Lash diary, Oct. 6, 1940; Lash, *Dealers and Dreamers*, 407; Ickes diary, Sept. 8, 1940; Ickes, *The Secret Diary: Vol. 3*, 311. On Sala, see *NYT*, Nov. 3, 1963.

9 *NYT*, Sept. 13, 1940; FHL, "Roosevelt Preferred: New York's Mayor States the Case for the President," *Life*, Oct. 21, 1940, 102–06.

10   Reminiscences of Paul Windels (1953 interview), CCOHC, 22; Westbrook Pegler, "Fair Enough," *WP*, Nov. 6, 1940. Copies of FHL's campaign speeches are in SF, "Roosevelt Campaign (1940)," NYMA.

11   Mark H. Leff, "Strange Bedfellows: The Utility Magnate as Politician," in James H. Madison, ed., *Wendell Willkie: Hoosier Internationalist* (Bloomington, IN, 1992),42; Steve Fraser, *Labor Will Rule: Sidney Hillman and the Rise of American Labor* (New York, 1991), 443; Ickes, *The Secret Diary: Vol. 3*, 221–23; *NYT*, Oct. 2, 12, 23, Nov. 2–3, 1940; Arthur Krock, "How National Unity Is Being Achieved," *NYT*, Oct. 25, 1940; Lewis W. Douglas to FHL, Oct. 17, 1940, SF, "Politics—Campaign of 1940," NYMA; *St. Louis Censor*, Nov. 21, 1940; Robert Appel, "Report of the Activities of the Illinois Committee of Independent Voters for Roosevelt and Wallace," OF 4142, FDRL; Anthony Arpaia to David K. Niles, Oct. 28, 1940, NCIV Papers, Box 3, FDRL. On class polarization in the 1940 election, see Samuel Lubell, *The Future of American Politics* (New York, 1952), 53–55, and David Montgomery, "The Mythical Man," *International Labor and Working-Class History* 74 (Fall 2008), 56.

12   *NYT*, Oct. 14–15, 1940; Robert Moses, "The Case Against Roosevelt," *Life*, Oct. 14, 1940, 105, 110–14; Robert E. Burke, "Election of 1940," in Arthur M. Schlesinger, Jr., ed., *History of American Presidential Elections, 1789–1968, Vol. 7: 1928–1940* (New York, 1985), 2925–2926, 2928; I. T. Hurts to FHL, Sept. 13, 1940; in SF, "Politics—Campaign of 1940," NYMA. See also other correspondence in the same file.

13   *NYT*, Oct. 22, Nov. 1–2, Dec. 20, 1940; Herbert Mitgang, *The Man Who Rode the Tiger: The Life and Career of Judge Samuel Seabury* (Philadelphia, 1963), 348, 354–55; Kessner, *Fiorello H. La Guardia*, 472, 481–82.

14   Ronald Bayor, *Neighbors in Conflict: The Irish, Germans, Jews, and Italians of New York City, 1929–1941* 2nd ed. (Urbana, IL, 1988), 110–14, 147–49, 213n75, 359–60, 426–28; Joshua M. Zeitz, *White Ethnic New York: Jews, Catholics, and the Shaping of Postwar Politics* (Chapel Hill, NC, 2007), 117–18; Ickes, *The Secret Diary: Vol. 2*, 86; Mike Wallace, *Gotham II* (New York, forthcoming). On Italian Americans in the 1940 election, see Stefano Luconi, "The Impact of World War II on the Political Behavior of the Italian-American Electorate in New York City," *New York History*, vol. 83, no. 4 (Fall 2002), 406–07, 417; "Survey of Italian Vote in New York City, Sept. 28 to Oct. 3, 1940," NCIV Papers, Box 4, FDRL; correspondence in OF 233a Miscel., FDRL; *PL*, 1072; *NYT*, June 12, Sept. 12–13, Nov. 6, 1940; and James Roe to FHL, Nov. 13, 1940, SF, "Politics—Campaign of 1940," NYMA. English-language drafts of FHL's radio scripts are in ibid.

15   *PPA: Vol. 10, 1941*, 3–6; FHL to Eleanor Roosevelt, Jan. 25, 1941, SF, "President," NYMA.

16   Berle and Jacobs, eds., *Navigating the Rapids*, 358; Ickes, *The Secret Diary: Vol. 3*, 383; Kessner, *Fiorello H. La Guardia*, 484–87; James Rowe, Jr., to FDR, Apr. 21,

1941, PSF 141, FDRL. See also Ralph Ingersoll, "What's Happened to Mayor La Guardia?" *PM*, Dec. 26, 1940.

17 Ickes diary, Nov. 9, 1940; Harold Smith, "Conferences with President Roosevelt" notes, Apr. 4, 22, 1941, Smith Papers, Box 3, FDRL; FDR to Charles Evans Hughes, Aug. 25, 1941, PPF 7590, FDRL. On various proposals for a home defense program, ultimately amalgamated to form the Office of Civilian Defense, see Richard W. Steele, "Preparing the Public for War: Efforts to Establish a National Propaganda Agency, 1940–1941," *AHR*, vol. 75, no. 6 (October 1970), 1641–1644; Robert E. Miller, "The War That Never Came: Civilian Defense, Mobilization, and Morale During World War II," PhD diss., University of Cincinnati, 1990, chap. 1; Philip J. Funigiello, *The Challenge to Urban Liberalism: Federal-City Relations During World War II* (Knoxville, TN, 1978), 39–49, and Laura McEnaney, *Civil Defense Begins at Home: Militarization Meets Everyday Life in the Fifties* (Princeton, 2000), 17–18.

18 Henry L. Stimson diary, Dec. 18, 1941, Stimson Papers, Sterling Library, Yale University; Lee Kennett, *For the Duration: The United States Goes to War, Pearl Harbor—1942* (New York, 1985), 28; FHL, "Presidential Address," in Paul V. Betters, ed., *City Problems of 1940: The Proceedings of the United States Conference of Mayors* (Washington, DC, 1940), 20; August Heckscher with Phyllis Robinson, *When La Guardia Was Mayor: New York's Legendary Years* (New York, 1978), 296; *New York Daily Mirror*, Jan. 15, 17, 1941; *Daily Worker*, Jan. 18, 1941; *NYP*, Jan. 18, 1941; *NYT*, Jan. 16, Feb. 19, Mar. 30, 1941; FHL to FDR, Feb. 5; FDR to FHL, Feb. 26, both in OF 148, FDRL; FHL to FDR, Jan. 31, 1941; "Preliminary Report for Civil Defense . . . Submitted . . . by F. H. La Guardia . . . January 31, 1941," both in OF 1892, FDRL.

19 Smith, "Conferences" notes, Apr. 22, 1941; Ickes, *The Secret Diary: Vol. 3*, 519; FHL to Edwin Watson, Apr. 25, 1941; FHL to FDR, Apr. 25, 1941, PSF 145, FDRL. For the executive order establishing the OCD, see *PPA: Vol. 10, 1941*, 162–66.

20 Pearson and Allen, "The Washington Merry-Go-Round," June 27, 1941; FHL, *Report of the Director of the Office of Civilian Defense* (Washington, DC, 1942), 10–26, 37; *Hearings Before the Committee on Military Affairs . . . on H.R. 5727*, House, 77th Cong., 1st Sess., 1–15; Miller, "The War That Never Came," 67–68, 110; Kennett, *For the Duration*, 33.

21 "Memorandum on Program and Organization, Office of Civilian Defense, November 6, 1941, Prepared by the Bureau of the Budget," OF 4422, FDRL; *Hearings Before the Select Committee Investigating the National Defense Migration . . . Pursuant to H. Res. 113 . . . Part 25*, House, 77th Cong., 2nd Sess., 9744; Miller, "The War That Never Came," 34n14; Kennett, *For the Duration*, 30; FHL to FDR, Apr. 25, 1941, PSF 145, FDRL. On La Guardia's staffing the OCD with mayors—his successor counted fifteen of them—see Reminiscences of James

Landis, CCOHC, 314, and Lash, *Franklin and Eleanor*, 645. Funigiello, *The Challenge to Urban Liberalism*, 47–55, is the best account of intergovernmental relations in the OCD, but says too little about how La Guardia's experience as a local official shaped his decisions. On mayors' support of La Guardia, see *WP*, Jan. 8, 1942.

22 Steele, "Preparing the Public for War," 1648–1651; Smith, "Conferences" notes, Apr. 18, 22, 1941; Richard W. Steele, *Propaganda in an Open Society: The Roosevelt Administration and the Media* (Westport, CT, 1985), 94–95; FHL to FDR, June 12, PSF 145, FDRL; LaMar Seal Mackay, "Domestic Operations of the Office of War Information in World War II," PhD diss., University of Wisconsin, 1966, 31; Ickes, *The Secret Diary: Vol. 3*, 519–20, 540, 572, 601.

23 McEnaney, *Civil Defense Begins at Home*, 17–18; Miller, "The War That Never Came," 103–04, 109–10; *NYHT*, Nov. 9, 16, 1941; *NYT*, July 25, 1941; FHL to FDR, Apr. 25, 1940; FHL to Eleanor Roosevelt, June 26, 1941, Eleanor Roosevelt Papers, Box 1608, FDRL.

24 Lash, *Eleanor and Franklin*, 640–42, 644–46; Manners, *Patience and Fortitude*, 258. On Eleanor Roosevelt's concept of civilian participation, see Funigiello, *The Challenge to Urban Liberalism*, 56–79.

25 Pearson and Allen, "The Washington Merry-Go-Round," Aug. 27, 1941; "Washington Notes," *Newsweek*, Aug. 18, 1941, 9; "OCD on the Fire," *Newsweek*, Sept. 8, 1941, 45–46; *WP*, Sept. 5, 1941; Ickes, *The Secret Diary, Vol. 3*, 572; Lash diary, Oct. 5, 1941; Lash, *Eleanor and Franklin*, 641.

26 Anthony S. Chen, *The Fifth Freedom: Jobs, Politics, and Civil Rights in the United States, 1941–1972* (Princeton, 2009), 36; Daniel Kryder, *Divided Arsenal: Race and the American State During World War II* (New York, 2000), 55–58, 66–67; "Total and Non-White Employment in New York City Establishments Employing Over 250 Workers—May 1941–May 1942," RG 211, Entry 91, Box 1, NA; Jervis Anderson, *A. Philip Randolph: A Biographical Portrait* (New York, 1972), 246–55; Walter White, *A Man Called White: The Autobiography of Walter White* (New York, 1948), 189; A. Philip Randolph to FDR, May 29, 1941; Stephen Early to Wayne Coy, June 6, 1941; both in OF 391, FDRL.

27 Dominic J. Capeci, Jr., "Fiorello H. La Guardia and Employment Discrimination, 1941–1943," *Italian Americana*, vol. 7, no. 2 (Spring–Summer 1983), 53–55, 49–63; Walter White to Byrnes McDonald, Oct. 3, 1940, SF, "N.A.A.C.P.," NYMA; Edwin Watson to FDR, June 14, 1941; Randolph to FDR, June 16, 1941; both in OF 391, FDRL; Anderson, *A. Philip Randolph*, 214, 251–52; Nat Brandt, *Harlem at War: The Black Experience in World War II* (Syracuse, NY, 1996), 76–79; *New York Amsterdam News*, June 21, 1941. Stimson's account also placed Aubrey Williams at the June 18 White House meeting—Stimson diary, June 18, 1941. On La Guardia's relationship with Randolph, see *Baltimore Afro-American*, Sept. 1, 1934,

Pittsburgh Courier, Sept. 1, 1940, and Andrew E. Kersten, *A. Philip Randolph: A Life in the Vanguard* (New York, 2007), 45–46.

28 Randolph to Eleanor Roosevelt, June 16, 1941, OF 391, FDRL; Lash, *Eleanor and Franklin*, 533–35; Anderson, *A. Philip Randolph*, 255–59, Stimson diary, June 18, 1941.

29 Kryder, *Divided Arsenal*, 64–65; Randolph to FDR, July 7, 1941; Walter White to FDR, July 8, 1941; White to Early, July 14, 1941; FHL to FDR, July 18, 1941; all in OF 4245g, FDRL; Capeci, "La Guardia and Employment Discrimination," 52.

30 Chen, *The Fifth Freedom*, 33; Kryder, *Divided Arsenal*, 74–87; William J. Collins, "Race, Roosevelt, and Wartime Production," *American Economic Review*, vol. 91, no. 1 (March 2001), 272–86.

31 Chen, *The Fifth Freedom*, chap. 3 and passim; Joshua Freeman, *Working-Class New York: Life and Labor Since World War II* (New York, 2000), 68–69; *New York Amsterdam News*, Feb. 24, 1945; *Baltimore Afro-American*, Mar. 3, 1945; *NYT*, Feb. 17, 1942, Feb. 21, 1945.

32 Jordan A. Schwarz, *Liberal: Adolf A. Berle and the Vision of an American Era* (New York, 1987), 158–59, 162–63; *NYT*, Mar. 27, May 22–24, June 8, July 7, 11–12, 1941; *NYP*, May 22, 1941; Smith, "Conferences" notes, Apr. 17, 1941; "La Guardia's Role," *Newsweek*, May 5, 1941, 11; Reminiscences of Edward J. Flynn, CCOHC, 20; Reminiscences of Paul O'Dwyer, CCOHC, 200; Will Chasan, "Can Tammany Come Back?," *The Nation*, Apr. 29, 1941, 466; Heckscher, *When La Guardia Was Mayor*, 323, 326. Smith noted that, shortly after meeting with Flynn, Roosevelt backed off momentarily from seeking La Guardia for the OCD job. "I gather by inference . . . ," Smith wrote, "that there was a possibility that La Guardia might be persuaded to run for mayor on the Democratic ticket."

33 *NYT*, Aug. 18, Sept. 13, 1941; William Spinrad, "New Yorkers Cast Their Ballots," PhD diss., Columbia University, 1955, 9.

34 Richard Norton Smith, *Thomas E. Dewey and His Times* (New York, 1982), 332–33, 339; Berle diary, Feb. 8, 1939; Reminiscences of Reuben Lazarus, CCOHC, 206.

35 Harvey Klehr, *The Heyday of American Communism* (New York, 1984), 386–99; Kenneth Waltzer, "The American Labor Party: Third Party Politics in New Deal–Cold War Era New York, 1936–1954," PhD diss., Harvard University, 1977, 123.

36 Joshua Freeman, *In Transit: The Transport Workers Union in New York City, 1933–1966* (New York, 1989), 197–223, esp. 216–17; Kessner, *Fiorello H. La Guardia*, 460–61; Minutes, Greater New York Industrial Union Council, May 8, Oct. 9, 1941, microfilm reel R-7419/1, Robert F. Wagner Labor Archives, New York University; Simon W. Gerson, "What Happened to La Guardia," *New Masses*, Oct. 22, 1940, 6–7; *NYT*, June 13, 16, 22, July 20, Aug. 24, Sept. 18–19, Oct. 6, 9, 16, 1941; *Politics for American Labor*, Oct. 25, 1941, copy in FHL Mayoral Papers, Box 4128, NYMA; Reminiscences of Paul O'Dwyer, CCOHC, 196; William O'Dwyer, *Beyond the Golden Door* (Jamaica, NY, 1986), 164–65.

37   *PM*, Sept. 2, 1941 (see also "The Shape of Things," *The Nation*, Aug. 16, 1941, 130); *Der Tog*, Oct. 13, 1941; "An Appeal for La Guardia," *NYHT*, Oct. 31, 1941. I owe the insight that concludes this paragraph to Ira Katznelson.

38   Lash diary, Oct. 5, 1941; Smith, "Conferences" notes, Oct. 9, 1941; *NYT*, Oct. 24, 1941; Kessner, *Fiorello H. La Guardia*, 497; *CPPC*, Oct. 21, 24, 1941; FHL to FDR, Oct. 24, 1941, PPF 1376, FDRL.

39   Bayor, *Neighbors in Conflict*, 139–45.

40   "June 5: Fiorello La Guardia," Special Survey, New York City, in Gallup, ed., *The Gallup Poll: Vol. 1*, 283.

41   *NYT*, Nov. 6, 8–9, 1941; *Cincinnati Post* clipping in OF 4422, FDRL; "La Guardia Out?" *Newsweek*, Dec. 22, 1941, 9; *NYHT*, Jan. 6, 1942.

42   David M. Kennedy, *Freedom from Fear: The American People in Depression and War, 1929–1945* (New York, 1999), 507–15; Dallek, *Franklin D. Roosevelt and American Foreign Policy*, 305; FHL to Hopkins, June 27, 1942; FHL to Colonel Franklin D'Olier et al., Nov. 8, 1941; both in Hopkins Papers, Box 161, FDRL; *NYT*, Nov. 30, 1941.

43   *NYT*, Dec. 8, 9, 1941; Kessner, *Fiorello H. La Guardia*, 501–02, 536–38; FHL to FDR, Dec. 7, 1941; and Edwin Watson to FDR, Dec. 8, 1941, OF 4422, FDRL; Eleanor Roosevelt, *This I Remember* (New York, 1949), 236.

44   Kennett, *For the Duration*, 27; Walter Lippmann, "Today and Tomorrow: Mayor La Guardia and Mrs. Roosevelt," *WP*, Dec. 16, 1941; Frank R. Kent, "The Great Game of Politics," *Baltimore Sun*, Dec. 21, 1941; Stimson diary, Dec. 18, 1941, Jan. 5, 1941; *NYHT*, Dec. 18, 1941; *NYWT*, Dec. 17, 19, 1941; *Brooklyn Eagle*, Dec. 21, 1941; *NYT*, Dec. 26, 1941, Jan. 5, 1942; Kessner, *Fiorello H. La Guardia*, 502–04; Lash, *Eleanor and Franklin*, 648; Funigiello, *The Challenge to Urban Liberalism*, 55–56; Wayne Coy to FDR, Dec. 13, 1941, OF 4422, Smith, "Conferences" notes, Dec. 19, 1941, Jan. 2, 1942.

45   Charles Garrett, *The La Guardia Years: Machine and Reform Politics in New York City* (New Brunswick, NJ, 1961), 282; Warren Moscow, *Politics in the Empire State* (New York, 1948), 28; *New York Daily Mirror*, Jan. 3, 1942; William Manchester, *The Glory and the Dream: A Narrative History of America, 1932–1972* (Boston, 1974), 258.

Chapter 9: The Battle of New York

1   *NYT*, Apr. 2, 1942; James Sparrow, *Warfare State: World War II Americans and the Age of Big Government* (New York, 2011), quote at 4.

2   Thomas Kessner, *Fiorello H. La Guardia and the Making of Modern New York* (New York, 1989), 508–76, is the best treatment of La Guardia's third-term failings.

3   Jon C. Teaford, *The Rough Road to Renaissance: Urban Revitalization in America, 1940–1985* (Baltimore, 1990), 14, 24; *Problems of American Small Business: Hear-*

ings Before the Special Committee to Study and Survey Problems of Small Business Enterprises . . . Part 10 . . . , Senate, 77th Cong., 2nd Sess., 1068, 1173–1174.

4   NYT, July 18, 1942; George A. Sloan, "New York City Attends to Its Own Business," Dun's Review (August 1942), 28; George A. Sloan to John Sloane, July 23, 1942, SF, "War Contracts—N.Y.C.," NYMA; M. P. Catherwood and Meredith B. Givens, "The Problem of War Production and Surplus Labor in New York City," May 13, 1942, RG 211, Entry 94, Box 2, NA. On the U-boats, see Mike Wallace, Gotham II (New York, forthcoming).

5   Catherwood and Givens, "Problems of War Production and Surplus Labor"; "Report of Inter-Departmental Staff Meeting on New York City Unemployment Situation . . . July 16, 1942 . . . "; "Effects of Curtailment Orders on Employment in the Metropolitan New York Area, July 1, 1942–January 1, 1943," all in RG 211, Entry 94, Box 2; Problems of American Small Business, 1049–1050, 1058; NYT, July 10, 12, 18, Aug. 27, Sept. 20, Nov. 10, 1942; John W. Hanes et al., Report of the Dewey Committee on Employment, May 15, 1943, reprinted in NYT, Apr. 12, 1943; Alan Brinkley, The End of Reform: New Deal Liberalism in Recession and War (New York, 1995), 192; Brian Waddell, The War Against the New Deal: World War II and American Democracy (DeKalb, IL, 2001), 96–98; Sloan, "New York City Attends to Its Own Business," 26; "Minutes of the Regional Labor Supply Committee Meeting, June 29, 1942"; J. J. Joseph to Louis Levine, June 4, 1942; both in RG 211, Entry 91, Box 1, NA; "Remarks by Mr. Jacob S. Potofsky . . . ," Feb. 11, 1942, SF, "War Contracts—N.Y.C.," NYMA.

6   New York City Department of Commerce, "Available Facilities for War Production in New York City, 1942," 2, copy in Henry A. Wallace Papers, Box 42, FDRL; "What's the Matter with New York?" NYP, July 1, 1942. In the NYHT series, see esp. "New York's Greatest Industry" and "New York Marches On: I," May 5, 1943. On "decentralization," see among others Teaford, The Rough Road to Renaissance, 10–25; Robert H. Armstrong and Homer Hoyt, Decentralization in New York City (Chicago, 1941); Leverett S. Lyon, "Economic Problems of American Cities," American Economic Review, vol. 32, no. 1, part 2 (March 1942), 307–22; Warren S. Thompson and P. K. Whelpton, "Changes in Regional and Urban Patterns of Population Growth," American Sociological Review, vol. 5, no. 6 (December 1940), 921–28.

7   August Heckscher with Phyllis Robinson, When La Guardia Was Mayor: New York's Legendary Years (New York, 1978), 293; Hanes et al., Report of the Dewey Committee; NYT, Nov. 30, 1939, June 9, 12, 1940, Sept. 14, Nov. 27, 1941, Jan. 30, June 14, 1942; FHL to Floyd Odlum, Feb. 21, 1942; FHL to Donald Nelson, Mar. 16, 1942; FHL to FDR, Mar. 16, 1943; FHL to Nelson, Apr. 6, 1942; Nelson to FHL, Apr. 7, 1942; Sloan to FHL, Apr. 8, 1942; FHL to Nelson, Apr. 28, 1942; FHL to Nelson, May 8, 1942; FHL to Paul McNutt, June 30, 1942; all in SF, "War

Contracts—N.Y.C.," NYMA; FHL to Leon Henderson, June 25, 1942; FHL to Lou Holland, July 18, 1942; in SF, "Correspondence with Federal Officials," NYMA.

8   Lehman to FHL, May 28, 1942, SF, "War Contracts—N.Y.C.," NYMA; Lehman and FHL to FDR, June 2, 1942; FDR to Lehman and FHL, June 10, 1942; FDR to FHL, July 22, 1942; all in OF 335-N, FDRL; *NYT*, May 29, 1942.

9   "Report of Inter-Departmental Meeting . . . July 16 . . ."; "Minutes of Meeting on New York Employment Situation, July 17, 1942, 10:00 am," in RG 211, Entry 94, Box 2, NA; James Forrestal to FHL, Oct. 20, 1942, SF, "War Contracts, N.Y.C.," NYMA; *NYT*, July 2, 7, 17–18, 24, 1942; FHL to FDR, June 22, 1942, OF 335-N, FDRL; F. H. Dryden to Marvin McIntyre, June 29, 1942, OF 444-C, FDRL; "Staging Area—Brooklyn," 7–10; Joshua Freeman, *Working-Class New York: Life and Labor Since World War II* (New York, 2000), 164.

10   Leonard A. Drake and Carrie Glasser, *Trends in the New York Clothing Industry* . . . (New York, 1942); Sloan, "New York City Attends to Its Own Business," 26; FHL to Sidney Hillman, May 10, 1941; Jacob S. Potofsky to Sloan, Feb. 16, 1942; Sloan to Potofsky, Feb. 18, 1942; Sloan to FHL, Feb. 19, 1942; FHL to Douglas C. MacKeachie, Feb. 19, 1942; MacKeachie to FHL, Mar. 3, 1942; FHL to Donald Nelson, Apr. 5, 1942; FHL to Nelson, Apr. 6, 1942; Sloan to FHL, Apr. 8, 1942; "Memorandum to Mr. Sloan, April 8, 1942"; Sloan, "Memorandum to Mayor La Guardia," Apr. 11, 1942; Sloan to FHL, Apr. 17, 1942; FHL to Nelson, May 8, 1942; FHL to Julius Levy, July 7, 1942; all in SF, "War Contracts—N.Y.C.," NYMA; "Minutes of the Regional Labor Supply Committee Meeting, June 29, 1942," RG 211, Entry 91, Box 1, NA; "Report of Inter-Departmental Meeting . . . July 16, 1942"; Lloyd Reynolds to William Haber, July 29, 1942; "Minutes of Meeting . . . July 17, 1942 . . . ," in RG 211, Entry 94, Box 2, NA.

11   Sloan to FHL, Apr. 17, 19, 1942; FHL to Julius Levy, July 7, 1942; "Notes on Meeting of Needle Trades Manufacturers . . . Held at Mayor's Office . . . June 24, 1942"; FHL to Superb Fashion Trousers et al., Aug. 25, 1942; Sloan to FHL, June 4, 1942; FHL to Sloan, July 9, 1942; FHL to David Dubinsky, Aug. 11, 1942; all in SF, "War Contracts—N.I.C.," NYMA; "Minutes of Meeting . . . July 17, 1942 . . . ," "Report of Inter-Departmental Meeting . . . July 16, 1942," RG 211, Entry 94, Box 2, NA; Sloan, "Plant Pools Urged for War Work Here," *NYT*, June 14, 1942; *NYT*, Aug. 6, 1942. The Amalgamated Clothing Workers agreed to drop their rates from ninety-five cents a pair to eighty-five cents for the purposes of making Army trousers, and though the Ladies Garment Workers announced no general policy, they privately indicated their willingness to help out contractors on an individual basis. In most cases the difference came out of wages, not profits.

12   Haber to Arthur Altmeyer, Aug. 6, 1942, Reynolds to Haber, July 18, 1942, both in RG 211, Entry 94, Box 2, NA; *Problems of American Small Business*, 1070–1073;

"Excerpts from Sloan's Remarks—New York Building Congress, November 25, 1942"; Lou Holland to Sloan, Dec. 5, 1942; FHL to Nelson, Dec. 21, 1942; FHL to Col. Oscar H. Fogg, Dec. 29, 1942; in SF, "War Contracts, N.Y.C.," NYMA; *NYT*, Nov. 10, 18, 1942, Apr. 12, 21, 1943; Rodney Gibson, "Future of New York," *WP*, Apr. 23, 1943; *NYHT*, June 27, 1943; *PL*, 1368.

13   Freeman, *Working-Class New York*, 144–45.

14   On inflation during the Second World War, see Lester V. Chandler, *Inflation in the United States, 1940–1948* (New York, 1951), and Seymour E. Harris, *Price and Related Controls in the United States* (New York, 1945).

15   Amy Porter, "Butch Says Cut It Out," *Collier's*, Apr. 28, 1945, 44.

16   *PPA: Vol. 11, 1941*, 284–88, 371–72; *CPPC*, May 23, 30, 1940.

17   Andrew H. Bartels, "The Politics of Price Control: The Office of Price Administration and the Dilemmas of Economic Stabilization, 1940–1946," PhD diss., Johns Hopkins University, 1980, 64–162; Harvey C. Mansfield, *Historical Reports on War Administration, Vol. 15: A Short History of OPA* (Washington, DC, 1947), chap. 2 (quote at 40).

18   *PPA: Vol. 11, 1942*, 216–24, 230–33, 356–67, 368–77; Mansfield, *A Short History of OPA*, 39–56; Richard Polenberg, *War and Society: The United States, 1941–1945* (Philadelphia, 1971), 22, 31; Meg Jacobs, *Pocketbook Politics: Economic Citizenship in Twentieth-Century America* (Princeton, 2005), 191–97; *NYT*, Jan. 11, 18, 21, 25, 31, Mar. 1, 3, 20, 28, 1943; *SB*, Feb. 28, 1943. See also Greater New York Industrial Union Council Minutes, Jan. 16, Aug. 6, Dec. 3, 1942, Reel 1, Wagner Labor Archives, New York University.

19   *PPA: Vol. 12, 1943*, 148–53; Mansfield, *A Short History of OPA*, 55–56, 147, 167–70; Meg Jacobs, "'How About Some Meat?': The Office of Price Administration, Consumption Politics, and State Building from the Bottom Up, 1941–1946," *JAH*, vol. 84, no. 3 (December 1997), 918; *SB*, Mar. 14, 1943.

20   Mansfield, *A Short History of OPA*, 261–62; Henderson to FHL, May 25, 1942, SF, "Correspondence with Federal Officials," NYMA.

21   Jacobs, "'How About Some Meat?'" 923; *NYT*, Dec. 31, 1943, Feb. 15, 1944; Lizabeth Cohen, *A Consumer's Republic: The Politics of Mass Consumption in Postwar America* (New York, 2003), 66; Freeman, *Working-Class New York*, 65.

22   FHL to Prentiss Brown and Claude Wickard, Jan. 29, 1943, in "48 Recommendations Made by Mayor F. H. La Guardia to Various Federal Agencies from Feb. 2, 1942 to Dec. 8, 1944," SF, "Food . . . ," NYMA; *NYT*, Apr. 12, 22, 27, 30, May 17, 1943, Nov. 27, 1944; *Hearings Before the Committee on Banking and Currency . . . on S. 1764, a Bill to Amend the Emergency Price Control Act of 1942 . . .* , Senate, 78th Cong., 2nd Sess., 657–58; *SB*, Apr. 23, 1944; Rebecca B. Rankin, ed., *New York Advancing: Victory Edition* (New York, 1945), 211; Mansfield, *A Short History of OPA*, 262.

23   D'Ann Campbell, *Women at War with America: Private Lives in a Patriotic*

Era (Cambridge, MA, 1984), 67; Betty Traunstein to FHL, Jan. 27, 1944, SF, "Food . . . ," NYMA; *SB*, Jan. 30, 1944; *NYT*, Feb. 15, Mar. 23, Apr. 1, 1944.

24 Michael Darrock, "What Happened to Price Control?: The OPA vs. the Inflationary Tide," *Harper's* (July 1943), 122, 124; Jacobs, *Pocketbook Politics*, 202–09; Jacobs, " 'How About Some Meat?' " 921; Cohen, *A Consumer's Republic*, 18–19 and passim.

25 *SB*, Feb. 28, 1943; *NYT*, Feb. 9, Sept. 28, 1943, Sept. 12, 1944, Jan. 16, 1945; Rankin, ed., *New York Advancing: Victory Edition*, 212.

26 John K. Hutchens, "His Honor: Radio Showman," *NYT Sunday Magazine*, July 16, 1944; Kessner, *Fiorello H. La Guardia*, 513–14; Bennett J. Parsteck, "A Rhetorical Analysis of Fiorello La Guardia's Weekly Radio Speeches, 1942–1945," PhD diss., New York University, 1969, 123, 132, 165, 187; Porter, "Butch Says Cut It Out," 23, 44; Oswald Garrison Villard, "Mr. La Guardia and the Union," *Christian Century*, Apr. 11, 1945, 462; Reminiscences of Reuben Lazarus, CCOHC, 209; Saul Nathaniel Scher, "Voice of the City: The History of WNYC, New York City's Municipal Radio Station, 1920–1962," PhD diss., New York University, 1965, 261–63, 266–67.

27 "La Guardia Assailed as Foe of Farmers," *NYT*, May 10, 1944; *SB*, Mar. 5, 1943, Mar. 19, 1944; *NYT*, Sept. 27–28, 1943, Apr. 24, 1944; FHL to South Carolina Peach Growers Association, July 21, 1945, SF, "Food . . . ," NYMA.

28 The Mayor's Office compiled a list of La Guardia's policy recommendations, "48 Recommendations Made by Mayor F. H. La Guardia to Various Federal Agencies from Feb. 2, 1942 to Dec. 8, 1944," SF, "Food . . . ," NYMA. See also *SB*, passim. Quotations from FHL to Prentiss Brown, May 15, 1943; Porter, "Butch Says Cut It Out," 44; *SB*, Apr. 18, 1943, Mar. 19, 1944.

29 Neil H. Lebowitz, " 'Above Party, Class, or Creed': Rent Control in the United States, 1940–1947," *Journal of Urban History*, vol. 7, no. 4 (August 1981), 442–52.

30 Mark Naison, "From Eviction Resistance to Rent Control: Tenant Activism in the Great Depression," in Ronald Lawson with Mark Naison, eds., *The Tenant Movement in New York City, 1904–1984* (New Brunswick, NJ, 1986), 128–29; [Charles Abrams et al.], "Report of the Special Committee of the Citizens' Housing Council on Rent Control for New York City," SF, "Rent Control," NYMA. Gilbert Osofsky, *Harlem, the Making of a Ghetto: Negro New York 1890–1930* (New York, 1966), 135–41, offers a good account of the problems Harlem residents had with landlords in the 1920s. Black community leaders were strong champions of the OPA in general, though they often had to push hard for adequate enforcement—see Cohen, *A Consumer's Republic*, 83–88.

31 Office of Price Administration, "Memorandum," July 26, 1943; Joseph Platzker, "Final Report on Rent Conditions in [the] City of New York," July 14, 1943; Platzker, "Report on 'Rental Conditions in New York City,' " June 23, 1943; [Abrams et al.], "Report . . . on Rent Control for New York City"; Platzker, "Sup-

plemental Report on 'Rental Conditions in the City of New York,'" Sept. 1, 1943; Louis G. Kibbe to FHL, July 14, 1943; Frederick K. Erdtmann to FHL, July 20, 1943; Douglas Elliman to FHL, Feb. 11, 1944; E. J. Marquart to FHL, July 2, 1943; Nathan Hoffmann to Platzker, July 13, 1943; A. B. Johnson to FHL, July 14, 1943; William I. Lerfeld to FHL, Sept. 2, 1943; all in SF, "Rent Control," NYMA; NYT, July 4, 16, Sept. 23–24, 1943; I. Berger, "The Rent Control Situation," Real Estate News (July 1943), 227–331.

32   FHL to Prentiss Brown, July 15, 1943; FHL to Sylvan Joseph, July 15, 1943; Office of Price Administration, "Memorandum," July 26, 1943; [Abrams et al.,] "Report . . . on Rent Control for New York City"; in SF, "Rent Control," NYMA; Naison, "From Eviction Resistance to Rent Control," 128–29; SB, Aug. 15, 1943. On the 1943 riot, see Dominic J. Capeci, Jr., The Harlem Riot of 1943 (Philadelphia, 1977).

33   Platzker, "Supplemental Report on the 'Rental Conditions in the City of New York'"; "Summary of OPA Maximum Rent Regulation for Housing in New York City," in SF, "Rent Control," NYMA; NYT, Sept. 29, 1943; Real Estate News (October 1943), 333; J. Adelman to FHL, Oct. 12, 1943; in SF, "Rent Control," NYMA. See also SB, Aug. 29, Sept. 5, 1943.

34   Freeman, Working-Class New York, 65–66; Jacob B. Ward et al., Report of the New York State Temporary Commission on Rental Housing, Vol. 1 (Albany, 1980), 46–54; New York State Division of Housing and Community Renewal, Office of Rent Administration, Rent Regulation After 50 Years: An Overview of New York State's Rent Regulated Housing, 1993 (n.p., 1994), 2–3; Emanuel Tobier and Barbara Gordon Espejo, "Housing," in Gerald Benjamin and Charles Brecker, eds., The Two New Yorks: State-City Relations in the Changing Federal System (New York, 1988), 453. On the demobilization of the OPA, see esp. Jacobs, "'How About Some Meat?'" 931–41, and Cohen, A Consumer's Republic, 100–08.

35   Max Lerner, "General Butch," PM, Apr. 7, 1943.

36   Bella Rodman, Fiorello La Guardia (New York, 1962), 215; Kessner, Fiorello H. La Guardia, 540; Heckscher, When La Guardia Was Mayor, 353.

37   Harold Ickes diary, Feb. 20, 1943, Ickes Papers, LC; FHL to Lieut. Gen. Stanley D. Embick, Nov. 19, 1942, SF, "Mayor's Office—FHL's Military Commission—WWII," NYMA.

38   FHL to FDR, Feb. 3, 1943, PPF 1376, FDRL.

39   NYT, Mar. 14, 1943; FHL to Hopkins, Mar. 17, 1943, Hopkins Papers, Box 161, FDRL. See correspondence in SF, "Mayor's Office—FHL's Military Commission—WWII," NYMA; George Martin, CCB: The Life and Century of Charles C. Burlingham, New York's First Citizen (New York, 2005), 474.

40   Kessner, Fiorello H. La Guardia, 544; Henry L. Stimson diary, Mar. 27–28, 30, Apr. 6, 1943, Stimson Papers, Sterling Library, Yale University. Harold Ickes's statement that "the Army felt that it might be very difficult to control this vol-

atile, outspoken and resourceful person" appears to be a projection of Ickes's own objections to the appointment. Stimson's diary and correspondence does not suggest this reservation—Ickes diary, Apr. 10, 1943.

41 Stimson to FDR, Apr. 6, 1943, Stimson Papers, Reel 107, Sterling Library.

42 Stimson diary, Apr. 7, 9, 10, 1943; FDR to Stimson, Apr. 8, 1943, Stimson Papers, Reel 107, Sterling Library.

43 Heckscher, *When La Guardia Was Mayor*, 349–51; Stimson diary, Apr. 11–13, 1943; Stimson to FDR, Apr. 13, 1943, Stimson Papers, Reel 107, Sterling Library.

44 FHL to FDR, June 6, 1943, PPF 1376, FDRL; Ickes diary, Apr. 10, 1943, Aug. 11, 20, 1944; Stimson diary, Apr. 6, 1943.

45 Kessner, *Fiorello H. La Guardia*, 519; James Byrnes to Ernest McFarland, Oct. 29, 1943; McFarland to FHL, Oct. 30, 1943; in SF, "Senate Correspondence," NYMA; Stefano Luconi, "The Impact of World War II on the Political Behavior of the Italian-American Electorate in New York City," *New York History*, vol. 83, no. 4 (Fall 2002), 412–16. For servicemen attesting to La Guardia's popularity in Europe, see, e.g., Elsie Krakower to FHL, [n.d.]; Lorna Berkeley to FHL, Oct. 21, 1944; in SF, "Mayor's Office—FHL's Military Commission—WWII," NYMA. The same folder contains editorials supporting the appointment in the *St. Louis Star-Times*, Sept. 26, 1944, and the *Raleigh News and Observer*, ca. Nov. 15, 1944. See also Stimson's comment upon learning of the plan: "[H]e [Roosevelt] thinks he [La Guardia] will have a good effect on the Italians both in Italy and America"—Stimson diary, Sept. 8, 1944.

46 FDR to Stimson, Sept. 4, 1944; FDR to Hopkins, Sept. 29, 1944; [Grace Tully] to FDR, Oct. 11, 1944; FHL to FDR, Oct. 18, 1944; all in PSF 141, FDRL; Stimson diary, Sept. 27–Oct. 1, Oct. 9, 1944; *NYT*, Sept. 25, 1944; Drew Pearson, "The Washington Merry-Go-Round," *New York Daily Mirror*, Sept. 28, 1944; Hopkins to FDR, Sept. 30, 1944, Hopkins Papers, Box 161, FDRL; *CPPC*, Oct. 3, 1944; *NYT*, Oct. 18, 1944; Ickes diary, Oct. 6, 1944; Pearson, "The Washington Merry-Go-Round," *WP*, Nov. 27, 1944; Villard, "Mr. La Guardia and the Union," 463.

Chapter 10: "I Hope Others Will Follow New York's Example"

1 For a similar framing, see Gary Gerstle, "The Crucial Decade: The 1940s and Beyond," *JAH*, vol. 92, no. 4 (March 2006), 1292–1299.

2 Among many others: Eric Goldman, *The Crucial Decade: America, 1945–1955* (New York, 1956); Alan Brinkley, *The End of Reform: New Deal Liberalism in Recession and War* (New York, 1995); David Plotke, *Building a Democratic Political Order: Reshaping American Liberalism in the 1930s and 1940s* (New York, 1996), chaps. 7–8; Nelson Lichtenstein, "From Corporatism to Collective Bargaining: Organized Labor and the Eclipse of Social Democracy in the Postwar Era," in Steven Fraser and Gary Gerstle, eds., *The Rise and Fall of the New Deal Order,*

1930–1980 (Princeton, 1989), chap. 5; Ira Katznelson, "Was the Great Society a Lost Opportunity?" in ibid., esp. 187, 189–94; Ira Katznelson and Bruce Pietry-kowski, "Rebuilding the American State: Evidence from the 1940s," *SAPD*, vol. 5, no. 2 (Fall 1991), 301–39; Margaret Weir, *Politics and Jobs: The Boundaries of Employment Policy in the United States* (Princeton, 1992), 41–58; Meg Jacobs, *Pocketbook Politics: Economic Citizenship in Twentieth-Century America* (Princeton, 2005), chap. 6.

3   Kenneth T. Jackson, *Crabgrass Frontier: The Suburbanization of the United States* (New York, 1985), esp. chap. 11; Christopher Howard, *The Hidden Welfare State: Tax Expenditures and Social Policy in the United States* (Princeton, 1997), chaps. 5–6; Jennifer Klein, *For All These Rights: Business, Labor, and the Shaping of America's Private-Public Welfare State* (Princeton, 2003), chap. 6.

4   *NYT*, Dec. 20, 1940; FHL to Lee Thompson Smith, Aug. 20, 1943, SF, "Postwar Problems," NYMA.

5   See, among others, Brinkley, *The End of Reform*, 227–29; Lizabeth Cohen, *A Consumers' Republic: The Politics of Mass Consumption in Postwar America* (New York, 2003), 112–19.

6   FHL to Jerome Frank et al., June 15, 1942; Robert Moses to FHL, June 4, 1942; FHL to City Planning Commission, Sept. 15, 1942; all in SF, "Post-War Building Program," NYMA.

7   FHL to Claude Pepper, June 4, 1942, in SF, "Post-War Building Program," NYMA; Adolf Sturmthal, "A Survey of Literature on Postwar Reconstruction," New York University, Institute of Postwar Reconstruction; "Legislation for Reconversion and Full Employment," submitted to the Senate Committee on Military Affairs, cited in James E. Murray, "A Practical Approach," *APSR*, vol. 39, no. 6 (December 1945), 1122; *Milwaukee Journal*, Dec. 18, 1944; Steve Fraser, *Labor Will Rule: Sidney Hillman and the Rise of American Labor* (New York, 1991), 495–96.

8   La Guardia, "New York's Postwar Program" (May 1, 1944), SF, "Post-War Building," NYMA; Citizens Budget Commission, *Annual Report: 1946* (New York, 1946), 7–9; *NYT*, May 2, 1944; Jon C. Teaford, *The Rough Road to Renaissance: Urban Revitalization in America, 1940–1985* (Baltimore, 1990), 39–40. See, e.g., Jesse Lewis to FHL, Sept. 2, 1944; FHL to Lewis, Sept. 8, 1944, SF, "Post-War Building," NYMA.

9   Jason Scott Smith, *Building New Deal Liberalism: The Political Economy of Public Works, 1933–1956* (New York, 2006), 234–37; "What This City Expects from Washington for 1945," *New York Sun*, Nov. 27, 1944.

10   Thomas Kessner, *Fiorello H. La Guardia and the Making of Modern New York* (New York, 1989), 560–61; Rexford G. Tugwell, *The Art of Politics as Practiced by Three Great Americans: Franklin Delano Roosevelt, Luis Muñoz Marín, and Fiorello H. La Guardia* (Garden City, NY, 1958), 29–30. See also Ester R. Fuchs, *Mayors and Money: Fiscal Policy in New York and Chicago* (Chicago, 1992), which makes a

related but more sophisticated argument. The New Deal, as we have seen, contributed to the structural expansion of municipal expenditures—through the growth of the parks and recreation system, the municipal hospital system, et cetera. The expansion of the public sphere during the 1930s was also a significant (but secondary) contributing factor in the attenuation of the tax base: the increase in tax-exempt property in New York between FY 1935 and FY 1946–47 accounted for 13.1 percent of the decrease in the assessed value of taxable property during that period.

11 T. Semmes Walmsley, "Presidential Address," in Paul V. Betters, ed., *City Problems of 1934: The Annual Proceedings of the United States Conference of Mayors* (Washington, DC, 1934), 3.

12 The fact that New York's budget shrank substantially in real terms during La Guardia's mayoralty has escaped some historians. Fred Siegel, for instance, notes that city expenditures grew in absolute terms by more than 40 percent during La Guardia's mayoralty; he does not note that, during the same period, inflation decreased the value of the dollar by more than 55 percent—an omission best described as sleight of hand—Fred Siegel, *The Future Once Happened Here: New York, D.C., L.A., and the Fate of America's Big Cities* (New York, 1997), 27.

13 Kessner, *Fiorello H. La Guardia*, 556; August Heckscher with Phyllis Robinson, *When La Guardia Was Mayor: New York's Legendary Years* (New York, 1978), 295, 343–45, 377–79; *NYT*, July 3–4, 1944, Feb. 12, 1945; *Hearings Before the Special Committee on Postwar Economic Policy and Planning . . . Pursuant to H. Res. 408 and H. Res. 60 . . . Part 6 . . .*, House, 79th Cong., 1st Sess., 1718. For a general overview of subway policy during and shortly after La Guardia's mayoralty, see Clifton Hood, *722 Miles: The Building of the Subways and How They Transformed New York* (New York, 1993), 224–48. For the liberal-left position, see, e.g., "Our Town's Living Room," *NYP*, July 5, 1944.

14 "Text of Mayor La Guardia's Address on the Change in Tax Methods," *NYT*, Jan. 11, 1940; *NYT*, Nov. 29, 1942; W. Brooke Graves, *American Intergovernmental Relations: Their Origins, Historical Development, and Current Status* (New York, 1964), 451–52, 458–59.

15 *NYP*, Aug. 7, 1942; City Planning Commission, "Proposed Post-War Works Program" (1942) and "Report of Scheduling on Postwar Improvements" (Sept. 14, 1943), in SF, "Post-War Building Program," NYMA.

16 FHL to Jerome Frank et al., June 15, 1942; FHL to Cornelius Scully, May 6, 1942; FHL to Maurice Tobin et al., May 12, 1942; FHL to Sam Rayburn et al., May 12, 1942; FHL to Claude Pepper, June 4, 1942; FHL to Harry Hopkins, Dec. 1, 1942; R. A. Hafner to FHL, Sept. 12, 1945; FDR to FHL, Mar. 1, 1943; FHL to New York Congressional delegation et al., Dec. 9, 1944; FHL, "New York City's Postwar Program," in City Planning Commission, *Proposed Post-War Works Program* (May 1944); all in SF, "Post-War Building," NYMA; Harry R. Betters, ed.,

City Problems of 1943–1944: The Annual Proceedings of the United States Conference of Mayors (Washington, DC, 1944), 31; Stephen Early to FHL, Mar. 5, 1943, PPF 1376, FDRL; *SB*, Mar. 7, 1943.

17   *Hearings Before a Subcommittee of the Committee on Education and Labor . . . on S. 1617 . . .* , Senate, 77th Cong., 1st Sess., 143; *Hearings Before the Special Committee on Postwar Economic Policy and Planning . . . Pursuant to H. Res. 408 and H. Res. 60 . . . Part 6 . . .* , House, 79th Cong., 1st Sess., 1710–1711, 1718, 1722.

18   Philip D. Funigiello, *The Challenge to Urban Liberalism: Federal-City Relations During World War II* (Knoxville, TN, 1978), 235–36, 243–45.

19   Jaap Kooijman, "Soon or Later On: Franklin D. Roosevelt and National Health Insurance, 1931–1945," *Presidential Studies Quarterly*, vol. 29, no. 2 (Spring 1999), 336–50; Daniel Hirschfield, *The Lost Reform: The Campaign for Compulsory Health Insurance in the United States from 1932–1943* (Cambridge, MA, 1970), 42–165; *PPA: Vol. 13, 1944–1945*, 41; Monte M. Poen, *Harry S Truman Versus the Medical Lobby* (Columbia, SC, 1979), 32–49; J. Joseph Huthmacher, *Senator Robert F. Wagner and the Rise of Urban Liberalism* (New York, 1968), 293; Paul Starr, *The Social Transformation of American Medicine* (New York, 1982), 266–80; Christine L. Compston, *Earl Warren: Justice for All* (New York, 2001), 53–54.

20   La Guardia, "Perspective in Postwar Planning," 10; *NYT*, Apr. 5, 1943, Feb. 20, Oct. 19, 1945; "Medical Care Plan of the City of New York as Proposed By F. H. La Guardia, Mayor" [*SB*, Apr. 30, 1944]; FHL to Eric Johnston, Sept. 23, 1943, in SF, "Health Insurance Plan," NYMA.

21   Charles Garrett, *The La Guardia Years: Machine and Reform Politics in New York City* (New Brunswick, NJ, 1961), 191; Freeman, *Working-Class New York*, 127; "Appendix B: Report of the Conference Committee," undated, SF, "Health Insurance Plan," NYMA; *NYT*, Oct. 6, 1944.

22   FHL to the Editors, *Fortune* (January 1945), 10, 18 (emphasis in the original).

23   "La Guardia versus Organized Medicine," *Medical Economics* (June 1944), 50–51; Starr, *The Social Transformation of American Medicine*, 299; "Meeting in Mayor's Office, April 24, 1944"; David Dubinsky to FHL, May 8, 1944; Michael Neylan to FHL, May 5, 1944; FHL to Arthur Hays Sulzberger, May 2, 1944; John J. Lamula to FHL, May 29, 1944, all in SF, "Health Insurance Plan," NYMA; *NYT*, Sept. 4, 1944. Lamula, a state assemblyman from Brooklyn's 1st AD, made a survey of his district and found that only two out of five hundred people asked about the plan disapproved of it.

24   "Medical Care Plan of the City of New York"; *NYT*, Oct. 6, 1944; FHL to the Editors, *Fortune* (January 1945), 10, 18. On compensatory federalism, see Martha Derthick's essay in Barry G. Rabe, ed., *Greenhouse Governance: Addressing Climate Change in America* (Washington, DC, 2010), chap. 3.

25   "La Guardia versus Organized Medicine," 48; McNutt to FHL, Apr. 20, 1944;

Celler to FHL, May 6, 1944; James V. King to FHL, May 18, 1944; Martin Cody to FHL, May 8, 1944; Samuel Neuberger to FHL, June 22, 1944; all in SF, "Health Insurance Plan," NYMA; Klein, *For All These Rights*, 160. See also *Health Council Digest*, vol. 1, no. 4 (Fall 1944); Hyman Blumberg to FHL, May 3, 1944, and Joseph Curran and Saul Mills to FHL, May 3, 1944, in SF, "Health Insurance Plan," NYMA; and "Our Town," *NYP*, Sept. 12, 1944.

26   Klein, *For All These Rights*, 118; Freeman, *Working-Class New York*. The trajectory of American health care financing posited in this paragraph draws heavily on Klein's book and also on Starr, *The Social Transformation of American Medicine*, bk 2, chap. 2, esp. pp. 331–34.

27   James MacGregor Burns, *Roosevelt: The Soldier of Freedom* (New York, 1970), 501–03; Richard Norton Smith, *Thomas E. Dewey and His Times* (New York, 1982), 383–405.

28   Fraser, *Labor Will Rule*, 511–17; *NYT*, Oct. 9, 1944; James Harten to Herman Shumlin, Aug. 18, 1944; FHL to Jo Davidson, Oct. 5, 1944; George Pellettieri to FHL, Sept. 26, 1944; "telephone message from Mr. Christenberry," Sept. 30, 1944; Mary McLeod Bethune to FHL, Oct. 3, 1944; James Harten to Bethune, Oct. 9, 1944; all in SF, "Campaign, Presidential (1944), NYMA. Correspondence regarding Roosevelt's weakness among Italian American and black voters may be found in the same file.

29   *NYT*, Oct. 15, 23, 28, 31, Nov. 3, 1944; Charles Olson to FHL, Nov. 13, 1944; Olson to FHL, "Proposed Itinerary for Mayor La Guardia," Oct. 25, 1944; Joe Kelly to FHL (copy to White House), Nov. 6, 1944; Walter J. Bayer to Olson, Nov. 1, 1944; transcript, La Guardia address to the *Herald Tribune* Forum, Oct. 18, 1944; all in SF, "Campaign, Presidential (1944)," NYMA; Henry A. Wallace diary, Dec. 14, 1945; June 11, 1946, in Reminiscences of Henry A. Wallace, CCOHC, 4351, 4769.

30   Hugh Gregory Gallagher, *FDR's Splendid Deception* (New York, 1985), chap. 17, (quote at 195); Samuel I. Rosenman, *Working with Roosevelt* (New York, 1952), 471–78, 482–83; *NYT*, Oct. 19, 22, 1944; "Route of President Roosevelt—October 21, 1944," in SF, "Campaign, Presidential (1944)," NYMA. See also correspon-dence in OF 200-3-Z, FDRL. Robert H. Ferrell, *The Dying President: Franklin D. Roosevelt, 1944–1945* (Columbia, MO, 1998), provides a comprehensive assess-ment of Roosevelt's health in the final year of his life.

31   Warren Moscow, *Politics in the Empire State* (New York, 1948), 18; *NYT*, Oct. 22, 1944; FDR to FHL, Oct. 24, 1944, PPF 1376, FDRL; William D. Hassett, *Off the Record with F.D.R., 1942–1945* (New Brunswick, NJ, 1958), 282.

32   Heckscher, *When La Guardia Was Mayor*, 388–89; NYT, Jan. 15, 1945.

33   *NYT*, Mar. 15, 22, Apr. 14, 22, 1945.

34   Fraser, *Labor Will Rule*, 500–06; Garrett, *The La Guardia Years*, 293–94; *NYT*, Aug. 30, 1943, Jan. 8, 11, 13, 21, Feb. 18, 1944.

35 *NYT*, Mar. 2, 4, 10, 14, 23–24, 28–31, 1944; Garrett, *The La Guardia Years*, 293–94; William Spinrad, "New Yorkers Cast Their Ballots," PhD diss., Columbia University, 1955, 109–10, 112–19; Spinrad, "New York's Third Party Voters," *Public Opinion Quarterly*, vol. 21, no. 4 (Winter 1957–58), 549–51; Martin Shefter, "Political Incorporation and Political Extrusion: Party Politics and Social Forces in Postwar New York," in Shefter, *Political Parties and the State: The American Historical Experience* (Princeton, 1994), 210–19. See also Hugh A. Bone, "Political Parties in New York City," *APSR*, vol. 40, no. 2 (April 1946), 272–82, and Robert Bower, "How New York City Labor Votes," *Public Opinion Quarterly*, vol. 11, no. 4 (Winter 1947–48), 614–15.

36 *NYP*, Apr. 13, 1945; *NYT*, Apr. 13, May 7, 1945; *SB*, Apr. 15, 1945; Harold Ickes diary, Feb. 26, 1944, Ickes Papers, LC; Reminiscences of Reuben Lazarus, CCOHC, 207; Chris McNickle, *To Be Mayor of New York: Ethnic Politics in the City* (New York, 1993), 54; Newbold Morris, *Let the Chips Fall: My Battles Against Corruption* (New York, 1955), 204; *NYHT*, May 7, 1945.

37 Robert G. Spivack, "New York's Mayoralty Race," *TNR*, July 9, 1945, 42; William O'Dwyer, *Beyond the Golden Door* (Jamaica, 1986), 210–18; Garrett, *The La Guardia Years*, 296–97; Morris, *Let the Chips Fall*, 209–10; Heckscher, *When La Guardia Was Mayor*, 400; *NYT*, June 2, 13, 27, Sept. 14, 28, 30, Oct. 11, Nov. 3, 1945; *PM*, Oct. 16, Nov. 4, 1945; McNickle, *To Be Mayor of New York*, 58–59; Bone, "Political Parties in New York City," 276–77, 281; David Dubinsky to Eleanor Roosevelt, Aug. 24, 1945, in Allida Black, ed., *The Eleanor Roosevelt Papers: The Human Rights Years, 1945–1948* (Detroit, 2007), 77–79.

38 *NYHT*, Nov. 7, 1945; Morris, *Let the Chips Fall*, 207; *NYT*, Sept. 28, Oct. 17, 1945; Garrett, *The La Guardia Years*, 295–96; Kessner, *Fiorello H. La Guardia*, 571; Moscow, *Politics in the Empire State*, 28. Spinrad, "New Yorkers Cast Their Ballots," though its methodology is both flawed and unsophisticated, remains the best analysis of the 1945 returns.

39 Martin Shefter, *Political Crisis/Fiscal Crisis: The Collapse and Revival of New York City* (New York, 1985), 29–36. On the marginalization of the left, see Martin Shefter, "Political Incorporation and Political Extrusion," 204–22, and Martha Biondi, *To Stand and Fight: The Struggle for Civil Rights in Postwar New York City* (Cambridge, MA, 2003), 47–54. McNickle, *To Be Mayor of New York*, and Joshua Zeitz, *White Ethnic New York: Jews, Catholics, and the Shaping of Postwar Politics* (Chapel Hill, NC, 2007), treat ethnic alignments. On the Reform Democrat movement, the classic work remains James Q. Wilson, *The Amateur Democrat: Club Politics in Three Cities* (Chicago, 1962). On the rising political power of professionally trained bureaucrats, see Theodore J. Lowi, "Machine Politics: Old and New," *Public Interest*, vol. 9 (1967), 86–90.

40 Staff of the *NYHT*, *New York City in Crisis* (New York, 1965), 78. For mid-thirties figures, see Table 5.3 in chapter 5.

41   John Kenneth Galbraith, *The Affluent Society* (Boston, 1958), chap. 17; Leonard Covello, *The Heart Is the Teacher* (New York, 1958), 275.

42   Shefter, *Political Crisis/Fiscal Crisis*, 29–36; McNickle, *To Be Mayor of New York*, 76; *NYT*, July 10, 18, Sept. 12, 1953; Bernard R. Gifford, "New York and Cosmopolitan Liberalism," *Political Science Quarterly*, vol. 93, no. 4 (Winter, 1978–79), 561. See esp. Freeman, *Working-Class New York*, chaps. 4, 7–8.

43   Stephen Berger, "Breaking the Governmental Habit: Proposals for the Mayor," *City Journal* (Winter 1993), 21. On the Fiscal Crisis and New York's political culture, see esp. Freeman, *Working-Class New York*, chap. 15; Roy Rosenzweig and Elizabeth Blackmar, *The Park and the People: A History of Central Park* (Ithaca, NY, 1992), 499–510; and, in another vein, Alice O'Connor, "The Privatized City: The Manhattan Institute, the Urban Crisis, and the Conservative Counterrevolution in New York," *Journal of Urban History*, vol. 34, no. 2 (January 2008), 333–53.

44   *NYT*, Dec. 13, 1945; Paul V. Betters, ed., *City Problems of 1945–1946: The Annual Proceedings of the United States Conference of Mayors* (Washington, DC, 1945), 159–63.

Epilogue

1   *Hearings Before the Committee on Labor and Public Welfare . . . on S. 55 and S.J. Res. 22 . . . Part 4 . . .* , Senate, 80th Cong., 1st Sess., 2021; Bella Rodman, *Fiorello La Guardia* (New York, 1962), 230; Thomas Kessner, *Fiorello H. La Guardia and the Making of Modern New York* (New York, 1989), 577.

2   See FHL's *PM* columns, Feb. 24, Mar. 17, Apr. 21, 28, June 16, 30, July 7, 14, Dec. 15, 22, 1946, Apr. 17, 27, June 1, 22, 1947; also Robert A. Caro, *The Power Broker: Robert Moses and the Fall of New York* (New York, 1974), 702; *Hearings Before the Committee on Banking and Currency . . . on H.R. 2549 . . .* , House, 80th Cong., 1st Sess., 365–83; *Hearings Before the Committee on Banking and Currency . . . on . . . Bills Pertaining to National Housing*, Senate, 80th Cong., 1st Sess., 140–59; *Hearings Before the Committee on Education and Labor . . . on S. 1606 . . .* , Senate, 79th Cong., 2nd Sess., 285–308; *Hearings Before a Subcommittee of the Committee on Foreign Relations . . . on S. 1875 . . .* , Senate, 80th Cong., 1st Sess., 47–51; *Hearings Before the Committee on Labor and Public Welfare . . . on S. 55 and S.J. Res. 22*, Senate, 80th Cong., 1st Sess., 2037–2039; George Kaplan, "The Labor Views of Fiorello H. La Guardia," PhD diss., New York University, 1962, 168–70, 190–91, 244–48.

3   *Hearings Before a Subcommittee of the Committee on Foreign Relations . . . on S. 1875 . . .* , Senate, 79th Cong., 2nd Sess., 51.

4   Truman and La Guardia's personal relationship ran hot and cold. The Missourian slighted La Guardia on one occasion by denying him the status of official representative when French authorities invited him to a 1945 Bastille Day cel-

ebration, but also did him the unprecedented honor of paying call to City Hall during a visit to the city. Truman wrote La Guardia of that visit, "I don't know when I have had a happier day or when I enjoyed a ride any more than the one I took with you around New York City. It makes the responsibility all the more binding and the inspiration all the stronger to do a good job"—Kessner, *Fiorello H. La Guardia*, 574; *NYT*, Oct. 28, 1945; Truman to FHL, Nov. 1, 1945, SF, "Post-War Building," NYMA.

5   Alonzo Hamby, *Beyond the New Deal: Harry S. Truman and American Liberalism* (New York, 1973), 53–85; Norman D. Markowitz, *The Rise and Fall of the People's Century: Henry A. Wallace and American Liberalism, 1941–1948* (New York, 1973), 136–54; FHL, "2 Headaches for Every Aspirin," *PM*, Nov. 10, 1946; FHL, "La Guardia's Program for Progressives," *PM*, Nov. 17, 1946; FHL, "How We Can Beat Inflation," *PM*, Apr. 27, 1947.

6   Reminiscences of Marie La Guardia, CCOHC, 50; Editorial, *Life*, Dec. 30, 1946, 18; Rodman, *Fiorello La Guardia*, 232–33; William Manners, *Patience and Fortitude: Fiorello La Guardia, a Biography* (New York, 1976), 269; Kessner, *Fiorello H. La Guardia*, 579–81, 583–84; Allan Nevins, *Herbert H. Lehman and His Era* (New York, 1963), 221–99; *NYT*, July 12, 15, 1946.

7   Kessner, *Fiorello H. La Guardia*, 585; Robert L. Beisner, *Dean Acheson: A Life in the Cold War* (New York, 2006), 46; *Hearings Before the Committee on Foreign Relations . . . on S. 938 . . .* , Senate, 80th Cong., 1st Sess., 120–43; FHL, "Let UN Handle Greek Crisis," *PM*, Mar. 16, 1947; FHL, "Don't Finance Foreign Armies," *PM*, Apr. 6, 1947; FHL, "Why Truman Plan Can't Work," *PM*, Apr. 20, 1947.

8   Eric Goldman, *The Crucial Decade—and After: America, 1945–1960* (New York, 1960), 39; Kessner, *Fiorello H. La Guardia*, 585; Reminiscences of Henry A. Wallace, CCOHC, 4989, 5185; Joseph and Stuart Alsop, "Matter of Fact: Wallace a Dewey Boon and Bane," *WP*, June 22, 1947; *NYT*, July 9, 1947; Wallace, "Fiorello," *TNR*, Sept. 29, 1947, 12. John C. Culver and John Hyde, *American Dreamer: A Life and Times of Henry A. Wallace* (New York, 2000), is the definitive biography of Wallace; on Wallace's foreign policy views, see Samuel Walker, *Henry A. Wallace and American Foreign Policy* (Westport, CT, 1976), and Hamby, "Henry A. Wallace, The Liberals, and Soviet American Relations," *Review of Politics*, vol. 30, no. 2 (April 1968), 157–65.

9   *NYT*, Dec. 29, 1946, Jan. 5, 1947; Hamby, *Beyond the New Deal*, 147–68.

10   FHL, "The REAL 3d Party Roots," *PM*, July 15, 1947. For the CP's activities after the war, see Joseph R. Starobin, *American Communism in Crisis, 1943–1957* (Cambridge, MA, 1972).

11   FHL to Eleanor Roosevelt, Apr. 2, 1947, in Allida Black, ed., *The Eleanor Roosevelt Papers: The Human Rights Years, 1945–1948* (Detroit, 2007), 522–23.

12   La Guardia: "Liberals Must Unite NOW," *PM*, May 18, 1947; FHL, "Crisis for Labor—and Liberals," *PM*, May 25, 1947; FHL, "We Can Still Save U.S. Labor,"

PM, June 15, 1947; FHL, "Blueprint for Total Labor Unity," *PM*, June 29, 1947; FHL, "The REAL 3d Party Roots," *PM*, July 15, 1947.

13 Reminiscences of George Baehr, CCOHC, 134–35; Robert Moses, *Public Works: A Dangerous Trade* (New York, 1970), 853; Newbold Morris, *Let the Chips Fall: My Battles Against Corruption* (New York, 1955), 213; I. F. Stone, "Tribute to a Great American," *PM*, Sept. 22, 1947; Rodman, *Fiorello La Guardia*, 236; Wallace, "Fiorello," 12.

14 Kessner, *Fiorello H. La Guardia*, 594; *PM*, Sept. 22, 1947; *NYT*, Sept. 21, 1947.

PHOTO CREDITS

1. "Franklin D. Roosevelt, James Roosevelt, and Sara Delano Roosevelt in Hyde Park, New York," 1891. Courtesy of the Franklin D. Roosevelt Presidential Library and Museum, Hyde Park, New York.

2. California Panorama Co., "Panorama of Prescott, Arizona," ca. 1909. Courtesy of the Library of Congress Prints and Photographs Division. PAN US GEOG— Arizona no. 31 (http://www.loc.gov/pictures/resource/pan.6a17228/).

3. "La Guardia in his cap and gown upon graduating from New York University Law School in June 1910." Courtesy of the La Guardia and Wagner Archives, La Guardia Community College, The City University of New York.

4. "Franklin D. Roosevelt, formal photo in Cambridge, Massachusetts," 1904. Courtesy of the Franklin D. Roosevelt Presidential Library and Museum, Hyde Park, New York.

5. La Guardia and Gianni Caproni, 1918. Courtesy of the La Guardia and Wagner Archives.

6. "Franklin D. Roosevelt and Al Smith in Albany, New York," 1930. Courtesy of the Franklin D. Roosevelt Presidential Library and Museum, Hyde Park, New York.

7. Robert Moses, Grover Whalen, and La Guardia, June 29, 1936. La Guardia and Wagner Archives. Reprinted with permission.

8. Franklin Roosevelt, La Guardia, Eleanor Roosevelt, and Edward Flynn, April 30, 1939. La Guardia and Wagner Archives. Reprinted with permission.

9. United States Public Works Administration, "Triborough Bridge, New York," 1939. Courtesy of the Library of Congress Prints and Photographs Division. NA712 .A5 1939.

10. La Guardia Airport Airday Military Celebration, 1939. The Port Authority of New York and New Jersey. Reprinted with permission.

11. Brooklyn College ca. 1940. Museum of the City of New York/Art Resource, NY. Reprinted with permission.

12. La Guardia, John L. Rice, and Brehon H. Somervell at dedication of baby health station, Queens, Dec. 8, 1938. La Guardia and Wagner Archives. Reprinted with permission.

13. "The nursery, or pre-school, at Harlem River Houses in a room that has what is probably a WPA mural, May 19, 1938." Reprinted with permission of the New York City Housing Authority. Image courtesy of the La Guardia and Wagner Archives.

14. "A couple poses in their living room at Harlem River Houses, March 7, 1939." Reprinted with permission of the New York City Housing Authority. Image courtesy of the La Guardia and Wagner Archives.

15. Manhattan: 40th Street [6th Avenue], 1935. Milstein Division of United States History, Local History & Genealogy, The New York Public Library, Astor, Lenox and Tilden Foundations. Reprinted with permission.

16. Astoria Park Pool. New York City Municipal Archives, Municipal Archives Collection. Reprinted with permission.

17. Still from 1938 film biography, *The March of Time—Fiorello La Guardia*. La Guardia and Wagner Archives. Reprinted with permission.

18. Rube Goldberg, "Fables of Franklin D.," *New York Sun*, Sept. 21, 1940, © Rube Goldberg, Inc. Reprinted with permission.

19. La Guardia, Edward J. Kelly, and Garnet Coulter stand in silent tribute, Dec. 12, 1945. Orig. © Acme News Pictures, Inc.; now public domain. Image courtesy of the La Guardia and Wagner Archives.

INDEX

Abrams, Charles, 351
accounting, 31
Acheson, Dean, 399
Actors Equity Association, 149
adult education, 17
advertising agencies, 149
Affiliated Young Democrats, 313–14
African Americans, 51, 75, 118, 209,
    232, 233–34, 239–43, 244, 245–46,
    309–10, 352
Agricultural Adjustment Act, 119, 144
Agricultural Adjustment Administration
    (AAA), 156–57, 173
agricultural legislation, 9
Agriculture Advisory Commission, 74
Agriculture Department, U.S., 282, 285,
    341, 343, 349
airports, xi, 154, 176, 197-98
air transport, 182, 207
Aldrich, Winthrop, 141
Allen, Robert, 283, 284, 307
Allied Progressives, 102, 105
Alsop, Joseph, 7, 275–76
Amalgamated Clothing Workers of Amer-
    ica (ACWA), 23, 215, 285, 295–96,
    298, 334
American Airlines, 309
American Construction Council, 64
American Federation of Labor (AFL), 121,
    230, 340
American Jewish Congress, 277, 278,
    313

American Journal of Public Health, 380
American Labor Party (ALP), 220, 222,
    223, 228, 229, 237, 245, 248, 296, 313,
    316, 351, 386–87, 388, 390, 401
American Legion, 267
American Liberty League, 217, 221
American Machine & Foundry, 309
Americans for Democratic Action (ADA),
    401, 402, 404
Amlie, Tom, 213
Amsterdam News, 242
Anderson, Paul Y., 275
anti-poll tax law, 396
antitrust laws, 121, 144
art, artists, 98, 201–4, 375
Association for Improving the Condition
    of the Poor (AICP), 97, 150–51
Atlantic, 250
Attlee, Clement, 405
Austria, 398
automobile industry, 249
automotive infrastructure, 77, 153, 176,
    182–85, 375

back-to-the-land movement, 106–8
Baehr, George, 404–5
Baker, Sara Josephine, 84
bakeries, 34
Baltimore, Md., 328
Bankers' Agreement, 117, 136, 139, 147,
    157, 170
Bankers' Trust, 97

banks, 102, 119
   runs on, 90
Bar Association, 112, 122
Barton, Bruce, 294
Baruch, Bernard, 281–82, 292, 308, 338
Battle of Britain, 304
Beard, Charles, 275
beef, 348–49
Beer, Samuel H., xii, 160
Bell, Daniel, 76
Bellanca, August, 23
Bellanca, Giuseppe, 23
Bell Labs, 309
Belt Parkway, ix, 183, 261
Benson, Elmer, 275
Berle, Adolf A., Jr., vii, 111, 119, 124, 130,
   142, 177, 186, 220, 250, 260, 269,
   282, 284, 313, 314
Berman, Marshall, 197
Berry, George L., 219
Bethlehem Steel, 309
Bethune, Mary McLeod, 382
Betters, Paul, 253, 254
Bingham, Alfred, 216
Birth of a Nation, The, 239–40
Black, Hugo, 301
Blackmar, Elizabeth, 176, 197
black markets, 336
Blanshard, Paul, 129–30
Bloom, Nicholas Dagen, 188
"Blue Eagle" propaganda, 147–48
Blue Network (NBC radio), 267
Bluestone, Daniel, 195–96
Board of Aldermen, NYC, 27, 37, 48, 116,
   128, 223, 226, 237
Board of Child Welfare, NYC, 150
Board of Education, NYC, 96, 193
Board of Estimate, NYC, 37–38, 43, 116,
   128, 140, 157, 180, 198, 205, 224, 247,
   266, 325
Board of Higher Education, NYC, 369
Board of Transportation, NYC, 155
Bolin, Jane, 233
Bolshevism, 401
Bonus Army, 105
"boss control," 11
Boston, Mass., 77, 84, 328
Bowers, Claude, 67
Brewster Aeronautical, 309
Bricker, John W., 381
bridges, xi, 84, 176, 177, 181, 185, 209, 321
Brinkley, Alan, 214
British Civil Service, 196

Bronx County, N.Y., 10, 77, 127, 147, 180,
   226, 248
Bronx Terminal Market, 38, 39, 84–85
Bronx Zoo, 150
Brookhart, Smith W., 57, 59
Brooklyn, N.Y., 77, 127, 128, 180, 226, 315
Brooklyn-Battery Tunnel, 373
Brooklyn College, 176, 185, 200, 373
Brooklyn Navy Yard, 14, 333, 352
Brooklyn Times Union, 211
Brotherhood of Sleeping Car Porters, 310
Broun, Heywood, 268
Brown, Prentiss, 348
Brownsville, 195, 231, 236, 389
Bryan, Charles W., 66
Bryan, William Jennings, 65, 111
Bryant Park, 155
budget balancing, 101, 102–3, 256
budget deficits, federal, 102, 104, 105, 143,
   255, 260
budget deficits, NYC, 139–41, 182, 372
budget making, 31
Buffalo, N.Y., 328
building and loan associations, 102
building trades, 178
Bulkley, Robert, 275
Bull Moose campaign, 25
Bureau of Labor Statistics, U.S., 242, 352
Bureau of Municipal Research (BMR),
   30–32, 154
Bureau of Public Roads, U.S., 262–63
Bureau of the Budget, U.S., 307
Bureau of Weights and Measures, NYC,
   344
Burke, Robert, 299
Burlingham, C. C., 357
Bushwick, 49
Butler, Nicholas Murray, 86
Byrnes, James, 256, 257–59, 360, 398

Cahan, Abraham, 237–39
Calitri, Antonio, 23
Campobello Island, 15
Canada, 282, 290–91, 293–94, 302
Canadians, 77
Canudo, Raimondo, 22, 23
capital, ratio of labor to, 168–69, 190
"Capital Parade," 275–76
capital reinvestment, 58, 369
Carnegie Hall, 203
Carter, Ledyard & Milburn, 7–8, 9
cash relief, 157
Castle Garden, 18

Catholics, 65
Causey, James, 295
Celler, Emanuel, 380
Center Theater, 202
centralized purchasing, 31
Central Park, 96, 177, 195, 197, 439
Central Park Zoo, 155
Chanler, William, 355
charity, 84, 97–98, 109
Charity Organization Society, 97
charter reform, 181
Chicago, Ill., 76, 84, 206, 221
Chicago Tribune, 224
child health clinics, 36, 199, 200
child labor, 34, 59, 65, 101, 121, 145, 229
Children's Aid Society, 97
child welfare, 371
Christadora settlement house, 150
Christian Front, 317
churches, 185, 244
Churchill, Winston, 290, 321, 355, 360
cities, 8, 55, 56
Citizens Budget Commission, 266, 368
Citizens Union, 39–40
City Center of Music and Drama, 202,
    203, 440
City College, 98, 200
City Council, 223, 248
City Defense Council, 303
City Fusion Party, 123–24
City Hall, New York, 96
City Industrial Relations Board, 229
city machines, 10–11, 191
    see also Tammany Hall
City Planning Commission, 222–23, 282,
    373
civic organizations, 178
Civil Defense Volunteer Organization, 343
Civilian Conservation Corps (CCC), 143,
    145, 148
civil rights, 297, 308–13
civil rights organizations, 244, 309
Civil Service, 22, 138, 139, 157, 193, 233,
    265, 316–17
Civil Works Administration (CWA), 152–
    59, 161, 166, 168, 170, 171, 172, 195,
    199, 253, 263
Clapper, Raymond, 273
Clark, Champ, 13
clergy, 122
Cleveland, Grover, 9
Cleveland, Ohio, 76, 328, 446
clothing, 34, 61, 328

Cohen, Lizabeth, 345
Cold War, 395
collective bargaining, 111, 215, 229
Collier's, 250
Colonial Park, 243
Commerce Department, U.S., 331–32, 335
Commission on Industrial Employment
    Stabilization, 105
Commission on Rural Homes, 107
Committee on Economic Security, 376
Committee on Industrial Organization,
    215–16
Commodity Credit Corporation, 148
Commonweal, 277
Communism, 316, 401–3
Communist Party, U.S., 161, 215, 223, 245,
    317, 390
compensatory federalism, 379
concentration camps, 292, 293
concerts, 34, 47, 201–3, 204
Coney Island, 196, 389
Conference of Progressive Political Action
    (CPPA), 60, 61
Congressional Record, 25
Congress of Industrial Organizations
    (CIO), 215–16, 228, 230, 264, 317,
    340, 343, 351, 366, 386, 388, 401
Conservative Party, British, 227
Conservatory Garden, 195
Consolidated Tenants League, 351
construction, 92, 158, 375
construction firms, 178
consumer groups, 244
Consumers' League, 8
Consumers Service Division, Department
    of Markets, 156–57
consuming classes, 144
Coolidge, Calvin, 58, 58, 59, 60
cooperative federalism, xiii–xv, 326
Copeland, Royal S., 226, 227–28, 229, 271,
    272, 444
Corsi, Edward, 50, 273
Costigan, Edward, 101, 110, 145
Coughlin, Charles E., 217, 218
Coulter, Garnet, 394
council of five, 225
Council of Parks, NYC, 154
county offices, 181
courthouses, 131
Covello, Leonard, 391
Cox, James M., 14
Coy, Wayne, 322
Crown Heights Consumer Council, 343

Cummings, Homer, 250
Curran, Henry, 42, 43, 203
Curran, Thomas J., 385
Currie, Lauchlin, 259
Curry, John F., 125, 225
Cutting, Bronson, 158, 212
Czechoslovakia, 398

Dailey, Vincent, 127
Daily Crimson, 6
dams, 166
Davies, John R., 315
Davis, John W., 66
Dayton, Kenneth, 355
decommodification, 33
defense industry, 264
defense spending, 327
deficits, federal, 102, 104, 105, 143, 255, 260
deflationary cycle, 143
deforestation, 44
Delaney, Hubert T., 233–34
Democratic National Committee, 126, 294, 295
Democratic National Conventions:
　of 1912, 266
　of 1920, 14
　of 1924, 65, 70
　of 1928, 70
　of 1932, 132, 226
　of 1936, 216
　of 1940, 266, 285, 294
Democratic Party, U.S., xi
　ethnic voters in, 75
　in New York, 68–70, 180–81
　in 1920s, 65–70
　1930s congressional majority of, 120
　as revived by Depression, 91
　and threat of third party, 268–71
　in upstate New York, 11, 12, 15
dental clinics, 34
Department of Housing and Buildings, NYC, 353
Department of Investigations, NYC, 296
Department of Markets, NYC, 47, 204, 343, 346
　Consumer Service Division of, 156–57
Department of Public Markets, Weights and Measures, NYC, 84–85
deposit insurance, 54
"Depression geniuses," 138
Dern, George, 198
Detroit, Mich., 76, 131–32, 183, 329
de Valera, Eamon, 405

Dewey, John, 214
Dewey, Thomas, 272–74, 276, 283, 284, 313, 331, 335, 360, 381–82, 385, 405
direct relief, 96
district clubs, 82
Division of Child Hygiene, NYC, 31, 84
docks, 321
dollar, devaluation of, 173
Domestic Relations Court, 264
Dooling, James J., 225, 226, 444
Doughton, Robert, 103
Douglas, Paul, 108, 214
Downes, Olin, 203
Dubinsky, David, 203, 219–20, 222, 224, 228, 340, 387, 405
Dulles, Allen, 272
Dunnigan, John J., 141

Early, Stephen, 310, 356
East Harlem, 17, 49, 50–51, 53, 61, 118, 289, 319, 321, 389
Eccles, Marriner, 259
Economy Act (1933), 119, 139, 145
Economy Bill, NY State, 139–42
education, xii, 153, 185, 200–201, 309, 366
　see also schools
efficiency movement, xi, 30–37, 38, 40, 123, 137
eggs, 348
Egypt, 398
Eighth Avenue Independent subway line, 182
Eisenhower, Dwight D., 357, 358
elections, New York, 232, 232
　of 1905, 319
　of 1921, 40–42
　of 1926, 70
　of 1928, 71–72
　of 1929, 80, 81, 82, 85–87, 88–89, 90, 113–14, 123, 248
　of 1930, 74, 108
　of 1933, 123–30, 232–33, 235–36, 424
　of 1937, 214, 225–26, 231–33, 247–49, 267, 272–73, 319
　of 1938, 272–75, 315
　of 1941, 210–11, 238–39, 313, 314–20, 354
　of 1942, 315
　of 1945, 385–90
　of 1949, 392–93
elections, U.S.:
　of 1914, 25–26
　of 1916, 26–27
　of 1920, 14, 67

of 1922, 49–50, 52–54
of 1924, 67, 70
of 1928, 70–71, 72, 74, 118, 320
of 1930, 101–2
of 1932, 73–74, 89, 109–10, 117, 118,
  145, 232–33, 235, 300, 301
of 1936, 213, 216–18, 219, 221–24, 228,
  231, 232–33, 300, 301, 383
of 1940, 175, 266, 283–85, 291, 294–
  301, 314, 319, 383
of 1944, 315, 381–85
of 1946, 397
of 1948, 400
electrical lighting, 107, 181
electric companies, 47
electricity, 34
electric transmission lines, 166
Elliott, Harriet, 338
Ellis Island, 22
Emergency Banking Act (1933), 119, 143
Emergency Employment Committee, 98
Emergency Price Control Act (1942), 339
Emergency Relief Appropriation Act
  (1935), 171, 217, 256
Emergency Relief Bureau, NYC, 265
"End Poverty in California" (EPIC), 164
environmental conservation, 9, 44
Espionage Act (1917), 27, 29
Ethridge, Mark, 312
Evening Graphic, 62
Evening Journal, 49
Executive Chamber, 115
Executive Order 8802, 312
executive reorganization bill, 257, 271
eye clinics, 34

Fabrizio, Giovanni, 23
factories, 147
factory safety regulations, 13
Fair Deal, 396
Fair Employment Practices Committee
  (FEPC), 308, 312, 396
Fair Labor Standards Act (1938), 270, 403
fair prices, 326
family insurance plans, 364
Farley, James A., 74, 126–27, 128, 140, 142,
  220, 225, 226, 248, 251, 284, 294,
  400, 444
Farley, Thomas, 115
farm aid, 44, 72, 98, 263
Farm Bloc, 60
Farm Bureau Federation, 263, 283
Farmer-Labor Party, 60, 214
farmers, 58–59, 101

Farm Holiday Association, 214
fascism, 289–90, 317, 318
Fay, James, 271
federal-city relations, 131
Federal Deposit Insurance Corporation,
  119
Federal Emergency Relief Act (1933), 119
Federal Emergency Relief Administration
  (FERA), 121, 149–50, 151, 153, 161,
  164, 168, 173
Federal Housing and Rent Act (1947), 353
Federal One arts project, 202, 203, 243
Federal Theater Project, 243, 263
Federal Works Agency, 263, 368
Fidelity & Deposit, 15, 63, 108
Filene, Edward, 222
financial institutions, 178
  see also banks
fireside chats, 73, 270, 301
Fisher, Irving, 162–63, 167
Fish Tuesday, 155–56
flood control, 143
Flynn, Edward J., 74, 81, 87, 116, 127, 140,
  142, 181, 225, 226, 294, 300, 314,
  383, 405
food, 34, 61, 345–49
  distribution of, 38–39
  prices of, 340, 346, 347
Ford, Henry, 59–60
Forrestal, James, 333
Fort Greene Health Center, 365
Forverts, 219, 237–38
"four freedoms," 301–2
France, 283, 289, 329, 337, 338
Frank, Dana, 27
Frankfurter, Felix, 104, 292
Franklin D. Roosevelt boardwalk, ix–x
Fraser, Steven, 226, 298
Freedmen's Bureau, 308
Freidel, Frank, 89
French, in NYC, 77
Full Employment bill, 397, 403
fusion movement, 112, 122–24, 129, 170,
  186, 230, 231
Fusion Party, 248, 273, 296

Galbraith, John Kenneth, 344, 391
Gallup, George, 252
gambling, 56
Gannon, Frances Foley, 156
garment industry, 236, 333–34, 335
Garner, John Nance, 103, 104–5, 261, 284
gas, 34
Gashouse District, 11

gasoline, 332
Gayda, Virginio, 320
General Maximum Price Regulation, 339, 340
George, Henry, 113
Georgia, 256, 271
Gerard, James W., 13
German American Bund, 247, 317
Germans, in NYC, 50, 77–78, 301, 319
Germany, 267, 283, 317, 376, 398
Gerson, Simon, 317
G.I. Bill, 363–64
Gibson, Harvey, 97
Gibson Committee, 97, 98, 155, 330
gift taxes, 103
Giornale D'Italia, Il, 320
Glass, Carter, 261–62
Glass-Steagall Act (1933), 119, 121
Glazer, Nathan, 78
gold, 143, 148, 173
gold standard, 143
Goldstein, Jonah, 388–89, 390
Goodyear Tire & Rubber, 331
grade-crossing removal projects, 184
Grand Central Terminal, 191
grants-in-aid, 149, 390
Great Britain, 283, 289, 291, 292, 316
Great Depression, ix, x, xii, xiii, 42, 72
    causes of, 99–101
    Democratic Party revived by, 91
    emergence from, 327
    Hoover's response to, 54, 111
    in New York, 90–132
    1933 expansion in, 148
Great Depression of 1890s, 96
Greater New York Industrial Union Council, 317
Great Society, 375
Greece, 398, 399
Greeks, in NYC, 77
Green, William, 340
Greenberg, Cheryl, 245
Greenpoint Hospital, 181
Greenwich Village, 49, 389
Griffith, D. W., 239–40
Gunther, John, 64, 73

Hamilton, Alexander, 67
Hannegan, Robert, 383
Harding administration, 60
Harlem, 79, 80, 186, 231, 235, 239, 240, 351
Harlem Hospital, 243
Harlem River Houses, 186, 187
harmony committee, 124

Harrison, Pat, 259
Hat, Cap, and Millinery Workers, 228
Hatch, Carl, 261–62
Hatch Act (1939), 261
Havana, Cuba, 43, 46, 130
health care, xii, xiv, 34, 84, 185, 204, 265, 363, 366, 373, 375, 376–81, 393
Health Department, NYC, 33–34, 185, 200, 369
Health Insurance Plan of Greater New York (HIP), 379–81
Hearst, William Randolph, 35, 38, 40, 49, 81, 226, 319
    charity of, 95
    Municipal Ownership League of, 113
Heffernan, John A., 211
Hell's Kitchen, 14
Henderson, Leon, 259, 333, 338, 341–42
Henry Hudson Drive, xi
Herald Tribune, 86, 135, 279, 289, 321, 330, 388
Hickok, Lorena, 148–49, 192
High, Stanley, 270
highway construction, 77, 153, 176, 182, 375
Hill, Arnold, 233
Hillman, Sidney, 218, 219, 220, 228, 295, 311, 386, 388
Hillquit, Morris, 36–37, 53, 151
Hitler, Adolf, 277, 278–79, 293, 301, 313, 317
Hodson, William, 161
Hold-the-Line order, 341, 342–43, 345
Holmes, Oliver Wendell, 117
home relief, 151
Home Relief Bureau, NYC, 149, 273
Hoover, Herbert, 54, 89, 108, 111, 173, 292, 331
    budget balancing of, 101, 102–3
    in election of 1928, 71, 72
    FDR's criticism of economic policies of, 105–6
    FDR's state relief program admired by, 110
    Garner program opposed by, 105
    Norris-La Guardia Anti-Injuction Act signed by, 104
    public works program of, 146
    voluntarist approach to recovery of, 101
Hopkins, Harry, 148, 160–61, 165, 190, 191, 192, 248, 254, 308, 356
    works relief projects of, 131, 150–52, 154, 158, 163, 166–67, 168, 169, 172, 209–10, 257, 258, 259

hospitals, 34, 83, 135, 177, 199, 371, 375, 392, 393
Hospitals Department, NYC, 142, 200, 265, 369
House of Representatives, U.S.:
    committee investigating relief in, 262
    Committee on Alcoholic Liquor Traffic of, 57
    Judiciary Committee of, 62
    public works program passed by, 171
    regional wage disparity bill in, 262, 263
    relief and public works bill in, 101
    Rules Committee of, 271
housing, xi, xii, 36, 52, 54, 61, 64, 97, 154, 166, 176, 182, 185–88, 204, 229, 364, 366, 375, 392
Housing Authority, U.S., 262
Howe, Frederic, xiii
Howe, Irving, 237
Howe, Louis, 64, 65, 87
Howe, Stanley, 161
How the Other Half Lives (Riis), 33
Hudson River, 181
Hughes, Charles Evans, 26, 86, 117
Hull, Cordell, 277–78, 279, 283
Hundred Days, 119, 121, 135, 145, 147, 152
Hungarians, in NYC, 77
Hunter College, 176, 185, 199, 200
Hyde Park, N.Y., xvii, 4, 6, 66, 163, 221, 234, 249, 253, 274, 283, 394
hydroelectric power, 59, 60, 72, 73
Hylan, John F., 38–39, 40, 41, 81, 82, 83, 84, 200, 239

iceworks, 34, 47
Ickes, Harold, 118, 131, 140, 147, 163, 166, 167, 168, 182–83, 186, 221, 252, 260, 266–67, 278, 284, 292, 294, 302, 305, 306, 308, 355, 359, 383, 405
Idlewild Airport, 374
"If It Comes" campaign, 303
Illinois, 75
immigration, immigrants, xv, 17, 18, 32, 56–57, 59, 62, 66, 78, 366
    restrictions on, 65
    as voters, 72
Impellitteri, Vincent, 392
income taxes, 13, 103, 234, 396
Independent Citizens' Committee of Artists, Scientists, and Professionals, 401
Independent Voters' Committee of the Arts and Sciences (IVCAS), 382
industrial employment, 92

industry, 146, 147, 158, 178, 366
infant health, 153
inflation, 155, 326, 336–38, 341–42, 345
inheritance taxes, 103
insurance companies, 102
International Ladies Garment Workers (ILGWU), 215, 219, 340, 387
International Pressmen's Union, 219
Irish, in NYC, 24, 26, 50, 51, 65, 77–78, 229, 232, 247, 301, 319, 320, 389
Isaacs, Stanley, 139
Italians, in NYC, 50, 51–52, 53, 77, 79, 85, 87, 88, 123, 128, 129, 222, 232, 235, 289, 300, 301, 319, 389
Italy, 29, 289, 318, 398
Ives, Irving, 313
Ives-Quinn bill, 313

Jacob Riis Beach, 195, 196, 204
Japan, 267, 321
Japanese Americans, 292, 293, 321–22
Jefferson, Thomas, 67, 96
Jefferson and Hamilton (Bowers), 67
Jensen, Richard, 163
Jersey City, N.J., 328
Jews, in NYC, 51, 77, 209, 232, 233, 234–36, 244
job creation, 143, 146, 162–65
jobs, "right" to, 161
jobs programs, 160–62
    see also specific programs
Johnson, Hiram, 103–4
Johnson, Hugh, 147, 191, 206, 278
Johnson, Lyndon, 375
Johnson-Reed bill, 56, 60
Joint Chiefs of Staff, 359
Joint Defense Board, 312
Joint Legislative Committee to Investigate the City of New York, 114
Jones, Jesse, 141, 164, 333
June Dairy, 395
Justice Department, U.S., 311

Kaiser, Henry J., 379
Kaiser Permanente, 379
Kelly, Edward, 183, 253, 382, 394
Kelly, Frank, 142, 225, 226, 382
Kennedy, David, 16
Kent, Frank, 259
Kessner, Thomas, 236, 293
Kieran, James, 271, 355
King, Mackenzie, 293, 294
Kingsbury, John, 151
Kings County, 10

Kings County League, 49
Kings County Medical Society, 149
Kintner, Robert, 275–76
Knox, Frank, 311, 333
Knudsen, William, 311
Koenig, Samuel, 41, 50
Kristallnacht, 280
Ku Klux Klan, 65

labor, ratio of capital to, 168–69, 190
labor costs, 144
labor regulations, 13, 59, 61
labor rights, 121
Labor's Non-Partisan League (LNPL), 219,
    220, 262
labor unions, 23, 35, 44, 59, 63, 85, 104,
    145, 185, 218–19, 228, 234, 237, 240,
    244, 309, 313, 316, 333–34, 350, 363,
    384
Labour Party, British, 61
Lafayette Theater, 243
La Follette, Phil, 212, 268, 275
La Follette, Robert M., Jr., 101, 145, 158,
    212–13, 214, 218, 250, 268–69, 275,
    282
La Follette, Robert M., Sr., 24, 56, 57–58,
    60–61, 117
La Guardia, Achille, 18, 20–21
La Guardia, Fiorello:
    as alleged demagogue, 210
    Allied cause supported by, 291
    ambition of, 21–22
    anti-gambling crusade of, 135, 155, 347
    appointees of, 137–39, 180, 233–34
    arts supported by, 202–4
    autobiography of, 17–18, 19
    basic economic vision of, 216
    blaze of activity of, 135–36
    as booster of aviation, 197–98
    in campaign of 1936, 221–22
    city jobs slashed by, 139–40
    Communism as viewed by, 401–3
    congressional projects of, 54–55,
        57–60, 62
    in consular service, 21–22
    consumer groups encouraged by,
        344–48
    and creation NYCHA, 185–86
    death of, 404–5
    and death of wife and child, 42–43
    Dewey viewed with suspicion by, 273
    early retirement considered by, 121–22
    Economy Bill of, 139–42
    education of, 19

    Eleanor Roosevelt esteemed by, 65
    in election of 1916, 25–27, 29, 49–50,
        52–54
    in election of 1929, 80, 81, 85–87,
        88–89, 90, 113–14, 123
    in election of 1933, 123–27, 128–29,
        230, 232–33, 424
    in election of 1937, 33, 214, 231–32,
        247–49, 267, 272–73, 319
    in election of 1940, 283–85
    in election of 1941, 210–11, 238–39,
        314–20, 354
    emotional issues of, 320–21
    ethnicity and votes for, 232–43, 232
    export subsidization plan of, 267,
        281–82
    FDR's second inaugural and, 224–25
    federal relief effort desired by, 108–9
    fourth term declined by, 245, 385–90
    fusionist support for, 124
    on Great Depression, 90–91, 99–101
    health insurance program of, 363, 366,
        376–81
    hydroelectric power supported by, 73
    immigration restrictions opposed by,
        17
    Jewish ancestry of, 277
    labor movement's support for, 228–29
    in labor party project, 220
    La Follette supported by, 60–61, 212–
        13, 214
    languages known by, 21
    law work of, 22–23
    Lehman supported by, 274–76
    in Madison Square Club, 24–25
    marriage of, 24
    mass purchasing power focused on by,
        106, 124–25
    Mayor's Advisory Committee on Busi-
        ness started by, 331–32
    Mayor's Poster Commission created by,
        155–56
    media profiles of, 250
    middle class support for, 129
    military post desired by, 354–61
    minorities appointed by, 233–34
    Nazis criticized by, 277–82
    as NCIV leader, 295–96
    New Deal as challenging to, 230–31
    newspaper columns of, 62, 395, 401
    on New York Boards, 37–38, 43, 48
    New York Democrats' disputes with,
        180–81
    and New York revenue, 370–72

and New York's engineering projects, 182–83
in 1920 mayoral primary, 40–42
1940 presidential run considered by, 266–68
pan-American cooperation desired by, 281
political philosophy of, 45–47
popularity of, 243–47
postwar planning by, 365–69, 372–74
as president of United States Conference of Mayors, 252–56
price ceilings enforced by, 343
and price controls, 326–27
Prohibition opposed by, 27, 56, 57
and proposed March on Washington, 310–13
on public authorities, 436–37
public works and relief projects of, 130–31
racial prejudice as seen by, 310–11
radio broadcasts of, 267, 296–97, 345, 346–49, 352, 388, 395–96
recreation space expanded by, 195–96
relief bill desired by, 104
rent control and, 352–53
Republican opposition to, 227–28
Republican Party joined by, 24
Republican support for, 227
retirement of, 394
Revenue Bill rewritten by, 103, 104
RFC denounced by, 102, 121
Rothstein case investigated by, 87–88
sales tax opposed by, 103
Senate testimony on project costs by, 263
"soak the rich" rhetoric of, 123
Tammany Hall opposed by, 18, 24, 29, 54, 125–26
taxes proposed by, 170
and threat of third party, 270–71
UNRRA run by, 398–99
urban air-raid defense plan of, 303–4
vacations of, 43, 46, 130
wartime liberal program endorsed by, 396–98
wealth enjoyed by, 395
western upbringing of, 18–19, 20
in World War I, 28–29
as worried about New York bombing, 303
WPA and, 175–76, 191, 193, 202–4, 206, 207, 252, 254–58, 261, 262
WPA defended by, 175–76, 252

see also Roosevelt-La Guardia relationship
La Guardia, Fioretta, 42–43
La Guardia, Marie Fisher, 23, 28, 38, 55, 64–65, 88, 130
La Guardia, Thea Almerigotti, 23, 37, 42–43, 53
La Guardia Airport, ix, 190, 197, 204, 257, 391
Land, Emory S., 333
Landis, James M., 323
Landon, Alf, 218
Lanzetta, James, 118
Latin America, 281
Latin Americans, in NYC, 77
Lazarus, Reuben, vii, 313
League for Independent Political Action (LIPA), 214–15
lease termination notices, 336
lectures, 34
legal aid, 210
LeHand, Missy, 127, 267
Lehman, Herbert, 71, 114, 117, 140, 142, 185, 235, 272, 274–76, 293, 332, 333, 398, 405
Lemke, William, 217, 218
Lerner, Max, 354
Lewis, David Levering, 234
Lewis, John L., 215, 219, 222, 278
Lexow Committee, 19
Liberal Party, 313, 387, 390
Liberty, 395
liberty of the community, 44
life insurance, 108
Lincoln Tunnel, ix, 183
Lindley, Ernest, 307–8
Lippmann, Walter, 39, 70, 322
Literary Digest, 14)
"Little Steel" policy, 340
London, 303
Long, Huey, 217
Long Island State Parks Commission, 154
Los Angeles, Calif., 206
Louis, Joe, 234
Lower East Side, 9, 50, 235, 236, 389
Lowi, Theodore J., 230
Luciano, Lucky, 273
Lundeen, Ernest, 224

MacArthur, Douglas, 381
Macy, Kingsland, 122–23, 124
Madison Square Garden, 278
Madison Square Republican Club, 24–25
Mahoney, Jeremiah, 226, 247

Mair, Norma, 242
Maney, Patrick, 268
Mann, Arthur, 88
Manufacturers Trust Company, 97
manufacturing, 92, 366, 393
Marcantonio, Vito, 53–54, 123
March of Time, 250
Maritime Commission, 333
Marshall, George, 306, 357, 405
Maryland, 271
mass media, 73
maternal health, 153
maternity clinics, 34
Maverick, Maury, 42
Mayo Clinic, 377
Mayor's Advisory Committee on Business,
    331–32
Mayor's Committee on City Planning, 200
Mayor's Committee on Plan and Survey,
    179
Mayor's Committee on Rent, 353
Mayor's Poster Commission, 155–56
McAdoo, William, 65
McCarren Pool, 204
McCloy, John J., 293, 305
McCooey, John H., 10, 225
McFarland, Ernest, 360
McGoldrick, Joseph, 141, 182
McGuinness, Peter J., 181
McKee, Joseph "Holy Joe," 116, 126–29,
    139, 140, 231
McKinley, William, 7
McManus, Thomas J., 14
McNary-Haugen Act, 59
McNutt, Paul, 332, 333
Mead, James, 274
means test, 172
Meany, George, 229–30
Mecca Temple, 203
medical care, 34
Mellon, Andrew, 58, 59, 60
merchant associations, 178
Mergenthaler Linotype, 309
meritocratization, 138–39
Metropolitan Opera House, 203
Mexico, 281
middle class, 240
military-industrial complex, 326–36
milk, 229
milk stations, 34, 46, 47
Miller, Nathan, 40, 45
Mills, Ogden, 86, 105
mineworkers, 55
Minnesota, 268

Mitchel, John Purroy, 25, 27, 38, 48, 82,
    84, 86, 150–51, 154
Mitchell, Billy, 55
Montgomery, David, 251–52
Moore, Deborah Dash, 234
Morgan, William Fellowes, Jr., 132, 264,
    355
Morgenthau, Henry, Jr., 74, 164, 257, 278,
    333, 388, 435
Morocco, 398
Morris, Newbold, 202, 203, 389, 390
mortgage companies, 102
mortgage debt, 143
Moscow, Warren, 323, 384
Moses, Robert, 40, 69, 130, 154–55, 156,
    179, 180, 185, 193, 195, 196–97, 233,
    264, 313, 331, 373, 396, 436–37, 439
Mosholu Consumers Group, 343
Moskowitz, Belle, 69
mosquito control, 76
Mugwumps, 113
"multiplier" effect, 145, 171
Mumford, Lewis, 155, 187
municipal beer gardens, 130, 154
municipal debt, 132
municipal governments, xiv–xv
Municipal Ownership League, 35, 113
municipal populism, 35
Murder, Inc., 315
Murphy, Charles Francis, 10, 11, 12, 13, 14,
    29, 38, 74, 81, 85, 126
Murphy, Frank, 131–32, 275
Murray, Philip, 340
Muscle Shoals dam, 60, 73
Musher, Sharon, 201
music, 176, 201–4
Mussolini, Benito, 91, 289, 291, 300

NAACP, 241, 310
Nation, 60, 129–30, 149, 250, 275
National Association of Manufacturers,
    366
National Citizens' Political Action Com-
    mittee, 382, 401
National Committee of Independent
    Voters for Roosevelt and Wallace
    (NCIV), 295–96, 382
National Emergency Council, 158
National Fair Rent Committee, 396
National Farmers' Union, 214
National Guard, 28
National Industrial Recovery Act (1933),
    119, 145–47, 152, 186, 215
nationalization, 326

National Labor Relations Act (1935), 217, 228, 229, 238, 311
National Negro Congress, 351
National Non-Partisan Committee for the Re-election of Roosevelt, 382
National Progressive League, 118, 295
National Progressives of America, 268–71
National Recovery Administration (NRA), 121, 144–45, 147–48, 173, 215, 228
National Resources Planning Board, 173
National Union, 217, 218
National War Labor Board, 339, 340, 341, 343
National Youth Administration, 310
Native Americans, 19–20
Nazis, 247, 277–82, 292
NBC, 267, 296, 383
Nearing, Scott, 29
needle trades unions, 23, 216, 219
    see also Amalgamated Clothing Workers of America; International Ladies Garment Workers Union
Neely, Matthew, 396
Nelson, Donald, 332
Nesbitt, C. T., 245–46
Neutrality Acts, 282
New Amsterdam, 4
Newark, N.J., 328
New Deal, 54, 129, 135
    alphabet agencies of, 126
    change in public attitudes and, xii–xiii
    as channeled through cities and counties, xi
    coalition of, xiii
    commitment to security of, 169
    Dewey's criticism of, 382
    as fractured by Cold War, 395
    freedom for creativity of, 120
    as issue in 1940 election, 296, 298, 299
    La Guardia on death of, 403, 404
    local states utilized in, xiv
    physical legacy of, ix–x
    as presenting challenges to La Guardia, 230–31
    purpose of, 172–73
    suburban, 364
    urban reform in, 30
    and withdrawal of federal resources from local public sectors, 364
    women mobilized by, 233
    in World War II, 325–26, 362
    see also New York, N.Y., New Deal in; specific programs
New England, 184

Newfoundland, 294
"new poor," 92–93
New Republic, 39, 130
newspapers, 178, 237, 244, 328, 330
New York, N.Y.:
    budget of, 83, 84, 467
    capital investment in, 180
    debt of, 141–42, 179
    Democratic Party's resurgence in, 11
    disease in, 79
    in election of 1940, 300–301
    engineering projects in, 182–83
    ethnic communities in, 77–79, 80
    FDR's dislike of, 7–8
    fiscal crises in, 39, 112, 126, 128, 136, 139–40
    food supply of, 156–57
    as global metropolis, 367
    Great Depression in, 90–132
    growing economy in, 80
    growth of, 76–77
    health insurance program in, 363
    manufacturing economy of, 328–30
    municipal bonds of, 112, 141–42, 234
    municipal spending in, 265
    municipal workers in, 392
    in 1929, 74–80
    in 1936 election, 222–24
    1945 capital budget of, 368–69
    1970s economic restructuring in, xvi
    parochialism of, 20
    rapid transit lines in, 77
    taxes in, 112, 170, 369–72
    wartime shortages in, 336
    wartime unemployment in, 327–28, 335, 351
New York, N.Y., New Deal in, xv, 129, 136, 364
    congressional opposition to, 256–59
    Democratic Party transformed by, 225–26
    municipal vulnerability in wake of, xv–xvi
    physical legacy in, ix–x
    postwar, 391–92, 393
    Republican Party reshaped by, 226–28
    WPA in, 189–211, 194, 260–61, 391, 441
New York Central, 83
New York City Corporation, 297
New York City Housing Authority (NYCHA), 185–86
New York Civilian Defense Volunteer Organization, 346
New York County, 10

New York Court of Appeals, 113
New York Democratic Committee, 127
New Yorker, 250
New York Federation of Churches, 313
New York Panorama, 243
New York Police Department, 19, 229, 315
New York Post, 330, 388
New York Public Library, 200
New York State, 256, 258
    budget of, 72–73, 83, 84
    FDR's Depression policies in, 105–11
    power gained by Republican Party in,
        40–41
New York State Board of Mediation, 229
New York State Federation of Labor, 229–30
New York State War Council, 344
New York Sunday World, 19
New York Supreme Court, 113
New York Times, 47, 60, 62, 88–89, 131,
        135, 155, 183, 203, 207, 218, 224,
        274–75, 289, 323, 368, 384
New York Tuberculosis and Health Soci-
        ety, 150
New York University, 98
New York Urban League, 90, 241
New York World, 17, 87–88
Niles, David, 118, 295, 335
Nixon, Richard, 381
Norris, George, 57, 59, 117, 119, 222, 224,
        275, 295
Norris-La Guardia Anti-Injuction Act
        (1932), 104
North Carolina, USS, 333
Novik, Morris, 199
NRA babies, 215
nurseries, 34
NYPD, 229

O'Brien, John, 116, 126, 127, 128, 129, 138,
        141, 147
O'Connor, John, 271–72, 276, 296, 451
O'Dwyer, William, 314–15, 317, 318, 372,
        388, 389, 390, 394
Office of Civilian Defense (OCD), 304–12,
        314, 320–24, 346
    Volunteer Participation Committee of,
        306
Office of Facts and Figures, 306
Office of Indian Affairs, 20
Office of Price Administration (OPA),
        327, 332, 338–42, 344, 345, 346, 348,
        349–54, 362
Office of Production Management, 311
Office of War Information, 306, 359

Office of War Mobilization, 359, 360
Official Committee for Relief of the
        Unemployed and Needy, 95–96
O'Gorman, James A., 12
Ohio, 75
Ohio Plan, 164
old-age assistance, 371
Olmsted, Frederick Law, 197
O'Neal, Ed, 283
one-world internationalism, 297
Orchard Beach, ix, 195, 204
Orsi, Robert, 52
Ottawa Journal, 291
Ottinger, Albert, 72
Oxford University, 196

Paige, Myles, 233
Paley, William S., 199
Panama Canal Zone, 130
parcel post, 107
parity-price program, 101
parks, 33, 34, 46, 47, 83–84, 154, 155, 177,
        182, 196–97, 229, 233, 373, 392, 393
Parks, Council of, NYC, 154
Parks Department, NYC, 154, 155, 193,
        195, 196
Parrish, Wayne, 160, 161
patronage, 82, 139, 271, 314, 315
Patterson, Robert, 333
Peabody, Endicott, 6
Pearl Harbor, Japanese attack on, 291,
        305, 308, 321, 322, 333, 338–39, 341,
        366, 374
Pearson, Drew, 283, 284, 307, 360
Pecora, Ferdinand, 127
Pelham Bay Park, 196
Pendergast, Tom, 70
Pennsylvania, 75, 192
pensions, 34
People's Committee, 351
People's Legislative Service, 60
People's Reconstruction League, 60
Perkins, Frances, 15, 63, 72, 74, 108, 219
Permanent Joint Board on Defense, 293–
        94, 302, 346
Philadelphia, Pa., 179, 183, 328
Piccirilli, Attilio, 23, 43
piers, 261
Pinchot, Amos, 117
Pittman, Key, 259
Pittsburgh, Pa., 76
Pittsburgh Courier, 234
playgrounds, 34, 83, 155, 177, 182, 196,
        229, 373, 392, 393

PM, 317, 354, 395, 401
Podair, Jerald, 196
point rationing, 341, 347
Poland, 398
Polenberg, Richard, 271
Popular Front, 386
Portal-to-Portal Act (1947), 403
Port Authority, 147, 185
post offices, 131
postwar planning, 362, 365–69, 372–74
poverty, xii
Powell, Adam Clayton, Jr., 243, 351
power plants, 321
Prescott, Ariz., xvii, 18, 20
price controls, 327, 338, 339–40, 343, 344,
    347, 349, 350, 353, 362
prices, xii, 27–28, 47, 144, 216
private opulence, 391
productivity, 58, 61, 216
profits, 144, 216
Progressive Citizens of America, 401
Progressive Era, x–xi, xiv, 29, 33, 35–37,
    45, 46, 83, 125, 137, 153, 369
Progressive National Committee (PNC),
    220, 295–96
Progressive Party, 248
Progressive Party, Wisconsin, 212, 214
Prohibition, 27, 56, 57, 62, 65, 66, 102,
    118
property taxes, 266, 319, 351, 352
"Proposed Planks for the Republican State
    Platform," 47
Prospect Park, 321
Prosser, Seward, 97
Prosser Committee, 97, 98, 330
Protestant fundamentalists, 65
public art projects, 154
public investment, 176–77, 325–26, 366–
    67, 378, 390
public power, 100, 101, 111, 117
public radio, 199
public terminal markets, 47
public utilities, 13, 34, 35, 83, 100, 217
Public Welfare Department, U.S., 265
Public Works Administration (PWA), 17,
    121, 131, 140, 146–47, 152, 153, 158,
    166, 167, 171, 172, 173, 178, 181, 182,
    183, 184, 185, 195, 198, 206, 221, 243,
    261
  consolidated into Federal Works
    Agency, 263, 368
  Housing Division of, 185–87, 188
  La Guardia's publicity work for, 252
  new appropriation for, 260

ratio of federal to local expenditures
    in, 257
public works programs, 44, 101, 108, 110,
    131, 145–46, 168, 169–70, 171–72, 174,
    370, 373–74
  public opposition to, 178–79
  see also specific programs
Puerto Rico, 118
Pulitzer, Joseph, 19

Quebec conference, 360
Queens College, 373
Queens County, 10, 128, 147
Queens-Midtown Tunnel, 183, 198, 221

racial discrimination, xiii
radio, 75, 107, 199, 204, 244
railroads, 59, 102, 321
Randall's Island Stadium, 195
Randolph, A. Philip, 310–12
rapid transit lines, 184 85
Raskob, John J., 71
rationing, 336
RCA Building, 396
recession of 1914–15, 96–97
recession of 1937, 159, 255, 268
Reconstruction Finance Corporation
    (RFC), 101, 102, 121, 141, 143
Recovery Party, 126, 129, 231
recreation, xii, 176, 265
Red Network (NBC radio), 296
refrigeration, 107
Regional Plan Association, 179
relief offices, 135
relief projects, 131
rent control, xii, 39, 47, 83, 327, 350–54,
    392–93
Republican Clubs, 49
Republican Party, U.S., 24
  federal work relief opposed by, 261
  middle class voters in, 76
  New York power gained by, 40–41
Republic Convention of 1940, 298
reservoirs, 321
Resettlement Administration, 166
resettlement programs, 106–7, 143, 146,
    164–66
Revenue Act (1942), 339
revenue bill, 102–3, 104
Rice, John, 185
Richberg, Donald, 104, 117
Ridder, Victor, 21, 191
"right to work" laws, 363
Riis, Jacob, 33

Rivington Street Settlement House, 8
roads, 83, 146, 177, 181, 185
    see also highway construction
Robinson, Joe, 259
Rockefeller Center, 202, 331
Rodgers, Daniel, 111, 172–73
Roe, James, 301
Roosevelt, Eleanor, 6, 7, 8–9, 16, 65, 69,
    220, 302, 306, 307, 310–11, 322, 345,
    384, 388, 402–3
Roosevelt, Franklin D.:
    as alleged demagogue, 210
    anti-Mussolini speech of, 290–91, 300
    as assistant secretary of Navy, 3, 10, 13, 14
    belief in civic responsibility of, 5
    "Black Cabinet" of, 233
    Byrnes confronted by, 258
    as contender for vice presidency, 14
    court-packing plan of, 249, 269
    death of, 387–88, 395
    Democratic Party as envisioned by,
        66–67
    Depression-era New York policies of,
        105–11
    Economy Act of, 139, 145
    education of, 4, 5–7
    in election of 1932, 89, 117, 145, 232–33
    in election of 1936, 219, 221–24, 231,
        232–33, 235
    in election of 1940, 285, 291, 294–301,
        319
    in election of 1944, 315, 381–85
    family history known by, 4–5, 18
    Farley removed by, 115
    federal relief efforts desired by, 108–9
    first inauguration of, 142–43
    in gubernatorial election of 1928,
        71–72
    in gubernatorial election of 1930, 74
    Hoover's economic policies criticized
        by, 105–6
    as ineffective governor, 72–73
    Jewish vote for, 235
    La Guardia airport supported by, 198
    at law firm, 7–8, 9, 14, 63
    localism utilized by, xiii
    marriage of, 7
    Nazis opposed by, 278
    and 1933 New York mayoral election,
        126–27
    paralysis of, 15–17, 63, 66, 70, 72
    polio contracted by, 15–16, 48, 63
    political philosophy of, 43–44
    political research by, 63–64

    popularity of, 243–47
    postwar vision of, 400
    poverty first seen by, 8–9
    and proposed March on Washington,
        310–13
    public works program of, 168, 169–70,
        171–72
    reformers seen as sanctimonious by, 114
    religious faith of, 6, 16, 43
    resettlement program of, 106–7, 143,
        146, 164–66
    retirement considered by, 282–83
    second bill of rights proposed by, 376
    second inaugural address of, 224–25
    Smith's relationship with, 69–70
    Smith supported at 1924 convention
        by, 70
    speech on Allied cause by, 289–91
    state relief program of, 109–10
    in state senate, 9–13
    Tammany opposed by, 11, 13, 14
    tenement district support for, 129
    third inaugural of, 301–2
    unemployment solutions of, 136–37,
        143, 146, 152–53, 162–63, 164–65,
        169–70, 173
    Walker's hearing and, 115–16
    as worried over New York City's
        finances, 140
    WPA regulations of, 190
Roosevelt, Theodore, 7, 9, 24, 25, 30, 117,
    120
Roosevelt, Theodore, Jr., 86
Roosevelt & O'Connor, 63
Roosevelt family, 4–5
Roosevelt-La Guardia relationship, ix, x,
    xiii–xiv, 48–49, 221
    anti-Nazi sentiment in, 278, 279,
        280–81
    beginning of alliance, 92
    early legislation in, 64–65
    FDR as wary of La Guardia's ascent,
        250–51
    and FDR's bid for third term, 175,
        296–301
    FDR's resettlement plan and, 165–66
    first meeting in, 3–4
    La Guardia dismissed as vice-presiden-
        tial candidate, 267
    La Guardia put as head of NCIV,
        295–96
    La Guardia put in charge of office of
        home defense by FDR, 302–13, 314,
        320–21

La Guardia removed from OCD, 322–24
and La Guardia's 1937 election victory,
248–49
La Guardia's campaigning for FDR's
fourth term, 382–85
and La Guardia's desire for military
position, 355–56, 357–361
and La Guardia's plan to succeed FDR,
282–83
La Guardia's radio broadcast in favor of
FDR, 296–97
La Guardia's support for FDR's foreign
policy, 291
La Guardia's tribute on death of FDR,
388
myth of, 206–8
and New York City's finances, 140–41
opposing styles in, 136
Republican mayors' references to, 206
World War II as damaging to, 292–93
and WPA deficiency, 261
Rose, Alex, 228, 387
Rosenberg, Anna, 307, 308, 310–11
Rosenman, Samuel, 74, 292
Rosenzweig, Roy, 176, 197
Rothstein, Arnold, 87–88
Royal Navy, 293
rubber rationing, 332
Ruotolo, Onorio, 23
Russia, 28, 29, 398
Ryan, Clendenin, 355

Sacco and Vanzetti case, 52
Sachs Furniture, 395
St. Louis Post-Dispatch, 104
Sala, J. Roland, 296
sales tax, 103, 170, 354–55, 371–72
Sara Delano Roosevelt Park, 155
Scandinavia, 166
Scandinavians, in NYC, 77
Schattschneider, E. E., 205
Schneiderman, Rose, 63
school lunches, 47
school nurses, 33
schools, 36, 46, 47, 64, 78, 83, 177, 181, 182,
185, 199, 204, 261, 368, 392
see also education
Schwartz, Maud, 63
science, 46
scientific progress, 32
Scots, 77
Seabury, Samuel, 112–16, 123, 124, 126,
128, 299, 315, 357
second bill of rights, 376

Second Hundred Days, 217
Second Popular Front, 343
Securities Act (1933), 119
Securities Exchange Commission, 119
security wages, 170
segregation, 310–13
Selective Service Act (1917), 28
Selective Training and Service Act (1940),
306
Senate, U.S.:
Agriculture Committee of, 59–60
Appropriations Committee of, 259
Banking and Currency Committee of,
127
direct election of, 11, 13
La Guardia's testimony on project costs
to, 263
in 1938 election, 275
public works program passed by, 171
Servicemen's Readjustment Act (1944),
363–64
settlement houses, 33
Seventeenth Amendment, 11
sewers, 83, 155, 182, 229
shantytowns, 94
Sheehan, William F., 11, 12
Shefter, Martin, 10
Shepard, Edward M., 11–12
shipbuilding, 146
Shipping Board, 55
Shipstead, Henrik, 57, 282
shortages, 336
Siegel, Fred, 467
Siegel, Isaac, 49
Siegel, Seymour, 199
Simkhovitch, Mary, 186
Simpson, Kenneth, 227
Sinatra, Frank, 383
Sinclair, Upton, 164, 167
sit-down strikes, 249
Skowronek, Stephen, 136
skyscrapers, 181
Sloan, George A., 331–32, 334
slot machines, 135, 155
slum clearance, 187, 229
slums, 34
Smaller War Plants Corporation (SWPC),
332, 334–35
Smith, Al, 14, 15, 48, 62, 69, 81, 116, 118,
137, 151, 154, 221, 225, 233, 235, 379,
388, 443–44
at 1924 convention, 65, 70
in election of 1928, 70–71, 72, 320
FDR's relationship with, 69–70

Smith, Harold, 322, 323
social insurance, 9, 34, 229, 262
socialism, 34, 236–38
Socialist Party, 24, 29, 34, 53, 61, 82, 128,
    219, 231, 235
social obligations, 109
social reformers, 32–33
social security, 169
Social Security Act (1935), 121, 153, 173,
    217, 363
social security bill, 396
social workers, 122
Socony-Vacuum Oil, 309
soldiers' bonus, 58, 59, 60
Somervell, Brehon, 191, 192, 265, 355
South America, 267, 281
South Brooklyn, 49
South Carolina, 257, 258, 271
South Carolina Peach Growers' Associa-
    tion, 348
Soviet Union, 203, 317
Spaniards, in NYC, 77
Spanish American War, 20
spending solution, 259–60
Sperry Gyroscope, 309
sports, 195
"spread of employment," 100
Stabilization Act (1942), 340
Star Casino, 53
State Department, U.S., 21, 55, 399
Staten Island County, 10, 128, 200
State Relief Commission of Ohio, 164
steam works, 47
Steffens, Lincoln, 61
Stein, Herbert, 171
Steingut, Irwin, 141
Stieglitz, Alfred, xi
Stimson, Henry L., 30, 86, 292, 311, 322,
    357–58, 359, 360
stock market, crash of, 90, 127
stock transfer taxes, 103
stockyards, 59
Stone, I. F., 405
storage facilities, 59
streets, 155
subsidiarity, 109
subsidization of jobs, 162–63
subway lines:
    construction of, 36, 97, 154, 176, 182,
        316
    five-cent fare on, 38, 39, 40, 41, 46, 83,
        372

Sullivan, Ed, 62, 81
Supreme Court, U.S., 249, 269, 301
swimming pools, 195, 196, 204, 233, 243
Swope, Gerard, 355
synagogues, 244

Taft, William Howard, 292
Taft-Hartley Act (1947), 403–4
Tammany Hall, 11, 19, 24, 40, 74, 81, 112,
        138, 225, 226, 227, 235, 237, 240, 248,
        249, 271, 347, 399
    collapse of, 214
    corruption in, 85, 87–88
    in Great Depression, 91
    loss of power of, xi
    opposition to, 10, 11, 13, 14, 24, 29, 35, 54,
        113–14, 122, 124, 125–26, 130, 139, 219
    origins of, 10
    Roosevelt's alliance with, 69
    see also Democratic Party, in New York
Tanner, Frederick, 24
taxes, 44, 58, 59, 60, 66, 77, 98, 102, 116,
        170, 217, 234, 255, 325, 329–30, 374
    gift, 103
    income, 13, 103, 234, 396
    inheritance, 103
    in New York, 106, 170, 369–72
    progressive, 101
    property, 266, 319, 351, 352
    sales, 103, 170, 354–55, 371–72
    utility, 141
Taxpayers Association of Greater New
        York, 353
Tchaikovsky, Pyotr Ilyich, 202
technology, 46
telephones, 107
Temporary Emergency Relief Administra-
        tion (TERA), 110, 149, 150, 151, 331
tenant groups, 244
tenements, 46, 235, 350, 369
Tennessee Valley Authority Act (1933), 119
Tennessee River Valley, 60, 121
terminal markets, 59
Textile Workers Organizing Committee,
        228
theaters, 34, 201–4, 440
Thomas, Norman, 86, 88, 136, 235, 424
Tilden, Samuel, 9
Time, 250
Times (London), 320
Tog, Der, 247, 317
tourism, 75

Townsend, Francis, 217
traffic accidents, 196
trains, 207
transportation, 77, 107, 153, 176, 182–85, 332–33, 375
Transport Workers Union, 316
Treasury, U.S., 27, 263
Tremont, 49
Triangle Shirtwaist Company, 13
Triborough Bridge, 83, 183, 198, 391
Triborough Bridge Authority, 147
Truman, Harry, 367, 381, 396, 397, 398–99, 404, 405
Tugwell, Rexford, 6–7, 190, 251, 282, 283, 285, 292
tunnels, xi, 83, 176, 182, 184, 185, 321
Turkey, 399
Turks, in NYC, 77
Tweed, William, 96

U-boats, 3, 327–28
unemployables, 168
unemployment, ix, xii, xvi, 34, 44, 51, 61, 96, 98–99, 120, 129, 130, 132, 143, 148–49, 154, 158, 159, 160, 173, 215, 264, 329, 330, 363, 374, 375
alleged "new normal" level of, 167
effects of, 93–94
FDR's plans for, 136–37, 143, 146, 152–53, 162–63, 164–65, 169–70, 173
manufacturing and, 163–64
by race, 425
in wartime New York, 327–28, 335, 351
unemployment insurance, 54, 101, 108, 110, 117, 118, 131, 379
Union for Democratic Action, 401
Union Pacific Railroad, 19
United Colored Democracy, 240
United Mine Workers, 219, 278
United Nations, 399–400
United Nations Relief and Rehabilitation Administration (UNRRA), 398–99
United States:
bonds of, 298
economic growth in, 159–60
as transformed from debtor to creditor nation, 75
United States Conference of Mayors, 132, 167–68, 252–56, 262, 266, 280–81, 303, 370, 374, 394
United States Housing Authority (USHA), 187–88

universities, 122, 375
urban air-raid defense, 303–4
U.S. Steel, 331
utility tax, 141

Vautrin, Murielle, 440
Vaux, Calvert, 197
Veiller, Lawrence, 33
Versailles peace settlement, 37
veterans' pensions, 371
Villard, Oswald Garrison, 60, 361
Virginia, University of, 289
Vitale, Albert H., 87
"Voodoo *Macbeth*," 243

WABC, 222
wage controls, 339–40
wage-labor capitalism, 34, 96
wages, 34, 52, 58, 59, 61, 121, 144, 145, 148, 169, 215, 216, 229, 237, 309, 333–34, 396
wages and hours bill, 269–70, 271
Wagner, Richard, 202
Wagner, Robert F., 13, 101, 105, 110, 145, 187, 222, 226, 235, 274, 372, 376, 381, 383, 384, 392–93
Wagner, Robert F., Jr., 372
Wagner Act (1935), 217, 228, 229, 238, 311
Wagner-Ellender-Taft housing bill, 396, 397
Wagner-Murray-Dingell health care, 376, 380, 396, 397
Walker, Jimmy, 11–12, 62, 81–85, 90, 122, 132, 137, 179, 235, 239–40, 248
Official Committee for Relief of the Unemployed and Needy created by, 95–96
scandals of, 87–88, 115–16, 123, 135, 137
Wallace, Henry A., 117, 132, 165, 221, 285, 294, 305, 388, 400, 403, 405
Walmsley, T. Semmes, 132, 370
Walsh, William J., 271
war, outlawing of, 98
war contracts, 292, 328, 328, 334–35, 367
Ward, Geoffrey C., 12–13
War Department, U.S., 198, 292, 294, 322, 360
War Manpower Commission, 312, 335
Warm Springs Foundation, 63, 66, 71, 387
war production, 176
War Production Board, 329, 332, 334
Warren, Earl, 376

Washington Post, 308
watchdog groups, 122
water, 36, 44, 182
water treatment plants, 375
wealth, 176–77
Weaver, Robert C., 312
Weil, La Guardia & Espen, 22–23
Weimar Republic, 162
Weiss, Nancy, 241
Welfare Department, New York, 142, 161
welfare state, 238
Wenger, Beth, 238
West Indies, xv, 79
WEVD, 219
Wheeler, Burton, 60
White, Walter, 310–11, 312
White, William Allen, 268
Whitney, Travis H., 153
WHOM, 300
widows' pensions, 13, 46
Wilgus, William J., 191
Wilkins, Roy, 233–34, 241
Williams, Aubrey, 311
Williams, Michael, 277
Williamsburg, 49, 235, 236
Williamsburg Houses, 186, 187
Willkie, Wendell, 294, 296, 297–99, 300,
    301, 302, 319–20, 379, 381
Wilson, Woodrow, 9, 13, 14, 26, 28, 30, 37,
    44, 113, 120, 235
Winchell, Walter, 62
Windels, Paul, 297
Wisconsin, 268–69, 379
Witte, Edwin, 104
WNYC, 176, 200, 233, 346, 347, 388
women, xv, 41–42, 75, 233
women's groups, 122
Women's Trade Union League, 97
Woodrum, Clifton, 262
Workers' Alliance, 255, 262
working hours, 9, 34, 101, 110, 118, 145,
    148, 169, 215, 229, 237
working standards, 144
Workmen's Circle, 219, 237

workmen's compensation, 9, 13, 34
work relief, 151–52, 158–59, 166–69, *174*,
    175–76, 231, 241–42, 258, 262, 362,
    370, 379
    reduction of spending on, 255
Works Progress Administration (WPA),
    157, 164, 168, 172, 173, 188–211, *189*,
    194, 253–66, 281, 306, 325, 346, 350,
    451
    African Americans and, 241–43
    arts, music, and theater projects of,
      201–4
    consolidated into Federal Works
      Agency, 262
    cuts in, 263–65
    increase in spending on, 260
    jobs allocated by formula, 205–6
    labor costs of, 190–93, 195
    La Guardia's defense of, 175–76, 252
    as polarizing agency, 251–52
    as publicized by Conference of Mayors,
      253–54
    seen as pro-urban, 256–58
    study on wages by, 262
World's Fair, 1939, 195, 250, 277
World-Telegram, 116
World War I, xiii, 14, 28–29, 34, 75, 237,
    279, 301, 337, 365
World War II, xii, xiii, 4, 45, 173, 291, 317,
    365, 374
    La Guardia's desire for role in, 354–61
    mobilization in, xi, 362
    war production for, 308–9
WOV, 300
WPA Guide to New York City, 243
WPA Poster Division, 156
WPA Radio Project, 200
WPA Writers Project, 75

Yearley, Clifton, 85
YMCA, 313
Young People's Socialist League, 237
youth movement, 237
Yugoslavia, 398